Journalizing and Posting

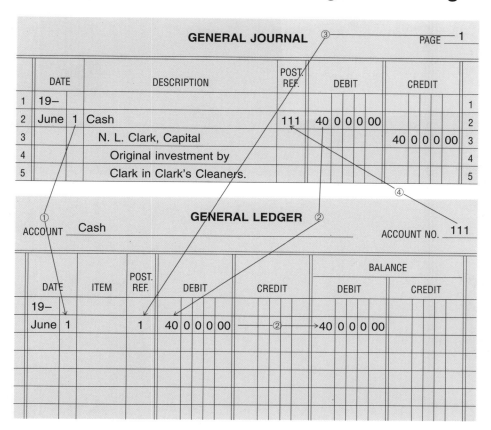

GENERAL JOURNAL   PAGE 1

	DATE	DESCRIPTION	POST. REF.	DEBIT	CREDIT	
1	19–					1
2	June 1	Cash	111	40 0 0 0 00		2
3		N. L. Clark, Capital			40 0 0 0 00	3
4		Original investment by				4
5		Clark in Clark's Cleaners.				5

GENERAL LEDGER

ACCOUNT __Cash__   ACCOUNT NO. __111__

DATE	ITEM	POST. REF.	DEBIT	CREDIT	BALANCE DEBIT	BALANCE CREDIT
19–						
June 1		1	40 0 0 0 00		40 0 0 0 00	

① Date of transaction
② Amount of transaction
③ Page numbers of the journal
④ Ledger account number

The Work Sheet

Account Name	Trial Balance Debit	Trial Balance Credit	Adjustments Debit	Adjustments Credit	Adjusted Trial Balance Debit	Adjusted Trial Balance Credit	Income Statement Debit	Income Statement Credit	Balance Sheet Debit	Balance Sheet Credit
	Assets ————————————→				Assets ——————→				Assets	
		Liabilities ——————→				Liabilities ——→				Liabilities
		Capital ——————————→				Capital ——————→				Capital
	Drawing ——————————→				Drawing ——————→				Drawing	
		Revenue ——————————→				Revenue ——→		Revenue		
	Expenses ————————→				Expenses ——→		Expenses			

Steps in the Closing Process

R Close the Revenue
E Close the Expenses
S Close the Income Summary Account and Transfer the Profit or Loss to the Capital Account
D Close the Drawing Account

24310   BAM110   11/20/97

Please Return to:
CALIFORNIA COAST UNIVERSITY
700 North Main Street
Santa Ana, CA.   92701

Contemporary College Accounting

Patricia A. Bille

Highline Community College

Douglas J. McQuaig

Wenatchee Valley College

Houghton Mifflin Company
Boston   Toronto
Geneva, Illinois   Palo Alto
Princeton, New Jersey

Senior Sponsoring Editor: Donald J. Golini
Senior Associate Editor: Joanne M. Dauksewicz
Senior Project Editor: Cynthia W. Harvey
Production/Design Coordinator: Carol J. Merrigan
Senior Manufacturing Coordinator: Marie Barnes
Marketing Manager: Robert D. Wolcott

Cover design by Edda Sigurdardottir, Greenwood Design Studio

Illustrations and photographs:
Page 4: Courtesy Pacioli Society, Seattle University; **17:** © John Coletti/The Picture Cube; **52:** © Zigy Kaluzny/Tony Stone Images; **65:** © Paul Conklin; **86:** © Bob Daemmrich/The Image Works; **106:** © John Coletti/The Picture Cube; **134:** © Mark E. Gibson; **146:** © Alan Carey/The Image Works; **192:** © Bob Daemmrich; **200:** © David R. Frazier Photolibrary; **240:** © Jeff Zaruha/Tony Stone Images; **244:** © Bob Daemmrich; **303:** © Bob Daemmrich; **344:** © Chronis Jons/Tony Stone Images; **379:** © Peter Le Grand/Tony Stone Images; **410:** © Mark E. Gibson; **453:** © Jim Cambon/Tony Stone Images; **501:** © Spencer Grant/Stock Boston; **528:** © Mark E. Gibson; **552:** © Mark Segal/Tony Stone Images.

Material in the **Computers at Work** feature on page 10 is reprinted by permission of *PC Novice*, 120 W. Harvest Drive, Lincoln, NE 68521. For subscription information, please call 800-472-4100, code number 4110.

Comments about *Contemporary College Accounting* can be sent to the authors at the following electronic-mail address: bille@pnw.com

Printed in the U.S.A.

Library of Congress Catalog Card No.: 93-78668

Student Book ISBN: 0-395-59288-7

Instructor's Annotated Edition ISBN: 0-395-59289-5

23456789-VH 99 98 97 96

Contents

COMPUTERS AT WORK **"X" Marks the Spot: Geographic Information Systems Turn Databases into Marketing Treasure Maps 209**

Chapter 6

Accounting for Merchandise: Purchases and Cash Payments Journals

236

PERFORMANCE OBJECTIVES 236 / PRACTITIONER'S CORNER 237

Chapter 7

Completing the Accounting Cycle for a Merchandising Business

290

PERFORMANCE OBJECTIVES 290 / PRACTITIONER'S CORNER 291

Douglas J. McQuaig
Patricia A. Bille

Preface

The goal for *Contemporary College Accounting* is to provide students with a sound basic knowledge of accounting terms, concepts, procedures, and computer applications, always taking into consideration students' widely varying objectives, whether they are planning more advanced studies in accounting or preparing to enter the job market in accounting or other business-related careers.

Based on more than 50 years of combined teaching experience, the authors have developed an up-to-date, understandable, and teachable basic accounting text. The text is logically organized, liberally illustrated, and paced in a manner that is easy for students to read and understand.

The text's scope and orientation were based on extensive reviews, campus visits, and conversations with many accounting instructors. The authors found that a growing number of instructors were looking for a more compact yet comprehensive textbook that could be used in one-semester or two-quarter courses. They were also looking for a textbook that reflected today's business environment in a more concrete way. This textbook was developed in response to all of these concerns.

The accounting principles described are those endorsed by the Financial Accounting Standards Board.

Chapter Coverage

Contemporary College Accounting is designed primarily for use in a course extending one semester or two quarters. The text may be divided into modules: Chapters 1 through 4 cover the full accounting cycle for a sole proprietorship service business. Chapters 5 through 7 cover special journals for a sole proprietorship merchandising business. Chapters 8 through 10 cover bank accounts and payroll accounting. Chapters 11 through 14 cover accounting for notes and receivables as well as the valuation of receivables, inventories, and plant assets.

The appendixes expand content coverage and increase the instructor's options for structuring the course. Because many students take only one quarter or one semester of accounting, Appendixes A through D offer brief exposure to the basics of financial statement analysis, valuation of inventories, modified accelerated Cost Recovery System of Depreciation, and statements of cash flows.

- **Appendix A: Financial Statement Analysis** (after Chapter 7) briefly describes percentages and ratios used to interpret information in financial statements.
- **Appendix B: Estimating the Value of Inventories** (after Chapter 13) describes the retail and gross profit methods.
- **Appendix C: Modified Accelerated Cost Recovery System of Depreciation** (after Chapter 14) presents definitions of and depreciation schedule for recovery property.
- **Appendix D: Statement of Cash Flows** (after Appendix C) briefly describes the indirect method of determining cash flows.

Characteristics of *Contemporary College Accounting*

Focus on the Fundamentals

Contemporary College Accounting presents the fundamentals of accounting in a practical, easy-to-understand manner that students will appreciate. Great stress is placed on developing a firm foundation of fundamental procedures. Appropriate repetition enables students to develop confidence in themselves and to make progress in manageable stages. This repetition is accomplished through extensive use of examples, illustrations, and photographs.

Recording business transactions is directly related to the fundamental accounting equation. Each newly introduced transaction is fully illustrated and is supported with T account examples. Comprehensive reviews of T accounts, organized in relation to the fundamental accounting equation, appear in the Working Papers to assist students as they review material and as they complete their assignments.

Reading Comprehension

Contemporary College Accounting is a very readable text. Using a direct approach, the authors write in short sentences that are supported by many illustrations and photographs to help students understand the discussion. Each chapter is well illustrated with business documents and report forms. As terms are introduced, they are defined thoroughly and are used in subsequent examples. Comprehension is also enhanced through the use of "Remember" and "FYI" notes. These short, marginal notations present a learning hint, a capsule summary, or a real-world example of a major point made in preceding paragraphs. End-of-chapter summaries review each learning objective presented in the chapter.

Terminology

The authors firmly believe that accounting is the language of business and that learning new terminology is an essential part of a first course. Each key term is printed in bold print and is explained when it is first introduced. The end-of-chapter glossary repeats the definitions of the terms presented in the chapter. In addition, page numbers are included for each glossary term, making it easy for students to refer to a term in the chapter.

Traditional and Innovative Questions, Exercises, and Problems

Contemporary College Accounting provides a wealth of exercise and problem material that is supported by the Working Papers, offering instructors a wide choice for classroom illustrations and assignments. Each chapter ends with a comprehensive review and study material consisting of a review of performance objectives, a glossary, eight discussion questions, eight exercises, three special critical thinking and communication questions, two sets of A and B problems, and a Challenge Problem.

- **Discussion Questions** Eight questions, based on the main points in the text, are included at the end of each chapter.
- **Classroom Exercises** For practice in applying concepts, eight exercises are provided with each chapter. Each exercise is described briefly in the margin. Exercises are also referenced in the margins of the Instructor's Annotated Edition.

- **Consider and Communicate** Each chapter contains a question that requires students to think about the concepts presented in the chapter. They are asked to explain and apply what they have learned, whether verbally or in writing.
- **What If . . .** Each chapter describes a situation in an accounting office that needs to be addressed. Students are required to write or discuss their opinions about how the situation should be handled.
- **A Question of Ethics** Each chapter describes an ethical situation that students must analyze. Students are asked to either discuss or write their reactions to the scenario and to form a judgment about the ethicality of the behavior or conduct described.
- **Problems** Each chapter contains four A problems and four B problems. The A and B problems are parallel in content and level of difficulty. They are arranged in order of difficulty, with Problems 1A and 1B in each chapter being the simplest and the last problem in each series being the most comprehensive.
- **Challenge Problems** Each chapter also contains a problem that requires a higher level of problem-solving skills.
- **Computer-based Assignments** Students may solve selected assignments by using a microcomputer and accompanying General Ledger and Spreadsheet software.

A Visual Approach to Understanding Transactions

The authors, in conjunction with Houghton Mifflin Company, have implemented a color-coded pedagogy that will hopefully help students recognize and remember key points. The pedagogical use of color also helps students to understand the flow of accounting data and recognize different types of documents and reports used in accounting. Finally, the use of color in this text will help students to identify the performance objective for each chapter, recognize the performance objectives called for in each exercise and problem, and review material efficiently and effectively.

Contemporary College Accounting consistently uses color in the treatment of accounting forms, financial statements, and documents in the text and end-of-chapter assignments.

- **Working papers, journals, ledgers, trial balances, and other forms and schedules** used as part of the internal accounting process are shown in light blue.
- **Financial statements,** including balance sheets, income statements, and statements of owner's equity, are shown in a darker shade of blue.
- **Source documents,** such as invoices, bank statement, facsimilies, and other material that originates with outside sources, are shown in gray.

This distinctive treatment differentiates these elements and helps students to see where each element belongs in the accounting cycle. Seeing these relationships helps students understand how accountants transform data into useful information.

Quality Control

The authors and the publisher of *Contemporary College Accounting* have taken a multi-step approach to ensure quality materials for classroom use. The quality control system begins with in-depth reviews of the original manuscript and concludes with accuracy reviews of page proof provided by instructors who are actively teaching the course.

Special Features

- **Practitioner's Corner**
  Accounting Practitioners, who also teach, share actual situations they have encountered in practice.
- **Extended Examples**
  Clark's Cleaners is used throughout Chapters 1 through 4 to illustrate the completion of the accounting cycle for a sole-proprietorship service business.

  Dodson Plumbing Supply is used throughout Chapters 5 through 7 to illustrate the completion of the accounting cycle, using special journals, for a sole-proprietorship merchandising business.

  Dodson Plumbing Supply is reintroduced at appropriate points in Chapters 11 through 14.
- **Accounting Cycle Review Problems**
  The review problem following Chapter 4 involves the full accounting cycle for Sun Spot Waterslides, a sole proprietorship service business. The review problem following Chapter 7 involves the full accounting cycle for Boyle Electronics, a sole proprietorship merchandising business.
- **Reviews of T Account Placement and Representative Transactions**
  Simple charts covering the accounts presented in Chapters 1-4, 5-7, 8-10, and 11-14 organize this crucial information for students. The charts are in the front of the Working Papers for handy reference when students complete their assignments. They are also found in the Instructor's Resource Manual with Solutions.
- **Computers at Work**
  Microcomputers have brought major changes to the work environment in which today's graduates are expected to function. The *Computers at Work* boxes offer instructors a springboard for explaining the impact of these changes to students. The boxed inserts are extracts from recent issues of *PC Novice* and *PC Today*, two popular and "user friendly" periodicals that inform readers about the latest technological advances in both hardware and software. Topics have been specially selected for their relevance to accounting in business.
- **Photographs**
  Each chapter contains photographs that expand and highlight chapter content and illustrate the world of business and technology.
- **Icons**
  End-of-chapter assignments have been coded with icons to indicate special features:

  Problems that can be solved using the General Ledger Program or Spread Sheet templates include these icons in the margin.

 Questions that involve critical thinking have been coded with a puzzle piece icon, to emphasize the importance of understanding how specific accounting procedures relate to the accounting process as a whole.

 Another important skill for today's students is the ability to communicate, whether verbally, within groups, or in writing. Assignments that can be used to help students practice and hone these skills have been coded with these icons in the margin.

Because many of the end-of-chapter assignments are multi-purpose, they are usually coded with more than one icon. The arrangement of the icons from left to right indicates the degree to which each question helps to develop a particular skill, with the first icon indicating the primary purpose of the question.

Supplementary Learning Aids for Students

For *Contemporary College Accounting*, we have assembled a most comprehensive package of student and instructor aids to complement a wide variety of teaching styles and course emphases.

Working Papers

The Working Papers include the performance objectives for each chapter, lists of key terms, study guide questions, an extended demonstration problem and solution for each chapter (which are reproduced in the Instructor's Resource Manual), forms for A and B problems and for the Review Problems following chapters 4 and 7, answers to study guide questions, a list of check figures, and additional blank working-paper forms. A Comprehensive Review Problem, to be completed after Chapter 14 is covered, involves end-of-period entries for Bell Draperies—notes receivable, notes payable, and valuation of receivables, inventories, and plant assets. Included in the Working Papers is a review of business mathematics, charts reviewing T Account placement and representative transactions, a 10-key calculator review, spreadsheet basics, tips on how to study accounting, how to solve accounting problems, and how to complete a practice set.

Practice Sets

A complete array of manual and computerized practice sets are available for use with this text. They are listed below with the appropriate chapters. Complete descriptions are found in the Instructor's Resource Manual with Solutions.

After Chapter 3   *Sailsports*

After Chapter 7   *Sounds Abound*, Second Edition

After Chapter 10   *The Book Loft*
May's Pet Center
The Oak Shoppe

After Chapter 14   *Carts Plus*

Software for Accounting

General Ledger Software

An easy-to-use general ledger package offers complete coverage of accounting concepts and procedures. Selected problems from *Contemporary College Accounting* can be completed with this package. An icon in the margin identifies these problems in text; instructions for working the problems with this software appear with the problem, making it easier for students to organize their work.

Contemporary College Accounting
Spreadsheet Templates

These templates allow students to solve end-of-chaper problems using Lotus® 1-2-3® or Microsoft® Excel spreadsheet software. An icon in the margin identifies problems in each chapter that can be done using either software.

Acknowledgments

We would sincerely like to thank the editorial staff of Houghton Mifflin for their continuous support. We thank our many students at Highline Community College and Wenatchee Valley College for their observations and evaluations. We also thank Suzanne M. Williamson, C.P.A., Olympic College, Ann Dawson, C.P.A., Seattle University, and Nancy Hansen, C.P.A., Highline Community College, for their contributions to special features, especially the Practitioner's Corner. The cooperation of Professors Audrey Chan-Nui and Geneva Knutson has also been most helpful.

During the writing of this text, we were greatly benefited by the suggestions and comments of academic reviewers throughout the country. We would also like to give a special note of thanks to the individuals who contributed by reviewing page proof and checking the end-of-chapter questions, exercises, and problems.

Anthony R. Carbone, Massachusetts Bay Community College
Sherrie Dusch, Barnes Business College
David Evans, Johnson County Community College
Judith Gaffney, Technical Career Institutes
Walter L. Griffin, Blinn College
James A. Hagan, Asheville-Buncombe Technical Community College
John Hartwick, Bucks County Community College
Jay S. Hallowell, Commonwealth College
Jane Howard, Barton County Community College
Gordon Linder, Prince George's Community College
Patricia P. McDaniel, Central Piedmont Community College
Patty Ann Michaelis, Northwest State Community College
Linda Scott, Indiana Vocational Technical College
William Serafin, Community College of Allegheny County—South Campus
Steven C. Teeter, Utah Valley State College
Cynthia Tomes, Des Moines Area Community College
Brad Tretten, Truckee Meadow Community College
Stan Weikert, College of the Canyons

As always, we would like to thank our families for their understanding and cooperation. Without their support, this text would never have been written. Love and gratitude to Bruce and Tracy Bille and Adeline Harris for their encouragement and assistance; to Deborah Boyle and Richard Lees for their dedication to task, loyalty, and laughter; and to the memory of Ryan Bille and Wesley Harris for their courage and inspiration. Heartfelt appreciation is extended to Beverlie McQuaig for her detailed proofreading and good humor. Pertinent suggestions for improving the material were given by Judith McQuaig Britton, C.P.A., of Smith, Bunday, Berman, and Briton, and John McQuaig, C.P.A., of McQuaig and Welk.

Patricia A. Bille
Douglas J. McQuaig

Dedication

This text is sincerely dedicated to the students who will use it. Every possible effort has been made to produce an understandable, up-to-date, and accurate presentation of the fundamentals of accounting. This text is intended to be an important element in your course, as well as an invaluable future reference for you in the preparation for your career in business.

Best wishes for your success.

Patricia A. Bille
Douglas J. McQuaig

chapter 1

Analyzing Business Transactions: Assets, Liabilities, Owner's Equity, Revenue and Expense Accounts, and Financial Statements

PERFORMANCE OBJECTIVES

After you have completed this chapter, you will be able to do the following:

1. Define accounting.

2. Record a group of business transactions, involving all five elements of the fundamental accounting equation, in column form.

3. Prepare an income statement.

4. Prepare a statement of owner's equity.

5. Prepare a balance sheet.

As a CPA in public accounting, I prepare financial statements for clients. Before I can release the statements to the client (to show to a bank's loan officer or to a potential buyer of the business), the statements must meet criteria set by the profession.

The headings of the statements must be accurate (name of company, title of the statement, date or period of time covered). The appearance must be neat and orderly. The statements need to "foot" or balance. The amounts in the statements must tie to, or equal, amounts shown in the accounting records. For example, the amount shown on the statement for cash must be the same amount shown in the Cash account. In other words, the statements must be accurate, reflecting the true financial activity of the company.

Without accurate financial statements, supported by accurate records, neither the client nor I am able to interpret the information necessary to make sound business decisions. As a practitioner, it is my goal to point out strengths and weaknesses for my clients to help make their businesses more efficient and profitable.

Definition of Accounting

Accounting is a process of analyzing, classifying, recording, summarizing, and interpreting business transactions in financial terms. A business **transaction** is an event that has a direct effect on the operation of an economic unit and has been expressed in terms of money. Examples of business transactions are buying and selling goods, renting a building, paying employees, and buying insurance. An **economic unit** includes not only business enterprises (companies or firms), but also nonprofit entities such as government bodies, churches, clubs, and fraternal organizations.

Accounting is an information system that measures financial activities. The information is processed and reported to decision-makers. Decision-makers act on the information and send new information for processing and reporting as the needs of the business demand. The cycle takes place over and over again to provide the best chance for success of an economic unit.

Accounting is the language of business that translates and communicates information about economic changes to users. As with any language, there is often more than one way to say something. You should begin now to develop your ability to be flexible as you see alternative words or forms used to accomplish the same results.

Performance Objective 1

Define accounting.

3

Fra Luca Pacioli is considered the father of double-entry accounting.

History of Accounting

Around 3000 B.C., peoples of the Middle East developed the first known business records—of farm production, taxes, and the exchange of goods. After A.D. 1200, the decimal numbering system aided those keeping records. It is believed that the Italians invented **double-entry accounting.** Not until 1494, however, did Fra Luca Pacioli, a Renaissance Franciscan monk and mathematician, include double-entry accounting in his book *Summa Arithmetica.* Pacioli formalized a system that is now the cornerstone of accounting. The system is called double-entry accounting because of the dual nature of the entries. Each entry into the system has at least two parts and these parts are equal and offsetting, as a result of which the system always stays in balance. **Single-entry accounting,** on the other hand, does not include the complete results of a transaction and thus is not considered an accounting system.

Bookkeeping and Accounting

The people who are involved in the process of accounting are broadly divided into bookkeepers and accountants, but their duties often overlap. Generally, **bookkeepers** are involved with the analyzing, classifying, and recording portions of the process, while **accountants** are primarily involved with the summarizing and interpreting portions of the process. An accountant sets up the system that a bookkeeper uses to record business transactions, supervises the bookkeeper, prepares financial statements and tax reports, and performs audit work. Although the work of the bookkeeper is more routine, it is sometimes hard to find the spot where the bookkeeper's work ends and the accountant's work begins. In any case, both the bookkeeper and accountant should understand the entire accounting system, exercise judgment in recording financial details, and organize and report the appropriate information.

Career Opportunities in Accounting

Newspaper classified advertisements are a starting point for familiarizing yourself with the variety of related accounting jobs that are available in your area, their requirements, and the wages and salaries offered. These jobs require varying amounts of education and experience. Computer skills are commonly required. You will see positions as accounting clerks, bookkeepers, or accountants offered. Let's take a look at the requirements and duties of several common accounting positions.

Accounting Clerk

An accounting clerk does routine recording of financial information either manually or by computer. The clerk's duties will vary with the size of the business. In small businesses, accounting clerks handle most of the record-keeping functions. In large businesses, clerks may specialize in one part of the accounting system, such as payroll, accounts receivable, or accounts payable. A minimum requirement for a position as an accounting clerk is one term of an accounting course.

General Bookkeeper

Many small- and medium-sized companies employ one person to oversee their bookkeeping operations. This person is called a general or full-charge bookkeeper. The general bookkeeper supervises the work of accounting clerks. Requirements for this job vary with the size of the company and the complexity of the accounting system. A minimum requirement for a general bookkeeper is one or two years of accounting education as well as experience as an accounting clerk.

Para-accountant

Para-accountants perform routine functions involving bookkeeping, taxation, and auditing while working directly under the supervision of a certified public accountant. They also may assist small business clients to set up their bookkeeping systems. A para-accountant would be required to have one to two years of accounting education and extensive experience in bookkeeping.

Accountant

The term *accountant* includes a broad range of tasks. The accountant may design and manage the entire accounting system for a business. The accountant may prepare the financial statements and tax returns. Accountants are employed in every kind of economic unit. Whatever their tasks may be, their

FYI

The want ads of newspapers cover only 7–8 percent of all jobs currently available. Effective job searches involve a proactive approach using many avenues besides newspaper ads.

work can be divided into three categories. The first category describes the certified public accountant, but CPAs are not limited to public accounting. They may also be employed in managerial or private accounting as well as not-for-profit accounting.

Public Accounting

Certified Public Accountants (CPAs) are at the top of their profession. To reach this high professional status, they must obtain at least a four-year college degree with accounting emphasis. CPAs must pass a rigorous, comprehensive four-part exam. This uniform, nationwide test includes sections on accounting practice, accounting theory, audit, and business law. Each State Board of Accountancy administers the CPA exam. Other requirements for certification may include an ethics exam and auditing experience.

Managerial or Private Accounting

Accountants who work for private business firms manage the accounting system, prepare budgets, determine costs of products, and provide financial information for managers and owners. Because of the importance of accounting, there are opportunities for accountants to advance into top management positions.

Not-for-Profit Accounting

Not-for-profit accounting procedures are used for government agencies, hospitals, religious institutions, and schools. Accountants in these organizations prepare budgets and maintain records of revenues and expenses to comply with the budget. Some not-for-profit organizations do make a profit; however, the profit is kept in the organization and is not distributed.

Rules for the Profession

You will not be surprised that with the level of responsibility required of those in the accounting profession, accountants' work is strictly monitored and there are many rules that the profession must follow. These rules and guidelines, which describe how the accounting process should be carried out, are known as **generally accepted accounting principles (GAAP).** To keep up with changes in the rules, CPAs are required to take Continuing Professional Education (CPE) credits to renew their licenses and maintain up-to-date practices.

The Financial Accounting Standards Board (FASB) is primarily responsible for developing and issuing rules and standards for the profession. Other groups that influence generally accepted accounting principles are shown at the top of the next page.

American Institute of Certified Public Accountants (AICPA)

Securities and Exchange Commission (SEC)

Internal Revenue Service (IRS)

Government Accounting Standards Board (GASB)

Users of Accounting Information

The following groups rely heavily on accounting information:

Owners Owners invest their money in a business. They require information about how much the business earns and spends. They need to know if they can pay their bills, and they must forecast the outcome of their business decisions.

Managers Managers supervise the operations of the business and make decisions that affect the future of the business.

Creditors Creditors lend money or extend credit to a company for the purchase of goods and services. They are interested in the company's ability to pay its debts.

Government agencies Regulatory agencies look at many kinds of accounting records and information relating to such areas as income taxes, sales taxes, and employment taxes.

The Fundamental Accounting Equation

Assets, Liabilities, and Owner's Equity

Double-entry accounting requires at least two equal and offsetting entries to keep the system in balance. The system is demonstrated by the **fundamental accounting equation.** This equation shows the relationship of assets, liabilities, and owner's equity.

Assets = Liabilities + Owner's Equity

Assets are properties or things of value—such as cash, equipment, buildings, and land—owned by an economic unit or business entity. A **business entity** (company or firm) is considered separate and distinct from the persons who supply the assets it uses. The owner's claim against the assets is called the **owner's equity** or investment.

You often hear the term **equity** used when a person wants to sell the ownership right to an asset such as a house or a car. Other terms that may be used include **capital,** *net worth*, or *proprietorship*.

Assets	=	Owner's Equity
Properties or things of value owned by the business		Owner's right to or investment in the business

Consider the following situations:

1. If a business has $10,000 worth of assets, and the business does not owe any amount against the assets, then

    Assets = Owner's Equity

    $10,000 = $10,000

2. Suppose that the assets consist of a truck that costs $18,000, of which the owner paid $12,000 down and borrowed $6,000 from a bank. In this case, the bank is called a **creditor** (one to whom money is owed). This can be shown as follows:

Assets	=	**Liabilities**	+	**Owner's Equity**
Items owned		Amounts owed		Owner's
Truck		to creditors		investment
$18,000	=	$6,000	+	$12,000

We have now introduced a new classification, **liabilities,** which represents debts and includes the amounts that the business entity owes to its creditors or the amount by which it is liable to its creditors.

Practice with the Equation

a. What is the amount of the assets?

    Assets = Liabilities + Owner's Equity   Solution: $ 6,000
       ? = $6,000 + $4,000   +4,000
             (L + OE = A) $10,000

b. What is the amount of the liabilities?

    Assets = Liabilities + Owner's Equity   Solution: $15,000
    $15,000 =   ?   + $8,000   −8,000
            (A − OE = L) $ 7,000

c. What is the amount of the owner's equity?

    Assets = Liabilities + Owner's Equity   Solution: $20,000
    $20,000 = $4,000   +   ?   −4,000
            (A − L = OE) $16,000

You have probably concluded by now that if you know two parts of the equation, you can compute the third part. It is important that you understand the relationship of these equation classifications. These classifications and their relationship will be the foundation of your accounting work.

Opening a New Business

Planning

Now that you have had some practice working with the fundamental accounting equation, it is time to place it in a business context. The business you will be following throughout the next three chapters is Clark's Cleaners. Neil Clark has been the manager of another cleaning business and has researched owning his own business. From his research, Clark prepared a business plan, using his personal computer (hardware) and a spreadsheet (software). **Hardware** is the computer equipment—the monitor or screen, the keyboard, the printer, and so forth. **Software**—in this case a spreadsheet—contains the instructions or programs that tell the computer to do certain tasks. The spreadsheet allows Neil to test different financial choices or "what ifs" before putting his decisions into effect. For example, what if he charges one amount to clean a suit coat instead of another amount? What if his rent is one amount or a higher amount? The computer software quickly recomputes the results of these changes. Neil can compare the results of one decision against another. Keep in mind that the decision may still be incorrect, but the spreadsheet software will allow many situations to be considered before a decision is made. It is thus possible to test corrective measures if the decision has not worked out satisfactorily.

Selecting the Business Form

Neil learned from his CPA that there are several different business forms:

Sole proprietorship   one owner contributes all resources and carries the burden of taxes and liability

Partnership   two or more owners contribute resources, providing tax benefits and organizational flexibility

Corporation   a number of owners buy stock in a business recognized by the state as a legal entity or artificial person, providing limited liability for the owners

Limited liability corporation   a hybrid entity that combines the tax benefits and organizational flexibility of a partnership with the liability-limiting characteristics of a corporation

Neil has decided that his business will be a sole proprietorship. Clark's Cleaners is the name of the new business. On the advice of his CPA, Neil has separated his personal holdings from those of the business. He has therefore opened a separate checking account for the business. This account is used exclusively for the business deposits and expenditures. In other words, the business is a distinct economic or accounting entity, separate from other businesses and from Clark's personal financial activities. This is known as the **separate entity concept.**

Neil intends that Clark's Cleaners will continue as an ongoing business. He has met the requirements of the accounting concept called the **going concern concept.**

Clark's Cleaners is a service business, not one that sells merchandise. The purpose of the new business is to clean fabric items, primarily clothing, but also draperies and other materials that require dry cleaning. Customers will pay for these services when they pick up the cleaned items.

FYI

Limited Liability Companies as a form of practice are being considered by states to provide an alternative form of business. This form of business is good for professionals who want to practice without risking personal liability.

Built to Last: Constructing a Solid Business Plan

The Eiffel Tower in Paris was quite an undertaking when Alexandre Gustave Eiffel began building it in the late 1800s. He formed almost 7,000 tons of iron into a gigantic tower 984 feet high. Needless to say, Eiffel must have spent many hours developing blueprints for his tower.

Starting a business can be a pretty momentous undertaking as well. You have to develop a product or service, get funding, market the business, and possibly hire employees. But no matter if your business entails aerospace consulting from a one-person office or word processing on your home PC, you also need to create a blueprint for your business—a business plan.

Without a plan that outlines objectives, strategies, operating procedures, growth, and financial forecasts, a business can easily fall victim to poor foresight or bad decisions. . . .

Simply stated, a business plan describes the concept behind the business, sets objectives, defines the market and the competition, documents development and production, and projects revenues, expenses, and the capital required. . . .

Planning with your PC. A number of software publishers offer programs to aid in the creation of business plans. . . . The majority of programs combine word processing features for you to input your textual information and spreadsheet features for you to input your numerical information. Most also have charting capabilities to illustrate your plan. . . . But keep in mind that your plan will only be as good as the ideas and information you put in it. Your ideas, your research, and your hard work are what will define your success.

Source: Excerpted from Cindy Krushenisky, "Built to Last: Constructing a Solid Business Plan," *PC Novice,* August 1994, pp. 68–71.

Constructing the Chart of Accounts

Neil's CPA helped him compile an official list of account titles called the **chart of accounts. Accounts** are the categories within the classifications of the fundamental accounting equation. The **account numbers** have been assigned to identify the accounts. The CPA has left room in the sequence of numbers to add new accounts as the business grows.

Each company develops its own chart of accounts to meet its individual needs. Rarely are two companies' chart of accounts identical. Usually, you will see assets beginning with a 1, liabilities with a 2, capital accounts with a 3, and revenue accounts with a 4. In a service business, such as Clark's Cleaners, expenses begin with a 5. Later you will see some variation in numbering, as well as higher numbers, depending on the type of company (service or merchandise), the preference of the designer of the system, or the way the software is organized.

Chart of Accounts

ASSETS	REVENUE
111 Cash	411 Income from Services
113 Accounts Receivable	
115 Supplies	EXPENSES
117 Prepaid Insurance	515 Advertising Expense
124 Equipment	521 Wages Expense
	524 Rent Expense
LIABILITIES	525 Utilities Expense
221 Accounts Payable	

OWNER'S EQUITY
311 N. L. Clark, Capital

Source Documents

Recall that the process of accounting begins by analyzing, classifying, and recording transactions. Transactions are recorded from **source documents.** Examples of source documents are checks, deposit slips, sales invoices, and purchase invoices.

R E M E M B E R
A source document is the evidence of a transaction.

Recording Business Transactions

As you record business transactions, you have to change the amounts listed under the headings Asset, Liabilities, and Owner's Equity. The total of one side of the equation must equal the total of the other side of the equation. You can think of the equation as a seesaw. If you add or subtract an amount on one side, you have to either add or subtract an equal amount on the other side or add or subtract an equal amount on the same side.

Performance Objective 2
Record a group of business transactions, involving all five elements of the fundamental accounting equation, in column form.

Analysis of a Transaction

Analyze each transaction by answering the following questions. Think of the word

ACID

to help you remember the four steps in analyzing a transaction.

A What *accounts* are involved?

C What are the *classifications* of the accounts involved?

I   Are the accounts *increased*?

D Are the accounts *decreased*?

The equation must be in balance after every transaction.

We will now look at a group of source documents and the resulting transactions. These transactions will illustrate common transactions seen in a service business. Clark's Cleaners is a **sole proprietorship,** or one-owner business. Each transaction is described, analyzed step by step, and illustrated. The first five transactions are accompanied by illustrations of source documents to emphasize that accounting transactions are generated by source documents. Study the source documents and ask yourself the questions listed above (ACID) for every transaction.

Transaction (a)   Owner invests cash in the business. N. L. Clark invests $40,000 cash in his new business. The source document is shown in Figure 1-1.

Figure 1-1

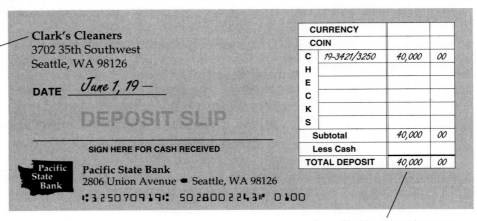

New business account

From Clark's personal account

Transaction (a) Analysis

A Accounts involved?   Cash and N. L. Clark, Capital

C Classifications involved?   Cash = Asset
                                   Capital = Owner's Equity

I   Account(s) increased?   Cash
                                   Capital

D Account(s) decreased?   none

Assets	=	Liabilities	+	Owner's Equity
Items owned	=	Amounts owed to creditors	+	Owner's investment
Cash	=			N. L. Clark, Capital
(a) +40,000	=			+40,000

An equal amount has been added to each side of the equation—it is in balance. Clark has no creditors, so his investment or claim on the assets is equal to the amount of the assets. This is the opening entry in the business's financial records. The account identified by the owner's name, followed by the word *Capital*, is used to record the amount of the owner's investment, or equity, in the business.

Transaction (b) **Company buys equipment paying cash.** To get ready to open, Clark's Cleaners buys equipment costing $22,000 from Drake Equipment Company and pays cash. The source document is shown in Figure 1-2.

Figure 1-2

DRAKE EQUIPMENT COMPANY
3006 Rogers Street • Seattle, WA • 98919

Invoice No. 289

INVOICE

Sold to: Clark's Cleaners
3702 35th Southwest
Seattle, WA 98126

Shipped to: Same

Customer's Order Number	Salesperson	Terms	F.O.B.	Date
2467C	*bb*	cash		June 1, 19—

Quantity	Description	Unit Price	Total
1	Model Z82 circular racks	3,285.38	3,285.38
4	Model 1184 tanks-automatic	3,183.00	12,732.00
1	Model 614 folder	4,935.00	4,935.00
	Subtotal		20,952.38
	Sales tax 5%		1,047.62
	Total		22,000.00

Transaction (b) Analysis

A Accounts involved?	Equipment and Cash
C Classifications involved?	Equipment = Asset Cash = Asset
I Account(s) increased?	Equipment
D Account(s) decreased?	Cash

Assets		= Liabilities	+ Owner's Equity
Items owned		= Amounts owed to creditors	+ Owner's investment
Cash + Equipment	=		N. L. Clark, Capital
(a) +40,000		=	+40,000
(b) −22,000	+22,000		
Bal. 18,000 +	22,000	=	40,000
40,000			40,000

Clark's Cleaners has exchanged one asset for another asset. The equation stayed in balance even though changes involved only one side of the equation. The two parts of the activity were equal and offsetting. The $22,000 price, which includes the sales tax that is part of the asset's cost, is known as the asset's **historical cost,** or the original cost of the asset at the time it is acquired.

Transaction (c) Company buys equipment on credit. Clark's Cleaners buys equipment on credit (on account) from Drake Equipment Company, $4,000. The source document is shown in Figure 1-3.

Figure 1-3

DRAKE EQUIPMENT COMPANY
3006 Rogers Street • Seattle, WA • 98919

Invoice No. 373

INVOICE

Sold to: Clark's Cleaners
3702 35th Southwest
Seattle, WA 98126

Shipped to: Same

Customer's Order Number	Salesperson	Terms	F.O.B.	Date
2468C	bb	net 30		June 2, 19—

Quantity	Description	Unit Price	Total
1	Model 3214 drapery ribber	3,809.52	3,809.52
		Sales tax 5%	190.48
		Total	4,000.00

Transaction (c) Analysis

A Accounts involved?   Equipment and Accounts Payable

C Classifications involved?   Equipment = Asset
                               Accounts Payable = Liability

I Account(s) increased?   Equipment
                               Accounts Payable

D Account(s) decreased?   None

Assets	=	Liabilities	+	Owner's Equity
Items owned	=	Amounts owed to creditors	+	Owner's investment
Cash + Equip.	=	Accounts Payable	+	N. L. Clark, Capital
PB 18,000 + 22,000 =				40,000
(c) + 4,000		+4,000		
NB 18,000 + 26,000 =		4,000	+	40,000
44,000			44,000	

The only difference between this transaction and transaction **(b)** is that Clark's Cleaners charged the equipment, promising to pay at a later date. The liability account, called **Accounts Payable,** is used for short-term liabilities or charge accounts, usually due in twenty-five to thirty days. Notice that we use PB to identify the previous balance and NB to identify the new balance (after the transaction has occurred).

Transaction (d) Company pays a creditor on account. Clark's Cleaners pays $1,000 to Drake Equipment Company to be applied against the firm's liability of $4,000. The source document is shown in Figure 1-4.

Figure 1-4

Clark's Cleaners
3702 35th Southwest
Seattle, WA 98126

NO. 100
19-7091/0100

June 4 19 ___

PAY TO THE ORDER OF *Drake Equipment Company* $ *1,000.00*

One thousand and no/100 DOLLARS

Pacific State Bank
2806 Union Avenue ▪ Seattle, WA 98126

For *Inv. #373 to apply on account* *Neil L. Clark*

Transaction (d) Analysis

A Accounts involved?	Cash and Accounts Payable
C Classifications involved?	Cash = Asset Accounts Payable = Liability
I Account(s) increased?	None
D Account(s) decreased?	Cash Accounts Payable

	Assets	= Liabilities	+	Owner's Equity
	Items owned	= Amounts owed to creditors	+	Owner's investment
	Cash + Equip.	= Accounts Payable	+	N. L. Clark, Capital
PB	18,000 + 26,000	= 4,000	+	40,000
(d)	− 1,000	−1,000		
NB	17,000 + 26,000	= 3,000	+	40,000
	43,000		43,000	

Clark paid part of the amount charged for equipment in transaction **(c)**.

Transaction (e)   Company buys supplies on credit. Clark's Cleaners buys cleaning fluid and garment bags on account from Blair and Company for $400. Cleaning fluid and garment bags are listed under Supplies instead of Equipment because these items are used up in a relatively short time. Equipment, on the other hand, normally lasts a number of years.

The source document, a purchase invoice, would be similar to the one shown with transaction **(b)**, except that Clark is buying supplies on account instead of equipment on account.

Transaction (e) Analysis

A Accounts involved?	Supplies and Accounts Payable
C Classifications involved?	Supplies = Asset Accounts Payable = Liability
I Account(s) increased?	Supplies Accounts Payable
D Account(s) decreased?	None

	Assets	= Liabilities	+	Owner's Equity
	Items owned	= Amounts owed to creditors	+	Owner's investment
	Cash + Equip. + Supplies	= Accounts Payable	+	N. L. Clark, Capital
PB	17,000 + 26,000	= 3,000	+	40,000
(e)	+400	+400		
NB	17,000 + 26,000 + 400	= 3,400	+	40,000
	43,400		43,400	

At a job interview, be prepared to discuss your experience, your skills, and how you work individually as well as with others.

This transaction is similar to the purchase of equipment on account, except Clark bought cleaning supplies on account.

Two important conclusions can be drawn from transactions **(a)–(e):**

1. Each transaction is analyzed in terms of increases or decreases in at least two accounts.

2. The equation remains in balance after each transaction.

Summary of Transactions

At this point, let us look back over the transactions we have recorded. To test your understanding of the recording procedure, describe what has taken place in each transaction.

	Assets			=	Liabilities	+	Owner's Equity
	Cash	+ Equip.	+ Supp.	=	Accounts Payable	+	N. L. Clark, Capital
(a)	+40,000			=			+40,000
(b)	−22,000	+ 22,000					
Bal.	18,000	+ 22,000		=			40,000
(c)		+4,000			+4,000		
Bal.	18,000	+ 26,000		=	4,000	+	40,000
(d)	−1,000				−1,000		
Bal.	17,000	+ 26,000		=	3,000	+	40,000
(e)			+400		+400		
Bal.	17,000	+ 26,000	+ 400	=	3,400	+	40,000
		43,400				43,400	

Recording these transactions serves as an introduction to double-entry accounting for assets, liabilities, and owner's equity. The "double" element is demonstrated by the fact that each transaction must be recorded in at least two accounts, and the accounting equation must be kept in balance.

Revenue and Expense Accounts

Clark's Cleaners is in business to make money—furthermore to make more money than it spends. **Revenue** is the amount earned by a business. Examples of revenue are fees earned for performing services, income from selling merchandise, rent income for providing the use of property, and interest income for lending money. Revenue may take the form of cash, checks, and credit card receipts, like those from VISA and MasterCard. Revenue may also result from credit sales to charge customers.

Expenses are the costs that relate to the earning of revenue (or the costs of doing business). Examples of expenses are wages expense for labor performed, rent expense for the use of property, interest expense for the use of money, and advertising expense for the use of various media. Expenses may be paid in cash when incurred (that is, immediately) or at a later time. If an expense is to be paid at a later time, the amount is classified as a liability.

Revenue and expenses directly affect owner's equity. If a business earns revenue, there is an increase in owner's equity. If a business incurs or pays an expense, there is a decrease in owner's equity. Consequently, we place revenue and expenses under the heading of owner's equity.

R E M E M B E R

The fundamental accounting equation is still $A = L + OE$. Revenue and expenses expand the equation to record increases and decreases to owner's equity separate from the capital account.

Chart of Accounts

With the introduction of revenue and expenses, we now have five basic classifications of accounts. Using these classifications, we can present the full chart of accounts for Clark's Cleaners, a service business. In the numbering of account titles, the 100s are used for assets, the 200s are used for liabilities, the 300s are used for owner's equity accounts, the 400s are used for revenue accounts, and the 500s are used for expense accounts.

R E M E M B E R

New accounts and account numbers may be added as needed. A chart of accounts should have elasticity or available numbers within each category.

Chart of Accounts

Clark's Cleaners

ASSETS	OWNER'S EQUITY
111 Cash	311 N. L. Clark, Capital
113 Accounts Receivable	REVENUE (INCREASE IN OWNER'S EQUITY)
115 Supplies	411 Income from Services
117 Prepaid Insurance	
124 Equipment	EXPENSES (DECREASE IN OWNER'S EQUITY)
	515 Advertising Expense
LIABILITIES	521 Wages Expense
221 Accounts Payable	524 Rent Expense
	525 Utilities Expense

The chart of accounts is custom-made to fit the company and represents the framework in which all of a company's transactions must be recorded using the exact account titles.

Transaction (f)   Company pays an expense in cash. Clark's Cleaners pays the month's rent of $500.

Transaction (f) Analysis

A Accounts involved?	Cash and Rent Expense
C Classifications involved?	Cash = Asset Rent Expense = Expense
I Account(s) increased?	Rent Expense
D Account(s) decreased?	Cash

	Assets			=	Liabilities	+		Owner's Equity		
	Cash + Equip. + Supp.			=	Accounts Payable	+	N. L. Clark, Capital	+ Revenue	− Expenses	
PB	17,000 + 26,000 +	400	=		3,400	+	40,000			
(f)	− 500								+500 (Rent)	
NB	16,500 + 26,000 +	400	=		3,400	+	40,000		− 500	
		42,900						42,900		

Clark's Cleaners incurred rent expense and paid for it.

It seems logical that if we add revenue to owner's equity, then an expense (the opposite of revenue) should be subtracted from owner's equity. We want to have a running total of the amount of expenses to be subtracted from owner's equity. To keep this running total, as each new expense is incurred (or comes into existence), it must be added to the previous total.

Transaction (g)   Company pays for insurance. Clark's Cleaners pays $360 for a one-year liability insurance policy. As it expires, the insurance will become an expense. However, because it is paid in advance for a period longer than one month, it has value and is therefore recorded as an asset called Prepaid Insurance.

Transaction (g) Analysis

A Accounts involved?	Cash and Prepaid Insurance
C Classifications involved?	Cash = Asset Prepaid Insurance = Asset
I Account(s) increased?	Prepaid Insurance
D Account(s) decreased?	Cash

Assets				=	Liabilities	+	Owner's Equity		
Cash +	Equip. +	Supp. +	Ppd. Ins.	=	Accounts Payable	+	N. L. Clark, Capital	+ Revenue	− Expenses
PB 16,500 +	26,000 +	400		=	3,400	+	40,000		− 500
(g) −360			+360						
NB 16,140 +	26,000 +	400 +	360	=	3,400	+	40,000		− 500
	42,900						42,900		

Again, one asset is exchanged for another. The amounts offset each other on one side of the equation.

Transaction (h) Company sells services for cash. For services performed, Clark's Cleaners receives $1,940 from cash customers.

Transaction (h) Analysis

<table>
<tr><td>A Accounts involved?</td><td>Cash and Income from Services</td></tr>
<tr><td>C Classifications involved?</td><td>Cash = Asset
Income from Services = Revenue</td></tr>
<tr><td>I Account(s) increased?</td><td>Cash increased
Revenue increased</td></tr>
<tr><td>D Account(s) decreased?</td><td>None</td></tr>
</table>

REMEMBER

When revenue is earned, it is recorded as an increase in owner's equity under the revenue heading and an increase in assets.

Assets				=	Liabilities	+	Owner's Equity		
Cash +	Equip. +	Supp. +	Ppd. Ins.	=	Accounts Payable	+	N. L. Clark, Capital	+ Revenue	− Expenses
PB 16,140 +	26,000 +	400 +	360	=	3,400	+	40,000		− 500
(h) +1,940								+1,940 (Income from Services)	
NB 18,080 +	26,000 +	400 +	360	=	3,400	+	40,000 +	1,940	− 500
	44,840						44,840		

Clark's Cleaners earned revenue for cleaning services and received cash.

Transaction (i) Company receives a bill for an expense. Clark's Cleaners receives a bill from the *City News* for newspaper advertising, $180. Clark's Cleaners has simply received the bill; it has not paid any cash.

Transaction (i) Analysis

<table>
<tr><td>A Accounts involved?</td><td>Accounts Payable and Advertising Expense</td></tr>
<tr><td>C Classifications involved?</td><td>Accounts Payable = Liability
Advertising Expense = Expense</td></tr>
<tr><td>I Account(s) increased?</td><td>Accounts Payable
Advertising Expense</td></tr>
<tr><td>D Account(s) decreased?</td><td>None</td></tr>
</table>

	Assets				=	Liabilities	+	Owner's Equity		
	Cash +	Equip. +	Supp. +	Ppd. Ins.	=	Accounts Payable	+	N. L. Clark, Capital	+ Revenue −	Expenses
PB	18,080 +	26,000 +	400 +	360	=	3,400	+	40,000 +	1,940 −	500
(i)						+180				+180 (Advertising)
NB	18,080 +	26,000 +	400 +	360	=	3,580	+	40,000 +	1,940 −	680
		44,840						44,840		

An expense has been incurred but not yet paid. Therefore, Clark's Cleaners owes the amount (a liability) and increases expenses. We can record an expense even though we didn't pay for it at the time because we are using the **accrual basis of accounting.** Expenses are recorded when they are incurred. An expense is incurred when a company becomes responsible for paying the expense. Also, under the accrual basis, revenue is recorded when it is earned, even if cash is not received at the time. Accrual-basis accounting allows revenue and expenses to be recorded in or matched with the appropriate accounting period. This is called the **matching principle.** Matching means that the expense incurred to earn the revenue is recorded in the same accounting period as the revenue.

Transaction (j) **Company pays an expense in cash.** Clark's Cleaners receives and pays a bill for electricity from City Power and Light, $220. The bill was not previously recorded as a liability. According to the company's chart of accounts, the electric bill is included as a Utilities Expense.

Transaction (j) Analysis

A	Accounts involved?	Cash and Utilities Expense
C	Classifications involved?	Cash = Asset Utilities Expense = Expense
I	Account(s) increased?	Utilities Expense
D	Account(s) decreased?	Cash

REMEMBER

Accrual-basis accounting allows us to record revenue when earned and record expenses when incurred.

	Assets				=	Liabilities	+	Owner's Equity		
	Cash +	Equip. +	Supp. +	Ppd. Ins.	=	Accounts Payable	+	N. L. Clark, Capital	+ Revenue −	Expenses
PB	18,080 +	26,000 +	400 +	360	=	3,580	+	40,000 +	1,940 −	680
(j)	−220									+220 (Utilities)
NB	17,860 +	26,000 +	400 +	360	=	3,580	+	40,000 +	1,940 −	900
		44,620						44,620		

Clark's Cleaners received a bill for utilities and paid it upon receipt of the bill.

Transaction (k)   Company sells services on account. Clark's Cleaners signs a contract with Formal Rentals to clean their for-hire formal garments on a credit basis. Clark's Cleaners completes a cleaning job and bills Formal Rentals $140 for services performed.

The **Accounts Receivable** account is used to record amounts due from charge customers—usually within twenty-five to thirty days.

Transaction (k) Analysis

A	Accounts involved?	Accounts Receivable and Income from Services
C	Classifications involved?	Accounts Receivable = Asset Income from Services = Revenue
I	Account(s) increased?	Accounts Receivable Income from Services
D	Account(s) decreased?	None

	Assets					=	Liabilities	+		Owner's Equity		
	Cash +	Equip. +	Supp. +	Ppd. Ins. +	Accts. Rec.	=	Accounts Payable	+	N. L. Clark, Capital +	Revenue	−	Expenses
PB	17,860 +	26,000 +	400 +	360		=	3,580	+	40,000 +	1,940	−	900
(k)					+140					+140 (Income from Services)		
NB	17,860 +	26,000 +	400 +	360 +	140	=	3,580	+	40,000 +	2,080	−	900
		44,760								44,760		

This transaction is the same as transaction **(i)**. Again, accrual-basis accounting allows us to record revenue when earned even though we have not received the cash but only the customer's promise to pay.

Transaction (l)   Company pays an expense in cash. Clark's Cleaners pays wages of part-time employee, $930. This additional expense of $930 is added to the previous balance of $900, resulting in a new running total of $1,830 in expenses.

Transaction (l) Analysis

A	Accounts involved?	Cash and Wages Expense
C	Classifications involved?	Cash = Asset Wages Expense = Expense
I	Account(s) increased?	Wages Expense
D	Account(s) decreased?	Cash

Assets					=	Liabilities	+	Owner's Equity			
Cash +	Equip. +	Supp. +	Ppd. Ins. +	Accts. Rec.	=	Accounts Payable	+	N. L. Clark, Capital	+ Revenue	− Expenses	
PB 17,860 +	26,000 +	400 +	360 +	140	=	3,580	+	40,000 +	2,080	−	900
(l) −930											+930 (Wages)
NB 16,930 +	26,000 +	400 +	360 +	140	=	3,580	+	40,000 +	2,080	−	1,830
		43,830						43,830			

This is the same as transaction **(f)** or **(j)**.

Transaction (m) **Company buys equipment on account (on credit) and makes a cash down payment.** Clark's Cleaners buys additional equipment from Drake Equipment Company costing $940, paying $140 down, with the remaining $800 on account.

Transaction (m) Analysis

A	Accounts involved?	Cash, Equipment, and Accounts Payable
C	Classifications involved?	Cash = Asset
		Equipment = Asset
		Accounts Payable = Liability
I	Account(s) increased?	Equipment
		Accounts Payable
D	Account(s) decreased?	Cash

Assets					=	Liabilities	+	Owner's Equity			
Cash +	Equip. +	Supp. +	Ppd. Ins. +	Accts. Rec.	=	Accounts Payable	+	N. L. Clark, Capital	+ Revenue	− Expenses	
PB 16,930 +	26,000 +	400 +	360 +	140	=	3,580	+	40,000 +	2,080	−	1,830
(m) −140	+940					+800					
NB 16,790 +	26,940 +	400 +	360 +	140	=	4,380	+	40,000 +	2,080	−	1,830
		44,630						44,630			

This entry is different from the others because it is recorded using multiple (more than two) accounts. This kind of entry is called a **compound entry.**

Transaction (n) **Company sells services for cash.** Clark's Cleaners receives revenue from cash customers for the remainder of the month, $1,790.

Transaction (n) Analysis

A	Accounts involved?	Cash and Income from Services
C	Classifications involved?	Cash = Asset
		Income from Services = Revenue
I	Account(s) increased?	Cash
		Income from Services
D	Account(s) decreased?	None

. . . .
R E M E M B E R
In recording revenue, part of the entry is always an increase in a revenue account.
. . . .

	Assets					=	Liabilities	+		Owner's Equity		
	Cash	+ Equip.	+ Supp.	+ Ppd. Ins.	+ Accts. Rec.	=	Accounts Payable	+	N. L. Clark, Capital	+	Revenue	− Expenses
PB	16,790	+ 26,940	+ 400	+ 360	+ 140	=	4,380	+	40,000	+	2,080	− 1,830
(n)	+1,790										+1,790 (Income from Services)	
NB	18,580	+ 26,940	+ 400	+ 360	+ 140	=	4,380	+	40,000	+	3,870	− 1,830
	46,420								46,420			

This is the same as transaction **(h)**.

Transaction (o)   **Company receives cash on account from credit customer.** Clark's Cleaners receives $90 from Formal Rentals to apply on account.

Transaction (o) Analysis

A Accounts involved?	Cash and Accounts Receivable
C Classifications involved?	Cash = Asset Accounts Receivable = Asset
I Account(s) increased?	Cash
D Account(s) decreased?	Accounts Receivable

Clark's Cleaners is receiving part of the cash that was promised in transaction **(k)**.

	Assets					=	Liabilities	+		Owner's Equity		
	Cash	+ Equip.	+ Supp.	+ Ppd. Ins.	+ Accts. Rec.	=	Accounts Payable	+	N. L. Clark, Capital	+	Revenue	− Expenses
PB	18,580	+ 26,940	+ 400	+ 360	+ 140	=	4,380	+	40,000	+	3,870	− 1,830
(o)	+90				−90							
NB	18,670	+ 26,940	+ 400	+ 360	+ 50	=	4,380	+	40,000	+	3,870	− 1,830
	46,420								46,420			

Transaction (p)   **Company pays creditor on account.** Clark's Cleaners pays Drake Equipment Company $1,980 on account.

Transaction (p) Analysis

A Accounts involved?	Cash and Accounts Payable
C Classifications involved?	Cash = Asset Accounts Payable = Liabilities
I Account(s) increased?	None
D Account(s) decreased?	Cash Accounts Payable

	Assets					=	Liabilities	+	Owner's Equity			
	Cash +	Equip. +	Supp. +	Ppd. Ins. +	Accts. Rec.	=	Accounts Payable	+	N. L. Clark, Capital	+ Revenue	− Expenses
PB	18,670 +	26,940 +	400 +	360 +	50	=	4,380	+	40,000 +	3,870	− 1,830
(p)	−1,980						−1,980				
NB	16,690 +	26,940 +	400 +	360 +	50	=	2,400	+	40,000 +	3,870	− 1,830
		44,440							44,440		

Both sides of the equation are reduced when Clark pays a creditor with cash.

Transaction (q)   **Owner makes a cash withdrawal.** N. L. Clark withdraws $1,200 to cover his personal living costs. Such a **withdrawal** may be considered the opposite of an investment to the owner's capital account. It is recorded as a minus under Capital and labeled Drawing.

Transaction (q) Analysis

A Accounts involved?	Cash and N. L. Clark, Capital
C Classifications involved?	Cash = Asset N. L. Clark, Capital = Owner's Equity
I Account(s) increased?	None
D Account(s) decreased?	Cash N. L. Clark, Capital

	Assets					=	Liabilities	+	Owner's Equity			
	Cash +	Equip. +	Supp. +	Ppd. Ins. +	Accts. Rec.	=	Accounts Payable	+	N. L. Clark, Capital	+ Revenue	− Expenses
PB	16,690 +	26,940 +	400 +	360 +	50	=	2,400	+	40,000 +	3,870	− 1,830
(q)	−1,200								−1,200 (Drawing)		
NB	15,490 +	26,940 +	400 +	360 +	50	=	2,400	+	38,800 +	3,870	− 1,830
		43,240							43,240		

Since a withdrawal is the opposite of an investment by the owner, it is not considered an expense. In Chapter 2, you will see a separate account introduced for withdrawals.

Summary of Transactions

Figure 1-5 summarizes transactions **(f)** through **(q)** for Clark's Cleaners. To test your understanding of the recording procedure, describe the nature of the transactions that have taken place.

Figure 1-5

	Assets					=	Liabilities	+	Owner's Equity			
	Cash +	Equip. +	Supp. +	Ppd. Ins. +	Accts. Rec.	=	Accounts Payable	+	N. L. Clark, Capital	+	Revenue	−	Expenses
Bal.	17,000 +	26,000 +	400			=	3,400	+	40,000				
(f)	−500												+500 (Rent)
Bal.	16,500 +	26,000 +	400			=	3,400	+	40,000			−	500
(g)	−360			+360									
Bal.	16,140 +	26,000 +	400 +	360		=	3,400	+	40,000			−	500
(h)	+1,940										+1,940 (Income from Services)		
Bal.	18,080 +	26,000 +	400 +	360		=	3,400	+	40,000	+	1,940	−	500
(i)							+180						+180 (Advertising)
Bal.	18,080 +	26,000 +	400 +	360		=	3,580	+	40,000	+	+1,940	−	680
(j)	−220												+220 (Utilities)
Bal.	17,860 +	26,000 +	400 +	360		=	3,580	+	40,000	+	1,940	−	900
(k)					+140						+140 (Income from Services)		
Bal.	17,860 +	26,000 +	400 +	360 +	140	=	3,580	+	40,000	+	2,080	−	900
(l)	−930												+930 (Wages)
Bal.	16,930 +	26,000 +	400 +	360 +	140	=	3,580	+	40,000	+	2,080	−	1,830
(m)	−140	+940					+800						
Bal.	16,790 +	26,940 +	400 +	360 +	140	=	4,380	+	40,000	+	2,080	−	1,830
(n)	+1,790										+1,790 (Income from Services)		
Bal.	18,580 +	26,940 +	400 +	360 +	140	=	4,380	+	40,000	+	3,870	−	1,830
(o)	+90				−90								
Bal.	18,670 +	26,940 +	400 +	360 +	50	=	4,380	+	40,000	+	3,870	−	1,830
(p)	−1,980						−1,980						
Bal.	16,690 +	26,940 +	400 +	360 +	50	=	2,400	+	40,000	+	3,870	−	1,830
(q)	−1,200								−1,200 (Drawing)				
Bal.	15,490 +	26,940 +	400 +	360 +	50	=	2,400	+	38,800	+	3,870	−	1,830

43,240 = 43,240

Left Side of Equal Sign

Cash	$15,490
Equipment	26,940
Supplies	400
Prepaid Insurance	360
Accounts Receivable	50
	$43,240

Right Side of Equal Sign

Accounts Payable	$ 2,400
N. L. Clark, Capital	38,800
Revenue	3,870
	$45,070
Expenses	−1,830
	$43,240

Major Financial Statements

A **financial statement** is a report prepared by accountants for owners, managers, and others both inside and outside the business. Three of the major financial statements consist of an income statement, a statement of owner's equity, and a balance sheet.

Note that the headings of all financial statements require three lines:

1. Name of the company (or owner, if there is no company name).

2. Title of the financial statement.

3. Period of time covered by the financial statement, or its date.

Also, note that dollar signs are placed at the head of each column and with each total. Single lines (drawn with a ruler) are used to show that figures above are being added or subtracted. Lines should be drawn across the entire column. Double lines are drawn under the final totals in a column.

The financial statements are all interconnected. Consequently, the income statement must be prepared first, followed by the statement of owner's equity, and then the balance sheet.

The Income Statement

Performance Objective 3
Prepare an income statement.

The **income statement** shows total revenue minus total expenses, which yields the net income or net loss. **The income statement shows the results of business transactions involving revenue and expense accounts over a period of time.** In other words, the income statement shows how the business has performed over a period of time, usually a month or a year. When total revenue exceeds total expenses over the period, the result is **net income,** or profit. Other terms that are identical with the name *income statement* are *statement of income and expenses* or *profit and loss statement*. If the total revenue is less than the total expenses, the result is a **net loss.**

The income statement in Figure 1-6 shows the results of the first month of operations for Clark's Cleaners. (Note that the net income figure presented here represents net income before adjustments. We will discuss adjustments in Chapter 4.) Note that, **as in all financial statements, the heading requires three lines:** name of the company, title of the financial statement, and period of time covered by the financial statement or its date.

For convenience, the individual expense amounts are recorded in the first amount column. In this way, the total expenses ($1,830) may be subtracted directly from the total revenue ($3,870).

The income statement covers a period of time, whereas the balance sheet has only one date: the end of the financial period. Look at the third line of the heading of the income statement shown in Figure 1-6. Then compare it with the third line of the balance sheet shown in Figure 1-8.

On the income statement, the revenue for June, less the expenses for June, shows the results of operations—a net income of $2,040. To the accountant, the term *net income* means "clear" income, or profit after all expenses have been deducted. Expenses are usually listed in the same order as in the chart of accounts, which is the official list of all the accounts in which transactions are recorded. Expense amounts are taken directly from the Expenses column of the accounting equation.

Figure 1-6

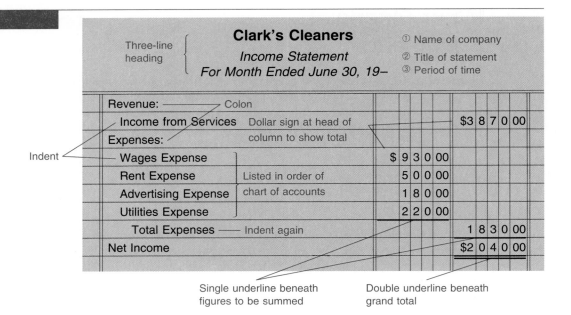

Clark's Cleaners
Income Statement
For Month Ended June 30, 19–

Three-line heading

① Name of company
② Title of statement
③ Period of time

Revenue: ———— Colon				
Income from Services Dollar sign at head of			$3 8 7 0 00
Expenses: column to show total			
Wages Expense	$ 9 3 0 00		
Rent Expense Listed in order of	5 0 0 00		
Advertising Expense chart of accounts	1 8 0 00		
Utilities Expense	2 2 0 00		
Total Expenses ——— Indent again		1 8 3 0 00	
Net Income		$2 0 4 0 00	

Indent

Single underline beneath figures to be summed

Double underline beneath grand total

Performance Objective 4

Prepare a statement of owner's equity.

The Statement of Owner's Equity

We said that revenue and expenses are connected with owner's equity through the medium of the financial statements. Now let's demonstrate this by a **statement of owner's equity,** shown in Figure 1-7, which the accountant prepares after he or she has determined the net income or net loss in the income statement. The statement of owner's equity shows how—and why—the owner's equity, or Capital, account has changed over a stated period of time (in this case, the month of June). Notice the third line in the heading of Figure 1-7. It shows that the statement of owner's equity covers the same period of time as the income statement.

Figure 1-7

REMEMBER

The income statement is prepared first, so that net income can be recorded in the statement of owner's equity. The statement of owner's equity is prepared second, so that the amount of capital at the end of the period can be recorded in the balance sheet, which is prepared last.

Clark's Cleaners
Statement of Owner's Equity
For Month Ended June 30, 19–

Three-line heading

① Name of company
② Title of statement
③ Period of time

N. L. Clark, Capital, June 1, 19– Dollar sign at		$40 0 0 0 00
Net Income for June head of columns	$2 0 4 0 00	
Less Withdrawals for June or to show total	1 2 0 0 00	
Increase in Capital		8 4 0 00
N. L. Clark, Capital, June 30, 19–		$40 8 4 0 00

Single underline beneath figures to be summed

Double underline beneath grand total

Now look at the body of the statement. The first line shows the balance in the Capital account at the beginning of the month. Two items have affected owner's equity during the month. A net income of $2,040 was earned, and the owner withdrew $1,200. To perform the calculations smoothly, move to the left one column and then list the two items, subtracting withdrawals from net income ($2,040 − $1,200 = $840). The difference ($840) represents an increase in capital. This difference is placed in the right-hand column to be added directly to the beginning capital. The final figure is the ending amount in the owner's Capital account.

The Balance Sheet

The amount of the owner's ending capital is now carried over to the balance sheet. The **balance sheet** summarizes the balances of the asset, liability, and owner's equity accounts on a given date (usually at the end of a month or year). It shows the **financial position** of the company. The date is a single day because the balance sheet is like a snapshot—it gives a picture of the business at that point in time. The picture will change with the next transaction.

The **report form** of the balance sheet, which will be used in this text, lists the assets, liabilities, and owner's equity vertically. The balance sheet prepared for Clark's Cleaners looks like this:

Performance Objective 5

Prepare a balance sheet.

R E M E M B E R

The balance sheet is a direct reflection of the accounting equation.

Figure 1-8

Three-line heading	**Clark's Cleaners**	① Name of company	
	Balance Sheet	② Title of statement	
	June 30, 19–	③ Date	

Assets ——— Main categories centered			
Cash		$15 4 9 0 00	
Accounts Receivable		5 0 00	
Supplies	Listed in order of	4 0 0 00	
Prepaid Insurance	chart of accounts	3 6 0 00	
Equipment		26 9 4 0 00	
Total Assets			$43 2 4 0 00
Liabilities	1 line space between main categories		
Accounts Payable			$ 2 4 0 0 00
Owner's Equity			
N. L. Clark, Capital			40 8 4 0 00
Total Liabilities and Owner's Equity			$43 2 4 0 00

Single underline beneath figures to be summed

Dollar sign at head of column or to show total

Double underline beneath grand total

R E M E M B E R

The amounts in the left column are used to calculate totals. Amounts in the right column are for grand totals.

The amount of the ending capital is recorded under the Owner's Equity heading. Also, a space of one line is used to separate Assets, Liabilities, and Owner's Equity.

Income Statement Involving More Than One Revenue Account

When a business firm or other economic unit has more than one distinct source of revenue, separate revenue accounts are set up for each source. See, for example, the income statement of The Regal Theater presented in Figure 1-9.

Figure 1-9

The Regal Theater
Balance Sheet Income Statement
For Month Ended September 30, 19–

Revenue:		
Admissions Income	$6 9 6 8 00	
Concessions Income	1 7 4 3 00	
Total Revenue		$8 7 1 1 00
Expenses:		
Film Rental Expense	$3 3 2 5 00	
Wages Expense	1 3 5 3 00	
Advertising Expense	9 2 5 00	
Utilities Expense	3 1 6 00	
Cleaning Expense	2 2 1 00	
Miscellaneous Expense	1 4 5 00	
Total Expenses		6 2 8 5 00
Net Income		$2 4 2 6 00

Statement of Owner's Equity Involving an Additional Investment with a Net Income or a Net Loss

Any additional investment by the owner during the period covered by the financial statements should be shown in the statement of owner's equity. Such a statement should show what has affected the Capital account from the *beginning* until the *end* of the period covered by the financial statements. For example, assume that the following information is true for the S. R. Hayes Company, which has a net income:

Balance of S. R. Hayes, Capital, on April 1	$86,000
Additional investment by S. R. Hayes on April 12	9,000
Net income for the month (from income statement)	1,500
Total withdrawals for the month	1,200

The statement of owner's equity in Figure 1-10 shows this information.

Figure 1-10

S. R. Hayes Company
Statement of Owner's Equity
For Month Ended April 30, 19–

S. R. Hayes, Capital, April 1, 19–			$86 0 0 0 00	
Additional Investment, April 12, 19–			9 0 0 0 00	
Total Investment			$95 0 0 0 00	
Net Income for April	$1 5 0 0 00			
Less Withdrawals for April	1 2 0 0 00			
Increase in Capital			3 0 0 00	
S. R. Hayes, Capital, April 30, 19–			$95 3 0 0 00	

The additional investment may be in the form of cash. Or the investment may be in the form of other assets, such as tools, equipment, and similar items. In the case of investments in assets other than cash, the assets should be recorded at their fair market value. **Fair market value** is the present worth of an asset, or the amount that would be received if the asset were sold to an outsider on the open market. Fair market value may differ greatly from the amount the owner originally paid for the asset.

As another example, assume the following for the T. C. Henry Company, which has a net loss:

T. C. Henry, Capital, on Oct. 1	$70,000
Additional investment by T. C. Henry on Oct. 25	6,000
Net loss for the month (from income statement)	250
Total withdrawals for the month	420

Again, the statement of owner's equity in Figure 1-11 shows this information.

Figure 1-11

T. C. Henry Company
Statement of Owner's Equity
For Month Ended October 31, 19–

T. C. Henry, Capital, October 1, 19–			$70 0 0 0 00	
Additional Investment, October 25, 19–			6 0 0 0 00	
Total Investment			$76 0 0 0 00	
Less: Net Loss for October	$ 2 5 0 00			
Withdrawals for October	4 2 0 00			
Decrease in Capital			6 7 0 00	
T. C. Henry, Capital, October 31, 19–			$75 3 3 0 00	

Accounting and the Computer

Computers perform routine record-keeping tasks and prepare financial statements. Because of their relatively low costs, computers are now an option for large and small businesses.

Whether accounting is done manually or on a computer, the rules and principles of accounting are the same. The process of analyzing, classifying, recording, and summarizing must still be performed in a systematic manner. The computer is fast and logical, but it requires accurate input to generate accurate output.

Input is the information entered into the accounting program or software. Printouts are output compiled by the instructions in the accounting program. You may have heard the phrase *Garbage In Garbage Out*. In other words, if the input is incorrect, the output will be incorrect. This is true whether the accounting is performed manually or on a computer.

Computer Application

One of the requirements of bookkeepers and accountants is that they be flexible—ready to learn new ways and variations of old ways. That is, their basic knowledge of accounting is essential, but they will encounter alternative language, forms, formats, and numbering of accounts. If you know your basics, you will be able to make these adjustments as well as to move from manual to computerized accounting.

Following is the chart of accounts, income statement, and balance sheet for Clark's Cleaners, printed from a commercial software package. Let's look at some of the similarities and differences between the manual illustrations and those produced by one of many commercial software packages. The goal is to build your confidence in your ability to adapt to different situations.

All Printouts

1. Titles on all three printouts include not only the name of the company, but the address.

2. The name of the printout and the date appear on the two statements.

The Chart of Accounts (Summary)

1. The account numbering for assets and liabilities are the same as in the manual illustrations.

2. The expenses begin with 6 instead of 5. This software reserves the numbers beginning with 5 for the accounts in a merchandising business.

3. The equity accounts begin with a 3, but then use an 8 or a 9 as the first digit in the second part of the number. These accounts are "hard-wired" into the program—in other words, the user of the software cannot change them as they can other numbers; they must use these numbers.

FYI

Software programs offer a variety of so-called standard charts of accounts, which businesses may adopt or adapt. In reality, however, there is no standard chart of accounts from one company to another. It depends on the needs of the company and the decisions of the system designer.

```
                    Clark's Cleaners
                   3702 35th Southwest
                   Seattle WA 98126

              Chart of Accounts [Summary]
                                                 Page 1

             Account
.................................................................

1-0000 Assets
       1-1110  Cash
       1-1130  Accounts Receivable
       1-1150  Supplies
       1-1170  Prepaid Insurance
       1-1240  Equipment
2-0000 Liabilities
       2-2210  Accounts Payable
3-0000 Equity
       3-3110  N. L. Clark, Capital
       3-3120  N. L. Clark, Drawing
       3-8000  Retained Earnings
       3-9000  Current Year Earnings
4-0000 Income
       4-4110  Income from Services
5-0000 Cost of Sales
6-0000 Expenses
       6-6150  Advertising Expense
       6-6210  Wages Expense
       6-6240  Rent Expense
       6-6250  Utilities Expense
8-0000 Other Income
9-0000 Other Expenses
```

The Profit and Loss Statement

1. The name of the statement is different, but it means the same thing as an Income Statement.

2. The date is printed June 199–, and it is assumed that June means for the month of June.

3. This software places dollar signs on every number following its own rules rather than the more common rules stated earlier.

4. In this software the underlining extends beyond the margin of the columns.

5. The difference between Total Income (Revenue) and Expenses is called Net Profit/(Loss) rather than Net Income or Net Loss. The terms mean the same thing.

6. This program does not double underline the grand totals.

```
                        Clark's Cleaners
                      3702 35th Southwest
                       Seattle WA 98126


                    Profit and Loss Statement

                           June 199–
.........................................................................

Income
     Income from Services            $3,870.00
Total Income                                         $3,870.00


Expenses
     Advertising Expense               $180.00
     Wages Expense                     $930.00
     Rent Expense                      $500.00
     Utilities Expense                 $220.00
Total Expenses                                       $1,830.00


Net Profit/(Loss)                                    $2,040.00
```

Balance Sheet

1. The date is printed as June 199– and it is assumed that June means June 30 or the end of the month.

2. The owner's equity section is just called Equity instead of Owner's Equity.

3. There is no separate statement of owner's equity. Look at the Equity section of the balance sheet. There you see the elements of the statement of owner's equity: beginning capital amount, minus amount withdrawn, plus current year's earnings (net income or net profit). The combined balance sheet and statement of owner's equity is common in accounting software.

4. This program does not double underline the grand totals.

```
                    Clark's Cleaners
                  3702 35th Southwest
                   Seattle WA 98126

                     Balance Sheet

                      June 199-

Assets
   Cash                              $15,490.00
   Accounts Receivable                   $50.00
   Supplies                             $400.00
   Prepaid Insurance                    $360.00
   Equipment                         $26,940.00
Total Assets                                      $43,240.00

Liabilities
   Accounts Payable                   $2,400.00
Total Liabilities                                  $2,400.00

Equity
   N.L. Clark, Capital               $40,000.00
   N.L. Clark, Drawing               ($1,200.00)
   Current Year Earnings              $2,040.00
Total Equity                                      $40,840.00

Total Liability & Equity                          $43,240.00
```

Summary

The amounts for assets, liabilities, capital, revenue, and expenses are the same in the manual illustrations and computerized printouts. There are some differences in language, form, and format. The biggest difference lies in the numbering of accounts. We hope you will begin to feel confident about your ability to adapt—that's your job—because change is normal. The certainty of change underscores the need for you to understand what you are doing and why you are doing it. You must be able to perform routine accounting duties as well as to see the larger picture and the flow of information in the accounting system. If you can do this, you will be far more valuable as an employee, manager, or owner.

CHAPTER REVIEW

R eview of Performance Objectives

1. Define accounting.

   Accounting is a process of analyzing, classifying, recording, summarizing, and interpreting business transactions in financial or monetary terms. It is also an information system and the language of business.

2. **Record a group of business transactions, involving all five elements of the fundamental accounting equation, in column form.**

   The accounting equation appears as follows:

   $$\text{Assets} = \text{Liabilities} + \text{Owner's Equity (Capital)} + \text{Revenue} - \text{Expenses}$$

   Accounts are classified and listed under each heading. Transactions are recorded by listing amounts as either additions to or deductions from the various accounts. The equation must always be in balance.

3. **Prepare an income statement.**

   The income statement shows the results of operations, or total revenue minus total expenses, which yields the net income or net loss. The heading consists of the name of the company, the title of the statement, and the period of time covered.

4. **Prepare a statement of owner's equity.**

   The statement of owner's equity shows how—and why—the owner's equity, or Capital account has changed over a stated period of time. The statement of owner's equity shows the beginning capital balance, plus net income (or minus net loss) taken from the income statement, minus any withdrawals. The heading consists of the name of the company, the title of the statement, and the period of time covered.

5. **Prepare a balance sheet.**

   The balance sheet consists of a listing of the final balances of the asset, liability, and owner's equity accounts. The balance sheet shows the financial position of the business. The heading of the balance sheet consists of the name of the company, the title of the statement, and the date. The balance sheet contains three sections: assets, liabilities, and owner's equity. The related accounts are listed under each section. Total assets equal total liabilities and owner's equity.

G lossary

Accountants Persons who are primarily involved with the summarizing and interpreting portions of the accounting process, as well as accounting system's design, taxes, and audit work. **(4)**

Accounting The process of analyzing, classifying, recording, summarizing, and interpreting business transactions in financial or monetary terms. **(3)**

Account numbers Numbers assigned to identify and separate the accounts numerically. **(10)**

Accounts The categories of the classifications of the fundamental accounting equation (Assets = Liabilities + Owner's Equity [+ Revenue − Expenses]). **(10)**

Accounts Payable A liability account used for short-term liabilities or charge accounts, usually due within twenty-five to thirty days. **(15)**

Accounts Receivable Account used to record the amounts owed by charge customers (legal claims against charge customers). **(22)**

Accrual basis of accounting Recognition of an expense when it is incurred—whether or not cash has been paid—or revenue when it has been earned—whether or not cash has been received. **(21)**

Assets Cash, properties, and other things of value owned by an economic unit or business entity. **(7)**

Balance sheet A financial statement showing the financial position of a firm or other economic unit on a given date, such as June 30 or December 31. The balance sheet lists the balances of the asset, liability, and owner's equity accounts. **(29)**

Bookkeepers Persons who are primarily involved with the process of analyzing, classifying, and recording of data. **(4)**

Business entity A business enterprise, separate and distinct from the persons who supply the assets it uses. Property acquired by a business is an asset of the business. The owner is separate from the business and in fact has claims on it. **(7)**

Capital The owner's investment or equity in an economic unit; also called *net worth* or *proprietorship*. **(7)**

Certified public accountant (CPA) An independent licensed professional who provides accounting services to clients for a fee. **(6)**

Chart of accounts The official list of account titles to be used to record the transactions of a business. **(10)**

Compound entry A transaction that requires multiple (more than two) accounts to record it. **(23)**

Creditor A person, company, or other organization to whom money is owed. **(8)**

Double-entry accounting The system by which each business transaction is recorded in at least two accounts and the accounting equation is kept in balance. **(4)**

Economic unit Includes business enterprises and also nonprofit entities, such as government bodies, religious institutions, clubs, and fraternal organizations. **(3)**

Equity The value of a right or claim to or financial interest in an asset or group of assets. **(7)**

Expenses The costs that relate to the earning of revenue (the costs of doing business). Examples are wages, rent, interest, and advertising; may be paid in cash or at a later time. **(18)**

Fair market value The present worth of an asset, or the amount that would be received if the asset were sold to an outsider on the open market. **(31)**

Financial position The resources or assets owned by an economic unit at a point in time, offset by the claims against those resources and owner's equity; shown by a balance sheet. **(29)**

Financial statement A report prepared by accountants that summarizes the financial affairs of a business. **(27)**

Fundamental accounting equation (Assets = Liabilities + Owner's Equity) An equation expressing the relationship of assets, liabilities, and owner's equity. **(7)**

Generally accepted accounting principles (GAAP) The rules or guidelines used for carrying out the accounting process. **(6)**

Going concern concept An accounting concept that identifies a business as an ongoing one whose intention is to remain in business and make a profit. **(9)**

Hardware The computer parts that you can see and touch, like the monitor or the keyboard. **(9)**

Income statement A financial statement showing the results of business transactions involving revenue and expense accounts over a period of time: total revenue minus total expenses. **(27)**

Liabilities Debts, or amounts owed to creditors. **(8)**

Matching principle Expenses for an accounting period are matched with the revenue for the same accounting period. **(21)**

Net income The results when total revenue exceeds total expenses over a period of time, also called a *profit*. **(27)**

Net loss The result when total expenses exceed total revenue over a period of time, also called a *loss*. **(27)**

Owner's equity The owner's right to or investment in the business. **(7)**

Para-accountants Persons who perform bookkeeping, taxation, and auditing services under the direct supervision of a public accountant. **(5)**

Report form The form of the balance sheet in which assets are placed at the top and liabilities and owner's equity are placed below. **(29)**

Revenue The amount a business earns. Examples are fees earned for performing services, sales, rent income, and interest income; may be in the form of cash, credit card receipts, or accounts receivable. **(18)**

Separate entity concept The idea that a business is a separate economic unit, apart from other business or personal entities. **(9)**

Single-entry accounting Does not include the complete results of a transaction as does double-entry accounting. **(4)**

Software The medium that contains the instructions that computer hardware requires to perform designated tasks, like accounting, word processing, and spreadsheet analysis. **(9)**

Sole proprietorship One of the three primary forms of business ownership; a one-owner business. **(12)**

Source documents The evidence that generates a transaction. Examples are deposit slips, checks, sales invoices, and purchase invoices. **(11)**

Statement of owner's equity A financial statement showing how and why the owner's equity, or Capital, account has changed over the accounting period. **(28)**

Transaction An event affecting an economic entity that can be expressed in terms of money and that must be recorded in the accounting records. **(3)**

Withdrawal The taking of cash or other assets out of a business by the owner for his or her own use. (This is also referred to as *drawing*.) A withdrawal is treated as a temporary decrease in the owner's equity, because it is anticipated that it will be offset by net income. **(25)**

QUESTIONS, EXERCISES, AND PROBLEMS

D iscussion Questions

1. Who are the users of accounting information?
2. What is meant by the fundamental accounting equation? Define assets, liabilities, and owner's equity.
3. What is a transaction, and what steps would you follow in analyzing a business transaction?
4. Briefly describe computer hardware and software.
5. What are revenue and expenses?
6. Describe how each of the three financial statements presented in the chapter are related to each other.
7. Why is a withdrawal not considered an expense?
8. What do we mean when we say that revenue and expenses are under the umbrella of owner's equity?

E xercises

Exercise 1-1 Complete the following equations:

a. Assets of $32,000 = Liabilities of $8,100 + Owner's Equity of $_____
b. Assets of $_____ − Liabilities of $21,000 = Owner's Equity of $30,000
c. Assets of $26,000 − Owner's Equity of $14,200 = Liabilities of $_____

P.O.2

Calculate missing items in the accounting equation.

Exercise 1-2 Determine the following amounts:

a. The amount of the liabilities of a business having $61,290 in assets and in which the owner has a $36,200 equity.
b. The equity of the owner of an automobile that cost $12,200 who owes $4,100 on an installment loan payable to the bank.
c. The amount of the assets of a business having $9,620 in liabilities and in which the owner has $22,000 equity.

P.O.2

Calculate missing items in the accounting equation.

Exercise 1-3 Label the following accounts as asset (A), liability (L), owner's equity (OE), revenue (R), or expense (E):

a. Supplies
b. Service Income
c. Prepaid Insurance
d. T. S. Bayne, Drawing
e. Accounts Receivable
f. Professional Fees
g. T. S. Bayne, Capital
h. Utilities Expense
i. Accounts Payable
j. Rent Expense

P.O.2

Classify accounts.

Exercise 1-4 Dr. T. R. Simms is an optometrist. As of November 30, Simms's Optometry Clinic owned the following property that related to her professional practice: Cash, $1,020; Supplies, $410; Professional Equipment, $21,500; Office Equipment, $5,130. On the same date, she owed the following business creditors: Barrett Supply Company, $1,880; Stanton Professional Equipment Sales, $960. Compute the following amounts in the accounting equation:

P.O.2

Formulate the accounting equation.

Assets $_____ = Liabilities $_____ + Owner's Equity $_____

P.O.2

Describe various transactions.

Exercise 1-5 T. L. Sinet is a consulting engineer. Describe the following transactions:

	Cash	+	Accts. Rec.	+	Supplies	+	Equip.	=	Accounts Payable	+	T. L. Sinet, Capital	+	Revenue	−	Expenses
Bal.	1,850	+	1,025	+	975	+	8,725	=	3,128	+	9,447				
(a)	+420		−420												
Bal.	2,270	+	605	+	975	+	8,725	=	3,128	+	9,447				
(b)	−795														+795 (Rent)
Bal.	1,475	+	605	+	975	+	8,725	=	3,128	+	9,447			−	795
(c)	+3,615												+3,615 (Income from Services)		
Bal.	5,090	+	605	+	975	+	8,725	=	3,128	+	9,447	+	3,615	−	795
(d)	−420								−420						
Bal.	4,670	+	605	+	975	+	8,725	=	2,708	+	9,447	+	3,615	−	795
(e)	−525														+525 (Wages)
Bal.	4,145	+	605	+	975	+	8,725	=	2,708	+	9,447	+	3,615	−	1,320
(f)	−1,400										−1,400 (Drawing)				
Bal.	2,745	+	605	+	975	+	8,725	=	2,708	+	8,047	+	3,615	−	1,320
(g)	−725								−725						
Bal.	2,020	+	605	+	975	+	8,725	=	1,983	+	8,047	+	3,615	−	1,320

Column group headers: **Assets** = **Liabilities** + **Owner's Equity**

P.O.2

Describe various transactions.

Exercise 1-6 Describe a transaction that resulted in the following for Sound Instrument Repair:

a. Repair Parts is increased by $77, and Accounts Payable is increased by $77.
b. Accounts Payable is decreased by $750, and Cash is decreased by $750.
c. Rent Expense is increased by $850, and Cash is decreased by $850.
d. Advertising Expense is increased by $126, and Accounts Payable is increased by $126.
e. Accounts Receivable is increased by $315, and Service Income is increased by $315.
f. Cash is decreased by $200, and L. J. Miller, Drawing, is increased by $200.
g. Equipment is increased by $322, Cash is decreased by $100, and Accounts Payable is increased by $222.
h. Cash is increased by $217, and Accounts Receivable is decreased by $217.

Exercise 1-7 From the following elements in a statement of owner's equity, determine the missing amounts.

P.O.4

Calculate statement of owner's equity items.

a. Capital, June 1 $22,000
Net Income for June   4,000
Withdrawals for June   3,000
Capital, June 30   ?

b. Capital, July 1 $41,000
Net Loss for July   2,000
Withdrawals for July   3,000
Capital, July 31   ?

c. Capital, August 1 $56,000
Net Income for August   4,000
Capital, August 31   58,000
Withdrawals for August   ?

d. Capital, September 1 $69,000
Net Loss for September   4,000
Capital, September 30   62,000
Withdrawals for September   ?

e. Capital, October 1 $76,000
Withdrawals for October   3,000
Capital, October 31   77,000
Net Income for October   ?

f. Capital, November 30 $95,000
Net Income for November   5,000
Withdrawals for November   4,000
Capital, November 1   ?

Exercise 1-8 From Exercise 1-5, present an income statement, a statement of owner's equity, and a balance sheet for the month ended August 31 of this year. List the expenses in the order in which they appear in the Expenses column; Rent Expense is first.

P.O.3,4

Prepare financial statements.

C onsider and Communicate

You are the bookkeeper for a new business and are presenting the financial statements to the owner. He is not familiar with accounting. He looks at the bottom line on the statement of owner's equity and is surprised to see that his capital has decreased. "How can that happen?" he exclaims. "I had a net income!" Explain to him how this could happen.

He looks at the bottom line of the income statement and says, "But the net income must be larger, I know we sold more than ever." How would you explain this result of operations?

Belinda Morez, CPA, has just met with a new client. The client, a sole proprietor, asked Ms. Morez about preparing a set of financial statements that he will take to his bank when he applies for a business loan. The client stated that he had done the preliminary work and would like Ms. Morez to review his work and make any appropriate suggestions for changes or corrections.

Included in the financial information is a summary of debts and items owned by the owner personally and in the business. These two items don't equal each other, but he doesn't seem to see a problem with it. In addition, the owner has included an "expense statement," where he has recorded all cash expenditures of the business as well as his personal expenditures. All cash deposits are recorded as income, no matter what the source.

What suggestions should Ms. Morez make to this business owner?

A Question of Ethics

One of your fellow students has just told you that he has taken a job as a bookkeeper in a small business. He has no previous accounting experience, and this is his first accounting class. He says he can learn as he goes through the class. The student does not feel that he lied to the employer, because he only implied that he knew about accounting and said he could do the job. Is he being ethical in accepting this job under these conditions?

P roblem Set A

P.O.2,3,4,5

Problem 1-1A On May 1 of this year, T. S. Ellen, D.C., established the Ellen Chiropractic Clinic. The organization's account headings are presented below. Transactions completed during the month of May follow.

Assets				=	Liabilities	+	Owner's Equity		
Cash +	Supplies +	Prof. Equip.	+ Office Equip.	=	Accounts Payable	+	T. S. Ellen, Capital	+ Revenue	− Expenses

a. Deposited $12,300 in a bank account entitled Ellen Chiropractic Clinic.
b. Paid office rent for the month, $950.
c. Bought supplies for cash, $1,375.
d. Bought professional equipment on account from Chiropractic Equipment West Supply, $15,300.
e. Bought a computer from A-Tech Computers, $3,870, paying $850 in cash and putting the remainder on account.
f. Received cash for professional fees earned, $1,280 (Professional Fees).
g. Paid A-Tech Computers $800 as part payment on amount owed on office equipment, recorded previously in transaction **(e).**
h. Received and paid bill for utilities, $273.
i. Paid salary of assistant, $1,450 (Salary Expense).
j. Earned professional fees, receiving $3,622 cash.
k. Ellen withdrew cash for personal use, $1,800.

Instructions

1. In the equation, list the owner's name above the term *Capital*.
2. Record the transaction and the balance after each transaction. Identify the accounts affected when the transaction involves revenue, expenses, or drawing.
3. Prepare an income statement and a statement of owner's equity for May and a balance sheet as of May 31. List the expenses, in the order in which they appear, in the Expenses column, with Rent Expense first.

Problem 1-2A Y. L. Nguyen, a surveyor, opened an office, Nguyen Surveys, on April 1. The account headings are presented below. Transactions completed during the month of April follow.

`P.O.2,3,4,5`

Assets					=	Liabilities	+	Owner's Equity		
Cash +	Supplies +	Prepaid Insurance	+ Prof. Equip.	+ Office Equip.	=	Accounts Payable	+	Y. L. Nguyen, Capital	+ Revenue	− Expenses

a. Deposited $15,200 in a bank account in the name of the business, Nguyen Surveys.
b. Bought professional equipment on account from Shilling Engineering Supplies, $8,400.
c. Invested personal computer and printer in the business, $5,326. (Increase the account for Office Equipment, and include in the statement of owner's equity as additional investment, as shown in Figure 1-10.)
d. Paid office rent for the month, $980.
e. Bought supplies for cash, $781.
f. Paid premium for a one-year insurance policy on professional equipment, $159.
g. Received $1,936 in professional fees for services rendered (Professional Fees).
h. Paid salary of assistant, $1,750 (Salary Expense).
i. Received and paid bill for telephone service, $78 (Telephone Expense).
j. Paid Shilling Engineering Supplies part of the amount owed on the purchase of professional equipment, $450.
k. Received $2,798 in professional fees for services rendered.
l. Paid for minor repairs to professional equipment (Repair Expense), $73.
m. Nguyen withdrew cash for personal use, $1,850.

Instructions

1. In the equation, complete the asset section, and list the owner's name above the term *Capital*.
2. Record the transactions and the balances after each transaction. Identify the account affected when the transaction involves revenue, expenses, or drawing.
3. Prepare an income statement and a statement of owner's equity for April and a balance sheet as of April 30. List expenses in the order in which they appear in the Expenses column. List Rent Expense first.

P.O.3,4,5 **Problem 1-3A** Chang and Associates hires an accountant, who determines the following account balances, listed in alphabetical order, as of September 30 of this year:

Accounts Payable	$ 4,817	Professional Fees	$10,950
Accounts Receivable	3,275	Rent Expense	1,650
Advertising Expense	385	Salary Expense	8,420
Appraisal Fees	2,950	Supplies	417
Cash	6,492	T. R. Chang, Capital, Sept. 1	17,226
Equipment	11,748	T. R. Chang, Drawing	3,200
Miscellaneous Expense	356		

Instructions

Prepare an income statement and a statement of owner's equity for September and a balance sheet as of September 30.

P.O.2,3,4,5 **Problem 1-4A** D. R. Fox started Fox Landscaping Service on May 1 of this year. The account headings are presented below. During May, Fox completed the transactions that follow:

Assets						=	Liabilities	+	Owner's Equity		
Cash +	Accts. Rec.	+ Supp.	+ Ppd. Ins.	+ Equip.	+ Truck	=	Accounts Payable	+	D. R. Fox, Capital	+ Revenue	− Expenses

a. Invested cash in the business, $8,000.
b. Bought a truck from Sherman Motors for $12,560, paying $1,300 in cash, with the remainder due in thirty days.
c. Bought equipment on account from Filbert Company, $2,000.
d. Paid rent for the month, $650.
e. Paid cash for insurance on truck for the year, $623.
f. Cash receipts for the first half of the month from cash customers, $1,565 (Income from Services).
g. Bought supplies for cash, $562.
h. Billed customers on account for services performed, $522.
i. Paid cash for utilities, $110.
j. Received bill for gas and oil used for the truck during the current month, $337 (Truck Expense).
k. Receipts for remainder of the month from cash customers, $1,497.
l. Fox withdrew cash for personal use, $1,200.
m. Paid wages to employees, $2,540.

Instructions

1. List the owner's name above the term *Capital* in the equation.
2. Record the transactions and the balances after each transaction. Identify the account affected when the transaction involves revenue, expenses, or drawing.
3. Prepare an income statement and a statement of owner's equity for May and a balance sheet as of May 31. List expenses in the order in which they appear in the Expenses column. Begin with Rent Expense.

Problem Set B

Problem 1-1B In April, S. L. Pasternak, D.V.M., established the Pasternak Veterinary Clinic. The organization's account headings are presented below. Transactions completed during the month of April follow.

P.O.2,3,4,5

Assets	=	Liabilities +	Owner's Equity
Cash + Supplies + Prof. + Office = Equip. Equip.		Accounts + Payable	S. L. Pasternak, + Revenue − Expenses Capital

a. Deposited $20,000 in a bank account entitled Pasternak Veterinary Clinic.
b. Paid rent for the month, $950.
c. Bought supplies on account from Hernandez and Company, $1,417.
d. Bought professional equipment on account from Terrel Company, $6,800.
e. Received bill from the *Daily Chronicle* for advertising, $394.
f. Paid $1,950 to Terrel Company as part payment on account for purchase of professional equipment recorded previously.
g. Received cash for professional services, $4,610 (Professional Fees).
h. Received and paid bill for utilities, $172.
i. Paid salary of assistant, $1,200.
j. Bought a copy machine from Ramsey Office Suppliers on account, $3,200.
k. Pasternak withdrew cash for personal use, $1,560.

Instructions

1. In the equation, list the owner's name above the term *Capital*.
2. Record the transactions and the balance after each transaction. Identify the accounts affected when the transaction involves revenue, expenses, or drawing.
3. Prepare an income statement and a statement of owner's equity for April and a balance sheet as of April 30. List expenses in the order in which they appear in the Expenses column, listing Rent Expense first.

Problem 1-2B C. W. Cavallini, Certified Public Accountant, opened her office on January 1. The account headings are presented below. Transactions completed during the month follow.

P.O.2,3,4,5

Assets	=	Liabilities +	Owner's Equity
Cash + Supplies + Ppd. + Office + Library = Ins. Equip.		Accounts + Payable	C. W. Cavallini, + Revenue − Expenses Capital

a. Deposited $24,000 in a bank account in the name of the business: C. W. Cavallini, C.P.A.
b. Bought equipment on account from Jellum Company, $15,200.
c. Cavallini invested her professional library, $6,300. (Increase the account for Library and the account of C. W. Cavallini, Capital, and include in the statement of owner's equity as Additional Investment, as shown in Figure 1-10.)
d. Paid office rent for the month, $830.
e. Bought office supplies for cash, $885.
f. Paid the premium for a one-year insurance policy on the equipment and the library, $220.
g. Received fees for services rendered, $2,800 (Professional Fees).
h. Received and paid bill for telephone service, $231 (Telephone Expense).

i. Paid salary of part-time receptionist, $1,100.
j. Paid automobile expense, $278 (Automobile Expense).
k. Received fees for services rendered, $2,950.
l. Paid Jellum Company part payment of amount owed for the purchase of office equipment recorded earlier, $1,500.
m. Cavallini withdrew cash for personal use, $2,300.

Instructions

1. In the equation, complete the asset section, and list the owner's name above the term *Capital*.
2. Record the transactions and the balances after each transaction. Identify the account affected when the transaction involves revenue, expenses, or drawing.
3. Prepare an income statement and a statement of owner's equity for January and a balance sheet as of January 31. List expenses in the order in which they appear in the Expenses column. List Rent Expense first.

P.O.3,4,5

Problem 1-3B An accountant determines the following balances, listed alphabetically, for Clearview Optical Clinic as of November 30:

Accounts Payable	$ 5,270	Equipment	$46,821
Accounts Receivable	8,820	Miscellaneous Expense	522
Advertising Expense	1,245	Professional Fees	15,202
Cash	6,274	Rent Expense	1,280
C. T. Sanchez,		Repair Income	2,862
Capital, Nov. 1	58,479	Supplies	1,960
C. T. Sanchez, Drawing	3,000	Wages Expense	11,891

Instructions

Prepare an income statement and a statement of owner's equity for November and a balance sheet as of November 30.

P.O.2,3,4,5

Problem 1-4B On August 1 of this year, T. L. Delano established Delano Termite Control. The account headings are presented below. During August, Delano completed the transactions listed.

Assets						=	Liabilities	+	Owner's Equity		
Cash +	Accts. Rec. +	Supp. +	Ppd. Ins. +	Equip. +	Truck	=	Accounts Payable	+	T. L. Delano, Capital	+ Revenue	− Expenses

a. Invested cash in the business, $15,200.
b. Bought a truck for use in the business from Sheraton Motors for $12,010, paying $3,500 in cash, with the balance due in thirty days.
c. Bought spraying equipment on account from Grace Company, $1,846.
d. Paid rent for the month, $560.
e. Cash receipts for the first half of the month from cash customers, $950 (Income from Services).
f. Paid cash for property and liability insurance on truck for the year, $443.
g. Bought supplies for cash, $181.
h. Received and paid heating bill, $162 (Utilities Expense).
i. Received bill from Smith Company for gas and oil used for the truck during the current month, $98 (Gas and Oil Expense).

j. Billed customers for services performed on account, $284.
k. Receipts for the remainder of the month from cash customers, $1,813.
l. Paid salary of assistant, $2,340.
m. Delano withdrew cash for personal use, $1,275.

Instructions

1. List the owner's name above the term *Capital* in the equation.
2. Record the transactions and the balances after each transaction. Identify the account affected when the transaction involves revenue, expenses, or drawing.
3. Prepare an income statement and a statement of owner's equity for August and a balance sheet as of August 31. List expenses in the order in which they appear in the Expenses column. Begin with Rent Expense.

CHALLENGE PROBLEM

John Page, a college student, plans to provide typing services to graduate students at the university near his home. He must determine how much money to deposit initially in his business account to cover the start-up of the new business. The deposit must cover the start-up costs and leave him with a balance of $5,000 in his business account. He plans to buy a computer/printer and a copier for $4,500 cash. The fax machine and the telephone system he needs are available for $2,500, and he will put down $300. He will buy paper for the copier for $275 on account. How much should John's investment be on June 1 if he is to meet his goal of having $5,000 in his business account after his anticipated transactions?

1. Use the practice grid to complete each transaction. Balance the fundamental accounting equation after each transaction.

Quality Typing Service

	Cash	Equipment	Supplies	Accounts Payable	J. Page, Capital

(a)   Make unknown beginning investment.

Balance

(b)   Buy equipment for cash, $4,500.

Balance

(c)   Buy equipment, $2,500, paying $300 down, and the remainder due in 90 days.

Balance

(d)   Buy supplies on account, $275.

Balance

2. Prepare a balance sheet for John's business as of June 10, 19–.

chapter 2

Recording Business Transactions:

T Account Form,

Debits and Credits,

and Trial Balance

PERFORMANCE OBJECTIVES

After you have completed this chapter, you will be able to do the following:

1. Present the fundamental accounting equation with the T account form, and label the debit and credit sides.

2. Present the fundamental accounting equation with the T account form, and label the plus and minus sides.

3. Record directly in T accounts a group of business transactions involving changes in asset, liability, owner's equity, revenue, and expense accounts for a service business.

4. Prepare a trial balance from the T accounts.

5. Recognize the effect of transpositions and slides on account balances.

Often textbooks show numerical data without the cents, that is, in whole dollars only. Whole dollars seem easier to work with in exercises and problems. This practice extends beyond the textbook. The Internal Revenue Service encourages using whole dollars. Financial statements are

frequently prepared using whole dollars. This is accomplished by rounding the figures up or down depending on the level of rounding. For example, when you round:

$178,573.86 to	ones	the result is	$178,574
	tens	the result is	178,570
	hundreds	the result is	178,600
	thousands	the result is	179,000

Usually only very large companies round at the thousand's level. Usually small businesses round to the one's level. In other words, $10,556.49 would be rounded down to $10,556 since the cents are less than 50.

Even when financial statements are presented rounded, the underlying financial records, the journals and ledgers, are maintained using cents. This is especially helpful when tracking specific amounts in case of an error or when people are asked to check or audit the accounting records.

When rounding, you must be careful to test that the rounded information has not caused a total to be off one dollar high or low. Prove your work and readjust those figures that were near the break point, that is, close to the midpoint of a range. Rounding is helpful since it provides financial statements that are easier to read and easier to compare if the statements are for more than one period. Comparative statements in rounded format are less cluttered.

Many computer programs have a rounding function and will do the work for you. Do remember to test that the work is accurate and balanced as rounded. Missing a place where a small adjustment should have been made can be embarrassing.

In Chapter 1, we described the fundamental accounting equation as Assets = Liabilities + Owner's Equity. Then we introduced Revenue and Expenses as extensions of the fundamental accounting equation to account for increases in owner's equity (revenue) and decreases to owner's equity (expenses). We introduced the recording of transactions involving all five classifications of accounts.

In this chapter, we will introduce the left and right side of the T account as debit and credit, respectively. We will also show the plus and minus signs that keep the equation in balance. Finally, we will enter the same series of transactions used in Chapter 1 in T accounts and prove the equality of debits and credits by means of a trial balance.

The T Account Form

In Chapter 1, we recorded business transactions in a column arrangement. For example, the Cash account column in the books of Clark's Cleaners is shown in Figure 1-5.

As an introduction to the recording of transactions, the use of columns has the following advantages:

1. In the process of analyzing the transaction, you
   a. Recognize the need to determine which accounts are involved (A).
   b. Determine the classification of the accounts involved (C).
   c. Decide whether the transaction results in an increase (I) or a decrease (D) in each of these accounts.

2. After each of the transactions has been recorded, the account balances can be added together to prove the equality of the two sides of the fundamental accounting equation. The total of one side of the accounting equation should equal the total of the other side of the equation.

Now, instead of recording transactions in a column for each account, we will use a **T account form** for each account, as shown in Figure 2-1. *The T account form has the advantage of providing two sides for each account: one side to record increases in the account, and the other to record decreases.* The T account form also takes up less space for illustration and for solving problems in actual practice.

After recording a group of transactions in an account, add both sides and record the totals in small figures called **footings.** (Use pencil because these footings are temporary.) Next, subtract the smaller footing from the larger footing to determine the balance of the account. For the account shown in Figure 2-1, the balance is $15,490 ($43,820 − $28,330).

Now record the balance on the side of the account having the larger footing, which, with a few minor exceptions, is the plus (+) side. The plus side of a T account is the side that represents the **normal balance** of the account.

Debit and Credit Sides

Here is the fundamental accounting equation expressed in T accounts (see Figure 2-2). The *left side* of a T account is called the **debit** side; the *right side* is called the **credit** side. Figure 2-2 repeats the accounting equation with the debit and credit sides identified in the Ts.

Figure 2-1

Cash Account Column

					Cash			
				+		**−**		
Transaction	**(a)**	+40,000	**(a)**	40,000	**(b)**	22,000		
Transaction	**(b)**	−22,000	**(h)**	1,940	**(d)**	1,000		
Balance		18,000	**(n)**	1,790	**(f)**	500		
Transaction	**(d)**	−1,000	**(o)**	90	**(g)**	360		
Balance		17,000			**(j)**	220		
Transaction	**(f)**	−500		43,820	**(l)**	930		
Balance		16,500			**(m)**	140		
Transaction	**(g)**	−360			**(p)**	1,980		
Balance		16,140			**(q)**	1,200		
Transaction	**(h)**	+1,940	Bal.	15,490		28,330		
Balance		18,080						
Transaction	**(j)**	−220						
Balance		17,860						
Transaction	**(l)**	−930						
Balance		16,930						
Transaction	**(m)**	−140						
Balance		16,790						
Transaction	**(n)**	+1,790						
Balance		18,580						
Transaction	**(o)**	+90						
Balance		18,670						
Transaction	**(p)**	−1,980						
Balance		16,690						
Transaction	**(q)**	−1,200						
Balance		15,490						

Figure 2-2

Assets		=	Liabilities		+	Owner's Equity		+	Revenue		−	Expenses	
Left	Right		Left	Right		Left	Right		Left	Right		Left	Right
Debit	Credit		Debit	Credit		Debit	Credit		Debit	Credit		Debit	Credit

Note that the left side is always the debit side, and the right side is always the credit side. This is true regardless of the transaction.

Present the fundamental accounting equation with the T account form, and label plus and minus sides.

Rules of Plus and Minus

Remember, as you record each business transaction, total amounts recorded on the debit side of accounts equal total amounts recorded on the credit side of the other accounts. Debits must equal credits. Let us now state this rule in terms of pluses and minuses. The amount placed on the left side of one account (or accounts) must equal the amount placed on the right side of another account (or accounts).

Memorize this equation.

Assets		=	Liabilities		+	Owner's Equity		+	Revenue		−	Expenses	
+	−		−	+		−	+		−	+		+	−
Left Debit	Right Credit		Left Debit	Right Credit		Left Debit	Right Credit		Left Debit	Right Credit		Left Debit	Right Credit

To assist you in your memorization, remember that *LEFT* is another word for *DEBIT* and *RIGHT* is another word for *CREDIT*. Notice that the DEBIT side is the increase side for assets and expenses, and the CREDIT side is the increase side for liabilities, owner's equity, and revenue. This arrangement of pluses and minuses explains how the equation stays in balance.

At this point, let's pause to determine the equality of the two sides of the equation by listing the balances of the accounts:

Account Name	Accounts with Normal Balances on the Left Side Assets Drawing Expenses	Accounts with Normal Balances on the Right Side Liabilities Capital Revenue
Cash	$17,000	
Supplies	400	
Equipment	26,000	
Accounts Payable		$ 3,400
N. L. Clark, Capital		40,000
	$43,400	$43,400

Accounting, like a building, has a foundation and a framework.

Let us take a more detailed look at owner's equity accounts. Since owner's equity consists of both a Capital account and a Drawing account, we will list them separately. The minus side of the Capital account is reserved for permanent withdrawals, either because the owner intends to reduce the size of the business permanently or because a net loss forces this reduction. However, amounts withdrawn for the owner's personal use are considered to be temporary, because the owner plans to replace these withdrawals with the net income earned by the firm. It is much more convenient to use a separate account to record these withdrawals. Therefore, withdrawals by the owner are recorded on the plus side of Drawing. Figure 2-3 illustrates this concept by showing the Drawing T account under the umbrella or wing of the Capital account.

Figure 2-3

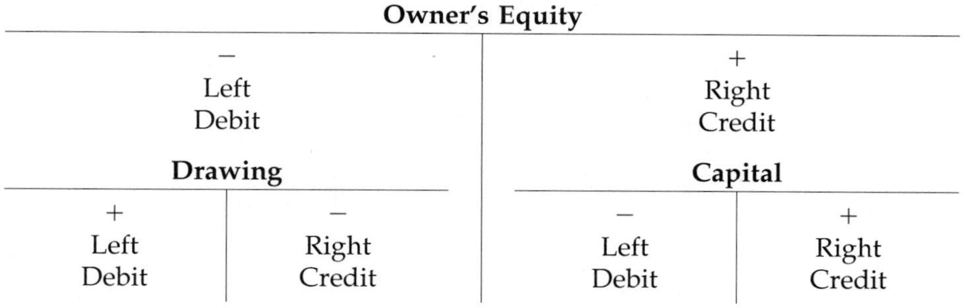

Owner's Equity

−	+
Left	Right
Debit	Credit

Drawing		**Capital**	
+	−	−	+
Left	Right	Left	Right
Debit	Credit	Debit	Credit

Drawing is placed under the heading of Owner's Equity because it appears in the statement of owner's equity. As you will recall, in the statement of owner's equity, we list beginning capital, plus net income, minus withdrawals. When we want to treat one account as a deduction from another, we reverse the plus and minus signs.

Let us take a further look at revenue and expenses as part of owner's equity. In Chapter 1 we placed revenue and expenses under the umbrella of owner's equity. Revenue increases owner's equity, and expenses decrease owner's equity. The T accounts for this situation are illustrated in Figure 2-4.

Figure 2-4

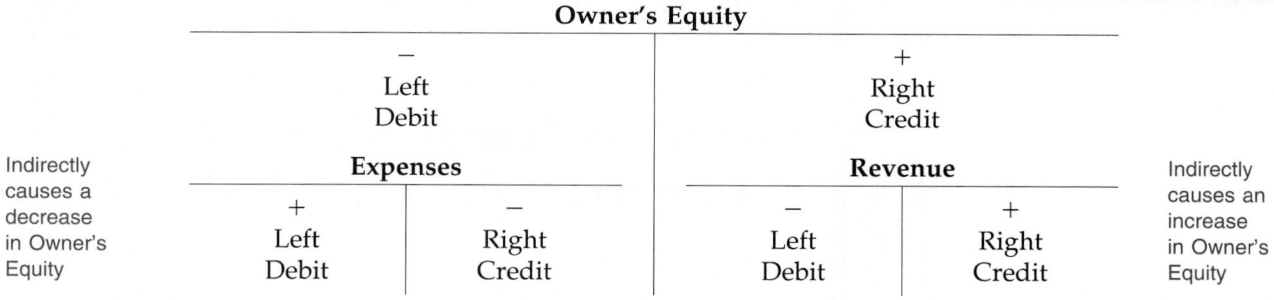

Owner's Equity

−	+
Left	Right
Debit	Credit

Indirectly causes a decrease in Owner's Equity

Expenses		**Revenue**	
+	−	−	+
Left	Right	Left	Right
Debit	Credit	Debit	Credit

Indirectly causes an increase in Owner's Equity

To summarize owner's equity:

Increases in owner's equity are recorded on the right side. Since revenue and investments of capital increase owner's equity, both are recorded on the right side of the accounts.

Decreases in owner's equity are recorded on the left side. Since expenses and withdrawals by the owner decrease owner's equity, both are recorded on the left side of the accounts.

Because revenue and expenses appear separately in the income statement, we will stretch out the equation to include them as separate headings, like this:

Assets		=	Liabilities		+	Owner's Equity, Capital		+	Revenue		−	Expenses	
+	−		−	+		−	+		−	+		+	−
Left Debit	Right Credit		Left Debit	Right Credit		Left Debit	Right Credit		Left Debit	Right Credit		Left Debit	Right Credit

Drawing	
+	−
Left Debit	Right Credit

To summarize debits and credits, increases and decreases

Debits Signify	*Credits Signify*
Increases in { Assets, Drawing, Expenses	Decreases in { Assets, Drawing, Expenses
Decreases in { Liabilities, Capital, Revenue	Increases in { Liabilities, Capital, Revenue
Assets	The *left* side is the *increase* side.
Liabilities	The *right* side is the *increase* side.
Owner's Equity (Capital)	The *right* side is the *increase* side.
Revenue	The *right* side is the *increase* side.
Expenses	The *left* side is the *increase* side.

Generally, you will not be using the minus side of expense or revenue accounts, since transactions involving revenue and expense accounts usually result in increases in these accounts. A possible exception to this statement occurs when errors have been made or in the case of closing entries (Chapter 4).

Recording Transactions in T Account Form

sing the accounts of Clark's Cleaners, we will now record in T accounts the same transactions described in Chapter 1.

Assets		=	Liabilities		+	Owner's Equity		+	Revenue		−	Expenses	
+	−		−	+		−	+		−	+		+	−
Left Debit	Right Credit		Left Debit	Right Credit		Left Debit	Right Credit		Left Debit	Right Credit		Left Debit	Right Credit

The fundamental accounting equation with T accounts for Clark's Cleaners is illustrated in Figure 2-5. We have given specific account titles for revenue and expense accounts, as stated in the company's chart of accounts. Also, we have changed the order of presentation of the asset accounts so that their sequence is now consistent with the chart of accounts. Accountants use the abbreviations Dr. for debit and Cr. for credit.

Figure 2-5

Assets	=	Liabilities	+	Owner's Equity	+	Revenue	−	Expenses

+	−
Dr.	Cr.

Cash

+	−
Dr.	Cr.

Accounts Receivable

+	−
Dr.	Cr.

Supplies

+	−
Dr.	Cr.

Prepaid Insurance

+	−
Dr.	Cr.

Equipment

+	−
Dr.	Cr.

−	+
Dr.	Cr.

Accounts Payable

−	+
Dr.	Cr.

−	+
Dr.	Cr.

N. L. Clark, Capital

−	+
Dr.	Cr.

N. L. Clark, Drawing

+	−
Dr.	Cr.

−	+
Dr.	Cr.

Income from Services

−	+
Dr.	Cr.

+	−
Dr.	Cr.

Advertising Expense

+	−
Dr.	Cr.

Wages Expenses

+	−
Dr.	Cr.

Rent Expense

+	−
Dr.	Cr.

Utilities Expense

+	−
Dr.	Cr.

Before we begin entering Clark's Cleaners' transactions into T accounts, let us again stress the steps in the analytical process of accounting; it may be helpful to review beginning steps in the process with the letters ACID and to add two steps to the process.

A 1. Decide which accounts are involved.

C 2. Classify the accounts involved as asset, liability, owner's equity (capital), revenue, or expense.

I 3. Decide which accounts are increased.
Decide which accounts are decreased.

D 4. After you have analyzed the transaction, prepare the entry as a debit to one account (or accounts) and a credit to another account (or accounts).

5. Check to see that at least one account is debited and at least one account is credited and that total amounts debited equal total amounts credited.

To prepare the entry, you must be able to visualize the fundamental accounting equation in the form of T accounts. Memorize it immediately if you have not done so already.

In order to help you determine how to record debits and credits in the foregoing transactions, we repeat the fundamental accounting equation prior to each transaction.

Use the ACID steps plus the two debit and credit steps to prepare each of the transactions for Clark's Cleaners. Be sure to check that the debits do equal credits after each transaction.

Transaction (a) **N. L. Clark invests $40,000 cash in his new business.** This transaction results in an increase in Cash and an increase in the Capital account.

Assets	=	Liabilities	+	Owner's Equity	+	Revenue	−	Expenses
+ −		− +		− +		− +		+ −
Debit Credit		Debit Credit		Debit Credit		Debit Credit		Debit Credit

Cash

+	−
(a) 40,000	

N. L. Clark, Capital

−	+
	(a) 40,000

Transaction (b) **Clark's Cleaners buys equipment costing $22,000 from Drake Equipment Company and pays cash.** This transaction results in an increase in Equipment and a decrease in Cash.

Assets	=	Liabilities	+	Owner's Equity	+	Revenue	−	Expenses
+ −		− +		− +		− +		+ −
Debit Credit		Debit Credit		Debit Credit		Debit Credit		Debit Credit

Cash

+	−
	(b) 22,000

Equipment

+	−
(b) 22,000	

Transaction (c) **Clark's Cleaners buys equipment on credit (on account) from Drake Equipment Company, $4,000.** This transaction results in an increase in Equipment and an increase in Accounts Payable.

Assets	=	Liabilities	+	Owner's Equity	+	Revenue	−	Expenses
+ −		− +		− +		− +		+ −
Debit Credit		Debit Credit		Debit Credit		Debit Credit		Debit Credit

Equipment

+	−
(c) 4,000	

Accounts Payable

−	+
	(c) 4,000

Transaction (d) **Clark's Cleaners pays $1,000 to Drake Equipment Company to be applied against the firm's liability of $4,000.** This transaction results in a decrease in Cash and a decrease in Accounts Payable.

Assets		=	Liabilities		+	Owner's Equity		+	Revenue		−	Expenses	
+	−		−	+		−	+		−	+		+	−
Debit	Credit		Debit	Credit		Debit	Credit		Debit	Credit		Debit	Credit

Cash		Accounts Payable	
+	−	−	+
	(d) 1,000	(d) 1,000	

Transaction (e) **Clark's Cleaners buys cleaning fluid and garment bags on account from Blair and Company for $400.** This transaction, in which the purchase is on a credit or charge account basis, results in an increase in Supplies and an increase in Accounts Payable.

Assets		=	Liabilities		+	Owner's Equity		+	Revenue		−	Expenses	
+	−		−	+		−	+		−	+		+	−
Debit	Credit		Debit	Credit		Debit	Credit		Debit	Credit		Debit	Credit

Supplies		Accounts Payable	
+	−	−	+
(e) 400			(e) 400

Transaction (f) **Clark's Cleaners pays the month's rent of $500.** Write $500 on the plus, or left, side of Rent Expense. **Rent Expense is increasing, therefore the amount is placed on the plus or debit side. The overall effect is to subtract the expense from the right side of the equation.** Also write $500 on the minus, or right, side of Cash.

Assets		=	Liabilities		+	Owner's Equity		+	Revenue		−	Expenses	
+	−		−	+		−	+		−	+		+	−
Debit	Credit		Debit	Credit		Debit	Credit		Debit	Credit		Debit	Credit

Cash		Rent Expense	
+	−	+	−
	(f) 500	(f) 500	

Transaction (g) **Clark's Cleaners pays $360 for a one-year liability insurance policy.** Write $360 on the plus, or debit, side of Prepaid Insurance and $360 on the minus, or credit, side of Cash.

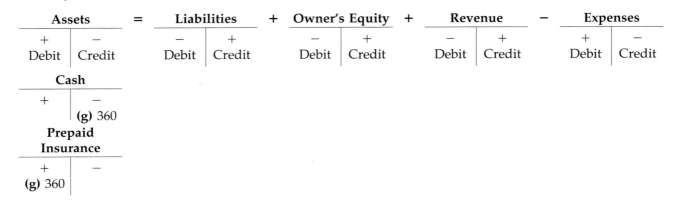

Assets		=	Liabilities		+	Owner's Equity		+	Revenue		−	Expenses	
+	−		−	+		−	+		−	+		+	−
Debit	Credit		Debit	Credit		Debit	Credit		Debit	Credit		Debit	Credit

Cash

+	−
	(g) 360

Prepaid Insurance

+	−
(g) 360	

Transaction (h)   For services performed, Clark's Cleaners receives $1,940 revenue from cash customers. Write $1,940 on the plus, or debit, side of Cash and $1,940 on the plus, or credit, side of Income from Services.

Assets		=	Liabilities		+	Owner's Equity		+	Revenue		−	Expenses	
+	−		−	+		−	+		−	+		+	−
Debit	Credit		Debit	Credit		Debit	Credit		Debit	Credit		Debit	Credit

Cash

+	−
(h) 1,940	

Income from Services

−	+
	(h) 1,940

Transaction (i)   Clark's Cleaners receives a bill from the *City News* for newspaper advertising, $180. Since there is an increase in Advertising Expense, we write $180 on the debit (plus) side of that account. Since there is an increase in Accounts Payable, we write $180 on the credit (plus) side of that account.

Assets		=	Liabilities		+	Owner's Equity		+	Revenue		−	Expenses	
+	−		−	+		−	+		−	+		+	−
Debit	Credit		Debit	Credit		Debit	Credit		Debit	Credit		Debit	Credit

Accounts Payable

−	+
	(i) 180

Advertising Expense

+	−
(i) 180	

Transaction (j)   Clark's Cleaners receives and pays a bill for electricity from City Power and Light, $220. Write $220 on the plus, or debit, side of Utilities Expense and $220 on the minus, or credit, side of Cash.

Assets		=	Liabilities		+	Owner's Equity		+	Revenue		−	Expenses	
+	−		−	+		−	+		−	+		+	−
Debit	Credit		Debit	Credit		Debit	Credit		Debit	Credit		Debit	Credit

Cash

+	−
	(j) 220

Utilities Expense

+	−
(j) 220	

C O M P U T E R S A T W O R K

Turning Time Into Money: CPA Tracks and Saves Billable Time with Timeslips

Time is money.

For some business owners, that's a lot more than a tired cliche. It literally describes how they make their living. Self-employed accountants, attorneys, and consultants make most of their money at the hands of the clock.

Peter Murphy, a self-employed CPA from Huntingburg, Ind., says old-fashioned methods of tracking time can waste it and cheat the client out of productive work hours.

Like many other entrepreneurs who bill by the hour, Murphy has reduced wasted hours, for both him and his clients, with the help of computer time management. Murphy uses *Timeslips*, a program costing about $300 that will time the work for clients, calculate time reports, bill clients, and track accounts receivable.

READY, SET, GO · An important feature of Timeslips is the "stopwatch." It's a terminate-and-stay resident (TSR) program that allows users to keep time regardless of the program they're using.

Murphy simply activates the program. Then he opens any program, document or account in which he wants to work, starts the timer and starts working. When he finishes, he turns off the timer, and Timeslips will record how long he worked on the account. . . .

LESS TIME BILLING · Now Murphy spends about 2 to 3 hours a month tracking and adding time on the computer. When he's done, he prints invoices to a laser printer. Secretaries spend virtually no time preparing bills beyond the stuffing of envelopes.

Overall, Timeslips saves the business about $3\frac{1}{2}$ hours a month. . . .

Regardless of the answer, time-tracking programs like Timeslips will benefit professionals who bill by the hour.

Source: Excerpted from Ryan Steeves, "Turning Time into Money," *PC Today*, July 1994, p. 30.

Transaction (k) Clark's Cleaners signs a contract with Formal Rentals to clean their for-hire formal garments on a credit basis. Clark's Cleaners completes a cleaning job and bills Formal Rentals $140 for services performed. Write $140 on the plus, or debit, side of Accounts Receivable and $140 on the plus, or credit, side of Income from Services.

Assets		=	Liabilities		+	Owner's Equity		+	Revenue		−	Expenses	
+	−		−	+		−	+		−	+		+	−
Debit	Credit		Debit	Credit		Debit	Credit		Debit	Credit		Debit	Credit

Accounts Receivable			Income from Services	
+	−		-	+
(k) 140				**(k)** 140

Transaction (l)   Clark's Cleaners pays wages of part-time employee, $930. Write $930 on the plus, or debit, side of Wages Expense and $930 on the minus, or credit, side of Cash.

Assets		=	Liabilities		+	Owner's Equity		+	Revenue		−	Expenses	
+	−		−	+		−	+		−	+		+	−
Debit	Credit		Debit	Credit		Debit	Credit		Debit	Credit		Debit	Credit

												Wages Expense	
Cash													
+	−											+	−
	(l) 930											**(l)** 930	

In describing the transactions of the business, notice that we say "Clark's Cleaners pays wages of part-time employee," not "N. L. Clark pays wages of part-time employee." Our reason for saying that Clark's Cleaners pays the wages is that we are treating the business as a separate economic or accounting entity. Clark's Cleaners is separate from any other businesses Clark might own and separate from his personal affairs. You may recall the separate entity concept from Chapter 1.

Transaction (m)   Clark's Cleaners buys from Drake Equipment Company additional equipment costing $940, paying $140 down, with the remaining $800 on account. Write $940 on the plus, or debit, side of Equipment. Write $140 on the minus, or credit, side of Cash and $800 on the plus, or credit, side of Accounts Payable. Recall from Chapter 1 that this is a compound entry.

Assets		=	Liabilities		+	Owner's Equity		+	Revenue		−	Expenses	
+	−		−	+		−	+		−	+		+	−
Debit	Credit		Debit	Credit		Debit	Credit		Debit	Credit		Debit	Credit

Cash			**Accounts Payable**										
+	−		−	+									
	(m) 140			**(m)** 800									
Equipment													
+	−												
(m) 940													

Transaction (n)   Clark's Cleaners receives revenue from cash customers for the remainder of the month, $1,790. Write $1,790 on the plus, or debit, side of Cash and $1,790 on the plus, or credit, side of Income from Services.

Assets		=	Liabilities		+	Owner's Equity		+	Revenue		−	Expenses	
+	−		−	+		−	+		−	+		+	−
Debit	Credit		Debit	Credit		Debit	Credit		Debit	Credit		Debit	Credit

Cash									**Income from Services**				
+	−								−	+			
(n) 1,790										**(n)** 1,790			

Transaction (o) **Clark's Cleaners receives $90 from Formal Rentals to apply on account (that is, to apply on the amount billed previously).** Write $90 on the plus, or debit, side of Cash and $90 on the minus, or credit, side of Accounts Receivable.

Assets	=	Liabilities	+	Owner's Equity	+	Revenue	−	Expenses
+ | −		− | +		− | +		− | +		+ | −
Debit | Credit		Debit | Credit		Debit | Credit		Debit | Credit		Debit | Credit

Cash

+	−
(o) 90	

Accounts Receivable

+	−
	(o) 90

Transaction (p) **Clark's Cleaners pays Drake Equipment Company $1,980 on account.** This means the money is to be applied against the firm's liability of $4,380. Write $1,980 on the minus, or debit, side of Accounts Payable and $1,980 on the minus, or credit, side of Cash.

Assets	=	Liabilities	+	Owner's Equity	+	Revenue	−	Expenses
+ | −		− | +		− | +		− | +		+ | −
Debit | Credit		Debit | Credit		Debit | Credit		Debit | Credit		Debit | Credit

Cash

+	−
	(p) 1,980

Accounts Payable

−	+
(p) 1,980	

Transaction (q) **Owner makes a cash withdrawal of $1,200.** At the end of the month, Clark withdraws from the business $1,200 in cash for his personal use. Write $1,200 on the minus, or credit, side of Cash and $1,200 on the plus, or debit, side of N. L. Clark, Drawing. Because the account N. L. Clark, Drawing, is used to record personal withdrawals by the owner, any additional amount should be recorded on the plus, or debit, side, of this account. Since the Drawing account is a deduction from Owner's Equity, the plus and minus signs are reversed.

Assets	=	Liabilities	+	Owner's Equity	+	Revenue	−	Expenses
+ | −		− | +		− | +		− | +		+ | −
Debit | Credit		Debit | Credit		Debit | Credit		Debit | Credit		Debit | Credit

Cash

+	−
	(q) 1,200

N. L. Clark, Drawing

+	−
(q) 1,200	

The Drawing account is used to record temporary decreases in Owner's Equity. The owner takes money out of the business for his or her living expenses hoping that the withdrawals will be offset by net income. In contrast, if the owner permanently reduces his or her investment in the business, the Capital account is debited.

Summary of Transactions

The transactions for Clark's Cleaners are summarized in the T accounts presented in Figure 2-6. **Note that, in recording expenses, one places the entries only on the plus, or debit, side. Also, in recording revenue, one places the entries only on the plus, or credit, side.**

Figure 2-6

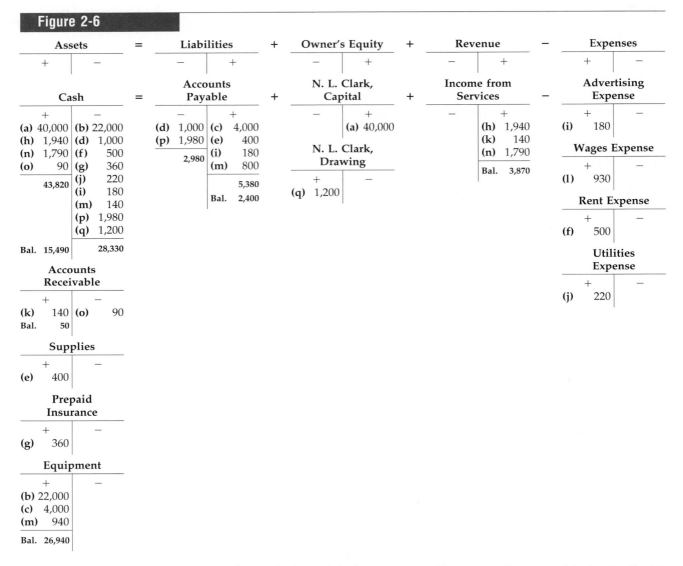

If you circle each balance, you will see that the normal balance of each account is on the plus side. An error can cause an abnormal balance. For example, writing checks for more cash than you have creates a credit balance in Cash, and overpaying your bills creates a debit balance in Accounts Payable. Train your eyes to look for abnormal balances. Your success and confidence with accounting will depend not only on your knowledge of the rules, but also on your ability to see things that just don't look right.

Now that we've seen how to record transactions in T accounts, let's prove the equality of debits and credits.

Preparation of the Trial Balance

You can now prepare a **trial balance** by simply recording the balances of the accounts. The trial balance is a listing of account balances in two columns labeled Debit and Credit. A trial balance is not considered a financial statement, but is, as the name implies, a trial run by the accountant to prove that the debit balances of the accounts equal the credit balances of the accounts. This is evidence of the equality of both sides of the fundamental accounting equation. The accountant must prove that the accounts are in balance before going on to make up the company's financial statements.

In preparing a trial balance, record the balances of the accounts in the same order as they are listed in the chart of accounts. The balance sheet accounts are listed first, followed by the income statement accounts, as shown in Figure 2-7.

- Assets
- Liabilities
- Owner's Equity
- Revenue
- Expenses

R E M E M B E R

Debits must equal credits. Also remember that even though debits equal credits, the work may be incorrect.

Performance Objective 4

Prepare a trial balance from the T accounts.

FYI

Spreadsheet software is ranked as the number one software used in business and government.

Figure 2-7

Clark's Cleaners

Trial Balance
June 30, 19–

Column heads identify information in each column

ACCOUNT NAME	DEBIT	CREDIT
Cash	15 4 9 0 00	
Accounts Receivable	5 0 00	
Supplies	4 0 0 00	
Prepaid Insurance	3 6 0 00	
Equipment	26 9 4 0 00	
Accounts Payable		2 4 0 0 00
N. L. Clark, Capital		40 0 0 0 00
N. L. Clark, Drawing	1 2 0 0 00	
Income from Services		3 8 7 0 00
Advertising Expense	1 8 0 00	
Wages Expense	9 3 0 00	
Rent Expense	5 0 0 00	
Utilities Expense	2 2 0 00	
	46 2 7 0 00	46 2 7 0 00

Accounts listed in order of chart of accounts

Dollar signs are not used on a trial balance

Single underline beneath figures to be summed

Double underline beneath column totals

The **normal balance of each account is on its plus side.** Remember that, when there is more than one entry in an account, we record the totals in footings and subtract one footing from the other to determine the balance. Record this balance on the side of the account having the larger footing. (Here we record the Drawing account balance in the debit column because it has a debit balance. We do not deduct Drawing from the Capital account at the time that we prepare the trial balance.) The table below indicates where each of the account balances would normally be shown in a trial balance.

	Trial Balance	
Account Titles	**Left or Debit Balances**	**Right or Credit Balances**
	Assets	
		Liabilities
		Capital
	Drawing	
		Revenue
	Expenses	
Totals	XXXX XX	XXXX XX

Errors Exposed by the Trial Balance

If the debit and credit columns are not equal, then it is evident that we have made an error. Possible causes of errors include the following:

- Making errors in arithmetic, such as errors in adding the trial balance columns or in finding the balances of the accounts.
- Recording only half an entry, such as a debit without a corresponding credit, or vice versa.
- Recording both halves of the entry on the same side, such as two debits rather than a debit and a credit.
- Recording one or more amounts incorrectly.

Procedure for Locating Errors

Suppose that you are in a business situation in which you have recorded transactions for a month in the account books, and the accounts do not balance. To save yourself time, you need to have a definite procedure for tracking down the errors. The best method is to do everything in reverse, as follows:

- Look for the pattern of balances to see if a normal balance was placed incorrectly.
- Re-add the trial balance columns.
- Check the transferring of the figures from the accounts to the trial balance.
- Verify the footings and balances of the accounts.

As an added precaution, form the habit of verifying all addition and subtraction as you go along. You can thus correct many mistakes *before* the time comes to make up a trial balance.

When the trial balance totals do not balance, the difference might indicate that you forgot to record half of an entry in the accounts. For example, if the difference in the trial balance totals is $20, you may have recorded $20 on the debit side of one account without recording $20 on the credit side of another account. Another possibility is to divide the difference by 2; this may provide a clue that you accidentally recorded half an entry twice. For example, if the difference in the trial balance is $600, you may have recorded $300 on the debit side of one account and an additional $300 on the debit side of another account. Look for a transaction that involved $300 and then see if you have recorded both a debit and a credit. By knowing which transactions to check, you can save a lot of time.

Transpositions and Slides

If the difference is evenly divisible by 9, the discrepancy may be either a transposition or a slide. A **transposition** means that the digits have been transposed, or switched around when copying from one place to another. For example, one transposition of digits in 916 can be written as 619.

Correct Number	Number Copied	Difference	Difference Divided by 9
916	619	297	$297 \div 9 = 33$

A **slide** is an error in placing the decimal point; in other words, a slide in the decimal point. For example, $163 could be inadvertently written as $1.63:

Correct Number	Number Copied	Difference	Difference Divided by 9
163.00	1.63	161.37	$161.37 \div 9 = 17.93$

Or the error may be a combination of transposition and slide, such as when $216 is written as $6.21:

Correct Number	Number Copied	Difference	Difference Divided by 9
216.00	6.21	209.79	$209.79 \div 9 = 23.31$

Again, the difference is evenly divisible by 9 (with no remainder).

CHAPTER REVIEW

R eview of Performance Objectives

1. **Present the fundamental accounting equation with the T account form, and label the debit and credit sides.**

Assets		=	Liabilities		+	Owner's Equity		+	Revenue		−	Expenses	
Left	Right		Left	Right		Left	Right		Left	Right		Left	Right
Debit	Credit		Debit	Credit		Debit	Credit		Debit	Credit		Debit	Credit

2. **Present the fundamental accounting equation with the T account form, and label the plus and minus sides.**

Assets		=	Liabilities		+	Owner's Equity		+	Revenue		−	Expenses	
+	−		−	+		−	+		−	+		+	−
Left	Right		Left	Right		Left	Right		Left	Right		Left	Right
Debit	Credit		Debit	Credit		Debit	Credit		Debit	Credit		Debit	Credit

3. **Record directly in T accounts a group of business transactions involving changes in asset, liability, owner's equity, revenue, and expense accounts for a service business.**

   The transactions are recorded by first recognizing and classifying the accounts involved. Next, decide whether the accounts involved are increased or decreased, and record the amounts as debits or credits in the accounts. The equation must always remain in balance.

4. **Prepare a trial balance from the T accounts.**

   A trial balance is prepared by listing the balance of each account in the Debit or Credit column to make certain that total debits equal total credits.

5. **Recognize the effect of transpositions and slides on account balances.**

   A possible error in a trial balance may be a transposition or a slide. The clue is that the difference in account balances or trial balance totals is evenly divisible by 9. With a transposition, the digits have been switched around. With a slide, the decimal point has been recorded in the wrong place.

Glossary

Credit The right side of a T account; to credit is to record an amount on the right side of a T account. Credits represent increases in liability, capital, and revenue accounts and decreases in asset, drawing, and expense accounts. **(50)**

Debit The left side of a T account; to debit is to record an amount on the left side of a T account. Debits represent increases in asset, drawing, and expense accounts and decreases in liability, capital, and revenue accounts. **(50)**

Footings The totals of each side of a T account, recorded in small, pencil-written figures. **(50)**

Normal balance The plus side of a T account. **(50)**

Slide An error in placing the decimal point in a number. **(65)**

T account form A form shaped like the letter T, in which increases and decreases in an account may be recorded. One side of the T is for entries on the debit or left side. The other side of the T is for entries on the credit or right side. **(50)**

Transposition An error that involves interchanging, or switching around, digits when recording a number. **(65)**

Trial balance A listing of all account balances in two columns to prove that the total of all the debit balances equals the total of all the credit balances. **(63)**

QUESTIONS, EXERCISES, AND PROBLEMS

Discussion Questions

1. List in order the steps in the analytical process of accounting.
2. Does the term *debit* always mean "increase"? Does the term *credit* always mean "decrease"? Explain.
3. What is meant by the separate entity concept?
4. What is the order of the accounts listed in the chart of accounts?
5. In a trial balance, if total debits equal total credits, does this mean that the recording of the transactions is absolutely accurate? Why or why not?
6. What is the difference between a trial balance and a balance sheet?
7. Give an example of a slide and a transposition. How can one quickly determine whether an error may involve a slide or a transposition?
8. What are the normal balances of Cash and Accounts Payable? How can Cash or Accounts Payable have an abnormal balance—that is, how can Cash have a credit balance or Accounts Payable have a debit balance?

Exercises

Exercise 2-1 On a sheet of paper, set up the fundamental accounting equation with T accounts under each of the five account classifications, noting plus and minus signs on the appropriate sides of each account. Under each classification, set up T accounts—again with the correct debit and credit sides and plus and minus signs—for each of the following accounts of Crystal Shoe Repair.

P.O.1,2

Draw T accounts and record debit and credit and plus and minus.

Cash	Accounts Payable	Rent Expense
Accounts Receivable	J. Robb, Capital	Wages Expense
Supplies	J. Robb, Drawing	Utilities Expense
Equipment	Income from Services	Miscellaneous Expense

P.O.3

Describe recorded transactions.

Exercise 2-2 During the first month of operation, Sherrard's Glass Supply recorded the following transactions. Describe transactions **(a)** through **(k)**.

Cash	
(a) 4,500	(b) 475
(k) 920	(c) 61
	(e) 82
	(g) 1,000
	(i) 81
	(j) 300

Accounts Receivable	
(h) 825	

Glass-Cutting Supplies	
(d) 370	

Glass-Cutting Equipment	
(f) 3,600	
(g) 1,750	

Accounts Payable	
	(d) 370
	(g) 750

C. S. Sherrard, Capital	
	(a) 4,500
	(f) 3,600

C. S. Sherrard, Drawing	
(j) 300	

Income from Services	
	(h) 825
	(k) 920

Rent Expense	
(b) 475	

Utilities Expense	
(i) 81	

Advertising Expense	
(c) 61	

Miscellaneous Expense	
(e) 82	

P.O.1,2

Draw T accounts and record transactions in them.

Exercise 2-3 S. L. Merritt operates Merritt Cleaners. The company has the following chart of accounts:

Chart of Accounts

ASSETS	OWNER'S EQUITY
Cash	S. L. Merritt, Capital
Accounts Receivable	S. L. Merritt, Drawing
Supplies	
Prepaid Insurance	REVENUE
Cleaning Equipment	Income from Services
Truck	
Office Equipment	EXPENSES
	Wages Expense
LIABILITIES	Truck Expense
Accounts Payable	Utilities Expense
	Advertising Expense

On a sheet of notebook paper, record the following transactions directly in pairs of T accounts. List the T account to be debited on the left side of the sheet and the account to be credited on the right side. Show the debit and credit sides and the plus and minus signs. (*Example:* Received and paid bill for advertising, $86.)

Advertising Expense		Cash	
Dr.	Cr.	Dr.	Cr.
+	−	+	−
86			86

a. Received and paid electric bill, $47.
b. Bought supplies on account, $127.
c. Received premium bill and paid liability insurance premium, $398.
d. Paid creditors on account, $595.
e. Returned defective supplies previously bought on account, $30.
f. Received and paid telephone bill, $26.
g. Charged customers for services rendered, $356.
h. Received and paid gasoline bill for truck, $210.
i. Received $898 from charge customers to apply on account.
j. Merritt withdrew cash for personal use, $200.

Exercise 2-4 List the classification of each of the following accounts. Write "Debit" or "Credit" to indicate the Increase Side, the Decrease Side, and the Normal Balance Side.

P.O.2

Classify accounts.

Account	Classification	Increase Side	Decrease Side	Normal Balance Side
0. Cash	Asset	Debit	Credit	Debit
1. Accounts Payable				
2. Wages Expense				
3. Fees Earned				
4. Equipment				
5. Rent Expense				
6. J. Doe, Capital				
7. Accounts Receivable				
8. Service Revenue				
9. J. Doe, Drawing				

Exercise 2-5 During the first month of operations, James Advertising Agency recorded transactions in T account form. Prepare a trial balance dated October 31 of this year.

P.O.4

Prepare trial balance.

	Cash		
(a)	6,200	(c)	400
(e)	4,000	(f)	700
		(h)	100
		(i)	3,200
		(j)	2,000

	Accounts Receivable
(g)	3,000

	Office Supplies
(c)	400

	Equipment
(b)	2,700
(d)	1,800

	Accounts Payable	
	(b)	2,700

	N. C. James, Capital	
	(a)	6,200
	(d)	1,800

	N. C. James, Drawing
(j)	2,000

	Advertising Fees	
	(e)	4,000
	(g)	3,000

	Salary Expense
(i)	3,200

	Rent Expense
(f)	700

	Utilities Expense
(h)	100

P.O.4

Prepare a corrected trial balance.

Exercise 2-6 ABC Copy Center hired a new accounting intern who is not entirely familiar with the process of preparing a trial balance. All the accounts have normal balances. Find the errors, and prepare a corrected trial balance for November 30 of this year.

ABC Copy Center

Trial Balance
November 30, 19–

ACCOUNT NAME	DEBIT	CREDIT
Accounts Receivable		14 4 0 0 00
Cash	2 8 0 0 00	
Accounts Payable	12 6 0 0 00	
Equipment	36 0 0 0 00	
R. C. Palmer, Capital		32 3 0 0 00
R. C. Palmer, Drawing		1 2 0 0 00
Prepaid Insurance		8 0 0 00
Income from Services		44 0 0 0 00
Rent Expense		3 6 0 0 00
Supplies	8 2 0 0 00	
Utilities Expense	1 1 0 0 00	
Wages Expense	20 8 0 0 00	
	81 5 0 0 00	96 3 0 0 00

P.O.5

Determine the effects of errors.

Exercise 2-7 Which of the following errors would cause a trial balance to have unequal totals? As a result of the errors, which accounts are either overstated (equal too much) or understated (equal too little)?

a. A purchase of office equipment for $490 was recorded as a debit to Office Equipment for $49 and a credit to Cash for $49.
b. A payment of $250 to a creditor was debited to Accounts Receivable and credited to Cash for $250 each.
c. A purchase of supplies for $225 was recorded as a debit to Equipment for $225 and a credit to Cash for $225.
d. A payment of $97 to a creditor was recorded as a debit to Accounts Payable for $97 and a credit to Cash for $79.

Exercise 2-8 Assume that a trial balance has been prepared and that the total of the debit balances is not equal to the total of the credit balances. On a sheet of paper, set up like the example below, note the amount by which the two totals would differ, and identify which column is understated or overstated. Item 0 is given as an example.

P.O.5

Determine the effects of errors.

Error	Amount of Difference	Debit or Credit Column Understated or Overstated
0. *Example:* A $271 debit to Accounts Receivable was not recorded.	$271	Debit column understated
a. A $23 debit to Supplies was recorded as $230.		
b. A $155 debit to Accounts Payable was recorded twice.		
c. A $77 debit to Prepaid Insurance was not recorded.		
d. A $52 credit to Cash was not recorded.		
e. A $260 debit to Equipment was recorded twice.		
f. A $73 debit to Supplies was recorded as a $73 debit to Miscellaneous Expense.		

C onsider and Communicate

Another accounting student is having difficulty understanding how the fundamental accounting equation stays in balance in a compound entry with one debit and two credits. Imagine, for example, that a business bought equipment for $5,000, paid $2,000 down, and charged the remainder.

In this transaction there are two credits and one debit—one debit and one credit on the left side of the equation and the other credit on the right side of the equation. How does the equation stay in balance?

W hat If . . .

What if the new bookkeeper notices that the financial statements for the company are presented in whole dollar amounts without any cents shown and then records next month's transactions in the journal in whole dollars to follow the pattern of the financial statements? Are the records in error? Will the financial statements be any different because of this?

A Question of Ethics

The new bookkeeper can't locate the errors that must be causing the month-end trial balance to be out of balance. Too shy to ask for help at the office, the bookkeeper takes the financial records home. There the bookkeeper asks her mother, a retired bookkeeper, to help her locate the errors. Is this ethical behavior?

P roblem Set A

P.O.1,2,3

Problem 2-1A During October of this year, C. S. Brady established the True-Cycle Repair Shop. The following asset, liability, and owner's equity accounts are included in the chart of accounts: Cash; Supplies; Shop Equipment; Store Equipment; Office Equipment; Accounts Payable; C. S. Brady, Capital. The following transactions occurred during the month of October:

a. Brady invested $22,000 cash in the business.
b. Bought shop equipment for cash, $1,875.
c. Bought supplies from Pearson Company, $651; payment is due in thirty days.
d. Bought store fixtures for $915 from Guizeth Hardware; payment is due in thirty days.
e. Bought a typewriter and calculator for $642 from Sherman Office Supply, paying $300 down; the balance is due in thirty days.
f. Paid $390 on account for the store fixtures in transaction **d.**
g. Brady invested in the business her personal tools with a fair market value of $478.

Instructions

1. Label the account titles under the appropriate headings in the fundamental accounting equation.
2. Correctly place the plus and minus signs under each T account, and label the debit and credit sides of the T account.
3. Record the amounts in the proper positions in the T accounts. Key each entry to the letter that identifies each transaction.

Problem 2-2A R. C. Talbot established Talbot Temp Agency during May of this year. The accountant prepared the following chart of accounts:

P.O.1,2,3,4

Chart of Accounts

ASSETS
Cash
Supplies
Computer Programs
Office Equipment
Neon Sign

LIABILITIES
Accounts Payable

OWNER'S EQUITY
R. C. Talbot, Capital
R. C. Talbot, Drawing

REVENUE
Income from Services

EXPENSES
Rent Expense
Utilities Expense
Wages Expense
Advertising Expense
Miscellaneous Expense

The following transactions occurred during the month:
a. Talbot invested $14,600 cash to establish the business.
b. Paid rent for the month, $675.
c. Bought office desks and a filing cabinet for cash, $1,376.
d. Bought a computer and printer for use in the business from Alpha Computers for $12,750; paid $2,500 down, with the balance due in thirty days (Office Equipment).
e. Bought a neon sign for $765; paid $300 down, with the balance due in thirty days.
f. Talbot invested in the business her personal computer software with a fair market value of $1,525 (Computer Programs).
g. Received bill for advertising from the *Urban Daily*, $121.
h. Received cash for services rendered, $729.
i. Received and paid electric bill, $212.
j. Paid bill for advertising, recorded previously in transaction **g.**
k. Received cash for services rendered, $1,197.
l. Paid wages to part-time employee, $795.
m. Received and paid for city business license, $45.
n. Talbot withdrew cash for personal use, $525.
o. Bought computer paper and company stationery from James, Inc., with payment due in thirty days, $159.

Instructions

1. Record the owner's name in the Capital and Drawing T accounts.
2. Record the plus and minus signs under each T account, and label the debit and credit sides of the T accounts.
3. Record the transactions in the T accounts. Key each entry to the letter that identifies each transaction.
4. Foot the T accounts and show balances.
5. Prepare a trial balance with a three-line heading, dated May 31.

P.O.1,2,3,4

Problem 2-3A A. L. Kubota, a dentist, opens an office for the practice of dentistry, A. L. Kubota, D.D.S. Her accountant recommends the following chart of accounts:

Chart of Accounts

ASSETS	REVENUE
Cash	Professional Fees
Accounts Receivable	
Office Equipment	EXPENSES
Office Furniture	Salary Expense
Professional Equipment	Rent Expense
	Utilities Expense
LIABILITIES	Miscellaneous Expense
Accounts Payable	
OWNER'S EQUITY	
A. L. Kubota, Capital	
A. L. Kubota, Drawing	

The following transactions occurred during July of this year:
a. Kubota invested $25,000 cash in her professional enterprise.
b. Bought a typewriter for $525 from Starling Office Machines, paying $250 down; the balance is due in thirty days.
c. Kubota invested in the enterprise her personal professional equipment with a fair market value of $9,400 (additional investment).
d. Bought waiting room chairs and carpets (Office Furniture), paying cash, $1,891.
e. Bought an intercom system on account from Triad Office Supply (Office Equipment), $419.
f. Received and paid telephone bill, $97.
g. Billed patients for professional services performed, $3,075.
h. Received and paid electric bill for heat and lights, $96.
i. Bought a copy machine on account from Triad Office Supply, $598.
j. Paid expenses for trip to local dental convention, $195.
k. Billed patients for additional professional services, $4,113.
l. Paid office rent for the month, $875.
m. Paid salary of assistant, $1,975.
n. Dr. Kubota withdrew cash for her personal use, $2,750.
o. Received $2,134 on account from patients who were billed previously.

Instructions

1. Record the owner's name in the Capital and Drawing T accounts.
2. Correctly place plus and minus signs under each T account, and label the debit and credit sides of the T accounts.
3. Record the transactions in the T accounts. Key each entry to the letter that identifies each transaction.
4. Foot the T accounts and show balances.
5. Prepare a trial balance as of July 31.
6. Prepare an income statement for July.

7. Prepare a statement of owner's equity for July.
8. Prepare a balance sheet as of July 31.

Problem 2-4A On September 1, T. M. Sizemore opened Tony's Video Arcade, an entertainment center. Sizemore's accountant listed the following account titles for the chart of accounts: Cash; Supplies; Prepaid Insurance; Equipment; Furniture and Fixtures; Accounts Payable; T. M. Sizemore, Capital; T. M. Sizemore, Drawing; Coin Box Revenue; Wages Expense; Rent Expense; Utilities Expense; Miscellaneous Expense. During September, the following transactions were completed:

`P.O.1,2,3,4`

a. Sizemore deposited $27,680 in a bank account in the name of the business.
b. Bought chairs and tables for cash, $1,310.
c. Bought supplies for the Arcade for $152 on account from Gramm Company.
d. Paid rent for the month, $825.
e. Bought video game equipment from Videotech and Vending Machines, Inc., $21,200; paid $8,200 down, with the remainder due in thirty days.
f. Paid $260 cash for a twelve-month liability insurance policy.
g. Received $1,595 from cash customers for the first half of the month.
h. Paid $2,250 as a part payment on account for the equipment purchased from Videotech and Vending Machines, Inc.
i. Received and paid electric bill, $171.
j. Paid wages to employees, $1,210.
k. Received $539 from cash customers for the second half of the month.
l. Sizemore withdrew cash for his personal use, $860.
m. Received bill for advertising in *Urban News and Views*, $128.
n. Paid $152 on account for the supplies acquired in transaction **c.**

Instructions

1. Record the owner's name in the Capital and Drawing T accounts.
2. Correctly place the plus and minus signs under each T account, and label the debit and credit sides of the T accounts.
3. Record the transactions in the T accounts. Key each entry to the letter that identifies each transaction.
4. Foot the T accounts and show balances.
5. Prepare a trial balance as of September 30.
6. Prepare an income statement for September.
7. Prepare a statement of owner's equity for September.
8. Prepare a balance sheet as of September 30.

P roblem Set B

Problem 2-1B During March of this year, K. P. Petrini established Petrini's Deli. The following asset, liability, and owner's equity accounts are included in the chart of accounts: Cash; Deli Supplies; Deli Equipment; Office Equipment; Truck; Accounts Payable; K. P. Petrini, Capital. During March, the following transactions occurred:

`P.O.1,2,3`

a. Petrini invested $29,600 in the business.
b. Bought used oven and ranges for $6,230, paying cash.
c. Bought deli supplies for cash, $729.

   d. Bought meats, cheeses, flour, and other supplies from J. R. Foods, with
      payment due in thirty days, $1,215.
   e. Bought a typewriter and filing cabinet for cash, $724.
   f. Bought a delivery truck for $10,830 from Byron Automotive, paying $1,000
      down, the balance due in thirty days.
   g. Paid $325 on account to J. R. Foods.

Instructions

   1. Label the account titles under the appropriate headings in the fundamental
      accounting equation.
   2. Correctly place the plus and minus signs under each T account, and label
      the debit and credit sides of the T account.
   3. Record the amounts in the proper positions in the T accounts. Key each
      entry to the letter that identifies each transaction.

P.O.1,2,3,4

Problem 2-2B S. W. Fraley established the Fraley Secretarial Service during
March of this year. The accountant prepared the following chart of accounts:

Chart of Accounts	
ASSETS	REVENUE
Cash	Income from Services
Supplies	
Computer Programs	EXPENSES
Office Equipment	Rent Expense
Neon Sign	Utilities Expense
	Wages Expense
LIABILITIES	Advertising Expense
Accounts Payable	Miscellaneous Expense
OWNER'S EQUITY	
S. W. Fraley, Capital	
S. W. Fraley, Drawing	

The following transactions occurred during the month:
   a. Fraley invested $14,800 cash to establish the business.
   b. Bought an office desk and filing cabinet for cash, $825.
   c. Bought computer software for use in the business from Shillings Computer
      Center for $8,950, paying $1,200 down; the balance is due in 30 days.
   d. Paid rent for the month, $720.
   e. Bought a neon sign for $958 from Ace Sign Company, with $250 as a down
      payment; the balance is due in thirty days.
   f. Received cash for services rendered, $565.
   g. Received bill for advertising, $371, from the *Daily Examiner*.
   h. Bought computer paper and stationery from J. T. Stallings Stationers, $244,
      with payment due in thirty days.
   i. Received and paid electric bill, $149.
   j. Received cash for services rendered, $2,010.
   k. Paid bill for advertising recorded previously in transaction **g.**
   l. Paid wages to part-time employee, $720.
   m. Fraley invested in the business his personal software (Computer Programs)
      with a fair market value of $719.

n. Fraley withdrew cash for personal use, $550.
o. Received and paid for city business license, $52.

Instructions

1. Record the owner's name in the Capital and Drawing T accounts.
2. Correctly place the plus and minus signs under each T account, and label the debit and credit sides of the accounts.
3. Record the transactions in the T accounts. Key each entry to the letter that identifies each transaction.
4. Foot the T accounts and show balances.
5. Prepare a trial balance, with a three-line heading, dated March 31.

Problem 2-3B J. T. Patten, an osteopath, opens the Patten Osteopathic Clinic. Her accountant recommends the following chart of accounts: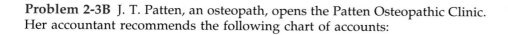

Chart of Accounts	
ASSETS	**REVENUE**
Cash	Professional Fees
Accounts Receivable	
Office Equipment	**EXPENSES**
Office Furniture	Salary Expense
Professional Equipment	Rent Expense
	Utilities Expense
LIABILITIES	Miscellaneous Expense
Accounts Payable	
OWNER'S EQUITY	
J. T. Patten, Capital	
J. T. Patten, Drawing	

The following transactions occurred during May of this year:
a. Patten invested $27,000 cash in her professional practice.
b. Bought telephone equipment on account from Parrett Office Supply (Office Equipment), $319.
c. Bought an electronic typewriter for $580 from Chang Office Machines, paying $180 down; the balance is due in thirty days.
d. Paid cash for chairs and carpets (Office Furniture) for the waiting room, $828.
e. Received and paid phone bill, $79.
f. Billed patients for professional services performed, $4,190.
g. Patten invested in the firm her professional equipment with a fair market value of $8,500 (additional investment).
h. Received and paid electric bill, $96.
i. Paid $225 in expenses for state osteopathic convention.
j. Received $1,710 from patients previously billed in transaction **f**.
k. Paid $150 as part payment on account for the telephone equipment purchased from Parrett Office Supply.
l. Paid office rent for the month, $850.
m. Paid salaries of staff, $2,025.
n. Received $2,575 from cash patients (not previously recorded).
o. Patten withdrew cash for personal use, $2,200.

Instructions

1. Record the owner's name in the Capital and Drawing T accounts.
2. Correctly place plus and minus signs under each T account, and label the debit and credit sides of the T accounts.
3. Record the transactions in the T accounts. Key each entry to the letter that identifies each transaction.
4. Foot the T accounts and show balances.
5. Prepare a trial balance as of May 31.
6. Prepare an income statement for May.
7. Prepare a statement of owner's equity for May.
8. Prepare a balance sheet as of May 31.

P.O.1,2,3,4

Problem 2-4B On August 1, J. C. Freeman opened a coin-operated laundry called Launder World. Freeman's accountant listed the following accounts in the chart of accounts: Cash; Supplies; Prepaid Insurance; Equipment; Furniture and Fixtures; Accounts Payable; J. C. Freeman, Capital; J. C. Freeman, Drawing; Coin Box Revenue; Wages Expense; Rent Expense; Utilities Expense; Miscellaneous Expense. During August, the following transactions were completed.

a. Freeman deposited $23,400 in a bank account in the name of the business.
b. Paid rent for the month, $725.
c. Bought chairs and tables for cash, $419.
d. Bought washers and dryers for $19,200, giving $3,300 cash as a down payment, with the remainder due in thirty days.
e. Bought washing supplies on account from Stryker Distributing Company, $521.
f. Received $819 from cash customers for the first half of the month.
g. Paid $297 for a one-year liability insurance policy.
h. Paid $350 as a partial payment on the equipment purchased in transaction **d.**
i. Received and paid electric bill, $245.
j. Paid $130 on account for the washing supplies acquired in transaction **e.**
k. Received $1,289 from cash customers for the second half of the month.
l. Paid $57 for license and other miscellaneous expenses.
m. Paid wages to employees, $1,057.
n. Freeman withdrew cash for personal use, $1,000.

Instructions

1. Record the owner's name in the Capital and Drawing T accounts.
2. Correctly place the plus and minus signs under each T account, and label the debit and credit sides of the T accounts.
3. Record the transactions in the T accounts. Key each entry to the letter that identifies each transaction.
4. Foot the T accounts and show balances.
5. Prepare a trial balance as of August 31.
6. Prepare an income statement for August.
7. Prepare a statement of owner's equity for August.
8. Prepare a balance sheet as of August 31.

CHALLENGE PROBLEM

You are a para-accountant for a CPA firm. You are interviewing a new client, J. O. Phillips, to set up his chart of accounts and the accounting records. Phillips Fax Service sends and receives facsimile (fax) messages and calls fax recipients to request that they pick up their documents. Phillips has already entered into some transactions prior to coming to you, but nothing has been journalized, because no accounting records exist yet.

Phillips describes the following events related to the new business: "I was able to pick up four fax machines for only $1,800, and I paid for them out of my personal account. I also bought a computer and printer for $2,500. I put $500 down and charged the rest to the business. I deposited $25,000 of my own money in the business account, leaving my personal savings at $6,000. The business check I wrote was for six months' rent in advance, $1,000 per month. I also took $600 cash from my savings just in case the business needs some quick cash. Certain customers will be allowed to put service fees on account. I will be advertising as well as hiring one employee. All utilities are included in my rent, but I do pay for the telephone."

Instructions

1. Create the chart of accounts you feel the client will need.
2. Draw T accounts required to contain the opening entry.
3. Enter the amounts of the opening entry into T accounts dated June 1. (Clue: Treat the rent paid in advance like insurance paid in advance.)

Chapter 3

Recording Business Transactions:

The General Journal and General Ledger

Documentation of accounting information is vital to a business. **Documentation** is a note or reference to a source document (i.e., check, invoice, loan document, etc.) or action taken.

Without these "chicken tracks" the financial records are incomplete. Individuals make mistakes on

financial transactions and could be unable to correct them later if they did not leave a trail. Imagine, if you were an accountant or bookkeeper, how difficult it would be for you to remember every transaction you recorded. Also, think of the dilemma you would face if you were asked to pick up where someone else left off and there were no notes or tracks to assist you.

Journal entries have explanations. The explanations may seem unnecessary when you prepare the entries, but six months later you'll be glad you made them as you review a file for past activity. The same documentation may help a CPA keep his or her license when reviews or audits are performed. Furthermore, having clear, concise, and complete documentation could protect a firm against loss from a lawsuit in which the accounting records play a part.

To review, make complete explanations for transactions, especially in the journal and also in the ledger if necessary. Write notes in the client's file about conversations with the client, actions taken, or any information that would leave a trail. That trail may have to be followed by a reviewer or auditor (private, state, or federal) or maybe by you when you need to track the activity in an account. Make tracks—it is essential.

In Chapter 2, we recorded business transactions as debits and credits to T accounts. We introduced T accounts because, in the process of formulating debits and credits for business transactions, it's easier to visualize the T accounts involved with their plus and minus sides. **Formulating the appropriate transaction debits and credits is the most important element in the accounting process.** It represents the very basic foundation of accounting, and all the superstructure represented by financial statements and other reports is entirely dependent upon it. After determining the debits and credits, the accountant records the transaction in a journal.

The initial steps in the accounting process are

1. Record business transactions in a journal.
2. Post entries to accounts in the ledger.
3. Prepare a trial balance.

In this chapter, we will present the general journal and the posting procedure.

Recording Transactions in the General Journal

We have seen that an accountant must keep a written record of each transaction. One could record the transactions directly in T accounts; however, only part of the transaction would be listed in each T account. A **journal** is a book for recording business transactions as they happen. The journal serves the function of recording both the debits and the credits of the entire transaction in one place. Actually, the journal is a diary for the business, in which one records in day-by-day order all the events involving financial affairs. A journal is called a **book of original entry.** In other words, a transaction is always recorded first in the journal and then in the ledger accounts. The process of recording a business transaction in the journal is called **journalizing.** You may recall that the information about transactions comes from business papers, such as checks, invoices, receipts, letters, and memos. These **source documents** furnish proof (objective evidence) that a transaction has taken place, so they should be identified in the journal entry whenever possible. Later we will introduce a variety of special journals. However, the basic form of journal is the **two-column general journal.** The term *two-column* refers to the two amount columns used for debit and credit amounts.

As an example of journalizing business transactions, let's use the transactions for Clark's Cleaners listed in Chapter 1. Each page of the journal is numbered in consecutive order. This is the first page, so we write a 1 in the space for the page number. Also, we must write the date of each transaction. Now let's begin with the first entry.

Transaction (a) June 1: N. L. Clark invests $40,000 cash in his new business.

First, let's show the complete journal entry.

Performance Objective 1

Record a group of transactions pertaining to a service enterprise in a two-column general journal.

GENERAL JOURNAL   PAGE 1

	DATE		DESCRIPTION	POST. REF.	DEBIT	CREDIT	
1	19–						1
2	June	1	Cash		40 0 0 0 00		2
3			N. L. Clark, Capital			40 0 0 0 00	3
4			Original investment by				4
5			Clark in Clark's Cleaners.				5

Now, to explain the entry, we will break it down line by line. On the Page line, record the page number. On the first line, record the year in the left part of the Date column. On the second line, record the month in the left part of the Date column and the day of the month in the right part of the Date column. We don't have to repeat the year and month until we start a new page, or until the year or month changes. (Because our illustrations are separated, however, they may repeat the month simply to eliminate confusion.)

This information is shown in color on the general journal below.

	DATE		DESCRIPTION	POST. REF.	DEBIT	CREDIT	
1	19–		⎤ Date				1
2	June	1	⎦				2
3							3

GENERAL JOURNAL — Page number — PAGE → 1

Decide which accounts should be debited and credited. We do this by first figuring out which accounts are involved and whether they are increased or decreased. We then visualize the accounts mentally with their respective plus and minus sides.

Cash is involved in our example. Cash is considered to be an asset because it falls within the definition of "things owned." Cash is increased, so we debit Cash.

N. L. Clark, Capital, is involved. This is an owner's equity account, because it represents the owner's investment. N. L. Clark, Capital, is increased, so we credit N. L. Clark, Capital. Let's show these entries by reverting back to our reliable fundamental accounting equation with the accompanying T accounts:

Assets	=	Liabilities	+	Owner's Equity	+	Revenue	–	Expenses
+ / –		– / +		– / +		– / +		+ / –
Debit / Credit		Debit / Credit		Debit / Credit		Debit / Credit		Debit / Credit

Cash		N. L. Clark, Capital
+ / –		– / +
40,000		40,000

As we said earlier, you perform this process mentally. If the transaction is more complicated, then use scratch paper and draw the T accounts. Using T accounts is the accountant's way of drawing a picture of the transaction. This is why we stressed the fundamental accounting equation, with the T accounts and plus and minus signs, so heavily in Chapter 2. You are urged to get in the T account habit; it will be a great help to you.

Always record the debit part of the entry first. Enter the account title—in this case, Cash—in the Description column. Record the amount—$40,000—in the Debit amount column.

GENERAL JOURNAL PAGE __1__

	DATE		DESCRIPTION	POST. REF.	DEBIT	CREDIT	
1	19–						1
2	June	1	Cash		40 0 0 0 00		2
3							3

Account title — (points to Cash / account title)

Debit amount — (points to 40 0 0 0 00)

Next, record the credit part of the entry. Enter the account title—in this case, N. L. Clark, Capital—on the line below the debit, in the Description column, indented about one-half inch. Do not let it extend into the Posting Reference column. On the same line, write the amount in the credit column. By custom, accountants don't generally abbreviate account titles.

GENERAL JOURNAL PAGE __1__

	DATE		DESCRIPTION	POST. REF.	DEBIT	CREDIT	
1	19–						1
2	June	1	Cash		40 0 0 0 00		2
3			N. L. Clark, Capital			40 0 0 0 00	3
4							4

Indent account title credited

You should now give a brief explanation, in which you may refer to business papers, such as check numbers or invoice numbers; you may also list names of charge customers or creditors, or terms of payment. Enter the explanation below the credit entry, indented an additional one-half inch.

GENERAL JOURNAL PAGE __1__

	DATE		DESCRIPTION	POST. REF.	DEBIT	CREDIT	
1	19–						1
2	June	1	Cash		40 0 0 0 00		2
3			N. L. Clark, Capital			40 0 0 0 00	3
4			Original investment by				4
5			Clark in Clark's Cleaners.				5
6							6

Indent again for explanation

For an entry in the general journal to be complete, it must contain (1) the date, (2) a debit entry, (3) a credit entry, and (4) an explanation. To anyone thoroughly familiar with the accounts, the explanation may seem to be quite obvious, but it is an integral part of the entry, whether recorded manually or as part of a computerized entry. To make the journal entries easier to read, leave one blank line between each transaction.

Transaction (b)   June 2: Clark's Cleaners buys equipment costing $22,000 from Drake Equipment Company and pays cash.

Decide which accounts are involved. Next, classify them under the five possible classifications. Visualize the plus and minus signs under the classifications. Now decide whether the accounts are increased or decreased. When you use T accounts to analyze the transaction, the results are as follows:

Equipment		Cash	
+	−	+	−
Debit	Credit	Debit	Credit
22,000			22,000

Now journalize this analysis below the first transaction. Record the day of the month in the Date column. Remember, you do not have to record the month and year again until the month or year changes or you use a new journal page.

REMEMBER

In trying to figure out how a transaction should be recorded, first decide on the accounts involved. Next, classify the accounts as A, L, OE, R, or E. Next ask yourself whether the accounts are increased or decreased, and think of the related accounts with their plus and minus sides. Now the debits and credits of the transaction will fall into place.

Skip a line between entries

GENERAL JOURNAL   PAGE 1

	DATE		DESCRIPTION	POST. REF.	DEBIT	CREDIT	
1	19–						1
2	June	1	Cash		40 0 0 0 00		2
3			N. L. Clark, Capital			40 0 0 0 00	3
4			Original investment by				4
5			Clark in Clark's Cleaners.				5
6							6
7		2	Equipment		22 0 0 0 00		7
8			Cash			22 0 0 0 00	8
9			Bought equipment for cash.				9

Transaction (c)   June 2: Clark's Cleaners buys equipment on credit (on account) from Drake Equipment Company, $4,000. To get organized, think of the T accounts first.

Equipment		Accounts Payable	
+	−	−	+
Debit	Credit	Debit	Credit
4,000			4,000

After skipping a line in the journal, record the day of the month and then the entry. In journalizing a transaction involving Accounts Payable, always state the name of the creditor in the explanation. Similarly, in journalizing a transaction involving Accounts Receivable, always state the name of the charge customer in the explanation.

	GENERAL JOURNAL				PAGE 1

	DATE	DESCRIPTION	POST. REF.	DEBIT	CREDIT	
10						10
11	2	Equipment		4 0 0 0 00		11
12		Accounts Payable			4 0 0 0 00	12
13		Bought equipment on account				13
14		from Drake Equipment				14
15		Company.				15

When a business buys an asset, the asset should be recorded at the actual cost (the agreed amount of a transaction). This is called the **cost principle.** For example, suppose that Clark's Cleaners bought the equipment from Drake Equipment Company at a real bargain price of $4,000. Drake Equipment Company had been asking $5,500 for the equipment. The day after Clark's Cleaners took possession of the equipment, it received an offer of $4,800 from another party, but the offer was declined. However, Clark's Cleaners *should record the equipment for the actual amount of the transaction that took place, which is $4,000.* This is true even though the fair market value may be $4,800.

Transaction (d) On June 4, Clark's Cleaners pays $1,000 to Drake Equipment Company to be applied against the firm's liability of $4,000. Picture the T accounts like this:

Accounts Payable		Cash	
−	+	+	−
Debit	Credit	Debit	Credit
1,000			1,000

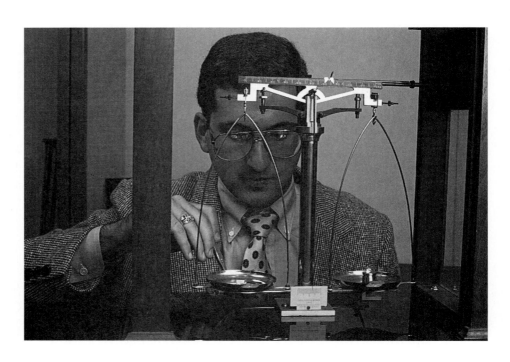

As the jeweler weighs precious metals on a balance scale, the accountant must also maintain accounts in balance with debits equaling credits. This is true whether the records are kept manually or electronically.

Cash is an easy account to recognize, so let's look at it first. In every transaction, ask yourself, "Is Cash involved?" If Cash is involved, determine whether it is coming in or going out. In this case, we see that cash is going out, so we record it on the minus side. We now have a credit to Cash and half of the entry. Next, we recognize that Accounts Payable is involved. We ask ourselves, "Do we owe more or less as a result of this transaction?" The answer is "less," so we record it on the minus, or debit, side of the account.

REMEMBER

Get in the T account habit. Picture the T accounts in your mind, or draw T accounts on paper with their plus and minus signs. The T account habit is a must.

GENERAL JOURNAL   PAGE ___1___

	DATE	DESCRIPTION	POST. REF.	DEBIT	CREDIT	
16						16
17	4	Accounts Payable		1 0 0 0 00		17
18		Cash			1 0 0 0 00	18
19		Paid Drake Equipment				19
20		Company on account.				20
21						21
22						22
23						23
24						24
25						25
26						26

Now let's list the transactions for June for Clark's Cleaners with the date of each transaction. The journal entries are illustrated on the following pages in Figures 3-1, 3-2, and 3-3.

REMEMBER

Six types of information must be entered in the general journal for each transaction: the date, the title of the account(s) to be debited, the amount of the debit, the title of the account(s) to be credited, the amount of the credit, and the explanation.

June   1 N. L. Clark invests $40,000 cash in his new business.

2 Buys equipment costing $22,000, paying cash.

2 Buys equipment on credit from Drake Equipment Company, $4,000.

4 Pays $1,000 to Drake Equipment Company to be applied against the firm's liability of $4,000.

4 Buys cleaning fluid and garment bags on account from Blair and Company, $400.

8 Pays rent for the month, $500.

10 Pays for a one-year liability insurance policy, $360.

14 Cash revenue received for second week, $1,940.

14 Receives bill for newspaper advertising, from the *City News*, $180.

15 Receives and pays bill for electricity, $220.

23 Clark's Cleaners signs a contract with Formal Rentals to clean their for-hire formal garments. Clark's Cleaners completes a cleaning job and bills Formal Rentals $140 for services performed.

24 Pays wages of part-time employee, $930, June 11 through June 24.

26 Buys from Drake Equipment Company additional equipment costing $940, paying $140 down, with the remaining $800 on account.

30 Cash revenue received for the remainder of the month, $1,790.

30 Receives $90 from Formal Rentals to apply on amount previously billed.

30 Pays $1,980 to Drake Equipment Company, to be applied against the firm's liability of $4,380.

30 Clark withdraws cash for personal living expenses, $1,200.

Figure 3-1

	DATE		DESCRIPTION	POST. REF.	DEBIT	CREDIT	
1	19–						1
2	June	1	Cash		40 0 0 0 00		2
3			N. L. Clark, Capital			40 0 0 0 00	3
4			Original investment by				4
5			Clark in Clark's Cleaners.				5
6							6
7		2	Equipment		22 0 0 0 00		7
8			Cash			22 0 0 0 00	8
9			Bought equipment for cash.				9
10							10
11		2	Equipment		4 0 0 0 00		11
12			Accounts Payable			4 0 0 0 00	12
13			Bought equipment on account				13
14			from Drake Equipment				14
15			Company.				15
16							16
17		4	Accounts Payable		1 0 0 0 00		17
18			Cash			1 0 0 0 00	18
19			Paid Drake Equipment				19
20			Company on account.				20
21							21
22		4	Supplies		4 0 0 00		22
23			Accounts Payable			4 0 0 00	23
24			Bought cleaning fluid and				24
25			garment bags on account				25
26			from Blair and Company.				26
27							27
28		8	Rent Expense		5 0 0 00		28
29			Cash			5 0 0 00	29
30			For month ended June 30.				30
31							31
32							32
33							33
34							34
35							35
36							36
37							37

GENERAL JOURNAL   PAGE 1

Figure 3-2

	DATE		DESCRIPTION	POST. REF.	DEBIT	CREDIT	
	GENERAL JOURNAL					PAGE 2	
1	19–						1
2	June	10	Prepaid Insurance		3 6 0 00		2
3			Cash			3 6 0 00	3
4			Premium for one-year liability				4
5			insurance policy.				5
6							6
7		14	Cash		1 9 4 0 00		7
8			Income from Services			1 9 4 0 00	8
9			For two weeks ended June 14.				9
10							10
11		14	Advertising Expense		1 8 0 00		11
12			Accounts Payable			1 8 0 00	12
13			Received bill for advertising				13
14			from *City News*.				14
15							15
16		15	Utilities Expense		2 2 0 00		16
17			Cash			2 2 0 00	17
18			Paid bill for electricity.				18
19							19
20		23	Accounts Receivable		1 4 0 00		20
21			Income from Services			1 4 0 00	21
22			Formal Rentals, for services				22
23			rendered.				23
24							24
25		24	Wages Expense		9 3 0 00		25
26			Cash			9 3 0 00	26
27			Paid wages, June 11 to				27
28			June 24.				28
29							29
30		26	Equipment		9 4 0 00		30
31			Cash			1 4 0 00	31
32			Accounts Payable			8 0 0 00	32
33			Bought equipment on account				33
34			from Drake Equipment				34
35			Company.				35
36							36
37							37

R E M E M B E R

You must enter the year and the month at the top of every page in the journal.

Figure 3-3

	DATE		DESCRIPTION	POST. REF.	DEBIT	CREDIT	
1	19–						1
2	June	30	Cash		1 7 9 0 00		2
3			Income from Services			1 7 9 0 00	3
4			For remainder of June, ended				4
5			June 30.				5
6							6
7		30	Cash		9 0 00		7
8			Accounts Receivable			9 0 00	8
9			Formal Rentals, to apply on				9
10			account.				10
11							11
12		30	Accounts Payable		1 9 8 0 00		12
13			Cash			1 9 8 0 00	13
14			Paid Drake Equipment				14
15			Company on account.				15
16							16
17		30	N. L. Clark, Drawing		1 2 0 0 00		17
18			Cash			1 2 0 0 00	18
19			Withdrawal for personal use.				19

GENERAL JOURNAL PAGE ___3___

The General Ledger

The **ledger** is a loose-leaf book or computer file containing the accounts of a business. The general ledger supplements the journal and makes it easy to determine the balance of each account. In this section, we'll see how this is accomplished.

The Chart of Accounts

One arranges the accounts in the ledger according to the chart of accounts. As we said previously, the chart of accounts is the official list of the ledger accounts in which transactions of a business are to be recorded. Assets are listed first, liabilities second, owner's equity third, revenue fourth, and expenses fifth. The chart of accounts for Clark's Cleaners is as follows:

Chart of Accounts

ASSETS (100–199)
111   Cash
113   Accounts Receivable
115   Supplies
117   Prepaid Insurance
124   Equipment

LIABILITIES (200–299)
211   Accounts Payable

OWNER'S EQUITY (300–399)
311   N. L. Clark, Capital
312   N. L. Clark, Drawing

REVENUE (400–499)
411   Income from Services

EXPENSES (500–599)
515   Advertising Expense
521   Wages Expense
524   Rent Expense
525   Utilities Expense

Notice that the arrangement of the chart of accounts consists of the balance sheet accounts followed by the income statement accounts. Accounts in the ledger are kept by numbers rather than by pages because it is hard to tell in advance how many pages to reserve for a particular account. When you use the number system, you can easily add sheets. The digits in the account numbers also indicate *classifications* of accounts. For most companies, assets start with 1, liabilities with 2, owner's equity with 3, revenue with 4, and expenses with 5.

Regarding the assets, notice the gaps in the account numbers between 111 and 124. These gaps allow space for additional accounts.

R E M E M B E R

When recording transactions for a business in the journal, one must use the exact account titles as listed in the company's chart of accounts.

The Ledger Account Form (Running Balance Format)

We have been looking at accounts in the simple T account form primarily because T accounts illustrate situations so well. The debit and credit sides are readily apparent. As we have said, accountants usually use the T account form to solve problems because it is such a good way to visualize accounts. However, the T account form is awkward when determining the balance of an account. One must add both columns and subtract the smaller total from the larger. To overcome this disadvantage, accountants generally use the four-column account form with Balance columns. Let's look at the Cash account of Clark's Cleaners in four-column form (Figure 3-4) compared with the T form. Temporarily, the Posting Reference column is left blank. The meaning and use of this column are described in the discussion of the posting process that follows.

Posting to the General Ledger

From this example, you can see that the journal is indeed the *book of original entry*. Each transaction must first be recorded in the journal in full. However, from the general journal entries, it is virtually impossible to determine readily the balance of any one account, such as Cash. So the **ledger account** has been devised to give us a complete record of the transactions recorded in each individual account. The process of transferring figures from the journal to the ledger accounts is called **posting.**

Figure 3-4

T ACCOUNT

Cash

+		−	
(a)	40,000	(b)	22,000
(h)	1,940	(d)	1,000
(n)	1,790	(f)	500
(o)	90	(g)	360
		(j)	220
	43,820	(l)	930
		(m)	140
		(p)	1,980
		(q)	1,200
Bal.	15,490		28,330

GENERAL LEDGER

ACCOUNT __Cash__   ACCOUNT NO. __111__

DATE		ITEM	POST. REF.	DEBIT	CREDIT	BALANCE DEBIT	BALANCE CREDIT
19–							
Jan.	1			40 000 00		40 000 00	
	2				22 000 00	18 000 00	
	4				1 000 00	17 000 00	
	8				500 00	16 500 00	
	10				360 00	16 140 00	
	14			1 940 00		18 080 00	
	15				220 00	17 860 00	
	24				930 00	16 930 00	
	26				140 00	16 790 00	
	30			1 790 00		18 580 00	
	30				90 00	18 670 00	
	30				1 980 00	16 690 00	
	30				1 200 00	15 490 00	

Transaction
Amount

Running
Balance

Note the determination of the running balance. In the abbreviated form, it looks like this:

ACCOUNT __Cash__   ACCOUNT NO. __111__

	DATE		ITEM	POST. REF.	DEBIT	CREDIT	BALANCE DEBIT	BALANCE CREDIT
	19–							
40,000	June	1			40 000 00		40 000 00	
−22,000		2				22 000 00	18 000 00	
18,000		4				1 000 00	17 000 00	
−1,000								
17,000								

The Posting Process

Performance Objective 2

Post entries from a two-column general journal to general ledger accounts.

In the posting process, you must transfer the following information from the journal to the ledger accounts: the *date of the transaction*, the *debit and credit amounts*, and the *page number* of the journal. Post each account separately, using the following steps. Post the debit part of the entry first. After locating the account in the ledger, you need to do the following:

1. Write the date of the transaction in the account's Date column.

2. Write the amount of the transaction in the Debit or Credit column and enter the new balance in the Balance columns under Debit or Credit.

3. Write the page number of the journal in the Posting Reference column of the ledger account. (This is a **cross-reference,** which tells where the amount came from.)

4. Record the ledger account number in the Posting Reference column of the journal. (This is also a cross-reference, which tells where the amount was posted.)

The first transaction for Clark's Cleaners is illustrated in Figure 3-5. Let's look first at the debit part of the entry.

Figure 3-5

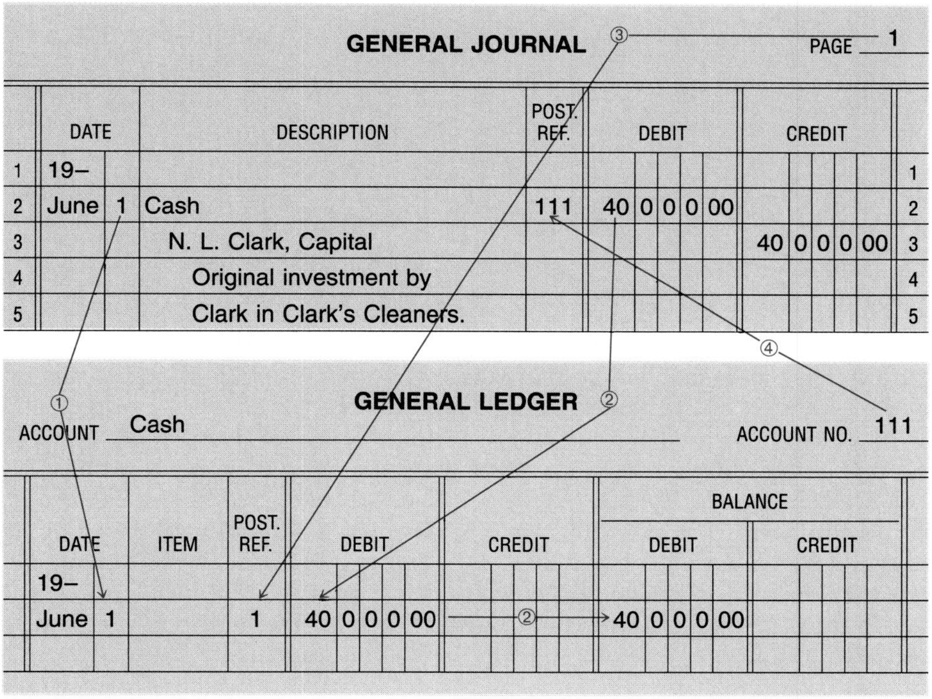

① Date of transaction
② Amount of transaction
③ Page numbers of the journal
④ Ledger account number

Entering the account number in the Posting Reference column of the journal should be the last step. It acts as a verification of the three preceding steps.

Next we post the credit part of the entry, as shown in Figure 3-6.

Figure 3-6

① Date of transaction
② Amount of transaction
③ Page numbers of the journal
④ Ledger account number

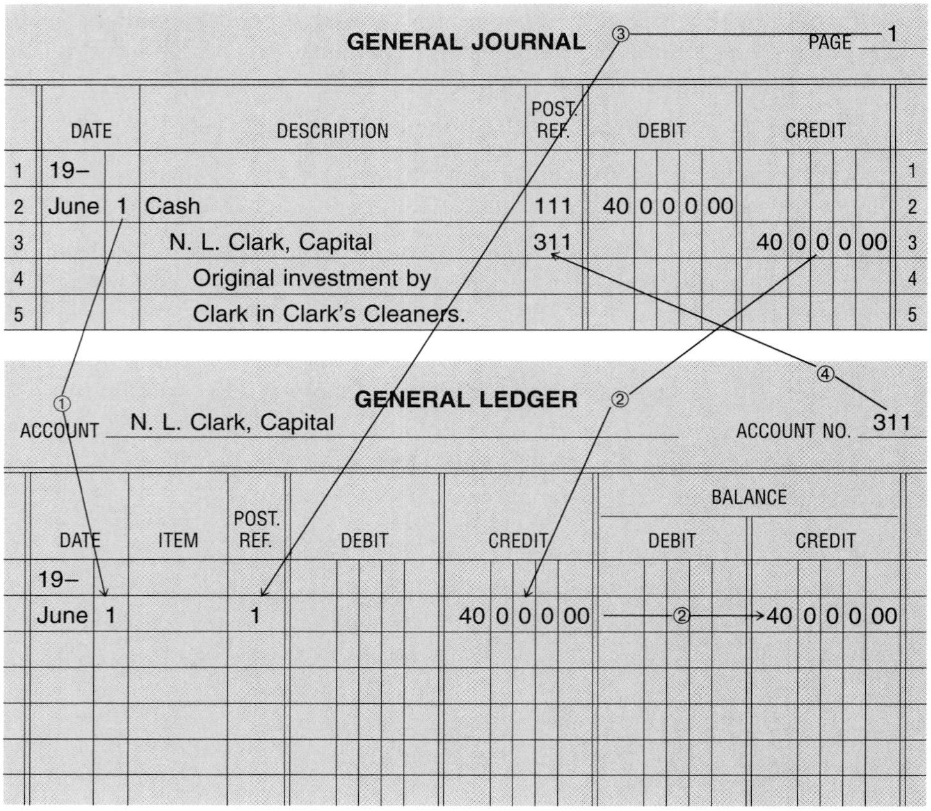

GENERAL JOURNAL   PAGE 1

	DATE	DESCRIPTION	POST. REF.	DEBIT	CREDIT	
1	19–					1
2	June 1	Cash	111	40 0 0 0 00		2
3		N. L. Clark, Capital	311		40 0 0 0 00	3
4		Original investment by				4
5		Clark in Clark's Cleaners.				5

GENERAL LEDGER

ACCOUNT N. L. Clark, Capital   ACCOUNT NO. 311

					BALANCE	
DATE	ITEM	POST. REF.	DEBIT	CREDIT	DEBIT	CREDIT
19–						
June 1		1		40 0 0 0 00		40 0 0 0 00

The accountant usually uses the Item column only at the end of a financial period. The words that may appear in this column are *balance, closing, adjusting,* and *reversing.* We will introduce these terms later.

Incidentally, some accountants use running balance–type ledger account forms having only one balance column. However, we have used the two-balance-column arrangement to designate clearly the appropriate balance of an account. For example, in Figure 3-5, Cash has a $40,000 balance recorded in the Debit column (normal balance). In Figure 3-6, N. L. Clark, Capital, has a $40,000 balance recorded in the Credit column (normal balance).

In the recording of the second transaction, shown in Figure 3-7, see if you can identify in order the four steps in the posting process.

Figure 3-7

GENERAL JOURNAL   PAGE ___1___

	DATE	DESCRIPTION	POST. REF.	DEBIT	CREDIT	
7	2	Equipment	124	22 0 0 0 00		7
8		Cash	111		22 0 0 0 00	8
9		Bought equipment for cash.				9
10						10

R E M E M B E R

Do not record account numbers in the Posting Reference column of the journal until the amounts have been posted to the ledger accounts as either debits or credits.

GENERAL LEDGER

ACCOUNT __Cash__   ACCOUNT NO. __111__

DATE	ITEM	POST. REF.	DEBIT	CREDIT	BALANCE DEBIT	BALANCE CREDIT
19–						
June 1		1	40 0 0 0 00		40 0 0 0 00	
2		1		22 0 0 0 00	18 0 0 0 00	

ACCOUNT __Equipment__   ACCOUNT NO. __124__

DATE	ITEM	POST. REF.	DEBIT	CREDIT	BALANCE DEBIT	BALANCE CREDIT
19–						
June 2		1	22 0 0 0 00		22 0 0 0 00	

R E M E M B E R

Posting is simply transferring or copying exactly the same date, as well as the debits and credits listed in the journal entry from the journal to the ledger.

Now let's look at the journal entries for the first month of operation for Clark's Cleaners. As you can see from the general journal and general ledger in Figure 3-8 (see pages 96–101), the Posting Reference column has been filled in, since the posting has been completed.

Figure 3-8

	DATE		DESCRIPTION	POST. REF.	DEBIT	CREDIT	
1	19–						1
2	June	1	Cash	111	40 0 0 0 00		2
3			N. L. Clark, Capital	311		40 0 0 0 00	3
4			Original investment by				4
5			Clark in Clark's Cleaners.				5
6							6
7		2	Equipment	124	22 0 0 0 00		7
8			Cash	111		22 0 0 0 00	8
9			Bought equipment for cash.				9
10							10
11		2	Equipment	124	4 0 0 0 00		11
12			Accounts Payable	211		4 0 0 0 00	12
13			Bought equipment on account				13
14			from Drake Equipment				14
15			Company.				15
16							16
17		4	Accounts Payable	211	1 0 0 0 00		17
18			Cash	111		1 0 0 0 00	18
19			Paid Drake Equipment				19
20			Company on account.				20
21							21
22		4	Supplies	115	4 0 0 00		22
23			Accounts Payable	211		4 0 0 00	23
24			Bought cleaning fluid and				24
25			garment bags on account				25
26			from Blair and Company.				26
27							27
28		8	Rent Expense	524	5 0 0 00		28
29			Cash	111		5 0 0 00	29
30			For month ended June 30.				30
31							31
32							32
33							33
34							34
35							35
36							36
37							37

GENERAL JOURNAL PAGE 1

Figure 3-8 (cont.)

	DATE		DESCRIPTION	POST. REF.	DEBIT	CREDIT	
1	19–						1
2	June	10	Prepaid Insurance	117	3 6 0 00		2
3			Cash	111		3 6 0 00	3
4			Premium for one-year liability				4
5			insurance policy.				5
6							6
7		14	Cash	111	1 9 4 0 00		7
8			Income from Services	411		1 9 4 0 00	8
9			For two weeks ended June 14.				9
10							10
11		14	Advertising Expense	515	1 8 0 00		11
12			Accounts Payable	211		1 8 0 00	12
13			Received bill for advertising				13
14			from *City News*.				14
15							15
16		15	Utilities Expense	525	2 2 0 00		16
17			Cash	111		2 2 0 00	17
18			Paid bill for electricity.				18
19							19
20		23	Accounts Receivable	113	1 4 0 00		20
21			Income from Services	411		1 4 0 00	21
22			Formal Rentals, for services				22
23			rendered.				23
24							24
25		24	Wages Expense	521	9 3 0 00		25
26			Cash	111		9 3 0 00	26
27			Paid wages through June 24.				27
28							28
29		26	Equipment	124	9 4 0 00		29
30			Cash	111		1 4 0 00	30
31			Accounts Payable	211		8 0 0 00	31
32			Bought equipment on account				32
33			from Drake Equipment				33
34			Company.				34
35							35
36							36
37							37

GENERAL JOURNAL   PAGE 2

Figure 3-8 (cont.)

GENERAL JOURNAL

PAGE 3

	DATE		DESCRIPTION	POST. REF.	DEBIT	CREDIT	
1	19–						1
2		30	Cash	111	1 7 9 0 00		2
3			Income from Services	411		1 7 9 0 00	3
4			For remainder of June, ended				4
5			June 30.				5
6							6
7		30	Cash	111	9 0 00		7
8			Accounts Receivable	113		9 0 00	8
9			Formal Rentals, to apply on				9
10			account.				10
11							11
12		30	Accounts Payable	211	1 9 8 0 00		12
13			Cash	111		1 9 8 0 00	13
14			Paid Drake Equipment				14
15			Company on account.				15
16							16
17		30	N. L. Clark, Drawing	312	1 2 0 0 00		17
18			Cash	111		1 2 0 0 00	18
19			Withdrawal for personal use.				19
20							20

GENERAL LEDGER

ACCOUNT Cash   ACCOUNT NO. 111

DATE		ITEM	POST. REF.	DEBIT	CREDIT	BALANCE DEBIT	BALANCE CREDIT
19–							
Jan.	1		1	40 0 0 0 00		40 0 0 0 00	
	2		1		22 0 0 0 00	18 0 0 0 00	
	4		1		1 0 0 0 00	17 0 0 0 00	
	8		1		5 0 0 00	16 5 0 0 00	
	10		2		3 6 0 00	16 1 4 0 00	
	14		2	1 9 4 0 00		18 0 8 0 00	
	15		2		2 2 0 00	17 8 6 0 00	
	24		2		9 3 0 00	16 9 3 0 00	
	26		2		1 4 0 00	16 7 9 0 00	
	30		3	1 7 9 0 00		18 5 8 0 00	
	30		3	9 0 00		18 6 7 0 00	
	30		3		1 9 8 0 00	16 6 9 0 00	
	30		3		1 2 0 0 00	15 4 9 0 00	

Figure 3-8 (cont.)

ACCOUNT __Accounts Receivable__   ACCOUNT NO. __113__

DATE		ITEM	POST. REF.	DEBIT	CREDIT	BALANCE	
						DEBIT	CREDIT
19—							
June	23		2	1 4 0 00		1 4 0 00	
	30		3		9 0 00	5 0 00	

ACCOUNT __Supplies__   ACCOUNT NO. __115__

DATE		ITEM	POST. REF.	DEBIT	CREDIT	BALANCE	
						DEBIT	CREDIT
19—							
June	4		1	4 0 0 00		4 0 0 00	

ACCOUNT __Prepaid Insurance__   ACCOUNT NO. __117__

DATE		ITEM	POST. REF.	DEBIT	CREDIT	BALANCE	
						DEBIT	CREDIT
19—							
June	10		2	3 6 0 00		3 6 0 00	

ACCOUNT __Equipment__   ACCOUNT NO. __124__

DATE		ITEM	POST. REF.	DEBIT	CREDIT	BALANCE	
						DEBIT	CREDIT
19—							
June	2		1	22 0 0 0 00		22 0 0 0 00	
	2		1	4 0 0 0 00		26 0 0 0 00	
	26		2	9 4 0 00		26 9 4 0 00	

Figure 3-8 (cont.)

ACCOUNT ___Accounts Payable___ ACCOUNT NO. __211__

DATE	ITEM	POST. REF.	DEBIT	CREDIT	BALANCE DEBIT	BALANCE CREDIT
19–						
June 2		1		4 0 0 0 00		4 0 0 0 00
4		1	1 0 0 0 00			3 0 0 0 00
4		1		4 0 0 00		3 4 0 0 00
14		2		1 8 0 00		3 5 8 0 00
26		2		8 0 0 00		4 3 8 0 00
30		3	1 9 8 0 00			2 4 0 0 00

ACCOUNT ___N. L. Clark, Capital___ ACCOUNT NO. __311__

DATE	ITEM	POST. REF.	DEBIT	CREDIT	BALANCE DEBIT	BALANCE CREDIT
19–						
June 1		1		40 0 0 0 00		40 0 0 0 00

ACCOUNT ___N. L. Clark, Drawing___ ACCOUNT NO. __312__

DATE	ITEM	POST. REF.	DEBIT	CREDIT	BALANCE DEBIT	BALANCE CREDIT
19–						
June 30		3	1 2 0 0 00		1 2 0 0 00	

ACCOUNT ___Income from Services___ ACCOUNT NO. __411__

DATE	ITEM	POST. REF.	DEBIT	CREDIT	BALANCE DEBIT	BALANCE CREDIT
19–						
June 14		2		1 9 4 0 00		1 9 4 0 00
23		2		1 4 0 00		2 0 8 0 00
30		3		1 7 9 0 00		3 8 7 0 00

Figure 3-8 (cont.)

ACCOUNT __Advertising Expense__   ACCOUNT NO. __515__

DATE	ITEM	POST. REF.	DEBIT	CREDIT	BALANCE DEBIT	BALANCE CREDIT
19–						
June 14		2	1 8 0 00		1 8 0 00	

ACCOUNT __Wages Expense__   ACCOUNT NO. __521__

DATE	ITEM	POST. REF.	DEBIT	CREDIT	BALANCE DEBIT	BALANCE CREDIT
19–						
June 24		2	9 3 0 00		9 3 0 00	

ACCOUNT __Rent Expense__   ACCOUNT NO. __524__

DATE	ITEM	POST. REF.	DEBIT	CREDIT	BALANCE DEBIT	BALANCE CREDIT
19–						
June 8		1	5 0 0 00		5 0 0 00	

ACCOUNT __Utilities Expense__   ACCOUNT NO. __525__

DATE	ITEM	POST. REF.	DEBIT	CREDIT	BALANCE DEBIT	BALANCE CREDIT
19–						
June 15		2	2 2 0 00		2 2 0 00	

In making a journal entry, you may get to the bottom of a page and there are not enough lines to record the entire entry. In this case, do not split up the entry; instead, record the entire entry on the next journal page. For ease of reading, leave one blank line between entries.

Performance Objective 3

Prepare a trial balance
from the ledger accounts.

Preparation of the Trial Balance

The trial balance is simply a list of the ledger accounts that have balances. A trial balance is presented in Figure 3-9.

Figure 3-9

Clark's Cleaners
Trial Balance
June 30, 19—

ACCOUNT NAME	DEBIT	CREDIT
Cash	15 4 9 0 00	
Accounts Receivable	5 0 00	
Supplies	4 0 0 00	
Prepaid Insurance	3 6 0 00	
Equipment	26 9 4 0 00	
Accounts Payable		2 4 0 0 00
N. L. Clark, Capital		40 0 0 0 00
N. L. Clark, Drawing	1 2 0 0 00	
Income from Services		3 8 7 0 00
Advertising Expense	1 8 0 00	
Wages Expense	9 3 0 00	
Rent Expense	5 0 0 00	
Utilities Expense	2 2 0 00	
	46 2 7 0 00	46 2 7 0 00

Remember that the trial balance only proves that the total ledger debit balances equal the total ledger credit balances. Even when the debit and credit balances are equal, two types of errors may slip through:

1. Posting the correct debit or credit amounts to the wrong account.

2. Neglecting to journalize or post an entire transaction.

If the balance of an account becomes zero, insert long dashes through both the Debit Balance and the Credit Balance columns. We'll use another business, the Madison Company, in this example. Its Accounts Receivable ledger account appears on the next page.

| ACCOUNT | Accounts Receivable | | | | | | ACCOUNT NO. | 113 | |

								BALANCE			
DATE		ITEM	POST. REF.	DEBIT		CREDIT		DEBIT		CREDIT	
19–											
Oct.	7		96	1 4 0 00				1 4 0 00			
	19		97	2 3 8 00				3 7 8 00			
	21		97			1 4 0 00		2 3 8 00			
	29		98			2 3 8 00		————		————	
	31		98	1 6 2 00				1 6 2 00			

FYI

The 500th anniversary celebration of the publication of the rules of double-entry accounting was held in 1994 in Italy. It honored Luca Pacioli, the father of double-entry accounting.

Correction of Errors

E rrors will occasionally be made in recording journal entries and posting to the ledger accounts. Never erase them, because it might look as if you were trying to conceal something. The method for correcting errors depends on how and when the error was made. There are two approved methods for correcting errors: the ruling method and the correcting entry method.

Ruling Method

You can use the ruling method to correct errors before or after an entry has been posted.

Correcting Errors Before Posting Has Taken Place   When an error has been made in recording an account title in a journal entry, draw a line through the incorrect account title in the journal entry, and write the correct account title immediately above. Include your initials with the correction. For example, an entry to record payment of $700 rent was incorrectly debited to Salary Expense.

Performance Objective 4
Correct entries using the ruling method.

	DATE		DESCRIPTION	POST. REF.	DEBIT		CREDIT		
1	19–		*Rent Expense*						1
2	Mar.	1	~~Salary Expense~~ *DJM*		7 0 0 00				2
3			Cash				7 0 0 00		3
4			Paid rent for the month.						4

When an error has been made in recording an amount, draw a line through the incorrect amount in the journal entry, and write the correct amount immediately above. For example, an entry for a $230 payment for office supplies was recorded as $320.

	DATE	DESCRIPTION	POST. REF.	DEBIT	CREDIT	
1	19–		DJM	230 00	DJM	1
2	Apr. 6	Office Supplies		320 00	230 00	2
3		Cash			320 00	3
4		Bought office stationery.				4
5						5

Correcting Errors After Posting Has Taken Place   When an entry was journalized correctly but one of the amounts was posted incorrectly, correct the error by ruling a single line through the amount, and record the correct amount above. For example, an entry to record cash received for professional fees was correctly journalized as $400. However, it was posted as a debit to Cash for $400 and a credit to Professional Fees for $4,000. In the Professional Fees account, draw a line through $4,000 and insert $400 above. Change the running balance of the account.

ACCOUNT **Professional Fees**   ACCOUNT NO. **411**

					BALANCE	
DATE	ITEM	POST. REF.	DEBIT	CREDIT	DEBIT	CREDIT
19–			DJM	400 00	DJM	25 600 00
Feb. 6		94		4000 00		29 200 00

Correcting Entry Method

You should use the correcting entry method when amounts have been posted to the wrong account. The correcting entry should *always* include an explanation. For example, a $620 payment for repairs was incorrectly journalized and posted as a debit to Miscellaneous Expense for $620 and a credit to Cash for $620.

	DATE		DESCRIPTION	POST. REF.	DEBIT	CREDIT	
1	19–						1
2	Jan.	9	Repair Expense		6 2 0 00		2
3			Miscellaneous Expense			6 2 0 00	3
4			To correct error of January 9				4
5			in which a payment for Repair				5
6			Expense was debited to				6
7			Miscellaneous Expense.				7
8							8

After the correcting entry has been journalized, the accounts would be posted like any other entry. After posting, the account balances should be correct. In a computerized system, the correcting entry method is probably the only method available after posting.

Computer Applications

In Chapter 1, you saw illustrations of the computer printouts of the chart of accounts, income statement or profit and loss statement, and balance sheet for Clark's Cleaners. In this chapter you saw how transactions are journalized and posted in a manual system. You also saw how to prepare a trial balance.

Journalizing

Computers can speed the process of journalizing and posting entries. For example, an accounting program requires a minimum amount of writing or keying.

Date. Frequently, you need only enter the date when it changes, because the program holds the last date you entered until you change it.

Account Number. When you enter the account number, the account name appears. In some programs you don't even need to key the account number; you select the account number from the chart of accounts by highlighting it, tapping enter, and the account number and name appear in the journal.

Debit and Credit Amounts. A tap of the tab key sends the **cursor** to the "debit" amount position. Some programs even repeat the last amount keyed in the "credit" position—after you indicate which account is to be credited. A further time-saving feature is the program's ability to place a decimal and two zeroes automatically when no cents are required. Most commercial programs have a proof box that indicates that you are in or out of balance. Some programs will not allow you to continue to journalize if you are out of balance—that is, if debits don't equal credits. Programs provide varying amounts of space for explanations. Some programs do not allow you to skip an explanation—and neither do some supervisors.

FYI

Microcomputer-based accounting software ranges from low-end systems costing $39 to high-end systems costing $1,000 per "module." Modules include accounts receivable, accounts payable, general ledger payroll, inventory, and fixed assets.

Posting

Some accounting programs post automatically as you journalize, whereas others require you to post each part of the transaction. Other programs require you to post by batches or groups of transactions, such as one day's business activities.

Error Correction

Most commercial programs do not allow deletion of a journal entry after it has been posted. As with a manual system, if you catch the error before it is posted, you can correct it, but past that point, you must first make a correcting entry to undo the error and then make the correct entry. This is one way accountants provide an **audit trail,** which is a series of references or tracks that allow someone to trace information or transactions through an accounting system.

Let's look at the printout from a commercial software package. You can see the journal, ledger, and trial balance for Clark's Cleaners. Again, let's look at some of the similarities and differences between the illustrations of manual accounting forms and those produced by a commercial software package. Remember, the goal is to build confidence in your ability to adapt to different situations, whether they involve manual or computerized accounting.

While computers and software are logical and rapidly perform routine tasks, they require skilled and thinking people for best performance. Computers are only one of many electronic tools used by accountants and their clients.

General Journal

Notice that each entry is dated and contains debit(s) and credit(s) that are equal in each entry. The account names are shown, and the page is numbered. However, differences include using dollar signs on all amounts, positioning the explanation first, and including the account number and an ID number indicating the journal and sequence number for each transaction. Manual systems also allow numbering of transactions; when used, that number, and not the account number, becomes the posting reference number. You will also notice the letters "Src" standing for Source. This indicates the book of original entry. You will see other journals called special journals. Whether the accounting system is manual or computerized, or the journal is general or special, the journal is a book of original entry listing each transaction in chronological order. A single transaction is entered in only one journal.

```
                              Clark's Cleaners
                             3702 35th Southwest
                             Seattle WA 98126

                              General Journal

                             6/1/9- to 6/30/9-
                                                                         Page 1

Src     Date      ID#              Account              Debit        Credit   Job

GJ     6/1/9-   Original investment by Clark in Clark's Cleaners.
                GJ000001   1-1110   Cash                $40,000.00
                GJ000001   3-3110   N. L. Clark, Capital              $40,000.00

GJ     6/2/9-   Bought equipment for cash.
                GJ000002   1-1240   Equipment           $22,000.00
                GJ000002   1-1110   Cash                                $22,000.00

GJ     6/2/9-   Bought equipment on account from Drake Equipment Company.
                GJ000003   1-1240   Equipment           $4,000.00
                GJ000003   2-2210   Accounts Payable                  $4,000.00

GJ     6/4/9-   Paid Drake Equipment Company on account.
                GJ000004   2-2210   Accounts Payable    $1,000.00
                GJ000004   1-1110   Cash                               $1,000.00

GJ     6/4/9-   Bought cleaning fluid and garment bags on account from Blair and Company.
                GJ000005   1-1150   Supplies            $400.00
                GJ000005   2-2210   Accounts Payable                  $400.00

GJ     6/8/9-   Paid rent for month ended June 30.
                GJ000006   6-6240   Rent Expense        $500.00
                GJ000006   1-1110   Cash                               $500.00

GJ     6/10/9-  Premium for one-year liability insurance policy.
                GJ000007   1-1170   Prepaid Insurance   $360.00
                GJ000007   1-1110   Cash                               $360.00

GJ     6/14/9-  Income for two weeks ended June 14.
                GJ000008   1-1110   Cash                $1,940.00
                GJ000008   4-4110   Income from Services              $1,940.00
```

(Continued on the next page)

```
                              Clark's Cleaners
                              3702 35th Southwest
                              Seattle WA 98126

                              General Journal

                              6/1/9- to 6/30/9-
                                                                        Page 2

  Src    Date    ID#                    Account              Debit      Credit    Job

  GJ    6/14/9-  Received bill for advertising from City News.
                 GJ000009   6-6150   Advertising Expense   $180.00
                 GJ000009   2-2210   Accounts Payable                  $180.00
  ........................................................................................
  GJ    6/15/9-  Paid bill for electricity.
                 GJ000010   6-6250   Utilities Expense      $220.00
                 GJ000010   1-1110   Cash                              $220.00
  ........................................................................................
  GJ    6/23/9-  Billed Formal Rentals for services rendered.
                 GJ000011   1-1130   Accounts Receivable    $140.00
                 GJ000011   4-4110   Income from Services              $140.00
  ........................................................................................
  GJ    6/24/9-  Paid wages through June 24.
                 GJ000012   6-6210   Wages Expense          $930.00
                 GJ000012   1-1110   Cash                              $930.00
  ........................................................................................
  GJ    6/26/9-  Bought equipment on account from Drake Equipment Company.
                 GJ000013   1-1240   Equipment              $940.00
                 GJ000013   1-1110   Cash                              $140.00
                 GJ000013   2-2210   Accounts Payable                  $800.00
  ........................................................................................
  GJ    6/30/9-  For two weeks ended June 30.
                 GJ000014   1-1110   Cash                 $1,790.00
                 GJ000014   4-4110   Income from Services            $1,790.00
  ........................................................................................
  GJ    6/30/9-  Formal Rentals paid to apply on account.
                 GJ000015   1-1110   Cash                   $90.00
                 GJ000015   1-1130   Accounts Receivable               $90.00
  ........................................................................................
  GJ    6/30/9-  Paid Drake Equipment Company on account.
                 GJ000016   2-2210   Accounts Payable     $1,980.00
                 GJ000016   1-1110   Cash                            $1,980.00
  ........................................................................................
  GJ    6/30/9-  Withdrawal for personal use.
                 GJ000017   3-3120   N. L. Clark, Drawing $1,200.00
                 GJ000017   1-1110   Cash                            $1,200.00
  ........................................................................................
                                     Grand Total:       $77,670.00  $77,670.00
```

Account Inquiry (General Ledger)

Both manual and computerized illustrations show account numbers, account name, date, and debit and credit amounts. Differences between the manual illustrations and the printouts from this software are that dollar signs are used, the memo column (called "Item" in the manual ledger forms) repeats 29 characters of the explanation. The ID# and Src are repeated. Again, the value of the Src (Source) column becomes more obvious when additional types of journals are used later in the text.

Clark's Cleaners
3702 35th Southwest
Seattle WA 98126

Account Inquiry

6/1/9- to 6/30/9-

Page 1

Account	ID#	Src	Date	Memo	Debit	Credit	Job
1-1110 Cash							
	GJ000001	GJ	6/1/9-	Original investment by Clark.	$40,000.00		
	GJ000002	GJ	6/2/9-	Bought equipment for cash.		$22,000.00	
	GJ000004	GJ	6/4/9-	Paid Drake Equipment Company.		$1,000.00	
	GJ000006	GJ	6/8/9-	Paid rent for month of June.		$500.00	
	GJ000007	GJ	6/10/9-	Premium for one-year liability.		$360.00	
	GJ000008	GJ	6/14/9-	Income: two weeks ended June 30.	$1,940.00		
	GJ000010	GJ	6/15/9-	Paid bill for electricity.		$220.00	
	GJ000012	GJ	6/24/9-	Paid wages through June 24.		$930.00	
	GJ000013	GJ	6/26/9-	Bought equipment on account.		$140.00	
	GJ000014	GJ	6/30/9-	For two weeks ended June 30.	$1,790.00		
	GJ000015	GJ	6/30/9-	Formal Rentals paid on account.	$90.00		
	GJ000016	GJ	6/30/9-	Paid Drake Equipment Company.		$1,980.00	
	GJ000017	GJ	6/30/9-	Withdrawal for personal use.		$1,200.00	
					$43,820.00	$28.330.00	
1-1130 Accounts Receivable							
	GJ000011	GJ	6/23/9-	Billed Formal Rentals.	$140.00		
	GJ000015	GJ	6/30/9-	Formal Rentals paid on account.		$90.00	
					$140.00	$90.00	
1-1150 Supplies							
	GJ000005	GJ	6/4/9-	Bought cleaning fluid and bags.	$400.00		
					$400.00	$0.00	
1-1170 Prepaid Insurance							
	GJ000007	GJ	6/10/9-	Premium for one-year liability.	$360.00		
					$360.00	$0.00	
1-1240 Equipment							
	GJ000002	GJ	6/2/9-	Bought equipment for cash.	$22,000.00		
	GJ000003	GJ	6/2/9-	Bought equipment on account.	$4,000.00		
	GJ000013	GJ	6/26/9-	Bought equipment on account.	$940.00		
					$26,940.00	$0.00	
2-2210 Accounts Payable							
	GJ000003	GJ	6/2/9-	Bought equipment on account.		$4,000.00	
	GJ000004	GJ	6/4/9-	Paid Drake Equipment Company.	$1,000.00		
	GJ000005	GJ	6/4/9-	Bought cleaning fluid and bags.		$400.00	
	GJ000009	GJ	6/14/9-	Received bill for advertising.		$180.00	
	GJ000013	GJ	6/26/9-	Bought equipment on account.		$800.00	
	GJ000016	GJ	6/30/9-	Paid Drake Equipment Company.	$1,980.00		
					$2,980.00	$5,380.00	

(Continued on the next page)

```
                              Clark's Cleaners
                             3702 35th Southwest
                             Seattle WA 98126

                              Account Inquiry

                             6/1/9- to 6/30/9-
                                                                         Page 2

   Account       ID#  Src   Date        Memo                Debit       Credit      Job

3-3110  N. L. Clark, Capital
        GJ000001  GJ  6/1/9-  Original investment by Clark.             $40,000.00

                                                            $0.00      $40,000.00


3-3120  N. L. Clark, Drawing
        GJ000017  GJ  6/30/9-  Withdrawal for personal use.  $1,200.00

                                                            $1,200.00     $0.00


4-4110  Income from Services
        GJ000008  GJ  6/14/9-  Income: two weeks ended June 30.          $1,940.00
        GJ000011  GJ  6/23/9-  Billed Formal Rentals.                      $140.00
        GJ000014  GJ  6/30/9-  For two weeks ended June 30.              $1,790.00

                                                            $0.00       $3,870.00


6-6150  Advertising Expense
        GJ000009  GJ  6/14/9-  Received bill for advertising.  $180.00

                                                             $180.00      $0.00


6-6210  Wages Expense
        GJ000012  GJ  6/24/9-  Paid wages through June 24.     $930.00

                                                             $930.00      $0.00


6-6240  Rent Expense
        GJ000006  GJ  6/8/9-   Paid rent for month of June.    $500.00

                                                             $500.00      $0.00


6-6250  Utilities Expense
        GJ000010  GJ  6/15/9-  Paid bill for electricity.     $220.00

                                                             $220.00      $0.00
```

FYI

Accounting and management software will become more user-friendly with built-in voice and video aids and help screens that know where you are in the program when you ask for help.

Summary Trial Balance

This trial balance looks quite a bit different from the trial balance you have seen. This trial balance also includes the account number. Notice the column headings: Beginning Balance (all zero, since Clark's Cleaners just began business), Total Debit and Total Credit, and Net Activity indicating the amount of difference between the debits and credits. Since the Beginning Balances are zero, the Ending Balance is the same as the Net Activity. The Total row represents total debits ($77,670) and total credits ($77,760), not the total of the balances of the accounts ($46,270), as shown in Figure 3-9. The important point to understand is that transactions were correctly journalized and the debits equal the credits.

```
                          Clark's Cleaners
                        3702 35th Southwest
                         Seattle WA 98126

                      Summary Trial Balance

                       6/1/9- to 6/30/9-
```

	Account	Beginning Balance	Total Debit	Total Credit	Net Activity	Ending Balance
1-1110	Cash	$0.00	$43,820.00	$28,330.00	$15,490.00	$15,490.00
1-1130	Accounts Receivable	$0.00	$140.00	$90.00	$50.00	$50.00
1-1150	Supplies	$0.00	$400.00	$0.00	$400.00	$400.00
1-1170	Prepaid Insurance	$0.00	$360.00	$0.00	$360.00	$360.00
1-1240	Equipment	$0.00	$26,940.00	$0.00	$26,940.00	$26,940.00
2-2210	Accounts Payable	$0.00	$2,980.00	$5,380.00	$2,400.00cr	$2,400.00cr
3-3110	N. L. Clark, Capital	$0.00	$0.00	$40,000.00	$40,000.00cr	$40,000.00cr
3-3120	N. L. Clark, Drawing	$0.00	$1,200.00	$0.00	$1,200.00	$1,200.00
4-4110	Income from Services	$0.00	$0.00	$3,870.00	$3,870.00cr	$3,870.00cr
6-6150	Advertising Expense	$0.00	$180.00	$0.00	$180.00	$180.00
6-6210	Wages Expense	$0.00	$930.00	$0.00	$930.00	$930.00
6-6240	Rent Expense	$0.00	$500.00	$0.00	$500.00	$500.00
6-6250	Utilities Expense	$0.00	$220.00	$0.00	$220.00	$220.00
	Total:		$77,670.00	$77,670.00		

Detail Trial Balance

To have this software print account balances in a trial balance, you would need to print a Detail Trial Balance. It looks like a combination of a ledger and a trial balance, providing a great deal of detail. The more sophisticated accounting software allows access to information in many formats and generates many reports in addition to the financial statements. This Detail Trial Balance gives you some idea of the variety and detail available for reports from computerized software.

```
                          Clark's Cleaners
                        3702 35th Southwest
                         Seattle WA 98126

                      Detail Trial Balance

                       6/1/9- to 6/30/9-
```

ID#	Src	Date	Memo	Debit	Credit	Net Activity	Ending Balance
1-1110 Cash					Beginning Balance:	$0.00	
GJ000001	GJ	6/1/9-	Original investment by Clark.	$40,000.00			
GJ000002	GJ	6/2/9-	Bought equipment for cash.		$22,000.00		
GJ000004	GJ	6/4/9-	Paid Drake Equipment Company.		$1,000.00		
GJ000006	GJ	6/8/9-	Paid rent for month of June.		$500.00		
GJ000007	GJ	6/10/9-	Premium for one-year liability.		$360.00		
GJ000008	GJ	6/14/9-	Income: two weeks ended June 30.	$1,940.00			
GJ000010	GJ	6/15/9-	Paid bill for electricity.		$220.00		
GJ000012	GJ	6/24/9-	Paid wages through June 2.		$930.00		
GJ000013	GJ	6/26/9-	Bought equipment on account.		$140.00		
GJ000014	GJ	6/30/9-	For two weeks ended June 30.	$1,790.00			
GJ000015	GJ	6/30/9-	Formal Rentals paid.	$90.00			
GJ000016	GJ	6/30/9-	Paid Drake Equipment Company.		$1,980.00		
GJ000017	GJ	6/30/9-	Withdrawal for personal use.		$1,200.00		
			Total:	$43,820.00	$28,330.00	$15,490.00	$15,490.00

(Continued on the next page)

```
                              Clark's Cleaners
                            3702 35th Southwest
                             Seattle WA 98126

                            Detail Trial Balance

                             6/1/9- to 6/30/9-
                                                                            Page 2
```

ID#	Src	Date	Memo	Debit	Credit	Net Activity	Ending Balance
1-1130 Accounts Receivable					Beginning Balance:	$0.00	
GJ000011	GJ	6/23/9-	Billed Formal Rentals.	$140.00			
GJ000015	GJ	6/30/9-	Formal Rentals paid on account.		$90.00		
			Total:	$140.00	$90.00	$50.00	$50.00
1-1150 Supplies					Beginning Balance:	$0.00	
GJ000005	GJ	6/4/9-	Bought cleaning fluid and bags.	$400.00			
			Total:	$400.00	$0.00	$400.00	$400.00
1-1170 Prepaid Insurance					Beginning Balance:	$0.00	
GJ000007	GJ	6/10/9-	Premium for one-year liability.	$360.00			
			Total	$360.00	$0.00	$360.00	$360.00
1-1240 Equipment					Beginning Balance:	$0.00	
GJ000002	GJ	6/2/9-	Bought equipment for cash.	$22,000.00			
GJ000003	GJ	6/2/9-	Bought equipment on account.	$4,000.00			
GJ000013	GJ	6/26/9-	Bought equipment on account.	$940.00			
			Total:	$26,940.00	$0.00	$26,940.00	$26,940.00
2-2210 Accounts Payable					Beginning Balance:	$0.00	
GJ000003	GJ	6/2/9-	Bought equipment on account.		$4,000.00		
GJ000004	GJ	6/4/9-	Paid Drake Equipment Company.	$1,000.00			
GJ000005	GJ	6/4/9-	Bought cleaning fluid and bags.		$400.00		
GJ000009	GJ	6/14/9-	Received bill for advertising.		$180.00		
GJ000013	GJ	6/26/9-	Bought equipment on account.		$800.00		
GJ000016	GJ	6/30/9-	Paid Drake Equipment Company.	$1,980.00			
			Total:	$2,980.00	$5,380.00	$2,400.00 cr	$2,400.00 cr
3-3110 N. L. Clark, Capital					Beginning Balance:	$0.00	
GJ000001	GJ	6/1/9-	Original investment by Clark.		$40,000.00		
			Total:	$0.00	$40,000.00	$40,000.00 cr	$40,000.00 cr
3-3120 N. L. Clark, Drawing					Beginning Balance:	$0.00	
GJ000017	GJ	6/30/9-	Withdrawal for personal use.	$1,200.00			
			Total:	$1,200.00	$0.00	$1,200.00	$1,200.00
4-4110 Income from Services					Beginning Balance:	$0.00	
GJ000008	GJ	6/14/9-	Income: two weeks ended June 30.		$1,940.00		
GJ000011	GJ	6/23/9-	Billed Formal Rentals.		$140.00		
GJ000014	GJ	6/30/9-	For two weeks ended June 30.		$1,790.00		
			Total:	$0.00	$3,870.00	$3,870.00 cr	$3,870.00 cr
6-6150 Advertising Expense					Beginning Balance:	$0.00	
GJ000009	GJ	6/14/9-	Received bill for advertising.	$180.00			
			Total:	$180.00	$0.00	$180.00	$180.00
6-6210 Wages Expense					Beginning Balance:	$0.00	
GJ000012	GJ	6/24/9-	Paid wages through June 24.	$930.00			
			Total:	$930.00	$0.00	$930.00	$930.00
6-6240 Rent Expense					Beginning Balance:	$0.00	
GJ000006	GJ	6/8/9-	Paid rent for month of June.	$500.00			
			Total:	$500.00	$0.00	$500.00	$500.00
6-6250 Utilities Expense					Beginning Balance:	$0.00	
GJ000010	GJ	6/15/9-	Paid bill for electricity.	$220.00			
			Total:	$220.00	$0.00	$220.00	$220.00
			Grand Total:	$77,670.00	$77,670.00		

COMPUTERS AT WORK

Accounting for Growth: Expanding a Business Often Requires More Complete Accounting Software

In 1964, Phillip Knight sold tennis shoes out of his basement and at track meets. That was the beginning of Nike.

More than 30 years ago, Frank and Dan Carney named their new small business after the product they sold and the dinky space where they operated. It was called Pizza Hut.

Most entrepreneurs have dreams of developing their small beginnings into multimillion-dollar enterprises. But the road from puny pizza parlor to pervasive pasta power is rough.

You may start off keeping records on paper. Soon your accountant, investor, or bank requires financial statements and you discover the convenience of a computer and a simple accounting package.

As your business grows, several employees need to have simultaneous access to accounts receivables. A huge hardware chain that buys your product starts requiring you to send electronic invoices.

Such growth is a welcome transformation in business, but you must handle the complex changes in technology and procedures. In the accounting arena, those changes often demand new, more comprehensive accounting software.

MOVING ON UP • Most financial software companies offer a wide range of accounting programs. Higher-end products are usually designed to decipher data from simpler programs. So when your business outgrows one level of software, you can convert to the next.

Don't go haywire with technology. . . . You usually don't need a topnotch system when starting out. Following logical progression from a simple accounting program to the more complex programs eases the transition. . . .

FACTORS TO CONSIDER • To decide which accounting package is best, you'll need to nail down your goals and think about where you plan to be in five years or so, and what kind of business you'll be operating. The answer will help guide you to the right family of software.

Check out software before you get started. Ask the company for a demonstration program.

Whatever you do, pick a reputable, financially sound company. . . . You don't want to buy from a company that doesn't present upgrades or that doesn't have more extensive programs to suit your future needs.

Source: Excerpted from Ryan Steeves, "Accounting for Growth," *PC Today*, February 1994, pp. 31–33.

Summary

The journal, ledger, and trial balance contain basically the same core of information in manual and computerized formats. Again, there are some differences in language, format, and detail. Continue to maintain your grasp of accounting basics. The contents of the transaction (input) will remain the same, but you will be able to adapt to the look of the forms (output).

CHAPTER REVIEW

R eview of Performance Objectives

1. **Record a group of transactions pertaining to a service enterprise in a two-column general journal.**

   From source documents, the transactions are analyzed to determine the accounts involved and whether the accounts are debited or credited. For each transaction, total debits must equal total credits. The journal is a book of original entry in which a day-by-day record of business transactions is maintained. The parts of a journal entry consist of the transaction date, the title of the account debited, the title of the account credited, the amounts recorded in the Debit and Credit columns, and an explanation.

2. **Post entries from a two-column general journal to general ledger accounts.**

   The ledger is a book that contains all the accounts arranged according to the chart of accounts. Posting is the process of transferring amounts from the journal to the ledger accounts. The posting process consists of four steps:
   1. Write the date of the transaction in the Date column.
   2. Write the amount of the transaction in the Debit or Credit column, and enter the new balance in the Balance columns under Debit or Credit.
   3. Write the page number of the journal in the Posting Reference column of the ledger account.
   4. Record the ledger account number in the Posting Reference column of the journal.

3. **Prepare a trial balance from the ledger accounts.**

   A trial balance is a list of all account balances in two columns labeled Debit and Credit. The trial balance shows that both sides of the accounting equation are equal. The heading consists of the company name, the title of the report (Trial Balance), and the date.

4. **Correct entries using the ruling method.**

   The ruling method can be used if an error is discovered before or after an entry has been posted. Draw a line through the incorrect account title or amount, and write the correct account title or amount immediately above. Include your initials with the correction.

5. **Correct entries using the correcting entry method.**

   The correcting entry method is used if an error is discovered after an entry has been posted. If the error consists of the wrong accounts, an entry is made canceling out the wrong account(s) and inserting the correct account(s).

G lossary

Audit trail A sequence of references that helps accountants trace information and transactions in an accounting system. **(106)**

Cost principle A purchased asset is recorded at its actual cost (the agreed amount of a transaction). **(86)**

Cross-reference The ledger account number in the Posting Reference column of the journal or the journal page number in the Posting Reference column of the ledger account. **(93)**

Cursor The indicator on the computer monitor that indicates where the next character will be keyed, usually a blinking line or box. **(105)**

Documentation A note or reference to a source document (e.g., check, invoice, loan document) or action taken. **(81)**

Journal The book in which a person makes the original record of a business transaction; commonly referred to as a *book of original entry*. **(82)**

Journalizing The process of recording a business transaction in a journal. **(82)**

Ledger A loose-leaf book or computer file containing the accounts of a business; commonly referred to as a *book of final entry*. **(90)**

Ledger account A complete record of the transactions recorded in each individual account. **(92)**

Posting The process of transferring figures from the journal to the ledger accounts. **(92)**

Two-column general journal The basic form of journal. **(82)**

QUESTIONS, EXERCISES, AND PROBLEMS

D iscussion Questions

1. What is the difference between a journal and a ledger?
2. In the posting process, what is meant by cross-referencing?
3. Before posting has taken place, how should a correction be made if the account titles have been recorded correctly in the journal but the amounts are wrong? After posting has taken place, how should the correction be made?
4. Why is a journal called a book of original entry?
5. In a chart of accounts having account numbers, list the first digit for each account:
   a. Service Income
   b. Rent Expense
   c. L. Cooke, Capital
   d. Accounts Payable
   e. Accounts Receivable
6. Briefly discuss how you would begin the selection process for accounting software. (Hint: See the "Computers at Work" box.)
7. What is the purpose of having a ledger account?
8. What is the sequence of the accounts in the general ledger?

E xercises

Exercise 3-1 In the two-column general journal below, the capital letters represent parts of a journal entry. On notebook paper, write the numbers 1 through 8. Alongside each number, write the letter that indicates where in the journal the items are recorded.

P.O.1

Label parts of a journal entry.

	DATE		DESCRIPTION	POST. REF.	DEBIT	CREDIT	
1	G						1
2	H	I J		O	M		2
3			K	P		N	3
4			L				4
5							5

GENERAL JOURNAL PAGE _____

1. Year
2. Month
3. Explanation
4. Title of account debited
5. Ledger account number of account credited
6. Amount of debit
7. Day of the month
8. Title of account credited

P.O.1

Journalize transactions.

Exercise 3-2 The following transactions of Shelby Company occurred during this year. Journalize the transactions in general journal form, including brief explanations.

July   1 Bought equipment for $8,300 from Marine Supply Company, paying $2,000 down; balance due in 30 days.
       9 Paid wages for the period July 1 through July 8, $1,375.
      14 Billed Harrison and Harrison Associates for services performed, $232.
      21 C. C. Shelby withdrew $1,750 for personal use.
      31 Paid Marine Supply Company account in full.

P.O.1

Journalize transactions.

Exercise 3-3 Northwest Landscaping Company completed the following selected transactions. Journalize the transactions in general journal form, including brief explanations.

Sept.   8 Collected $626 from S. Galb, a charge customer.
       14 Issued a check in full payment of an account payable to Billings Company, $109.
       19 T. R. Tyler (the owner) withdrew cash for personal use, $1,300.
       21 Purchased store supplies, $940, and office supplies, $270, on account from First Mercantile. Payment is due in 30 days.
       29 T. R. Tyler made an additional investment consisting of $4,000 in cash and $6,400 in equipment.

Exercise 3-4 The following T account shows the cash transactions for a month.

P.O.2

Post to a ledger account.

	Cash	No. 111	
4/1	12,000	4/2	800
4/8	1,800	4/6	500
4/15	6,300	4/10	2,100
4/21	800	4/22	5,200
4/30	5,100		

Post the amounts to the ledger account for Cash. Assume that all transactions appear on page 6 of the journal.

ACCOUNT __Cash__   ACCOUNT NO. __111__

DATE	ITEM	POST. REF.	DEBIT	CREDIT	BALANCE	
					DEBIT	CREDIT

Exercise 3-5 Arrange the following steps in the posting process in proper order:

P.O.2

Determine steps in the posting process.

a. The ledger account number is recorded in the Posting Reference column of the journal.
b. The amount of the balance of the ledger account is recorded in the Debit Balance or Credit Balance column.
c. The date of the transaction is recorded in the Date column of the ledger account.
d. The amount of the transaction is recorded in the Debit or Credit column of the ledger account.
e. The page number of the journal is recorded in the Posting Reference column of the ledger account.

P.O.3

Prepare a corrected trial balance.

Exercise 3-6 The bookkeeper for McNeilly Company has prepared the following trial balance:

McNeilly Company
Trial Balance
May 31, 19–

ACCOUNT NAME	DEBIT	CREDIT
Cash		2 6 0 0 00
Accounts Receivable	8 4 0 0 00	
Supplies	7 0 0 00	
Prepaid Insurance	6 5 0 00	
Equipment	16 4 0 0 00	
Accounts Payable		3 8 0 0 00
S. McNeilly, Capital		12 0 0 0 00
S. McNeilly, Drawing	2 0 0 0 00	
Income from Services		19 6 5 0 00
Rent Expense	6 0 0 0 00	
Miscellaneous Expense	1 9 0 0 00	
	36 0 5 0 00	38 0 5 0 00

The bookkeeper has asked for your help. In examining the firm's journal and ledger, you discover the following:
a. The debits to the Cash account total $7,000, and the credits total $4,400.
b. A $400 payment to a creditor was entered in the journal but was not posted to the Accounts Payable account. Cash was properly posted.
c. The first two digits in the balance of the Accounts Receivable account were transposed in copying the balance from the ledger to the trial balance.
Prepare a corrected trial balance.

P.O.4,5

Journalize correcting entries.

Exercise 3-7 Record correcting entries for each of the following errors:
a. A cash purchase of office equipment for $420 was journalized as a cash purchase of store equipment for $420. (Use the ruling method: assume the entry was not posted.)
b. An entry for a $360 cash payment for office supplies was journalized as $306. (Use the ruling method: assume the entry was not posted.)
c. A $730 payment for repairs was journalized and posted as a debit to Building instead of a debit to Repair Expense. (Use the correcting method to journalize the correction.)
d. A $630 premium for liability insurance was journalized as $360. (Use the correcting method to journalize the correction.)

P.O.4,5

Determine the effect of errors.

Exercise 3-8 Determine the effect of the following errors on a company's total revenue, total expenses, and net income. Indicate the effect by listing O for "overstated (too much)," U for "understated (too little)," or NA for "not affected." Item 0 is provided as an example.

	Total Revenue	Total Expenses	Net Income
0. *Example:* A check for $326 was written in payment of a charge account. The accountant debited Utilities Expense for $326 and credited Cash for $326.	NA	O	U
a. $440 was received from charge customers. The accountant debited Cash for $440 and credited Income from Services for $440.			
b. The owner withdrew $930 for personal use. The accountant debited Salary Expense for $930 and credited Cash for $930.			
c. A check for $1,540 was written to pay rent for the month. The accountant debited Rent Expense for $1,450 and credited Cash for $1,450.			
d. $2,400 was received from cash customers. The accountant debited Cash for $2,400 and credited the owner's Capital account for $2,400.			
e. A check for $96 was written in payment of the owner's personal clothing bill. The accountant debited Miscellaneous Expense for $96 and credited Cash for $96.			

 onsider and Communicate

You are the new bookkeeper in a small business. The bookkeeper whose job you are taking is training you on the business's manual system. As he journalizes, he writes the account number in the Posting Reference column because he thinks it's easier. Then, when he posts, he thinks he doesn't have to be bothered writing the account numbers. How would you explain why he should resist the urge to write the account number in the Posting Reference column immediately and should instead enter the account number after he has posted the amount to the ledger?

 hat If . . .

The firm's new bookkeeper understands that revenue less expenses equals net income or net loss. The bookkeeper is concerned about entering amounts into the proper expense accounts, but he is really rushed. What if the bookkeeper correctly identifies an amount as an expense, but enters the amount in the incorrect expense account? What is the effect on the bottom line of the income statement? Does it really matter whether the correct expense account is used as long as the amount is recorded in one of the expense accounts? Briefly state how you would clean up this problem.

Question of Ethics

You work part time as an accounting intern at a large firm. You observe that your supervisor is struggling to balance a trial balance. Finally, in desperation, she exclaims, "Well, I'm just going to MICOR it." You ask what she means by MICOR. She replies, "Make It Come Out Right." In other words, she's going to plug a number—that is, she will enter a number that will force the trial balance to balance.

Is your supervisor behaving in an ethical manner by forcing the numbers to balance? Do you have any ethical concerns? Should you feel responsible to question your supervisor's ethics directly, or should you mention it to your supervisor's boss?

roblem Set A

P.O.1

Problem 3-1A The chart of accounts for the Fremont Driving School is given below, followed by the transactions that took place during July of this year.

Chart of Accounts

ASSETS	REVENUE
111 Cash	411 Driving Revenue
112 Accounts Receivable	
117 Prepaid Insurance	EXPENSES
121 Cars	511 Salary Expense
123 Equipment	512 Rent Expense
	513 Gas and Oil Expense
LIABILITIES	514 Advertising Expense
211 Accounts Payable	515 Repair Expense
	516 Telephone Expense
OWNER'S EQUITY	529 Miscellaneous Expense
311 T. R. Fremont, Capital	
312 T. R. Fremont, Drawing	

July 1 Paid $1,430 for one year's liability insurance.
2 Paid rent for office and garages for the month, $850.
4 Received bill for advertising from the *City Daily*, $215.
5 Received bill for auto repair from Jensen's Automotive, $212.
8 Billed students for driving lessons, $795.
10 Received and paid telephone bill, $76.
14 Bought overhead projector on account from Tubman Company, $286, payment due in 30 days.
17 T. R. Fremont withdrew $700 for personal use.
19 Paid bill for advertising, charged previously on July 4.
21 Received bill from Barton Oil Company for gas and oil used in the firm's operations, $213.

24 Received cash from students, $310 (students were not billed previously).
25 Paid salary of assistant, $1,490.
26 Bought a desk and chair from Baxter Furniture, $259, with payment due in 30 days.
29 Received $575 in cash from students previously billed.
30 Billed students for driving lessons, $835.
30 Paid $186 in expenses for travel to Defensive Driving Seminar.
30 T. R. Fremont withdrew $725 for personal use.

Instructions

Record the transactions in a general journal, including a brief explanation for each entry. Number the journal pages 30, 31, and 32.

Problem 3-2A The journal entries in the Working Papers relate to Clark's Cleaners' second month of operation. The balances of the accounts as of July 1 have been entered in the accounts in the ledger. A check mark has been placed in the Posting Reference column to indicate that this is a balance brought forward. However, when posting entries for July, record page numbers in the ledger accounts.

P.O.2,3

Instructions

1. Post the journal entries to the ledger accounts.
2. Prepare a trial balance as of July 31.
3. Prepare an income statement for the two months ended July 31.
4. Prepare a statement of owner's equity for the two months ended July 31.
5. Prepare a balance sheet as of July 31.

Problem 3-3A The chart of accounts of B. L. Hintzen, a chiropractor, is shown below.

P.O.1,2,3

Chart of Accounts

ASSETS	REVENUE
111 Cash	411 Professional Fees
113 Accounts Receivable	
115 Supplies	EXPENSES
117 Prepaid Insurance	515 Advertising Expense
124 Equipment	520 Salary Expense
	524 Rent Expense
LIABILITIES	525 Utilities Expense
221 Accounts Payable	
OWNER'S EQUITY	
311 B. L. Hintzen, Capital	
312 B. L. Hintzen, Drawing	

Dr. Hintzen completed the following transactions during February:

Feb. 1 Paid office rent for the month, $700.
2 Bought professional equipment from Health-Tech Company on account, $1,085, payment due in 30 days.
3 Bought plastic gloves and other supplies on account from Burns Company, $71.65, payment due in 30 days.

5 Paid cash to Sports Therapy Products Plus (a creditor) on account, $1,275.

6 Received cash on account from patients, $2,800.

9 Received and paid bill for advertising, $245.50.

11 Paid cash for premium on a one-year liability insurance policy, $1,142.

12 Billed patients on account for professional services rendered, $2,450.

14 Part of the professional equipment purchased on February 2 was defective. Returned the equipment and received a reduction in the bill, $179.

16 Received cash for professional services, $1,420.

27 Paid monthly salary of part-time chiropractic assistant, $1,216.

28 Received and paid telephone bill for the month, $83.

28 Billed patients on account for professional services rendered, $1,570.

28 Dr. Hintzen withdrew $1,620 in cash for personal use.

Instructions

1. Journalize the transactions for February, beginning with page 27.
2. Post the entries to the ledger accounts. (Because the professional enterprise was in operation previously, the balances have been recorded in the ledger accounts. A check mark has been placed in the Posting Reference column to indicate that this is a balance brought forward.)
3. Prepare a trial balance as of February 28 for B. L. Hintzen, D.C.

Instructions for General Ledger Software

1. Journalize the transactions in the general journal.
2. Post the entries to the general ledger.
3. Print a trial balance as of February 28.

P.O.1,2,3

Problem 3-4A Finley Land Surveys uses the following chart of accounts:

Chart of Accounts

ASSETS	REVENUE
111 Cash	411 Professional Fees
113 Accounts Receivable	
115 Supplies	EXPENSES
124 Equipment	518 Truck Expense
126 Truck	521 Wages Expense
	524 Rent Expense
LIABILITIES	525 Utilities Expense
221 Accounts Payable	
OWNER'S EQUITY	
311 A. R. Finley, Capital	
312 A. R. Finley, Drawing	

The following transactions were completed during March:

Mar. 1 Finley transferred $14,200 from a personal bank account to an account to be used in the business.

1 Paid rent for the month, $640.

2 Bought a transit and level on account from Carnes Engineering Supplies, $3,220. Payment is due in 30 days. (Debit Equipment)

3 Paid cash for stationery, pencils, and other incidental supplies, $126.40.

4 Bought a used truck from Lehman Motors for $12,400, paying $4,000 down, with the balance due in 30 days.

4 Finley invested his own personal drafting table and filing cabinet, valued at $610, in the business.

7 Billed Bradford Construction for services rendered, $2,410.

8 Received bill from Sterling Auto Repair for minor repairs to the truck, $182.

8 Billed C. B. Carlson for services rendered, $2,011.

10 Bought survey chains and stakes from Miller, Inc., $226.40. Payment is due in 30 days. (Debit Supplies)

14 Received $1,000 from Bradford Construction as part payment on account.

15 Returned defective chains to Miller, Inc., and received a $42 reduction in amount owed.

19 Billed Hendricks Development for services rendered, $3,450.

22 Received $2,011 from C. B. Carlson in full payment of account.

26 Paid Sterling Auto Repair $182 as full payment.

30 Received and paid telephone bill, $92.

31 Paid wages of assistant, $1,200.

31 Received and paid bill for gas and oil for the truck, $91.

31 Finley withdrew cash for personal use, $1,400.

Instructions

1. Record the transactions in the general journal, beginning with page 1 and giving a brief explanation for each entry.
2. In the general ledger, record the account titles and numbers.
3. Post the entries to the ledger accounts.
4. Prepare a trial balance dated March 31.

Instructions for General Ledger Software

1. Journalize the transactions in the general journal.
2. Post the entries to the general ledger.
3. Print a trial balance as of March 31.

P roblem Set B

Problem 3-1B The chart of accounts for Health Systems Plus, an aerobics dance studio, is given below, followed by the transactions that took place during November of this year.

P.O.1

Chart of Accounts

ASSETS	REVENUE
111 Cash	411 Aerobics Class Revenue
112 Accounts Receivable	
117 Supplies	EXPENSES
118 Prepaid Insurance	511 Wages Expense
121 Equipment	512 Advertising Expense
122 Furniture	513 Rent Expense
	514 Utilities Expense
LIABILITIES	519 Miscellaneous Expense
211 Accounts Payable	
OWNER'S EQUITY	
311 N. S. Chan, Capital	
312 N. S. Chan, Drawing	

Nov. 1 Bought a sound system on account from Barron Electronics, $3,200. Paid $1,200 as a down payment with the balance due in 30 days.

3 Paid $69 for business stationery.

4 Bought chairs on account from Bixby Furniture, $631, with the balance due in 30 days.

6 Paid rent for the month, $575.

7 Received cash for aerobics classes, $435 (students not billed previously).

10 Received and paid electric bill, $76.

13 Billed students for aerobics classes, $1,475.

15 Paid wages to part-time assistants, $750.

17 Chan invested in the business her personal camcorder having a fair market value of $1,042.

19 Paid cash for one-year liability insurance premium, $360.

21 Received bill from Lacy Advertising Agency to be paid in 30 days, $164.

22 Received cash for aerobics classes, $435. (Students were not billed previously.)

24 Paid wages to part-time assistants, $490.

27 Received and paid telephone bill, $89.

29 Billed students for aerobics classes, $975.

29 Paid wages to part-time assistants, $785.

30 Chan withdrew cash for personal use, $1,450.

Instructions

Record the transactions in a general journal, including a brief explanation for each entry. Number the journal pages 21, 22, and 23.

P.O.2,3

Problem 3-2B The journal entries in the Working Papers relate to Hale's Appliance Repair's second month of operation. The balances of the accounts as of July 1 have been recorded in the accounts in the ledger. A check mark has been placed in the Posting Reference column to indicate that this is a balance brought forward. However, when posting entries for July, record page numbers in the ledger accounts.

Instructions

1. Post the journal entries to the ledger accounts.
2. Prepare a trial balance as of July 31.
3. Prepare an income statement for the two months ended July 31.
4. Prepare a statement of owner's equity for the two months ended July 31.
5. Prepare a balance sheet as of July 31.

P.O.1,2,3

Problem 3-3B Following is the chart of accounts of B. L. Hintzen, chiropractor:

Chart of Accounts

ASSETS
111 Cash
113 Accounts Receivable
115 Supplies
117 Prepaid Insurance
124 Equipment

LIABILITIES
221 Accounts Payable

OWNER'S EQUITY
311 B. L. Hintzen, Capital
312 B. L. Hintzen, Drawing

REVENUE
411 Professional Fees

EXPENSES
515 Advertising Expense
520 Salary Expense
524 Rent Expense
525 Utilities Expense

Dr. Hintzen completed the following transactions during February:

Feb.
2 Bought professional equipment on account from Peyton and Rogers, $1,285.50, payment due in 30 days.
3 Paid office rent for the month, $800.
3 Received cash on account from patients, $2,095.50.
6 Received and paid bill for advertising, $269.50.
9 Bought plastic gloves and other supplies on account from Tuttle Company, $93.95. Payment is due in 30 days.
12 Billed patients on account for professional services rendered, $2,481.
13 Paid cash for one-year property insurance policy, $144.
15 Received cash for professional services, $376. (Patients were not billed previously.)
17 Part of the professional equipment purchased on February 2 from Peyton and Rogers was defective; returned equipment and received a reduction in bill, $186.
27 Paid monthly salary of part-time chiropractic assistant, $1,090.
28 Received and paid telephone bill for the month, $51.
28 Billed patients on account for professional services rendered, $1,719.
28 Dr. Hintzen withdrew cash for personal use, $1,082.

Instructions

1. Journalize the transactions for February, beginning with page 27.
2. Post the entries to the ledger accounts. (Because the professional enterprise was in operation previously, the balances have been recorded in the ledger accounts. A check mark has been placed in the Posting Reference column to indicate that this is a balance brought forward.)
3. Prepare a trial balance as of February 28 for B. L. Hintzen, D.C.

Instructions for General Ledger Software

1. Journalize the transactions in the general journal.
2. Post the entries to the general ledger.
3. Print a trial balance as of February 28.

P.O.1,2,3

Problem 3-4B Bishop Telephone Answering Service uses the following chart of accounts:

Chart of Accounts

ASSETS	REVENUE
111 Cash	411 Income from Fees
113 Accounts Receivable	
115 Supplies	EXPENSES
117 Prepaid Insurance	521 Wages Expense
124 Office Equipment	524 Rent Expense
	525 Utilities Expense
LIABILITIES	526 Equipment Rental Expense
221 Accounts Payable	
OWNER'S EQUITY	
311 L. D. Bishop, Capital	
312 L. D. Bishop, Drawing	

The following transactions were completed during May:

May 1 Bishop transferred $3,800 from a personal bank account to an account to be used in the business.
 2 Paid $352 as rental for telephone equipment for the month of May.
 3 Bought a filing cabinet for cash, $147.
 3 Paid rent for the month, $650.
 3 Bought desk and chair on account from Herman and Company, $496. Payment is due in 30 days.
 6 Billed charge customers for services rendered, $528.
 7 Paid cash for stationery and other supplies, $216.
 10 Bought typewriter for $428 from Drake Office Supply, paying $128 down, with the balance due in 30 days.
 14 Billed charge customers for services rendered, $681.
 19 Paid Herman Company account, in full, $496.
 19 Paid 12-month premium for property and liability insurance, $152.
 22 Collected $376 from charge customers to apply on account.
 29 Received and paid electric bill, $72.
 29 Billed charge customers for services rendered, $892.
 31 Paid wages of part-time employees, $516.
 31 Bishop withdrew $400 for personal use.
 31 Collected $614 from charge customers to apply on account.
 31 Received bill from Ace Communications for rental of telephone equipment, $200.

Instructions

1. Record the transactions in the general journal, beginning with page 1 and giving a brief explanation for each entry.
2. In the general ledger, record the account titles and numbers.
3. Post the entries to the ledger accounts.
4. Prepare a trial balance dated May 31, 19—.

Instructions for General Ledger Software
1. Journalize the transactions in the general journal.
2. Post the entries to the general ledger.
3. Print a trial balance as of May 31.

CHALLENGE PROBLEM

The Fleming Company has the following balances in the general ledger. All balances are normal balances.

Accounts Payable	$ 1,700	D. D. Fleming, Capital	$12,000
Accounts Receivable	4,300	D. D. Fleming, Drawing	1,000
Cash	3,200	Prepaid Insurance	430
Equipment	15,000	Rent Expense	3,000
Income from Services	15,800	Supplies	670
Miscellaneous Expense	1,900		

1. Prepare a correct trial balance for June 30, 19— from the information above.
2. What is the net income for this company as shown by this trial balance?
3. Listed below are facts uncovered after you prepared the trial balance. Record in general journal form the necessary additional or correcting journal entries to reflect the new information. Show the letter and date for each entry.
   a. Customers were billed at the end of the month for $1,500 for services rendered, but the event was not recorded in the general journal.
   b. The business bought a new piece of equipment originally advertised for $10,000, but they received a 10 percent discount and will pay the full amount due in 30 days.
   c. The company received a notice that the monthly rent will be increased from $750 per month to $800 per month beginning next month.
   d. A payment of $3,000 by the charge customers was credited to the revenue account.
   e. The payment of $1,500 for Advertising Expense was charged to Miscellaneous Expense.
4. What is the correct net income for the business? Show your calculations.

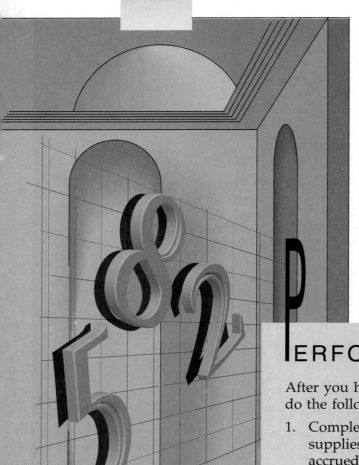

chapter 4

Completing the Accounting Cycle for a Service Enterprise: The Work Sheet, Adjusting and Closing Entries, and Post-Closing Trial Balance

PERFORMANCE OBJECTIVES

After you have completed this chapter, you will be able to do the following:

1. Complete a work sheet involving adjustments for supplies used, expired insurance, depreciation, and accrued wages for a service enterprise.

2. Prepare an income statement, a statement of owner's equity, and a balance sheet directly from the work sheet of a service business.

3. Journalize and post the adjusting entries.

4. Journalize and post closing entries for a service enterprise.

5. Prepare a post-closing trial balance for any type of enterprise.

6. Define the following methods of accounting: accrual basis, cash-receipts-and-disbursements basis, modified cash basis.

7. Prepare interim statements.

One of the first surprises I had when I became a tax accountant was finding out how many bookkeepers and accountants do not know how to close the books at the end of the year.

Their records appear neat and orderly, but at the end of the accounting cycle when I examine the records, the revenue, expense, income summary, and drawing accounts are still "open." That is, the accounts still have balances. It becomes a real problem for me the next year, because transactions from the prior year and the current year are all lumped together. This violates the matching principle.

Imagine the problem for the business owner if the records are not corrected. The owner could conceivably pay income taxes twice. In other words, last year's revenue and expenses are still in the records (because the books were never closed) along with the current year's revenue and expenses.

Now, as a precaution, I call the bookkeeper or accountant and ask, "What is the January 1, 19— balance in the Capital account?" If the records of the previous year end have been properly closed as of December 31, 19—, the bookkeeper's balance and mine "tie" or are the same. I may then proceed with the tax preparation.

So far you have practiced analyzing, journalizing, and posting transactions as well as preparing a trial balance. Let's look at how each step fits into the accounting cycle.

The Accounting Cycle

The **accounting cycle** represents the sequence of steps in the accounting procedure. Figure 4-1 shows how we introduce these steps on a chapter-by-chapter basis. This outline brings us up to date on what we have accomplished so far and how each chapter fits into the steps in the accounting cycle.

Figure 4-1

Chapter 1

Analyze Business Transactions.
Assets = Liabilities + Capital + Revenue − Expenses
Prepare Financial Statements.

Chapter 2

Analyze Business Transactions.

$$\text{Assets} = \text{Liabilities} + \text{Capital} + \text{Revenue} - \text{Expenses}$$

+	−		−	+		−	+		−	+		+	−
Dr.	Cr.		Dr.	Cr.		Dr.	Cr.		Dr.	Cr.		Dr.	Cr.

Prepare a Trial Balance from T Accounts.

Chapter 3

Journalize and Post Business Transactions.
Prepare a Trial Balance from the General Ledger.

Chapter 4

Gather the Adjustment Data.
Complete a Work Sheet.
Prepare Financial Statements.
Journalize and Post Adjusting Entries.
Journalize and Post Closing Entries.
Prepare a Post-Closing Trial Balance.

Fiscal Period

fiscal period is any period of time covering a complete accounting cycle. A fiscal year is a fiscal period consisting of twelve consecutive months. It does not have to coincide with the calendar year. For example, the fiscal period of a resort that is operated during the summer months may be October 1 of one year to September 30 of the next year. State and local governments usually have a fiscal period from July 1 of one year to June 30 of the next year. For income tax purposes, any period of twelve consecutive months may be selected. However, you have to be consistent and use the same fiscal period from year to year.

The Work Sheet

t the moment, we are concerned with the work sheet. The **work sheet** is a working paper used by accountants to record necessary adjustments and provide up-to-date account balances needed to prepare the financial statements. The work sheet is simply a tool used to help accountants prepare the financial statements. As a tool, the work sheet serves as a central place for bringing together the information needed to record the adjustments. Once he or she has up-to-date account balances, the accountant can prepare the financial statements. (As you may recall, we said that the income statement and balance sheet that we looked at in Chapter 1 were tentative because adjustments had not been recorded at that time.)

First, we will present the work sheet form, so that you can see what you will be working with. Next, we will describe and show examples of adjustments. Finally, we will show how the adjustments are entered on the work sheet and how the work sheet is completed.

For our purposes, we will use a ten-column work sheet—so called because two amount columns are provided for each of the work sheet's five major sections, or pairs of columns. We will explain the function of each of these sections, again basing our discussion on the accounting activities of Clark's Cleaners. But first we need to fill in the heading, which consists of three lines: (1) the name of the company, (2) the title of the working paper, and (3) the period of time covered.

Clark's Cleaners
Work Sheet
For Month Ended June 30, 19—

ACCOUNT NAME	TRIAL BALANCE		ADJUSTMENTS		ADJUSTED TRIAL BALANCE		INCOME STATEMENT		BALANCE SHEET	
	DEBIT	CREDIT	DEBIT	CREDIT	DEBIT	CREDIT	DEBIT	CREDIT	DEBIT	CREDIT

Next, we want to point out the classification of accounts that are placed in each column. We are going to start with the Trial Balance columns and then move across the work sheet, discussing each pair of columns separately.

REMEMBER
You have already done a trial balance. Record the normal balances in the Trial Balance Debit or Credit column.

The Columns of the Work Sheet

Trial Balance Columns   When you use a work sheet, you do not have to prepare a trial balance on a separate sheet of paper. Instead, you enter the account balances in the first two columns of the work sheet. List the accounts in the Account Name column in the same order that they appear in the chart of accounts. Assuming normal balances, the account classifications are listed in the Trial Balance columns below. We presented a trial balance in Chapter 2. The same classifications are recorded in the Debit and Credit columns of the work sheet.

FYI
You may take a trial balance at any time to verify the equality of debits and credits. It may be handwritten, produced on a calculator tape, or printed from a spreadsheet program.

Account Name	Trial Balance		Adjustments		Adjusted Trial Balance		Income Statement		Balance Sheet	
	Debit	Credit	Debit	Credit	Debit	Credit	Debit	Credit	Debit	Credit
	Assets →				→ Assets					
		Liabilities				→ Liabilities				
		Capital →				→ Capital				
	Drawing				→ Drawing					
		Revenue →				→ Revenue				
	Expenses →				→ Expenses					

As we move along in this chapter, we will discuss the adjustments. The Adjusted Trial Balance columns contain the same account classifications as the Trial Balance columns. **The Adjusted Trial Balance columns are merely extensions of the Trial Balance columns after the amounts of the adjustments have been included.** If an adjustment is required, the amounts are carried over from the Trial Balance columns through the Adjustments columns and into the Adjusted Trial Balance columns.

Income Statement Columns An income statement simply contains the revenue minus the expenses. Revenue accounts have credit balances, so they are recorded in the Income Statement Credit column. Expense accounts, on the other hand, have debit balances, so they are recorded in the Income Statement Debit column.

Account Name	Trial Balance		Adjustments		Adjusted Trial Balance		Income Statement		Balance Sheet	
	Debit	Credit	Debit	Credit	Debit	Credit	Debit	Credit	Debit	Credit
	Assets →				→ Assets					
		Liabilities				→ Liabilities				
		Capital →				→ Capital				
	Drawing				→ Drawing					
		Revenue →				→ Revenue →		→ Revenue		
	Expenses →				→ Expenses →		→ Expenses			

Balance Sheet Columns As you recall, the balance sheet is a statement showing assets, liabilities, and owner's equity. Asset accounts have debit balances, so they are recorded in the Balance Sheet Debit column. Liability accounts have credit balances, so they are recorded in the Balance Sheet Credit column. The Capital account has a credit balance, so it is recorded in the Balance Sheet Credit column. Because the Drawing account is a deduction from Capital, it has a debit balance and is recorded in the Balance Sheet Debit column (the opposite column from that in which Capital is recorded).

Account Name	Trial Balance		Adjustments		Adjusted Trial Balance		Income Statement		Balance Sheet	
	Debit	Credit	Debit	Credit	Debit	Credit	Debit	Credit	Debit	Credit
	Assets ———				→ Assets ———				→ Assets	
		Liabilities				→ Liabilities				→ Liabilities
		Capital ——				→ Capital ——				→ Capital
	Drawing				→ Drawing				→ Drawing	
		Revenue ——				→ Revenue ——		→ Revenue		
	Expenses				→ Expenses ——		→ Expenses			

Adjustments

Adjustments are a means or way of updating the ledger accounts. Adjustments may be considered *internal transactions*. Adjustments are determined after the trial balance has been prepared.

Only a few accounts are adjusted. After you have acquired experience in accounting, these accounts will be easy to recognize. To describe the reasons for making adjustments, let's return to Clark's Cleaners. First, we will select the accounts that require adjustments. Next, we will show the adjustments recorded in T accounts. However, bear in mind that the adjustments are ordinarily first recorded on the work sheet in a manual set of records.

Supplies

In the trial balance, the Supplies account has a balance of $400. Each time Clark's Cleaners bought supplies, Clark wrote the entry as a debit to Supplies and a credit to either Cash or Accounts Payable. Thus he recorded each purchase of supplies as an increase in the Supplies account.

As long as supplies are unused, they are considered to be an asset. But we have not taken into consideration the fact that any business continually uses up supplies in the process of carrying on its activities. For Clark's Cleaners, the items recorded under Supplies consist of cleaning fluid, plastic garment bags, hangers, and similar items. Rather than going to the trouble of keeping a day-by-day record of the supplies used, Clark's Cleaners waits until the end of the month and then takes a physical count of the supplies left over. **To find out the amount of supplies used, subtract the amount left from the total supplies that were on hand.**

When Clark takes an inventory on June 30, he finds that there are $90 worth of supplies left over. The situation looks like this:

Had	$400	(Recorded under Supplies)
− Have left	−90	(Determined by taking an inventory)
Used	$310	(The amount used is an expense of doing business. This is Supplies Expense.)

R E M E M B E R

For the adjustment of supplies, first find the amount used by subtracting the amount left from the balance of the Supplies account. In the adjusting entry, take the amount used out of Supplies and put it into Supplies Expense.

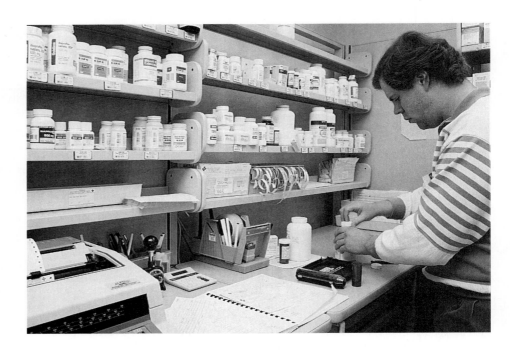

Pharmacists purchase many kinds of supplies—labels, bottles, pens, adhesives, as well as tapes for cash registers and adding machines.

To record the amount of the supplies used, Clark has to make an **adjusting entry.** The purpose of an adjusting entry is to bring the books up to date at the end of the fiscal period. Let's look at this in the form of T accounts. We need to take the amount of supplies used ($310) out of the Supplies account, because we no longer have that much of the asset. Also, we need to put the amount used ($310) into Supplies Expense, because Clark's Cleaners has increased its supplies expense.

(a)

	Supplies			Supplies Expense	
	+	−		+	−
(Old) Balance	400	Adjusting 310		Adjusting 310	
(New) Balance	90				

Prepaid Insurance

The $360 balance in Prepaid Insurance stands for the premium paid in advance for a 12-month liability insurance policy. One month's premium, which amounts to $30, has now expired.

$$12 \text{ months } \overline{)\ \$360}^{\ \$ 30 \text{ per month}}$$

In the adjustment, Clark's Cleaners deducts the expired or used portion from Prepaid Insurance and adds it to Insurance Expense.

(b)

	Prepaid Insurance			Insurance Expense	
	+	−		+	−
(Old) Balance	360	Adjusting 30		Adjusting 30	
(New) Balance	330				

The new balance of Prepaid Insurance, $330 ($360 − $30), represents the cost of insurance that is now paid in advance and should therefore appear in the balance sheet. The $30 figure in Insurance Expense represents the cost of insurance that has expired and should therefore appear in the income statement.

Depreciation of Equipment

We have followed the policy of recording durable items, such as appliances and fixtures, under Equipment because they will last longer than one year. The benefits derived from these assets will eventually be used up (they will either wear out or become obsolete). Therefore, we should systematically spread out their costs over the period of their useful lives. In other words, we write off the cost of the assets as an expense over the *estimated useful life of the equipment* and call it **depreciation** because such equipment loses its usefulness. A part of depreciation expense is allotted to each fiscal period. In the case of Clark's Cleaners, the Equipment account has a balance of $26,940. Suppose we estimate that the equipment will have a useful life of eight years, with a trade-in value of $2,940 at the end of that time. The amount of depreciation for one month is figured like this:

1. Subtract the trade-in (salvage) value from the cost to get the full depreciation.

   $26,940 − $2,940 = $24,000

2. Divide the full depreciation by the number of years in the asset's estimated life to get the depreciation for one year.

   $$\frac{\$\ 3,000 \text{ per year}}{8 \text{ years} \overline{)\$24,000 \text{ full depreciation}}}$$

3. Divide the depreciation for one year by 12 to get the depreciation for one month.

   $$\frac{\$\ 250 \text{ per month}}{12 \text{ months} \overline{)\$3,000}}$$

When depreciation is recorded, we do not take away or subtract directly from the asset account. In asset accounts, such as Equipment or Building, we must keep the original cost recorded in the account intact. Consequently, the amount of depreciation has to be recorded in another account; that account is **Accumulated Depreciation.** Accumulated Depreciation, Equipment, is contrary to, or a deduction from, Equipment, so we call it a **contra account.**

One always records the adjusting entry for depreciation as a debit to Depreciation Expense (an income statement item) and a credit to Accumulated Depreciation (a balance sheet item), because both accounts are increased. The adjustment in T account form would appear as follows:

(c)

Depreciation Expense, Equipment		Accumulated Depreciation, Equipment	
+	−	−	+
Adjusting 250			Adjusting 250

On the balance sheet, the balance of Accumulated Depreciation is deducted from the balance of the related asset account as illustrated below on the partial balance sheet for Clark's Cleaners. The net figure shown, $26,690, is referred to as the **book value** of the asset. Thus, book value is the cost of an asset minus accumulated depreciation.

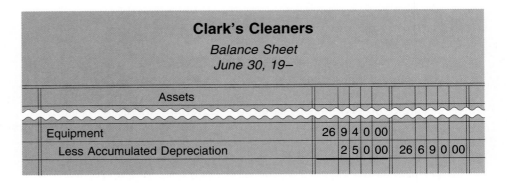

Clark's Cleaners

Balance Sheet

June 30, 19–

Assets			
Equipment	26 9 4 0 00		
Less Accumulated Depreciation	2 5 0 00	26 6 9 0 00	

To show the accounts under their proper headings, let's look at the fundamental accounting equation. (Brackets indicate that Accumulated Depreciation, Equipment, is a deduction from the Equipment account. Note that the plus and minus signs are switched around.)

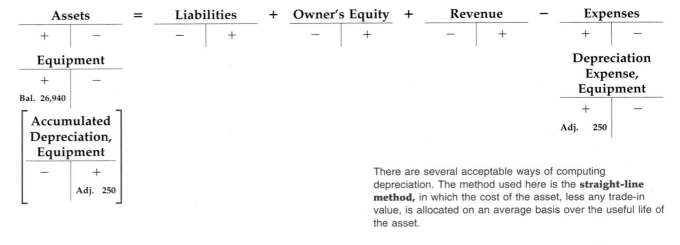

There are several acceptable ways of computing depreciation. The method used here is the **straight-line method,** in which the cost of the asset, less any trade-in value, is allocated on an average basis over the useful life of the asset.

Accumulated Depreciation, Equipment, as the title implies, is the total depreciation that the company has taken since the original purchase of the asset. Rather than crediting the Equipment account, Clark's Cleaners keeps track of the total depreciation taken since it first acquired the asset in a separate account. The maximum depreciation it could take would be the cost of the equipment, $26,940 less trade-in value of $2,940. So, for the first year, Accumulated Depreciation, Equipment, will increase at the rate of $250 per month, assuming that no additional equipment has been purchased. For example, at the end of the second month, Accumulated Depreciation, Equipment, will amount to $500 ($250 + $250). At the end of the second month, the book value will be $26,440 ($26,940 − $500).

. . . .
R E M E M B E R

The book value of an asset equals the cost of the asset minus the accumulated depreciation. Also, book value is not the same as market value.
. . . .

Wages Expense

The end of the fiscal period and the end of the employee's payroll period rarely fall on the same day. A diagram of the situation looks like this:

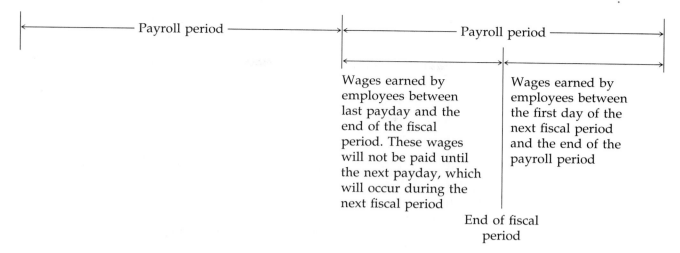

In brief, we are faced with a situation where the last day of the fiscal period falls in the middle of the payroll period. So, we have to split up the wages earned between the fiscal period just ending and the new fiscal period.

We will use another company for this example. Assume that this firm pays its employees a total of $400 per day and that payday falls on Friday throughout the year. When the employees pick up their paychecks on Friday, at the end of the work day, the checks include their wages for that day as well as for the preceding four days. The employees work a five-day week. And suppose that the last day of the fiscal period falls on Wednesday, December 31. We can diagram this as shown in the illustration below.

				Dec. 26	Dec. 29	Dec. 30	Dec. 31	Jan. 1	Jan. 2
Mon	**Tue**	**Wed**	**Thur**	**Fri**	**Mon**	**Tue**	**Wed**	**Thur**	**Fri**
$400	$400	$400	$400	$400	$400	$400	$400	$400	$400

End of Fiscal Year

Payroll period → ← Payroll period →

Payday $2,000 (Dec. 26) $1,200 $800   Payday $2,000 (Jan. 2)

December						
S	M	T	W	T	F	S
	1	2	3	4	⑤	6
7	8	9	10	11	⑫	13
14	15	16	17	18	⑲	20
21	22	23	24	25	㉖	27
28	29	30	31			

— Paydays

> **R E M E M B E R**
>
> If the end of the fiscal period (year) occurs during the middle of a payroll period, Wages Expense must be adjusted to bring it up to date. In the adjusting entry, add the amount employees have earned between the last payroll period and the end of the fiscal period.

To have the Wages Expense account reflect an accurate balance for the fiscal period, you need to add $1,200 for the cost of labor between the last payday, December 26, and the end of the year, December 31 ($400 for December 29; $400 for December 30; $400 for December 31). Because the $1,200 will not be paid at this time but is owed to the employees on December 31, you also need to add $1,200 to Wages Payable, a liability account.

Wages Expense				Wages Payable	
+		−		−	+
Balance 102,800					Adjusting 1,200
Adjusting 1,200					

Returning to our illustration of Clark's Cleaners, the last payday was June 24. Between June 24 and the end of the month, Clark's Cleaners owes an additional $100 in wages to its employee. Accountants refer to this extra amount that has not been recorded at the end of the month as **accrued wages.** In accounting terms, **accrual means recognition of an expense or a revenue that has been incurred or earned but has not yet been recorded.** Here, we are concerned with an expense only, which in this case is Wages Expense.

Wages Expense				Wages Payable	
+		−		−	+
(Old) Balance 930					Adjusting 100
Adjusting 100					
(New) Balance 1,030					

R E M E M B E R

In the adjusting entry for accrued wages, increase both the Wages Expense and the Wages Payable accounts.

One always records the adjusting entry for accrued wages as a debit to Wages Expense and a credit to Wages Payable because both accounts are increased.

Net Income (or Net Loss)

Net income (or net loss) is the difference between revenue and expenses. It is used to balance off the Income Statement columns; and since revenue is normally larger than expenses, the balancing-off amount must be added to the expense side. Net income (or net loss) is also used to balance off the Balance Sheet columns. As on the statement of owner's equity, one adds net income to the owner's beginning Capital balance. Since the Capital balance is located in the Balance Sheet Credit column, net income must also be added to that side. The following diagram shows these relationships:

Account Name	Trial Balance		Adjustments		Adjusted Trial Balance		Income Statement		Balance Sheet	
	Debit	Credit	Debit	Credit	Debit	Credit	Debit	Credit	Debit	Credit
	A + Draw. + E	Accum. Depr. + L + Cap. + R			A + Draw. + E	Accum. Depr. + L + Cap. + R	E	R	A + Draw.	Accum. Depr. + L + Cap.
Net Income							NI			NI

On the other hand, if expenses are larger than revenue, the result is a net loss. One must add net loss to the revenue side to balance off the Income Statement columns. Also, because one deducts a net loss from the owner's equity, one includes net loss in the debit side of the Balance Sheet columns, thereby balancing off these columns. To show this, let's look at the Income Statement and Balance Sheet columns diagrammed here.

	Income Statement		Balance Sheet	
	Debit	**Credit**	**Debit**	**Credit**
	E	R	A + Draw.	Accum. Depr. + L + Cap.
Net Loss		NL	NL	

Summary of Adjustments by T Accounts

To test your understanding, describe why the following adjustments are necessary. The answers are shown below the accounts.

(a)

Supplies				Supplies Expense			
+		−		+		−	
Balance	400	Adjusting	310	Adjusting	310		

(b)

Prepaid Insurance				Insurance Expense			
+		−		+		−	
Balance	360	Adjusting	30	Adjusting	30		

(c)

Depreciation Expense, Equipment				Accumulated Depreciation, Equipment			
+		−		−		+	
Adjusting	250					Adjusting	250

(d)

Wages Expense				Wages Payable			
+		−		−		+	
Balance	930					Adjusting	100
Adjusting	100						

a. To record the cost of supplies used during June, $310.

b. To record the insurance expired during June, $30.

c. To record the depreciation for the month of June, $250.

d. To record accrued wages owed at the end of June, $100.

At this point, take particular notice of the fact that **each adjusting entry contains an income statement account (revenue or expense) and a balance sheet account (asset or liability).**

Recording the Adjustments on the Work Sheet

In the examples above, we used T accounts to explain how to handle adjustments. T accounts, as you are aware, represent a reliable method of organizing any type of accounting entry into debits and credits. Now it is time to record adjustments on the work sheet. To help you remember which classifications of accounts appear in each column of the work sheet, we will label the columns by letter; for example, A for assets and L for liabilities.

After completing the trial balance in the first two columns of the work sheet, enter the adjustments directly in the Adjustments columns. Note that the trial balance for Clark's Cleaners is the same as the one presented in Chapter 3.

Adjustments Columns of the Work Sheet

When we enter the adjustments, we identify them as **(a), (b), (c),** and **(d)** to indicate the relationships between the debit and credit sides and the sequence of the individual adjusting entries, as shown in Figure 4-2.

Note that Supplies Expense; Insurance Expense; Depreciation Expense, Equipment; Accumulated Depreciation, Equipment; and Wages Payable did not have a balance in the trial balance. Some people leave these accounts out of the trial balance and add them to the bottom of the work sheet as needed for adjusting.

Here is a brief review of the adjustments:

a. To record the $310 cost of supplies used during June.

b. To record the $30 cost of insurance expired during June.

c. To record $250 depreciation for the month of June.

d. To record $100 of accrued wages owed at the end of June.

Figure 4-2

Clark's Cleaners
Work Sheet
For Month Ended June 30, 19–

	ACCOUNT NAME	TRIAL BALANCE DEBIT A + DRAW. + E	TRIAL BALANCE CREDIT ACCUM. DEPREC. + L + C + R	ADJUSTMENTS DEBIT	ADJUSTMENTS CREDIT
1	Cash	15 4 9 0 00			
2	Accounts Receivable	5 0 00			
3	Supplies	4 0 0 00			(a) 3 1 0 00
4	Prepaid Insurance	3 6 0 00			(b) 3 0 00
5	Equipment	26 9 4 0 00			
6	Accumulated Depreciation, Equipment				(c) 2 5 0 00
7	Accounts Payable		2 4 0 0 00		
8	Wages Payable				(d) 1 0 0 00
9	N. L. Clark, Capital		40 0 0 0 00		
10	N. L. Clark, Drawing	1 2 0 0 00			
11	Income from Services		3 8 7 0 00		
12	Advertising Expense	1 8 0 00			
13	Wages Expense	9 3 0 00		(d) 1 0 0 00	
14	Supplies Expense			(a) 3 1 0 00	
15	Rent Expense	5 0 0 00			
16	Utilities Expense	2 2 0 00			
17	Insurance Expense			(b) 3 0 00	
18	Depreciation Expense, Equipment			(c) 2 5 0 00	
19		46 2 7 0 00	46 2 7 0 00	6 9 0 00	6 9 0 00
20					

Steps in the Completion of the Work Sheet

Before proceeding to the completion of the work sheet, let's list the recommended steps to follow.

1. Complete the Trial Balance columns, total, and rule.

2. Complete the Adjustments columns, total, and rule.

3. Complete the Adjusted Trial Balance columns, total, and rule.

4. Record balances in the Income Statement and Balance Sheet columns.

5. Record net income or net loss in the Income Statement columns, total, and rule.

6. Record net income or net loss in the Balance Sheet columns, total, and rule.

Figure 4-3

Clark's Cleaners

Work Sheet

For Month Ended June 30,–

	ACCOUNT NAME	TRIAL BALANCE DEBIT A + DRAW. + E					TRIAL BALANCE CREDIT ACCUM. DEPREC. + L + C + R				
1	Cash	15	4	9	0	00					
2	Accounts Receivable			5	0	00					
3	Supplies		4	0	0	00					
4	Prepaid Insurance		3	6	0	00					
5	Equipment	26	9	4	0	00					
6	Accumulated Depreciation, Equipment										
7	Accounts Payable							2	4	0	0	00
8	Wages Payable										
9	N. L. Clark, Capital						40	0	0	0	00
10	N. L. Clark, Drawing	1	2	0	0	00					
11	Income from Services							3	8	7	0	00
12	Advertising Expense		1	8	0	00					
13	Wages Expense		9	3	0	00					
14	Supplies Expense										
15	Rent Expense		5	0	0	00					
16	Utilities Expense		2	2	0	00					
17	Insurance Expense										
18	Depreciation Expense, Equipment										
19		46	2	7	0	00	46	2	7	0	00
20											

(a) Supplies used, $310
(b) Insurance expired, $30
(c) Additional depreciation, $250
(d) Accrued wages, $100

Step 1

Now let's look at the work sheet shown in Figure 4-3 above. To reinforce the idea of adjusting entries, we have added a brief explanation of each adjustment at the bottom of the work sheet. The completed work sheet is shown in Figure 4-4 on pages 144 and 145.

After the first fiscal period, Accumulated Depreciation will always have a balance until the related asset is sold or disposed of. In the demonstration problem shown in your Working Papers, you can see an example of a work sheet for a company that was in business before the present fiscal year.

Regarding the work sheet, again, let us emphasize that it is strictly a working paper or tool that is used to gather together all the up-to-date information needed to prepare the financial statements. **The adjustments are always recorded in the work sheet first.**

ADJUSTMENTS DEBIT	ADJUSTMENTS CREDIT	ADJUSTED TRIAL BALANCE DEBIT A + DRAW. + E	ADJUSTED TRIAL BALANCE CREDIT ACCUM. DEPREC. + L + C + R	INCOME STATEMENT / BALANCE SHEET	
		15 4 9 0 00		No adjustment, carry amount over directly	1
		5 0 00		No adjustment, carry amount over directly	2
(a) 3 1 0 00		9 0 00		Adjustment involved, subtract $310 (used) from $400	3
	(b) 3 0 00	3 3 0 00		Adjustment involved, subtract $30 (expired) from $360	4
		26 9 4 0 00		No adjustment, carry amount over directly	5
	(c) 2 5 0 00		2 5 0 00	Adjustment involved, carry $250 over to the same column	6
			2 4 0 0 00	No adjustment, carry amount over directly	7
	(d) 1 0 0 00		1 0 0 00	Adjustment involved, carry $100 over to the same column	8
			40 0 0 0 00	No adjustment, carry amount over directly	9
		1 2 0 0 00		No adjustment, carry amount over directly	10
			3 8 7 0 00	No adjustment, carry amount over directly	11
		1 8 0 00		No adjustment, carry amount over directly	12
(d) 1 0 0 00		1 0 3 0 00		Adjustment involved, add $100 (accrued) to $930	13
(a) 3 1 0 00		3 1 0 00		Adjustment involved, carry $310 over to the same column	14
		5 0 0 00		No adjustment, carry amount over directly	15
		2 2 0 00		No adjustment, carry amount over directly	16
	(b) 3 0 00	3 0 00		Adjustment involved, carry $30 over to the same column	17
(c) 2 5 0 00		2 5 0 00		Adjustment involved, carry $250 over to the same column	18
6 9 0 00	6 9 0 00	46 6 2 0 00	46 6 2 0 00		19
					20

Step 2   Step 3

Mixed Accounts   Accountants refer to accounts like Supplies and Prepaid Insurance, as they appear in the trial balance, as **mixed accounts**—accounts with balances that are partly income statement amounts and partly balance sheet amounts. For example, Supplies is recorded as $400 in the Trial Balance, but after adjustment, this amount is split up or apportioned as $310 in Supplies Expense in the Income Statement columns and $90 in Supplies in the Balance Sheet columns. Similarly, Prepaid Insurance is recorded at $360 in the Trial Balance columns but apportioned as $30 in Insurance Expense in the Income Statement columns and as $330 in Prepaid Insurance in the Balance Sheet columns. In other words, portions of these trial balance amounts are recorded in each section.

Figure 4-4

REMEMBER

A net income amount is recorded in the Income Statement Debit column and the Balance Sheet Credit column (same side as the increase side of Capital). A net loss is recorded in the Income Statement Credit column and the Balance Sheet Debit column (same side as the decrease side of Capital).

Clark's Cleaners

Work Sheet

For Month Ended June 30,–

		TRIAL BALANCE	
	ACCOUNT NAME	DEBIT A + DRAW. + E	CREDIT ACCUM. DEPREC. + L + C + R
1	Cash	15,490.00	
2	Accounts Receivable	50.00	
3	Supplies	400.00	
4	Prepaid Insurance	360.00	
5	Equipment	26,940.00	
6	Accumulated Depreciation, Equipment		
7	Accounts Payable		2,400.00
8	Wages Payable		
9	N. L. Clark, Capital		40,000.00
10	N. L. Clark, Drawing	1,200.00	
11	Income from Services		3,870.00
12	Advertising Expense	180.00	
13	Wages Expense	930.00	
14	Supplies Expense		
15	Rent Expense	500.00	
16	Utilities Expense	220.00	
17	Insurance Expense		
18	Depreciation Expense, Equipment		
19		46,270.00	46,270.00
20	Net Income		
21			
22			

(a) Supplies used, $310
(b) Insurance expired, $30
(c) Additional depreciation, $250
(d) Accrued wages, $100

Step 1
List the accounts in the chart of accounts. Record the account balances in the Trial Balance columns. Total and rule the columns. Drs. must equal Crs.

ADJUSTMENTS DEBIT	ADJUSTMENTS CREDIT	ADJUSTED TRIAL BALANCE DEBIT A + DRAW. + E	ADJUSTED TRIAL BALANCE CREDIT ACCUM. DEPREC. + L + C + R	INCOME STATEMENT DEBIT E	INCOME STATEMENT CREDIT R	BALANCE SHEET DEBIT A + DRAW.	BALANCE SHEET CREDIT ACCUM. DEPREC. + L + C	
		15 4 9 0 00				15 4 9 0 00		1
		5 0 00				5 0 00		2
(a) 3 1 0 00		9 0 00				9 0 00		3
	(b) 3 0 00	3 3 0 00				3 3 0 00		4
		26 9 4 0 00				26 9 4 0 00		5
	(c) 2 5 0 00		2 5 0 00				2 5 0 00	6
			2 4 0 0 00				2 4 0 0 00	7
	(d) 1 0 0 00		1 0 0 00				1 0 0 00	8
			40 0 0 0 00				40 0 0 0 00	9
		1 2 0 0 00				1 2 0 0 00		10
			3 8 7 0 00		3 8 7 0 00			11
		1 8 0 00		1 8 0 00				12
(d) 1 0 0 00		1 0 3 0 00		1 0 3 0 00				13
(a) 3 1 0 00		3 1 0 00		3 1 0 00				14
		5 0 0 00		5 0 0 00				15
		2 2 0 00		2 2 0 00				16
(b) 3 0 00		3 0 00		3 0 00				17
(c) 2 5 0 00		2 5 0 00		2 5 0 00				18
6 9 0 00	6 9 0 00	46 6 2 0 00	46 6 2 0 00	2 5 2 0 00	3 8 7 0 00	44 1 0 0 00	42 7 5 0 00	19
				1 3 5 0 00			1 3 5 0 00	20
				3 8 7 0 00	3 8 7 0 00	44 1 0 0 00	44 1 0 0 00	21
								22

Step 2
Record the adjustments, labeling each adjustment as (a), (b), (c), and so on. Total and rule the columns. Drs. must equal Crs.

Step 3
Carry amounts across from the Trial Balance columns plus or minus any amounts in the Adjustments columns. Total and rule the columns. Drs. must equal Crs.

Step 4
From the top of the Adjusted Trial Balance columns, go down line by line carrying each amount over to the Income Statement or Balance Sheet columns. Total the columns. Debits do not equal credits, since revenue is usually unequal to expenses.

Step 5
Record Net Income or Net Loss in the Account Name column and put the amount in the appropriate Income Statement column. Total and rule the columns.

Step 6
Record the net income or net loss amount in the appropriate Balance Sheet column. Total, balance, and rule the columns.

This video rental store depreciates office equipment (the computer and the printer), display racks, and the video tapes.

. . . .
R E M E M B E R

When a work sheet requires two pages, the totals at the bottom of the first sheet do not have to be equal. Debits must equal credits by the end of the second page.
. . . .

Work Sheet Requiring Two Pages

If a large number of accounts are involved, it may be necessary to continue the work sheet to a second page.

	(First Page)			
Account Name	**Trial Balance**		**Adjustments**	
Wages Expense	3,240 00		(c) 220 50	
Totals carried forward	98,312 00	91,146 10	962 50	126 50

Note the totals at the bottom of the first page are labeled "Totals carried forward" in the Account Name column. At the top of the second page, the totals are repeated and labeled "Totals brought forward" in the Account Name column. Continue listing account names and balances below the totals brought forward.

	(Second Page)			
	Trial Balance		**Adjustments**	
Account Name	**Debit**	**Credit**	**Debit**	**Credit**
Totals brought forward	98,312 00	91,146 10	962 50	126 50
Wages Payable				(c) 220 50

Finding Errors in the Income Statement and Balance Sheet Columns

The amount of the net income or net loss must be recorded in both an Income Statement column and a Balance Sheet column. After adding the net income to the Balance Sheet Credit column, let's say that the Balance Sheet columns are not equal. To find the error, follow this procedure:

1. Verify the addition of all the columns.

2. Check to see that the amount of the net income or loss is recorded in the correct columns. For example, net income is placed in the Income Statement Debit column and the Balance Sheet Credit column.

3. Look to see if the appropriate amounts have been recorded in the Income Statement and Balance Sheet columns. For example, asset amounts should be listed in the Balance Sheet Debit column, expense amounts should be listed in the Income Statement Debit column, and so forth.

4. Verify, by adding or subtracting across a line, that the amounts carried over from the Trial Balance columns through the Adjustments columns into the Adjusted Trial Balance columns and either the Income Statement or the Balance Sheet columns are correct.

Generally, one of these steps will expose the error.

Completion of the Financial Statements

As we stated, the purpose of the work sheet is to help the accountant prepare the financial statements. Since we have completed the work sheet for Clark's Cleaners, we can now prepare the income statement, the statement of owner's equity, and the balance sheet by taking the figures directly from the work sheet. These statements are shown in Figure 4-5 on page 148.

Note that one records Accumulated Depreciation, Equipment, in the asset section of the balance sheet as a direct deduction from Equipment. Accountants refer to this as a contra account because it is contrary to its companion account. The difference, $26,690, is called the book value because it represents the cost of the assets after Accumulated Depreciation has been deducted.

When preparing the statement of owner's equity, always remember to check the beginning balance of Capital against the balance shown in the Capital account in the general ledger. An additional investment may have been made during the fiscal period, and you need to record this additional investment in the statement of owner's equity, as shown on page 31 in Chapter 1.

Performance Objective 2

Prepare an income statement, a statement of owner's equity, and a balance sheet directly from the work sheet of a service business.

Journalizing Adjusting Entries

To change the balance of a ledger account, you need a journal entry as evidence of the change. So far, we have been listing adjustments only in the Adjustments columns of the work sheet. Since the work sheet is not a journal, we must journalize the adjustments to bring the ledger accounts up to date. Take the information for these entries directly from the Adjustments columns of the work sheet, debiting and crediting exactly the same accounts and amounts in the journal entries.

Performance Objective 3

Journalize and post the adjusting entries.

Figure 4-5

REMEMBER

Money columns are not labeled Debit or Credit. Each column simply shows account balances. Amounts in these columns are either added or subtracted.

REMEMBER

Ruling columns correctly is very important. Always draw a single rule below a column to be added. Draw double rules below the totals.

Clark's Cleaners

Income Statement

For Month Ended June 30, 19–

Revenue:		
Income from Services		$3,870.00
Expenses:		
Advertising Expense	$ 180.00	
Wages Expense	1,030.00	
Supplies Expense	310.00	
Rent Expense	500.00	
Utilities Expense	220.00	
Insurance Expense	30.00	
Depreciation Expense, Equipment	250.00	
Total Expenses		2,520.00
Net Income		$1,350.00

Clark's Cleaners

Statement of Owner's Equity

For Month Ended June 30, 19–

N. L. Clark, Capital, June 1, 19–		$40,000.00
Net Income for June	$1,350.00	
Less Withdrawals for June	1,200.00	
Increase in Capital		150.00
N. L. Clark, Capital, June 30, 19–		$40,150.00

Clark's Cleaners

Balance Sheet

June 30, 19–

Assets		
Cash		$15,490.00
Accounts Receivable		50.00
Supplies		90.00
Prepaid Insurance		330.00
Equipment	$26,940.00	
Less Accumulated Depreciation	250.00	26,690.00
Total Assets		$42,650.00
Liabilities		
Accounts Payable	$ 2,400.00	
Wages Payable	100.00	
Total Liabilities		$ 2,500.00
Owner's Equity		
N. L. Clark, Capital		40,150.00
Total Liabilities and Owner's Equity		$42,650.00

In the Description column of the general journal, write "Adjusting Entries" before you begin making these entries. This eliminates the need to write explanations for each entry. The adjusting entries for Clark's Cleaners are shown in Figure 4-6 below.

Figure 4-6

GENERAL JOURNAL   PAGE ___3___

	DATE		DESCRIPTION	POST. REF.	DEBIT	CREDIT	
21			Adjusting Entries				21
22	June	30	Supplies Expense	523	3 1 0 00		22
23			Supplies	115		3 1 0 00	23
24							24
25		30	Insurance Expense	529	3 0 00		25
26			Prepaid Insurance	117		3 0 00	26
27							27
28		30	Depreciation Expense, Equipment	533	2 5 0 00		28
29			Accum. Depreciation, Equipment	125		2 5 0 00	29
30							30
31		30	Wages Expense	521	1 0 0 00		31
32			Wages Payable	223		1 0 0 00	32

R E M E M B E R

Each adjusting entry consists of an income statement account and a balance sheet account.

When you post the adjusting entries to the ledger accounts, write the word "Adjusting" in the Item column of the ledger account. For example, the adjusting entry for Supplies is posted as shown below:

GENERAL LEDGER

ACCOUNT __Supplies__   ACCOUNT NO. __115__

DATE		ITEM	POST. REF.	DEBIT	CREDIT	BALANCE DEBIT	BALANCE CREDIT
19–							
June	4		1	4 0 0 00		4 0 0 00	
	30	Adjusting	3		3 1 0 00	9 0 00	

ACCOUNT __Supplies Expense__   ACCOUNT NO. __523__

DATE		ITEM	POST. REF.	DEBIT	CREDIT	BALANCE DEBIT	BALANCE CREDIT
19–							
June	30	Adjusting	3	3 1 0 00		3 1 0 00	

In the adjusting entries, notice that the intent is to make sure that the expenses are recorded to match up or compare with the revenue for the same period of time. In other words, for the month of June, we record all the revenue for June and all the expenses for June. Thus the revenue and expenses for the same time period are matched. This is the same matching principle discussed in Chapter 1.

Businesses with More Than One Revenue Account and More Than One Accumulated Depreciation Account

The only revenue account for Clark's Cleaners is Income from Services. However, a business may have several distinct sources of revenue. For example, Luna Veterinary Clinic has two revenue accounts: Professional Fees and Boarding Fees. Figure 4-7 illustrates the placement of these accounts in the income statement.

Figure 4-7

Luna Veterinary Clinic
Income Statement
For Year Ended December 31, 19–

Revenue:		
Professional Fees	$ 111 720 00	
Boarding Fees	22 080 00	
Total Revenue		$ 133 800 00
Expenses:		
Salaries Expense	$ 84 000 00	
Depreciation Expense, Building	6 480 00	
Depreciation Expense, Equipment	3 840 00	
Supplies Expense	3 720 00	
Insurance Expense	720 00	
Miscellaneous Expense	2 160 00	
Total Expenses		100 920 00
Net Income		$ 32 880 00

In Figure 4-7, also note that the company has two assets subject to depreciation: Building and Equipment. In the financial statements, Depreciation Expense and Accumulated Depreciation must be listed for each asset.

Land supposedly will last forever; consequently, land is not depreciated. Separate adjustments would already have been recorded in the work sheet for depreciation of equipment and building. Here's the balance sheet for Luna Veterinary Clinic, shown in Figure 4-8.

Figure 4-8

Luna Veterinary Clinic

Balance Sheet
December 31, 19–

Assets					
Cash				$	6 2 4 0 00
Supplies					2 0 0 00
Land					4 4 0 0 00
Building	$ 117 7 0 0 00				
Less Accumulated Depreciation	36 4 0 0 00			81 3 0 0 00	
Office Equipment	$ 42 6 0 0 00				
Less Accumulated Depreciation	29 2 0 0 00			13 4 0 0 00	
Total Assets				$ 105 5 4 0 00	
Liabilities					
Accounts Payable				$	2 8 0 0 00
Owner's Equity					
Doris P. Luna, Capital				102 7 4 0 00	
Total Liabilities and Owner's Equity				$ 105 5 4 0 00	

Closing Entries

Adjusting entries, closing entries, and the post-closing trial balance are usually prepared only at the end of a twelve-month fiscal period. However, to expose you to these final steps in the accounting cycle, we have assumed that the fiscal period for Clark's Cleaners consists of only one month. We made this assumption so that we could thoroughly cover the material and give you a chance to practice its application. The entire accounting cycle is outlined in Figure 4-9 on page 152.

We know that the income statement, as stated in the third line of its heading, covers a definite period of time. The income statement consists of revenue minus expenses for this period of time only. So, when this period is over, we should start from zero for the next period. In other words, we wipe the slate clean, so that we can start all over again next period.

Purpose of Closing Entries

This brings us to the *purpose* of the **closing entries**, which is to close off the revenue and expense accounts. We do this because their balances apply to only one fiscal period. Closing entries are made after the last adjusting entry. With the coming of the next fiscal period, we want to start from scratch, recording revenue and expenses for the new fiscal period. After closing entries we have this:

$$\text{Assets} = \text{Liabilities} + \underset{\text{(Capital)}}{\text{Owner's Equity}} + \overset{\text{(closed)}}{\cancel{\text{Revenue}}} - \overset{\text{(closed)}}{\cancel{\text{Expenses}}}$$

The assets, the liabilities, and the owner's Capital account remain open. The balance sheet, with its one date in the heading, gives the present balances of these accounts. The accountant carries the asset, liability, and capital account balances over to the next fiscal period.

Figure 4-9

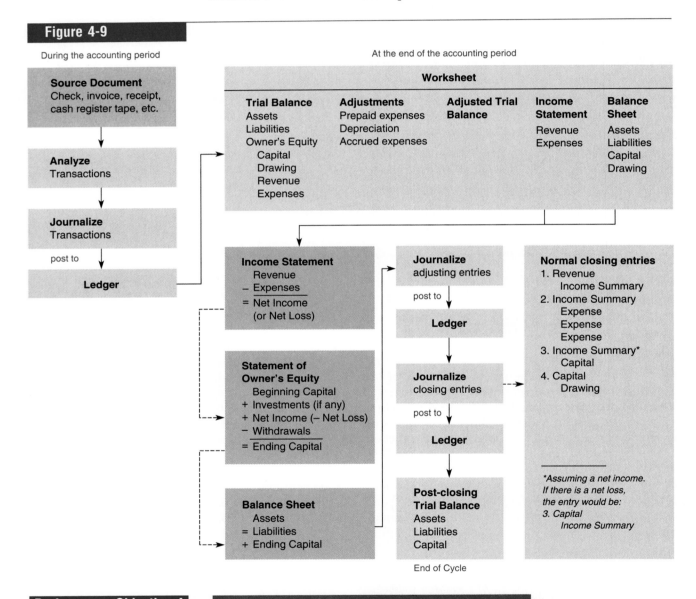

End of Cycle

Performance Objective 4

Journalize and post closing entries for a service enterprise.

Procedure for Closing

The procedure for closing is simply to balance off the account; in other words, to make the balance *equal to zero*. Let's illustrate this first with T accounts.

Suppose an account has a debit balance of $960; then, to make the balance equal to zero, we *credit* the account for $960. We write "Closing" in the Item column of the ledger account.

Debit		Credit	
Balance	960	Closing	960

To take another example, suppose an account has a credit balance of $1,200; then, to make the balance equal to zero, we *debit* the account for $1,200.

Debit		Credit	
Closing	1,200	Balance	1,200

Every entry must have both a debit and a credit. So, to record the other half of the closing entry, we bring into existence **Income Summary**. The Income Summary account does not have plus and minus signs.

There are four steps in the closing procedure:

1. **Close the revenue accounts into Income Summary.**

2. **Close the expense accounts into Income Summary.**

3. **Close the Income Summary account into the Capital account, transferring the net income or loss to the Capital account.**

4. **Close the Drawing account into the Capital account.**

To illustrate, we return to Clark's Cleaners. We'll first make the entries directly in T accounts. We have the following T account balances in the revenue and expense accounts after the adjustments have been posted.

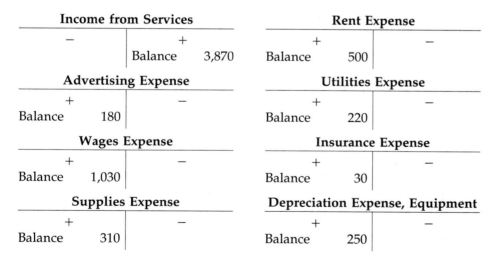

Step 1 **Close the revenue account, or accounts, into Income Summary.** In order to make the balance of Income from Services equal to zero, we *balance it off*, or debit it, in the amount of $3,870. Because we need an offsetting credit, we credit Income Summary for the same amount.

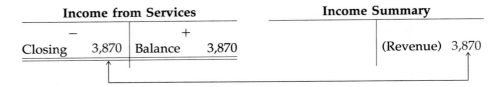

The balance of Income from Services is transferred to Income Summary.

Step 2 **Close the expense accounts into Income Summary.** To make the balances of the expense accounts equal to zero, we need to balance them off, or credit them. In essence, the total of all the individual balances of the expense accounts is transferred to Income Summary, as shown in these T accounts:

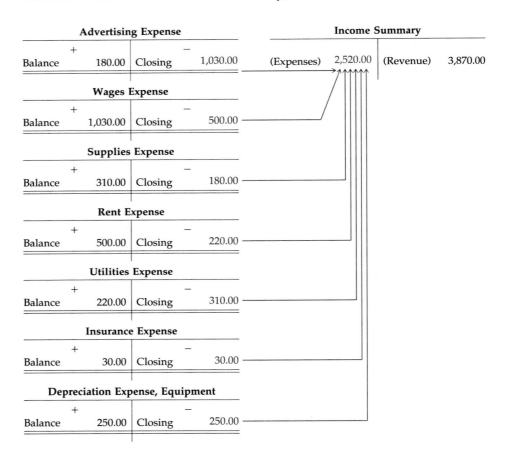

Step 3 **Close the Income Summary Account into Capital.** Recall that we created Income Summary so that we could have a debit and a credit with each closing entry. Now that it has done its job, we close it out. We use the same procedure as before, in that we make the balance equal to zero, or balance off the account. We transfer, or close, the balance of the Income Summary account into the Capital account, as shown in the T accounts.

Income Summary				N. L. Clark, Capital	
(Expenses) 2,520	(Revenue) 3,870		−	+	
Closing 1,350				Balance	40,000
				(Net Inc.)	1,350

Income Summary is always closed into the Capital account by the amount of the net income (Revenue minus Expenses) or the net loss. Comparing net income or net loss with the closing entry for Income Summary can serve as a check point or verification for you.

Net income is added or credited to the Capital account because, in the statement of owner's equity, net income is treated as an addition. Net loss, on the other hand, should be subtracted from or debited to the Capital account, because net loss is treated as a deduction in the statement of owner's equity. Here's how one would close Income Summary for J. Doe Company, which had a net loss of $200:

Income Summary				J. Doe, Capital		
(Expenses)	900	(Revenue)	700	(Net Loss) 200	Balance	30,000
		Closing	200			

The entry to close Income Summary into Doe's Capital account would look like this:

GENERAL JOURNAL   PAGE 3

DATE	DESCRIPTION	POST. REF.	DEBIT	CREDIT
	Closing Entries			
31	J. Doe, Capital		2 0 0 00	
	Income Summary			2 0 0 00

Step 4 **Close the Drawing Account into Capital.** Let us return to the example of Clark's Cleaners. The Drawing account applies to only one fiscal period, so it too must be closed. You may recall from Chapter 2 that Drawing is not an expense, because no money is paid to anyone outside the business. And because Drawing is not an expense, it cannot affect net income or net loss. It appears in the statement of owner's equity as a deduction from the Capital account, so it is closed directly into the Capital account. We balance off the Drawing account, or make the balance of it equal to zero. The balance of Drawing is transferred to the Capital account.

N. L. Clark, Drawing				N. L. Clark, Capital		
+		−		−	+	
Balance	1,200	Closing	1,200	1,200	Balance	40,000
					(Net Inc.)	1,350

The journal entries in the closing procedure are shown in Figure 4-10. Notice how writing "Closing Entries" in the Description column eliminates the need to write explanations for all the closing entries. Closing entries are made after the last adjusting entry.

Figure 4-10

	DATE		DESCRIPTION	POST. REF.	DEBIT	CREDIT	
			GENERAL JOURNAL			PAGE 4	
1	19–		Closing Entries				1
2	June	30	Income from Services		3 8 7 0 00		2
3	Step 1		Income Summary			3 8 7 0 00	3
4							4
5		30	Income Summary		2 5 2 0 00		5
6			Advertising Expense			1 8 0 00	6
7			Wages Expense			1 0 3 0 00	7
8			Supplies Expense			3 1 0 00	8
9	Step 2		Rent Expense			5 0 0 00	9
10			Utilities Expense			2 2 0 00	10
11			Insurance Expense			3 0 00	11
12			Depreciation Expense,				12
13			Equipment			2 5 0 00	13
14							14
15	Step 3	30	Income Summary		1 3 5 0 00		15
16			N. L. Clark, Capital			1 3 5 0 00	16
17							17
18	Step 4	30	N. L. Clark, Capital		1 2 0 0 00		18
19			N. L. Clark, Drawing			1 2 0 0 00	19
20							20

As a memory tool to learn the sequence of steps in the closing procedure, one can use the letters of the closing elements, **REID: R**evenue, **E**xpenses, **I**ncome Summary, **D**rawing.

These closing entries show that Clark's Cleaners has net income of $1,350, the owner has withdrawn $1,200 for personal expenses, and $150 has been retained, or plowed back into the business, thereby increasing capital.

Closing Entries Taken Directly from the Work Sheet

One can gather the information for the closing entries either directly from ₁e ledger accounts or from the work sheet. Since the Income Statement col-mns of the work sheet consist entirely of revenues and expenses, one can ick up the figures for three of the four closing entries from these columns. igure 4-11 shows a partial work sheet for Clark's Cleaners.

You may formulate the closing entries by simply balancing off all the figures that appear in the Income Statement columns. For example, in the Income Statement column, there is a credit for $3,870 (Income from Services), so we debit that account for $3,870 and credit Income Summary for $3,870.

Figure 4-11

	ACCOUNT NAME	TRIAL BALANCE		ADJUSTMENTS		INCOME STATEMENT	
1	Cash	15 4 9 0 00					
2	Accounts Receivable	5 0 00					
3	Supplies	4 0 0 00			(a) 3 1 0 00		
4	Prepaid Insurance	3 6 0 00			(b) 3 0 00		
5	Equipment	26 9 4 0 00					
6	Accumulated Depr.,						
7	Equipment				(c) 2 5 0 00		
8	Accounts Payable		2 4 0 0 00				
9	Wages Payable				(d) 1 0 0 00		
10	N. L. Clark, Capital		40 0 0 0 00				
11	N. L. Clark, Drawing	1 2 0 0 00					
12	Income from Services		3 8 7 0 00				3 8 7 0 00
13	Advertising Expense	1 8 0 00				1 8 0 00	
14	Wages Expense	9 3 0 00		(d) 1 0 0 00		1 0 3 0 00	
15	Supplies Expense			(a) 3 1 0 00		3 1 0 00	
16	Rent Expense	5 0 0 00				5 0 0 00	
17	Utilities Expense	2 2 0 00				2 2 0 00	
18	Insurance Expense			(b) 3 0 00		3 0 00	
19	Depreciation Expense,						
20	Equipment			(c) 2 5 0 00		2 5 0 00	
21		46 2 7 0 00	46 2 7 0 00	6 9 0 00	6 9 0 00	2 5 2 0 00	3 8 7 0 00
22	Net Income					1 3 5 0 00	
23						3 8 7 0 00	3 8 7 0 00

GENERAL LEDGER

ACCOUNT Income Summary   ACCOUNT NO. 399

DATE	ITEM	POST. REF.	DEBIT	CREDIT	BALANCE DEBIT	BALANCE CREDIT
19–						
June 30		4		3 8 7 0 00		3 8 7 0 00
30		4	2 5 2 0 00			1 3 5 0 00
30	Closing	4	1 3 5 0 00			

ACCOUNT ___Income from Services___ ACCOUNT NO. ___411___

DATE		ITEM	POST. REF.	DEBIT	CREDIT	BALANCE DEBIT	BALANCE CREDIT
19–							
June	7		1		9 6 0 00		9 6 0 00
	14		2		9 8 0 00		1 9 4 0 00
	21		2		8 3 0 00		2 7 7 0 00
	23		2		1 4 0 00		2 9 1 0 00
	30		3		9 6 0 00		3 8 7 0 00
	30	Closing	4	3 8 7 0 00		—	—

ACCOUNT ___Advertising Expense___ ACCOUNT NO. ___515___

DATE		ITEM	POST. REF.	DEBIT	CREDIT	BALANCE DEBIT	BALANCE CREDIT
19–							
June	14		2	1 8 0 00		1 8 0 00	
	30	Closing	4		1 8 0 00	—	—

ACCOUNT ___Wages Expense___ ACCOUNT NO. ___521___

DATE		ITEM	POST. REF.	DEBIT	CREDIT	BALANCE DEBIT	BALANCE CREDIT
19–							
June	10		1	4 4 0 00		4 4 0 00	
	24		3	4 9 0 00		9 3 0 00	
	30	Adjusting	4	1 0 0 00		1 0 3 0 00	
	30	Closing	4		1 0 3 0 00	—	—

ACCOUNT ___Supplies Expense___ ACCOUNT NO. ___523___

DATE		ITEM	POST. REF.	DEBIT	CREDIT	BALANCE DEBIT	BALANCE CREDIT
19–							
June	30	Adjusting	3	3 1 0 00		3 1 0 00	
	30	Closing	4		3 1 0 00	—	—

ACCOUNT ___Rent Expense___ ACCOUNT NO. __524__

DATE		ITEM	POST. REF.	DEBIT	CREDIT	BALANCE DEBIT	BALANCE CREDIT
19—							
June	8		1	5 0 0 00		5 0 0 00	
	30	Closing	4		5 0 0 00	—	—

ACCOUNT ___Utilities Expense___ ACCOUNT NO. __525__

DATE		ITEM	POST. REF.	DEBIT	CREDIT	BALANCE DEBIT	BALANCE CREDIT
19—							
June	15		2	2 2 0 00		2 2 0 00	
	30	Closing	4		2 2 0 00	—	—

ACCOUNT ___Insurance Expense___ ACCOUNT NO. __529__

DATE		ITEM	POST. REF.	DEBIT	CREDIT	BALANCE DEBIT	BALANCE CREDIT
19—							
June	30	Adjusting	3	3 0 00		3 0 00	
	30	Closing	4		3 0 00	—	—

ACCOUNT ___Depreciation Expense, Equipment___ ACCOUNT NO. __531__

DATE		ITEM	POST. REF.	DEBIT	CREDIT	BALANCE DEBIT	BALANCE CREDIT
19—							
June	30	Adjusting	3	2 5 0 00		2 5 0 00	
	30	Closing	4		2 5 0 00	—	—

The Post-Closing Trial Balance

Performance Objective 5

Prepare a post-closing trial balance for any type of enterprise.

After posting the closing entries and before going on to the next fiscal period, one should verify the balances of the accounts that remain open. To do so, make up a **post-closing trial balance, using the final balance figures from the ledger accounts.** The purpose of the post-closing trial balance is to make absolutely sure that the debit balances equal the credit balances.

Note that the accounts listed in the post-closing trial balance (assets, liabilities, and Capital) are the **real** or **permanent accounts** (see Figure 4-12). The accountant carries forward the balances of the permanent accounts from one fiscal period to another.

Contrast this to the handling of **nominal** or **temporary-equity accounts** (revenue, expenses, Income Summary, and Drawing), which, as you have seen, are closed at the end of each fiscal period.

If the totals of the post-closing trial balance are not equal, here's a recommended procedure for tracking down the error:

1. Re-add the trial balance columns.

2. Check to see that the figures were correctly transferred from the ledger accounts to the post-closing trial balance.

3. Verify the posting of the adjusting entries and the recording of the new balances.

4. Make sure the closing entries have been posted and all revenue, expense, Income Summary, and Drawing accounts have zero balances.

Figure 4-12

Clark's Cleaners
Post-Closing Trial Balance
June 30, 19–

ACCOUNT NAME	DEBIT	CREDIT
Cash	15 4 9 0 00	
Accounts Receivable	5 0 00	
Supplies	9 0 00	
Prepaid Insurance	3 3 0 00	
Equipment	26 9 4 0 00	
Accumulated Depreciation, Equipment		2 5 0 00
Accounts Payable		2 4 0 0 00
Wages Payable		1 0 0 00
N. L. Clark, Capital		40 1 5 0 00
	42 9 0 0 00	42 9 0 0 00

The Accrual Basis of Accounting

Define the following methods of accounting: accrual basis, cash-receipts-and-disbursements basis, modified cash basis.

Up to this time, we have been dealing with the accrual basis of accounting, mentioned briefly in Chapter 1. Let us take a more thorough look at accrual-basis accounting along with the cash-receipts-and-disbursements basis, and the modified cash basis.

Recall that when we use the **accrual basis** of accounting, we record revenue when it is earned and expenses when they are incurred. An expense is incurred when a company becomes responsible for paying the expense. Under the accrual basis, when a bill is received or service is performed, revenue and expenses are matched up with the appropriate fiscal period. For example, Clark's Cleaners' transactions were recorded on the accrual basis; as proof, let us recall two transactions that we first looked at in Chapter 1.

Transaction (i) Received the bill for newspaper and advertising, $180. The expense was recorded before it was paid in cash. The expense was matched up with the fiscal period in which it was incurred.

Advertising Expense			Accounts Payable	
(i)	180		**(i)**	180

Transaction (k) Entered into a contract with Formal Rentals to clean their for-hire garments on a credit basis. Billed Formal Rentals for services performed.

Accounts Receivable			Income from Services	
(k)	140		**(k)**	140

The revenue was recorded before it was received in cash. The revenue was matched up with the fiscal period in which it was earned. Accountants feel strongly that the accrual basis gives the most realistic picture of the revenue and expense accounts and hence the net income.

Cash-Receipts-and-Disbursements Basis

When the **cash-receipts-and-disbursements basis** is used, all revenue is recorded only when it is received in cash, and all expenses are recorded only when they are paid in cash. *The cash-receipts-and-disbursements basis is not appropriate for most business firms.* This is true because most companies do have some equipment, and the Internal Revenue Service requires that equipment be depreciated over a period of years, resulting in an expense that does not involve cash.

The cash-receipts-and-disbursements basis is used predominantly by individuals for their personal tax returns. Here, revenue in the form of salaries or wages, interest, and similar items is reported only when received in cash, and expenses to be included as personal deductions are reported only when paid in cash.

Modified Cash Basis

Professional enterprises are not alone in using a **modified cash basis;** many small businesses, particularly service-type firms, use it as well. **Revenue is not recorded by the firm until it receives cash** from the customer. Here we are concerned with situations in which services are performed in one fiscal period although the cash for these same services is not received until a later fiscal period. Under the modified cash basis, the revenue is recorded in the later period, when the cash is actually received.

Expenses are also recorded only when they are paid in cash. Consequently, an expense may be incurred in one fiscal period and paid in a later period. Under the modified cash basis, the expense is recorded in the later period, when it is actually paid. For example, an employee's earnings for the month of December are paid on January 5. Under this basis, no entry is made for accrued salaries, but on January 5, an entry is made debiting Salary Expense and crediting Cash.

However, under the modified cash basis, **exceptions are made for expenditures on items having an economic life of more than one year and on some prepaid items.** This is where the "modified" element comes into the picture. Examples of such expenditures and prepaid items are equipment, supplies, and insurance. Costs of these items must be prorated or spread out over their useful lives, so adjusting entries are made for depreciation of equipment, supplies used up, and expiration of insurance. As we stated, there is no need to make additional adjusting entries, such as an adjustment for accrued salaries or other accrued adjustments that we will introduce later. The Internal Revenue Service publications refer to the modified cash basis as a hybrid method, because it blends some of the characteristics of the accrual basis and the cash-receipts-and-disbursements basis of accounting.

Interim Statements

Performance Objective 7

Prepare interim statements.

As we said previously, a firm's fiscal period generally consists of twelve consecutive months. However, it is understandable that the owner of the business does not want to wait until the end of the twelve-month period to find out how the company is doing financially. Instead, most owners want financial statements at the end of each month. The financial statements prepared during the fiscal year for periods of less than twelve months are called **interim statements.** (They are given this name because they are prepared in the in-between times.) For example, a business may prepare the income statement, the statement of owner's equity, and the balance sheet *monthly*. These statements provide up-to-date information about the results and status of operations. Suppose a company has a fiscal period extending from January 1 of one year through December 31 of the same year; it might have the following interim statements:

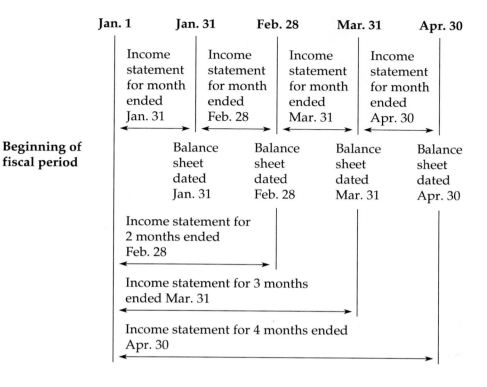

In this case, the accountant would prepare a work sheet at the end of each month. Next, based on these work sheets, he or she would prepare the financial statements. *However, the remaining steps—journalizing the adjusting and closing entries and preparing the post-closing trial balance—would be performed only at the end of the year.*

Computer Application

In Chapter 1 you saw computer printouts of the income statement (profit and loss statement) and balance sheet for Clark's Cleaners. In Chapter 3 you saw the general journal, general ledger (account inquiry), and trial balance printouts. As you have seen in Chapter 4, some accounts require adjustment because Clark has used some of the assets (supplies and insurance), equipment has depreciated or lost usefulness, and wages have accrued since the last payroll. While the earlier statments were close to accurate, they were preadjusted statements. In this chapter they have been brought up to date with the adjustments that fine-tune the financial picture provided by those earlier statements.

You will notice that no work sheet is illustrated. Some computerized accounting software may provide a screen for organizing the adjustments. One of the beauties of computerized accounting is that there is no work sheet to prepare, but you must still key in the adjusting entries.

Trial Balance Before Adjustments

Notice that Figure 4-2 shows the steps for preparing a trial balance in the first two columns of the work sheet, formulating the data for the adjusting entries, and completing the work sheet. Whether you are using a computer or not, you must prepare or print out a trial balance, which is a preadjusted or unadjusted (before adjustments) trial balance. You need this trial balance to formulate the adjusting entries. We repeat this unadjusted trial balance shown on page 111 so that you can trace the steps in its preparation.

```
                          Clark's Cleaners
                        3702 35th Southwest
                        Seattle WA 98126

                       Summary Trial Balance

                        6/1/9- to 6/30/9-
                                                                    Page 1

         Account    Beginning Balance   Total Debit   Total Credit   Net Activity   Ending Balance

1-1110 Cash              $0.00          $43,820.00    $28,330.00    $15,490.00      $15,490.00
1-1130 Accounts Receivable $0.00           $140.00        $90.00        $50.00          $50.00
1-1150 Supplies          $0.00             $400.00         $0.00       $400.00         $400.00
1-1170 Prepaid Insurance $0.00             $360.00         $0.00       $360.00         $360.00
1-1240 Equipment         $0.00          $26,940.00         $0.00    $26,940.00      $26,940.00
2-2210 Accounts Payable  $0.00           $2,980.00     $5,380.00    $2,400.00cr     $2,400.00cr
3-3110 N. L. Clark, Capital $0.00            $0.00    $40,000.00   $40,000.00cr    $40,000.00cr
3-3120 N. L. Clark, Drawing $0.00        $1,200.00         $0.00     $1,200.00       $1,200.00
4-4110 Income From Services $0.00            $0.00     $3,870.00    $3,870.00cr     $3,870.00cr
6-6150 Advertising Expense $0.00           $180.00         $0.00       $180.00         $180.00
6-6210 Wages Expense     $0.00             $930.00         $0.00       $930.00         $930.00
6-6240 Rent Expense      $0.00             $500.00         $0.00       $500.00         $500.00
6-6250 Utilities Expense $0.00             $220.00         $0.00       $220.00         $220.00
                                         ..........     ..........

              Total:                    $77,670.00    $77,670.00
                                         ..........     ..........
```

The Accounting Cycle (Computerized)

The accounting cycle changes slightly when we use a computerized system, since we need not complete the work sheet. The computerized accounting cycle is pictured in Figure 4-13.

The statements would be prepared after the adjusting entries have been journalized and posted. Then, if it is the end of the fiscal period, the closing entries would be made and the books prepared for the new fiscal period. These illustrations assume monthly adjustment and closing at the end of the fiscal period. Some businesses adjust only at the end of the year and prepare interim unadjusted statements for internal use.

Figure 4-13

THE ACCOUNTING CYCLE

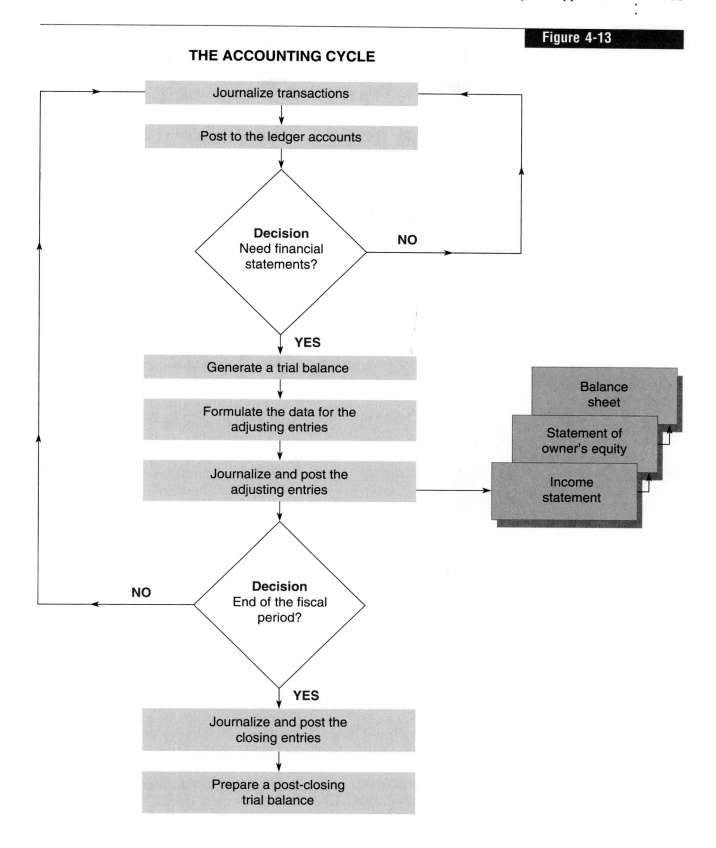

How to Choose an Accounting Package: Issues to Consider and Questions to Ask

"It's a jungle out there" might be the catchword for someone trying to choose the ideal accounting software program for their business. So many different packages exist, each designed for distinct needs and types of businesses. . . .

DO YOU REALLY NEED ONE? • Before you even consider which accounting package to buy, give some thought to whether computerizing your accounting functions is actually what you need. . . .

• **Why do you want to computerize?** . . . What do you want to accomplish—do you want to do your general ledger, payroll, or all your accounting functions on a computer? How simple or complex are your firm's accounting needs, and what aspects do you want to computerize? . . .

• **Are you flexible?** You will probably need to be flexible to accommodate the way that your accounting software does things. . . .

• **You will need help at times.** . . . You might need to practice the commands, and chances are good that you'll find yourself contacting technical support for help at least once.

WHAT ARE THE BENEFITS? •

Automatic Updating. . . . If you enter a figure in one segment . . . , most accounting programs will then revise the same information in other parts.

Easier Reporting. Accounting programs offer . . . the option of using either standard or user-defined formats when writing reports.

Professional Reports, Documents, Invoices. . . . Many packages provide flexibility in allowing you to custom-design some of the reports and documents to your needs and liking.

Tax Preparation. Once you've set up an organized accounting system, you have all the records needed to prepare your tax returns.

View Multiple Programs. When using *Windows* programs, you can switch between different applications, including your word processor,

spreadsheet, database, or accounting software, without having to exit one application. . . .

WHAT CONSIDERATIONS? • There are a number of considerations you should look at when selecting an accounting package. These include the kinds of accounting the package can do, the accounting functions it can perform, the type and availability of forms and reports, the ability to import and export data to and from other programs, and also the availability of technical support.

Single vs. double-entry accounting. . . . The first question to ask is whether you want a basic, single entry "checkbook" type program, or a double-entry accounting system.

Choice of accounting functions. Some of the accounting functions included in DOS and Windows accounting software include General Ledger, Accounts Payable, Accounts Receivable, Inventory, Order Entry and Invoicing, Point-of-Sale Billing, Sales Analysis, Payroll, Job Costing, Cash Management, Purchase Order, Bank Reconciliation and letter writing. . . .

Reports and forms. . . . How does it structure different forms and reports? Do the sequence and format of the reports generated meet with the needs of your business?

Import/export capabilities. Can the program send and receive information from other software? . . .

Whatever your needs, there are accounting packages out there that can help you do your accounting with greater ease and efficiency. While they are easy to use and offer great computing power, the multitude of packages makes it necessary for you to examine carefully your needs and match them to the right program.

Source: Excerpted from Jeffrey Hsu, "How to Choose an Accounting Package," *PC Today*, Premium Issue, pp. 24–26.

General Journal

Below is the continuation of Clark's general journal containing the four adjusting entries you saw entered first in the work sheet.

```
                            Clark's Cleaners
                            3702 35th Southwest
                            Seattle WA 98126

                            General Journal

                            6/1/9- to 6/30/9-

                                                                      Page 1

  Src   Date     ID#              Account             Debit       Credit    Job
  GJ    6/30/9-  Adjusting entry for supplies
                 GJ000018  6-6190  Supplies Expense   $310.00
                 GJ000018  1-1230  Supplies                       $310.00

  GJ    6/30/9-  Adjusting entry for insurance
                 GJ000019  6-6210  Insurance Expense  $30.00
                 GJ000019  1-1270  Prepaid Insurance              $30.00

  GJ    6/30/9-  Adjusting entry for equipment depreciation
                 GJ000020  6-6230  Depreciation Expense, Equipment $250.00
                 GJ000020  1-1560  Accum. Depreciation, Equipment           $250.00

  GJ    6/30/9-  Adjustment for wages earned but not yet paid
                 GJ000021  6-6110  Wages Expense       $100.00
                 GJ000021  2-2130  Wages Payable                  $100.00
```

General Ledger (Account Inquiry)

The general ledger accounts affected by the adjusting entries are shown on page 168. Notice that all of the account inquiry is shown so that you can see the trail of the activity for the month. Also, the ledger accounts have been arranged in pairs by adjustment rather than actual general ledger order. This way you can better see the changes the adjusting entries made. Notice that whether the entries are made manually or keyed into a computer, one amount goes to an income statement account and the other amount goes to a balance sheet account—thus the term mixed accounts.

The Financial Statements (After Adjustments)

Compare these financial statements with those on pages 28 and 29 in Chapter 1. The accounts that have changed are only the ones affected by adjusting entries—Supplies and Supplies Expense; Prepaid Insurance and Insurance Expense; Equipment and Accumulated Depreciation, Equipment; and Wages Expense and Wages Payable.

```
                           Clark's Cleaners
                          3702 35th Southwest
                          Seattle WA 98126

                           Account Inquiry

                          6/1/9- to 6/30/9-
                                                                        Page 1

   Account      ID#   Src   Date        Memo              Debit      Credit    Job

6-6190  Supplies Expense
        GJ000018  GJ  6/30/9-  Adjusting entry for supplies    $310.00    .........
                                                               $310.00      $0.00

1-1230  Supplies
        GJ000005  GJ   6/4/9-  Bought cleaning fluid and bags.  $400.00
        GJ000018  GJ  6/30/9-  Adjusting entry for supplies               $310.00
                                                               $400.00    $310.00

6-6210  Insurance Expense
        GJ000019  GJ  6/30/9-  Adjusting entry for insurance     $30.00    .........
                                                                $30.00      $0.00

1-1270  Prepaid Insurance
        GJ000007  GJ  6/10/9-  Premium for one-year insurance   $360.00
        GJ000019  GJ  6/30/9-  Adjusting entry for insurance               $30.00
                                                               $360.00     $30.00

6-6230  Depreciation Expense, Equipment
        GJ000020  GJ  6/30/9-  Adjusting entry for equipment depr. $250.00  .........
                                                               $250.00      $0.00

1-1560  Accum. Depreciation, Equipment
        GJ000020  GJ  6/30/9-  Adjusting entry for equipment depr.          $250.00
                                                                 $0.00     $250.00

6-6110  Wages Expense
        GJ000012  GJ  6/24/9-  Paid wages through June 24.       $930.00
        GJ000021  GJ  6/30/9-  Adjustment for wages earned       $100.00
                                                             $1,030.00      $0.00

2-2130  Wages Payable
        GJ000021  GJ  6/30/9-  Adjustment for wages earned                 $100.00
                                                                 $0.00     $100.00
```

The Profit and Loss Statement (Income Statement)

Again, the date is different from the manual illustrations. This program assumes June 19– means "for the period ended June 19–." First, look at the difference between the unadjusted and adjusted net profit (net income). Before adjustments for supplies, insurance, depreciation, and wages expenses, the net profit was $2,040.00. After adjustments were made, the net profit is $1,350. The goal is that the records be accurate. Had the adjustments been ignored, Clark's would have understated four expenses totaling $690 (Supplies Expense, $310.00; Insurance Expense, $30.00; Depreciation Expense, $250.00; and Wages Expense, $100.00).

```
                      Clark's Cleaners
                      3702 35th Southwest
                      Seattle WA 98126

                   Profit & Loss Statement

                        June 199-


Income
      Income from Services           $3,870.00
   Total Income                                  $3,870.00

Expenses
      Advertising Expense              $180.00
      Wages Expense                  $1,030.00
      Supplies Expense                 $310.00
      Rent Expense                     $500.00
      Utilities Expense                $220.00
      Insurance Expense                 $30.00
      Depreciation Expense, Equip.     $250.00
   Total Expenses                                $2,520.00

Net Profit/(Loss)                                $1,350.00
```

The Balance Sheet

The adjusting entries not only affected the profit and loss (income) statement, but also the balance sheet totals. Before adjustments, Total Assets amounted to $43,240.00. After adjustments, Total Assets amount to $42,650.00. Had the adjustments been ignored, Clark's would have overstated Total Assets by $590.00 (Supplies reduced by the $310.00 used, Prepaid Insurance reduced by the $30.00 expired, and Accumulated Depreciation increased by the $250.00 estimated to be the loss of usefulness.) Remember that the Equipment account maintains the original cost; the book value of the Equipment may be computed by subtracting accumulated depreciation from the asset amount.

Before adjustments, Total Liabilities amounted to $2,400.00. Had the adjustments been ignored, Clark's would have understated Total Liabilities by $100—the amount of the adjustment for accrued wages (Wages Payable).

Before adjustments, Total Equity (capital) was $40,840.00. After adjustments, Clark's equity is $40,150, a difference of $690.00—the amount by which the net profit was reduced when the adjustments were entered.

The goal of the adjustments, whether done manually or on computer is accuracy. Yes, the profit (and income taxes) went down, as did the owner's equity, but the statements did not present an accurate picture of the business before adjustments were made.

```
                          Clark's Cleaners
                        3702 35th Southwest
                         Seattle WA 98126

                           Balance Sheet

                            June 199-

.....................................................................

Assets
    Cash                                   $15,490.00
    Accounts Receivable                        $50.00
    Supplies                                   $90.00
    Prepaid Insurance                         $330.00
    Equipment                              $26,940.00
    Accum. Depreciation, Equipment           ($250.00)*
Total Assets                                               $42,650.00

Liabilities
    Accounts Payable                        $2,400.00
    Wages Payable                             $100.00
Total Liabilities                                          $2,500.00

Equity
    N. L. Clark, Capital                   $40,000.00
    N. L. Clark, Drawing                    ($1,200.00)*
    Current Year Earnings                   $1,350.00
Total Equity                                              $40,150.00

Total Liability & Equity                                  $42,650.00

*Amounts in ( ) are deducted.
```

Closing Entries

There is no illustration for closing entries because the software did not require that closing entries be keyed. Instead, users select a menu item for closing either end-of-month or end-of-fiscal period. Usually, before the program will automatically zero out all temporary owner's equity accounts (revenue, expense, drawing, and income summary accounts), a series of questions are asked. For example, Have you saved your work to date? Have you made backup copies of your files? Have you made printouts of everything you need? If you answer no to any of the questions, the program may not let you proceed with closing. These answers are important, because some of the less expensive programs will not allow you to go back to prior periods to make printouts. This is another thing to check when shopping for accounting software packages.

Assuming all answers are yes, the program will proceed automatically—and almost instantly—to close the temporary owner's equity accounts, compute the net profit (or net loss), and send the profit (or loss) to the capital account. Some accounting software packages require keying of the closing entries.

Summary Trial Balance (Post-Closing Trial Balance)

The printout of the post-closing trial balance for Clark's Cleaners will be the same as the manual post-closing trial balance except for the differences in language and format that have been discussed. The only accounts open (or containing balances greater than zero) will be the real or permanent accounts (assets, liabilities, and owner's equity capital account). The temporary (or nominal) accounts are closed or have zero balances in preparation for the new fiscal period.

CHAPTER REVIEW

R eview of Performance Objectives

1. **Complete a work sheet involving adjustments for supplies used, expired insurance, depreciation, and accrued wages for a service enterprise.**

   Adjustment for supplies used: debit Supplies Expense and credit Supplies.

   Adjustment for expired insurance: debit Insurance Expense and credit Prepaid Insurance.

   Adjustment for depreciation: debit Depreciation Expense and credit Accumulated Depreciation.

   Adjustment for accrued wages: debit Wages Expense and credit Wages Payable.

2. **Prepare an income statement, a statement of owner's equity, and a balance sheet directly from the work sheet of a service business.**

   Prepare the income statement directly from the amounts listed in the Income Statement Debit and Credit columns. The net income should equal the net income shown on the work sheet. For the statement of owner's equity, use the amount of the beginning capital listed in the Balance Sheet Credit column, the amount of the net income from the Balance Sheet Credit column, and the amount of Drawing from the Balance Sheet Debit column.

3. **Journalize and post the adjusting entries.**

   The adjusting entries are taken directly from the Adjustments columns of the work sheet.

4. **Journalize and post closing entries for a service enterprise.**

   The four steps in the closing procedure as are as follows:
   1. Close the revenue accounts into Income Summary.
   2. Close the expense accounts into Income Summary.
   3. Close the Income Summary account into the Capital account, transferring the net income or loss to the Capital account.
   4. Close the Drawing account into the Capital account.

5. **Prepare a post-closing trial balance for any type of enterprise.**

   A post-closing trial balance consists of the final balances of the accounts remaining open. It is the final proof that the debit balances equal the credit balances before the posting for the new fiscal period commences.

6. **Define the following methods of accounting: accrual basis, cash-receipts-and-disbursements basis, modified cash basis.**

   Under the accrual basis of accounting, revenue is recorded when earned, even if cash is received at a later date, and expenses are recorded when incurred, even if cash is to be paid at a later date. Under the cash-receipts-and-disbursements basis, revenue is recorded only when cash is received, and expenses are recorded only when paid in cash. This basis is used mainly by individuals for their income taxes. Under the modified cash basis, revenue and expenses are recorded in the same manner as under the cash basis, but expenditures for assets having a useful life of more than one year and certain prepaid items are adjusted.

7. **Prepare interim statements.**

   Interim statements consist of year-to-date income statements and statements of owner's equity as well as balance sheets as of various dates during the fiscal period.

G lossary

Accounting cycle The sequence of steps in the accounting process that is completed during the fiscal period. **(129)**

Accrual Recognition of an expense or a revenue that has been incurred or earned but has not yet been recorded. **(138)**

Accrual basis An accounting method by which revenue is recorded when it is earned, regardless of when it is received, and expenses are recorded when they are incurred, regardless of when they are paid. **(161)**

Accrued wages The amount of unpaid wages owed to employees for the time between the last payday and the end of the fiscal period. **(138)**

Accumulated Depreciation A contra-asset account, or a deduction from an asset such as equipment or building, representing the estimated depreciation built up against the cost of the asset. **(135)**

Adjusting entry An entry to help bring the books up to date at the end of the fiscal period. **(134)**

Adjustments Internal transactions that bring ledger accounts up to date as a planned part of the accounting procedure. They are first recorded in the Adjustments columns of the work sheet. **(133)**

Book value The cost of an asset minus the accumulated depreciation. **(136)**

Cash-receipts-and-disbursements basis An accounting method by which all revenue is recorded only when it is received in cash, and all expenses are recorded only when they are paid in cash. **(161)**

Closing entries Entries made at the end of a fiscal period to close off the revenue and expense accounts; that is, to make the balances of the temporary-equity account equal to zero. Closing is also called *clearing the accounts.* **(151)**

Contra account An account that is contrary to, or a deduction from, another account; for example, Accumulated Depreciation, Equipment, entered as a deduction from Equipment. **(135)**

Depreciation An expense based on the expectation that an asset will gradually decline in usefulness as a result of time, wear and tear, or obsolescence; the cost of the asset is therefore spread out over its estimated useful life. A part of depreciation expense is apportioned to each fiscal period. **(135)**

Fiscal period Any period of time covering a complete accounting cycle, generally consisting of twelve consecutive months. **(130)**

Income Summary An account brought into existence in order to have a debit and credit for each closing entry. **(153)**

Interim statements Financial statements prepared during the fiscal year, covering a period of time less than the entire twelve months. **(162)**

Mixed accounts Certain accounts that appear in the trial balance that are partly income statement amounts and partly balance sheet amounts—for example, Prepaid Insurance and Supplies. **(143)**

Modified cash basis An accounting method by which revenue is recorded only when it is received in cash. Expenditures classified as expenses are recorded only when they are paid in cash. Exceptions are made for expenditures on items having a useful life of more than one year and for certain prepaid items. For example, expenditures for supplies and insurance premiums can be *prorated*, or spread out over the fiscal periods covered. Expenditures for long-lived items are recorded as assets and later depreciated or written off as an expense during their useful lives. **(162)**

Nominal or **temporary-equity accounts** Accounts that apply to only one fiscal period and that are closed at the end of a fiscal period, such as revenue, expense, Income Summary, and Drawing accounts. This category may also be described as all accounts except assets, liabilities, and the Capital account. **(160)**

Post-closing trial balance The listing of the final balances of the real accounts at the end of the fiscal period. **(160)**

Real or **permanent accounts** The accounts that remain open (assets, liabilities, and the Capital account in owner's equity) and that have balances that will be carried over to the next fiscal period. **(160)**

Straight-line method A means of calculating depreciation in which the cost of an asset, less any trade-in value, is allocated on an average basis over the useful life of the asset. **(136)**

Work sheet A working paper used by accountants to record necessary adjustments and provide up-to-date account balances needed to prepare the financial statements. **(130)**

QUESTIONS, EXERCISES, AND PROBLEMS

Discussion Questions

1. What is the amount of the adjusting entry for supplies, if the balance of the account before adjustment is $1,450 and the amount on hand at the end of the fiscal period is $640?
2. What is a mixed account? Give an example. What is a contra account? Give an example.
3. If wages are paid for work performed for the period Monday through Friday, and the accounting period ends on Wednesday, why is it necessary to make an adjustment?
4. Why is it necessary to journalize adjusting entries?
5. At the end of the fiscal period, the adjusting entry to record accrued wages was accidentally omitted. What is the effect of the omission on (a) the amount of net income for the accounting period and (b) the balance sheet as of the end of the period? Explain.
6. a. What is the purpose of the post-closing trial balance?
   b. What is the difference between a trial balance and a post-closing trial balance?
7. List the four steps in the closing procedure.
8. List two ways closing entries are completed using accounting software.

Exercises

P.O.1

Classify accounts and indicate normal balances.

Exercise 4-1 Classify each of the accounts listed below as assets (A), liabilities (L), owner's equity (OE), revenue (R), or expenses (E). Indicate the normal debit or credit balance of each account. Indicate either the Income Statement columns (I) or the Balance Sheet columns (B) in which each account balance will appear in the work sheet. Item 0 is given as an example.

Account	Classification	Normal Balance	Income Statement or Balance Sheet Columns
0. *Example:* Rent Expense	E	Debit	I
a. Accounts Payable			
b. Supplies			
c. Equipment			
d. C. Jones, Capital			
e. Accounts Receivable			
f. Accumulated Depreciation, Equipment			
g. C. Jones, Drawing			
h. Commissions Income			
i. Prepaid Insurance			
j. Depreciation Expense, Equipment			

P.O.1

Record adjusting entries in T accounts.

Exercise 4-2 Using T accounts, record the adjusting entries for each of the situations listed below. The last day of the accounting period is December 31.

a. Salaries for two days are unpaid at December 31. Salaries are $30,000 for a five-day week.
b. On August 1, a $1,200 premium was paid on a twelve-month insurance policy. The amount of the premium was debited to Prepaid Insurance.
c. Before adjustments, the Supplies account has a balance of $3,460. The count of supplies on hand amounts to $2,110.
d. Equipment was purchased on March 3 for $24,000. The expected life of office equipment is ten years, with no trade-in value.

P.O.2

Place accounts on financial statements.

Exercise 4-3 Indicate whether each of the following would appear on the income statement, the statement of owner's equity, or the balance sheet. The first item is provided as an example.

Item	Income Statement	Statement of Owner's Equity	Balance Sheet
0. *Example:* The total liabilities of the business at the end of the year.			X
a. The amount paid for supplies on hand at the end of the year.			
b. Total insurance expired during the year.			
c. Total accounts receivable at the end of the year.			
d. Total revenue earned during the year.			
e. Total withdrawals by the owner.			
f. The book value of the company's equipment.			
g. The amount of the owner's investment at the end of the year.			
h. The amount of depreciation taken on equipment during the year.			
i. The cost of supplies used during the year.			
j. The amount of the owner's investment at the beginning of the year.			
k. The amount of the company's net income for the year.			

Exercise 4-4 Journalize the adjusting entries (a) through (e) from the following T accounts. Normally, the Adjustments columns of the work sheet are used as a basis for journalizing adjusting entries. This exercise is only for practice.

P.O.3

Journalize adjusting entries.

Insurance Expense	
(a) 550	

Wages Expense	
19,420	
(e) 490	

Rent Expense	
(d) 600	

Wages Payable	
	(e) 490

Prepaid Rent	
1,800	(d) 600

Supplies	
2,140	(c) 420

Depreciation Expense, Equipment	
(b) 910	

Accumulated Depreciation, Equipment	
	5,220
	(b) 910

Prepaid Insurance	
1,450	(a) 550

Supplies Expense	
(c) 420	

P.O.3

Journalize adjusting entries.

Exercise 4-5 Journalize the year-end adjusting entry for each of the following for the fiscal year ending December 31:

a. The payment of the $720 insurance premium for three years in advance was originally recorded as Prepaid Insurance. One year of the policy has now expired.

b. All employees earn a total of $800 per day for a five-day week beginning on Monday and ending Friday. They were paid for the work week ending December 27. They worked on Monday, December 30, and Tuesday, December 31.

c. The Supplies account had a balance of $348 on January 1. During the year, $1,000 of supplies were bought. A year-end inventory shows that $540 worth of supplies are still on hand.

d. Equipment costing $57,900 has a useful life of five years with a $6,000 trade-in value at the end of five years. Record the depreciation for the year.

P.O.3,4

Journalize adjusting and closing entries from account balances.

Exercise 4-6 Record the adjusting and closing journal entries that support the amounts recorded in T accounts.

Miscellaneous Expense		Income Summary		Wages Payable	
240	240	4,900	4,800	(a)	180
			100		

Insurance Expense		Income from Services		Depreciation Expense, Equipment	
(c) 480	480	4,800	400	(b) 800	800
			3,600		
			800		

Wages Expense		Accumulated Depreciation, Equipment		Prepaid Insurance	
1,600	3,380		3,200	960	(c) 480
1,600		(b)	800	160	
(a) 180					

J. Riegle, Drawing		J. Riegle, Capital	
600	600	100	26,000
		600	

P.O.4

Journalize closing entries from work sheet columns.

Exercise 4-7 The Income Statement columns of the work sheet of P. J. Manson Company for the fiscal year ended June 30 appears below. During the year, P. J. Manson withdrew $42,000. Journalize the closing entries.

ACCOUNT NAME	INCOME STATEMENT	
	DEBIT	CREDIT
Service Revenue		72 0 0 0 00
Concession Income		14 0 0 0 00
Wages Expense	31 0 0 0 00	
Advertising Expense	3 0 0 0 00	
Rent Expense	8 0 0 0 00	
Supplies Expense	2 0 0 0 00	
Taxes Expense	2 0 0 0 00	
Miscellaneous Expense	1 0 0 0 00	
	47 0 0 0 00	86 0 0 0 00
Net Income	39 0 0 0 00	
	86 0 0 0 00	86 0 0 0 00

Exercise 4-8 Classify the accounts listed below as real (permanent) or nominal (temporary), and indicate whether or not each account is closed. Also, indicate the financial statement in which each account will appear. The Building account is given as an example.

P.O.2,4,5

Classify accounts and show where they are listed on a work sheet.

				Closed			
Account Title	Real	Nominal	Yes	No	Balance Sheet	Income Statement
0. *Example:* Building	X			X	X	
a. Rent Expense						
b. Prepaid Insurance						
c. Accounts Payable						
d. Supplies Expense						
e. Accumulated Depreciation, Equipment						
f. Wages Payable						
g. Income from Fees						

C onsider and Communicate

You are the bookkeeper for a busy, small service business. You have asked the owner for the information you need for adjusting entries for depreciation, insurance, supplies, and wages. The owner responds, "What you've done so far is close enough. Don't bother with adjusting or closing entries. They take too much time. Besides, I really only look at the checkbook anyway." Explain to the owner the need for adjusting entries and how they affect his balance sheet as well as his income statement. Also convince him that closing entries are necessary.

W hat If . . .

As the firm accountant, you have prepared the unadjusted trial balance on the worksheet. You begin to compute the depreciation expense for the current month of July, before recording the adjustments on the worksheet. You find that equipment was purchased on credit on July 1 and not recorded in the journal. Should you record the purchase as an adjustment on July 31, or should you journalize and post the purchase of equipment and date the entry July 1? What difference does it make as long as the equipment is recorded in the books? Does the date matter? Is there a difference between adjusting entries and correcting entries?

A Question of Ethics

Your client is preparing financial statements for the bank. You know that he has incurred a computer repair expense during the month, but you see no such expense on the books. When you question the client, he tells you that he has not received the official bill although he knows the expense was $1,250. Your client is on the accrual basis of accounting. He does not want the computer expense on the books as of the end of the month because that will lower the profit for the period and he has to show the statements to his bank. Is your client behaving ethically by suggesting that the computer expense not be booked until the official bill is presented? Are you behaving ethically if you go along with the client's request? What principle is involved here?

P roblem Set A

P.O.1,3

Problem 4-1A The trial balance of Holly's Upholstery at December 31, the end of the current year, is shown on the next page. Data for the year-end adjustments are as follows:

a. Inventory of supplies at December 31, $1,211.
b. Insurance expired at the rate of $25 per month.
c. Equipment has a life of five years with an estimated trade-in value of $6,000. Use the straight-line rate to determine the amount of depreciation for the year.

d. Wages are paid at the rate of $320 per week for a five-day week. Two day's wages have accrued.

Instructions

1. Complete the work sheet.
2. Journalize the adjusting entries.

Holly's Upholstery

Trial Balance
December 31, 19—

ACCOUNT NAME	DEBIT	CREDIT
Cash	2 4 1 0 00	
Supplies	3 4 7 6 00	
Prepaid Insurance	4 0 0 00	
Equipment	40 3 2 0 00	
Accumulated Depreciation, Equipment		20 5 9 2 00
Accounts Payable		4 3 5 00
S. Holly, Capital		22 1 3 0 00
S. Holly, Drawing	15 0 3 3 00	
Income from Services		42 0 2 0 00
Wages Expense	16 5 1 2 00	
Rent Expense	4 2 0 0 00	
Utilities Expense	1 7 8 0 00	
Advertising Expense	6 2 1 00	
Miscellaneous Expense	4 2 5 00	
	85 1 7 7 00	85 1 7 7 00

Problem 4-2A The trial balance of Springer Video Games, a video game store, as of August 31 is given in the work sheet in the Working Papers. Data for the month-end adjustments are as follows: `P.O.1,2,3`

a. Inventory of supplies at August 31, $869.
b. Insurance expired during the month, $180.
c. Depreciation of building for the month, $420.
d. Depreciation of game equipment for the month, $2,600.
e. Depreciation of furniture and fixtures for the month, $20.
f. Wages accrued at August 31, $398.

Instructions

1. Complete the work sheet for the month.
2. Prepare an income statement, a statement of owner's equity, and a balance sheet. Assume that no additional investments were made during August.
3. Journalize the adjusting entries.

Instructions for General Ledger Software

1. Journalize the adjusting entries in the general journal. (No work sheet is required on the computer.)
2. Post the adjusting entries.
3. Print an income statement, a statement of owner's equity, and a balance sheet. Assume no additional investments were made during August.

L.O.3,4,5

Problem 4-3A The completed work sheet for Lakeview Insurance Agency is presented in the Working Papers.

Instructions

1. Record the December 31 balances in the ledger accounts. Record "Balance" in the Item columns and a check mark in the Post. Ref. column. Complete the titles of the Capital, Drawing, and revenue accounts.
2. Journalize and post the adjusting entries.
3. Journalize and post the closing entries with the four steps in the proper sequence, using the order of accounts in the general ledger.
4. Prepare a post-closing trial balance.

P.O.1,2,3,4

Problem 4-4A The trial balance of Perrini Janitorial Service is recorded in the work sheet in the Working Papers for the fiscal period September 1 of one year through August 31 of the next year. Data for the adjustments are as follows:

a. Inventory of cleaning supplies, $310.
b. Depreciation of cleaning equipment, $717.
c. Depreciation of truck, $920.
d. Accrued wages, $276.

Instructions

1. Complete the work sheet.
2. Prepare an income statement.
3. Prepare a statement of owner's equity assuming that no additional investments were made during the year.
4. Prepare a balance sheet.
5. Journalize the adjusting entries. (To save time, do not post.)
6. Journalize the closing entries with the four steps in the proper sequence. (To save time, do not post.)

Instructions for General Ledger Software

1. Journalize the adjusting entries in the general journal. (No work sheet is required on the computer.)
2. Post the adjusting entries.
3. Print an income statement, a statement of owner's equity, and a balance sheet.
4. Journalize the closing entries in the general journal.
5. Post the closing entries.
6. Print a post-closing trial balance.

P roblem Set B

P.O.1,3

Problem 4-1B The trial balance of Sarah's Elegant Nails as of December 31, the end of the current year, is presented on the next page. Data for the year-end adjustments are as follows:

a. Inventory of Beauty/Nail Supplies at December 31, $10,617.
b. Insurance expired during the year at the rate of $20 per month.
c. Equipment has a life of five years with zero trade-in value. Using the straight-line method, record one year's depreciation.

Sarah's Elegant Nails
Trial Balance
December 31, 19–

ACCOUNT NAME	DEBIT	CREDIT
Cash	4 8 5 2 00	
Beauty/Nail Supplies	13 0 8 9 00	
Prepaid Insurance	3 2 0 00	
Equipment	31 1 0 0 00	
Accumulated Depreciation, Equipment		12 4 4 0 00
Accounts Payable		1 8 3 8 00
S. T. Winter, Capital		23 2 7 9 00
S. T. Winter, Drawing	9 8 0 0 00	
Income from Services		34 8 8 0 00
Wages Expense	9 5 0 0 00	
Rent Expense	2 8 0 0 00	
Utilities Expense	6 1 4 00	
Telephone Expense	1 8 0 00	
Miscellaneous Expense	1 8 2 00	
	72 4 3 7 00	72 4 3 7 00

Instructions

1. Complete the work sheet.
2. Journalize the adjusting entries.

Problem 4-2B The trial balance of Elliott Luxury Lanes, a bowling alley, as of March 31, is given in the work sheet in the Working Papers. Data for the month-end adjustments are as follows:

P.O.1,2,3

a. Inventory of supplies at March 31, $731.
b. Insurance expired during the month, $220.
c. Depreciation of building for the month, $750.
d. Depreciation of bowling equipment during the month, $1,500.
e. Depreciation of furniture and fixtures for the month, $162.
f. Wages accrued at March 31, $466.

Instructions

1. Complete the work sheet for the month.
2. Prepare an income statement, a statement of owner's equity, and a balance sheet. Assume that no additional investments were made during March.
3. Journalize the adjusting entries.

Instructions for General Ledger Software

1. Journalize the adjusting entries in the general journal. (No work sheet is required on the computer.)
2. Post the adjusting entries.
3. Print an income statement, a statement of owner's equity, and a balance sheet. Assume no additional investments were made during March.

P.O.3,4,5

Problem 4-3B The completed work sheet for Working Systems, a career counseling agency, is presented in the Working Papers.

Instructions

1. Record the December 31 balances in the ledger accounts. Record "Balance" in the Item columns and a check mark in the Post. Ref. column. Complete the titles of the Capital, Drawing, and revenue accounts.
2. Journalize and post the adjusting entries.
3. Journalize and post the closing entries with the four steps in the proper sequence, using the order of accounts in the general ledger.
4. Prepare a post-closing trial balance.

P.O.1,2,3,4

Problem 4-4B The trial balance of Kaplan Recycling Services is recorded in the work sheet in the Working Papers for the fiscal period November 1 of one year through October 31 of the next year. Data for the adjustments are as follows:

a. Inventory of supplies, $257.
b. Depreciation of equipment, $860.
c. Depreciation of truck, $1,655.
d. Accrued wages, $295.

Instructions

1. Complete the work sheet.
2. Prepare an income statement.
3. Prepare a statement of owner's equity assuming that no additional investments were made during the year.
4. Prepare a balance sheet.
5. Journalize the adjusting entries. (To save time, do not post.)
6. Journalize the closing entries with the four steps in the proper sequence. (To save time, do not post.)

Instructions for General Ledger Software

1. Journalize the adjusting entries in the general journal. (No work sheet is required on the computer.)
2. Post the adjusting entries.
3. Print an income statement, a statement of owner's equity, and a balance sheet.
4. Journalize the closing entries in the general journal.
5. Post the closing entries.
6. Print a post-closing trial balance.

CHALLENGE PROBLEM

Here is the partial work sheet for Haig's Recreation Outlet:

Haig's Recreation Outlet
Work Sheet
For Year Ended December 31, 19–

ACCOUNT NAME	BALANCE SHEET DEBIT	BALANCE SHEET CREDIT
Cash	31 1 1 3 60	
Notes Receivable	11 5 2 0 00	
Accounts Receivable	137 2 1 4 72	
Merchandise Inventory	181 4 3 0 40	
Supplies	1 5 1 6 80	
Prepaid Taxes	1 9 6 3 20	
Prepaid Insurance	2 0 1 6 00	
Land	26 8 8 0 00	
Building	201 6 0 0 00	
Accumulated Depreciation, Building		69 1 2 0 00
Office Equipment	17 3 5 6 80	
Accumulated Depreciation, Office Equipment		13 3 4 4 00
Store Equipment	21 0 2 4 00	
Accumulated Depreciation, Store Equipment		15 9 8 4 00
Delivery Equipment	17 8 0 8 00	
Accumulated Depreciation, Delivery Equipment		13 7 7 6 00
Notes Payable		17 3 7 6 00
Mortgage Payable (current portion)		8 6 4 0 00
Accounts Payable		94 6 9 3 44
Mortgage Payable		178 2 8 1 60
R. D. Haig, Capital		208 1 8 8 48
R. D. Haig, Drawing	80 6 2 0 80	
Wages Payable		4 0 8 9 60
	732 0 6 4 32	623 4 9 3 12
Net Income		108 5 7 1 20
	732 0 6 4 32	732 0 6 4 32

Instructions

1. Prepare a statement of owner's equity (no additional investment).
2. Prepare a balance sheet.

Accounting Cycle Review Problem

This problem is designed to enable you to apply the knowledge you have acquired in the preceding chapters. In accounting, the ultimate test is being able to handle data in real-life situations. This problem will give you valuable experience.

Chart of Accounts

ASSETS
111   Cash
113   Accounts Receivable
115   Supplies
117   Prepaid Insurance
121   Land
122   Building
123   Accumulated Depreciation, Building
124   Pool/Slide Facility
125   Accumulated Depreciation, Pool/Slide Facility
126   Pool Furniture
127   Accumulated Depreciation, Pool Furniture

LIABILITIES
221   Accounts Payable
223   Wages Payable
241   Mortgage Payable

OWNER'S EQUITY
311   S. Beidel, Capital
312   S. Beidel, Drawing
399   Income Summary

REVENUE
411   Income from Services
412   Concession Income

EXPENSES
515   Advertising Expense
517   Pool Maintenance Expense
521   Wages Expense
523   Supplies Expense
525   Utilities Expense
529   Insurance Expense
531   Depreciation Expense, Building
533   Depreciation Expense, Pool/Slide Facility
535   Depreciation Expense, Pool Furniture
538   Interest Expense
539   Miscellaneous Expense

You are to record transactions in a two-column general journal. Assume that the fiscal period is one month. You will then be able to complete all the steps in the accounting cycle.

When you are analyzing the transactions, think them through by visualizing the T accounts or by writing them down on scratch paper. Specific instructions are provided for recording some transactions, but reason them out for yourself as well. Check off each transaction as it is recorded.

July   1   Beidel deposited $310,000 in a bank account for the purpose of buying Sun Spot Waterslides. The business is a public recreation area offering three large waterslides (called "tubes"), one children's slide, an inner tube run, and a hot tub area.

         2   Bought Sun Spot Waterslides in its entirety for a total price of $542,800. The assets include pool furniture, $4,500; the pool/slide facility (includes filter system, pools, pump, and slides), $147,800; building, $95,500; and land, $295,000. Paid $135,000 down and signed a mortgage note for the remainder. (Debit the assets, and credit Cash and Mortgage Payable.)

         2   Received and paid the bill for property and liability insurance for the coming year, $14,050.40.

         2   Bought 125 inner tubes from Wright's Tires for $3,325 paying $1,700 down, with the remainder due in twenty days. (Debit Supplies instead of an Equipment account, because inner tubes generally last only a month or so.)

         3   Signed a contract with a video game company to lease them space for their video games and to provide a food concession. The rental income agreed upon is 10 percent of the revenue generated from their machines and food sales, with the estimated monthly rental income paid in advance. Received cash payment for July, $532 (Debit Cash and credit Concession Income.)

         5   Received bills totaling $1,666 for the grand opening/Fourth of July party. The bill from Party Promotions for the promotional handouts, balloons, decorations, and prizes was $868 and the newspaper advertising bills were $798 from the *City Star*. (These expenses should all be considered advertising expense.)

         6   Signed a one-year contract for pool maintenance with Crystal Clean Maintenance and paid the maintenance fee for July of $708.40.

         6   Paid cash for employee picnic food and beverages, $144.54 (Debit Miscellaneous Expense.)

         7   Received $19,678.40 in cash as income for the use of the facilities. (Credit Income from Services.)

         9   Bought parts for the filter system on account from Applewood Pool Supply, $1,338.40. (Debit Pool Maintenance Expense.)

        14   Received $12,854.80 in cash as income from the use of the facilities. (Credit Income from Services.)

        15   Paid wages to employees for the period ending July 14, $14,112.

        16   Paid the bills for advertising expenses already recorded on July 5.

        16   Beidel withdrew cash for personal use, $2,350.

        17   Bought additional pool furniture from Leisure Products for $2,972, payment due in thirty days.

18 Paid cash to seamstress for alterations and repairs to the character costumes, $69.44 (Debit Miscellaneous Expense.)

21 Received $17,010 in cash as income for the use of the facilities.

21 Paid cash to Wright's Tires as partial payment on account, $1,137.50.

23 Received a $315 allowance from Leisure Products for lawn chairs received in damaged condition (a reduction in the outstanding bill, by $315).

25 Received and paid telephone bill, $246.40.

30 Paid wages for the period July 15 through 29 of $16,184.

31 Received $19,558 in cash as income for the use of the facilities.

31 Paid cash to Applewood Pool Supply to apply on account, $669.20.

31 Received and paid water bill, $2,840.60.

31 Paid cash as an installment payment on the mortgage, $6,700. Of this amount, $2,390.80 represents a reduction in the principal, and the remainder is interest. (Debit Mortgage Payable, debit Interest Expense, and credit Cash.)

31 Received and paid electric bill, $1,370.60.

31 Bought additional inner tubes from Wright's Tires for $750.40, paying $100 down, with the remainder due in thirty days.

31 Beidel withdrew cash for personal use, $3,350.

31 Sales for the video and food concession amounted to $7,938; ten percent of $7,938 equals $793.80. Since you have already recorded $532 as concession income, record the additional $261.80 revenue due from the concessionaire (cash was not received).

Instructions

1. Journalize the transactions, starting on page 1 of the general journal.
2. Post the transactions to the ledger accounts.
3. Prepare a trial balance in the first two columns of the work sheet.
4. Complete the work sheet. Data for the adjustments are as follows:
   a. Insurance expired during the month, $1,170.40.
   b. Depreciation of pool furniture for the month, $70.
   c. Depreciation of pool/slide facility for the month, $798.
   d. Depreciation of building for the month, $490.
   e. Wages accrued at July 31, $824.60.
   f. Inner tubes on hand (supplies) at July 31, $1,694.
5. Prepare the income statement.
6. Prepare the statement of owner's equity.
7. Prepare the balance sheet.
8. Journalize adjusting entries.
9. Post adjusting entires to the ledger accounts.
10. Journalize closing entries.
11. Post closing entries to the ledger accounts.
12. Prepare a post-closing trial balance.

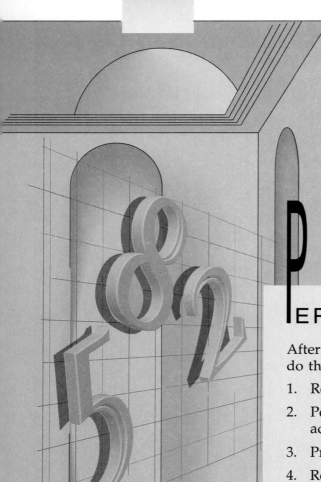

Chapter 5

Accounting for Merchandise: Sales and Cash Receipts Journals

PERFORMANCE OBJECTIVES

After you have completed this chapter, you will be able to do the following:

1. Record transactions in a sales journal.

2. Post from a sales journal to a general ledger and an accounts receivable ledger.

3. Prepare a schedule of accounts receivable.

4. Record and post sales returns and allowances and sales returns and allowances involving sales tax to the ledger accounts.

5. Post directly from sales invoices to an accounts receivable ledger, and journalize and post a summarizing entry in the general journal.

6. Record transactions for a retail merchandising business in a cash receipts journal.

7. Post from a cash receipts journal to a general ledger and an accounts receivable ledger.

8. Calculate cash discounts according to credit terms, and record cash receipts from charge customers who are entitled to deduct the cash discount.

O ne of the most dramatic "quick fixes" to a firm's financial problems I have ever experienced took place at a company struggling with cash-flow problems. This firm did not have enough cash inflow to meet the needs of cash outflow. This situation may sound familiar—it happens

to individuals and to businesses. At this company all sales were made on account, and although the terms were n/30, the money just wasn't coming in quickly enough.

When I questioned the bookkeeper, he explained that his procedure at the end of the month included reviewing each customer's account, computing the balance, and typing out the statement. In a good month, the statements were mailed by the tenth of the next month. If he got behind, however, the statements to customers went out much later.

The solution was relatively easy. For a modest cost, the cash receipts journal and accounts receivable ledger, which had been updated manually, were computerized. The month-end-statement project, instead of dragging on for weeks, became a last-day-of-the-month project with a few keystrokes on the computer.

The dollar savings in labor easily justified the cost, but the real bonus was that the accounts receivable payments started coming in much faster! The lag time between receiving payments from customers and paying bills to creditors was shortened. The company could tell when customer accounts were late and start collection reminders sooner. And, the bookkeeper and others responsible for cash could breathe a sigh of relief.

By now you have had enough experience to complete the full accounting cycle for service and professional enterprises. To expand your accounting knowledge, let's introduce accounting systems for merchandising enterprises. The same general principles of double-entry accounting apply.

This chapter describes specific accounts and journals related to sales in merchandising firms. A merchandising firm could be anything from a toy shop to a department store. The chapter introduces the sales journal and cash receipts journal as well as the subsidiary accounts receivable ledger. Just as we used Clark's Cleaners as a continuing example of a service business, we will use Dodson Plumbing Supply as a continuing example of a merchandising business.

Special Journals

ny accounting system must be as efficient as possible. As a matter of fact, accounting is a means, or tool, used to measure efficiency in a business. Consequently, one should take short cuts wherever one can without sacrificing internal control. Briefly, **internal control** is a system of rules and procedures that a business follows to (1) protect assets against fraud and waste, (2) provide for accurate accounting data, (3) promote an efficient operation, and (4) encourage adherence to management policies. We will also discuss internal control in Chapters 6 and 8, which relate to purchasing merchandise and handling cash.

As we will see, **special journals**—books of original entry used to record specialized types of repetitive transactions—provide one more shortcut. Using a two-column general journal for recording transactions that take place day after day is extremely time consuming, because each individual credit and debit account and amount must be posted separately. Special journals are generally introduced as the business grows and departments are formed to handle specialized accounting activities. Some of the advantages of using special journals are:

1. They speed journalizing by eliminating repetitive writing or rekeying.

2. They speed posting by allowing column totals to be posted as summary entries.

3. They increase accuracy by reducing the amount of journalizing and posting.

4. They promote the division of labor, so that work can be delegated as the business grows.

5. They allow most entries to be placed on only one line.

The following table provides an overview of the four special journals that we will introduce in chapters 5 and 6:

Chapter	Special Journal	Specialized Transaction	Letter Designation
5	Sales	Sales of merchandise on account only	S
5	Cash receipts	All increases to cash received from any source	CR
6	Purchases	Purchases of merchandise on account only	P
6	Cash payments	All cash decreases to cash for any purpose	CP

When any of these four journals is used, the general journal must also be used to record any nonspecialized transaction—in other words, any transactions that the special journals cannot handle. **The letter designation for the general journal is J.** When more than one journal is used in a business, the posting reference must include the letter in addition to the page number of the journal. For example, a business would use J4 to identify page 4 of the general journal and S6 to identify page 6 of the sales journal. With this method, the source of each entry is easily identified so that activity may be tracked.

Sales-Related Accounts for Merchandising Firms

A merchandising business depends on the sale of goods or merchandise for its revenue. The business records the amount of the sale under the account titled **Sales** or another sales account describing the product. A number of other specialized accounts are used by merchandising firms.

Merchandise Inventory consists of a stock of goods that a company buys and intends to resell, in the same physical condition, at a profit. Merchandise should be differentiated from other assets, such as equipment and supplies, that are acquired for use in the business and are not for resale.

The **Sales Returns and Allowances** account is used to record the physical return of merchandise by customers or a reduction in a bill because merchandise was damaged. It is treated as a deduction from Sales.

The **Sales Discount** account is used to record cash discounts granted for prompt payments, in accordance with the credit terms. We will discuss this account in more detail when we introduce the cash receipts journal.

Sales Tax Payable is an account used to record the state or local tax levied on the buyer of merchandise.

FYI

The Merchandise Inventory account is only involved during merchandise adjustment under the periodic method (Chapter 7). The account is heavily involved under the perpetual inventory method (Chapter 13).

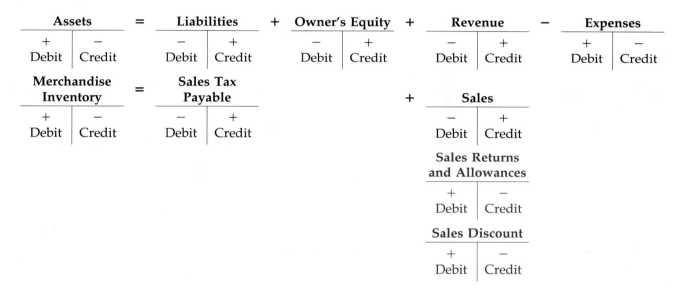

The T accounts for Sales Returns and Allowances and for Sales Discount are shown in color to emphasize that we are treating them as deductions from the Sales account placed above them. Sales Returns and Allowances and Sales Discount appear as deductions from Sales in a merchandiser's financial statements. Their relationship is similar to that between the Drawing account and the Capital account; remember that we deduct Drawing from Capital in the statement of owner's equity.

The firm's accountant makes entries involving Merchandise Inventory only when the firm takes an actual physical count of the goods in stock; otherwise the accountant leaves this account strictly alone. Changing the balance of the Merchandise Inventory account requires adjusting entries made at the end of the fiscal period. We will show these adjusting entries in Chapter 7.

The type of transaction most frequently encountered in a merchandising business is the sale of merchandise. Sales transactions may involve cash, credit cards, or charge accounts.

Customers can purchase almost anything with credit cards, including gasoline, stamps, and telephone calls.

Handling Sales on Account

Sales are recorded only in response to a customer order. The routines for processing orders and recording sales vary with the type and size of the business. The larger the business, the more likely it is that a sales journal will be used for sales on account. Any sale of merchandise involving cash would be recorded in the cash receipts journal, which is illustrated later in the chapter.

In a retail business, a salesperson usually prepares a sales ticket—in either duplicate or triplicate—for a sale on account. One copy is given to the customer and another to the accounting department, where it will serve as the basis for an entry in the sales journal. A third copy may be used as a record of sales—when one is computing sales commissions or is involved in inventory control, for example.

In a wholesale business, the company usually receives a written order from a customer or from a salesperson who obtained the order from the customer. The order must then be approved by the credit department, after which it is sent to the billing department, where the sales **invoice** is prepared.

Invoices are prepared in multiple copies. For example, Figure 5-1 shows one possible distribution of sales invoice copies to various parties. Figure 5-2 shows an invoice of our model business, Dodson Plumbing Supply—a wholesaler.

We will introduce the sales journal by looking at three transactions on the books of Dodson Plumbing Supply:

Aug. 1 Sold merchandise on account to C. P. Landis Company, invoice no. 320, $580.92.
3 Sold merchandise on account to Milne, Inc., invoice no. 321, $116.
6 Sold merchandise on account to Alvarez Construction, invoice no. 322, $394.

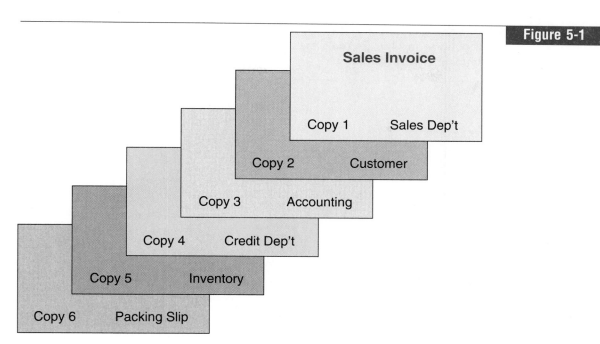

Figure 5-1

Figure 5-2

Copy 1	Sales Dep't
Copy 2	Customer
Copy 3	Accounting
Copy 4	Credit Dep't
Copy 5	Inventory
Copy 6	Packing Slip

DODSON PLUMBING SUPPLY
1400 Jackson Avenue • San Diego, CA • 92102

Invoice No. 320

INVOICE

Sold to: C. P. Landis Company
5210 Gilman Avenue
San Diego, CA 92102

Shipped by: Their truck

Customer's Order Number	Salesperson	Terms	F.O.B.	Date
5384	*h.t.*	2/10,n/30		August 1, 19—

Quantity	Description	Unit Price	Total
6	Olin single-control tub shower faucet #44B652	51.50	309.00
6	Olin dual-control washerless lavoratory faucet #59B641	22.20	133.20
12	Olin massage shower head, antique brass #37B411	11.56	138.72
		Total	580.92

If the transactions were recorded in a general journal, they would appear as they do in Figure 5-3, shown on the next page. Next, the journal entries would be posted to the accounts in the general ledger. (Assume there were no beginning balances in the ledger accounts.) Obviously, there is a great deal of repetition in both journalizing and posting. Using a sales journal eliminates much of the repetition.

Figure 5-3

GENERAL JOURNAL   PAGE 23

	DATE		DESCRIPTION	POST. REF.	DEBIT	CREDIT	
1	19–						1
2	Aug.	1	Accounts Receivable	113	5 8 0 92		2
3			Sales	411		5 8 0 92	3
4			Invoice no. 320, C. P. Landis				4
5			Company.				5
6							6
7		3	Accounts Receivable	113	1 1 6 00		7
8			Sales	411		1 1 6 00	8
9			Invoice no. 321, Milne, Inc.				9
10							10
11		6	Accounts Receivable	113	3 9 4 00		11
12			Sales	411		3 9 4 00	12
13			Invoice no. 322, Alvarez				13
14			Construction.				14

GENERAL LEDGER

ACCOUNT Accounts Receivable   ACCOUNT NO. 113

					BALANCE	
DATE	ITEM	POST. REF.	DEBIT	CREDIT	DEBIT	CREDIT
19–						
Aug. 1		23	5 8 0 92		5 8 0 92	
3		23	1 1 6 00		6 9 6 92	
6		23	3 9 4 00		1 0 9 0 92	

ACCOUNT Sales   ACCOUNT NO. 411

					BALANCE	
DATE	ITEM	POST. REF.	DEBIT	CREDIT	DEBIT	CREDIT
19–						
Aug. 1		23		5 8 0 92		5 8 0 92
3		23		1 1 6 00		6 9 6 92
6		23		3 9 4 00		1 0 9 0 92

The Sales Journal (Without Sales Tax)

The **sales journal** is used to record the sales of merchandise on account only. This specialized type of transaction results in a debit to Accounts Receivable and a credit to Sales. Let's look at Figure 5-4 to see how Dodson Plumbing Supply would record transactions in the sales journal instead of in the general journal.

Figure 5-4

	DATE		INV. NO.	CUSTOMER'S NAME	POST. REF.	ACCOUNTS RECEIVABLE DR., SALES CR.	
1	19–						1
2	Aug.	1	320	C. P. Landis Company		5 8 0 92	2
3		3	321	Milne, Inc.		1 1 6 00	3
4		6	322	Alvarez Construction		3 9 4 00	4
5							5

SALES JOURNAL　　　　PAGE __38__

REMEMBER

The sales journal is a book of original entry. It is not necessary to record the transaction in the general journal.

Because one special column is headed Accounts Receivable Dr./Sales Cr., each transaction requires only a single line. Repetition is avoided, and all entries for sales of merchandise on account are found in one place. Listing the invoice number makes it easier to check the details of a particular sale at a later date.

Posting from the Sales Journal

Using the sales journal also saves time and space in posting to the ledger accounts. Because every entry is a debit to Accounts Receivable and a credit to Sales, Dodson Plumbing Supply can make a single posting to these accounts for the amount of the total as of the last day of the month. This entry is called a **summarizing entry,** because it summarizes one month's transactions. Accountants refer to this as a summary posting. In the Post. Ref. columns of the ledger accounts, the letter S designates the sales journal. The transactions involving the sales of merchandise on account for the entire month of August are shown in Figure 5-5 on page 196.

After posting to the Accounts Receivable account, go back to the sales journal and record the account number in parentheses directly below the total. The account number for the account being debited (Accounts Receivable) goes on the left. The account number for the account being credited (Sales) goes on the right of the account number being debited. Don't record these account numbers until you have completed the postings.

If you should find an error, do not erase it. The same procedure for error correction described in Chapter 3 applies to special journals. If you catch the error in the journal entry before it is posted to the ledger, simply draw a single line through the error (with a ruler), write in the correct information, and add

Performance Objective 2

Post from a sales journal to a general ledger and an accounts receivable ledger.

your initials. If an amount is entered incorrectly in the ledger (although the journal entry is correct), follow the same procedure. However, if an entry included the incorrect accounts, then you must prepare a new journal entry correcting the first entry.

Figure 5-5

SALES JOURNAL   PAGE ___38___

	DATE	INV. NO.	CUSTOMER'S NAME	POST. REF.	ACCOUNTS RECEIVABLE DR., SALES CR.	
1	19–					1
2	Aug. 1	320	C. P. Landis Company		5 8 0 92	2
3	3	321	Milne, Inc.		1 1 6 00	3
4	6	322	Alvarez Construction		3 9 4 00	4
13	31	331	C. P. Landis Company		3 7 5 50	13
14	31	332	F. A. Barnes, Inc.		8 6 1 00	14
15	31				6 9 8 9 88	15
16					(113)(411)	16
17						17

GENERAL LEDGER

ACCOUNT __Accounts Receivable__   ACCOUNT NO. __113__

					BALANCE	
DATE	ITEM	POST. REF.	DEBIT	CREDIT	DEBIT	CREDIT
19–						
Aug. 31		S38	6 9 8 9 88		6 9 8 9 88	

ACCOUNT __Sales__   ACCOUNT NO. __411__

					BALANCE	
DATE	ITEM	POST. REF.	DEBIT	CREDIT	DEBIT	CREDIT
19–						
Aug. 31		S38		6 9 8 9 88		6 9 8 9 88

• • • • • • • • • • • •
R E M E M B E R

The purpose of posting reference numbers is to tell where in the ledger an amount was posted or the journal from which it came.
• • • • • • • • • • • • •

The Sales Journal (With Sales Tax)

Most states and some cities levy a **sales tax** on retail sales of goods and services. The retailer collects the sales tax from customers and later pays it to the tax authorities.

When goods or services are sold on credit, the sales tax is charged to the customer and recorded at the time of the sale. To handle this type of transaction, the sales journal includes a Sales Tax Payable column. Later, when the sales tax is paid to the government, the accountant debits Sales Tax Payable and credits Cash.

Right now, because we want to illustrate a sales journal for a retail merchandising firm operating in a state having a sales tax, we will talk about the transactions of Angel Toy Center. Its sales journal is presented in Figure 5-6.

Figure 5-6

SALES JOURNAL   PAGE 96

	DATE	INV. NO.	CUSTOMER'S NAME	POST. REF.	ACCOUNTS RECEIVABLE DEBIT	SALES TAX PAYABLE CREDIT	SALES CREDIT	
1	19–							1
2	Apr. 1	9382	B. A. Bates		1 6 64	64	1 6 00	2
3	1	9383	Mary's Day					3
4			Care		2 2 88	88	2 2 00	4
5	1	9384	Paula Dunn		5 2 00	2 00	5 0 00	5
6	2	9385	B. E. Kunz		1 2 48	48	1 2 00	6
18	30	10121	S. T. Lucero		1 2 4 80	4 80	1 2 0 00	18
19	30				2 5 1 6 80	9 6 80	2 4 2 0 00	19
20					(1 1 3)	(2 2 5)	(4 1 1)	20
21								21

Each column total is posted to the appropriate ledger account as a total at the end of the month. After posting the figures, the accountant records the account numbers in parentheses immediately below the totals. Note that Angel Toy Center's charge customers owe the total amount of the sales plus the sales tax, $2,516.80 ($2,420 + $96.80 = $2,516.80).

GENERAL LEDGER

ACCOUNT Accounts Receivable   ACCOUNT NO. 113

						BALANCE	
DATE	ITEM	POST. REF.	DEBIT	CREDIT	DEBIT	CREDIT
19–						
Apr. 30		S96	2 5 1 6 80		2 5 1 6 80	

REMEMBER

With a sales journal having more than one column, use the column totals to prove that the total debits equal the total credits. Do this before posting to the general ledger accounts.

ACCOUNT __Sales Tax Payable__ ACCOUNT NO. __225__

DATE	ITEM	POST. REF.	DEBIT	CREDIT	BALANCE DEBIT	BALANCE CREDIT
19–						
Apr. 30		S96		9 6 80		9 6 80

ACCOUNT __Sales__ ACCOUNT NO. __411__

DATE	ITEM	POST. REF.	DEBIT	CREDIT	BALANCE DEBIT	BALANCE CREDIT
19–						
Apr. 30		S96		2 4 2 0 00		2 4 2 0 00

The Accounts Receivable Ledger

As we have seen, Accounts Receivable represents the total amount owed to a business by its charge customers. This account, however, fails to provide a business with one essential piece of information. The business can't tell from the totals in the Accounts Receivable account how much each individual charge customer owes. Businesses thus keep a separate account for each charge customer.

When a business has only a few charge customers, it is possible to have a separate Accounts Receivable account in the general ledger for each charge customer. However, when there are more than a few charge customers, this arrangement is too awkward.

It is more practical to have a separate book (or computer file) containing a list of all the charge customers with their balances. This is called the **accounts receivable ledger**. In the accounts receivable ledger, the individual charge customer accounts can be listed in alphabetical order and/or assigned an account number. If the company is not computerized, accountants prefer a loose-leaf binder, so that they can insert accounts for new customers and remove accounts that have been closed.

The Accounts Receivable account must still be maintained in the general ledger. When all the postings are up to date, the balance of this account should equal the total of the individual balances of the charge customers. The Accounts Receivable account in the general ledger is called a **controlling account**. The accounts receivable ledger is really a special ledger, called a **subsidiary ledger**. Figure 5-7 diagrams the connection between the general ledger and the accounts receivable ledger.

Figure 5-7

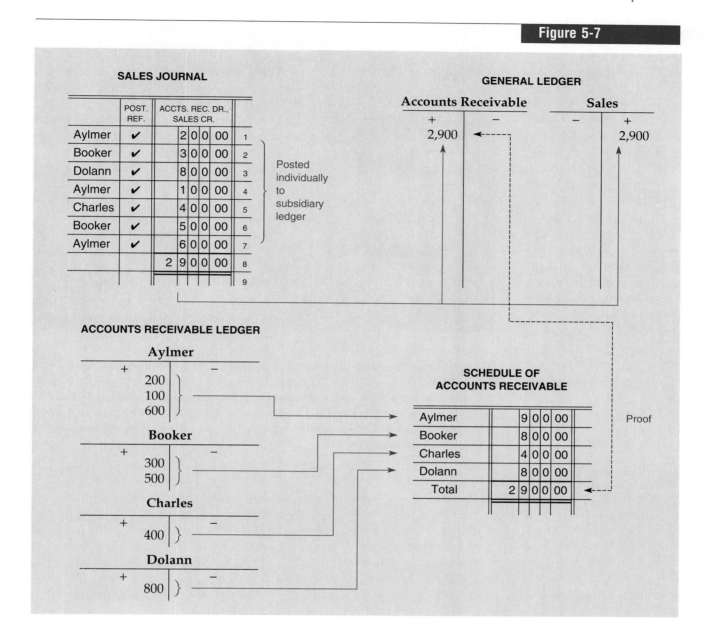

The accountant posts the individual amounts to the accounts receivable ledger every day. As a result, this ledger will have up-to-date information for use within the business or for outside inquiries. At the end of the month, the accountant posts the total of the sales journal (in Figure 5-7, $2,900) to the general ledger accounts as a debit to the Accounts Receivable controlling account and a credit to the Sales account. As indicated in Figure 5-7, the balance of the Accounts Receivable controlling account at the end of the month must equal the total of the balances of the charge customer accounts in the accounts receivable ledger. The **schedule of accounts receivable** is a listing of charge customers' individual balances.

Because no payments were received from charge customers in our simplified illustration, the total of the sales journal equals the balance of Accounts Receivable. This is not the normal situation. For example, if $1,200 had been received from charge customers, the balance of both the Accounts Receivable

Hand-held scanners are used to "read" the price tag or bar code on a product, simultaneously recording the sale and adjusting the inventory.

controlling account and the total of the schedule of accounts receivable would be $1,700 ($2,900 − $1,200). The total of the sales journal would still be $2,900.

After you post the amount from the sales journal to a charge customer's account in the accounts receivable ledger, put a check mark (√) in the Post. Ref. column of the sales journal. Figure 5-8 shows the posting procedure for a single-column sales journal.

Figure 5-8

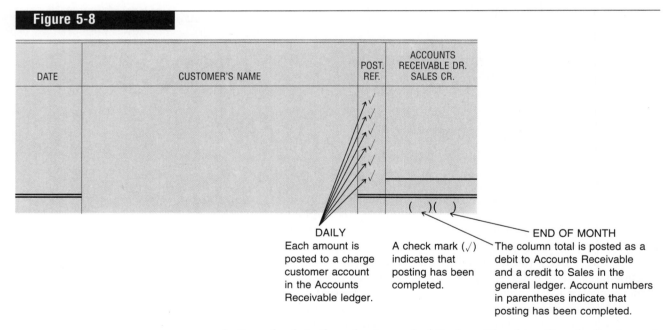

DATE	CUSTOMER'S NAME	POST. REF.	ACCOUNTS RECEIVABLE DR. SALES CR.

DAILY
Each amount is posted to a charge customer account in the Accounts Receivable ledger.

A check mark (√) indicates that posting has been completed.

END OF MONTH
The column total is posted as a debit to Accounts Receivable and a credit to Sales in the general ledger. Account numbers in parentheses indicate that posting has been completed.

Let's go back to the sales journal of Dodson Plumbing Supply for August. We will cover the daily postings that its accountant has made to the accounts receivable ledger. Then we'll see the schedule of accounts receivable. These entries are shown in Figure 5-9 in the sales journal and the ledger accounts that follow. Note that the ruling consists of a single line under the amount column and double lines extended through the Date, Post. Ref., and Amount columns. The last day of the month is recorded on the same line as the total.

Figure 5-9

SALES JOURNAL   PAGE ___38___

	DATE	INV. NO.	CUSTOMER'S NAME	POST. REF.	ACCOUNTS RECEIVABLE DR., SALES CR.	
1	19–					1
2	Aug. 1	320	C. P. Landis Company	√	5 8 0 92	2
3	3	321	Milne, Inc.	√	1 1 6 00	3
4	6	322	Alvarez Construction	√	3 9 4 00	4
5	9	323	Mitchell Service Company	√	9 6 1 00	5
6	11	324	Cozart Hardware	√	7 7 2 24	6
7	16	325	Hewitt and Sons, Inc.	√	4 4 1 00	7
8	20	326	Hazen Plumbing and Heating	√	7 1 0 00	8
9	23	327	Barlow Building Supplies	√	3 8 4 00	9
10	24	328	Cozart Hardware	√	2 9 3 22	10
11	28	329	Hewitt and Sons, Inc.	√	4 8 7 00	11
12	30	330	Barlow Building Supplies	√	6 1 4 00	12
13	31	331	C. P. Landis Company	√	3 7 5 50	13
14	31	332	F. A. Barnes, Inc.	√	8 6 1 00	14
15	31				6 9 8 9 88	15
16					(113)(411)	16
17						17

ACCOUNTS RECEIVABLE LEDGER

NAME ___Alvarez Construction___
ADDRESS ___3680 Paseo Avenue___
___San Diego, CA 92103___

DATE	ITEM	POST. REF.	DEBIT	CREDIT	BALANCE
19–					
Aug. 6		S38	3 9 4 00		3 9 4 00

NAME ___Barlow Building Supplies___
ADDRESS ___2242 Mission Avenue___
___San Diego, CA 92103___

DATE	ITEM	POST. REF.	DEBIT	CREDIT	BALANCE
19–					
Aug. 23		S38	3 8 4 00		3 8 4 00
30		S38	6 1 4 00		9 9 8 00

Figure 5-9 (cont.)

NAME _____ F. A. Barnes, Inc.
ADDRESS _____ 424 Fifteenth Street
San Diego, CA 92104

DATE		ITEM	POST. REF.	DEBIT	CREDIT	BALANCE
19–						
Aug.	31		S38	8 6 1 00		8 6 1 00

NAME _____ Cozart Hardware
ADDRESS _____ 2168 Tenth Street
San Diego, CA 92103

DATE		ITEM	POST. REF.	DEBIT	CREDIT	BALANCE
19–						
Aug.	11		S38	7 7 2 24		7 7 2 24
	24		S38	2 9 3 22		1 0 6 5 46

NAME _____ Hazen Plumbing and Heating
ADDRESS _____ 1620 Salazar Road
San Diego, CA 92105

DATE		ITEM	POST. REF.	DEBIT	CREDIT	BALANCE
19–						
Aug.	20		S38	7 1 0 00		7 1 0 00

NAME _____ Hewitt and Sons, Inc.
ADDRESS _____ 4142 Lucientes Avenue
San Diego, CA 92105

DATE		ITEM	POST. REF.	DEBIT	CREDIT	BALANCE
19–						
Aug.	16		S38	4 4 1 00		4 4 1 00
	28		S38	4 8 7 00		9 2 8 00

Figure 5-9 (cont.)

NAME _____ C. P. Landis Company
ADDRESS _____ 5210 Gilman Avenue
_____ San Diego, CA 92102

DATE		ITEM	POST. REF.	DEBIT	CREDIT	BALANCE
19–						
Aug.	1		S38	5 8 0 92		5 8 0 92
	31		S38	3 7 5 50		9 5 6 42

NAME _____ Milne, Inc.
ADDRESS _____ 1457 Megler Avenue
_____ San Diego, CA 92103

DATE		ITEM	POST. REF.	DEBIT	CREDIT	BALANCE
19–						
Aug.	3		S38	1 1 6 00		1 1 6 00

NAME _____ Mitchell Service Company
ADDRESS _____ 5196 Eighteenth Street
_____ San Diego, CA 92104

DATE		ITEM	POST. REF.	DEBIT	CREDIT	BALANCE
19–						
Aug.	9		S38	9 6 1 00		9 6 1 00

Assuming that these were the only transactions involving charge customers, the accountant prepares a schedule of accounts receivable, listing the balance of each charge customer.

Performance Objective 3

Prepare a schedule of accounts receivable.

Dodson Plumbing Supply
Schedule of Accounts Receivable
August 31, 19–

Alvarez Construction	$	3 9 4 00
Barlow Building Supplies		9 9 8 00
F. A. Barnes, Inc.		8 6 1 00
Cozart Hardware		1 0 6 5 46
Hazen Plumbing and Heating		7 1 0 00
Hewitt and Sons, Inc.		9 2 8 00
C. P. Landis Company		9 5 6 42
Milne, Inc.		1 1 6 00
Mitchell Service Company		9 6 1 00
Total Accounts Receivable	$6	9 8 9 88

Again we assume that there were no previous balances in the customers' accounts. Under this circumstance, the Accounts Receivable controlling account in the general ledger will have the same balance, $6,989.88, as the schedule of accounts receivable.

GENERAL LEDGER

ACCOUNT __Accounts Receivable__   ACCOUNT NO. __113__

| | | | | | | | | BALANCE | |
DATE	ITEM	POST. REF.	DEBIT		CREDIT		DEBIT		CREDIT
19–									
Aug. 31		S38	6 9 8 9 88				6 9 8 9 88		

Sales Returns and Allowances

Performance Objective 4

Record and post sales returns and allowances and sales returns and allowances involving sales tax to the ledger accounts.

The Sales Returns and Allowances account handles two types of transactions having to do with merchandise that has previously been sold. A *return* is a physical return of the goods. An *allowance* is a reduction from the original price because the goods were defective or damaged. It may not be economically worthwhile to have customers return the goods; each situation is a special case. To avoid writing a separate letter each time to inform customers of their account adjustments, businesses use a special form called a **credit memorandum**. A credit memorandum, as shown in Figure 5-10, is a written statement indicating a seller's willingness to reduce the amount of a buyer's debt.

Figure 5-10

DODSON PLUMBING SUPPLY
1400 Jackson Avenue • San Diego, CA • 92102

No.
69

CREDIT MEMORANDUM

Credit to: Barlow Building Supplies   **Date:**   September 2, 19—
2242 Mission Avenue
San Diego, CA 92103

WE CREDIT YOUR ACCOUNT AS FOLLOWS:

Quantity	Description	Total
1	Olin pop-up tub drain, antique finish 1½-inch brass overflow tube #46C72	54.00

The Sales Returns and Allowances account is considered to be a deduction from Sales. Using an account separate from Sales provides a better record of the total returns and allowances. Accountants deduct Sales Returns and Allowances from Sales in the income statement, as we will see later.

Using T accounts, here's an example of a return. The original sale is shown first and is followed by the issuance of a credit memorandum.

Transaction (a) On August 30, Dodson Plumbing Supply sold merchandise on account to Barlow Building Supplies, $614, and recorded the sale in the sales journal.

Transaction (b) On September 2, Barlow Building Supplies returned $54 worth of the merchandise. Dodson Plumbing Supply issued credit memorandum no. 69 (see Figure 5-10).

Assets	=	Liabilities	+	Owner's Equity	+	Revenue	−	Expenses
+ | −		− | +		− | +		− | +		+ | −
Debit | Credit		Debit | Credit		Debit | Credit		Debit | Credit		Debit | Credit

Accounts Receivable

+	−
(a) 614	**(b)** 54

Sales

−	+
	(a) 614

Sales Returns and Allowances

+	−
(b) 54	

Dodson Plumbing Supply's accountant debits Sales Returns and Allowances, because Dodson Plumbing has more returns and allowances than it had before. The accountant credits Accounts Receivable because the charge customer, Barlow Building Supplies, owes less than before. One uses the word *credit* in "credit memorandum" because the seller has to credit Accounts Receivable.

The general journal is used because these returns do not belong in the sales journal. Remember, the sales journal is for sales on account only—not for sales returns and allowances. If the balance of the Accounts Receivable controlling account is to equal the total of the individual balances in the accounts receivable ledger, one must post to both the Accounts Receivable controlling account in the general ledger and the account of Barlow Building Supplies in the accounts receivable ledger. To accomplish this dual posting, draw a line from the lower left corner to the upper right corner of the square in the Post. Ref. column. When the amount has been posted as a credit to the general ledger account, write the account number of Accounts Receivable (controlling account) in the upper part of the Post. Ref. column. After the account of Barlow Building Supplies has been posted as a credit, put a check mark in the lower portion of the Post. Ref. column. Sales Returns and Allowances is posted to the general ledger in the usual manner. Figure 5-11 shows the entries after posting is complete.

R E M E M B E R

Since Sales Returns and Allowances is a deduction from Sales, the plus and minus signs are reversed.

R E M E M B E R

When a credit memo is issued, it means we have given the customer permission to return the goods or receive an allowance.

Figure 5-11

GENERAL JOURNAL
PAGE __27__

	DATE		DESCRIPTION	POST. REF.	DEBIT	CREDIT	
1	19–						1
2	Sept.	2	Sales Returns and Allowances	412	5 4 00		2
3			Accounts Receivable, Barlow				3
4			Building Supplies	113 ✓		5 4 00	4
5			Issued credit memo no. 69.				5
6							6
7		2	Sales Returns and Allowances	412	1 2 7 00		7
8			Accounts Receivable, Mitchell				8
9			Service Company	113 ✓		1 2 7 00	9
10			Issued credit memo no. 70.				10

GENERAL LEDGER

ACCOUNT __Accounts Receivable__   ACCOUNT NO. __113__

DATE		ITEM	POST. REF.	DEBIT	CREDIT	BALANCE DEBIT	BALANCE CREDIT
19–							
Aug.	31		S38	6 9 8 9 88		6 9 8 9 88	
Sept.	2		J27		5 4 00	6 9 3 5 88	
	2		J27		1 2 7 00	6 8 0 8 88	

ACCOUNT __Sales Returns and Allowances__   ACCOUNT NO. __412__

DATE		ITEM	POST. REF.	DEBIT	CREDIT	BALANCE DEBIT	BALANCE CREDIT
19–							
Sept.	2		J27	5 4 00		5 4 00	
	2		J27	1 2 7 00		1 8 1 00	

ACCOUNTS RECEIVABLE LEDGER

NAME __Barlow Building Supplies__
ADDRESS __2242 Mission Avenue__
__San Diego, CA 92103__

DATE		ITEM	POST. REF.	DEBIT	CREDIT	BALANCE
19–						
Aug.	23		S38	3 8 4 00		3 8 4 00
	30		S38	6 1 4 00		9 9 8 00
Sept.	2		J27		5 4 00	9 4 4 00

NAME _____ Mitchell Service Company

ADDRESS _____ 5196 Eighteenth Street

San Diego, CA 92104

DATE		ITEM	POST. REF.	DEBIT	CREDIT	BALANCE
19–						
Aug.	9		S38	9 6 1 00		9 6 1 00
Sept.	2		J27		1 2 7 00	8 3 4 00

Sales Return Involving a Sales Tax

If a customer who returns merchandise to a retail store was originally charged sales tax, the sales tax must be returned to the customer. To illustrate, first refer to the sales journal of Angel Toy Center (Figure 5-6 on page 197), which has a column for recording the sales taxes collected. On April 3, assume that B. A. Bates returns the merchandise bought on April 1 for $16 plus $.64 sales tax. Angel Toy Center no longer owes the $.64 sales tax to the revenue department, sales have been reduced by $16, and Bates' individual account is reduced by $16.64.

GENERAL JOURNAL   PAGE ____12____

	DATE		DESCRIPTION	POST. REF.	DEBIT	CREDIT	
1	19–						1
2	Apr.	3	Sales Returns and Allowances		1 6 00		2
3			Sales Tax Payable		64		3
4			Accounts Receivable, B. A. Bates			1 6 64	4
5			Issued credit memo no. 371.				5
6							6
7							7

Procedure for Locating Errors

Suppose you are facing a situation where the total of the schedule of accounts receivable does not equal the balance of the Accounts Receivable controlling account. As we stated before, to locate possible errors, do everything in reverse. Here is a suggested order:

1. Re-add the schedule of accounts receivable.

2. Check the balances transferred from the customer accounts in the accounts receivable ledger to the schedule of accounts receivable.

3. Verify the postings from the sales and general journals to the Accounts Receivable controlling account.

4. Re-add the sales journal.

5. Verify the balances of the customer accounts in the accounts receivable ledger.

6. Check the postings from the sales and general journals to the customer accounts in the accounts receivable ledger.

Posting Directly from Sales Invoices (An Alternative to Using a Sales Journal)

Performance Objective 5

Post directly from sales invoices to an accounts receivable ledger, and journalize and post a summarizing entry in the general journal.

Companies that have a large volume of sales on account sometimes use duplicate copies of their sales invoices as a sales journal. The accountant posts daily to the charge customer accounts in the accounts receivable ledger, working directly from the duplicate copies of the sales invoices or sales slips. He or she writes the invoice number rather than the journal page in the Posting Reference column of the customer's account. A file is maintained for the copies of the sales invoices. Then, at the end of the month, the accountant brings the Accounts Receivable controlling account up to date by totaling all the sales invoices for the month and then making a general journal entry debiting Accounts Receivable and crediting Sales.

Let's use a different firm to show how this procedure works. Dawson Sports Equipment Company posts directly from its sales invoices; the total of its sales invoices for December is $37,426. Its accountant journalizes and posts the entry as follows:

GENERAL JOURNAL PAGE 36

	DATE		DESCRIPTION	POST. REF.	DEBIT	CREDIT	
1	19–						1
2	Dec.	31	Accounts Receivable	121	37 4 2 6 00		2
3			Sales	411		37 4 2 6 00	3
4			Summarizing entry for the total				4
5			of the sales invoices for the				5
6			month.				6
7							7

GENERAL LEDGER

ACCOUNT Accounts Receivable   ACCOUNT NO. 113

DATE		ITEM	POST. REF.	DEBIT	CREDIT	BALANCE DEBIT	BALANCE CREDIT
19–							
Dec.	31		J36	37 4 2 6 00		37 4 2 6 00	

"X" Marks the Spot: Geographic Information Systems Turn Databases into Marketing Treasure Maps

A quick quiz: name one piece of software that will tell you where to find your current customers, where to find new customers, how to cut marketing costs, and how to boost sales.

Give yourself five points for answering **geographic information system.** Geographic information systems, or GIS, combine the power of computerized maps with databases to let users literally see their data.

In a typical GIS application, the owner of a boutique feeds information from a customer database into a GIS, which plots each customer's address as a point on a map. The retailer then overlays color-coded Census data on the map to see a demographic profile of customers' neighborhoods including factors like household income. The boutique can use the GIS to find other neighborhoods with similar demographics and reach them with target marketing tools such as direct mail and billboards. . . .

Traditional beneficiaries of GIS include the Environmental Protection Agency, which uses GIS to find and keep track of hazardous waste sites. During last summer's Midwest floods, federal relief agencies superimposed satellite images on top of GIS maps to direct relief efforts. In the corporate world, GIS is used for everything from plotting utility lines to choosing sites for fast-food restaurants.

Recent advances in IBM-compatible PCs have put GIS within the reach of small and mid-sized companies. . . .

Assigning sales territories and market areas is one of the principal uses of desktop GIS. Say, for example, that you want to divide a market area equally among your sales force. With a desktop GIS, you can plot all of your current and potential customers on a map. Using links to the database, you could then find out how many customers/ prospects are located in each ZIP code, Census tract, city, county, or other geographic area.

Source: Excerpted from *PC Today*, January 1994, pp. 16–17.

ACCOUNT ___Sales___ ACCOUNT NO. __411__

DATE		ITEM	POST. REF.	DEBIT	CREDIT	BALANCE	
						DEBIT	CREDIT
19–							
Dec.	31		J36		37 4 2 6 00		37 4 2 6 00

The above journal entry can be recognized as a *summarizing entry*, because it summarizes the credit sales for one month. Because the company's accountant posts the entry to the accounts in the general ledger, there is no need for a sales journal; the one summarizing entry in the general journal records the total sales for the month.

Figure 5-12 shows an invoice and the corresponding entry in the accounts receivable ledger for Dawson Sports Equipment Company. The $855 would be posted to the general ledger as a part of the total comprising the monthly summarizing entry.

Figure 5-12

DAWSON SPORTS EQUIPMENT COMPANY
1620 Santa Maria Avenue • San Francisco, CA • 94133

INVOICE

Invoice No.
6075

Sold to: Guzman Sporting Goods
225 N.W. Satsop Avenue
Portland, OR 97201

Shipped by: Express Collect

Customer's Order Number	Salesperson	Terms	F.O.B.	Date
359	N. D.	2/10,n/30		Dec. 4, 19—

Quantity	Description	Unit Price	Total
10	Fentris cartop bicycle carrier No. 561N	85.50	855.00

ACCOUNTS RECEIVABLE LEDGER

NAME __Guzman Sporting Goods__
ADDRESS __225 N.W. Satsop Ave.__
__Portland, OR 97201__

DATE	ITEM	POST. REF.	DEBIT	CREDIT	BALANCE
19—					
Dec. 4		6075	8 5 5 00		8 5 5 00

We have seen that using a sales journal enables an accountant to journalize and post transactions involving the sale of merchandise on account very efficiently. The cash receipts journal further illustrates the advantages of using special journals.

The Cash Receipts Journal

The **cash receipts journal** contains all transactions in which Cash is debited. It may be used for a service as well as a merchandising business. To get acquainted with the cash receipts journal, let's list some typical transactions of a retail merchandising business that result in an increase in cash. To get a better picture of the transactions, let's record them initially in T accounts.

Performance Objective 6

Record transactions for a retail merchandising business in a cash receipts journal.

May   3 Sold merchandise for cash, $100, plus $4 sales tax.

Cash		Sales		Sales Tax Payable	
+	−	−	+	−	+
104			100		4

May   4 Sold merchandise, $100, plus $4 sales tax, and the customer used a **bank charge card.** Millions of people use these cards every day. The bank issuing the card bills the customer directly each month. The business, on the other hand, deposits the bank credit card receipts every day. The bank *deducts a discount* and credits the firm's account with cash. This discount is usually between 4 and 6 percent of the total of sales plus sales tax. We will assume the discount is 4 percent. The firm therefore records the amount of the discount under Credit Card Expense. (From the amount that would ordinarily be debited to Cash, deduct the bank charge, consisting of 4 percent of the total of sales plus sales tax, and debit this amount to Credit Card Expense instead of to Cash: $104 × .04 = $4.16 credit card expense; $100 + $4 − $4.16 = $99.84.)

Cash		Credit Card Expense		Sales		Sales Tax Payable	
+	−	+	−	−	+	−	+
99.84		4.16			100		4

May   5 Collected cash on account from C. P. Ray, a charge customer, $208.

Cash		Accounts Receivable	
+	−	+	−
208			208

May   7 The owner, N. D. Cole, invested cash in the business, $3,000.

Cash		N. D. Cole, Capital	
+	−	−	+
3,000			3,000

May   8 Sold Equipment for cash at cost, $150.

Cash		Equipment	
+	−	+	−
150			150

The same transactions are shown in general journal form in Figure 5-13.

Figure 5-13

GENERAL JOURNAL   PAGE _____

	DATE		DESCRIPTION	POST. REF.	DEBIT	CREDIT	
1	19–						1
2	May	3	Cash		1 0 4 00		2
3			Sales			1 0 0 00	3
4			Sales Tax Payable			4 00	4
5			Sold merchandise for cash.				5
6							6
7		4	Cash		9 9 84		7
8			Credit Card Expense		4 16		8
9			Sales			1 0 0 00	9
10			Sales Tax Payable			4 00	10
11			Sold merchandise involving				11
12			a bank charge card.				12
13							13
14		5	Cash		2 0 8 00		14
15			Accounts Receivable, C. P. Ray			2 0 8 00	15
16			Collected cash on account.				16
17							17
18		7	Cash		3 0 0 0 00		18
19			N. D. Cole, Capital			3 0 0 0 00	19
20			Owner invested cash.				20
21							21
22		8	Cash		1 5 0 00		22
23			Equipment			1 5 0 00	23
24			Sold equipment at cost.				24
25							25
26							26
27							27
28							28

Now let's appraise these five transactions: The first three would occur frequently; the last two could conceivably take place, but they would be less frequent. If one is designing a cash receipts journal, it is logical to include a Cash Debit column, because all the transactions involve an increase in cash. If a business regularly collects cash from charge customers, there should be an Accounts Receivable Credit column. If a firm often sells merchandise for cash and collects a sales tax, there should be a Sales Credit column and a Sales Tax Payable Credit column. If the business honors bank charge cards and wants to record the amount on a timely basis, there should be a Credit Card Expense Debit column to take care of the amount deducted by the bank.

However, the credit to N. D. Cole, Capital, and the credit to Equipment occur very seldom, so it would not be practical to set up special columns for these credits. They can be handled adequately by an Other Accounts Credit column, which can be used for credits to all accounts that have no special column.

As an alternative, many firms postpone recording the amount of bank credit card expense until they actually receive notification by their bank on their bank statement. For example, total credit card sales for a restaurant for a time period amount to $1,600 plus 4 percent sales tax. The entry is

Cash		Sales		Sales Tax Payable	
+	−	−	+	−	+
1,664			1,600		64

The restaurant's next bank statement includes a debit memorandum for credit card charges of $66.56, using an assumed 4 percent discount rate ($1,664 × .04). The firm handles this in a similar manner to a check service charge:

Credit Card Expense		Cash	
+	−	+	−
66.56			66.56

Now let's return to the transactions described previously and record them in a cash receipts journal (see Figure 5-14 on page 214). First, we will repeat the transactions:

May 3 Sold merchandise for cash, $100, plus $4 sales tax.
   4 Sold merchandise, $100, plus $4 sales tax, and the customer used a bank charge card. Discount charged by the bank is 4 percent of the amount of the total of sales plus sales tax.
   5 Collected cash on account from C. P. Ray, a charge customer, $208.
   7 The owner, N. D. Cole, invested cash in the business, $3,000.
   8 Sold equipment for cash at cost, $150.

REMEMBER
The amount of credit card expense is based on the total of sales *plus* sales tax payable.

Figure 5-14

	DATE		ACCOUNT CREDITED	POST. REF.	OTHER ACCOUNTS CREDIT	ACCOUNTS RECEIVABLE CREDIT	SALES CREDIT	SALES TAX PAYABLE CREDIT	CREDIT CARD EXPENSE DEBIT	CASH DEBIT	
1	19–										1
2	May	3	———				1 0 0 00	4 00		1 0 4 00	2
3		4	———				1 0 0 00	4 00	4 16	9 9 84	3
4		5	C. P. Ray			2 0 8 00				2 0 8 00	4
5		7	N. D. Cole,								5
6			Capital		3 0 0 0 00					3 0 0 0 00	6
7		8	Equipment		1 5 0 00					1 5 0 00	7
8											8

CASH RECEIPTS JOURNAL — PAGE 41

Performance Objective 7

Post from a cash receipts journal to a general ledger and an accounts receivable ledger.

Posting from the Cash Receipts Journal

Here are some other transactions made during the month that involve increases in cash. (Remember that these transactions are for a retail business.)

May 11 Borrowed $300 from the bank, receiving cash and giving the bank a promissory note.

16 Sold merchandise for cash, $200, plus $8 sales tax.

21 Sold merchandise for cash, $50, plus $2 sales tax; customer used a bank charge card. Credit card expense charge is 4 percent of sales plus tax.

26 Collected cash from L. Romero, a charge customer, on account, $62.40.

28 Sold merchandise for cash, $40, plus $1.60 sales tax.

31 Sold merchandise for cash, $150, plus $6 sales tax; customer used a bank charge card. Credit card expense charge is 4 percent of sales plus tax.

31 Collected cash from T. Henson, a charge customer, on account, $26.

In the transaction of May 11, in which $300 was borrowed from the bank, the bank was given a promissory note as evidence of the debt. The account Notes Payable, instead of Accounts Payable, is used to represent the amount owed on the promissory note (a written promise to pay at a specified time). The Accounts Payable account is reserved for charge accounts with creditors, which are normally paid on a thirty-day basis.

Let's assume that all the month's transactions involving debits to Cash have now been recorded in the cash receipts journal. The cash receipts journal (Figure 5-15) and the T accounts on the next page illustrate the postings to the general ledger and the accounts receivable ledger.

Figure 5-15

CASH RECEIPTS JOURNAL
PAGE 41

	DATE	ACCOUNT CREDITED	POST. REF.	OTHER ACCOUNTS CREDIT	ACCOUNTS RECEIVABLE CREDIT	SALES CREDIT	SALES TAX PAYABLE CREDIT	CREDIT CARD EXPENSE DEBIT	CASH DEBIT	
1	19—									1
2	May 3	——	—			100 00	4 00		104 00	2
3	4	——	—			100 00	4 00	4 16	99 84	3
4	5	C. P. Ray	✓		208 00				208 00	4
5	7	N. D. Cole,								5
6		Capital	311	3000 00					3000 00	6
7	8	Equipment	124	150 00					150 00	7
8	11	Notes								8
9		Payable	222	300 00					300 00	9
10	16	——	—			200 00	8 00		208 00	10
11	21	——	—			50 00	2 00	2 08	49 92	11
12	26	L. Romero	✓		62 40				62 40	12
13	28	——	—			40 00	1 60		41 60	13
14	31	——	—			150 00	6 00	6 24	149 76	14
15	31	T. Henson	✓		26 00				26 00	15
16	31			3450 00	296 40	640 00	25 60	12 48	4399 52	16
17				(X)	(113)	(411)	(225)	(534)	(111)	17

Accounts Receivable Ledger

T. Henson

+	−	
	May 31	26

L. Romero

+	−	
	May 26	62.40

C. P. Ray

+	−	
	May 5	208

General Ledger

Cash   111

+	−
May 4,399.52 31	

Accounts Receivable   113

+	−
	May 31 296.40

Equipment   124

+	−
	May 8 150

Sales Tax Payable   225

−	+
	May 31 25.60

Notes Payable   222

−	+
	May 11 300

N. D. Cole, Capital   311

−	+
	May 7 3,000

Sales   411

−	+
	May 31 640

Credit Card Expense   534

+	−
May 31 12.48	

Individual amounts in the Accounts Receivable Credit column of the cash receipts journal are usually posted daily. Individual amounts in the Other Accounts Credit column may also be posted daily. The Other Accounts column is used when none of the special columns can handle the transaction. If the same account appears frequently in the Other Accounts column, consider including the account as a special column heading in the future. Remember, one of the goals of special journals is to save time.

At the end of the month, we can post the special column totals in the cash receipts journal to the general ledger accounts. These columns include Accounts Receivable Credit, Sales Credit, Sales Tax Payable Credit, Credit Card Expense Debit, and Cash Debit.

In the Post. Ref. column, the check marks ($\sqrt{}$) indicate that the amounts in the Accounts Receivable Credit column have been posted to the individual charge customers' accounts as credits. The account numbers show that the amounts in the Other Accounts Credit column have been posted separately to the accounts described in the Account Credited column. An (X) goes under the total of the Other Accounts column, where it means "do not post—the figures have already been posted separately." This column is totaled only to make it easier to prove that the debits equal the credits.

Note the ruling. A single rule is placed above the column totals, and double rules extend through all but the Account Credited column. Also, on the last line, the last day of the month is recorded in the Date column.

Let's say it's the end of the month. Total the columns first. Then begin **crossfooting** the journal by proving that the sum of the debit totals equals the sum of the credit totals. This process must be done before one posts the totals to the general ledger accounts.

Debit Totals		Credit Totals	
Cash	$4,399.52	Other Accounts	$3,450.00
Credit Card Expense	12.48	Accounts Receivable	296.40
	$4,412.00	Sales	640.00
		Sales Tax Payable	25.60
			$4,412.00

Debits = Credits

Post the special column totals to the general ledger, using the letters *CR* as the posting reference. Next, write the general ledger account number in parentheses below the total in the appropriate column.

Private Credit Card Companies In regard to credit card sales, it should be mentioned that many firms also accept credit cards of private companies, such as American Express, Diners Club, and Carte Blanche. Transactions involving this type of credit card are treated as sales on account. For example, total revenue involving private companies' credit cards for a hotel over a given time period amounts to $900, plus 8 percent hotel tax. The entry is

Accounts Receivable		Hotel Tax Payable		Hotel Revenue	
+	−	−	+	−	+
972			72		900

Private credit card companies charge a fee or discount for their services. In this case, assume a discount rate of 6 percent ($972 × .06 = $58.32). When $913.68 ($972 − $58.32) is received from the credit card company, the entry is

Cash		Credit Card Expense		Accounts Receivable	
+	−	+	−	+	−
913.68		58.32			972

Credit Terms

Performance Objective 8

Calculate cash discounts according to credit terms, and record cash receipts from charge customers who are entitled to deduct the cash discount.

The seller always stipulates credit terms: How much credit can a customer be allowed? And how much time should the customer be given to pay the full amount? The **credit period** is the time the seller allows the buyer before full payment has to be made. Retailers generally allow twenty-five to thirty days.

Wholesalers and manufacturers often specify a **cash discount** in their credit terms. A cash discount is the amount a customer can deduct for paying a bill within a short time. The discount is based on the *total amount of the invoice after any returns and allowances and freight charges billed on the invoice have been deducted.* Naturally, this discount acts as an incentive for charge customers to pay their bills promptly.

Let's say that a wholesaler offers customers credit terms of 2/10, n/30. These terms mean that the customer gets a 2 percent discount if the bill is paid within ten days after the invoice date. The discount period begins the day after the invoice date. If the bill is not paid within the ten days, then the entire amount is due within thirty days after the invoice date. Other cash discounts that may be used are the following:

- **1/15, n/60**   The seller offers a 1 percent discount if the bill is paid within fifteen days after the invoice date or the whole bill must be paid within sixty days after the invoice date.
- **2/10, EOM, n/60**   The seller offers a 2 percent discount if the bill is paid within ten days after the end of the month, and the whole bill must be paid within sixty days after the last day of the month.

A wholesaler or manufacturer offering a cash discount adopts a single cash discount as a credit policy and makes this available to all its customers. The seller considers cash discounts as **sales discounts**; the buyer, on the other hand, considers a cash discount as a purchases discount. In this section we are concerned with the sales discount. *Recall that the Sales Discount account, like Sales Returns and Allowances, is a deduction from Sales.*

To illustrate, we return to Dodson Plumbing Supply. We will record the following transactions in T accounts.

Transaction (a)   August 1: Sold merchandise on account to C. P. Landis Company, invoice no. 320; terms 2/10, n/30; $580.92.

Transaction (b)   August 10: Received check from C. P. Landis Company for $569.30 in payment of invoice no. 320, less cash discount ($580.92 × .02 = $11.62; $580.92 − $11.62 = $569.30).

Assets		=	Liabilities		+	Owner's Equity		+	Revenue		−	Expenses	
+	−		−	+		−	+		−	+		+	−
Debit	Credit		Debit	Credit		Debit	Credit		Debit	Credit		Debit	Credit
Accounts Receivable									**Sales**				
									−	+			
+	−									(a) 580.92			
(a) 580.92	(b) 580.92												
Cash									**Sales Discount**				
+	−								+	−			
(b) 569.30									(b) 11.62				

Since Dodson Plumbing Supply offers this cash discount to all its customers, and since charge customers often pay their bills within the discount period, Dodson Plumbing sets up a Sales Discount Debit column in the cash receipts journal. Note that Dodson Plumbing Supply is a wholesaler. Therefore, a column for Sales Tax Payable is not used since few states levy a tax on sales at the wholesale level.

	DATE		ACCOUNT CREDITED	POST. REF.	OTHER ACCOUNTS CREDIT	ACCOUNTS RECEIVABLE CREDIT	SALES CREDIT	SALES DISCOUNT DEBIT	CASH DEBIT	
1	19–									1
2	Aug.	10	C. P. Landis Co.			5 8 0 92		1 1 62	5 6 9 30	2
3										3

CASH RECEIPTS JOURNAL — PAGE 18

Several other transactions of Dodson Plumbing Supply involve increases in cash during August. Remember that the standard credit terms for all charge customers are 2/10, n/30.

Aug. 15 Cash sales for first half of the month, $1,460.
16 Received check from Alvarez Construction for $386.12 in payment of invoice no. 322, less cash discount ($394.00 − $7.88 = $386.12).
17 Received payment on a promissory note given by John R. Bryant, $300 principal, plus $3 interest. (The amount of the interest is recorded in Interest Income.)
21 Received check from Cozart Hardware for $756.80 in payment of invoice no. 324, less cash discount ($772.24 − $15.44 = $756.80).
23 Sold equipment for cash at cost, $126.
26 L. E. Dodson, the owner, invested an additional $4,000 cash in the business.
26 Received a check from Hewitt and Sons, Inc., for $432.18 in payment of invoice no. 325, less the cash discount ($441.00 − $8.82 = $432.18).

31 Cash sales for second half of the month, $1,620.
31 Received check from Milne, Inc., in payment of invoice no. 321, for $116. (This is longer than the ten-day period, so they missed the cash discount.)

Dodson Plumbing records these transactions in its cash receipts journal (Figure 5-16 on the next page). After that has been done, the company's accountant proves the equality of debits and credits:

R E M E M B E R

When journalizing a cash receipt involving a sales discount, be sure to credit Accounts Receivable for the total amount of the sales transaction.

Debit Totals			**Credit Totals**	
Cash	$10,465.20		Other Accounts	$ 4,429.00
Sales Discount	57.96		Accounts Receivable	3,014.16
	$10,523.16		Sales	3,080.00
				$10,523.16

Debits = Credits

Figure 5-16

CASH RECEIPTS JOURNAL   PAGE ___18___

	DATE	ACCOUNT CREDITED	POST. REF.	OTHER ACCOUNTS CREDIT	ACCOUNTS RECEIVABLE CREDIT	SALES CREDIT	SALES DISCOUNT DEBIT	CASH DEBIT	
1	19–								1
2	Aug. 10	C. P. Landis Co.	✓		5 80 92		1 1 62	5 69 30	2
3	15	————————	—			1 4 60 00		1 4 60 00	3
4	16	Alvarez Construction	✓		3 94 00		7 88	3 86 12	4
5	17	Notes Receivable	112	3 00 00					5
6		Interest Income	451	3 00				3 03 00	6
7	21	Cozart Hardware	✓		7 72 24		1 5 44	7 56 80	7
8	23	Equipment	155	1 26 00				1 26 00	8
9	26	L. E. Dodson, Capital	311	4 00 00 00				4 00 00 00	9
10	26	Hewitt and Sons, Inc.	✓		4 41 00		8 82	4 32 18	10
11	30	Hazen Plumbing/Heat.	✓		7 10 00		1 4 20	6 95 80	11
12	31	————————	—			1 6 20 00		1 6 20 00	12
13	31	Milne, Inc.	✓		1 16 00			1 16 00	13
14	31			4 4 29 00	3 0 14 16	3 0 80 00	5 7 96	10 4 65 20	14
15				(X)	(1 1 3)	(4 1 1)	(4 1 3)	(1 1 1)	15

Sales Returns and Allowances and Sales Discount on an Income Statement

In the fundamental accounting equation, to be consistent with the income statement, we place Sales Returns and Allowances and Sales Discount under Sales with the plus and minus signs reversed. Both accounts are considered contra revenue accounts, and so we subtract their totals from Sales on the income statement. As an example, here is the Revenue from the Sales section of the annual income statement of Dodson Plumbing Supply, taken from the illustration in Chapter 7.

Dodson Plumbing Supply

Income Statement
For Year Ended December 31, 19–

Revenue from Sales:			
Sales		$ 195 1 80 00	
Less: Sales Returns and Allowances	$ 8 40 00		
Sales Discount	1 8 80 00	2 7 20 00	
Net Sales			$ 192 4 60 00

Accounting and the Computer

Commercial software programs frequently provide accounts receivable modules. This feature allows a business to integrate or link the general ledger with the accounts receivable ledger. This means that when a sale on account, a return of merchandise, or a customer's payment is entered into the program, it is posted not only to the customer's account but also to the general ledger. This is a major time-saving feature.

Sales and Receivables Journal

The sales and receivables journal in this software provides basically the same information as the sales journal shown earlier in Figure 5-5. The difference is the amount of time involved in preparing the manual sales journal over the computerized sales journal. The printout on page 221 shows the sales on account of Dodson Plumbing Supply entered into an accounting software program. Each entry required a minimum amount of keying: the day, the customer name, and the amount are entered once into the appropriate space or field on the screen. Had sales tax been levied or an immediate discount applied, the program would have computed the amounts and arrived at the amount due.

Card File (Schedule of Accounts Receivable)

FYI

Not all accounting programs post automatically. Some require the operator to prompt the posting after an entry or a group of entries.

FYI

Errors in entries will usually post as quickly as correct entries if debits equal credits. The good news is that you can make correcting entries which will also integrate.

Once transactions are entered in the sales journal, the amounts are posted to the accounts receivable ledger as well as to the general ledger. Furthermore, these entries also produced a schedule of accounts receivable called a Card File shown on page 222. This list of customers with their current balances is called a card file in this software because each customer has an electronic card. The card, which appears on the screen, contains information about the customer—address, telephone, contact person, and sales information. Software producers are continuing to try to make the screen more recognizable and friendly.

With the card file or schedule of accounts receivable, the bookkeeper or accountant can verify that the total of the schedule of accounts receivable is equal to the total of the general ledger control account. At this time, the billing statements can be prepared by computer and mailed to customers.

In these illustrations, we have emphasized sales on account. No payments have been made by customers. Therefore, the sales journal total also shows the same total as the schedule of accounts receivable.

```
                        Dodson Plumbing Supply
                          1400 Jackson Avenue
                          San Diego, CA 92102

                        Sales & Receivables Journal

                          8/1/9- to 8/31/9-
                                                              Page 1

 Src    Date     ID#              Account           Debit      Credit   Job

 SJ    8/1/9-    Sale; C. P. Landis Company
                 00000320   1-1130   Accounts Receivable   $580.92
                 00000320   4-4110   Sales                           $580.92

 SJ    8/3/9-    Sale; Milne, Inc.
                 00000321   1-1130   Accounts Receivable   $116.00
                 00000321   4-4110   Sales                           $116.00

 SJ    8/6/9-    Sale; Alvarez Construction
                 00000322   1-1130   Accounts Receivable   $394.00
                 00000322   4-4110   Sales                           $394.00

 SJ    8/9/9-    Sale; Mitchell Service Company
                 00000323   1-1130   Accounts Receivable   $961.00
                 00000323   4-4110   Sales                           $961.00

 SJ    8/11/9-   Sale; Cozart Hardware
                 00000324   1-1130   Accounts Receivable   $772.24
                 00000324   4-4110   Sales                           $772.24

 SJ    8/16/9-   Sale; Hewitt and Sons, Inc.
                 00000325   1-1130   Accounts Receivable   $441.00
                 00000325   4-4110   Sales                           $441.00

 SJ    8/20/9-   Sale; Hazen Plumbing and Heating
                 00000326   1-1130   Accounts Receivable   $710.00
                 00000326   4-4110   Sales                           $710.00

 SJ    8/23/9-   Sale; Barlow Building Supplies
                 00000327   1-1130   Accounts Receivable   $384.00
                 00000327   4-4110   Sales                           $384.00

 SJ    8/24/9-   Sale; Cozart Hardware
                 00000328   1-1130   Accounts Receivable   $293.22
                 00000328   4-4110   Sales                           $293.22

 SJ    8/28/9-   Sale; Hewitt and Sons, Inc.
                 00000329   1-1130   Accounts Receivable   $487.00
                 00000329   4-4110   Sales                           $487.00

 SJ    8/30/9-   Sale; Barlow Building Supplies
                 00000330   1-1130   Accounts Receivable   $614.00
                 00000330   4-4110   Sales                           $614.00

 SJ    8/31/9-   Sale; C. P. Landis Company
                 00000331   1-1130   Accounts Receivable   $375.50
                 00000331   4-4110   Sales                           $375.50

 SJ    8/31/9-   Sale; F. A. Barnes, Inc.
                 00000332   1-1130   Accounts Receivable   $861.00
                 00000332   4-4110   Sales                           $861.00

                                 Total:    $6,989.88    $6,989.88
```

Dodson Plumbing Supply
1400 Jackson Avenue
San Diego, CA 92102

Card File

8/1/9–   Page 1

Name	Phone	Type	Current Balance	Identifiers
Alvarez Construction		Customer	$394.00	
Barlow Building Supplies		Customer	$998.00	
C. P. Landis Company		Customer	$956.42	
Cozart Hardware		Customer	$1,065.46	
F. A. Barnes, Inc.		Customer	$861.00	
Hazen Plumbing and Heating		Customer	$710.00	
Hewitt and Sons, Inc.		Customer	$928.00	
Milne, Inc.		Customer	$116.00	
Mitchell Service Company		Customer	$961.00	
Total			$6,989.88	

Cash Receipts Journal

The cash receipts journal printed from this software looks different in format from the journal in Figure 5-16, but the same changes will occur in the general ledger and the accounts receivable ledger after posting. By now you may have become accustomed to the format of accounting program printouts. Notice the similarity between the input and the output, and that regardless of whether input and output is manual or electronic, you must know the rules and procedures of accounting.

Dodson Plumbing Supply
1400 Jackson Avenue
San Diego, CA 92102

Cash Receipts Journal

8/1/9– To 8/31/9–

Page 1

Src	Date	ID#		Account	Debit	Credit	Job
CR	8/10/9–	Payment; C. P. Landis Company					
		CR000000	1-1110	Cash	$569.30		
		CR000000	4-4130	Sales Discount	$11.62		
		CR000000	1-1130	Accounts Receivable		$580.92	
CR	8/15/9–						
		CR000006	1-1110	Cash	$1,460.00		
		CR000006	4-4110	Sales		$1,460.00	
CR	8/16/9–	Payment; Alvarez Construction					
		CR000001	1-1110	Cash	$386.12		
		CR000001	4-4130	Sales Discount	$7.88		
		CR000001	1-1130	Accounts Receivable		$394.00	
CR	8/17/9–						
		CR000007	1-1110	Cash	$303.00		
		CR000007	1-1120	Notes Receivable		$300.00	
		CR000007	4-4990	Interest Income		$3.00	

```
CR    8/21/9-   Payment; Cozart Hardware
                CR000002   1-1110   Cash                         $756.80
                CR000002   4-4130   Sales Discount                $15.44
                CR000002   1-1130   Accounts Receivable                           $772.24

CR    8/23/9-
                CR000008   1-1110   Cash                         $126.00
                CR000008   1-1240   Equipment                                     $126.00

CR    8/26/9-   Payment; Hewitt and Sons, Inc.
                CR000003   1-1110   Cash                         $432.18
                CR000003   4-4130   Sales Discount                 $8.82
                CR000003   1-1130   Accounts Receivable                           $441.00

CR    8/26/9-
                CR000009   1-1110   Cash                       $4,000.00
                CR000009   3-8000   L. E. Dodson, Capital                       $4,000.00

CR    8/30/9-   Payment; Hazen Plumbing and Heating
                CR000004   1-1110   Cash                         $695.80
                CR000004   4-4130   Sales Discount                $14.20
                CR000004   1-1130   Accounts Receivable                           $710.00

CR    8/31/9-   Payment; Milne, Inc.
                CR000005   1-1110   Cash                         $116.00
                CR000005   1-1130   Accounts Receivable                           $116.00

CR    8/31/9-
                CR000010   1-1110   Cash                       $1,620.00
                CR000010   4-4110   Sales                                       $1,620.00
```

CHAPTER REVIEW

R eview of Performance Objectives

1. **Record transactions in a sales journal.**

   The sales journal is used for recording sales of merchandise on account only. An entry can be recorded on one line. The date, invoice number, and customer's name are listed, as well as the amount of the invoice in the Accounts Receivable Dr./Sales Cr. column.

2. **Post from a sales journal to a general ledger and an accounts receivable ledger.**

   The entries are posted daily to the accounts receivable ledger. At the end of the month, the total is posted to the general ledger as a debit to the Accounts Receivable controlling account and a credit to the Sales account.

3. **Prepare a schedule of accounts receivable.**

   The schedule of accounts receivable consists of a listing of the individual balances of the charge customers taken from the accounts receivable ledger.

4. **Record and post sales returns and allowances and sales returns and allowances involving sales tax to the ledger accounts.**

   When a customer returns merchandise that he or she has bought, or when his or her bill is reduced to allow for defective or damaged merchandise, the Sales Returns and Allowances account is debited and the Accounts Receivable account is credited. The entry is recorded in the general journal and posted to both the general ledger and the accounts receivable ledger.

5. **Post directly from sales invoices to an accounts receivable ledger, and journalize and post a summarizing entry in the general journal.**

   Another shortcut uses sales invoices or sales slips as a sales journal, thereby doing away with the sales journal. One posts to the charge customer accounts in the accounts receivable ledger directly from the sales invoices. At the end of the month, one adds all the sales invoices and makes a summarizing entry in the general journal for the amount of the total. This entry is a debit to Accounts Receivable and a credit to Sales.

6. **Record transactions for a retail merchandising business in a cash receipts journal.**

   A transaction for a retail merchandising business can be recorded on one line in a cash receipts journal. The cash receipts journal contains the following columns: Date, Account Credited, Post. Ref., Other Accounts Credit, Accounts Receivable Credit, Sales Credit, Sales Tax Payable Credit, Credit Card Expense Debit, and Cash Debit.

7. **Post from a cash receipts journal to a general ledger and an accounts receivable ledger.**

   The accountant posts daily from the Accounts Receivable Credit column to the individual charge customers' accounts in the accounts receivable ledger. After posting, the accountant puts a check mark ($\checkmark$) in the Post. Ref. column. The accountant also posts the amounts in the Other Accounts Credit column daily. After these entries are posted, the account numbers are recorded in the Post. Ref. column. The special columns are posted as totals at the end of the month. After posting, the accountant writes the account numbers in parentheses under the totals. He or she writes an (X) below the total of the Other Accounts Credit column to show that amounts are posted individually and not the total.

8. **Calculate cash discounts according to credit terms, and record cash receipts from charge customers who are entitled to deduct the cash discount.**

   The same cash discount is available to all customers. The amount of the discount is determined by multiplying the invoice total (excluding freight charges and any returns and allowances) by the cash discount rate (usually 1 or 2 percent). The amount of the discount is recorded as a debit to Sales Discount.

G lossary

Accounts receivable ledger A subsidiary ledger that lists the individual accounts of charge customers in alphabetical order. **(198)**

Bank charge card A bank credit card, like the credit cards used by millions of private citizens. The cardholder pays what she or he owes directly to the issuing bank. The business firm deposits the credit card receipts; the amount of the deposit equals the total of the receipts, less a discount deducted by the bank. **(210)**

Cash discount The amount a customer can deduct for paying a bill within a specified period of time; usually to encourage prompt payment. Not all sellers offer cash discounts. **(217)**

Cash receipts journal A special journal used to record all transactions in which cash comes in, or increases. **(210)**

Controlling account An account in the general ledger that summarizes the balances of a subsidiary ledger. **(198)**

Credit memorandum A business form provided by the seller to a buyer who has either returned a purchase (or part of a purchase) for credit or been granted an allowance for damaged goods. **(204)**

Credit period The time the seller allows the buyer before full payment on a charge sale has to be made. **(217)**

Crossfooting Horizontal addition of column totals to prove that the total debits equal the total credits. **(216)**

Internal control Rules and procedures that a business follows to (1) protect assets against fraud and waste, (2) provide accurate accounting data, (3) promote an efficient operation, and (4) encourage adherence to management policies. **(190)**

Invoice A business form prepared by the seller that lists the items shipped, their cost, terms of the sale, and the mode of shipment. The buyer considers it a purchase invoice; the seller considers it a sales invoice. **(192)**

Merchandise Inventory A stock of goods that a company buys and intends to resell, in the same physical condition, at a profit. **(191)**

Sales A revenue account for recording the sale of merchandise. **(191)**

Sales Discount An account that records a deduction from the original price granted by the seller to the buyer for the prompt payment of an invoice. **(191)**

Sales journal A special journal for recording the sale of merchandise on account only. **(195)**

Sales Returns and Allowances The account a seller uses to record the physical return of merchandise by customers or a reduction in a bill because merchandise was damaged. Sales Returns and Allowances is treated as a deduction from Sales. This account is usually evidenced by a credit memorandum issued by the seller. **(191)**

Sales tax A tax levied by a state or city government on the retail sale of goods and services. The tax is paid by the consumer but collected by the retailer. **(197)**

Sales Tax Payable An account that identifies funds collected by the business and transmitted to tax authorities. **(191)**

Schedule of accounts receivable A listing of the balances of each customer shown in the accounts receivable ledger. **(199)**

Special journals Books of original entry in which one records specialized types of repetitive transactions. **(190)**

Subsidiary ledger A group of accounts representing individual subdivisions of a controlling account. **(198)**

Summarizing entry An entry made to post the column totals of the special journals to the appropriate accounts in the general ledger. It is also used when individual sales invoices are posted directly to the accounts receivable ledger. The summarizing entry represents the one entry made in the general journal to record the total sales on account for a period of time and posted to the general ledger. **(195)**

QUESTIONS, EXERCISES, AND PROBLEMS

D iscussion Questions

1. Describe the posting procedure from the sales journal to the accounts receivable ledger.
2. Why is an accounts receivable ledger necessary for a business with a large number of charge customers?
3. Why is it worthwhile to set up an account for sales returns and allowances, when one could just debit the Sales account for any transaction involving a return or an allowance?
4. What is the purpose of a schedule of accounts receivable?

5. Because of mistakes in adding the columns of a cash receipts journal, the totals of both the Accounts Receivable Credit column and the Cash Debit column were $100 too low. How will this error be discovered?
6. What are the normal balances of (a) Sales, (b) Sales Discount, and (c) Sales Returns and Allowances?
7. Explain the following credit terms: (a) n/30, (b) 2/10, n/60, (c) 1/15 EOM, n/30.
8. Briefly describe what is meant by integration in accounting software.

Exercises

P.O.1,2

Journalize to a sales journal; total, prove, and rule; and describe posting.

Exercise 5-1 Journalize the following two sales of merchandise on account on page 93 of the Sales Journal.

Oct. 22 Sold merchandise on account to D. Fleming, invoice no. 419, $576.40, plus a 5 percent sales tax.
31 Sold merchandise on account to D. Boyle, invoice no. 420, $1,626.00, plus a 5 percent sales tax.

Total, prove, and rule the sales journal. Describe how this sales journal would be posted to the general ledger and the accounts receivable ledger.

	DATE	INV. NO.	CUSTOMER'S NAME	POST. REF.	ACCOUNTS RECEIVABLE DEBIT	SALES TAX PAYABLE CREDIT	SALES CREDIT	
1	19–							1
2	Oct. 3	414	Andersal Co.		403 83	19 23	384 60	2
3	4	415	D. Fleming		723 45	34 45	689 00	3
4	7	416	Nortle Co.		1501 50	71 50	1430 00	4
5	11	417	D. Boyle		762 85	36 33	726 52	5
6	16	418	C. T. Oscar		726 18	34 58	691 60	6
7								7
8								8
9								9
10								10
11								11

SALES JOURNAL — PAGE 93

P.O.2

Post sales on account to general and accounts receivable ledgers.

Exercise 5-2 Post the individual amounts and the column totals from the completed Exercise 5-1 to the general ledger, accounts receivable ledger, and T accounts below.

Accounts Receivable 121	Sales Tax Payable 213	Sales 411
+ −	− +	− +

Andersal Co.	D. Boyle	D. Fleming	Nortle Co.	C. T. Oscar
+ −	+ −	+ −	+ −	+ −

Exercise 5-3 Record the following transactions in a general journal for Masters Company:

Oct. 10 Hale Company returned $420 of merchandise (wrong color) previously purchased on account. Issued credit memo no. 104. Hale's original purchase was for $2,460.

17 Franco Company returned $370 of defective merchandise previously purchased on account. Issued credit memo no. 105. Franco's original purchase was for $640.

23 Masters Company issued credit memo no. 106 to Wells Company for $130 as an allowance for damaged merchandise. Wells' original purchase was for $3,650.

P.O.4

Entries involving sales returns and allowances.

Exercise 5-4 Prepare a schedule of accounts receivable from the accounts receivable ledger after completion of Exercise 5-2. Compare the total of the schedule of accounts receivable with the balance of the Accounts Receivable account.

P.O.3

Prepare a schedule of accounts receivable.

Exercise 5-5 A business firm uses duplicate copies of its sales invoices to record sales of merchandise on account and duplicate copies of its credit memorandums to record sales returns and allowances. During November, the company issued 327 invoices for $156,119.32 and 17 credit memorandums for $9,110.16. Present the summarizing entries, dated November 30, in general journal form to record the sales and sales returns and allowances.

P.O.5

Summarize entries for directly posting sales and sales returns.

Exercise 5-6 Label the blanks below the account names in the column heads as either Debit or Credit. Record the following entries in the cash receipts journal, page 27.

June 10 Received check from R. Lees for $343 in payment of invoice no. 861 for $350 less cash discount.

12 C. Green, the owner, invested an additional $3,500 cash in the business.

30 Cash sales for the month, $2,485.

P.O.6

Label column headings and journalize entries in a cash receipts journal.

CASH RECEIPTS JOURNAL   PAGE _____

DATE	ACCOUNT CREDITED	POST. REF.	OTHER ACCOUNTS	ACCOUNTS RECEIVABLE	SALES	SALES DISCOUNT	CASH

Exercise 5-7

a. Total, prove, and rule the cash receipts journal from Exercise 5-6.
b. Post the amounts in the T accounts.

P.O.7

Total, prove, and rule and post amounts from cash receipts journal to ledgers.

Cash	111	Accts. Rec.	113	C. Green, Capital	311	Sales	411	Sales Discount	413
+	−	+	−	−	+	−	+	+	−
Bal. 3,000.00		Bal. 350.00			Bal. 3,000.00				

R. Lees	
+	−
Bal. 350.00	

P.O.8

Calculate due date,
discount, and amount due
on sales invoices.

Exercise 5-8 Complete the following chart by calculating the due date, applicable discount, and amount due for each invoice.

	Sales Invoice No.	Sales Invoice Date	Credit Terms	Amount of Sales Invoice	Sales Returns and Allowances	Date Payment Received	Amount of Sales Discount	Amount Due	Date Due to Receive Discount
a	410	July 1	2/10,n/30	450.00	0.00	July 10			
b	411	July 10	1/10,n/30	660.00	50.00	July 18			
c	412	July 15	2/10,n/30	980.00	0.00	July 29			
d	413	July 22	n/30	830.00	35.00	July 24			
e	414	July 30	1/10,n/30	780.00	0.00	Aug. 7			

Consider and Communicate

After you finished the month's posting, the total of the schedule of accounts receivable matched the balance of the Accounts Receivable controlling account in the general ledger. You therefore mailed the statements to customers. You have received a phone call from Customer A who is irritated and claims he was overcharged $52.86. Customer B calls to ask why her bill does not include her purchase of a blender for $52.86. She says she lost her original sales slip and needs a copy of the itemized bill so that she can return the item. Assume that the customers are correct. Explain how this could happen.

What If . . .

As the accountant for a large retail firm, you have been tracking the increase in Sales Returns and Allowances, which in the past had remained in the range of 5 to 7 percent of sales. For the last three months, Sales Returns and Allowances as a percentage of sales has been 10 percent, 12 percent, and 15 percent. In an effort to determine the cause of this increase in Sales Returns and Allowances, you must investigate the situation. Who will you ask about this?

A Question of Ethics

Ms. Hap, an employee, accidentally dropped a pallet of boxes off the forklift she was driving in the warehouse. No one saw what happened. She couldn't see (or hear) any damage to the televisions, so she reloaded the boxes and did not tell her supervisor. Is Ms. Hap behaving in an ethical manner when she withholds this information? Assume the sets were damaged and were delivered to the stores and sold to customers. How might this unreported accident show up in the accounting records? What should Ms. Hap have done?

Problem Set A

Problem 5-1A Whiley Wholesale Office Supply had the following sales of merchandise on account and sales returns and allowances during September:

Sept.   2 Sold merchandise on account to Thomas Office Machines, invoice no. 121, $279.

7 Sold merchandise on account to Sheldon and Turner, invoice no. 122, $416.50.

10 Sold merchandise on account to Best Supplies, Inc., invoice no. 123, $512.51.

14 Sold merchandise on account to Allied Office Products, invoice no. 124, $148.90.

17 Issued credit memo no. 15, $75.16, to Sheldon and Turner for merchandise returned.

22 Sold merchandise on account to Thomas Office Machines, invoice no. 125, $411.25.

24 Issued credit memo no. 16, $125.76, to Best Supplies, Inc., for merchandise returned.

26 Sold merchandise on account to Sheldon and Turner, invoice no. 126, $253.20.

27 Sold merchandise on account to Allied Office Products, invoice no. 127, $375.15.

29 Sold merchandise on account to Thomas Office Machines, invoice no. 128, $162.75.

30 Issued credit memo no. 17, $75.35, to Best Supplies, Inc., for merchandise damaged in transit.

Instructions

1. Record these sales of merchandise on account in the sales journal (page 41). Record the sales returns and allowances in the general journal (page 69).
2. Immediately after recording each transaction, post to the accounts receivable ledger.
3. Post the amounts from the general journal daily. Post the sales journal amount as a total at the end of the month.
4. Prepare a schedule of accounts receivable. Compare the balance of the Accounts Receivable controlling account with the total of the schedule of accounts receivable.

Exercise 5-2A Paula's Palette and Brush sells art supplies on a retail basis. Most of the sales are for cash. However, a few steady customers have charge accounts. The sales staff fills out a sales slip for each sale. The state government levies a 5 percent retail sales tax, which is collected by the retailer. Charge sales for the month of May are as follows:

May   3 Sold clay to C. Lambert, sales slip no. 326, $38.00 plus sales tax of $1.90, total $39.90.

7 Sold acrylic paints on account to R. W. Cook, sales slip no. 361, $36.95 plus sales tax of $1.85, total $38.80.

12 Sold beads and watercolor paints to Clara's Boutique for $79 plus sales tax, sales slip no. 385.

18 Winnie's Child Care bought construction paper on account, sales slip no. 391, $210 plus sales tax.

22 First Community Church bought finger paints and incidental supplies for $225 plus sales tax, sales slip no. 399.

23 Winnie's Child Care returned construction paper, which was water damaged during delivery. Full credit was allowed on the sale of $54 and the sales tax of $2.70. Issued credit memo no. 36.

23 Sold an easel on account to L. C. Scheib, sales slip no. 424, $22.95 plus sales tax.

24 Allowed First Community Church credit of $22 plus sales tax for return of art supplies. Issued credit memo no. 37.

Instructions

1. Record these transactions in either the sales journal (page 34) or the general journal (page 79).
2. Immediately after recording each transaction, post to the accounts receivable ledger.
3. Post the amounts from the general journal daily. Post the sales journal amount as a total at the end of the month.
4. Prepare a schedule of accounts receivable.

Instructions for General Ledger Software

1. Record these transactions in either the sales journal or the general journal and print the entries. Analyze the entries, mark the journal in which each entry belongs, and enter the entries in two batches.
2. Post the amounts from the sales journal and the general journal.
3. Print a schedule of accounts receivable.

P.O.1,6,8

Problem 5-3A Henderson Beauty Products sells on a wholesale basis. Terms of sales on account are 2/10, n/30. The following transactions involving cash receipts and sales of merchandise took place in April of this year.

Apr. 2 Received $1,960 cash from Allure Nails in payment of March 22 invoice of $2,000, less 2 percent cash discount.

5 Received $1,584 cash in payment of $1,420 note receivable and interest of $164.

6 Received $1,372 cash from Emanual's in payment of March 29 invoice of $1,400, less 2 percent cash discount.

8 Sold merchandise on account to Dora's Beauty Salon, invoice no. 371, $516.

15 Cash sales for first half of April, $4,372.

18 Received cash from Dora's Beauty Salon in payment of invoice no. 371, less 2 percent cash discount.

20 Received $541 cash from S. D. Weiser in payment of March 21 invoice, no discount.

22 Sold merchandise on account to Moderne Hair Salon, invoice no. 384, $722.

25 Received $406 refund for return of defective equipment that was originally bought for cash.

27 Sold merchandise on account to Crystal Products, invoice no. 391, $627.

30 Cash sales for second half of April, $4,565.

Instructions

1. Journalize the transactions for April in the cash receipts journal and the sales journal.
2. Total and rule the journals.
3. Prove the equality of debit and credit totals of the cash receipts journal.

Problem 5-4A Athletics Unlimited, a sporting goods shop, uses duplicate copies of its charge sales invoices as a sales journal and posts to the accounts receivable ledger directly from the sales invoices. The invoices are totaled at the end of the month, and an entry is made in the general journal to summarize the charge sales for the month. The charge sales invoices for October are as follows:

P.O.3,5

Oct.　4 Goff Athletic Supply, invoice no. 6216, $492.
　　　8 S. L. Singer Company, invoice no. 6240, $681.
　　 11 M. M. Davis, invoice no. 6252, $421.
　　 17 Chadwick and Martin, invoice no. 6277, $1,317.
　　 23 Barden and Howell, invoice no. 6303, $452.
　　 27 Gifford Specialty Company, invoice no. 6321, $598.
　　 28 Chase and Company, invoice no. 6339, $365.
　　 31 S. L. Singer Company, invoice no. 6347, $329.

Instructions

1. Post to the accounts receivable ledger directly from the sales invoices, listing the invoice number in the Posting Reference column.
2. Record the summarizing entry in the general journal (page 33) for the total amount of the sales invoices.
3. Post the general journal entry to the appropriate accounts in the general ledger.
4. Prepare a schedule of accounts receivable.

P roblem Set B

Problem 5-1B Whiley Wholesale Office Products had the following sales of merchandise on account and sales returns and allowances during September:

P.O.1,2,3,4

Sept.　4 Sold merchandise on account to Allied Office Products, invoice no. 91, $261.80.
　　　8 Sold merchandise on account to Sheldon and Turner, invoice no. 92, $272.75.
　　 11 Sold merchandise on account to Best Supplies, Inc., invoice no. 93, $386.50.
　　 14 Sold merchandise on account to Sheldon and Turner, invoice no. 94, $420.15.
　　 16 Issued credit memo no. 24, $37.25, to Allied Office Products for merchandise returned.
　　 21 Sold merchandise on account to Thomas Office Machines, invoice no. 95, $513.20.
　　 23 Issued credit memo no. 25, $32.75, to Best Supplies, Inc., for merchandise returned.
　　 26 Sold merchandise on account to Allied Office Products, invoice no. 96, $354.95.
　　 28 Sold merchandise on account to Sheldon and Turner, invoice no. 97, $314.82.

29 Sold merchandise on account to Thomas Office Machines, invoice no. 98, $139.28.

30 Issued credit memo no. 26 to Thomas Office Machines for damage done to merchandise during shipment, $42.15.

Instructions

1. Record these sales of merchandise on account in the sales journal (page 41). Record the sales returns and allowances in the general journal (page 69).
2. Immediately after recording each transaction, post to the accounts receivable ledger.
3. Post the amounts from the general journal daily. Post the sales journal amount as a total at the end of the month.
4. Prepare a schedule of accounts receivable. Compare the balance of the Accounts Receivable controlling account with the total of the schedule of accounts receivable.

P.O.1,2,3,4

Problem 5-2B Bed of Roses, a floral shop, sells flowers on a retail basis. Most of the sales are for cash. However, a few steady customers have charge accounts. Bed of Roses' sales staff fills out a sales slip for each sale. The state government levies a 5 percent retail sales tax, which is collected by the retailer. The following represent Bed of Roses' charge sales for May:

May 4 Sold floral arrangement on account to R. W. Cook, sales slip no. 342, $42 plus sales tax of $2.10, total $44.10.

6 Sold potted plants on account to C. Lambert, sales slip no. 367, $34 plus sales tax of $1.70, total $35.70.

12 Winnie's Child Care bought several floral arrangements on account for an open house, sales slip no. 379, $286 plus sales tax of $14.30, total $300.30.

15 Sold wreath on account to Clara's Boutique, sales slip no. 396, $74 plus sales tax of $3.70, total $77.70.

17 Sold corsage on account to L. C. Scheib, sales slip no. 404, $17 plus sales tax.

17 Winnie's Child Care returned a flower spray. Delivery of the spray occurred after the open house was over. Bed of Roses allowed full credit on the sale of $56 and the sales tax of $2.80. Issued credit memo no. 18.

23 Sold flower arrangements to First Community Church on account for their anniversary, $120 plus sales tax, sales slip no. 439.

24 Allowed First Community Church credit, $24 plus sales tax, because of withered blossoms in floral arrangements. Issued credit memo no. 19.

Instructions

1. Record these transactions in either the sales journal (page 34) or the general journal (page 79).
2. Immediately after recording each transaction, post to the accounts receivable ledger.
3. Post the amounts from the general journal daily. Post the sales journal amount as a total at the end of the month.
4. Prepare a schedule of accounts receivable.

Instructions for General Ledger Software

1. Record these transactions in either the sales journal or the general journal and print the entries. Analyze the entries, mark the journal in which each entry belongs, and enter the entries in two batches.

2. Post the amounts from the sales journal and the general journal.
3. Print a schedule of accounts receivable.

Problem 5-3B The R. E. Ritchie Company sells snacks primarily to vending machine operators. Terms of sales on account are 2/10, n/30. The following transactions involving cash receipts and sales of merchandise took place in June of this year:

P.O.1,6,8

June 3 Received $1,715 cash from C. P. Rodda in payment of May 24 invoice of $1,750, less 2 percent cash discount.
  5 Received $2,475 cash in payment of $2,250 note receivable and interest of $225.
  8 Sold merchandise on account to P. Snider, invoice no. 964, $1,050.
  9 Received $1,960 in cash from D. E. Molina in payment of May 31 invoice of $2,000, less 2 percent cash discount.
  14 Received cash from P. Snider in payment of invoice no. 964, less 2 percent cash discount.
  16 Cash sales for first half of June, $8,617.50.
  19 Received $622.50 in cash from C. N. Hull in payment of May 20 invoice, no discount.
  22 Sold merchandise on account to A. L. Jordan, invoice no. 989, $1,462.50.
  25 Received $815 cash refund for return of defective equipment bought in May for cash.
  29 Sold merchandise on account to F. C. Mosher, invoice no. 1012, $1,820.
  30 Cash sales for the second half of June, $8,485.

Instructions

1. Journalize the transactions for June in the cash receipts journal and the sales journal.
2. Total and rule the journals.
3. Prove the equality of debit and credit totals of the cash receipts journal.

Problem 5-4B Adventures Unlimited, a hobby shop, uses duplicate copies of its charge sales invoices as a sales journal and posts to the accounts receivable ledger directly from the sales invoices. The invoices are totaled at the end of the month, and an entry is made in the general journal to summarize the charge sales for the month. The charge sales invoices for October are as follows:

P.O.3,5

Oct. 2 Goff Athletic Supply, invoice no. 6237, $590.
  8 M. M. Davis, invoice no. 6241, $782.
  11 S. L. Singer Company, invoice no. 6253, $345.
  14 Barden and Howell, invoice no. 6270, $788.
  17 Chadwick and Martin, invoice no. 6296, $694.
  20 Gifford Specialty Company, invoice no. 6309, $535.
  24 Chase and Company, invoice no. 6315, $1,012.
  30 S. L. Singer Company, invoice no. 6354, $1,415.

Instructions

1. Post to the accounts receivable ledger directly from the sales invoices, listing the invoice number in the Posting Reference column.
2. Record the summarizing entry in the general journal (page 33) for the total amount of the sales invoices.
3. Post the general journal entry to the appropriate accounts in the general ledger.
4. Prepare a schedule of accounts receivable.

CHALLENGE PROBLEM

You have given an accounting test to an applicant for an accounting position at Lindsay Beauty Supply. The applicant has journalized and posted March transactions shown below and has prepared a schedule of accounts receivable.

Mar.   2 Sold merchandise on account to Wave and Curl, invoice no. 318, $281.

        9 Sold merchandise on account to Hairlocks, invoice no. 319, $603.

    12 Issued credit memorandum no. 18 to Wave and Curl, for merchandise returned, $27.

    17 Sold merchandise on account to Cut & Style, invoice no. 320, $436.

    28 Sold goods on account to Beauty Barn, invoice no. 321, $119.

    31 Issued credit memorandum no. 19 to Cut & Style, for merchandise returned, $19.

The applicant's work is shown below and on the next page.

Instructions

1. Before evaluating the applicant's answers, prepare a correct solution to the employment test by recording all transactions and preparing a new schedule of accounts receivable on the forms in the working papers.
2. Check the applicant's work, and make a list of the errors by journal.
3. Check your solution to see that the total of the schedule of accounts receivable is equal to the balance of the accounts receivable control account in the general ledger.

SALES JOURNAL   PAGE _____

	DATE	INV. NO.	CUSTOMER'S NAME	POST. REF.	ACCOUNTS RECEIVABLE DR., SALES CR.	
1	19–					1
2	Mar. 2	318	Wave and Curl	✓	2 1 8 00	2
3	9	319	Hairlocks	✓	6 0 3 00	3
4	17	320	Cut & Style	✓	4 3 6 00	4
5	31				1 3 2 0 00	5
6					(113)(411)	6
7						7

GENERAL JOURNAL   PAGE _____

	DATE	DESCRIPTION	POST. REF.	DEBIT	CREDIT	
1	19–					1
2	Mar. 12	Accounts Receivable, Wave and				2
3		Curl	113 ✓	2 7 00		3
4		Sales Returns and Allowances	412		2 7 00	4
5		Issued credit memo no. 18.				5
6						6
7	31	Accounts Receivable, Cut & Style	113 ✓	1 9 00		7
8		Sales Returns and Allowances	412		1 9 00	8
9		Issued credit memo no. 19.				9
10						10

Partial General Ledger

Accounts Receivable   113

+		–
27		
19		
1,257		
Bal. 1,303		

Sales   411

–		+
		1,257

Sales Returns and Allowances   412

+		–
27		
19		
	Bal. 46	

Accounts Receivable Ledger

Beauty Barn

+		–

Cut & Style

+		–
436		
19		
Bal. 455		

Hairlocks

+		–
603		

Wave and Curl

+		–
218		
27		
Bal. 245		

Lindsay Beauty Supply
Schedule of Accounts Receivable
March 31, 19–

Cut & Style	4 5 5 00
Hairlocks	6 0 3 00
Wave and Curl	2 4 5 00
	1 3 0 3 00

chapter 6

Accounting for Merchandise:

Purchases and Cash

Payments Journals

PERFORMANCE OBJECTIVES

1. Record transactions in a three-column purchases journal.

2. Post from a three-column purchases journal to an accounts payable ledger and a general ledger.

3. Record transactions involving purchases returns and allowances in a general journal.

4. Prepare a schedule of accounts payable.

5. Record transactions in a multicolumn purchases journal.

6. Post from a multicolumn purchases journal to an accounts payable ledger and a general ledger.

7. Post directly from purchase invoices to an accounts payable ledger, and journalize and post a summarizing entry in the general journal and general ledger.

8. Record transactions in a cash payments journal for a service enterprise.

9. Record transactions involving cash discounts in a cash payments journal for a merchandising enterprise.

A s manager of the accounts payable department, I know how important timely and accurate recordkeeping is when it comes to paying suppliers or vendors. My company purchases close to two million dollars of merchandise each year, and about half our suppliers offer

cash discounts for early payment. That can mean annual savings of close to $30,000 if our department stays on its toes by paying those suppliers within the discount period. It means we have to monitor carefully the accounts payable accounts and get bills that offer discounts processed as soon as possible so that the discount period doesn't expire.

We have been talking about the procedures, accounts, and special journals used to record the selling of merchandise and the receipt of cash. Now let's discuss those same elements as they apply to the *buying* of merchandise and the payment of cash. Again, we will use Dodson Plumbing Supply as an example of a merchandising business.

Purchasing Procedures

W hen you think of the variety in types and sizes of merchandising firms, it comes as no surprise to learn that there is also considerable variety in the procedures used to buy goods for resale. Some purchases may be for cash; however, in most cases, purchases are on a credit basis. In a small retail store, the owner may do the buying. In large retail and wholesale concerns, department heads or division managers do the buying, after which the Purchasing Department places purchase orders, follows up the orders, receives the goods, and sees that deliveries are made to the right departments. The Purchasing Department also acts as a source of information on current prices, price trends, quality of goods, prospective suppliers, and reliability of suppliers.

The Purchasing Department normally requires that any buying orders be in writing, in the form of a **purchase requisition.** After the purchase requisition is approved, the Purchasing Department sends a **purchase order** to the supplier. A purchase order is the company's written offer to buy certain goods. The accountant does not make any entry at this point, because the supplier has not yet indicated acceptance of the order. In most larger companies, a purchase order is made out with at least five copies. One copy goes to the supplier, one stays in the Purchasing Department (as proof of what was ordered), one goes to the department that sent out the requisition (telling them that the goods they wanted have been ordered), one goes to the Accounting Department, and a blind copy (with quantities omitted) goes to Receiving.

To continue with the accounts of Dodson Plumbing Supply, the Fixtures Department submits a purchase requisition to the Purchasing Department, as shown in Figure 6-1. The Purchasing Department completes the rest of the purchase requisition and then sends out the purchase order shown in Figure 6-2.

Figure 6-1

DODSON PLUMBING SUPPLY

1400 Jackson Avenue • San Diego, CA • 92102

No. C-726

PURCHASE REQUISITION

Department __Fixtures__   Date of request __July 2, 19—__
Advise on delivery __C. Fenwick__   Date required __August 5,19—__

Quantity	Description
50	Drominex shower heads #772R

Approved by *D.M. Bruce*   Requested by *J.C. Garcia*

FOR PURCHASING DEPT. USE ONLY

Purchase order no. __7918__   Issued to: Colvin, Inc.
Date __July 5, 19—__   1614 Olivera St.
San Francisco, CA 94129

Figure 6-2

DODSON PLUMBING SUPPLY

1400 Jackson Avenue • San Diego, CA • 92102

PURCHASE ORDER

To: Colvin, Inc.   Shipped by:
1614 Olivera St.
San Francisco, CA 94129

Order Number	Terms	Date
7918	2/10, n/30	July 5, 19—

Quantity	Description	Unit Price	Total
50	Drominex shower heads #772R	14.20	710.00
	Total		710.00

D.M. Bruce

The seller then sends an invoice to the buyer. This invoice should arrive in advance of the goods (or at least *with* the goods). From the seller's point of view, this is a sales invoice. If the sale is on credit, as we saw in Chapter 5, the seller's accountant makes an entry debiting Accounts Receivable and crediting Sales. To the buyer, this is a purchase invoice. Customarily, when the merchandise is received, the buyer's accountant makes an entry debiting Purchases and crediting Accounts Payable. Dodson Plumbing Supply receives the invoice shown in Figure 6-3 from Colvin, Inc.

Figure 6-3

COLVIN, INC.
1614 Olivera Street • San Francisco, CA • 94129

Invoice No. 2706

I N V O I C E

Sold to: Dodson Plumbing Supply
1400 Jackson Avenue
San Diego, CA 92102

Date: July 31, 19—
Shipped by: Western Freight Line

Your Order Number	Salesperson	Terms	F.O.B.	Date Shipped
7918	*C.L.*	2/10, n/30	San Francisco	July 31, 19—

Quantity	Description	Unit Price	Total
50	Drominex shower heads #772R	14.20	710.00
	Freight		49.00
	Total		759.00

Let's review the fundamental accounting equation with the T accounts involved in selling merchandise introduced in Chapter 5 plus the accounts we will be introducing.

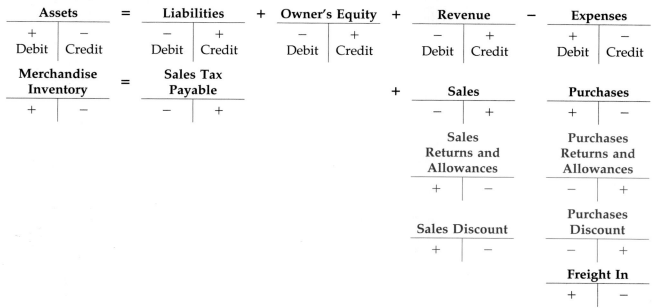

Goods intended for resale are checked against orders with a hand-held scanner. This records the item description and the quantity received. The Freight In account is used to record the transportation charges on this incoming delivery.

Bear in mind that the Purchases account is used exclusively for the buying of merchandise intended for resale. If the firm buys anything else, the accountant records the amount under the appropriate asset or expense account.

Purchases-Related Accounts for Merchandising Firms

A merchandising business must purchase goods to sell, ideally at a low enough price that it can make a profit. Let's look at some new accounts related to a merchandising business. Notice that these accounts begin with the number 5, indicating a cost account. We will discuss these accounts further in Chapter 7 as part of the Cost of Goods Sold section of the income statement. Some businesses continue to number their operating expenses beginning with 5; others use the number 6.

The **Purchases** account is used to record the cost of merchandise bought for resale. Remember that the Purchases account is used strictly for the buying of merchandise. The plus and minus signs are the same as the signs for Merchandise Inventory. Purchases is placed under the heading of Expenses because the accountant closes this account, along with the expense accounts, at the end of the fiscal period. Also, like expenses, the amount of Purchases reduces net profit.

The **Purchases Discount** account is used to record cash discounts granted for prompt payments, in accordance with the credit terms.

The **Purchases Returns and Allowances** account is a deduction from Purchases. A separate account is set up to keep track of the returns and the reductions in bills because of damaged merchandise. On the income statement, we treat Purchases Returns and Allowances and Purchases Discount as deductions from Purchases. For consistency, both accounts are presented below Purchases in the fundamental accounting equation.

The **Freight In** account is used to record the transportation charges on incoming merchandise intended for resale. Debits to this account increase the cost of purchases. Since you may be wondering, the cost of sending merchandise to customers is an operating expense called Delivery Expense, whereas Freight In, like the other purchases-related accounts, is part of the cost of goods sold section.

FYI

Freight In is a purchases-related account for transportation costs on incoming merchandise. Delivery Expense is an operating expense for costs of outgoing merchandise to customers.

Freight Charges on Incoming Merchandise

As mentioned, Freight In is an expense account used to record the transportation costs of merchandise purchased for resale. Companies use this account to keep a record of all separately charged delivery costs on incoming merchandise. Some accountants call this account *Transportation In.*

Freight costs are expressed as FOB (free on board) destination or shipping point. (Destination is the buyer's location; shipping point is the seller's location.) In both cases, the supplier loads the goods free on board the carrier. Beyond that point, there must be an understanding as to who is responsible for ultimately paying the freight charges. If the seller assumes the entire cost of transportation, without any reimbursement from the buyer, the terms are **FOB destination**. If the buyer is responsible for paying the freight cost, the shipping terms are called **FOB shipping point**.

Briefly, in FOB destination the freight charges are not stated, and the buyer simply pays the amount of the bill. For example, Dodson Plumbing Supply (remember, it's in San Diego) buys fittings from a supplier in Chicago with shipping terms of FOB San Diego listed on the invoice. The total of the invoice is $1,740, and there is no separate listing of freight charges. In other words, the seller has included the transportation costs in the price.

On the other hand, FOB shipping point, in which the buyer is responsible for paying the freight charges, may come in two ways.

1. The freight charges may be paid separately by the buyer to the transportation company. For example, an automobile dealer in Houston buys cars FOB Detroit. In this case, the automobile dealer makes one check payable to the manufacturer and another check payable to the carrier for the freight charges.

2. The transportation costs may be listed separately on the invoice. For example, suppose a person orders a refrigerator from a mail order company. The freight charges are listed on the bill or invoice, and the mail order company has prepaid (paid in advance) the freight charges as a favor or convenience for the buyer. However, the buyer is still responsible for reimbursing the mail order company for the freight charges. Similarly, a business buys merchandise, and the amount of the freight charges may be listed separately on the invoice.

Look again at the invoice of Colvin, Inc. shown in Figure 6-3. Note that the freight cost is listed separately, so the terms are FOB shipping point. Colvin paid the transportation cost, but Dodson must reimburse Colvin for this cost. Incidentally, unless the title to the goods is expressly reserved by the seller, whoever pays the freight charges customarily has title to the goods.

Let's proceed with three other transactions for Dodson Plumbing. As in Chapter 5, we will first record the transctions in a general journal. Then, as a means of reemphasizing the advantages of special journals as opposed to a general journal, we will record the same transactions in a special journal.

During the first week in August, the following transactions took place:

Aug.   2   Bought merchandise on account from Colvin, Inc., $710, their invoice no. 2706, dated July 31; terms 2/10, n/30, FOB San Francisco; freight prepaid and added to the invoice, $49 (total $759).
       3   Bought merchandise on account from Richter and Son, $772, their invoice no. 982, dated August 2; terms net 30 days; FOB Cleveland; freight prepaid and added to the invoice, $57 (total $829).
       5   Bought merchandise on account from Adams Manufacturing Company, $564, their invoice no. 10611, dated August 3; terms 2/10, n/30, FOB Los Angeles.

Notice that the transactions with Colvin, Inc., and Richter and Son are both FOB shipping point, with the freight charges listed separately. Consequently, the buyer (Dodson) must reimburse the sellers for the transportation costs by paying the total of the invoices.

If these transactions are recorded in a general journal, they look like Figure 6-4. Next the general journal entries would be posted to the general ledger.

Figure 6-4

GENERAL JOURNAL   PAGE __22__

	DATE		DESCRIPTION	POST. REF.	DEBIT	CREDIT	
1	19–						1
2	Aug.	2	Purchases	511	7 1 0 00		2
3			Freight In	514	4 9 00		3
4			Accounts Payable	221		7 5 9 00	4
5			Colvin, Inc., their invoice				5
6			no. 2706, dated July 31,				6
7			terms 2/10, n/30.				7
8							8
9		3	Purchases	511	7 7 2 00		9
10			Freight In	514	5 7 00		10
11			Accounts Payable	221		8 2 9 00	11
12			Richter and Son, their				12
13			invoice no. 982, dated				13
14			August 2, terms net 30 days.				14
15							15
16		5	Purchases	511	5 6 4 00		16
17			Accounts Payable	221		5 6 4 00	17
18			Adams Manufacturing Co.,				18
19			their invoice no. 10611, dated				19
20			August 3, terms 2/10, n/30.				20
21							21
22							22

GENERAL LEDGER

ACCOUNT ___Accounts Payable___ ACCOUNT NO. __221__

DATE		ITEM	POST. REF.	DEBIT	CREDIT	BALANCE DEBIT	BALANCE CREDIT
19–							
Aug.	1	Balance	✓				5 0 4 00
	2		J22		7 5 9 00		1 1 1 5 00
	3		J22		8 2 9 00		1 9 4 4 00
	5		J22		5 6 4 00		2 5 0 8 00

ACCOUNT ___Purchases___ ACCOUNT NO. __511__

DATE		ITEM	POST. REF.	DEBIT	CREDIT	BALANCE DEBIT	BALANCE CREDIT
19–							
Aug.	1	Balance	✓			20 6 1 2 00	
	2		J22	7 1 0 00		21 3 2 2 00	
	3		J22	7 7 2 00		22 0 9 4 00	
	5		J22	5 6 4 00		22 6 5 8 00	

ACCOUNT ___Freight In___ ACCOUNT NO. __514__

DATE		ITEM	POST. REF.	DEBIT	CREDIT	BALANCE DEBIT	BALANCE CREDIT
19–							
Aug.	1	Balance	✓			1 5 0 2 00	
	2		J22	4 9 00		1 5 5 1 00	
	3		J22	5 7 00		1 6 0 8 00	

Let's take a minute to explain the terms in the transactions. The notation "net 30 days" or "n/30" means that the bill is due within 30 days after the date of the invoice. The notation "2/10, n/30" refers to the purchases discount or cash discount. It means that the seller offers a 2 percent discount if the bill is paid within 10 days after the date of the invoice. Otherwise the whole bill must be paid within 30 days after the invoice date. We will be working with these credit terms later in the chapter.

The cost of delivering goods sold to customers is debited to Delivery Expense, an operating expense. Sometimes these costs are included in the price of the goods, while other times the amount is charged separately to the customer.

Purchases Journal (Three-Column)

Performance Objective 1

Record transactions in a three-column purchases journal.

The repetition illustrated in our example can be avoided if the accountant uses a **purchases journal** instead of the general journal. This purchases journal is used to record the purchase of merchandise *on account only:*

		PURCHASES JOURNAL								PAGE 29	
	DATE	SUPPLIER'S NAME	INVOICE NO.	INVOICE DATE	TERMS	POST. REF.	ACCOUNTS PAYABLE CREDIT	FREIGHT IN DEBIT	PURCHASES DEBIT	
1	19–									1
2	Aug. 2	Colvin, Inc.	2706	7/31	2/10, n/30		7 5 9 00	4 9 00	7 1 0 00	2
3	3	Richter and Son	982	8/2	n/30		8 2 9 00	5 7 00	7 7 2 00	3
4	5	Adams Manufacturing Co.	10611	8/3	2/10, n/30		5 6 4 00		5 6 4 00	4
5										5
6										6

Posting from the Purchases Journal to the General Ledger

Performance Objective 2

Post from a three-column purchases journal to an accounts payable ledger and a general ledger.

Figure 6-5 shows the journal entries for all transactions involving the purchase of merchandise on account for August and the related ledger accounts for the same time period. In the Post. Ref. column of the ledger accounts, P designates the purchases journal. After posting to the ledger accounts, the accountant goes back to the purchases journal and records the account numbers in parentheses directly below the total.

Figure 6-5

PURCHASES JOURNAL

PAGE 29

	DATE		SUPPLIER'S NAME	INVOICE NO.	INVOICE DATE	TERMS	POST. REF.	ACCOUNTS PAYABLE CREDIT	FREIGHT IN DEBIT	PURCHASES DEBIT	
1	19–										1
2	Aug.	2	Colvin, Inc.	2706	7/31	2/10,n/30		7 5 9 00	4 9 00	7 1 0 00	2
3		3	Richter and Son	982	8/2	n/30		8 2 9 00	5 7 00	7 7 2 00	3
4		5	Adams Manufacturing Co.	10611	8/3	2/10, n/30		5 6 4 00		5 6 4 00	4
5		9	Spargo Products Co.	B643	8/6	1/10, n/30		1 6 5 00	1 0 00	1 5 5 00	5
6		18	L. C. Waters	46812	8/17	n/60		2 2 8 00		2 2 8 00	6
7		25	Delaney and Cox	1024	8/23	2/10, n/30		3 7 6 00	1 4 00	3 6 2 00	7
8		26	Colvin, Inc.	2801	8/25	2/10, n/30		4 0 6 00	2 2 00	3 8 4 00	8
9		31						3 3 2 7 00	1 5 2 00	3 1 7 5 00	9
10								(2 2 1)	(5 1 4)	(5 1 1)	10
11											11
12											12

GENERAL LEDGER

ACCOUNT Accounts Payable   ACCOUNT NO. 221

					BALANCE	
DATE	ITEM	POST. REF.	DEBIT	CREDIT	DEBIT	CREDIT
19–						
Aug. 1	Balance	√				5 0 4 00
31		P29	3 3 2 7 00			3 8 3 1 00

ACCOUNT Purchases   ACCOUNT NO. 511

					BALANCE	
DATE	ITEM	POST. REF.	DEBIT	CREDIT	DEBIT	CREDIT
19–						
Aug. 1	Balance	√			20 6 1 2 00	
31		P29	3 1 7 5 00		23 7 8 7 00	

ACCOUNT Freight In   ACCOUNT NO. 514

					BALANCE	
DATE	ITEM	POST. REF.	DEBIT	CREDIT	DEBIT	CREDIT
19–						
Aug. 1	Balance	√			1 5 0 2 00	
31		P29	1 5 2 00		1 6 5 4 00	

R E M E M B E R

Transactions involving the buying of supplies or other assets should not be recorded in the three-column purchases journal, because this purchases journal may be used only for the purchases of merchandise for resale.

The Accounts Payable Ledger

n Chapter 5 we called the Accounts Receivable account in the general ledger a controlling account. We saw that the accounts receivable ledger consists of the individual accounts for the company's charge customers. We also saw that the accountant usually posts to the accounts receivable ledger every day.

Figure 6-6

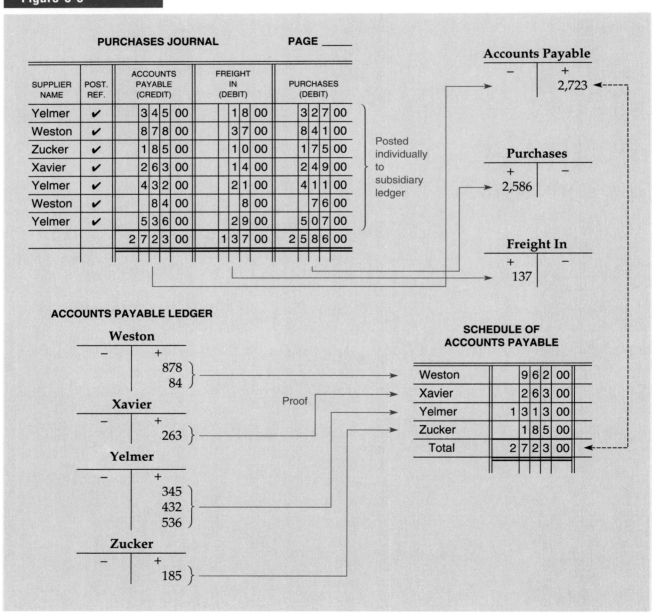

Accounts Payable is the other side of the coin; it is also a controlling account in the general ledger. The **accounts payable ledger** is a subsidiary ledger, and it consists of individual accounts for all the creditors. Posting is usually done daily to the accounts payable ledger. After posting to the individual creditors' accounts, the accountant puts a check mark (√) in the Post. Ref. column of the purchases journal. After the accountant has finished all the posting to the controlling account at the end of the period, the total of the schedule of accounts payable should equal the balance of the Accounts Payable account. The three-column form is used for the accounts payable ledger. Figure 6-6 diagrams the connection between the general ledger and the accounts payable subsidiary ledger.

Because no payments were made to creditors, the total of the purchases journal equals the balance of Accounts Payable in the simplified illustration shown in Figure 6-6 on page 246. This is not the normal situation. For example, if we had paid creditors $900, the balance of both the Accounts Payable controlling account and the total of the schedule of accounts payable would be $1,823 ($2,723 − $900). The total of the purchases journal would still be $2,723.

Now let's see the purchases journal (shown in Figure 6-7) and the postings to the ledger (shown in Figure 6-8 on pages 248 and 249). Note that in the accounts payable ledger—as in the accounts receivable ledger—the accounts of the individual creditors are listed in alphabetical order. Firms that handle all of their bookkeeping and accounting on computer may assign account numbers to each individual account.

> **R E M E M B E R**
>
> Increases in Accounts Payable are recorded in the Credit column. Decreases in Accounts Payable are recorded in the Debit column.

Figure 6-7

PURCHASES JOURNAL

PAGE 29

	DATE		SUPPLIER'S NAME	INVOICE NO.	INVOICE DATE	TERMS	POST. REF.	ACCOUNTS PAYABLE CREDIT	FREIGHT IN DEBIT	PURCHASES DEBIT	
1	19–										1
2	Aug.	2	Colvin, Inc.	2706	7/31	2/10, n/30	√	759 00	49 00	710 00	2
3		3	Richter and Son	982	8/2	n/30	√	829 00	57 00	772 00	3
4		5	Adams Manufacturing Co.	10611	8/3	2/10, n/30	√	564 00		564 00	4
5		9	Spargo Products Co.	B643	8/6	1/10, n/30	√	165 00	10 00	155 00	5
6		18	L. C. Waters	46812	8/17	n/60	√	228 00		228 00	6
7		25	Delaney and Cox	1024	8/23	2/10, n/30	√	376 00	14 00	362 00	7
8		26	Colvin, Inc.	2801	8/25	2/10, n/30	√	406 00	22 00	384 00	8
9		31						3327 00	152 00	3175 00	9
10								(221)	(514)	(511)	10
11											11
12											12
13											13
14											14
15											15

Figure 6-8

ACCOUNTS PAYABLE LEDGER

NAME _Adams Manufacturing Company_

ADDRESS _254 Calle Mancha_

Los Angeles, CA 90025

DATE		ITEM	POST. REF.	DEBIT	CREDIT	BALANCE
19—						
Aug.	5		P29		5 6 4 00	5 6 4 00

NAME _Colvin, Inc._

ADDRESS _1614 Olivera Street_

San Francisco, CA 94129

DATE		ITEM	POST. REF.	DEBIT	CREDIT	BALANCE
19—						
Aug.	2		P29		7 5 9 00	7 5 9 00
	26		P29		4 0 6 00	1 1 6 5 00

NAME _Delaney and Cox_

ADDRESS _2426 Reilly Way, N.E._

Seattle, WA 98102

DATE		ITEM	POST. REF.	DEBIT	CREDIT	BALANCE
19—						
Aug.	25		P29		3 7 6 00	3 7 6 00

NAME _Richter and Son_

ADDRESS _142 Grant Road_

Cleveland, OH 44102

DATE		ITEM	POST. REF.	DEBIT	CREDIT	BALANCE
19—						
July	27		P28		1 8 0 00	1 8 0 00
Aug.	3		P29		8 2 9 00	1 0 0 9 00

NAME __Spargo Products Company__
ADDRESS __2154 Springer St.__
__Boston, MA 02107__

DATE		ITEM	POST. REF.	DEBIT	CREDIT	BALANCE
19–						
Aug.	9		P29		1 6 5 00	1 6 5 00

NAME __L. C. Waters__
ADDRESS __1620 Minard St.__
__San Jose, CA 95101__

DATE		ITEM	POST. REF.	DEBIT	CREDIT	BALANCE
19–						
July	29		P28		3 2 4 00	3 2 4 00
Aug.	18		P29		2 2 8 00	5 5 2 00

Purchases Returns and Allowances

As its title implies, the Purchases Returns and Allowances account handles either a return of merchandise previously purchased or an allowance made for merchandise that arrived in damaged condition. In both cases there is a reduction in the amount owed to the supplier. The buyer sends a letter or printed form to the supplier, who acknowledges the reduction by sending a credit memorandum. The buyer should wait for notice of the agreed deduction before making an entry.

The Purchases Returns and Allowances account is considered to be a deduction from Purchases. Using a separate account provides a better record of the total returns and allowances. Purchases Returns and Allowances is deducted from the Purchases account on the income statement. (This point is illustrated later.) For now, let's look at an example consisting of two entries on the books of Dodson Plumbing Supply.

Transaction (a) On August 5, bought merchandise on account from Adams Manufacturing Company, $564, their invoice no. 10611 of August 3; terms 2/10, n/30, FOB Los Angeles. Recorded this as a debit to Purchases and a credit to Accounts Payable. On August 6 returned merchandise costing $70. Made no entry.

Transaction (b) On August 8, received credit memorandum no. 629 from Adams Manufacturing Company for $70. Recorded this as a debit to Accounts Payable and a credit to Purchases Returns and Allowances.

Assets		=	Liabilities		+	Owner's Equity		+	Revenue		−	Expenses	
+	−		−	+		−	+		−	+		+	−
Debit	Credit		Debit	Credit		Debit	Credit		Debit	Credit		Debit	Credit

Accounts Payable

	+		**Purchases**	
			+	−
(b) 70	(a) 564		(a) 564	

Purchases Returns and Allowances

−	+
	(b) 70

Purchases Returns and Allowances is credited because Dodson Plumbing has more returns and allowances than before. Accounts Payable is debited because Dodson Plumbing owes less than before.

During August, suppose that Dodson Plumbing Supply also received a credit memo from Spargo Products Company for $42 as an allowance for damaged merchandise. The entries in the general journal for recording the two credit memos are shown below.

Performance Objective 3

Record transactions involving purchases returns and allowances in a general journal.

GENERAL JOURNAL PAGE 27

	DATE		DESCRIPTION	POST. REF.	DEBIT	CREDIT	
1	19–						1
2	Aug.	8	Accounts Payable, Adams				2
3			Manufacturing Company		7 0 00		3
4			Purchases Returns and				4
5			Allowances			7 0 00	5
6			Credit memo no. 629 for				6
7			return of merchandise.				7
8							8
9		12	Accounts Payable, Spargo				9
10			Products Company		4 2 00		10
11			Purchases Returns and				11
12			Allowances			4 2 00	12
13			Credit memo no. 482 as an				13
14			allowance for damaged				14
15			merchandise.				15

In these entries, Accounts Payable is followed by a comma and the name of the individual creditor's account. **The accountant must post to both the Accounts Payable controlling account and the individual creditor's account in the accounts payable ledger.** The journal entries are shown here as they appear when the posting is completed. The account numbers in the Post. Ref. column indicate postings to the accounts in the general ledger, and the check marks indicate postings to the accounts in the accounts payable ledger.

GENERAL JOURNAL   PAGE __27__

	DATE		DESCRIPTION	POST. REF.	DEBIT	CREDIT	
1	19–						1
2	Aug.	8	Accounts Payable, Adams				2
3			Manufacturing Company	221 ✓	7 0 00		3
4			Purchases Returns and				4
5			Allowances	512		7 0 00	5
6			Credit memo no. 629 for				6
7			return of merchandise.				7
8							8
9		12	Accounts Payable, Spargo				9
10			Products Company	221 ✓	4 2 00		10
11			Purchases Returns and				11
12			Allowances	512		4 2 00	12
13			Credit memo no. 482 as an				13
14			allowance for damaged				14
15			merchandise.				15

GENERAL JOURNAL

ACCOUNT __Accounts Payable__   ACCOUNT NO. __221__

	DATE		ITEM	POST. REF.	DEBIT	CREDIT	BALANCE DEBIT	BALANCE CREDIT
	19–							
	Aug.	1	Balance	✓				5 0 4 00
		8		J27	7 0 00			4 3 4 00
		12		J27	4 2 00			3 9 2 00

ACCOUNT __Purchases Returns and Allowances__   ACCOUNT NO. __512__

	DATE		ITEM	POST. REF.	DEBIT	CREDIT	BALANCE DEBIT	BALANCE CREDIT
	19–							
	Aug.	1	Balance	✓				6 4 0 00
		8		J27		7 0 00		7 1 0 00
		12		J27		4 2 00		7 5 2 00

R E M E M B E R

From the viewpoint of the buyer, a credit memo is recorded as a debit to Accounts Payable and a credit to Purchases Returns and Allowances. From the viewpoint of the seller, a credit memo is recorded as a debit to Sales Returns and Allowances and a credit to Accounts Receivable.

ACCOUNTS PAYABLE LEDGER

NAME _____ Adams Manufacturing Company

ADDRESS _____ 254 Calle Mancha

Los Angeles, CA 90025

DATE		ITEM	POST. REF.	DEBIT	CREDIT	BALANCE
19–						
Aug.	5		P29		5 6 4 00	5 6 4 00
	8		J27	7 0 00		4 9 4 00

NAME _____ Spargo Products Company

ADDRESS _____ 2154 Springer St.

Boston, MA 02107

DATE		ITEM	POST. REF.	DEBIT	CREDIT	BALANCE
19–						
Aug.	9		P29		1 6 5 00	1 6 5 00
	12		J27	4 2 00		1 2 3 00

Schedule of Accounts Payable

Performance Objective 4

Prepare a schedule of accounts payable.

Assuming that no other transactions involved Accounts Payable, the **schedule of accounts payable**—a list of the amounts owed to creditors —would appear as follows. Note that the balances of the creditors' accounts, with the exception of the accounts for Adams Manufacturing Company and Spargo Products Company, are taken from the accounts payable ledger shown in Figure 6-8.

Dodson Plumbing Supply

Schedule of Accounts Payable
August 31, 19–

Adams Manufacturing Company	$ 4 9 4 00
Colvin, Inc.	1 1 6 5 00
Delaney and Cox	3 7 6 00
Richter and Son	1 0 0 9 00
Spargo Products Company	1 2 3 00
L. C. Waters	5 5 2 00
Total Accounts Payable	$3 7 1 9 00

The Accounts Payable controlling account in general ledger at the top of the next page is now posted up to date.

GENERAL LEDGER

ACCOUNT Accounts Payable   ACCOUNT NO. 221

DATE		ITEM	POST. REF.	DEBIT	CREDIT	BALANCE DEBIT	BALANCE CREDIT
19–							
Aug.	1	Balance	✓				5 0 4 00
	8		J27	7 0 00			4 3 4 00
	12		J27	4 2 00			3 9 2 00
	31		P29		3 3 2 7 00		3 7 1 9 00

Subsidiary Ledgers

The place of subsidiary ledgers in the accounting cycle is shown in Figure 6-9. The figure also shows how the schedules of accounts receivable and accounts payable fit into the accounting cycle.

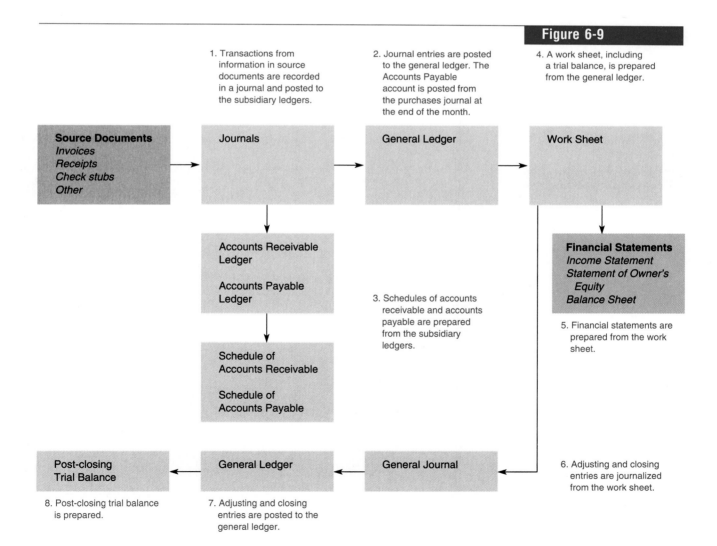

Figure 6-9

1. Transactions from information in source documents are recorded in a journal and posted to the subsidiary ledgers.

2. Journal entries are posted to the general ledger. The Accounts Payable account is posted from the purchases journal at the end of the month.

4. A work sheet, including a trial balance, is prepared from the general ledger.

Source Documents
Invoices
Receipts
Check stubs
Other

Journals

General Ledger

Work Sheet

Accounts Receivable Ledger

Accounts Payable Ledger

Schedule of Accounts Receivable

Schedule of Accounts Payable

3. Schedules of accounts receivable and accounts payable are prepared from the subsidiary ledgers.

Financial Statements
Income Statement
Statement of Owner's Equity
Balance Sheet

5. Financial statements are prepared from the work sheet.

Post-closing Trial Balance

General Ledger

General Journal

6. Adjusting and closing entries are journalized from the work sheet.

8. Post-closing trial balance is prepared.

7. Adjusting and closing entries are posted to the general ledger.

Multicolumn Purchases Journal (Invoice Register)

Instead of the three-column purchases journal we have shown, some businesses prefer to use a multicolumn purchases journal or invoice register, which will handle not only freight charges and purchases of merchandise but **anything bought on account.** Items other than merchandise usually consist of supplies and equipment acquired for use in the firm. The advantage of a multicolumn purchases journal is that all types of purchases on account are recorded in one journal.

As an illustration, we will use another company, Melissa's Gift Shop. Here are three transactions occurring during the first week in May:

May 2 Bought merchandise on account from Cordez Specialty Company, $610, their invoice no. L311, dated May 1; terms 2/10, n/30, FOB shipping point, freight prepaid and added to the invoice $36 (total $646).

Purchases		Freight In		Accounts Payable	
+	–	+	–	–	+
610		36			646

May 4 Bought paper sacks on account from BB Paper Products, their invoice no. 962D, dated May 4, terms n/30, $98.

Store Supplies		Accounts Payable	
+	–	–	+
98			98

Figure 6-10

PURCHASES JOURNAL

	DATE	SUPPLIER'S NAME	INVOICE NO.	INVOICE DATE	TERMS	POST. REF.	ACCOUNTS PAYABLE CREDIT	
1	19–							
2	May 2	Cordez Specialty						
3		Company	L311	5/1	2/10, n/30	✓	6 4 6 00	
4	4	BB Paper Products	962D	5/4	n/30	✓	9 8 00	
5	5	Noll Cabinet Shop	4273	5/5	n/30	✓	6 2 9 00	
6	9	C. B. Boles Company	C-349	5/7	1/10, n/30	✓	4 1 6 00	
7	16	Gable and Son	124-9	5/15	2/10, n/30	✓	3 9 2 00	
8	24	Moore Office Machines	N92	5/23	n/30	✓	5 1 5 71	
9	27	Curtis, Inc.	517R	5/26	1/15, n/60	✓	3 0 4 00	
10	30	Coe Office Supplies	5119	5/30	n/30	✓	4 2 36	
11	31	Brice Corporation	D274	5/29	2/10, n/30	✓	2 7 7 20	
12	31						3 3 2 0 27	
13							(2 2 1)	
14								

May 5 Bought a display case on account from Noll Cabinet Shop, their invoice no. 4273, dated May 5; terms n/30, $629.

Store Equipment		Accounts Payable	
+	−	−	+
629			629

These transactions, as well as other transactions during the month, are now recorded in the multicolumn purchases journal shown in Figure 6-10 at the bottom of the page.

For each transaction recorded in the multicolumn purchases journal, the amount to be credited is entered in the Accounts Payable Credit column. The next three columns are used to record the particular accounts most frequently affected. These are called special columns because one special account is involved. The final set of columns, under the heading Other Accounts Debit, is used to record the buying of items not provided for in the special debit columns.

Posting from the Multicolumn Purchases Journal

Posting to the creditors' accounts in the accounts payable ledger is similar to posting from a three-column purchases journal. Posting is done daily, and the check marks (√) in the Post. Ref. column indicate that the amounts have been posted separately.

Performance Objective 6

Post from a multicolumn purchases journal to an accounts payable ledger and a general ledger.

PAGE ___62___

PURCHASES DEBIT	FREIGHT IN DEBIT	STORE SUPPLIES DEBIT	OTHER ACCOUNTS DEBIT				
			ACCOUNT	POST. REF.	AMOUNT		
							1
							2
6 1 0 00	3 6 00						3
		9 8 00					4
			Store Equipment	118	6 2 9 00		5
4 0 4 00	1 2 00						6
3 9 2 00							7
			Office Equipment	117	5 1 5 71		8
3 0 4 00							9
			Office Supplies	116	4 2 36		10
2 6 4 20	1 3 00						11
1 9 7 4 20	6 1 00	9 8 00			1 1 8 7 07		12
(5 1 1)	(5 1 4)	(1 1 5)			(X)		13
							14

The amounts listed in the Other Accounts Debit column are posted separately—usually on a daily basis. The posting process is the same as that for posting from a general journal. The account numbers recorded in the Post. Ref. column indicate that the amounts have been posted.

At the end of the month, first prove that the sum of the debit totals equals the total of the Accounts Payable Credit column. This process is referred to as crossfooting the journal.

	Debit Totals		**Credit Total**
Purchases	$1,974.20	Accounts Payable	$3,320.27
Freight In	61.00		
Store Supplies	98.00		
Other Accounts	1,187.07		
	$3,320.27		

Debits = Credits

Next, the accountant posts the special columns as totals. After posting the total amount, he or she records the ledger account number in parentheses below the total in the appropriate column. The (X) placed below the total of the Other Accounts Debit column means "this amount was not posted"—since the figures have already been posted separately.

Posting Directly from Purchase Invoices

Performance Objective 7

Post directly from purchase invoices to an accounts payable ledger, and journalize and post a summarizing entry in the general journal.

Posting from purchase invoices is a shortcut like posting from sales invoices (described in Chapter 5). The accountant posts to the individual creditors' accounts daily, directly from the purchase invoices. The suppliers' invoice numbers rather than journal page numbers are recorded in the Post. Ref. column. The Accounts Payable controlling account in the general ledger is brought up to date at the end of the month by making a summarizing entry in the general journal. The accountant debits Purchases and Freight In, as well as any assets the company bought on account, and credits Accounts Payable.

Since posting directly from purchase invoices is a variation of the accounting system, we will use a different example: Engle Tire Center. This firms sorts its invoices for the month and finds that the totals are as follows: purchases of merchandise, $9,164; freight charges on merchandise, $291; store supplies, $168; office supplies, $126; store equipment, $520. The accountant then makes a summarizing entry in the general journal, as follows.

			GENERAL JOURNAL											PAGE __37__				
	DATE		DESCRIPTION	POST. REF.		DEBIT					CREDIT					
1	19–																	1
2	Oct.	31	Purchases	511	9	1	6	4	00									2
3			Freight In	514		2	9	1	00									3
4			Store Supplies	116		1	6	8	00									4
5			Office Supplies	115		1	2	6	00									5
6			Store Equipment	128		5	2	0	00									6
7			Accounts Payable	221							10	2	6	9	00			7
8			Summarizing entry for total															8
9			purchase of goods															9
10			on account.															10
11																		11

The accountant posts the above entry to the general ledger accounts.

		GENERAL LEDGER													

ACCOUNT __Office Supplies__ ACCOUNT NO. __115__

								BALANCE					
DATE		ITEM	POST. REF.	DEBIT		CREDIT		DEBIT			CREDIT		
19–													
Oct.	31		J37	1 2 6 00				1 2 6 00					

ACCOUNT __Store Supplies__ ACCOUNT NO. __116__

								BALANCE					
DATE		ITEM	POST. REF.	DEBIT		CREDIT		DEBIT			CREDIT		
19–													
Oct.	31		J37	1 6 8 00				1 6 8 00					

ACCOUNT __Store Equipment__   ACCOUNT NO. __128__

DATE		ITEM	POST. REF.	DEBIT	CREDIT	BALANCE DEBIT	BALANCE CREDIT
19–							
Oct.	31		J37	5 2 0 00		5 2 0 00	

ACCOUNT __Accounts Payable__   ACCOUNT NO. __221__

DATE		ITEM	POST. REF.	DEBIT	CREDIT	BALANCE DEBIT	BALANCE CREDIT
19–							
Oct.	31		J37		10 2 6 9 00		10 2 6 9 00

ACCOUNT __Purchases__   ACCOUNT NO. __511__

DATE		ITEM	POST. REF.	DEBIT	CREDIT	BALANCE DEBIT	BALANCE CREDIT
19–							
Oct.	31		J37	9 1 6 4 00		9 1 6 4 00	

ACCOUNT __Freight In__   ACCOUNT NO. __514__

DATE		ITEM	POST. REF.	DEBIT	CREDIT	BALANCE DEBIT	BALANCE CREDIT
19–							
Oct.	31		J37	2 9 1 00		2 9 1 00	

This procedure does away with the need for a purchases journal, and it also includes the buying of any assets on account in the same summarizing entry. An example of an invoice is shown in Figure 6-11.

Figure 6-11

PASHINSKI BROTHERS
9600 Alhambra Street • San Francisco, CA • 94132

Invoice No. 13168

INVOICE

Sold to: Engle Tire Center
2716 Brighton Road
Burlingame, CA 94011

Rec'd October 7, 19—

Date: Oct. 4, 19—
Shipped by: Pacific Express Co.

Order Number	Salesperson	Terms	F.O.B.	Date Shipped
1635	J.K.	1/10, n/30	Burlingame	Oct. 4, 19—

Quantity	Description	Unit Price	Total
10	Pico, motorcycle front, raised letters RL 90-19 3.25 x 19	52.20	522.00
10	Pico, motorcycle rear, raised letters RP 90-14 5.10 x 16	52.20	522.00
		Total	1,044.00

Engle Tire Center posts the amount of the invoice to the account of the supplier in the accounts payable ledger:

ACCOUNTS PAYABLE LEDGER
NAME _Pashinski Brothers_
ADDRESS _9600 Alhambra St._
San Francisco, CA 94132

DATE		ITEM	POST. REF.	DEBIT	CREDIT	BALANCE
19—						
Oct.	7		13168		1 0 4 4 00	1 0 4 4 00

Engle Tire Center will also include the $1,044 figure in the summarizing entry recorded in the general journal, debiting Purchases and crediting Accounts Payable. Note that the supplier's invoice number is recorded in the Post. Ref. column in the Pashinski Brothers account.

Transportation Charges on the Buying of Assets Other than Merchandise

Any freight charges involved in the buying of any other assets, such as supplies or equipment, should be debited to their respective asset accounts. As an illustration, let's return to Dodson Plumbing Supply and assume this company bought display cases on account from C and C Cabinet Shop, at a cost of $2,700 plus freight charges of $90. As a convenience, the seller of the display cases prepaid the transportation costs for Dodson Plumbing Supply and then added the $90 to the invoice price of the cases. Let's visualize this by means of T accounts.

Store Equipment		Accounts Payable	
+	–	–	+
2,790			2,790

On the other hand, if Dodson Plumbing had paid the freight charges separately, the entry for the payment would be a debit to Store Equipment for $90 and a credit to Cash for $90.

R E M E M . B E R

Freight In is only used to record the transportation charges on merchandise intended for resale.

Internal Control of Purchases

Purchases is one area in which internal control is essential. Efficiency and security require most companies to work out careful plans and procedures for buying and paying for goods. This is understandable, as large sums of money are usually involved. The control aspect generally involves the following measures:

1. Purchases are made only after proper authorization is given. Purchase requisitions and purchase orders are all prenumbered, so that each form can be accounted for.

2. The receiving department carefully checks and counts all goods upon receipt. Later the report of the receiving department is verified against the purchase order and the purchase invoice.

3. The person who authorizes the payment is neither the person doing the ordering nor the person actually writing the check. Payment is authorized only after the verifications have been made.

4. The person who actually writes the check has not been involved in any of the foregoing purchasing procedures.

Cash Payments Journal: Service Enterprise

The **cash payments journal,** as the name implies, is used to record all transactions in which cash goes out, or decreases. Cash payments are made by check, a document directing the bank to transfer funds from the business's account to the recipient. When the cash payments journal is used, all transactions in which cash is credited *must* be recorded in it. This journal may be used for a service as well as a merchandising business.

To get acquainted with the cash payments journal, let's list some typical transactions of a service firm (such as a dry cleaner or a bowling alley) or of a professional enterprise (such as a lawyer's office) that result in a decrease in cash. To illustrate, we will record the following transactions in the general journal to see where there is repetition.

May 2 Paid C. N. Brown Company, a creditor, on account, Ck. No. 63, $220.
     4 Paid cash for supplies, Ck. No. 64, $90.
     5 Paid wages for two weeks, Ck. No. 65, $1,216.
     6 Paid rent for the month, Ck. No. 66, $350.

GENERAL JOURNAL PAGE _____

	DATE		DESCRIPTION	POST. REF.	DEBIT	CREDIT	
1	19–						1
2	May	2	Accounts Payable,				2
3			C. N. Brown Co.		2 2 0 00		3
4			Cash			2 2 0 00	4
5			Paid on account, Ck. No. 63.				5
6							6
7		4	Supplies		9 0 00		7
8			Cash			9 0 00	8
9			Paid cash for supplies,				9
10			Ck. No. 64.				10
11							11
12		5	Wages Expense		1 2 1 6 00		12
13			Cash			1 2 1 6 00	13
14			Paid wages for two weeks,				14
15			Ck. No. 65.				15
16							16
17		6	Rent Expense		3 5 0 00		17
18			Cash			3 5 0 00	18
19			Paid rent for month,				19
20			Ck. No. 66.				20
21							21

Now let's appraise these four transactions. The first one would occur very often, as payments to creditors are made several times a month. Of the last three transactions, the debit to Wages Expense might occur twice a month, the debit to Rent Expense once a month, and the debit to Supplies only occasionally.

It is logical to include a Cash Credit column in a cash payments journal, because all transactions recorded in it involve a decrease in cash. Since payments to creditors are made often, there should also be an Accounts Payable Debit column. One can set up any other column that is used often enough to warrant it. Otherwise, an Other Accounts Debit column takes care of all the other transactions.

Now let's record these same transactions in the cash payments journal shown in Figure 6-12 and include a column titled Ck. No., which will be discussed in Chapter 8. If you think a moment, you will see that this is consistent with good management of cash. All expenditures but Petty Cash expenditures should be paid for by check. First let's repeat the transactions.

> **Performance Objective 8**
>
> Record transactions in a cash payments journal for a service enterprise.

May 2 Paid C. N. Brown Company, a creditor, on account, Ck. No. 63, $220.
4 Paid cash for supplies, Ck. No. 64, $90.
5 Paid wages for two weeks, Ck. No. 65, $1,216.
6 Paid rent for the month, Ck. No. 66, $350.

Figure 6-12

CASH PAYMENTS JOURNAL PAGE 62

	DATE	CK. NO.	ACCOUNT DEBITED	POST. REF.	OTHER ACCOUNTS DEBIT	ACCOUNTS PAYABLE DEBIT	CASH CREDIT	
1	19–							1
2	May 2	63	C. N. Brown Co.			2 2 0 00	2 2 0 00	2
3	4	64	Supplies		9 0 00		9 0 00	3
4	5	65	Wages Expense		1 2 1 6 00		1 2 1 6 00	4
5	6	66	Rent Expense		3 5 0 00		3 5 0 00	5
6								6

Note that you list all checks in consecutive order. In this way, *every* check is accounted for, which is necessary for internal control.

At the end of the month, post the special columns as totals to the general ledger accounts; do not post the total of the Other Accounts Debit column. An (X) is written below the total of the Other Accounts Debit column to indicate that the total amount is not posted. Post the figures in this column individually, then place the account number in the Post. Ref. column. Post the amounts in the Accounts Payable Debit column separately to individual accounts in the accounts payable ledger. After posting, put a check mark ($\sqrt{}$) in the Post. Ref. column. The posting letter designation for the cash payments journal is CP. Other transactions involving decreases in cash during May are as follows:

> · · · · · · · · · · · · · ·
> R E M E M B E R
>
> In the Post. Ref. column, a check mark indicates that the amount has been posted to the creditor's account in the accounts payable ledger. In the Post. Ref. column a dash indicates that the amounts will be posted as part of the totals of the special columns. In the Post. Ref. column an X indicates that the amount is posted as part of the column total.
> · · · · · · · · · · · · · ·

May 7 Paid a one-year premium for fire insurance, Ck. No. 67, $360.
9 Paid Madison, Inc., a creditor, on account, Ck. No. 68, $418.
11 Issued Ck. No. 69 in payment of delivery expense, $62.
14 Paid Rankin and Son, a creditor, on account, Ck. No. 70, $110.
16 Issued Ck. No. 71 to the Taylor State Bank, for a note payable, $660, $600 on the principal and $60 interest.

19 Bought equipment from Smith Company for $800, paying $200 down. Issued Ck. No. 73. The rest of this entry is recorded in the general journal, as explained below.

20 Paid wages for two weeks, Ck. No. 74, $1,340.

22 Issued Ck. No. 75 to Clara C. Shaw Advertising Agency for advertising, $94 (not previously recorded).

26 Paid telephone bill, Ck. No. 76, $26.

31 Issued check for freight bill on equipment purchased on May 19, Ck. No. 77, $28.

31 Paid Lusk and Travis, a creditor, on account, Ck. No. 78, $160.

These transactions are recorded in the cash payments journal illustrated in Figure 6-13. Notice that an X is placed in the Post. Ref. column when no individual amounts are posted.

Figure 6-13

CASH PAYMENTS JOURNAL

PAGE 62

	DATE	CK. NO.	ACCOUNT DEBITED	POST. REF.	OTHER ACCOUNTS DEBIT	ACCOUNTS PAYABLE DEBIT	CASH CREDIT	
1	19–							1
2	May 2	63	C. N. Brown Co.	✓		2 2 0 00	2 2 0 00	2
3	4	64	Supplies	115	9 0 00		9 0 00	3
4	5	65	Wages Expense	521	1 2 1 6 00		1 2 1 6 00	4
5	6	66	Rent Expense	524	3 5 0 00		3 5 0 00	5
6	7	67	Prepaid					6
7			Insurance	117	3 6 0 00		3 6 0 00	7
8	9	68	Madison, Inc.	✓		4 1 8 00	4 1 8 00	8
9	11	69	Delivery Expense	530	6 2 00		6 2 00	9
10	14	70	Rankin and Son	✓		1 1 0 00	1 1 0 00	10
11	16	71	Notes Payable	210	6 0 0 00			11
12			Interest Expense	529	6 0 00		6 6 0 00	12
13	19	72	Void	—				13
14	19	73	Equipment	X	2 0 0 00		2 0 0 00	14
15	20	74	Wages Expense	521	1 3 4 0 00		1 3 4 0 00	15
16	22	75	Advertising					16
17			Expense	515	9 4 00		9 4 00	17
18	26	76	Telephone					18
19			Expense	519	2 6 00		2 6 00	19
20	31	77	Equipment	124	2 8 00		2 8 00	20
21	31	78	Lusk and Travis	✓		1 6 0 00	1 6 0 00	21
22	31				4 4 2 6 00	9 0 8 00	5 3 3 4 00	22
23					(X)	(2 2 1)	(1 1 1)	23
24								24

FYI

If an asset is purchased with a cash payment and the remainder on account, the entry may be made in two journals. Place the amount of the down payment in the cash payments journal (put an X in the Posting Reference column for the asset) and the remainder in the general journal (put an X in the Posting Reference column for Cash). An alternative is to record the entire entry in the cash payments journal, placing parentheses around the amount in the Accounts Payable debit column. The parentheses indicate "the opposite," in this case a credit to Accounts Payable.

. . . .

R E M E M B E R

The (X) below the total of the Other Accounts Debit column means "do not post."

. . . .

After totaling the columns at the end of the month, check the accuracy of the footings by proving that the sum of the debit totals equals the sum of the credit totals. Since you have posted the individual amounts in the Other Accounts Debit column to the general ledger, the only posting that remains is the credit to the Cash account for $5,334 and the debit to the Accounts Payable (controlling) account for $908.

	Debit Totals		Credit Total	
Other Accounts	$4,426.00		Cash	$5,334.00
Accounts Payable	908.00			
	$5,334.00			

Debits = Credits

The posting process for the cash payments journal is similar to the posting process for the cash receipts journal. Individual amounts in the Accounts Payable Debit column and the general journal are usually posted daily to the subsidiary ledger. Individual amounts in the Other Accounts Debit column of the special journal and individual amounts in the general journal are usually posted daily to the general ledger. Totals of the Cash Credit column and the Accounts Payable Debit column are posted at the end of the month.

Cash Payments Journal: Merchandising Enterprise

Performance Objective 9

Record transactions involving cash discounts in a cash payments journal for a merchandising enterprise.

A cash payments journal for a merchandising enterprise is a special journal used to record all transactions in which cash goes out, or decreases. There is one slight difference between the cash payments journal for a merchandising enterprise and that for a service enterprise. This difference has to do with the cash discounts available to a merchandising business. Recall that a cash discount is the amount that the buyer may deduct from the bill; this acts as an incentive to make the buyer pay the bill promptly. The buyer considers the cash discount to be a Purchases Discount, because it relates to the buyer's purchase of merchandise. The Purchases Discount account, like Purchases Returns and Allowances, is treated as a deduction from Purchases on the buyer's income statement.

Let us return to Dodson Plumbing Supply and assume that the following transactions take place. To demonstrate the debits and credits, let's show some typical transactions in the form of T accounts.

. . . .

R E M E M B E R

The cash discount does not apply to freight charges billed separately on an invoice.
. . . .

Transaction (a) August 2: Bought merchandise on account from Colvin, Inc., $710, their invoice no. 2706, dated July 31; terms 2/10, n/30; FOB San Francisco; freight prepaid and added to the invoice, $49 (total $759).

Transaction (b) August 8: Issued Ck. No. 76 to Colvin, Inc., in payment of invoice no. 2706 less the cash discount of $14.20, $744.80 ($759 − $14.20), which is recorded in the cash payments journal. Notice that the discount applies only to the amount billed for the merchandise (2 percent of $710). Here are the transactions shown in T accounts:

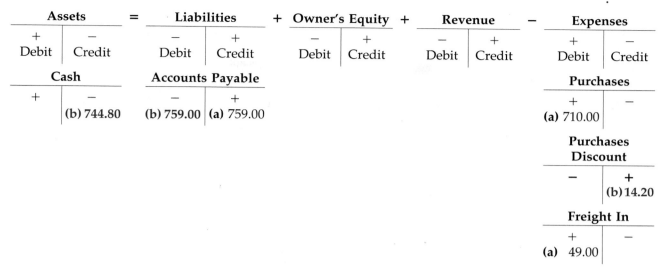

Any well-managed business takes advantage of a purchases discount whenever possible. So, if a discount is generally available to the business, it is worthwhile to set up a special Purchases Discount Credit column in the cash payments journal. Transaction **(b)**, August 8, looks like this in the cash payments journal:

	DATE	CK. NO.	ACCOUNT NAME	POST. REF.	OTHER ACCOUNTS DEBIT	ACCOUNTS PAYABLE DEBIT	PURCHASES DISCOUNT CREDIT	CASH CREDIT	
			CASH PAYMENTS JOURNAL					PAGE __26__	
1	19–								1
2	Aug. 8	76	Colvin, Inc.			7 5 9 00	1 4 20	7 4 4 80	2
3									3

Here are some other transactions of Dodson Plumbing Supply involving decreases in cash during August. Note that credit terms vary among the different creditors. Detailed information on the purchase invoices paid below is available in the purchases journal shown in Figure 6-5 (on page 245).

Aug. 10 Paid wages for two-week period, Ck. No. 77, $1,680.

   11 Issued Ck. No. 78 to Adams Manufacturing Company, in payment of invoice no. 10611 ($564), less return ($70); less cash discount, 2/10, n/30; $484.12 ($564 − $70 = $494; $494.00 × .02 = $9.88; $494.00 − $9.88 = $484.12).

   12 Bought supplies for cash; issued Ck. No. 79 payable to Davenport Office Supplies, $70.

   15 Issued Ck. No. 80 to Spargo Products Company in payment of their invoice no. B643 ($165) less return ($42); less cash discount, 1/10, n/30; $121.87 [$165 − $42 = $123; freight charges totaled $10.00 ($123 − $10 = $113); $113.00 × .01 = $1.13; $123.00 − $1.13 = $121.87].

   16 Bought merchandise for cash, Ck. No. 81, payable to Jones and Son, $200.

R E M E M B E R

After posting to the accounts payable subsidiary ledger from the cash payments journal, record a check mark in the Post. Ref. column in the cash payments journal.

19 Received bill and issued Ck. No. 82 to Monroe Express for freight charges on merchandise purchased earlier from Adams Manufacturing Company, $60.

23 Issued Ck. No. 84 to American Fire Insurance Company for insurance premium for one year, $420.

25 Paid wages for two-week period, Ck. No. 85, $1,750.

27 Paid F. P. Franz for merchandise he returned on a cash sale, Ck. No. 86, $51.

31 Issued Ck. No. 87 to Richter and Son in payment of invoice no. 902, net 30 days, $180.

The transaction of August 19 paying the freight bill to Monroe Express increases the Freight In account, as the transportation charges are for merchandise purchased.

Now let's record these transactions in the cash payments journal (Figure 6-14). After that has been done, Dodson Plumbing's accountant proves the equality of debits and credits:

	Debit Totals			**Credit Totals**	
Other Accounts	$4,231.00		Cash	$5,761.79	
Accounts Payable	1,556.00		Purchases Discount	25.21	
	$5,787.00			$5,787.00	

Debits = Credits

Figure 6-14

CASH PAYMENTS JOURNAL   PAGE 26

	DATE	CK. NO.	ACCOUNT NAME	POST. REF.	OTHER ACCOUNTS DEBIT	ACCOUNTS PAYABLE DEBIT	PURCHASES DISCOUNT CREDIT	CASH CREDIT	
1	19–								1
2	Aug. 8	76	Colvin, Inc.	✓		7 5 9 00	1 4 20	7 4 4 80	2
3	10	77	Wages Expense	521	1 6 8 0 00			1 6 8 0 00	3
4	11	78	Adams Manufacturing Company	✓		4 9 4 00	9 88	4 8 4 12	4
5	12	79	Supplies	115	7 0 00			7 0 00	5
6	15	80	Spargo Products Company	✓		1 2 3 00	1 13	1 2 1 87	6
7	16	81	Purchases	511	2 0 0 00			2 0 0 00	7
8	19	82	Freight In	514	6 0 00			6 0 00	8
9	23	83	Void	—					9
10	23	84	Prepaid Insurance	117	4 2 0 00			4 2 0 00	10
11	25	85	Wages Expense	521	1 7 5 0 00			1 7 5 0 00	11
12	27	86	Sales Returns and Allowances	412	5 1 00			5 1 00	12
13	31	87	Richter and Son	✓		1 8 0 00		1 8 0 00	13
14	31				4 2 3 1 00	1 5 5 6 00	2 5 21	5 7 6 1 79	14
15					(X)	(2 2 1)	(5 1 3)	(1 1 1)	15
16									16

Internal Control of Cash

n a small business, the owner or manager usually signs all the checks. However, if the owner delegates the authority to sign checks to some other person, that person should *not* have access to the accounting records. This helps to prevent fraud, because an employee could conceal a cash disbursement in the accounting records. In other words, for a medium-sized to large-size business, it's worth a manager's while to keep a separate book, which in this case is the cash payments journal. One person writes the checks; another person records the checks in the cash payments journal. In this way, one person acts as a check on the other. There would have to be agreement between the two people for embezzlement to take place. Again, this precaution is consistent with a good system of internal control, because it is less likely embezzlement will occur if several people are involved in handling different parts of the cash transactions.

R E M E M B E R

To the seller, a cash discount is a sales discount and is recorded in the cash receipts journal as a debit. To the purchaser, a cash discount is a purchases discount and is recorded in the cash payments journal as a credit.

Purchases Returns and Allowances, Purchases Discounts, and Freight In

n the fundamental accounting equation, to be consistent with the income statement, we placed Purchases Returns and Allowances and Purchases Discounts under Purchases with the plus and minus signs reversed. Both accounts are considered contra accounts and are subtracted from Purchases on the income statement. Since Freight In increases the cost of purchases, it must be added. A portion of the Cost of Goods Sold section of the annual income statement of Dodson Plumbing Supply, as well as the Revenue from Sales section (taken from Figure 7-4 in the next chapter), is presented below. We will discuss the Cost of Goods Sold in detail in Chapter 7.

Dodson Plumbing Supply
Income Statement
For Year Ended December 31, 19–

Revenue from Sales:			
Sales		$ 195 1 8 0 00	
Less: Sales Returns and Allowances	$ 8 4 0 00		
Sales Discount	1 8 8 0 00	2 7 2 0 00	
Net Sales			$ 192 4 6 0 00
Cost of Goods Sold:			
Merchandise Inventory, January 1, 19–		$ 67 0 0 0 00	
Purchases	$87 1 4 0 00		
Less: Purchases Returns and			
Allowances	$ 832.00		
Purchases Discount	1,248.00	2 0 8 0 00	
Net Purchases	$85 0 6 0 00		
Add Freight In	2 4 6 0 00		
Delivered Cost of Purchases		87 5 2 0 00	
Goods Available for Sale		$ 154 5 2 0 00	

Trade Discounts

Manufacturers and wholesalers of many lines of products publish catalogs listing their products at retail prices. These firms offer their customers substantial reductions from the list or catalog prices. The reductions from the list price are called **trade discounts.** These discounts are *not related* to cash payments. Firms list these trade discounts on sheets showing trade discounts that may be applied to the catalog prices. This saves the cost of reproducing the catalogs.

Firms may quote trade discounts as a single percentage such as 40 percent off the listed catalog price of $8,000. In this case, the selling price is calculated as follows:

List or catalog price	$8,000
Less trade discount of 40% ($8,000 × .4)	3,200
Selling price	$4,800

Firms may also quote trade discounts as a chain, or series, of percentages. For example, a distributor of automobile parts grants discounts of 30 percent, 10 percent, and 10 percent off the listed catalog price of $900. In this case, the selling price is calculated as follows:

List or catalog price	$900.00
Less first trade discount of 30% ($900 × .3)	270.00
Remainder after first discount	$630.00
Less second trade discount of 10% ($630 × .1)	63.00
Remainder after second discount	$567.00
Less third discount of 10% ($567 × .1)	56.70
Selling price	$510.30

Neither the seller nor the buyer records trade discounts in the accounts. They enter only the selling price after the single discount or the chain discount has been applied.

Remember, firms can apply cash discounts after the trade discounts. In either of the above situations, if the buyer pays the invoice within ten days, the seller applies the cash discount to the selling price (which is the price after the trade discount has been applied).

Comparison of Entries for Two Companies' Purchases and Sales

Figure 6-15 compares purchases and sales of merchandise by two companies. Each event is journalized first on the books of the purchaser and then on the books of the seller.

Purchaser's Books — Able Company

Seller's Books — Baker Company

Figure 6-15

Bought merchandise from Baker Company, $500; terms 2/10, n/30.

Dr. Purchases, $500
  Cr. Accounts Payable, $500

Sold merchandise to Able Company, $500; terms 2/10, n/30.

Dr. Accounts Receivable, $500
  Cr. Sales, $500

Received credit memo from Baker Company for return of merchandise, $100.

Dr. Accounts Payable, $100
  Cr. Purchases Returns and
    Allowances

Issued credit memo to Able Company for return of merchandise, $100.

Dr. Sales Returns and
    Allowances, $100
  Cr. Accounts Receivable, $100

Paid Baker Company within the discount period, $392 ($500 − $100 = $400; $400 x .02 = $8; $400 − $8 = $392).

Dr. Accounts Payable, $400
  Cr. Cash, $392
  Cr. Purchases Discount, $8

Received cash from Able Company within the discount period, $392.

Dr. Cash, $392
Dr. Sales Discount, $8
  Cr. Accounts Receivable, $400

FYI

The recommended order of posting to the subsidiary ledgers and general ledger is (1) sales journal, (2) purchases journal, (3) the cash receipts journal, and (4) the cash payments journal. General journal entries are posted on the specific dates of the transactions.

FYI

Special journals are set up to save time and improve accuracy and efficiency. A company may use any combination of journals. One company may use a cash payments journal and a general journal. Another company may use all five journals. Size and needs of the company will determine the journals used.

Comparison of the Five Types of Journals

We have now looked at four special journals and the general journal. It is very important for a business to select and use the journals that will provide the most efficient accounting system possible. Figure 6-16 summarizes the applications of and correct procedures for using the journals we have discussed.

Figure 6-16

Types of Transactions

Sale of merchandise on account	Purchase of merchandise on account	Receipt of cash	Payment of cash	All other

Evidenced by Source Documents

Sales invoice	Purchase invoice	Credit card receipts / Cash register tape / Checks	Check stub	Miscellaneous

Types of Journals

Sales journal	Purchases journal	Cash receipts journal	Cash payments journal	General journal

Posting to Ledger Accounts

Individual amounts posted daily to the accounts receivable ledger and the total posted monthly to the general ledger.	*Individual amounts posted daily to the accounts payable ledger and the totals of the special columns posted monthly to the general ledger.*	*Individual amounts in the Accounts Receivable Credit column posted daily to the accounts receivable ledger.* *Individual amounts in the Other Accounts columns posted daily to the general ledger.* *Totals of special columns posted monthly.*	*Individual amounts in the Accounts Payable Debit column posted daily to the accounts payable ledger.* *Individual amounts in the Other Accounts columns posted daily to the general ledger.* *Totals of special columns posted monthly.*	*Entries posted daily to the subsidiary ledgers and the general ledger.*

Computer Applications

Commercial software programs frequently provide accounts payable modules. This feature allows a business to integrate or link the general ledger with the accounts payable ledger. This means that when a purchase on account, a return of merchandise, or a payment to a vendor is entered into the program, it is posted not only to the vendor's account, but also to the general ledger. This is a major time-saving feature, as was the integration of accounts receivable transactions.

Purchases and Payables Journal

The purchases and payables journal in this software provides basically the same information as the purchases journal shown earlier in Figure 6-5. The difference again is the amount of time involved in preparing the manual purchases journal over the computerized purchases journal. Figure 6-17 shows the purchase of merchandise for resale on account by Dodson Plumbing Supply entered into an accounting software program. Each entry required a minimum amount of keying; the day, selecting the vendor name, and keying once the amount entered into the appropriate space or field on the screen. Notice that the program split the purchase of merchandise and the charge for freight into two entries, but the outcome will be the same.

Figure 6-17

```
                        Dodson Plumbing Supply
                        1400 Jackson Avenue
                        San Diego, CA  92102

                        Purchases & Payables Journal

                        8/1/9- to 8/31/9-
                                                                    Page 1

Src    Date    ID#              Account              Debit        Credit   Job
PJ    8/2/9-   Purchase; Colvin, Inc.
               00000001  2-2210  Accounts Payable                 $710.00
               00000001  2-2210  Accounts Payable                 $49.00
               00000001  5-5110  Purchases           $710.00
               00000001  5-5140  Freight In          $49.00

PJ    8/3/9-   Purchase; Richter and Son
               00000002  2-2210  Accounts Payable                 $772.00
               00000002  2-2210  Accounts Payable                 $57.00
               00000002  5-5110  Purchases           $772.00
               00000002  5-5140  Freight In          $57.00

PJ    8/5/9-   Purchase; Adams Manufacturing Co.
               00000003  2-2210  Accounts Payable                 $564.00
               00000003  5-5110  Purchases           $564.00

PJ    8/9/9-   Purchase; Spargo Products Co.
               00000004  2-2210  Accounts Payable                 $155.00
               00000004  2-2210  Accounts Payable                 $10.00
               00000004  5-5110  Purchases           $155.00
               00000004  5-5140  Freight In          $10.00

PJ    8/18/9-  Purchase; L. C. Waters
               00000005  2-2210  Accounts Payable                 $228.00
               00000005  5-5110  Purchases           $228.00

PJ    8/25/9-  Purchase; Delaney and Cox
               00000006  2-2210  Accounts Payable                 $362.00
               00000006  2-2210  Accounts Payable                 $14.00
               00000006  5-5110  Purchases           $362.00
               00000006  5-5140  Freight In          $14.00

PJ    8/26/9-  Purchase; Colvin, Inc.
               00000007  2-2210  Accounts Payable                 $384.00
               00000007  2-2210  Accounts Payable                 $22.00
               00000007  5-5110  Purchases           $384.00
               00000007  5-5140  Freight In          $22.00

                                                                 $3,327.00
```

Card File (Schedule of Accounts Payable)

FYI

While we can use a computer program to stay on top of due dates, it can also be done with a tickler file. A tickler file consists of a series of folders numbered 1 through 31. A copy of the invoice is placed in the folder for the date on which it needs to be paid to receive the discount. Either way, manual or computerized, paying on time pays off.

As a result of the entries in the purchases and payables journal, the amounts are posted to the accounts payable ledger as well as to the general ledger. Furthermore, these entries also produce a schedule of accounts payable called a card file in this software because each vendor has an electronic card or record containing information about the vendor—address, telephone, contact person, merchandise information, and balance due (see Figure 6-18). You will see more and more software in which screens simulate index cards, a check, a deposit slip—all in an attempt to make the user more comfortable when they see familiar forms on the screen.

With the card file or schedule of accounts payable, the bookkeeper or accountant can verify that the total of the schedule of accounts payable is equal to the total of the general ledger control account. Then, when the statements are received from vendors, they can be checked for accuracy against the schedule of accounts payable.

In these illustrations, we have emphasized purchases on account. No payments have been made to vendors yet, but there were two returns. The total of the card file is the same as the Accounts Payable total shown on page 253.

Figure 6-18

```
                          Dodson Plumbing Supply
                           1400 Jackson Avenue
                          San Diego, CA  92102

                                Card File

                                                                 Page 1

        Name              Phone        Type      Current Balance   Identifiers

Adams Manufacturing Co.                Vendor         $494.00
Colvin, Inc.                           Vendor       $1,165.00
Delaney and Cox                        Vendor         $376.00
L. C. Waters                           Vendor         $552.00
Richter and Son                        Vendor       $1,009.00
Spargo Products Co.                    Vendor         $123.00

Total Accounts Payable                              $3,719.00
```

Cash Payments Journal

The Cash Payments (or Cash Disbursements) Journal printed from this software (Figure 6-19) looks different from the one in Figure 6-14, but the same changes will occur in the general ledger and the accounts payable after posting. Again, you should be seeing the similarity of the formats of the purchases and payables journal compared to the sales journal; the card files for schedules of accounts receivable and payable, and the similarity of the formats of the cash payments journal and the cash receipts journal. An even more important similarity is what you are learning manually compared to the electronic output you see illustrated here.

Figure 6-19

```
                        Dodson Plumbing Supply
                         1400 Jackson Avenue
                         San Diego, CA  92102

                       Cash Disbursements Journal

                          8/1/9- to 8/31/9-
```
                                                                    Page 1

Src	Date	ID#		Account	Debit	Credit	Job
CD	8/8/9-		Payment; Colvin, Inc.				
		76	1-1110	Cash		$744.80	
		76	5-5130	Purchases Discount		$14.20	
		76	2-2210	Accounts Payable	$759.00		
CD	8/10/9-		Payroll				
		77	1-1110	Cash		$1,680.00	
		77	2-2230	Wages Expense	$1,680.00		
CD	8/11/9-		Payment; Adams Manufacturing Co.				
		78	1-1110	Cash		$484.12	
		78	5-5130	Purchases Discount		$9.88	
		78	2-2210	Accounts Payable	$494.00		
CD	8/12/9-		Davenport				
		79	1-1110	Cash		$70.00	
		79	1-1150	Supplies	$70.00		
CD	8/15/9-		Payment; Spargo Products Co.				
		80	1-1110	Cash		$121.87	
		80	5-5130	Purchases Discount		$1.13	
		80	2-2210	Accounts Payable	$123.00		
CD	8/16/9-		Jones and Son				
		81	1-1110	Cash		$200.00	
		81	5-5110	Purchases	$200.00		
CD	8/19/9-		Monroe Express				
		82	1-1110	Cash		$60.00	
		82	5-5140	Freight In	$60.00		
CD	8/23/9-		Void				
		83	1-1110	Cash	$0.00		
CD	8/23/9-		American Fire Insurance Co.				
		84	1-1110	Cash		$420.00	
		84	1-1170	prepaid Insurance	$420.00		
CD	8/25/9-		Payroll				
		85	1-1110	Cash		$1,750.00	
		85	2-2230	Wages Expense	$1,750.00		
CD	8/27/9-		F. P. Franz				
		86	1-1110	Cash		$51.00	
		86	4-4120	Sales Returns and Allow.	$51.00		
CD	8/31/9-		Payment; Richter and Son				
		87	1-1110	Cash		$180.00	
		87	2-2210	Accounts Payable	$180.00		

CHAPTER REVIEW

R eview of Learning Objectives

1. **Record transactions in a three-column purchases journal.**

   The three-column purchases journal handles the purchase of merchandise on account with the freight charge being prepaid by the seller and included in the invoice total. A transaction can be recorded on one line including the date, supplier's name, invoice number, invoice date, terms, Accounts Payable Credit, Freight In Debit, and Purchases Debit.

2. **Post from a three-column purchases journal to an accounts payable ledger and a general ledger.**

   Amounts in the Accounts Payable Credit column are posted daily to the accounts payable ledger. At the end of the month, the totals are posted to the general ledger as a debit to Purchases, a debit to Freight In, and a credit to Accounts Payable.

3. **Record transactions involving purchases returns and allowances in a general journal.**

   When a credit memo is received for the return of merchandise or as an allowance for damaged merchandise, the buyer credits Purchases Returns and Allowances. If the merchandise was bought on account, the buyer debits Accounts Payable. The transaction is recorded in the general journal.

4. **Prepare a schedule of accounts payable.**

   A schedule of accounts payable, listing the balance of each individual creditor's account, is prepared from the accounts payable ledger.

5. **Record transactions in a multicolumn purchases journal.**

   A multicolumn purchases journal handles transactions involving the buying of anything on account, as well as freight charges prepaid by suppliers on behalf of the buyer. Transactions can be recorded on one line. There are special columns for the most frequently used accounts as well as an Other Accounts Debit column.

6. **Post from a multicolumn purchases journal to an accounts payable ledger and a general ledger.**

   Amounts in the Accounts Payable Credit column are posted daily to the accounts payable ledger. Amounts in the Other Accounts Debit column are posted to the general ledger. At the end of the month, the totals of the special columns are posted to the general ledger.

7. **Post directly from purchase invoices to an accounts payable ledger, and journalize and post a summarizing entry in the general journal.**

   As a further shortcut, the firm may post to the accounts of the individual creditors in the accounts payable ledger directly from invoices for purchases of merchandise bought on credit. At the end of the month, the accountant makes a summarizing entry in the general journal, debiting Purchases, Freight In, and assets that were acquired and crediting Accounts Payable for the total of the invoices.

8. **Record transactions in a cash payments journal for a service enterprise.**

A cash payment for a service enterprise can be handled on one line in a cash payments journal. The cash payments journal contains the following columns: Date, Ck. No., Account Debited, Post. Ref., Other Accounts Debit, Accounts Payable Debit, and Cash Credit.

9. **Record transactions involving cash discounts in a cash payments journal for a merchandising enterprise.**

A cash payment for a merchandising enterprise including purchases discounts can be recorded on one line in a cash payments journal. The cash payments journal contains the following columns: Date, Ck. No., Account Name, Post. Ref., Other Accounts Debit, Accounts Payable Debit, Purchases Discount Credit, and Cash Credit.

G lossary

Accounts payable ledger A subsidiary ledger consisting of individual accounts for all the creditors. **(247)**

Cash payments journal A special journal used to record all transactions in which cash goes out, or decreases. **(261)**

FOB destination The seller pays the freight charges and includes them in the selling price. **(241)**

FOB shipping point The buyer pays the freight charges between the point of shipment and the destination. Payment may be made directly to the carrier upon receiving the goods or to the supplier if the supplier prepaid the freight charges on behalf of the buyer. **(241)**

Freight In The account used to record transportation charges on incoming merchandise intended for resale. **(241)**

Purchase order A written order from the buyer of goods to the supplier, listing items wanted as well as terms of the transaction. **(237)**

Purchase requisition A form used to request that the Purchasing Department buy something. This form is intended for internal use within a company. **(237)**

Purchases An account for recording the cost of merchandise acquired for resale. **(240)**

Purchases Discount An account that records cash discounts granted by suppliers in return for prompt payment; it is treated as a deduction from Purchases. **(240)**

Purchases journal A special journal used to record the buying of goods on account. It may be used to record the purchase of merchandise only. Or, it may be a multicolumn journal, or invoice register, used to record the buying of anything on account. **(244)**

Purchases Returns and Allowances An account that records a company's return of merchandise it has purchased or a reduction in the bill because of damaged or unacceptable merchandise; it is treated as a deduction from Purchases. **(240)**

Schedule of accounts payable A listing of the balances of each supplier shown in the accounts payable ledger. **(252)**

Trade discount Substantial reduction from the list or catalog prices of goods, granted by the seller; not recorded by the buyer or the seller. **(268)**

QUESTIONS, EXERCISES, AND PROBLEMS

D iscussion Questions

1. Explain the process of proving the totals of a multicolumn purchases journal. What is this process called?
2. Explain the purpose of the purchase requisition, the purchase order, and the purchase invoice. Which item is used as the basis for a journal entry?
3. How can a computer be considered as merchandise by one company and office equipment by another?
4. Explain the meaning and importance of the shipping terms FOB destination and FOB shipping point. Who has title to the goods once they have been shipped?
5. Why is it worthwhile to post to the accounts payable ledger on a daily basis?
6. Explain the handling of payment of delivery costs for (a) merchandise sold, (b) merchandise purchased, and (c) store equipment purchased.
7. An electronics business purchased speakers for resale. The total of the invoice is $2,440, and it is subject to trade discounts of 15, 10, and 5. Compute the amount the dealer will pay for the speakers.
8. What are the normal balances of (a) Purchases, (b) Purchases Returns and Allowances, and (c) Purchases Discount?

E xercises

P.O.1

Journalize to a three-column purchases journal; total, prove, and rule it; and describe posting.

Exercise 6-1 Journalize the following two purchases of merchandise on p. 87 of the purchases journal below. Total, prove, and rule the purchases journal. Describe how this purchases journal would be posted to the general ledger and the accounts payable ledger.

June 25 Bought merchandise on account from Lodi Inc., $726.52, their invoice no. J335 dated June 23; terms 2/10, n/30, FOB Chicago; freight prepaid and added to the invoice, $36.33 (total $762.85).
28 Bought merchandise on account from Miracle Co., $691.60, their invoice no. 1848, dated June 26; terms, 1/10, n/30, FOB St. Louis; freight prepaid and added to the invoice, $34.58 (total $726.18).

PURCHASES JOURNAL   PAGE __87__

	DATE		SUPPLIER'S NAME	INVOICE NO.	INVOICE DATE	TERMS	POST. REF.	ACCOUNTS PAYABLE CREDIT	FREIGHT IN DEBIT	PURCHASES DEBIT	
1	19–										1
2	June	2	Miracle Co.	1822	5/31	2/10, n/30		4 0 3 83	1 9 23	3 8 4 60	2
3		3	Sports Co.	945	6/2	n/30		7 2 3 45	3 4 45	6 8 9 00	3
4		9	Sports Co.	950	6/6	1/10, n/30		1 5 0 1 50	7 1 50	1 4 3 0 00	4
5											5
6											6
7											7
8											8

Exercise 6-2 Complete the journal you began in Exercise 6-1 to show its appearance after posting the individual amounts and the column totals to the general ledger and accounts payable ledger T acounts below:

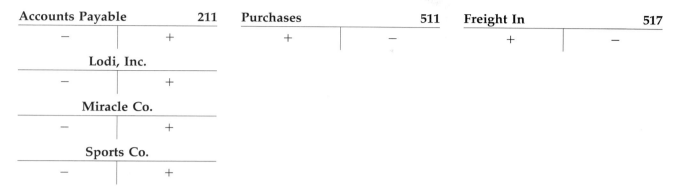

Accounts Payable	211
−	+

Lodi, Inc.	
−	+

Miracle Co.	
−	+

Sports Co.	
−	+

Purchases	511
+	−

Freight In	517
+	−

Exercise 6-3 Journalize the following entry on general journal page 92:

March   3 Received credit memo no. 185 from Alice's Loft, for merchandise returned, $37.

Post to the general ledger and accounts payable ledger T accounts.

	DATE	DESCRIPTION	POST. REF.	DEBIT	CREDIT	
GENERAL JOURNAL					PAGE 92	
1	19−					1
2						2
3						3
4						4
5						5
6						6
7						7
8						8
9						9

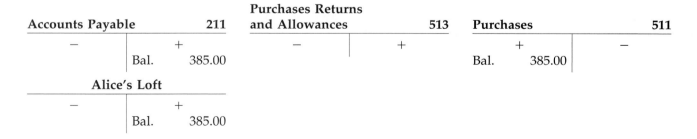

Accounts Payable	211
−	+
	Bal. 385.00

Alice's Loft	
−	+
	Bal. 385.00

Purchases Returns and Allowances	513
−	+

Purchases	511
+	−
Bal. 385.00	

P.O.4

Prepare a schedule of accounts payable.

Exercise 6-4 Prepare a schedule of accounts payable from the accounts payable ledger after completion of Exercise 6-2. Compare the total of the schedule of accounts payable with the balance of the Accounts Payable account in Exercise 6-2.

P.O.3,5,6

Describe purchases-related entries.

Exercise 6-5 Describe the transactions posted in the following general ledger T accounts:

	Cash		
+		−	
		(c)	1,176

	Accounts Payable		
−		+	
(b)	150	(a)	1,350
(c)	1,200		

	Purchases		
+		−	
(a)	1,350		

Purchases Returns and Allowances			
−		+	
		(b)	150

Purchases Discount			
−		+	
		(c)	24

P.O.7

Record and post purchases directly from invoices.

Exercise 6-6 A business firm posts directly from its purchase invoices. After sorting the invoices for the month, the totals are as follows: purchases of merchandise, $9,319; freight charges on merchandise, $184; store supplies, $147; office supplies, $102; store equipment, $1,226. Record the summarizing entry in the general journal.

P.O.8

Calculate amounts paid for merchandise purchases.

Exercise 6-7 For the following purchases of merchandise, determine the amount of cash to be paid:

Purchases	Invoice Date	Credit Terms	FOB	Amount of Purchase	Freight Charges	Total Invoice Amount	Returns and Allowances	Date Paid
a.	June 1	2/10, n30	Destination	$450	———	$ 450	———	June 30
b.	June 12	1/10, n/30	Destination	600	———	600	$100	June 21
c.	June 14	2/10, n/30	Shipping point	940	$60	1,000	———	June 20
d.	June 21	n/30	Shipping point	830	70	900	130	July 12
e.	June 24	1/10, n/30	Shipping point	760	50	810	90	July 3

P.O.1,5,8,9

Designate the appropriate journal.

Exercise 6-8 Indicate the journal in which each of the following transactions should be recorded. Assume a three-column purchases journal.

Transaction	Journal				
	S	P	CR	CP	J
a. Paid a creditor on account.					
b. Bought merchandise on account.					
c. Sold merchandise for cash.					
d. Adjusted for insurance expired.					
e. Received payment on account from a charge customer.					
f. Received a credit memo for merchandise returned.					
g. Bought equipment on credit.					
h. Sold merchandise on account.					
i. Recorded a customer's NSF checks.					
j. Invested personal noncash assets in the business.					
k. Withdrew cash for personal use.					

C onsider and Communicate

You are the manager of the Accounts Receivable Department for a merchandising business. Your billing clerk sent a bill for $2 to a customer who charged $100 in goods (including sales tax) with terms 2/10, n/30. The customer has called and indicated his displeasure. He can't understand an error like this since he paid in time. Explain to your billing clerk why Accounts Receivable is credited for $100 and not $98. How was permission given to send less than the full amount?

W hat If . . .

You have asked your client, a florist, to prepare a list of her Accounts Receivable by customer name, so that you may compare the balance with the balance of the control account in the general ledger.

She sent you the following list: Wholesale Florists, $1,250; Florist's Supply, $575; Pacific Petals, $340.

You recognize the names as those of her suppliers and not her customers. You ask her again for the Accounts Receivable list; and she sends the same list, adding that those are the people that need to *receive* a payment from her. When you list a few of her customers' names, she tells you that these are the Accounts Payable because those are people who need to *pay* her.

Is she confused? If so, explain how she is confused about Accounts Receivable and Accounts Payable. Also suggest ways to avoid communication problems in the future.

A Question of Ethics

You work in a retail store selling computers. One of the employees asks you to write up the sales invoice for the sale of a computer to him at cost without the owner's approval. The employee knows that the owner sometimes sells computers to the employees at a discount, but this employee insists that it will not be any money out of the owner's pocket if you do this. Can you do this for the employee? If the owner only approves the sale at a smaller discount, are you behaving ethically if you write up the sale at cost?

P roblem Set A

P.O.1,2,4

Problem 6-1A Malone Athletic Supply uses a three-column purchases journal. The company is located in St. Louis. On January 1 of this year, the balances of the ledger accounts are Accounts Payable, $4,443.33; Purchases, zero; Freight In, zero. In addition to a general ledger, the company also uses an accounts payable ledger. Transactions for January related to the purchase of merchandise are as follows:

Jan.   4 Bought twenty-four Keep-fit Treadmills from Full-Cycle Equipment Company, $12,396, invoice no. 791J, dated January 2; terms 1/10, n/30; FOB St. Louis.

6 Bought forty-eight Bauch Steppers from Kobe, Inc., $14,247.56, invoice no. L1015, dated Janaury 4; terms 2/10, n/30; FOB St. Louis.

7 Bought twenty-four programmable air resistance cycles from Kalama Company, $7,167.36, invoice no. AC969, dated January 6, terms net 30 days; FOB St. Louis.

10 Bought thirty-six Cascade-Country Skiers from Hercules, Inc., $8,969.76, invoice no. 9116D, dated January 8; terms 2/10, n/30; FOB St. Paul, freight prepaid and added to the invoice, $297 (total $9,266.76).

12 Bought sixty 58"-by-24" exercise mats from Kobe, Inc., $984.60, invoice no. L1196, dated January 10, terms 2/10, n/30; FOB St. Louis.

16 Bought seventy-two 1-pound wrist weights from Bascom, Inc., $524.88, invoice no. PE242, dated January 15; terms 1/10, n/30; FOB St. Louis.

20 Bought seventy-two 1.5-pound ankle weights from Bascom, Inc., $586.08, invoice no. PE316, dated January 19; terms 1/10, n/30; FOB St. Louis.

27 Bought thirty-six three-weight dumbbell racks from Hunter and Finch, $808.92, invoice no. N9226, dated January 24; terms net 30 days; FOB Chicago, freight prepaid and added to the invoice, $46 (total $854.92).

Instructions

1. Open the following creditor accounts in the accounts payable ledger and record the January 1 balances, if any, as given: Bascom, Inc., $917.50; Full-Cycle Equipment Company, $729.42; Hercules, Inc.; Hunter and Finch; Kalama Company, $2,796.41; Kobe, Inc. For the accounts having balances, write "Balance" in the Item column, and place a check mark in the Post. Ref. column.

2. Record the balance of $4,443.33 in the Accounts Payable controlling account as of January 1. Write "Balance" in the Item column and place a check mark in the Post. Ref. column.

3. Record the transactions in the purchases journal beginning with page 79.

4. Post to the accounts payable ledger daily.
5. Post to the general ledger at the end of the month.
6. Prepare a schedule of accounts payable, and compare the balance of the Accounts Payable controlling account with the total of the schedule of accounts payable.

Problem 6-2A Gretchen's Fine Leathers is located in Galway, Iowa. The company had the following purchases of merchandise and other assets and related returns and allowances during July of this year:

P.O.4,5,6

July   3 Bought merchandise on account from Vaughn, Inc., $933.40, invoice no. 4681, dated July 2; terms 2/10, n/30; FOB Galway.

        6 Bought merchandise on account from Foster Brothers, $827.86, invoice no. L433, dated July 5; terms net 30 days; FOB Chicago, freight prepaid and added to the invoice, $41 (total $868.86).

    10 Bought store supplies on account from Rivera Company, $261.74, invoice no. B187, dated July 9; terms net 30 days; FOB Chicago.

    12 Bought office supplies on account from Jones Office Supply, $183.92, invoice no. 4675, dated July 11; terms net 30 days; FOB Omaha, freight prepaid and added to the invoice, $5 (total $188.92). (Record Office Supplies for $188.92.)

    14 Received credit memo from Pettit Company for merchandise returned, $48, credit memo no. 717.

    16 Bought merchandise on account from Vaughn, Inc., $1,039.34, invoice no. 4699, dated July 14; terms 2/10, n/30; FOB Galway.

    22 Bought merchandise on account from Koch and Sons, $1,041, invoice no. N468, dated July 21; terms net 30 days; FOB Des Moines, freight prepaid and added to the invoice, $59 (total $1,100).

    26 Bought merchandise on account from Dorn and Kelly, $986.25, invoice no. 7347, dated July 24; terms 1/10, n/30; FOB Chicago.

    29 Received credit memo from Foster Brothers for merchandise returned, $92, credit memo no. 359.

    30 Bought merchandise on account from Pettit Company, $1,292.54, invoice no. R288, dated July 28; terms 2/10, n/30; FOB Newark, freight prepaid and added to the invoice, $117 (total $1,409.54).

    31 Bought merchandise on account from Dorn and Kelly, $772.12, invoice no. 7398, dated July 29; terms net 30 days; FOB Chicago.

    31 Bought merchandise on account from Foster Brothers, $516.56, invoice no. L512, dated July 30; terms net 30 days; FOB Chicago, freight prepaid and added to the invoice, $40 (total $556.56).

    31 Bought a microcomputer from Jones Office Supply, $3,119, invoice no. 5112, dated July 30, terms net 30 days; FOB Omaha, freight prepaid and added to the invoice, $16 (total $3,135). (Record Equipment for $3,135.)

Instructions

1. Open the following accounts in the accounts payable ledger and record the July 1 balances, if any, as given: Dorn and Kelly, $912.10; Foster Brothers; Jones Office Supply; Koch and Sons; Pettit Company, $1,846.20; Rivera Company; Vaughn, Inc., $424.15. For the accounts having balances, write

"Balance" in the Item column, and place a check mark in the Post. Ref. column.

2. Record the transactions in either the general journal, starting on page 29, or page 7 of the purchases journal as appropriate.

3. Post the entries to the creditors' accounts in the accounts payable ledger immediately after you make each journal entry.

4. Post the entries in the general journal and the Other Accounts Debit column of the purchases journal immediately after you make each journal entry.

5. In the space below the purchases journal, show proof that the sum of the debit totals equals the total of the Accounts Payable Credit column.

6. Post the totals of the special columns of the purchases journal at the end of the month.

7. Prepare a schedule of accounts payable, and compare the balance of the Accounts Payable controlling account with the total of the schedule of accounts payable.

P.O.7

Problem 6-3A Briggs Sash and Door, Houston, records sales of merchandise daily by posting directly from its sales invoices to the accounts receivable ledger. At the end of the month, it makes a summarizing entry in the general journal. It records purchases of goods on account the same way, daily, posting directly from the invoices to the accounts payable ledger and making a summarizing entry in the general journal at the end of the month. Sales of merchandise and purchases of goods on account during November of this year were as follows:

Sales of merchandise on account
Nov.   2 Moore Glass Specialties, no. 4122, $616.20.
        6 Philip Mason Construction, no. 4123, $712.46.
       10 Brent and Fry, no. 4124, $809.64.
       14 Henwood Lumber Products, no. 4125, $1,276.50.
       19 Branson and Clarkston, no. 4126, $1,042.27.
       24 L. C. Moreno, Inc., no. 4127, $871.56.
       27 Silverman Fine Homes, no. 4128, $2,927.64.
       29 Branard and Goods, no. 4129, $1,329.14.
       30 Hogan Paint and Glass, no. 4130, $1,803.93.
       30 Wardell and Company, no. 4131, $625.52.

Purchases of goods on account
Nov.   2 Warner Manufacturing Company, merchandise, $716.21, FOB Houston.
        7 Strutzel and Zale, merchandise, $2,962, FOB Houston.
       10 Briggs Wholesale Hardware, merchandise, $3,112; FOB Dallas; freight prepaid and added to the invoice, $242 (total $3,354).
       12 Ringle Custom Printing, office supplies, $79, FOB Houston.
       18 C and P Manufacturing Company, merchandise, $4,669.50; FOB El Paso; freight prepaid and added to the invoice, $114 (total $4,783.50).
       22 Ramsey Paper Company, store supplies, $119.72, FOB Houston.
       27 Reese Wood Products, merchandise, $3,942, FOB Houston.
       30 James Office Furniture, office equipment, $706.59, FOB Houston.

Instructions

1. Record the summarizing entry for the sale of merchandise on account in the general journal.
2. Record the summarizing entry for the purchases of goods on account in the general journal.

Problem 6-4A The following transactions were completed by Frodsham Decorating during January of this fiscal year. Terms of sale are 2/10, n/30.

P.O.1,2,3,4

Jan. 2 Paid rent for the month, $900, Ck. No. 921.

2 E. M. Frodsham, the owner, invested an additional $4,000 in the business.

3 Received check from Vantage Fabrics for $1,470 in payment of invoice, $1,500, less 2 percent cash discount.

3 Bought merchandise on account from Vincent and Company, $4,695, invoice no. 446; terms 2/10, n/30; dated Janaury 2.

6 Received check from Price and Shepard for $935.90 in payment of $955 invoice, less 2 percent cash discount.

7 Bought supplies on account from Davis Office Supply, $227, invoice no. 146; terms net 30 days.

7 Sold merchandise on account to Eckhardt and Stedman, $1,835, invoice no. 724.

11 Paid Vincent and Company $4,601.10, CK. No. 922, in payment of their $4,695 invoice, less cash discount.

14 Sold merchandise on account to Vantage Fabrics, $2,605, invoice no. 725.

15 Cash sales for January 1 through January 15, $10,300.

18 Bought merchandise on account from Coldman Products, $7,250, invoice no. 284, dated January 17; terms 2/10, n/30; FOB shipping point, freight prepaid and added to invoice, $200 (total $7,450).

18 Issued credit memorandum no. 41 to Vantage Fabrics, $85 for merchandise returned.

20 Issued Ck. No. 923, $463, for services of Bedrock Agency, not recorded previously (Miscellaneous Expense).

22 Received credit memorandum no. 117, $537.50, from Coldman Products for merchandise returned.

23 Received bill and paid Fast Track Freight, Ck. No. 924, $149, for freight charges on merchandise purchased January 3.

29 Sold merchandise on account to Borden Supply, $2,875, invoice no. 726.

31 Cash sales for January 16 through Janaury 31, $9,098.

31 Issued Ck. No. 925, $8,950.14, for salaries for the month (Debit Salary Expense.)

31 E. M. Frodsham, the owner, withdrew $1,040 for personal use, Ck. No. 926.

Instructions

1. Record the transactions for January using a sales journal, page 93; a purchases journal, page 76; a cash receipts journal, page 61; a cash payments journal, page 72; a general journal, page 18. The chart of accounts appears on the next page.

Chart of Accounts

111 Cash	412 Sales Returns and Allowances
113 Accounts Receivable	413 Sales Discount
114 Merchandise Inventory	511 Purchases
115 Supplies	512 Purchases Returns and
117 Prepaid Insurance	Allowances
124 Equipment	513 Purchases Discount
221 Accounts Payable	514 Freight In
311 E. M. Frodsham, Capital	520 Salary Expense
312 E. M. Frodsham, Drawing	524 Rent Expense
411 Sales	539 Miscellaneous Expense

2. Post daily all entries involving customer accounts to the accounts receivable ledger.
3. Post daily all entries involving creditor accounts to the accounts payable ledger.
4. Post daily those entries involving the Other Accounts columns and the general journal to the general ledger.
5. Add the columns of the special journals, and prove the equality of debit and credit totals at the bottom of each journal.
6. Post the appropriate totals of the special journals to the general ledger.
7. Prepare a trial balance.
8. Prepare a schedule of accounts receivable and a schedule of accounts payable. Do the totals equal the balances of the related controlling accounts?

Instructions for General Ledger Software

1. Record the transactions in the sales journal, purchases journal, cash receipts journal, cash payments journal, and general journal.
    a. Since the program uses a single-column purchases journal, add the amount of the freight to the amount of purchases.
    b. Note that Sundry Accounts and Other Accounts mean the same thing.
2. Print the journals.
3. Post the amounts from the sales, purchases, cash receipts, cash payments, and general journals.
4. Print a trial balance.
5. Print a schedule of accounts receivable and compare the total with the balance of the Accounts Receivable controlling account.
6. Print a schedule of accounts payable and compare the total with the balance of the Accounts Payable controlling account.

Problem Set B

P.O.1,2,4

Problem 6-1B Bingham Light Fixtures uses a three-column purchases journal. The company is located in Tampa, Florida. On January 1 of this year, the balances of the ledger accounts are Accounts Payable, $1,358.08; Purchases, zero; Freight In, zero. In addition to a general ledger, Bingham Light Fixtures also uses an accounts payable ledger. Transactions for January relating to the buying of merchandise are as follows:

Jan. 3 Bought twelve six-light crystal chandeliers (no shades) from Wagner Manufacturing Company, $3,025.92, invoice no. 797N, dated January 2; terms net 30 days; FOB Tampa.

5 Bought twenty-four two-light crystal wall sconces from Wagner Manufacturing Company, $898.80, invoice no. 869N, dated January 3; terms net 30 days; FOB Tampa.

9 Bought twenty-four one-light cane and wood-look swag lamps from Gable and Reiter, $867.60, invoice no. 19662, dated January 5; terms 1/10, n/30; FOB Dallas; freight prepaid and added to the invoice, $64 (total $931.60).

11 Bought 36 two-light, 360-degree swivel ceiling fixtures from Sebring Electric, $876.96, invoice no. 8712E, dated January 10; terms net 60 days; FOB Tampa.

15 Bought twenty-four six-light oak bath bars, $650.88, from Mannion Electric, invoice no. 71161, dated January 14; terms net 30 days; FOB Tampa.

19 Bought twenty-four oak frame fluorescent ceiling fixtures, including two rapid-start bulbs from Powell Manufacturing Company, $984, invoice no. 1692R, dated January 17; terms net 30 days; FOB Atlanta.

26 Bought twelve chain-hung shop lights, two-light fixtures, including 13″ plug-in and two 40-watt bulbs from Sebring Electric, $150.72, invoice no. 9164E, dated January 23; terms net 30 days; FOB Tampa.

30 Bought twelve cast iron post-top lanterns, one-light, 12″ diameter, 14″ high polyethylene globe from Fuller and Son, $288; invoice no. DR72, dated January 28; terms net 30 days; FOB Pensacola; freight prepaid and added to the invoice, $19 (total $307).

Instructions

1. Open the following accounts in the accounts payable ledger and record balances, if any, as given as of January 1: Fuller and Son; Gable and Reiter, $641.58; Mannion Electric; Powell Manufacturing Company, $716.50; Sebring Electric; Wagner Manufacturing Company.
2. Record the balance of $1,358.08 in the Accounts Payable controlling account as of January 1. Write "Balance" in the Item column and place a check mark in the Post. Ref. column.
3. Record the transactions in the purchases journal beginning with page 92.
4. Post to the accounts payable ledger daily.
5. Post to the general ledger at the end of the month.
6. Prepare a schedule of accounts payable, and compare the balance of the Accounts Payable controlling account with the total of the schedule of accounts payable.

Problem 6-2B Maria's Health Foods is located in Tucson. The company bought the following merchandise and other assets and had the following returns and allowances during July of this year:

P.O.4,5,6

July 2 Bought merchandise on account from Durham Natural Foods, $995, invoice no. L4620, dated July 1; terms 2/10, n/30; FOB Phoenix; freight prepaid and added to the invoice, $31 (total $1,026).

3 Bought merchandise on account from Neil and Sloan, $526.40, invoice no. 124D, dated July 2; terms 1/10, n/30; FOB Tucson.

6 Bought merchandise on account from Ringer, Inc., $894, invoice no. 7144, dated July 5; terms net 30 days; FOB Tucson.

10 Bought office supplies on account from Mercer and Company, $216, invoice no. 6247, dated July 10; terms net 30 days; FOB Tucson.

12 Received a credit memo from Neil and Sloan for merchandise returned, $73, credit memo no. 73.

15 Bought merchandise on account from Alvarez and Company, $847, invoice no. 5327, dated July 14; terms 1/10, n/30; FOB Los Angeles; freight prepaid and added to invoice, $52 (total $899).

21 Bought display cases on account from Reyes Company, $1,001, invoice no. D247, dated July 19; terms net 30 days; FOB Tucson.

26 Bought merchandise on account from Neil and Sloan, $1,293, invoice no. 310D, dated July 25; terms 1/10, n/30; FOB Tucson.

27 Received a credit memo from Ringer, Inc., for merchandise returned, $94, credit memo no. 306.

28 Bought merchandise on account from Durham Natural Foods, $1,985, invoice no. L4811, dated July 27; terms 2/10, n/30; FOB Phoenix; freight prepaid and added to the invoice, $106 (total $2,091).

29 Bought store supplies on account from F. C. Rollins, Inc., $105, invoice no. 6207, dated July 29; terms net 30 days; FOB Tucson.

31 Bought merchandise on account from Alvarez and Company, $784, invoice no. 5619, dated July 30; terms 1/10, n/30; FOB Los Angeles; freight prepaid and added to invoice, $49 (total $833).

31 Bought display shelving from Reyes Company, $319, invoice no. D329, dated July 29; terms net 30 days; FOB Tucson.

Instructions

1. Open the following accounts in the accounts payable ledger and record the July 1 balances, if any, as given: Alvarez and Company, $502.60; Durham Natural Foods, $1,321.10; Mercer and Company; Neil and Sloan; Reyes Company; Ringer, Inc., $1,358.75; F. C. Rollins, Inc. For the accounts having balances, write "Balance" in the Item column, and place a check mark in the Post. Ref. column.

2. Record the transactions in either the general journal, starting on page 46 or the purchases journal, on page 21, as appropriate.

3. Post the entries to the creditors' accounts in the accounts payable ledger immediately after you make each journal entry.

4. Post the entries in the Other Accounts Debit column of the purchases journal and in the general journal immediately after you make each of those journal entries.

5. In the space below the purchases journal, show proof that the sum of the debit totals equals the total of the Accounts Payable Credit column.

6. Post the totals of the special columns of the purchases journal at the end of the month.

7. Prepare a schedule of accounts payable, and compare the balance of the Accounts Payable controlling account with the total of the schedule of accounts payable.

P.O.7

Problem 6-3B The Bingham Company records sales of merchandise daily by posting directly from its sales invoices to the accounts receivable ledger. The firm is located in Boston. At the end of the month, a summarizing entry is made in the general journal. The purchase of goods on account is recorded in a similar manner. Each day's posting is done directly from the invoices to the accounts payable ledger, and a summarizing entry is made in the general journal at the end of the month. Sales of merchandise and purchases of goods on account during March of this year were as follows:

Sales of merchandise on account

Mar. 3 Sedwick Corporation, no. 4279, $1,762.14.
 7 C. R. Parsons, no. 4280, $4,410.10.
 11 N. D. McGinnin and Company, no. 4281, $2,011.06.
 16 Cline and Sharp, no. 4282, $1,864.50.
 20 Stanley Graves, no. 4283, $2,859.20.
 23 P. T. Isaacs, no. 4284, $2,164.24.
 25 Miller and Parks, no. 4285, $2,385.16.
 27 Stella Thielen, no. 4286, $1,729.42.
 28 R. C. Brooks, no. 4287, $761.60.
 29 Pickerill and Company, no. 4288, $1,942.
 30 L. C. Toomey, no. 4289, $2,106.14.

Purchases of goods on account

Mar. 2 Torres, Inc., merchandise, $3,616.19; FOB Boston.
 6 Lindsay and Stewart, merchandise, $2,727.41; FOB New York; freight prepaid and added to the invoice, $105 (total $2,832.41).
 8 Hein and French, store supplies, $641.10, FOB Boston.
 10 Keller Mills, merchandise, $3,624, FOB Boston.
 16 Magee and Son, merchandise, $961.15, FOB Boston.
 21 Halgren and Rogers, merchandise, $4,099, FOB Manchester, freight prepaid and added to the invoice, $227 (total $4,326).
 27 Moller Computer World, office equipment, $3,117.72, FOB Boston.
 30 Heller and Boyd, Inc., merchandise, $1,692.40, FOB Boston.

Instructions

1. Record the summarizing entry for the sale of merchandise on account in the general journal.
2. Record the summarizing entry for the purchase of goods on account in the general journal.

Problem 6-4B The following transactions were completed by Frodsham Decorating during January of this fiscal year. Terms of sale are 2/10, n/30.

P.O.1,2,3,4

Jan. 3 Paid rent for the month, $850, Ck. No. 421.
 3 E. M. Frodsham, the owner, invested an additional $4,630 in the business.
 4 Received check from Vantage Fabrics for $1,176 in payment of invoice, $1,200, less 2 percent cash discount.
 4 Bought merchandise on account from Vincent and Company, $4,125; invoice no. 555; terms 2/10, n/30; dated January 2.
 6 Received check from Price and Shepard for $784 in payment of $800 invoice, less 2 percent cash discount.
 8 Bought supplies on account from Davis Office Supply, $109.30; invoice no. 196; terms net 30 days.
 8 Sold merchandise on account to Eckhardt and Stedman, $1,925, invoice no. 924.

11 Paid Vincent and Company $4,042.50, Ck. No. 422, in payment of their $4,125 invoice, less cash discount.

14 Sold merchandise on account to Vantage Fabrics, $2,580, invoice no. 925.

15 Cash sales for January 1 through January 15, $9,630.90.

19 Bought merchandise on account from Coldman Products, $5,560; invoice no. 924, dated January 16; terms 2/10, n/60; FOB shipping point, freight prepaid and added to invoice, $250 (total $5,810).

19 Issued credit memorandum no. 51 to Vantage Fabrics, $73, for merchandise returned.

24 Received credit memorandum no. 147, $194, from Coldman Products for merchandise returned.

25 Issued Ck. No. 423, $367, for services to Bedrock Agency, not recorded previously (Miscellaneous Expense).

26 Sold merchandise on account to Borden Supply, $3,106, invoice no. 926.

27 Received bill and paid Fast Track Freight, Ck. No. 424, $98, for freight charges on merchandise purchased January 4.

31 Cash sales for January 16 through January 31, $7,910.50.

31 Issued Ck. No. 425, $7,298.16, for salaries for the month.

31 E. M. Frodsham, the owner, withdrew $1,250 for personal use, Ck. No. 426.

Instructions

1. Record the transactions for January using a sales journal, page 93; a purchases journal, page 76; a cash receipts journal, page 61; a cash payments journal, page 72; a general journal, page 18. The chart of accounts appears below.

Chart of Accounts

111	Cash	412	Sales Returns and Allowances
113	Accounts Receivable	413	Sales Discount
114	Merchandise Inventory	511	Purchases
115	Supplies	512	Purchases Returns and
117	Prepaid Insurance		Allowances
124	Equipment	513	Purchases Discount
221	Accounts Payable	514	Freight In
311	E. M. Frodsham, Capital	520	Salary Expense
312	E. M. Frodsham, Drawing	524	Rent Expense
411	Sales	539	Miscellaneous Expense

2. Post daily all entries involving customer accounts to the accounts receivable ledger.

3. Post daily all entries involving creditor accounts to the accounts payable ledger.

4. Post daily those entries involving the Other Accounts columns and the general journal to the general ledger.

5. Add the columns of the special journals, and prove the equality of debit and credit totals at the bottom of each journal.

6. Post the appropriate totals of the special journals to the general ledger.

7. Prepare a trial balance.

8. Prepare a schedule of accounts receivable and a schedule of accounts payable. Do the totals equal the balances of the related controlling accounts?

Instructions for General Ledger Software

1. Record the transactions in the sales journal, purchases journal, cash receipts journal, cash payments journal, and general journal.
   a. Since the program uses a single-column purchases journal, add the amount of the freight to the amount of purchases.
   b. Note that Sundry Accounts and Other Accounts mean the same thing.
2. Print the journals.
3. Post the amounts from the sales, purchases, cash receipts, cash payments, and general journals.
4. Print a trial balance.
5. Print a schedule of accounts receivable and compare the total with the balance of the Accounts Receivable controlling account.
6. Print a schedule of accounts payable and compare the total with the balance of the Accounts Payable controlling account.

CHALLENGE PROBLEM

Following are the schedules of accounts receivable and accounts payable for Grady Company, as well as the balances of the Accounts Receivable and Accounts Payable controlling accounts on July 31.

Schedule of Accounts Receivable		Schedule of Accounts Payable	
R. Axel	$ 716	L. Boro	$2,132
K. Jahn	1,330	C. Drake	941
W. Rizo	865	F. Hogg	1,018
T. Wigg	221	J. Lorn	956
Total	$3,132	Total	$5,047

It was found that the following errors were made in the accounts receivable ledger and the accounts payable ledger during the July transactions:

a. An error was made in posting a $280 payment that was applied to R. Axel's account. The $280 should have been posted to K. Jahn's account.
b. Our check to J. Lorn for $402 was written and journalized correctly but posted as $204.
c. Wigg's account was incorrectly balanced due to an addition error and should be $212, not $221.
d. A check for $100 from W. Rizo was not posted to his account.
e. Our check to C. Drake for $300 was posted to L. Boro's account by mistake.

Instructions

1. Correct the accounts receivable ledger account balances, and prepare a new schedule of accounts receivable. Compare the balance of the new schedule of accounts receivable with the correct balance of the controlling account, which is $2,743.
2. Correct the accounts payable ledger account balances, and prepare a new schedule of accounts payable. Compare the balance of the new schedule of accounts payable with the correct balance of the controlling account, which is $4,345.

chapter 7

Completing the Accounting Cycle for a Merchandising Business

PERFORMANCE OBJECTIVES

After you have completed this chapter, you will be able to do the following:

1. Prepare an adjustment for merchandise inventory.

2. Prepare an adjustment for unearned revenue.

3. Record adjustment data in a work sheet (including merchandise inventory, unearned revenue, supplies used, expired insurance, depreciation, and accrued wages).

4. Complete the work sheet.

5. Journalize the adjusting entries for a merchandising business.

6. Prepare a classified income statment for a merchandising firm.

7. Prepare a classified balance sheet.

8. Compute working capital and current ratio.

9. Journalize the closing entries for a merchandising firm.

10. Determine which adjusting entries should be reversed, and journalize the reversing entries.

If the 'bottom line' is still the same, what difference does it make?" This is a common question new business owners ask when I try to explain the proper classification of merchandising income statements.

True, the "bottom line" is still the same, but it is just as critical to an outside

user, such as a lender or an investor, to know how that profit was earned as to know the amount of the profit. For example, some companies that have never made a dime from their normal operations show a profit the year they decide to get out of business. Why? The company is selling off assets.

Chicken Bob's Restaurant is a good example. Business profits from selling fried chicken (the restaurant's income from operations) had always been poor, so Bob finally decided to sell the business. But no one wanted to buy a business that had never made much of a profit. One investor bought the building owned by the company. The building was sold for a whopping gain (the amount received was well above the original cost), and the income statement that period looked terrific. But let's face it—the sale of the building was a one-time-only situation. If Chicken Bob's had been able to call the building's profit "income from operations," an outside investor could be misled into thinking the restaurant was producing healthy profits. Not so. It was the Other Income—that is, the sale of the building—that gave Bob his profit and his first and only positive looking income statement. In the income statement, the Other Income classification should be recorded below income from operations, not in operating income.

In Chapters 5 and 6 you became familiar with the concept of special journals, which are used to separate bodies of information and to save time. As we stated, special journals can be manually prepared or computer generated.

Now we shall proceed to complete the accounting cycle for a merchandising business. First, we must determine the value of the ending merchandise inventory. To do this, we shall introduce an adjustment that is used only in merchandising firms. In Chapter 13 we shall look at another type of adjustment used by merchandising firms—especially those that use computers to help count and value their inventory.

Adjustment for Merchandise Inventory

Prepare an adjustment for merchandise inventory.

When we introduced the Merchandise Inventory account in Chapter 5, we put it under the heading of assets and said that, in our example, the balance of the account is changed only after a **physical inventory** (or actual count of the stock of goods on hand) has been taken. This is consistent with a system of **periodic inventories,** in which one records the purchase of merchandise as a debit to Purchases for the amount of the cost and the sale of merchandise as a credit to Sales for the amount of the selling price. A company operating with a periodic inventory system takes an inventory count periodically (at least once a year). Next, adjusting entries are made to the Merchandise Inventory account to take off the beginning inventory and add on the ending inventory.

Consider this example. A firm has a Merchandise Inventory balance of $27,000, which represents the cost of the inventory at the beginning of the fiscal period. At the end of the fiscal period, the firm takes an actual count of the stock on hand and determines the cost of the ending inventory to be $31,000. Naturally, in any business, goods are constantly being bought, sold, and replaced, as Figure 7-1 illustrates. Evidently the reason that the cost of the ending inventory is larger than the cost of the beginning inventory is that the firm in our example bought more than it sold. When we adjust the Merchandise Inventory account, we want to place the new figure of $31,000 in the account. We do this by a two-step process.

Step 1 Credit the Merchandise Inventory account by the amount of the beginning inventory into Income Summary. This makes the value of Merchandise Inventory zero. In other words, take off the beginning inventory. The offsetting debit is to Income Summary, representing the beginning inventory amount.

Let's look at this entry in the form of T accounts.

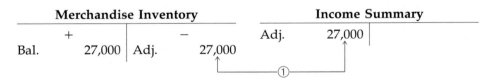

We handle this just as we handle the closing of any other account, by balancing off the account, or making the balance equal to zero. We treat the entry as a credit to Merchandise Inventory and a debit to Income Summary.

Step 2 Debit the ending Merchandise Inventory, because one must record on the books the cost of the asset remaining on hand. In other words, add on the ending inventory. The offsetting credit is to Income Summary, representing the ending inventory amount.

Let's repeat the T accounts, showing step 1 and adding step 2.

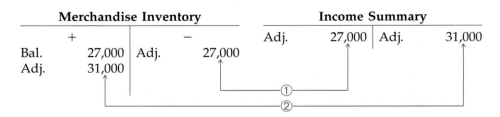

R E M E M B E R

The Income Summary account is the same Income Summary that we used to record closing entries. Income Summary now has the extra function of being the balancing or offsetting account in the adjustment of Merchandise Inventory.

| Why the merchandise inventory changes during the fiscal period | **Figure 7-1** |

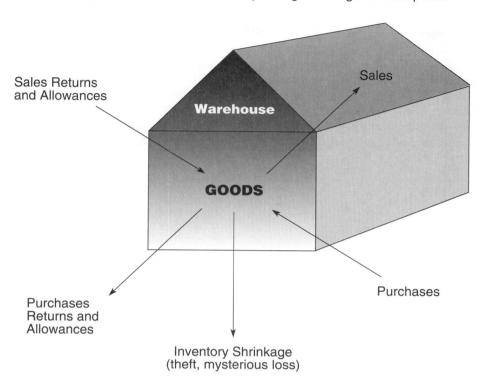

In step 2, we debit Merchandise Inventory (recording the asset on the plus side of the account), and we do the opposite to Income Summary.

The reason for adjusting the Merchandise Inventory account in these two steps is that both the beginning and the ending amounts appear as distinct figures in the Income Statement columns of a work sheet. The Income Statement columns are used as the basis for preparing the income statement (see Figure 7-2 on pages 298 and 299).

Adjustment for Unearned Revenue

Prepare an adjustment for unearned revenue.

Now let's introduce another adjusting entry: **unearned revenue,** which is revenue received in advance for goods or services to be delivered or performed later. As we said, this entry could pertain to a service as well as to a merchandising business. Frequently, cash is received in advance for services to be performed in the future. For example, a dining hall sells meal tickets in advance, a concert association sells season tickets in advance, a magazine publisher receives subscriptions in advance, teams sell season tickets, and an insurance company receives premiums in advance. If the amounts received by each of these organizations will be earned during the present fiscal period, the amounts should be credited to revenue accounts. On the other hand, if the amounts received will *not* be earned during the present fiscal period, the amounts should be credited to unearned revenue accounts. **An unearned revenue account is classified as a liability,** because an organization is liable for the amount received in advance until it is earned.

To illustrate, assume that on April 1 Ness Publishing Company receives $72,000 in cash for subscriptions covering two years and records them originally as debits to Cash and credits to Unearned Subscriptions. At the end of the year, Ness finds that $30,000 of the subscriptions have been earned. Accordingly, Ness's accountant makes an adjusting entry, debiting Unearned Subscriptions and crediting Subscriptions Income. In other words, the accountant takes the earned portion out of Unearned Subscriptions and adds it to Subscriptions Income. T accounts show the situation as follows:

Cash				Unearned Subscriptions		
+		−		−		+
Apr. 1	72,000			Dec. 31 Adj.	30,000	Apr. 1	72,000

Subscriptions Income	
−	+
	Dec. 31 Adj. 30,000

As another example, suppose that Dodson Plumbing Supply offers a course in plumbing repairs for home owners and apartment managers. On November 1, Dodson Plumbing receives $1,200 in fees for a three-month course. Because Dodson Plumbing's present fiscal period ends on December 31, the three months' worth of fees received in advance will not be earned during this fiscal period. Therefore, Dodson Plumbing's accountant records the transaction as a debit to Cash of $1,200 and a credit to Unearned Course Fees of $1,200. Unearned Course Fees is a liability account, because Dodson Plumbing must complete the how-to course or refund a portion of the money it collected. **Any account beginning with the word *Unearned* is always a liability.**

On December 31, because two months' worth of course fees have now been earned, Dodson Plumbing's accountant makes an adjusting entry to transfer $800 $\left(\frac{2}{3} \text{ of } \$1,200\right)$ from Unearned Course Fees to Course Fees Income. By T accounts, the situation looks like this:

Cash				Unearned Course Fees		
+		−		−		+
Nov. 1	1,200			Dec. 31 Adj. 800		Nov. 1	1,200
				(2 months)		(3 months)

Course Fees Income	
−	+
	Dec. 31 Adj. 800
	(2 months)

Dodson Plumbing Supply's chart of account is presented on the next page.

Before we demonstrate how to record adjustments, let's first look at the trial balance section of Dodson Plumbing Supply's work sheet. See Figure 7-2 on pages 298 and 299.

Chart of Accounts

ASSETS (100–199)
111   Cash
112   Notes Receivable
113   Accounts Receivable
114   Merchandise Inventory
115   Supplies
117   Prepaid Insurance
121   Land
122   Building
123   Accumulated Depreciation, Building
124   Equipment
125   Accumulated Depreciation, Equipment

LIABILITIES (200–299)
211   Notes Payable
221   Accounts Payable
223   Wages Payable
232   Unearned Course Fees
241   Mortgage Payable

OWNER'S EQUITY (300–399)
311   L. E. Dodson, Capital
312   L. E. Dodson, Drawing
399   Income Summary

REVENUE (400–499)
411   Sales
412   Sales Returns and Allowances
413   Sales Discount
450   Course Fees Income
451   Interest Income

EXPENSES (500–599)
511   Purchases
512   Purchases Returns and Allowances
513   Purchases Discount
514   Freight In
521   Wages Expense
523   Supplies Expense
529   Insurance Expense
531   Depreciation Expense, Building
533   Depreciation Expense, Equipment
538   Taxes Expense
539   Miscellaneous Expense
540   Interest Expense

Data for the Adjustments

Performance Objective 3
Record adjustment data in a work sheet (including merchandise inventory, unearned revenue, supplies used, expired insurance, depreciation, and accrued wages).

Listing the adjustment data appears to be a relatively minor task. In a business situation, however, one must take actual physical counts of the inventories and match them up with costs. One must check insurance policies to determine the amount of insurance that has expired. Finally, one must systematically write off, or depreciate, the cost of equipment and buildings.

For income tax and accounting purposes, land cannot be depreciated. Even if the building and lot were bought as one package for one price, the buyer must separate the cost of the building from the cost of the land. For real estate taxes, the county assessor appraises the building and the land separately. If there is no other qualified appraisal available, one can use the assessor's ratio or percentage as a basis for separating building cost and land cost.

Here are the adjustment data for Dodson Plumbing Supply. We will show the adjustments recorded in T accounts.

a–b. Ending merchandise inventory, $65,800

Merchandise Inventory				Income Summary			
+		−		(a) Adj.	67,000	(b) Adj.	65,800
Bal.	67,000	(a) Adj.	67,000				
(b) Adj.	65,800						

c. Course fees earned, $800

Unearned Course Fees				Course Fees Income			
−		+		−		+	
(c) Adj.	800	Bal.	1,200			(c) Adj.	800

· · · · · · · · · · · ·
R E M E M B E R

The amount of the adjusting entry for supplies used equals the balance of the Supplies account minus the amount of the ending inventory.

d. Ending supplies inventory, $412

Supplies				Supplies Expense			
+		−		+		−	
Bal.	1,440	(d) Adj.	1,028	(d) Adj.	1,028		

e. Insurance expired, $320

Prepaid Insurance				Insurance Expense			
+		−		+		−	
Bal.	960	(e) Adj.	320	(e) Adj.	320		

f. Additional year's depreciation of building, $4,000

Accumulated Depreciation, Building				Depreciation Expense, Building			
−		+		+		−	
		Bal.	32,000	(g)	4,000		
		(g)	4,000				

g. Additional year's depreciation of equipment, $4,800

Accumulated Depreciation, Equipment				Depreciation Expense, Equipment			
−		+		+		−	
		Bal.	16,400	(f) Adj.	4,800		
		(f) Adj.	4,800				

h. Wages owed but not paid to employees at end of year, $1,120

Wages Payable				Wages Expense			
−		+		+		−	
		(h)	1,120	Bal.	45,800		
				(h)	1,120		

We now record these in the Adjustments columns of the work sheet, using the same letters to identify the adjustments (see Figure 7-2 on pages 298 and 299).

FYI

Some government agencies and businesses have arranged their pay periods to avoid accrued wages, their adjustment, and the reversal of the adjusting entry. Payroll taxes will be covered in Chapters 9 and 10.

Completion of the Work Sheet

Performance Objective 4
Complete the work sheet.

Previously, in introducing work sheets, we included the Adjusted Trial Balance columns as a means of verifying that the accounts were in balance after recording the adjusting entries. At this time, to reduce the number of columns in the work sheet, we will eliminate the Adjusted Trial Balance columns. The account balances after the adjusting entries will be carried directly into the Income Statement and Balance Sheet columns.

The completed work sheet looks like Figure 7-2 on pages 298 and 299.

Observe in particular the way we carry forward the figures for Merchandise Inventory and Income Summary. **Income Summary is the only account in which we don't combine the debit and credit figures. Instead, we carry them into the Income Statement columns in Figure 7-2 as two distinct figures.** As we said, the reason is that both figures appear in the income statement itself. The amount listed as Income Summary in the Income Statement Debit column is the beginning merchandise inventory. The amount listed as Income Summary in the Income Statement Credit column is the ending merchandise inventory. We will talk about this topic in greater detail later in the chapter.

When developing the work sheet, complete one step at a time:

1. Record the trial balance, and make sure that the total of the Debit column equals the total of the Credit column.

2. Record the adjustments in the Adjustments columns, and make sure that the totals are equal.

3. Complete the Income Statement and Balance Sheet columns by recording the adjusted balance of each account. Here are the accounts and classifications pertaining to a merchandising business that appear in these columns:

Income Statement		Balance Sheet	
Debit	**Credit**	**Debit**	**Credit**
Expenses	Revenues	Assets	Liabilities
+	+	+	+
Sales Returns and Allowances	Purchases Returns and Allowances	Drawing	Capital
+	+		+
Sales Discount	Purchases Discount		Accumulated Depreciation
+	+		
Purchases	Income Summary		
+			
Freight In			
+			
Income Summary			

Study the example shown at the top of page 300, noting especially the way we treat these special accounts for a merchandising business.

Figure 7-2

Dodson Plumbing Supply
Work Sheet
For Year Ended December 31, 19—

	ACCOUNT NAME	TRIAL BALANCE DEBIT	TRIAL BALANCE CREDIT	ADJUSTMENTS DEBIT	ADJUSTMENTS CREDIT
1	Cash	19 1 5 4 00			
2	Notes Receivable	4 0 0 0 00			
3	Accounts Receivable	29 4 4 6 00			
4	Merchandise Inventory	67 0 0 0 00		(b) 65 8 0 0 00	(a) 67 0 0 0 00
5	Supplies	1 4 4 0 00			(d) 1 0 2 8 00
6	Prepaid Insurance	9 6 0 00			(e) 3 2 0 00
7	Land	12 0 0 0 00			
8	Building	90 0 0 0 00			
9	Accumulated Depreciation, Building		32 0 0 0 00		(f) 4 0 0 0 00
10	Equipment	33 6 0 0 00			
11	Accumulated Depreciation, Equipment		16 4 0 0 00		(g) 4 8 0 0 00
12	Notes Payable		3 0 0 0 00		
13	Accounts Payable		36 4 0 0 00		
14	Wages Payable				(h) 1 1 2 0 00
15	Unearned Course Fees		1 2 0 0 00	(c) 8 0 0 00	
16	Mortgage Payable		8 0 0 0 00		
17	L. E. Dodson, Capital		140 5 7 4 00		
18	L. E. Dodson, Drawing	36 9 0 0 00			
19	Income Summary			(a) 67 0 0 0 00	(b) 65 8 0 0 00
20	Sales		195 1 8 0 00		
21	Sales Returns and Allowances	8 4 0 00			
22	Sales Discount	1 8 8 0 00			
23	Course Fees Income				(c) 8 0 0 00
24	Interest Income		1 2 0 00		
25	Purchases	87 1 4 0 00			
26	Purchases Returns and Allowances		8 3 2 00		
27	Purchases Discount		1 2 4 8 00		
28	Freight In	2 4 6 0 00			
29	Wages Expense	45 8 0 0 00		(h) 1 1 2 0 00	
30	Supplies Expense			(d) 1 0 2 8 00	
31	Insurance Expense			(e) 3 2 0 00	
32	Depreciation Expense, Building			(f) 4 0 0 0 00	
33	Depreciation Expense, Equipment			(g) 4 8 0 0 00	
34	Taxes Expense	1 9 6 0 00			
35	Miscellaneous Expense				
36	Interest Expense	3 7 4 00			
37		434 9 5 4 00	434 9 5 4 00	144 8 6 8 00	144 8 6 8 00
38	Net Income				
39					

	INCOME STATEMENT		BALANCE SHEET		
	DEBIT	CREDIT	DEBIT	CREDIT	
			19 1 5 4 00		1
			4 0 0 0 00		2
			29 4 4 6 00		3
			65 8 0 0 00		4
			4 1 2 00		5
			6 4 0 00		6
			12 0 0 0 00		7
			90 0 0 0 00		8
				36 0 0 0 00	9
			33 6 0 0 00		10
				21 2 0 0 00	11
				3 0 0 0 00	12
				36 4 0 0 00	13
				1 1 2 0 00	14
				4 0 0 00	15
				8 0 0 00	16
				140 5 7 4 00	17
			36 9 0 0 00		18
	67 0 0 0 00	65 8 0 0 00			19
		195 1 8 0 00			20
	8 4 0 00				21
	1 8 8 0 00				22
		8 0 0 00			23
		1 2 0 00			24
	87 1 4 0 00				25
		8 3 2 00			26
		1 2 4 8 00			27
	2 4 6 0 00				28
	46 9 2 0 00				29
	1 0 2 8 00				30
	3 2 0 00				31
	4 0 0 0 00				32
	4 8 0 0 00				33
	1 9 6 0 00				34
					35
	3 7 4 00				36
	218 7 2 2 00	263 9 8 0 00	291 9 5 2 00	246 6 9 4 00	37
	45 2 5 8 00			45 2 5 8 00	38
	263 9 8 0 00	263 9 8 0 00	291 9 5 2 00	291 9 5 2 00	39

Account Name	Location in Work Sheet			
	Income Statement		Balance Sheet	
	Debit	Credit	Debit	Credit
Merchandise Inventory			65,800 00	
Sales		195,180 00		
Sales Returns and Allowances	840 00			
Sales Discount	1,880 00			
Purchases	87,140 00			
Purchases Returns and Allowances		832 00		
Purchases Discount		1,248 00		
Freight In	2,460 00			
Income Summary	67,000 00	65,800 00		

Adjusting Entries

 igure 7-3 (at the top of the next page) shows the way the adjusting entries look when they are taken from the Adjustments columns of the work sheet and recorded in the general journal.

Financial Statements and the Work Sheet

n Chapter 4, we discussed at length the income statements for a service and a professional enterprise, respectively. Then in Chapters 5 and 6, we discussed the specialized accounts and journals for merchandising enterprises; thus far in Chapter 7, we have discussed the work sheet and adjusting entries for merchandise inventory and unearned revenue.

We will now demonstrate how to formulate financial statements directly from a work sheet. We will also review closing entries—but this time for a merchandising business—and introduce reversing entries. To do this, we will look again at Figure 7-2, the work sheet for Dodson Plumbing Supply shown on pages 298 and 299. First we will look at the financial statements in their entirety, and then we will explain their various subdivisions.

The Income Statement

 s you know, the work sheet is merely a tool used by accountants to prepare the financial statements. Look at the Income Statement columns of the work sheet for Dodson Plumbing Supply shown in Figure 7-2. Of course, **each of the amounts that appear in the Income**

Figure 7-3

	DATE		DESCRIPTION	POST. REF.	DEBIT	CREDIT	
1	19–		Adjusting Entries				1
2	Dec.	31	Income Summary		67 0 0 0 00		2
3			Merchandise Inventory			67 0 0 0 00	3
4							4
5		31	Merchandise Inventory		65 8 0 0 00		5
6			Income Summary			65 8 0 0 00	6
7							7
8		31	Unearned Course Fees		8 0 0 00		8
9			Course Fees Income			8 0 0 00	9
10							10
11		31	Supplies Expense		1 0 2 8 00		11
12			Supplies			1 0 2 8 00	12
13							13
14		31	Insurance Expense		3 2 0 00		14
15			Prepaid Insurance			3 2 0 00	15
16							16
17		31	Depreciation Expense, Building		4 0 0 0 00		17
18			Accumulated Depreciation,				18
19			Equipment			4 0 0 0 00	19
20							20
21		31	Depreciation Expense, Equipment		4 8 0 0 00		21
22			Accumulated Depreciation,				22
23			Building			4 8 0 0 00	23
24							24
25		31	Wages Expense		1 1 2 0 00		25
26			Wages Payable			1 1 2 0 00	26
27							27
28							28

GENERAL JOURNAL — PAGE 96

Statement columns of the work sheet will also be used in the income statement. Notice that the amounts for the beginning and ending merchandise inventory now appear separately on the Income Summary line. Figure 7-4 shows the entire income statement. Pause for a while and look it over carefully before studying how we will break it down into its components.

The outline of the income statement follows a logical pattern that is much the same for any type of merchandising business. The ability to interpret the income statement and extract parts from it is very useful when one is gathering information for decisions. To realize the full value of an income statement, however, you need to know the skeleton outline of an income statement backward and forward; you must be able to visualize it. So, let's look at the statement section by section.

Figure 7-4

Dodson Plumbing Supply
Income Statement
For Year Ended December 31, 19–

Revenue from Sales:			
Sales		$ 195 1 8 0 00	
Less: Sales Returns and Allowances	$ 8 4 0 00		
Sales Discount	1 8 8 0 00	2 7 2 0 00	
Net Sales			$ 192 4 6 0 00
Cost of Goods Sold:			
Merchandise Inventory, January 1, 19–		$ 67 0 0 0 00	
Purchases	$ 87 1 4 0 00		
Less: Purchases Returns and			
Allowances $ 832.00			
Purchases Discount 1,248.00	2 0 8 0 00		
Net Purchases	$ 85 0 6 0 00		
Add Freight In	2 4 6 0 00		
Delivered Cost of Purchases		87 5 2 0 00	
Goods Available for Sale		$ 154 5 2 0 00	
Less Merchandise Inventory, December 31, 19–		65 8 0 0 00	
Cost of Goods Sold			88 7 2 0 00
Gross Profit			$ 103 7 4 0 00
Operating Expenses:			
Wages Expense		$ 46 9 2 0 00	
Supplies Expense		1 0 2 8 00	
Insurance Expense		3 2 0 00	
Depreciation Expense, Building		4 0 0 0 00	
Depreciation Expense, Equipment		4 8 0 0 00	
Taxes Expense		1 9 6 0 00	
Total Operating Expenses			59 0 2 8 00
Income from Operations			$ 44 7 1 2 00
Other Income:			
Course Fees Income		$ 8 0 0 00	
Interest Income		1 2 0 00	
Total Other Income		$ 9 2 0 00	
Other Expenses:			
Interest Expense		3 7 4 00	5 4 6 00
Net Income			$ 45 2 5 8 00

Net Sales	$192,460
− Cost of Goods Sold	88,720
Gross Profit	$103,740
− Operating Expenses	59,028
Income from Operations	$ 44,712

Accountants perform audits (checking the business accounting records) on site using laptop computers.

To put forth the concepts of **gross** and **net,** here is an example of a simple single-sale transaction:

Several years ago, Diane Hanks bought an antique table at a second-hand store for $90. She decided to sell the table for $170. She advertised in the daily newspaper at a cost of $5. How much did she make as clear profit?

Sale of table	$170
Less cost of table	90
Gross Profit	$ 80
Less Advertising Expense	5
Net Income or Net Profit (gain on the sale)	$ 75

Gross profit is the profit on the sale of the table before any expense has been deducted, which in this case is $80. **Net income,** or *net profit,* is the final or clear profit after all expenses have been deducted. In a single-sale situation such as this, we refer to the final outcome as the net profit. But for a business that has many sales and expenses, most accountants prefer the term *net income.* Regardless of which word one uses, *net* refers to clear profit—after all expenses have been deducted.

Revenue from Sales

Now let's look at the Revenue from Sales section in the income statement of Dodson Plumbing Supply.

Revenue from Sales:					
Sales				$ 195 1 8 0 00	
Less: Sales Returns and Allowances	$	8 4 0 00			
Sales Discount		1 8 8 0 00	2 7 2 0 00		
Net Sales					$ 192 4 6 0 00

When we introduced Sales Returns and Allowances and Sales Discount, we treated them as deductions from Sales. You can see that in the income statement they are deducted from Sales to give us **net sales.** Note that we recorded these items in the same order in which they appear in the ledger.

REMEMBER

Returns and Allowances (Sales or Purchases) is listed on one line, and Discount (Sales or Purchases) is listed below.

Cost of Goods Sold

The section of the income statement that requires the greatest amount of concentration is the **Cost of Goods Sold.** Let us therefore repeat it in its entirety:

Cost of Goods Sold:				
Merchandise Inventory, January 1, 19–			$ 67 0 0 0 00	
Purchases	$ 87 1 4 0 00			
Less: Purchases Returns and				
Allowances	$ 832.00			
Purchases Discount	1,248.00	2 0 8 0 00		
Net Purchases	$ 85 0 6 0 00			
Add Freight In	2 4 6 0 00			
Delivered Cost of Purchases			87 5 2 0 00	
Goods Available for Sale			$ 154 5 2 0 00	
Less Merchandise Inventory, December 31, 19–			65 8 0 0 00	
Cost of Goods Sold				$ 88 7 2 0 00

First, let's look closely at the Purchases section.

Purchases	$87 1 4 0 00		
Less: Purchases Returns and			
Allowances	$ 832.00		
Purchases Discount	1,248.00	2 0 8 0 00	
Net Purchases	$85 0 6 0 00		
Add Freight In	2 4 6 0 00		
Delivered Cost of Purchases		87 5 2 0 00	

Note the parallel to the Revenue from Sales section. To arrive at **Net Purchases,** we deduct the sum of Purchases Returns and Allowances and Purchases Discount from Purchases. To complete the Purchases section we add Freight In to Net Purchases to get **Delivered Cost of Purchases.**

Now let's look at the full Cost of Goods Sold section. You might think of Cost of Goods Sold like this:

Amount we started with (beginning inventory)	$ 67,000
+ Net amount we purchased, including freight charges	87,520
Total amount that could have been sold (available)	$154,520
− Amount left over (ending inventory)	65,800
Cost of the goods that were actually sold	$ 88,720

Here's the Cost of Goods Sold expressed in proper wording.

Merchandise Inventory, January 1, 19–	$ 67,000
+ Delivered Cost of Purchases	87,520
Goods Available for Sale	$154,520
− Merchandise Inventory, December 31, 19–	65,800
Cost of Goods Sold	$ 88,720

Operating Expenses

Operating expenses, as the name implies, are the regular expenses of doing business. As we stated in Chapter 4, we will list the accounts and their respective balances in the order that they appear in the ledger.

Many firms use subclassifications of operating expenses, such as the following:

1. **Selling expenses** Any expenses directly connected with the selling activity, such as
   - Sales Salaries Expense
   - Sales Commissions Expense
   - Advertising Expense
   - Store Supplies Expense
   - Delivery Expense
   - Depreciation Expense, Store Equipment

2. **General expenses** Any expenses related to the office or administration, or any expense that cannot be directly connected with a selling activity:
   - Office Salaries Expense
   - Taxes Expense
   - Depreciation Expense, Office Equipment
   - Rent Expense
   - Insurance Expense
   - Office Supplies Expense

In preparing the income statement, classifying expense accounts as selling expenses or general expenses is a matter of judgment. The only reason we're not using this breakdown here is that we're trying to keep the number of accounts to a minimum. In other words, getting bogged down in a large number of accounts could make it more difficult for you to understand the main concepts.

Income from Operations

Now let's repeat the skeleton outline:

Net Sales
− Cost of Goods Sold

Gross Profit
− Operating Expenses

Income from Operations

If the Operating Expenses are the regular, recurring expenses of doing business, then Income from Operations should be the regular or recurring income from normal business operations. When you are comparing the results of operations over a number of years, Income from Operations is the most significant figure to use each year as a basis for comparison.

Other Income

The Other Income classification, as the name implies, records any revenue account other than revenue from sales. What we are trying to do is to isolate Sales at the top of the income statement as the major revenue account, so that the Gross Profit figure represents the profit made on the sale of merchandise *only*. Additional accounts that may appear under the heading of Other Income are Rent Income (the firm is subletting part of its premises); Interest Income (the firm holds an interest-bearing note or contract); Gain on Disposal of Plant and Equipment (the firm makes a profit on the sale of plant and equipment), Miscellaneous Income.

Other Expenses

The classification of Other Expenses records various nonoperating expenses, such as Interest Expense or Loss on Disposal of Plant and Equipment.

The Statement of Owner's Equity and the Balance Sheet

Figure 7-2 (shown on pages 298 and 299) is a work sheet for Dodson Plumbing Supply. Here again we find that **every figure in the Balance Sheet columns of the work sheet is used in either the statement of owner's equity or the balance sheet.**

The preparation of the financial statements follows the same order that we presented before: first, the income statement; second, the statement of owner's equity; third, the balance sheet. The statement of owner's equity shows why the balance of the Capital account has changed from the beginning of the fiscal period to the end of it. In preparing the statement of owner's equity, one should always look into the ledger for the owner's capital account to find any changes, such as additional investments, made during the year.

In Figure 7-5 we observe the balance of L. E. Dodson, Capital, listed on the work sheet as $140,574. We also note a credit of $8,000 in the ledger account representing an additional investment. Therefore, the beginning balance of L. E. Dodson, Capital, was $132,574 ($140,574 − $8,000).

REMEMBER

Net income appears on both the income statement and the statement of owner's equity.

Balance Sheet Classifications

Balance sheet classifications are generally uniform for all types of business enterprises. You are strongly urged to take the time to learn the following definitions of the classifications and the order of accounts within them. If you do, you will have a standard routine for compiling

Performance Objective 7

Prepare a classified balance sheet.

Figure 7-5

Dodson Plumbing Supply
Statement of Owner's Equity
For Year Ended December 31, 19–

L. E. Dodson, Capital, January 1, 19–			$ 132 5 7 4 00
Additional Investment, August 26, 19–			8 0 0 0 00
Total Investment			$ 140 5 7 4 00
Net Income for the Year	$ 45 2 5 8 00		
Less Withdrawals for the Year	36 9 0 0 00		
Increase in Capital			8 3 5 8 00
L. E. Dodson, Capital,			
December 31, 19–			$ 148 9 3 2 00

a balance sheet. This routine will save you a lot of time and confusion. As you read, refer to Figure 7-6 on page 308.

Current Assets

Current assets consist of cash and any other assets or resources that are expected to be realized in cash or to be sold or consumed during the normal operating cycle of the business (or one year, unless the normal operating cycle is less than twelve months).

Accountants list current assets in the order of their convertibility into cash; in other words, their **liquidity.** (If you've got an asset such as a car or a stereo and you sell it quickly and turn it into cash, you are said to be turning it into a *liquid* state.) If the first four accounts under Current Assets (see Figure 7-6) are present, always record them in the same order: (1) Cash, (2) Notes Receivable, (3) Accounts Receivable, and (4) Merchandise Inventory.

Notes receivable (current) are short-term (one year or less) promissory notes (promise-to-pay notes) held by the firm. A note is generally received from a customer as a substitute for a charge account.

Notes Receivable is generally placed ahead of Accounts Receivable, because promissory notes are considered to be more convertible into cash than Accounts Receivable. (*Reason:* The holder of the note can raise more cash by borrowing from a bank, pledging the notes as security for the loan.)

Supplies and Prepaid Insurance are considered prepaid items that will be used up or will expire within the following operating cycle or year. That's why they appear at the bottom of the Current Assets section. There is no particular reason to list Supplies before Prepaid Insurance. Prepaid Insurance could just as easily have preceded Supplies.

Plant and Equipment

Plant and equipment are relatively long-lived assets that are held for use in the production or sale of other assets or services; some accountants refer to them as *fixed assets.* The three types of accounts that usually appear in this category are Land, Building, and Equipment (refer to Figure 7-6 again). Note that the Building and Equipment accounts are followed by their respective Accumulated Depreciation accounts. Incidentally, the order of listing of plant and equipment is not uniform in practice. However, in keeping with modern

R E M E M B E R
Since Accumulated Depreciation is a contra account, it is deducted from the appropriate asset.

Figure 7-6

Dodson Plumbing Supply

Balance Sheet
December 31, 19–

Assets					
Current Assets:					
Cash			$ 19 1 5 4 00		
Notes Receivable			4 0 0 0 00		
Accounts Receivable			29 4 4 6 00		
Merchandise Inventory			65 8 0 0 00		
Supplies			4 1 2 00		
Prepaid Insurance			6 4 0 00		
Total Current Assets				$ 119 4 5 2 00	
Plant and Equipment:					
Land			$ 12 0 0 0 00		
Building	$ 90 0 0 0 00				
Less Accumulated Depreciation	36 0 0 0 00		54 0 0 0 00		
Equipment	$ 33 6 0 0 00				
Less Accumulated Depreciation	21 2 0 0 00		12 4 0 0 00		
Total Plant and Equipment				78 4 0 0 00	
Total Assets				$ 197 8 5 2 00	
Liabilities					
Current Liabilities:					
Notes Payable			$ 3 0 0 0 00		
Mortgage Payable (current portion)			2 0 0 0 00		
Accounts Payable			36 4 0 0 00		
Wages Payable			1 1 2 0 00		
Unearned Course Fees			4 0 0 00		
Total Current Liabilities				$ 42 9 2 0 00	
Long-Term Liabilities:					
Mortgage Payable				6 0 0 0 00	
Total Liabilities				$ 48 9 2 0 00	
Owner's Equity					
L. E. Dodson, Capital				148 9 3 2 00	
Total Liabilities and Owner's Equity				$ 197 8 5 2 00	

practice, we will list these assets in order of their length of life, with the longest-lived asset being placed first.

Current Liabilities

Current liabilities are debts that will become due within the normal operating cycle of the business, usually within one year; they normally will be paid, when due, from current assets. List current liabilities in the order of their expected payment. Notes Payable (current) is placed ahead of Accounts Payable, just as Notes Receivable is placed ahead of Accounts Receivable. The Mortgage Payable (current portion), which may be placed ahead of Accounts Payable, is the payment one makes to reduce the principal of the mortgage in a given year. Wages Payable and any other accrued liabilities, such as Commissions Payable and the current portion of unearned revenue accounts, usually fall at the bottom of the list of current liabilities.

Long-Term Liabilities

Long-term liabilities are debts that are payable over a comparatively long period, usually more than one year. Ordinarily, Mortgage Payable is the only account in this category for a sole-proprietorship (or one-owner) type of business. One single amount in a category can be recorded in the column on the extreme right.

Working Capital and Current Ratio

Both the management and the short-term creditors of a firm are vitally interested in two questions:

1. Does the firm have a sufficient amount of capital to operate?

2. Does the firm have the ability to pay its debts?

Two measures used to answer these questions are a firm's working capital and its current ratio; the necessary data are taken from a classified balance sheet.

Working capital is determined by subtracting current liabilities from current assets; thus

> Working capital = Current assets − Current liabilities

| **Performance Objective 8** |
| Compute working capital and current ratio. |

The normal operating cycle for most firms is one year. Because current assets equal cash—or items that can be converted into cash or used up within one year—and current liabilities equal the total amount that the company must pay out within one year, working capital is appropriately named. It is the amount of capital the company has available to use or to work with. The working capital for Dodson Plumbing Supply is as follows:

> Working capital = $119,452 − $42,920 = $76,532

Current ratio is useful in revealing a firm's ability to pay its bills. The current ratio is determined by dividing current assets by current liabilities:

$$\text{Current ratio} = \frac{\text{Current assets (amount coming in within one year)}}{\text{Current liabilities (amount going out within one year)}}$$

The current ratio for Dodson Plumbing Supply is calculated like this:

$$\text{Current ratio} = \frac{\$119,452}{\$42,920} = 2.78 \qquad 42,920\overline{)119,452} = 2.78 \ \ = 2.78\!:\!1$$

In the case of Dodson Plumbing Supply, $2.78 is available to pay every dollar currently due on December 31.

When banks are considering granting loans to merchandising firms, a minimum current ratio of 2:1 is generally required.

Closing Entries

In Chapter 4, we discussed closing entries for a service business; now let's look at closing entries for a merchandising business. The same methods apply to both types of business. You follow the same four steps to close or zero out the revenue, expense, and Drawing accounts.

At the end of a fiscal period, you close the revenue and expense accounts so that you can start the next fiscal period with a clean slate. You also close the Drawing account because it, too, applies to one fiscal period. As you recall from our discussion in Chapter 4, these accounts are called **temporary-equity accounts,** or *nominal accounts*.

You can speed up the preparation of closing entries by balancing off each figure in the Income Statement columns of the work sheet. Figure 7-2 shows the Income Statement columns (see page 299). After you have looked them over, let's take up the four steps of the closing procedure.

Four Steps in the Closing Procedure

Performance Objective 9

Journalize the closing entries for a merchandising firm.

To repeat, these four steps should be followed when closing:

1. Close the revenue accounts, as well as the other accounts appearing in the income statement and having credit balances. **(Debit the figures that are credited in the Income Statement columns of the work sheet, except the figure on the Income Summary line.)** This entry is illustrated as follows:

			GENERAL JOURNAL						PAGE	97			
	DATE		DESCRIPTION	POST. REF.		DEBIT				CREDIT			
1	19–		Closing Entries										1
2	Dec.	31	Sales		195	1	8	0	00				2
3			Course Fees Income			8	0	0	00				3
4			Interest Income			1	2	0	00				4
5			Purchase Returns and										5
6			Allowances			8	3	2	00				6
7			Purchases Discount		1	2	4	8	00				7
8			Income Summary							198	1	8 0 00	8
9													9

2. Close the expense accounts as well as the other accounts appearing in the income statement that have debit balances. **(Check the figures that are debited in the Income Statement columns of the work sheet, except the figure on the Income Summary line.** This entry appears on the next page.)

Note that you close Purchases Discount and Purchases Returns and Allowances in step 1 along with the revenue accounts. Note also that in step 2 you close Sales Discount and Sales Returns and Allowances along with the expense accounts.

	DATE		DESCRIPTION	POST. REF.	DEBIT	CREDIT	
9	Dec.	31	Income Summary		151 7 2 2 00		9
10			Sales Returns and Allowances			8 4 0 00	10
11			Sales Discount			1 8 8 0 00	11
12			Purchases			87 1 4 0 00	12
13			Freight In			2 4 6 0 00	13
14			Wages Expense			46 9 2 0 00	14
15			Supplies Expense			1 0 2 8 00	15
16			Insurance Expense			3 2 0 00	16
17			Depreciation Expense, Building			4 0 0 0 00	17
18			Depreciation Expense,				18
19			Equipment			4 8 0 0 00	19
20			Taxes Expense			1 9 6 0 00	20
21			Interest Expense			3 7 4 00	21
22							22

3. Close the Income Summary account into L. E. Dodson, Capital. **(Debit Income Summary by the amount of the net income; credit it by the amount of a net loss.)**

	DATE		DESCRIPTION	POST. REF.	DEBIT	CREDIT	
22	Dec.	31	Income Summary		45 2 5 8 00		22
23			L. E. Dodson, Capital			45 2 5 8 00	23
24							24

Here is what the T accounts look like. Bear in mind that the Income Summary account already contains adjusting entries for merchandise inventory.

Income Summary					L. E. Dodson, Capital		
Adjusting (Beginning Merchandise Inventory)	67,000	Adjusting (Ending Merchandise Inventory)	65,800	−		+	
(Expenses)	151,722	(Revenue)	198,180		Balance	140,574
(Net Income)	45,258				(Net Income)	45,258

4. Close the Drawing account into the Capital account.

	DATE	DESCRIPTION	POST. REF.	DEBIT	CREDIT	
25	Dec. 31	L. E. Dodson, Capital		36 9 0 0 00		25
26		L. E. Dodson, Drawing			36 9 0 0 00	26
27						27
28						28
29						29

GENERAL JOURNAL PAGE 97

Here is what the T accounts would look like:

L. E. Dodson, Drawing

+		−	
Balance	36,900	Closing	36,900

L. E. Dodson, Capital

−		+	
(Drawing)	36,900	Balance	140,574
		(Net Income)	45,258

Reversing Entries

Reversing entries are general journal entries that are the exact reverse of certain adjusting entries. A reversing entry enables the accountant to record routine transactions in the usual manner, *even though* an adjusting entry affecting one of the accounts involved in the transaction has intervened. We can see this concept best by looking at an example.

Suppose there is an adjusting entry for accrued wages owed to employees at the end of the fiscal year. (We talked about this in Chapter 4.) Assume that all the employees of a certain firm are paid, altogether, $400 per day for a five-day week and that payday occurs every Friday throughout the year. When the employees get their checks at 5:00 P.M. on Friday, the checks include their wages for that day as well as for the preceding four days. Assume that, one year, the last day of the fiscal year happens to fall on Wednesday, December 31. A diagram of this situation would look like this:

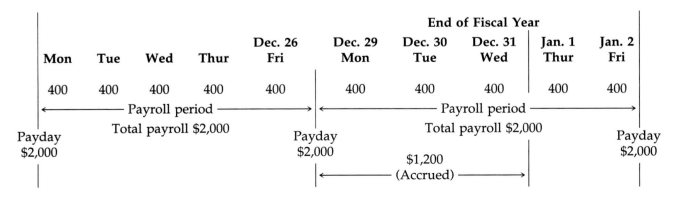

Each Friday during the year, the payroll has been debited to the Wages Expense account and credited to the Cash account. As a result, Wages Expense has a debit balance of $102,800. Here is the adjusting entry in T account form:

Wages Expense					Wages Payable			
+		**−**			**−**		**+**	
Balance	102,800					Dec. 31 Adjust.	1,200	
Dec. 31 Adjust.	1,200							

Next, along with all the other expense accounts, Wages Expense is closed by crediting it for $104,000. However, Wages Payable continues to have a credit balance of $1,200. The $2,000 payroll on January 2 must be split up by debiting Wages Payable $1,200, debiting Wages Expense $800, and crediting Cash $2,000.

The employee who records the payroll not only has to record this particular payroll differently from all other weekly payrolls for the year but also has to refer back to the adjusting entry to determine what portion of the $2,000 is debited to Wages Payable and what portion is debited to Wages Expense. In many companies, however, the employee who records the payroll does not have access to the adjusting entries.

There is a solution to this problem. The need to refer to the earlier entry and divide the debit total between the two accounts is eliminated *if a reversing entry is made on the first day of the following fiscal period.* Many accounting software packages will automatically reverse specified adjusting entries at the beginning of the new fiscal period. Manually, one makes an entry that is the exact reverse of the adjusting entry, as follows:

GENERAL JOURNAL   PAGE 118

	DATE		DESCRIPTION	POST. REF.	DEBIT	CREDIT	
27							27
28	19—		Reversing Entries				28
29	Jan.	1	Wages Payable		1 2 0 0 00		29
30			Wages Expense			1 2 0 0 00	30

Now let's bring the T accounts up to date.

Wages Expense				Wages Payable			
+		**−**		**−**		**+**	
Balance	102,800	Dec. 31 Closing	104,000	Jan. 1 Reversing	1,200	Dec. 31 Adjust.	1,200
Dec. 31 Adjust.	1,200						
		Jan. 1 Reversing	1,200				

The reversing entry has the effect of transferring the $1,200 liability from Wages Payable to the credit side of Wages Expense. Wages Expense will temporarily have a credit balance until the next payroll is recorded in the routine manner. In our example this occurs on January 2 for $2,000. Here are the T accounts:

Wages Expense				Wages Payable			
+		**−**		**−**		**+**	
Balance	102,800	Dec. 31 Closing	104,000	Jan. 1 Reversing	1,200	Dec. 31 Adjust.	1,200
Dec. 31 Adjust.	1,200						
Jan. 2	2,000	Jan. 1 Reversing	1,200				

There is now a *net debit balance* of $800 in Wages Expense, which is the correct amount ($400 for January 1 and $400 for January 2). To see this, look at the following ledger accounts. December 26 was the last payday of one year, and January 2 is the first payday of the next year.

GENERAL LEDGER

ACCOUNT **Wages Expense**   ACCOUNT NO. **521**

DATE		ITEM	POST. REF.	DEBIT	CREDIT	BALANCE DEBIT	BALANCE CREDIT
Dec.	26		CP16	2 0 0 0 00		102 8 0 0 00	
	31	Adjusting	J116	1 2 0 0 00		104 0 0 0 00	
	31	Closing	J117		104 0 0 0 00	—	—
19—							
Jan.	1	Reversing	J118		1 2 0 0 00		1 2 0 0 00
	2		CP17	2 0 0 0 00		8 0 0 00	

ACCOUNT **Wages Payable**   ACCOUNT NO. **223**

DATE		ITEM	POST. REF.	DEBIT	CREDIT	BALANCE DEBIT	BALANCE CREDIT
19—							
Dec.	31	Adjusting	J116		1 2 0 0 00		1 2 0 0 00
19—							
Jan.	1	Reversing	J118	1 2 0 0 00		—	—

The reversing entry for accrued salaries or wages applies to service companies as well as to merchandising ones. You can see that a reversing entry simply switches around an adjusting entry. Which adjusting entries should be reversed? Here are two handy rules for reversing. **If an adjusting entry is to be reversed, it must meet all of the following qualifications:**

Performance Objective 10

Determine which adjusting entries should be reversed, and journalize the reversing entries.

1. **It must increase an asset or liability account.**

2. **The asset or liability account must not have had a previous balance.**

With the exception of the first year of operations, Merchandise Inventory and contra accounts—such as Accumulated Depreciation—always have previous balances. Consequently, adjusting entries involving these accounts should never be reversed. Let's apply these rules to the adjusting entries for Dodson Plumbing Supply on page 299. The only adjustment to be reversed is the one for Wages Payable—a liability that both was increased and had no previous balance. None of the other adjustments are reversed because each had a decrease or a previous balance.

Computer Applications

Work Sheet

Commercial accounting software programs usually do not have a work sheet, unless it is a screen provided to assist the accountant in preparing adjustments. In either case, the unadjusted trial balance provides vital information for preparing some adjustments.

After the adjusting entries are keyed (journalized and posted), the program computes the new balances, the profit or loss is calculated, and financial statements are ready to be printed. Like other accounting procedures, adjusting must be done accurately. If not, the errors will flow into the records—just more quickly when done electronically.

Financial Statements (Profit and Loss Statement and Balance Sheet)

Figure 7-7 is a software printout of an income statement, the Profit & Loss Statement. Figure 7-8 is a computerized printout of the Balance Sheet. However, you'll note there is no Statement of Owner's Equity. The income statement format is two column, one for the Year-to-Date totals and one for the Percent of Sales (% of Sales) computed by dividing each amount by the Total Income (Net Sales). The Percent of Sales figures assist management in

Figure 7.7

Dodson Plumbing Supply

Profit & Loss Statement

December 199–

	Year to Date	% of Sales
Income		
Sales	$195,180.00	101.4%
Sales Rets. and Allow.	(840.00)	(0.4%)
Sales Discount	(1,880.00)	(1.0%)
Total Income	$192,460.00	100.0%
Cost of Sales		
Beginning Inventory	$67,000.00	
Purchases	87,140.00	45.3%
Purchases Rets. and Allow.	(832.00)	(0.4%)
Purchases Discount	(1,248.00)	(0.6%)
Freight In	2,460.00	1.3%
Ending Inventory	(65,800.00)	
Total Cost of Sales	$88,720.00	45.5%
Gross Profit	$103,740.00	54.5%
Expenses		
Wages Expense	$46,920.00	24.4%
Supplies Expense	1,028.00	0.5%
Insurance Expense	320.00	0.2%
Depr. Expense, Building	4,000.00	2.1%
Depr. Expense, Equipment	4,800.00	2.5%
Taxes Expense	1,960.00	1.0%
Total Expenses	$59,028.00	30.7%
Operating Profit	$44,712.00	23.9%
Other Income		
Course Fees Income	$800.00	0.4%
Interest Income	120.00	0.1%
Total Other Income	$920.00	0.5%
Other Expenses		
Interest Expense	$374.00	0.2%
Total Other Expenses	$374.00	0.2%
Net Profit/(Loss)	$45,258.00	24.1%

Figure 7.8

```
                        Dodson Plumbing Supply

                            Balance Sheet

                           December 199-


.........................................................................
Assets
    Cash                              $19,154.00
    Notes Receivable                    4,000.00
    Accounts Receivable                29,446.00
    Merchandise Inventory              65,800.00
    Supplies                              412.00
    Prepaid Insurance                     640.00
    Land                               12,000.00
    Building                           90,000.00
    Accum. Depr., Building            (36,000.00)
    Equipment                          33,600.00
    Accum. Depr., Equipment           (21,200.00)
Total Assets                                            $197,852.00

Liabilities
    Notes Payable                      $3,000.00
    Accounts Payable                   36,400.00
    Wages Payable                       1,120.00
    Unearned Course Fees                  400.00
    Mortgage Payable                    8,000.00
Total Liabilities                                        $48,920.00

Equity
    L. E. Dodson, Capital            $140,574.00
    L. E. Dodson, Drawing             (36,900.00)
    Current Year Earnings              45,258.00
Total Equity                                            148,932.00

Total Liability & Equity                               $197,852.00
```

analyzing changes from one period to another. Most commercial software packages offer this column, as well as other reports to aid comparative analysis.

You will find the elements of the statement of owner's equity at the bottom of the Balance Sheet (beginning Capital, including additional investments, minus Drawing plus Current Year Earnings [Net Income]). These amounts have been computed by the program and are automatically sent to the appropriate places.

Closing Entries

Some commercial software packages require that the closing entries be keyed into the program. Other packages have closing as a menu item or item to select. If closing is a menu item, you are likely to encounter several questions before you are allowed to close—Have you saved your files? Have you backed up your files? Have you printed your financial statements? These questions act as a safety net to avoid premature closing. Remember, closing means that the balances of the revenue, expenses, and drawing accounts are zeroed and their balances sent to the summary account, and its balance to the capital account as a net income or a net loss. Computerized closing can be fast, but again, if debits do not equal credits, errors will be carried along whether manually or electronically entered.

CHAPTER REVIEW

Review of Performance Objectives

1. **Prepare an adjustment for merchandise inventory.**

   The adjustment for merchandise inventory requires two adjusting entries. In the first adjusting entry (to take off the beginning inventory), debit Income Summary and credit Merchandise Inventory. In the second adjusting entry (to add on the ending inventory), debit Merchandise Inventory and credit Income Summary.

2. **Prepare an adjustment for unearned revenue.**

   For revenue received in advance, an adjustment is required to separate the portion that has been earned from the portion that is unearned. We assumed the amount of revenue received in advance was originally recorded as unearned revenue, which is a liability. In the adjusting entry for the amount actually earned, debit the unearned revenue account (Unearned Course Fees) and credit the revenue account (Course Fees Income).

3. **Record adjustment data in a work sheet (including merchandise inventory, unearned revenue, supplies used, expired insurance, depreciation, and accrued wages).**

   In the Adjustments columns of the work sheet, record the following adjusting entries:
   For merchandise inventory: first, debit Income Summary and credit Merchandise Inventory (to take off the beginning inventory); next, debit Merchandise Inventory and credit Income Summary (to add on the ending inventory).
   For unearned revenue: debit the unearned revenue account and credit the revenue account (to record revenue earned).
   For supplies used: debit Supplies Expense and credit Supplies.
   For expired insurance: debit Insurance Expense and credit Prepaid Insurance.
   For depreciation: debit Depreciation Expense and credit Accumulated Depreciation.
   For accrued wages or salaries: debit the Salaries Expense or Wages Expense account and credit the Salaries Payable or Wages Payable account.

4. **Complete the work sheet.**

   Regarding the accounts introduced in the chapter, in the work sheet carry the Income Summary account as two separate figures from the Adjustments columns into the Income Statement columns. For merchandise inventory, record the amount of the ending inventory in the Balance Sheet Debit column. For unearned revenue, record the unearned revenue account in the Balance Sheet Credit column and the revenue account in the Income Statement Credit column.

5. **Journalize the adjusting entries for a merchandising business.**

   The adjusting entries recorded in the journal are taken directly from the Adjustments columns of the work sheet.

6. **Prepare a classified income statement for a merchandising firm.**

   The skeleton outline of the income statement looks like this:

Revenue from Sales

$\left\{\begin{array}{l}\text{Gross Sales} \\ -\ \text{Sales Returns and Allowances} \\ -\ \text{Sales Discount} \\ \hline =\ \text{Net Sales}\end{array}\right.$

− Cost of Goods Sold

$\left\{\begin{array}{l}\text{Beginning Merchandise Inventory} \\[6pt] +\ \text{Delivered Cost of Purchases} \qquad \left\{\begin{array}{l}\text{Gross Purchases} \\ -\ \text{Purchases Returns and Allowances} \\ -\ \text{Purchases Discount} \\ +\ \text{Freight In} \\ \hline =\ \text{Delivered Cost of Purchases}\end{array}\right. \\[6pt] \hline =\ \text{Goods Available for Sale} \\ -\ \text{Ending Merchandise Inventory} \\ \hline =\ \text{Cost of Goods Sold}\end{array}\right.$

= Gross Profit

− Operating Expenses $\left\{\begin{array}{l}\text{Selling Expenses} \\ \text{General Expenses}\end{array}\right.$

= Income from Operations

+ Other Income $\left\{\begin{array}{l}\text{Interest Income} \\ \text{Rent Income} \\ \text{Gain on Disposal of Plant and Equipment}\end{array}\right.$

− Other Expenses $\left\{\begin{array}{l}\text{Interest Expense} \\ \text{Loss of Disposal of Plant and Equipment}\end{array}\right.$

= Net Income

7. **Prepare a classified balance sheet.**

The skeleton outline of the balance sheet looks like this:

Assets **Current Assets** (listed in the order of their convertibility into cash)

1. Cash
2. Notes Receivable
3. Accounts Receivable
4. Merchandise Inventory
5. Prepaid items (Supplies; Prepaid Insurance)

Plant and Equipment (listed in the order of their length of life; the asset with the longest life is placed first)

1. Land
2. Buildings
3. Equipment

Liabilities **Current Liabilities** (listed in the order of their urgency of payment; the most pressing obligation is placed first)

1. Notes Payable
2. Mortgage Payable or Contracts Payable (current portion)
3. Accounts Payable
4. Accrued liabilities (Wages Payable; Commissions Payable)
5. Unearned Revenue

Long-Term Liabilities (Contracts Payable; Mortgage Payable)

Owner's Equity Capital balance at end of the fiscal year

8. **Compute working capital and current ratio.**

These two measures help analysts determine whether a firm has enough capital to operate and whether it can pay its debts.

Working capital = Current assets − Current liabilities

$$\text{Current ratio} = \frac{\text{Current assets}}{\text{Current liabilities}}$$

9. **Journalize the closing entries for a merchandising firm.**

There are four steps in making closing entries for a merchandising business:
Step 1 Close all revenue accounts, Purchases Discount, and Purchases Returns and Allowances into Income Summary (any accounts listed as credits in the work sheet Income Statement columns except Income Summary).
Step 2 Close all expense accounts, Sales Discount, and Sales Returns and Allowances into Income Summary (any accounts listed as debits in the work sheet Income Statement columns except Income Summary).
Step 3 Close Income Summary into Capital (transfer net income or net loss into the owner's Capital account).
Step 4 Close Drawing into Capital.

10. **Determine which adjusting entries should be reversed, and journalize the reversing entries.**

Reverse the adjusting entries that increase either asset or liability accounts and do not have previous balances. A contra account like Accumulated Depreciation should not be reversed. Reversing entries are dated as of the first day of the next fiscal period.

 **lossary**

Cost of Goods Sold Merchandise Inventory at beginning of the fiscal period, plus delivered cost of purchases, minus Merchandise Inventory at the end of the fiscal period. Terms often used to describe the same thing are *cost of merchandise sold* and *cost of sales*. **(304)**

Current assets Cash and any other assets or resources that are expected to be realized in cash or to be sold or consumed during the normal operating cycle of the business (or one year, if the normal operating cycle is less than twelve months). **(307)**

Current liabilities Debts that will become due within the normal operating cycle of a business, usually within one year, and that are normally paid from current assets. **(308)**

Current ratio A firm's current assets divided by its current liabilities. Portrays a firm's short-term debt-paying ability. **(309)**

Delivered Cost of Purchases Net Purchases plus Freight In. **(304)**

General expenses Expenses incurred in the administration of a business, including office expenses and any expenses that are not wholly classified as Selling Expenses or Other Expenses. **(305)**

Gross Profit Net Sales minus Cost of Goods Sold, or profit before deducting expenses. **(303)**

Liquidity The ability of an asset to be turned into cash quickly, either by selling it or by putting it up as security for a loan. **(307)**

Long-term liabilities Debts payable over a comparatively long period, usually more than one year. **(309)**

Net income The final figure on an income statement after all expenses have been deducted from revenues. Also called *net profit*. **(303)**

Net purchases Total Purchases minus Purchases Returns and Allowances and minus Purchases Discount. **(304)**

Net sales Sales, minus Sales Returns and Allowances minus Sales Discounts. **(304)**

Notes receivable (current) Written promises to pay an amount due in a period of less than one year. **(307)**

Periodic inventory Taking an actual count of the stock of goods on hand at intervals and computing its value; also referred to as a *physical inventory*. **(292)**

Physical inventory Taking an actual count of the stock of goods on hand; also referred to as a *periodic inventory*. **(292)**

Plant and equipment Long-lived assets that are held for use in the production or sale of other assets or services; also called *fixed assets*. **(307)**

Reversing entries The reverse of certain adjusting entries, recorded as of the first day of the following fiscal period. **(312)**

Selling expenses Expenses directly connected with the selling activity, such as salaries of sales staff, advertising expenses, and delivery expenses. **(305)**

Temporary-equity accounts Accounts whose balances apply to one fiscal period only, such as revenues, expenses, and the Drawing account. Temporary-equity accounts are also called *nominal accounts*. **(310)**

Unearned revenue Revenue received in advance for goods or services to be delivered later; considered to be a liability until the revenue is earned. **(293)**

Working capital A firm's current assets less its current liabilities. The amount of capital a firm has available to use or to work with during a normal operating cycle. **(309)**

QUESTIONS, EXERCISES, AND PROBLEMS

Discussion Questions

1. What is a physical or periodic inventory? What does the word *periodic* mean in the term *periodic inventory*?
2. On the Income Summary line of a work sheet, $126,200 appears in the Income Statement debit column, and $126,100 appears in the Income Statement Credit column. Which figure represents the beginning inventory?
3. Explain what is meant by unearned revenue and why it is treated as a liability?

4. When a college receives one semester's dormitory rent in advance, an entry is made debiting Cash and crediting Unearned Rent. At the end of the year, a large portion of the rent has been earned. What adjusting entry would you suggest?
5. What is the difference between the cost of goods available for sale and the cost of goods sold?
6. Explain the calculations of net sales and cost of net purchases.
7. On an income statement, what is the difference between income from operations and net income? Which is the most useful in comparing the results of operations over a number of years?
8. What is the rule for recognizing whether or not an adjusting entry should be reversed?

E xercises

Exercise 7-1 On December 31, the Maxlin Company counted its inventory and valued it at $180,600. The January balance of the Inventory account shows $135,329. Journalize the adjusting entry as of December 31, and list the title and new balance that will appear on the balance sheet.

| P.O.1,2 |

Journalize adjustments for merchandise inventory and unearned revenue.

On October 31, the Vermillion Igloos Hockey Club received $800,000 in cash in advance for season tickets for eight home games. The transaction was recorded as a debit to Cash and a credit to Unearned Admissions. By December 31, the end of the fiscal year, the team had played three home games and received an additional $450,000 cash admissions income at the gate.

Journalize the adjusting entry as of December 31, and list the title of the account and the related balance that will appear on the income statement. List the title of the account and the related balance that will appear on the balance sheet.

Exercise 7-2 Indicate the work sheet columns (Income Statement Debit, Income Statement Credit, Balance Sheet Debit, Balance Sheet Credit) in which the balances of the following accounts should appear:

| P.O.3,4 |

Place account balances in work sheet column.

a. F. Dexter, Drawing
b. Advertising Expense
c. Merchandise Inventory (ending)
d. Purchases Discount
e. Unearned Fees
f. Sales Returns and Allowances
g. Accumulated Depreciation, Building
h. Income Summary
i. Fees Income
j. Prepaid Rent

Exercise 7-3 On December 31, the end of the fiscal year, the accountant for *Fidelity Magazine* was called away suddenly due to an emergency. However, before leaving, the accountant jotted down a few notes pertaining to the adjustments. Record the necessary adjusting entries.

| P.O.1,2,5 |

Journalize adjusting entries.

a. Subscriptions received in advance amounting to $136,400 were recorded as Unearned Subscriptions. At the end of the year, $90,200 had been earned.
b. Depreciation of equipment for the year is $18,600.
c. The amount of expired insurance for the year is $916.
d. The balance of Prepaid Rent is $2,800, representing four months' rent. Three months' rent has now expired.
e. Three days' salaries will be unpaid at the end of the year; total weekly (five days') salaries are $3,600.
f. Beginning inventory, $18,362; ending inventory, $19,294.

P.O.6

Provide missing amounts on an income statement.

Exercise 7-4 Calculate the missing items in the following:

	Sales	Sales Returns and Allowances	Net Sales	Beginning Merchandise Inventory	Net Purchases	Goods Available for Sale	Ending Merchandise Inventory	Cost of Goods Sold	Gross Profit
a.	$248,000	$ 6,000	—	$148,000	$170,000	—	$136,000	$182,000	—
b.	304,000	—	$296,000	144,000	—	$404,000	196,000	208,000	—
c.	—	12,000	628,000	—	412,000	496,000	92,000	—	—

P.O.6

Prepare Cost of Goods Sold section.

Exercise 7-5 Using the following information, prepare the Cost of Goods Sold section of an income statement.

Purchases Discount	$ 9,000
Merchandise Inventory, December 31	191,000
Purchases	491,000
Merchandise Inventory, January 1	188,000
Purchases Returns and Allowances	16,000
Freight In	27,000

P.O.6,7

Classify income statement and balance sheet accounts.

Exercise 7-6 **Part 1:** Identify each of the following items relating to sections on an income statement as Revenue from Sales (S), Cost of Goods Sold (CGS), Selling Expenses (SE), General Expenses (GE), Other Income (OI), or Other Expense (OE).

a. Advertising Expense
b. Rent Expense
c. Purchases Discount
d. Sales Returns and Allowances
e. Interest Income
f. Freight In
g. Depreciation Expense, Building
h. Interest Expense
i. Insurance Expense
j. Delivery Expense

Classify balance sheet items.

Part 2: Identify each of the following items relating to sections of a balance sheet as Current Assets (CA), Plant and Equipment (PE), Current Liabilities (CL), Long-Term Liabilities (LTL), or Owner's Equity (OE):

a. Accounts Receivable
b. Building
c. Wages Payable
d. Prepaid Taxes
e. Mortgage Payable (current)
f. Supplies
g. Mortgage Payable (due May 31, 19x8)
h. Unearned Fees
i. D. Mann, Capital
j. Notes Payable

Exercise 7-7 On December 31, the following selected accounts and amounts appeared in the balance sheet. Determine the amount of the working capital and the current ratio.

Building	$160,000
Prepaid Insurance	600
Merchandise Inventory	72,000
Store Equipment	14,000
Unearned Fees	700
Notes Payable	7,000
Accumulated Depreciation, Building	72,000
Accounts Payable	22,000
Land	40,000
Store Supplies	1,000
Cash	9,000
Accumulated Depreciation, Store Equipment	6,000
Notes Receivable	4,000
Mortgage Payable (current portion)	4,400
Salaries Payable	2,000
C. Ruhl, Capital	101,500
Mortgage Payable (due June 30, 19x9)	85,000

Exercise 7-8 From the following T accounts, journalize the closing entries dated December 31:

Salary Expense		N. Hale, Drawing		Purchases Returns and Allowances	
68,000		54,000			7,600

Purchases		Miscellaneous Expense		Rent Expense	
236,800		13,200		24,000	

Sales Returns and Allowances		Freight In		Sales	
8,000		15,200			504,000

Income Summary		N. Hale, Capital		Purchases Discount	
88,000	104,000		336,000		5,600

 onsider and Communicate

You have a friend who is a seamstress specializing in wedding ensembles. She receives cash, not only to purchase material, but to cover her labor. She receives this cash well in advance of the wedding date, often in the fiscal period prior to the date of delivery of the ensemble. She always debits Cash and credits Revenue. First, explain to her why this entry violates the matching principle. Second, explain to her what kind of account Unearned Revenue is. Third, explain when the Unearned Revenue account is used.

W hat If . . .

What if there is an error in recording an ending inventory. The correct amount of the inventory should be $12,500 but the entry reads $1,250. You prepare the financial statements and give a rough draft to the accounting supervisor without realizing the error. She quickly notes that something must be wrong to have such a low profit and points out the ending inventory as the number she suspects. What else could have alerted her to the ending inventory as the problem?

A Question of Ethics

You work in the accounting department of a large retail firm. Your neighbor asks you about the profits of the firm where you work, suggesting that they must be doing well as your boss just bought a new boat. How can you/should you/would you respond?

Problem Set A

P.O.1,2,3,4,5

Problem 7-1A For Ben's Auto Supply, the work sheet for the fiscal year ended December 31 of this year is presented in the Working Papers. The Trial Balance columns have been completed.

Data for the adjustments are as follows:

a.–b. Merchandise inventory at December 31, $152,514.
  c. Salaries accrued at December 31, $2,934.
  d. Supplies inventory at December 31, $1,116.
  e. Depreciation of store equipment, $8,829.
  f. Depreciation of office equipment, $2,598.
  g. Insurance expired during the year, $948.
  h. Rent earned, $3,600.

Instructions

1. Complete the work sheet, including the heading.
2. Journalize the adjusting entries.

P.O.1,3,5,6,7

Problem 7-2A A portion of the work sheet of Byrum and Company for the year ended December 31 is shown below.

	ACCOUNT NAME		INCOME STATEMENT DEBIT	INCOME STATEMENT CREDIT	BALANCE SHEET DEBIT	BALANCE SHEET CREDIT	
1	Cash				10 6 9 6 24		1
2	Merchandise Inventory				66 8 6 8 20		2
3	Supplies				2 6 8 20		3
4	Prepaid Insurance				2 2 5 00		4
5	Store Equipment				34 1 6 4 00		5
6	Accumulated Depreciation, Store Equipment					26 4 9 6 00	6
7	Accounts Payable					12 3 8 4 00	7
8	Salaries Payable					5 2 9 20	8
9	C. L. Byrum, Capital					67 6 2 7 80	9
10	C. L. Byrum, Drawing				27 7 2 0 00		10
11	Income Summary		65 1 2 4 00	66 8 6 8 20			11
12	Sales			169 6 3 4 40			12
13	Sales Returns and Allowances		1 2 9 0 60				13
14	Purchases		87 2 8 0 16				14
15	Purchases Returns and Allowances			8 6 7 60			15
16	Purchases Discount			1 4 7 2 40			16
17	Salary Expense		34 0 6 6 80				17
18	Supplies Expense		7 9 5 60				18
19	Rent Expense		12 9 6 0 00				19
20	Insurance Expense		4 9 6 80				20
21	Depreciation Expense, Store Equipment		3 9 2 4 00				21
22			205 9 3 7 96	238 8 4 2 60	139 9 4 1 64	107 0 3 7 00	22

Instructions

1. Determine the entries that appeared in the Adjustments columns, and present them in general journal form.
2. Determine the net income for the year and the amount of the owner's capital at the end of the year (assuming that no capital contributions were made during the year).

Instructions for General Ledger Software

1. Record the adjusting entries in the general journal.
2. Print the journal.
3. Post the general journal amounts to the general ledger.
4. Print a trial balance.
5. Print the income statement, statement of owner's equity, and balance sheet.

Problem 7-3A Here is the partial work sheet for Haig's Recreation Outlet: P.O.7,8

Haig's Recreation Outlet
Work Sheet
For Year Ended December 31, 19–

	ACCOUNT NAME	BALANCE SHEET DEBIT	BALANCE SHEET CREDIT	
1	Cash	31 1 1 3 60		1
2	Notes Receivable	11 5 2 0 00		2
3	Accounts Receivable	137 2 1 4 72		3
4	Merchandise Inventory	181 4 3 0 40		4
5	Supplies	1 5 1 6 80		5
6	Prepaid Taxes	1 9 6 3 20		6
7	Prepaid Insurance	2 0 1 6 00		7
8	Land	26 8 8 0 00		8
9	Building	201 6 0 0 00		9
10	Accumulated Depreciation, Building		69 1 2 0 00	10
11	Office Equipment	17 3 5 6 80		11
12	Accumulated Depreciation, Office Equipment		13 3 4 4 00	12
13	Store Equipment	21 0 2 4 00		13
14	Accumulated Depreciation, Store Equipment		15 9 8 4 00	14
15	Delivery Equipment	17 8 0 8 00		15
16	Accumulated Depreciation, Delivery Equipment		13 7 7 6 00	16
17	Notes Payable		17 3 7 6 00	17
18	Mortgage Payable (current portion)		8 6 4 0 00	18
19	Accounts Payable		94 6 9 3 44	19
20	Wages Payable		4 0 8 9 60	20
21	Mortgage Payable		178 2 8 1 60	21
22	R. D. Haig, Capital		208 1 8 8 48	22
23	R. D. Haig, Drawing	80 6 2 0 80		23
24		732 0 6 4 32	623 4 9 3 12	24
25	Net Income		108 5 7 1 20	25
26		732 0 6 4 32	732 0 6 4 32	26

Instructions

1. Prepare a statement of owner's equity (no additional investment).
2. Prepare a classified balance sheet.
3. Determine the amount of the working capital.
4. Determine the amount of the current ratio (carry to two decimal places).

P.O.1,3,4,5,6 7,8,9,10

Problem 7-4A The following accounts appear in the ledger of Kesti and Company as of April 30. Their fiscal year extends from May 1 of one year through April 30 of the following year.

Cash	$ 6,524.64
Accounts Receivable	22,365.00
Merchandise Inventory	77,220.00
Store Supplies	1,103.28
Prepaid Insurance	1,462.50
Store Equipment	44,460.00
Accumulated Depreciation, Store Equipment	11,820.00
Accounts Payable	16,627.50
Salaries Payable	
S. P. Kesti, Capital	153,292.50
S. P. Kesti, Drawing	42,390.00
Income Summary	
Sales	303,945.00
Sales Returns and Allowances	3,960.00
Purchases	205,575.00
Purchases Returns and Allowances	6,592.50
Purchases Discount	3,847.92
Freight In	13,890.00
Advertising Expense	12,225.00
Salary Expense	49,650.00
Store Supplies Expense	
Rent Expense	15,300.00
Insurance Expense	
Depreciation Expense, Store Equipment	

The data needed for the adjustments on April 30 are as follows:

a.–b. Merchandise inventory, April 30, $72,294.
   c. Store supplies inventory, April 30, $403.80.
   d. Insurance expired for the year, $960.
   e. Depreciation for the year, $9,435.
   f. Accrued salaries on April 30, $708.

Instructions

1. Prepare a work sheet for the fiscal year ended April 30.
2. Prepare an income statement.
3. Prepare a statement of owner's equity. No additional investments were made during the year.
4. Prepare a classified balance sheet.
5. Journalize the adjusting entries.
6. Journalize the closing entries.
7. Journalize the reversing entry.
8. Determine the amount of (a) the working capital and (b) the current ratio.
9. Comment on the financial condition of the company.

Instructions for General Ledger Software

1. Record the adjusting entries in the general journal and print a copy of the entries.
2. Post the general journal amounts to the general ledger.
3. Print an adjusted trial balance.
4. Print the income statement, statement of owner's equity, and balance sheet.
5. Record the closing entries in the general journal and print a copy of the entries.
6. Post the general journal amounts to the general ledger.
7. Print a post-closing trial balance.
8. Record the reversing entry in the general journal at the beginning of the next month.

P roblem Set B

Problem 7-1B The work sheet for Beal's Fine Antiques for the fiscal year ended December 31 of this year is presented in the Working Papers. The Trial Balance columns have been completed.   P.O.1,2,3,4,5

Data for the adjustments are as follows:

a.–b. Merchandise inventory at December 31, $76,400.
   c. Salaries accrued at December 31, $960.
   d. Insurance expired during the year, $600.
   e. Supplies inventory at December 31, $190.
   f. Depreciation of store equipment, $2,500.
   g. Depreciation of office equipment, $1,300.
   h. Rent earned, $1,500.

Instructions

1. Complete the work sheet, including the heading.
2. Journalize the adjusting entries.

Problem 7-2B A portion of the work sheet of Hogan and Company for the year ended December 31 is shown on the next page.   P.O.1,3,5,6,7

Instructions

1. Determine the entries that appeared in the Adjustments columns, and present them in general journal form (page 41).
2. Determine the net income for the year and the amount of the owner's capital at the end of the year (assuming that no capital contributions were made during the year).

Instructions for General Ledger Software

1. Record the adjusting entries in the general journal.
2. Print the journal.
3. Post the general journal amounts to the general ledger.
4. Print a trial balance.
5. Print the income statement, statement of owner's equity, and balance sheet.

	ACCOUNT NAME	INCOME STATEMENT		BALANCE SHEET		
		DEBIT	CREDIT	DEBIT	CREDIT	
1	Cash			11 675 00		1
2	Merchandise Inventory			96 175 00		2
3	Supplies			3 20 00		3
4	Prepaid Insurance			3 00 00		4
5	Store Equipment			49 100 00		5
6	Accumulated Depreciation, Store Equipment				32 775 00	6
7	Accounts Payable				18 250 00	7
8	Salaries Payable				7 00 00	8
9	M. L. Hogan, Capital				86 175 00	9
10	M. L. Hogan, Drawing			34 500 00		10
11	Income Summary	82 100 00	96 175 00			11
12	Sales		216 775 00			12
13	Sales Returns and Allowances	1 900 00				13
14	Purchases	105 325 00				14
15	Purchases Returns and Allowances		1 175 00			15
16	Purchases Discount		2 000 00			16
17	Salary Expense	46 950 00				17
18	Supplies Expense	1 180 00				18
19	Rent Expense	18 500 00				19
20	Insurance Expense	9 50 00				20
21	Depreciation Expense, Store Equipment	5 050 00				21
22		261 955 00	316 125 00	192 070 00	137 900 00	22
23						23
24						24
25						25
26						26
27						27
28						28

P.O.7,8 **Problem 7-3B** A partial work sheet for Suarez Electrical Supply is shown below and on the next page.

Suarez Electrical Supply
Work Sheet
For Year Ended December 31, 19–

	ACCOUNT NAME	BALANCE SHEET		
		DEBIT	CREDIT	
1	Cash	20 664 00		1
2	Notes Receivable	10 080 00		2
3	Accounts Receivable	53 232 00		3
4	Merchandise Inventory	88 550 40		4
5	Supplies	6 72 00		5
6	Prepaid Taxes	1 008 00		6
7	Prepaid Insurance	8 64 00		7

	Account	Debit	Credit	
8	Land	12 48 0 00		8
9	Building	96 00 0 00		9
10	Accumulated Depreciation, Building		30 24 0 00	10
11	Office Equipment	7 02 7 20		11
12	Accumulated Depreciation, Office Equipment		2 67 8 40	12
13	Store Equipment	11 56 8 00		13
14	Accumulated Depreciation, Store Equipment		8 67 8 40	14
15	Truck	8 64 0 00		15
16	Accumulated Depreciation, Truck		7 15 2 00	16
17	Notes Payable		6 74 4 00	17
18	Mortgage Payable (current portion)		2 88 0 00	18
19	Accounts Payable		45 02 4 00	19
20	Wages Payable		1 57 4 40	20
21	Mortgage Payable		88 32 0 00	21
22	G. P. Suarez, Capital		107 70 2 40	22
23	G. P. Suarez, Drawing	35 90 4 00		23
24		346 68 9 60	300 99 3 60	24
25	Net Income		45 69 6 00	25
26		346 68 9 60	346 68 9 60	26
27				27
28				28
29				29
30				30
31				31
32				32
33				33

Instructions

1. Prepare a statement of owner's equity (no additional investment).
2. Prepare a classified balance sheet.
3. Determine the amount of the working capital.
4. Determine the amount of the current ratio (carry to two decimal places).

Problem 7-4B The following accounts appear in the ledger of The Grater Company on October 31. Their fiscal year extends from November 1 of one year through October 31 of the following year.

P.O.1,3,4,5,6
7,8,9,10

Cash	$ 7,560
Accounts Receivable	19,740
Merchandise Inventory	77,700
Store Supplies	966
Prepaid Insurance	1,512
Store Equipment	39,060
Accumulated Depreciation, Store Equipment	13,780
Accounts Payable	19,320
Salary Payable	
L. I. Grater, Capital	159,068
L. I. Grater, Drawing	50,400
Income Summary	
Sales	303,600
Sales Returns and Allowances	4,200
Purchases	238,000
Purchases Returns and Allowances	4,830

Purchases Discount	3,360
Freight In	9,800
Advertising Expense	5,460
Salary Expense	37,800
Store Supplies Expense	
Rent Expense	11,760
Insurance Expense	
Depreciation Expense, Store Equipment	

The data needed for the adjustments on October 31 are as follows:

a.–b. Merchandise inventory, October 31, $74,760.
   c. Store supplies inventory, October 31, $546.
   d. Insurance expired for the year, $861.
   e. Depreciation for the year, $8,953.
   f. Accrued salary on October 31, $1,778.

Instructions

1. Prepare a work sheet for the fiscal year ended October 31.
2. Prepare an income statement.
3. Prepare a statement of owner's equity. No additional investments were made.
4. Prepare a classified balance sheet.
5. Journalize the adjusting entries.
6. Journalize the closing entries.
7. Journalize the reversing entry.
8. Determine the amount of (a) the working capital and (b) the current ratio.
9. Comment on the financial condition of the company.

Instructions for General Ledger Software

1. Record the adjusting entries in the general journal and print a copy of the entries.
2. Post the general journal amounts to the general ledger.
3. Print an adjusted trial balance.
4. Print the income statement, statement of owner's equity, and balance sheet.
5. Record the closing entries in the general journal and print a copy of the entries.
6. Post the general journal amounts to the general ledger.
7. Print a post-closing trial balance.
8. Record the reversing entry in the general journal at the beginning of the next month.

CHALLENGE PROBLEM

Complete a cost of goods sold section of a classified income statement using the form provided in the Working Papers and selecting from the following information:

Freight In	$ 1,500
Sales	200,000
Purchases Returns and Allowances	3,410
Beginning Inventory (January 1, 19–)	131,800
Total of Purchases Returns and Allowances and Purchases Discount	4,290
Sales Returns and Allowances	8,320
Sales Discount	1,103
Ending Inventory	91,050
Cost of Goods Sold	127,440

Accounting Cycle Review Problem

This problem is designed to get you to review and apply the knowledge that you have acquired in Chapters 5 through 7.

You are to record transactions completed by Boyle Electronics during the month of January of this year. This company is located in Dallas. To gain practice in completing the steps in the accounting cycle for this merchandising business, assume that the fiscal period consists of one month. Here is the chart of accounts. Following that you will find the transactions for the month.

Chart of Accounts

ASSETS
111 Cash
113 Accounts Receivable
114 Merchandise Inventory
115 Supplies
117 Prepaid Insurance
124 Equipment
125 Accumulated Depreciation, Equipment

LIABILITIES
221 Accounts Payable

OWNER'S EQUITY
311 D. L. Boyle, Capital
312 D. L. Boyle, Drawing
399 Income Summary

REVENUE
411 Sales
412 Sales Returns and Allowances
413 Sales Discount

COST OF GOODS SOLD
511 Purchases
512 Purchases Returns and Allowances
513 Purchases Discount
514 Freight In

OPERATING EXPENSES
521 Salary Expense
523 Supplies Expense
524 Rent Expense
529 Insurance Expense
533 Depreciation Expense, Equipment
539 Miscellaneous Expense

JOURNALS
Sales Journal, page 84
Purchases Journal, page 67
Cash Receipts Journal, page 47
Cash Payments Journal, page 56
General Journal, pages 112–113

ACCOUNTS RECEIVABLE
Burke Supply
Eaton and Sievert
F. C. Parket
Pike and Secord
Vanguard Appliance

ACCOUNTS PAYABLE
Collins Products
Dempsey Office Supply
Franz Company
Vargas and Company

Jan.   2 Paid rent for the month, $900; Ck. No. 921.
       2 D. L. Boyle, the owner, invested an additional $3,300 cash in the business.
       3 Bought merchandise on account from Vargas and Company, $4,260; their invoice no. 446; terms 2/10, n/30; dated January 2.
       3 Received check from Vanguard Appliance for $1,470 in payment of invoice for $1,500, less discount.
       4 Sold merchandise on account to F. C. Parket, $1,125, invoice no. 723.
       6 Received check from Pike and Secord for $955.50 in payment of $975 invoice, less 2 percent cash discount.

6 Issued Ck. No. 922, $735, to Franz Company, in partial payment of their invoice no. 727, for $750, less 2 percent discount.

7 Bought supplies on account from Dempsey Office Supply, $147, their invoice no. 146, terms net 30 days.

7 Sold merchandise on account to Eaton and Sievert, $1,335, invoice no. 724.

10 Issued credit memorandum no. 39 to F. C. Parket, $75, for merchandise returned.

11 Cash sales for January 1 through 10, $6,771.

11 Paid Vargas and Company $4,174.80; Ck. No. 923, in payment of their $4,260 invoice, less cash discount.

14 Sold merchandise on account to Vanguard Appliance, $2,925, invoice no. 725.

14 Received check from F. C. Parket, $1,029, in payment of $1,125 invoice, less return of $75, less 2 percent cash discount.

18 Bought merchandise on account from Collins Products, $7,170; their invoice no. 284, dated January 17; terms 2/10, n/30; FOB shipping point, freight prepaid and added to invoice, $225 (total, $7,395).

20 Issued Ck. No. 924, $423, for advertising to Sempert Agency, not previously recorded.

21 Cash sales for January 11 through 20, $5,985.

22 Received credit memo no. 117, $637.50, from Collins Products for merchandise returned.

23 Received bill and paid Davis Fast Freight $129, Ck. No. 925, for freight charges on merchandise purchased January 3.

29 Sold merchandise on account to Burke Supply, $2,910, invoice no. 726.

31 Cash sales for January 21 through 31, $6,642.

31 Issued Ck. No. 926, $73.50, to R. Salazar for miscellaneous expenses not previously recorded.

31 Issued Ck. No. 927, $7,590.02, for salaries for the month.

31 D. L. Boyle, the owner, withdrew $1,425 for personal use, Ck. No. 928.

Instructions

1. Record the following transactions for January for Boyle Electronics using the chart of accounts and special journals listed above. Terms of sale are 2/10, n/30.
2. Post daily all entries involving customer accounts to the accounts receivable ledger.
3. Post daily all entries involving creditor accounts to the accounts payable ledger.
4. Post daily those entries involving the Other Accounts columns and the general journal to the general ledger.
5. Add the columns of the special journals, and show the proof of equality of debit and credit totals at the bottom of each journal.
6. Post the appropriate totals of the special journals to the general ledger.
7. Prepare a schedule of accounts receivable and a schedule of accounts payable. Do the totals equal the balances of the related controlling accounts?
8. Complete the work sheet for January.
9. Data for the month-end adjustments are as follows:

   a.–b. Merchandise Inventory at January 31, $32,465.
   c. Supplies inventory at January 31, $472.
   d. Insurance expired during January, $40.
   e. Depreciation of equipment during January, $105.

10. Journalize and post the adjusting entries.
11. Prepare a classified income statement.
12. Prepare a statement of owner's equity. (No additional investment was made during the month.)
13. Prepare a classified balance sheet.
14. Journalize and post the closing entries.
15. Prepare a post-closing trial balance.

Instructions for General Ledger Software

1. Record the transactions in the sales journal, purchases journal, cash receipts journal, cash payments journal, and general journal.
   a. Use acct. no. 221 for Accounts Payable.
   b. Since the program uses a single-column purchases journal, add the amount of the freight to the amount of purchases.
   c. Note that Sundry Accounts and Other Accounts mean the same thing.
2. Print the journals.
3. Post the amounts from the sales, purchases, cash receipts, cash payments, and general journals.
4. Print a trial balance.
5. Print a schedule of accounts receivable and compare the total with the balance of the Accounts Receivable controlling account.
6. Print a schedule of accounts payable and compare the total with the balance of the Accounts Payable controlling account.

Appendix A

Financial Statement Analysis

PERFORMANCE OBJECTIVES

After you have completed this appendix, you will be able to do the following:

1. Determine gross profit percentage.
2. Determine Merchandise Inventory turnover.
3. Determine Accounts Receivable turnover.
4. Determine return on investment.

An important function of accounting is to provide tools for interpreting the financial statements or the results of operations. This appendix presents a number of percentages and ratios that are frequently used for analyzing financial statements.

Kenwood Card Shop will serve as our example (see the comparative income statement on page 335).

For each year, net sales is the base (100 percent). Every other item on the income statement can be expressed as a percentage of net sales for the particular year involved. For example, let's look at the following percentages:

Performance Objective 1

Determine gross profit percentage.

$$\text{Gross profit \% (19x8)} = \frac{\text{Gross profit for 19x8}}{\text{Net sales for 19x8}} = \frac{\$150,000}{\$428,000} = .35 = 35\%$$

$$\text{Gross profit \% (19x7)} = \frac{\text{Gross profit for 19x7}}{\text{Net sales for 19x7}} = \frac{\$152,000}{\$400,000} = .38 = 38\%$$

$$\text{Sales salary expense (19x8)} = \frac{\text{Sales salary expense for 19x8}}{\text{Net sales for 19x8}}$$

$$= \frac{\$63,600}{\$428,000} = .1486 = 15\%$$

$$\text{Sales salary expense (19x7)} = \frac{\text{Sales salary expense for 19x7}}{\text{Net sales for 19x7}}$$

$$= \frac{\$58,000}{\$400,000} = .145 = 15\%$$

Here's how one might interpret a few of the percentages:

19x8

- For every $100 in net sales, gross profit amounted to $35.
- For every $100 in net sales, sales salary expense amounted to $15.
- For every $100 in net sales, net income amounted to $4.

Kenwood Card Shop

Comparative Income Statement
For Years Ended January 31, 19x8, and January 31, 19x7

	19x8		19x7	
	AMOUNT	PERCENT	AMOUNT	PERCENT
Revenue from Sales:				
Sales	$ 453 600 00	106	$ 420 000 00	105
Less Sales Returns and Allowances	25 600 00	6	20 000 00	5
Net Sales	$ 428 000 00	100	$ 400 000 00	100
Cost of Goods Sold:				
Merchandise Inventory, February 1	$ 116 000 00	27	$ 64 000 00	16
Delivered Cost of Purchases	320 000 00	75	300 000 00	75
Goods Available for Sale	$ 436 000 00	102	$ 364 000 00	91
Less Merchandise Inventory, January 31	158 000 00	37	116 000 00	29
Cost of Goods Sold	$ 278 000 00	65	$ 248 000 00	62
Gross Profit	$ 150 000 00	35	$ 152 000 00	38
Operating Expenses:				
Sales Salary Expense	$ 63 600 00	15	$ 58 000 00	15
Rent Expense	24 000 00	6	24 000 00	6
Advertising Expense	21 400 00	5	16 000 00	4
Depreciation Expense, Equipment	20 000 00	5	18 000 00	5
Insurance Expense	2 000 00	——	2 000 00	——
Store Supplies Expense	1 000 00	——	1 000 00	——
Miscellaneous Expense	1 000 00	——	1 000 00	——
Total Operating Expenses	$ 133 000 00	31	$ 120 000 00	30
Net Income	$ 17 000 00	4	$ 32 000 00	8

19x7

- For every $100 in net sales, gross profit amounted to $38.
- For every $100 in net sales, sales salary expense amounted to $15.
- For every $100 in net sales, net income amounted to $8.

Merchandise Inventory Turnover

Merchandise inventory turnover is the number of times a firm's average inventory is sold during a given year.

Performance Objective 2

Determine Merchandise Inventory turnover.

$$\text{Merchandise inventory turnover} = \frac{\text{Cost of goods sold}}{\text{Average merchandise inventory}}$$

Average merchandise inventory

$$= \frac{\text{Beginning merchandise inventory} + \text{Ending merchandise inventory}}{2}$$

19x8

$$\text{Average merchandise inventory} = \frac{\$116,000 + \$158,000}{2}$$

$$= \frac{\$274,000}{2} = \underline{\underline{\$137,000}}$$

$$\text{Merchandise inventory turnover} = \frac{\$278,000}{\$137,000} = \underline{\underline{2.03}} \text{ times per year}$$

19x7

$$\text{Average merchandise inventory} = \frac{\$64,000 + \$116,000}{2}$$

$$= \frac{\$180,000}{2} = \underline{\underline{\$90,000}}$$

$$\text{Merchandise inventory turnover} = \frac{\$248,000}{\$90,000} = \underline{\underline{2.76}} \text{ times per year}$$

With each turnover of merchandise, the company makes a gross profit, so the higher the turnover, the better.

Accounts Receivable Turnover

Performance Objective 3

Determine Accounts Receivable turnover.

Accounts receivable turnover is the number of times charge accounts are turned over (paid off) during a given year. A turnover implies a sale on account followed by payment of the debt.

$$\text{Accounts receivable turnover} = \frac{\text{Net sales on account}}{\text{Average accounts receivable}}$$

$$\text{Average accounts receivable} = \frac{\text{Beginning accounts receivable} + \text{Ending accounts receivable}}{2}$$

Going back to Kenwood Card Shop, let's assume the following information for 19x8 and 19x7:

	19x8	*19x7*
Net sales on account (from the sales journal)	$330,000	$302,000
Beginning accounts receivable (from Accounts Receivable account)	39,680	37,500
Ending accounts receivable (from Accounts Receivable account)	45,840	39,680

19x8

$$\text{Average accounts receivable} = \frac{\$39{,}680 + \$45{,}840}{2} = \frac{\$85{,}520}{2} = \underline{\underline{\$42{,}760}}$$

$$\text{Accounts receivable turnover} = \frac{\$330{,}000}{\$42{,}760} = \underline{\underline{7.72}} \text{ times per year}$$

19x7

$$\text{Average accounts receivable} = \frac{\$37{,}500 + \$39{,}680}{2} = \frac{\$77{,}180}{2} = \underline{\underline{\$38{,}590}}$$

$$\text{Accounts receivable} = \frac{\$302{,}000}{\$38{,}590} = \underline{\underline{7.83}} \text{ times per year}$$

A lower turnover rate indicates that a firm is experiencing greater difficulty in collecting charge accounts. In addition, more investment capital is tied up in accounts receivable.

Return on Investment (Yield)

 eturn on investment represents the earning power of the owner's investment in the business.

Performance Objective 4
Determine return on investment.

$$\text{Return on investment} = \frac{\text{Net income for the year}}{\text{Average capital}}$$

$$\text{Average capital} = \frac{\text{Beginning capital} + \text{Ending capital}}{2}$$

Getting back to Kenwood Card Shop, let's assume the following information for 19x8 and 19x7:

	19x8	*19x7*
Beginning balance of owner's Capital account	$176,920	$181,440
Ending balance of owner's Capital account	184,780	176,920

19x8

$$\text{Average capital} = \frac{\$176{,}920 + \$184{,}780}{2} = \frac{\$361{,}700}{2} = \underline{\underline{\$180{,}850}}$$

$$\text{Return on investment} = \frac{\$17{,}000}{\$180{,}850} = .094 = \underline{\underline{9.4\%}}$$

19x7

$$\text{Average capital} = \frac{\$181{,}440 + \$176{,}920}{2} = \frac{\$358{,}360}{2} = \underline{\underline{\$179{,}180}}$$

$$\text{Return on investment} = \frac{\$32{,}000}{\$179{,}180} = .179 = \underline{\underline{17.9\%}}$$

As a result, we can state the following:

- In 19x8, for an average investment of $100, the business earned $9.40.
- In 19x7, for an average investment of $100, the business earned $17.90.

Problems

P.O.1

Problem A-1 Rivas Company's abbreviated comparative income statement for years 19x8 and 19x7 is shown below.

Instructions

1. For the years 19x8 and 19x7, determine gross profit as a percentage of net sales.
2. For the years 19x8 and 19x7, determine net income as a percentage of net sales.

Rivas Company
Comparative Income Statement
For Years Ended December 31, 19x8 and December 31, 19x7

	19x8	19x7	
Net Sales	$ 487 2 0 0 00	$ 462 0 0 0 00	
Cost of Goods Sold	287 4 0 0 00	277 2 0 0 00	
Gross Profit	199 8 0 0 00	184 8 0 0 00	
Total Operating Expenses	152 2 4 0 00	146 1 6 0 00	
Net Income	$ 47 5 6 0 00	$ 38 6 4 0 00	

P.O.2

Problem A-2 Rivas Company's merchandise inventory figures are:

	19x8	*19x7*
Beginning merchandise inventory (January 1)	$ 88,420	$106,110
Ending merchandise inventory (December 31)	103,210	88,420

Determine the merchandise inventory turnover for the years 19x8 and 19x7.

Problem A-3 R. A. Rivas, Capital account balances are as follows:

P.O.4

January 1, 19x7	$375,670
January 1, 19x8	$493,970
December 31, 19x8	$526,820

Determine the return on investment for the years 19x8 and 19x7.

Chapter 8

Bank Accounts and Cash Funds

PERFORMANCE OBJECTIVES

After you have completed this chapter, you will be able to do the following:

1. Describe the procedure for depositing checks.

2. Reconcile a bank statement.

3. Record the required journal entries directly from the bank reconciliation.

4. Record journal entries to establish and reimburse Petty Cash Fund.

5. Complete petty cash vouchers and petty cash payments records.

6. Record the journal entry to establish a Change Fund.

7. Record journal entries for transactions involving Cash Short and Over.

Believe it or not, company owners are the worst offenders when it comes to violating internal control procedures for cash.

One of my first accounting assignments was to straighten out the Cash account for a hardware store. The checking account had not been reconciled to the bank

statement for six months—there had been valiant attempts, but they fizzled. Shortly after I got started, I could see why. Here are just a few of the reasons:

- The owner would grab a handful of checks in case he needed them, but would forget to record the ones he used or to return the blank checks.
- En route to the bank, the owner would find himself short of cash and help himself to a few twenties from the bank bag. (Deposits per the cash journal never matched the deposits reflected on the bank statement.)
- The owner paid vendors directly from the cash register. (Payables were a mess, too!)

It took three days on my part and cost hundreds of dollars for my fees to straighten out the mess. But the owner soon mended his ways—not long after he got my bill.

A requirement of any system of financial accounting, either for an individual or for a business enterprise, is the accurate and efficient management of cash. For a business of any size, all cash received during a working day should be deposited by the end of the day, and all disbursements—with the exception of payments from Petty Cash—should be made by check. When we talk about cash, we mean currency, coins, checks, money orders, traveler's checks, and bank drafts or bank cashier's checks. Personal checks are accepted on a conditional-payment status; that is, based on the condition that they're valid. In other words, we consider checks to be good until they are proven to be invalid.

In this chapter, besides discussing bank accounts, we are going to talk about **cash funds**—petty cash funds and change funds—which are separately held amounts of cash set aside for specific purposes.

Using a Checking Account

Although you may be familiar with the process of opening a checking account, making deposits, and writing checks, let's review these and other procedures associated with opening and maintaining a business checking account. We will discuss signature cards, deposit slips, automated teller machines, night deposits, and ways of endorsing checks.

Signature Card

Donna A. Whitman founded Whitman Video, a video rental firm, and opened a checking account in the name of the business. When she made her first deposit, she filled out a **signature card** for the bank's files. Whitman gave her assistant the authority to sign checks, too, so the assistant also signed the card. Figure 8-1 shows a typical signature card.

Figure 8-1

Title		Account Number
Whitman Video		5008-3007

In consideration of the acceptance by   PRIME NATIONAL BANK   of my/our account of the type indicated below, I/we agree to be bound by such rules and regulations and/or such schedules of interest, fees and charges applicable to such account as may now or hereafter be adopted by and in effect at said Bank, and also by the provisions printed hereon. It is understood that the acceptance by said Bank of my/our account is subject to the receipt by said Bank of satisfactory credit information.

(1) Sign Here   *Donna A. Whitman*

(2) Sign Here   *Alicia C. Rodriguez*

Address   1424 Garber Avenue

City	State	Zip
San Diego	California	92109

☑ CHECKING   ☐ MULTIPLE MATURITY   ☐ CASH MANAGER
☐ SAVINGS   ☐ GUARANTEED INTEREST   ☐ SAFE DEPOSIT   ☐ OTHER _____
                        (Multiple Maturity)

IF THIS IS A JOINT ACCOUNT, BOTH OWNERS MUST SIGN ABOVE
Each of the signers guarantees the genuineness of the signature of the other. Each signer also agrees with the other and the Bank that deposits now or hereafter made to this account may be withdrawn in whole or part by either or survivor, and that each may endose for deposit to this account any instrument payable to the order of either or both. Provisions respecting this agreement shall be modified only upon receipt by the Bank of written notice, signed by both.

Deposit Slips

Performance Objective 1

Describe the procedure for depositing checks.

The bank provides printed **deposit slips** or deposit tickets on which customers record the amount of coins and currency they are depositing and list each individual check being deposited. A typical deposit slip is shown in Figure 8-2.

For identification purposes, each check should be listed according to its American Bankers Association (ABA) transit number. The **ABA number** is the small fraction located in the upper right corner of a check. The numerator (top of the fraction) indicates the city or state in which the bank is located and the specific bank on which the check is drawn. The denominator (bottom of the fraction) indicates the Federal Reserve District in which the check is cleared and the routing number used by the Federal Reserve Bank. For example,

$$\frac{68\text{-}420}{1210}$$

When the bank receives the deposited checks, it prints the amount of each check on the lower right side of the check in a very distinctive script called **MICR,** which stands for *magnetic ink character recognition.* The routing number used by the Federal Reserve Bank was previously printed on the lower left side of the blank check. The reason banks use this MICR script is that the electronic equipment used to process the checks is able to read the script identifying the bank on which the check is drawn, as well as the amount of the check. Clearing checks electronically greatly speeds up the process.

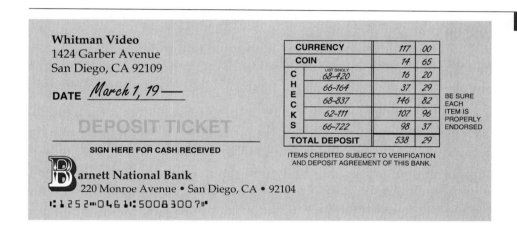

Figure 8-2

Automated Teller Machines

Deposits and withdrawals can be made at all hours at banks having automated teller machines **(ATMs)**. Each depositor uses a plastic card that resembles a bank credit card and contains a code number. The amount to be deposited or withdrawn is keyed in by the depositor and shows up on a screen. To make a deposit, the customer inserts an envelope containing cash and/or checks and a copy of the deposit slip into the ATM. To make a withdrawal, the customer removes the cash requested from the machine. When all transactions are completed, the automated teller machine returns the customer's plastic card and prints out a slip that lists the type and amount of each transaction. Customers can also check balances of accounts and transfer money from one account to another.

Endorsements

The bank refuses to accept for deposit a check made out to a firm until someone from the firm has endorsed the check. The **endorsement** may be made by signature or by stamp. The endorsement must appear on the back of

ATMs offer a variety of services twenty-four hours a day and provide instructions in more than one language. For convenience and security, some ATMs are accessible from the user's vehicle.

the left end of a check above the line as it does in Figure 8-3. The endorsement (1) transfers title to the money and (2) guarantees the payment of the check. In other words, if the check is not good, an **NSF check** (not sufficient funds), then the bank, in order to protect itself, will deduct the amount of the check from the depositor's account.

Restrictive Endorsement Whitman Video endorses all incoming checks by stamping on the back of the checks "Pay to the Order of Barnett National Bank, For Deposit Only, Whitman Video, 5008-3007." This is called a **restrictive endorsement** because it restricts or limits any further transferring of the check

Figure 8-3

FYI

If you receive an NSF check from a customer, resubmit the check to the bank. If it does not clear, call the writer of the check. You can also call the bank on which it was drawn and ask if there are sufficient funds to cover the check. If there are and the check is local, you may want to go directly to that bank and cash it. To avoid the losses that result from accepting bad checks, some vendors subscribe to the services of companies that maintain records of people who have poor credit histories.

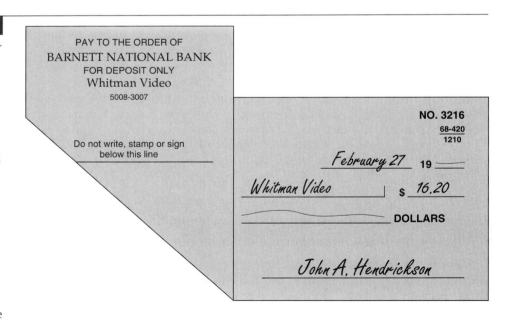

Figure 8-4

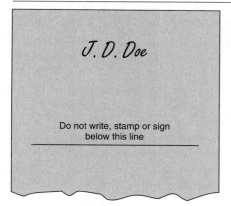

Blank Endorsement

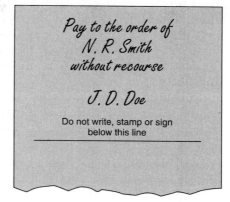

Qualified Endorsement

by endorsement. This endorsement also forces the deposit of the check, because the endorsement is not valid for any other purpose, like cashing all or part of the check.

Blank Endorsement   When the party to whom a check is made payable (the payee) endorses the check by signing only her or his name on the back of the check, the party makes what is known as a **blank endorsement** (Figure 8-4). With a blank endorsement, there are no restrictions attached.

Qualified Endorsement   A third type of endorsement is a **qualified endorsement**, which generally includes the phrase "Pay to the order of," followed by the name of the person to whom the check is being transferred and then followed by the phrase "without recourse." Such an endorsement frees the endorser of future liability in case the drawer of the check does not have sufficient funds to cover the check.

Writing Checks

People generally use a check to withdraw money from a bank checking account. The party who writes the check is called the **drawer.** A check represents an order by the depositor, directing the bank to pay a designated person or company. The party to whom payment is to be made is the **payee.**

Checks should be written carefully so that no dishonest person can successfully alter them. Write the payee's name on the first long line. Write the amount of the check in figures close to the dollar sign, then write the amount in words at the extreme left of the line provided for this information. Write cents as a fraction of 100. For example, write $727.50 as "seven hundred twenty-seven and 50/100," or $89.00 as "eighty-nine and 00/100." From a legal standpoint, if there is a discrepancy between the amount in figures and the written amount, the written amount prevails. However, as a general practice, the bank gets in touch with the depositor and asks what the correct amount should be.

Some firms use a **check writer,** which is a device used to imprint the amount in figures and words on the check itself with a combination of inks that make it more difficult to alter the check. Many more firms print their

FYI

Do not destroy voided checks. It has happened that an employee who tore up two checks that had errors on them had to sift through two days of office trash to recover the pieces. Fortunately, the office building bagged trash, numbered the bags, and kept it for 72 hours. The physical check had to be accounted for; it had to be listed on the bank statement as cleared, be marked void, or still be in the checkbook.

checks on the printer connected to their computer. Large firms may use laser checkprinters that print the MICR coding most banks require.

Finally, the depositor's signature on the face of the check should match that on the signature card on file at the depositor's bank. Some signatures, particularly in large firms or in governmental bodies, are computer-generated signatures.

Figure 8-5 shows a check, with the accompanying stub, drawn on the account of Whitman Video. A description of the script appears in Figure 8-6.

Figure 8-5

Figure 8-6

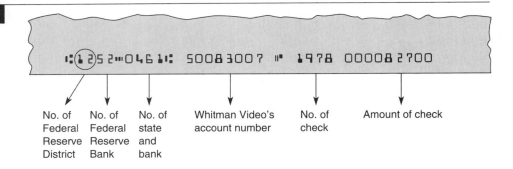

| No. of Federal Reserve District | No. of Federal Reserve Bank | No. of state and bank | Whitman Video's account number | No. of check | Amount of check |

Check Register

Instead of recording payments of cash in a cash payments journal (like the one presented in Chapter 6), some accountants prefer using a check register. The **check register** is merely a large checkbook with perforations that make it easy to tear out the checks. The page opposite the checks has columns labeled for special situations, such as Bank Name Credit (instead of Cash), Accounts Payable Debit, and so on. Each check is recorded in the special columns. Check registers are also found in accounting software, which offers the added advantage of preparing the checks on the attached printer.

Assuming that Dodson Plumbing Supply used a check register in place of a cash payments journal, the check register would look like Figure 8-7.

Figure 8-7

	DATE	CK. NO.	PAYEE	ACCOUNT DEBITED	POST. REF.	OTHER ACCOUNTS DEBIT	ACCOUNTS PAYABLE DEBIT	PURCHASES DISCOUNT CREDIT	VALLEY BANK CREDIT	
1	19–									1
2	Aug. 8	76	Colvin, Inc.	Colvin, Inc.	✓		759 00	14 20	744 80	2
3	10	77	Payroll	Wages Expense	521	1 680 00			1 680 00	3
4	11	78	Adams							4
5			Manufacturing	Manufacturing	✓		494 00	9 88	484 12	5
6	12	79	Davenport	Supplies	115	70 00			70 00	6
7	15	80	Spargo	Spargo						7
8			Products Co.	Products Co.	✓		123 00	1 13	121 87	8
9	16	81	Jones and Son	Purchases	511	200 00			200 00	9
10	19	82	Monroe Express	Freight In	514	60 00			60 00	10
11	23	83	Void		—					11
12	23	84	American Fire	Prepaid						12
13			Ins. Co.	Insurance	117	420 00			420 00	13
14	25	85	Payroll	Wages Expense	521	1 750 00			1 750 00	14
15	27	86	F. P. Franz	Sales Ret. and						15
16				Allow.	412	51 00			51 00	16
17	31	87	Richter and Son	Richter and Son	✓		180 00		180 00	17
18	31					4 231 00	1 556 00	25 21	5 761 79	18
19						(X)	(221)	(513)	(111)	19
20										20

CHECK REGISTER — PAGE _____

Some check registers also contain a Bank Deposits column.

Bank Statements

Once a month the bank sends all its customers a **bank statement.** This statement provides the following information about each customer's accounts:

- The balance at the beginning of the month
- Additions in the form of deposits and credit memos
- Deductions in the form of checks and debit memos
- The final balance at the end of the month

A bank statement for Whitman Video is shown in Figure 8-8 on page 349. The following code of symbols is listed on the bottom of the statement:

- **CM (credit memo)** Increases or credits to the account, such as notes or accounts left with the bank for collection.
- **DM (debit memo)** Decreases or debits to the account, such as NSF checks, automated teller withdrawals, and service charges. Service charges are based on the number of items processed and the average account balance. Special charges may also be levied against the account for collections and other services performed.

- **EC (error correction)** Corrections of errors made by the bank, such as mistakes in transferring figures.
- **OD (overdraft)** An overwithdrawal, resulting in a negative balance in the account.

The bank usually mails statements to its depositors shortly after the end of the month. The **canceled checks** (checks that have been cashed or cleared by the bank) are listed on the bank statement. They are called canceled checks because they are canceled by a stamp or perforation, indicating that they have been paid. Debit or credit memos are generally mailed in the same envelope with the statement. As we mentioned before, debit memos represent deductions from and credit memos represent additions to a bank account.

Recording Deposits or Withdrawals on the Bank's Books

Each business entity keeps its accounts from its own point of view. Let's take a brief look from the bank's point of view to help understand debit and credit memos seen on bank statements. Each customer's deposits are liabilities, in that the bank owes the customer the amount of the deposits. Using T accounts, it looks like this on the bank's books:

Liabilities

−	+
Debits	Credits

Deposits Payable

−	+

	Debits	Credits	
	Checks written	Deposits	
Debit	Service charges	Notes	**Credit**
memos	NSF checks	collected	**memos**
	ATM withdrawals		

Recording Deposits or Withdrawals on the Customer's Books

The customer uses the account titled Cash, or Cash in Bank, or simply the name of the bank. Deposits are recorded as debits, and withdrawals are recorded as credits in the account. On a bank reconciliation, the balance of the account is listed as the **ledger balance of cash.**

Need for Reconciling Bank Balance and Book Balance of Cash

Performance Objective 2

Reconcile a bank statement.

Since the bank statement balance and the ledger balance of cash are not equal, a firm makes a **bank reconciliation** to uncover the reasons for the difference between the two balances and to correct any errors that may have been made by either the bank or the firm. This makes it possible to reach the same balance in each account, which is called the *adjusted balance,* or *true balance,* of the Cash account.

Figure 8-8

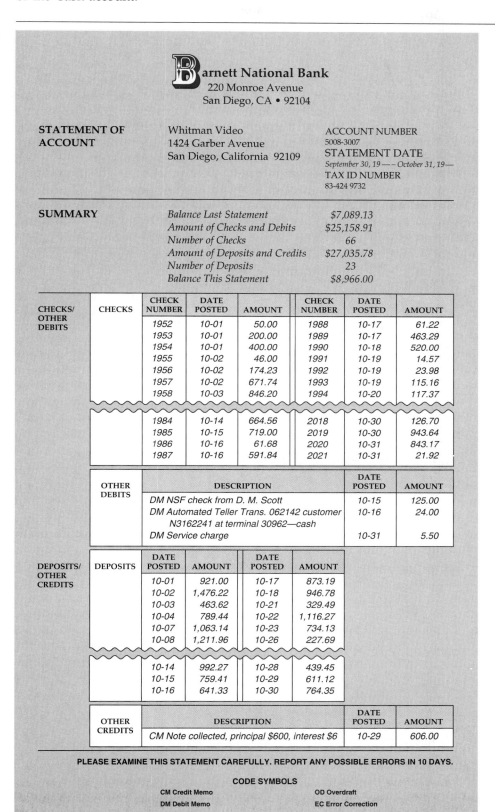

Barnett National Bank
220 Monroe Avenue
San Diego, CA • 92104

STATEMENT OF ACCOUNT

Whitman Video
1424 Garber Avenue
San Diego, California 92109

ACCOUNT NUMBER
5008-3007
STATEMENT DATE
September 30, 19—–October 31, 19—
TAX ID NUMBER
83-424 9732

SUMMARY

Balance Last Statement	$7,089.13
Amount of Checks and Debits	$25,158.91
Number of Checks	66
Amount of Deposits and Credits	$27,035.78
Number of Deposits	23
Balance This Statement	$8,966.00

CHECKS/ OTHER DEBITS — CHECKS

CHECK NUMBER	DATE POSTED	AMOUNT	CHECK NUMBER	DATE POSTED	AMOUNT
1952	10-01	50.00	1988	10-17	61.22
1953	10-01	200.00	1989	10-17	463.29
1954	10-01	400.00	1990	10-18	520.00
1955	10-02	46.00	1991	10-19	14.57
1956	10-02	174.23	1992	10-19	23.98
1957	10-02	671.74	1993	10-19	115.16
1958	10-03	846.20	1994	10-20	117.37
1984	10-14	664.56	2018	10-30	126.70
1985	10-15	719.00	2019	10-30	943.64
1986	10-16	61.68	2020	10-31	843.17
1987	10-16	591.84	2021	10-31	21.92

OTHER DEBITS

DESCRIPTION	DATE POSTED	AMOUNT
DM NSF check from D. M. Scott	10-15	125.00
DM Automated Teller Trans. 062142 customer N3162241 at terminal 30962—cash	10-16	24.00
DM Service charge	10-31	5.50

DEPOSITS/ OTHER CREDITS — DEPOSITS

DATE POSTED	AMOUNT	DATE POSTED	AMOUNT
10-01	921.00	10-17	873.19
10-02	1,476.22	10-18	946.78
10-03	463.62	10-21	329.49
10-04	789.44	10-22	1,116.27
10-07	1,063.14	10-23	734.13
10-08	1,211.96	10-26	227.69
10-14	992.27	10-28	439.45
10-15	759.41	10-29	611.12
10-16	641.33	10-30	764.35

OTHER CREDITS

DESCRIPTION	DATE POSTED	AMOUNT
CM Note collected, principal $600, interest $6	10-29	606.00

PLEASE EXAMINE THIS STATEMENT CAREFULLY. REPORT ANY POSSIBLE ERRORS IN 10 DAYS.

CODE SYMBOLS

CM Credit Memo   OD Overdraft
DM Debit Memo   EC Error Correction

There are a variety of reasons for differences between the bank statement balance and the customer's cash balance. Here are some of the more usual ones:

- **Outstanding checks** Checks that have been written but not yet received for payment (cleared) by the time the bank sends out its statement. The depositor, when writing out his or her checks, deducted the amounts from the Cash account in the company's books, which explains the difference.
- **Deposit in transit** A deposit made after the bank statement was issued. The depositor has naturally already added the amount to the Cash account in his or her books, but the deposit has not been recorded by the bank.
- **Service charge** A bank charge for services rendered: for issuing checks, for collecting money, for receiving payment of notes turned over to it by the customer for collection, and for other such services. The bank notifies the depositor with a debit memorandum and immediately deducts the fee from the balance of the bank account.
- **Collections** When the bank acts as a collection agent for its customers by accepting payments on promissory notes, installment accounts, and charge accounts, it adds the proceeds to the customer's bank account and sends a credit memorandum to notify the customer of the transaction.
- **NSF (Not Sufficient Funds) check** When a bank customer deposits a check, she or he counts it as cash. Occasionally, however, a check is not paid (bounces), and then the bank notifies the customer. The customer must then make a deduction from the Cash account. An NSF check may also be called a *dishonored check.*
- **Errors** In spite of internal control and systems designed to double-check against errors, sometimes either the customer or the bank makes a mistake. Often these errors do not become evident until the bank reconciliation is performed.

Steps in Reconciling the Bank Statement

Follow these steps in reconciling a bank statement:

1. **Canceled checks**
   a. Compare the amount of each canceled check with the bank statement and note any differences.
   b. In the checkbook beside the check number, list the date of the bank statement.

2. **Deposits**
   a. Compare the deposits shown on the bank statement with the deposits in transit (not recorded by the bank at the time of the statement) listed on last month's bank reconciliation. By this time all of last month's deposits in transit should be listed on this month's bank statement. If not, notify the bank immediately.
   b. Compare the remaining deposits listed on this month's bank statement with deposits written in the company's accounting records. Consider any deposits not shown on the bank statement as deposits in transit.

3. **Outstanding checks**
   a. Arrange the canceled checks that may accompany the bank statement in the order of the check numbers. Otherwise look at the list of checks identified by number on the bank statement.

b. Identify any outstanding checks from prior months, and note the checks that have not been returned or cleared.

c. For each canceled (or cleared) check, compare the amount recorded at the lower right-hand corner of the check or listed on the bank statement with the amount written on the check. Next, compare the canceled checks with the checkbook. Use a check mark ($\checkmark$) to indicate that the check has cleared and that the amount is correct. Any checks that have not been checked off, including the outstanding checks from prior months, are still outstanding checks.

4. **Bank memoranda** Trace the credit and debit memos to the journal. If the memos have not been recorded, make separate entries for them.

A large firm should require that the reconciliation be prepared by an employee who is not involved in recording business transactions or in handling cash receipts and disbursements.

Many banks offer telephone access to account information and activities, including deposits, checks cleared, and last transaction. Automated teller machines (ATMs) sometimes offer current statements, balances, as well as cash deposits and withdrawals.

Example of a Bank Reconciliation

Let's look at an example of a bank reconciliation for Whitman Video.

The bank statement of Whitman Video shows a final balance of $8,966 as of October 31 (see Figure 8-8). The present balance of the Cash account in the ledger, after Whitman's accountant has posted from the journal, is $8,030.50. The accountant took the following steps:

1. Verified that canceled checks were recorded correctly on the bank statement.

2. Discovered that a deposit of $1,003 made on October 31 was not recorded on the bank statement.

3. Noted outstanding checks: no. 1916, $461; no. 2022, $119; no. 2023, $827; no. 2024, $67.

4. Noted that a credit memo for a note collected by the bank from Lee and Brock, $600 principal plus $6 interest, was not recorded in the journal.

5. Found that check no. 2001 for $523, payable to Davis, Inc., on account was recorded in the journal as $532. (The correct amount is $523.)

6. Noted that a debit memo for a collection charge and service charge of $5.50 was not recorded in the journal.

7. Noted that a debit memo for an NSF check for $125 from D. M. Scott was not recorded.

8. Noted that a $20 personal withdrawal by Donna A. Whitman, the owner, using an automated teller, was not recorded.

- - - - - - - - - - - - -
R E M E M B E R

For placing each item on the bank reconciliation, ask yourself if it has been recorded only by the bank, or only by the depositor. If an item has been recorded by both the bank and the depositor, there is nothing to do. If an item has been recorded by the bank only, then record it in a similar manner in the Ledger Balance of Cash section. If an item has been recorded by the depositor only, then record it in a similar manner in the Bank Statement Balance section.
- - - - - - - - - - - - -

The note received from Lee and Brock is called a **promissory note.** A promissory note is a written promise to pay a definite amount at a definite future time. Let's assume that Whitman Video received the sixty-day non-interest-bearing note from Lee for services performed. In recording the transaction, Whitman's accountant debited Notes Receivable and credited Income from Services. The account, Notes Receivable, is similar to Accounts Receivable. However, Accounts Receivable is reserved for customer charge accounts with payments usually due in thirty days. Next, Whitman Video turned the note over to its bank for collection.

Look at Figure 8-9 to see how each of steps 1–8 on page 351 relates to the bank reconciliation.

Figure 8-9

Whitman Video
Bank Reconciliation
October 31, 19 —

Bank Statement Balance		$8,966.00
Add: Deposit in transit (October 31)		1,003.00
		$9,969.00
Deduct: Outstanding checks		
No. 1916	$461.00	
No. 2022	119.00	
No. 2023	827.00	
No. 2024	67.00	1,474.00
Adjusted Bank Statement Balance		$8,495.00
Ledger Balance of Cash		$8,030.50
Add: Note collected (principal $600.00, interest $6.00, Lee and Brock)	$606.00 ←	
Error in recording Check No. 2001 payable to Davis, Inc.	9.00	615.00
		$8,645.50
Deduct: Bank service and collection charges	$ 5.50 ←	
NSF check from D. M. Scott	125.00 ←	
Cash withdrawal by Donna A. Whitman	20.00 ←	150.50
Adjusted Ledger Balance of Cash		$8,495.00

Require journal entries

The accountant makes journal entries for the items indicated in Figure 8-9 to change the Cash account from the present balance of $8,030.50 to the actual balance of $8,495.00. Again, those items that require journal entires are highlighted in Figure 8-9 and shown in Figure 8-10.

Figure 8-10

	DATE		DESCRIPTION	POST. REF.	DEBIT				CREDIT				
1	19–												1
2	Oct.	31	Cash			6	0	6	00				2
3			Notes Receivable							6	0	0	00	3
4			Interest Income									6	00	4
5			Bank collected note signed by											5
6			Lee and Brock.											6
7														7
8		31	Cash					9	00					8
9			Accounts Payable									9	00	9
10			Error in recording check no.											10
11			2001 payable to Davis, Inc.											11
12														12
13		31	Miscellaneous Expense					5	50					13
14			Cash									5	50	14
15			Bank service charge and											15
16			collection charge.											16
17														17
18		31	Accounts Receivable			1	2	5	00					18
19			Cash							1	2	5	00	19
20			NSF check received from											20
21			D. M. Scott.											21
22														22
23		31	D. A. Whitman, Drawing				2	0	00					23
24			Cash								2	0	00	24
25			Withdrawal for personal use.											25
26														26

GENERAL JOURNAL PAGE 23

The account Interest Income is classified as an other revenue account. It represents the amount received on the promissory note that is over and above the face value of the note.

Regarding the NSF check, upon being notified by the bank, Whitman Video calls its customer (D. M. Scott). Scott can now take steps to cover the check. Let's back up and review Whitman's transaction with D. M. Scott. In return for recording services, Whitman received Scott's check for $125. At that time, Whitman's accountant recorded the transaction as a debit to Cash for $125 and a credit to Income from Services for $125. Now, assume that the bank, through its debit memorandum, notifies Whitman Video about Scott's NSF check. To avoid overdrawing its own bank account, Whitman makes an entry crediting Cash (to correct its record of Cash) and debiting Accounts Receivable since D. M. Scott owes the money to Whitman Video.

The Petty Cash Fund

Day after day, business firms are confronted with transactions involving small immediate payments, such as the cost of delivery charges, postage due, or even larger charges—depending on what the management considers to be a petty or small amount in relation to the size of the business. If the firm had to go through the usual procedure of making all payments by check, the time consumed would be frustrating and the whole process unduly expensive. For many firms, the cost of writing each check is considerable when one considers the cost of an employee's time in writing and reconciling the check. Suppose you buy a stamp from an employee for $.29, and you want to reimburse her for that money. To write a check would be ridiculous. It only makes sense to pay in cash, out of the **Petty Cash Fund.** *Petty* means "small," so the firm sets a maximum amount that can be paid immediately out of petty cash. Payments that exceed this maximum must be processed by regular check through the journal.

Performance Objective 4

Record journal entries to establish and reimburse Petty Cash Fund.

Establishing the Petty Cash Fund

After the firm has decided on the maximum amount of a payment from petty cash, the next step is to estimate how much cash will be needed during a given period of time, such as a month. Small payments are made during the month from the Petty Cash Fund.

It is also important to consider the element of security when keeping cash in the office. If the risk is great, the amount kept in the fund should be small.

Whitman Video decides to establish a Petty Cash Fund of $50 and put it under the control of the administrative assistant. Accordingly, their accountant writes a check, cashes it at the bank, and records this transaction in the journal as follows:

	DATE	DESCRIPTION	POST. REF.	DEBIT	CREDIT	
1	19–					1
2	Sept. 1	Petty Cash Fund		5 0 00		2
3		Cash			5 0 00	3
4		Established a Petty Cash Fund.				4
5						5

GENERAL JOURNAL PAGE _____

T accounts for the entry look like this:

Petty Cash Fund		Cash	
+	−	+	−
50			50

Because the Petty Cash Fund is an asset account, it is listed in the balance sheet immediately below Cash.

Once the fund has been created, it is not debited again unless the original amount is not large enough to handle the necessary transactions. In that case, the accountant has to make the Petty Cash Fund bigger—perhaps increasing the amount of the fund from $50 to $75. **But, barring such a change in the size of the fund, Petty Cash Fund is debited only once.**

After the accountant cashes that original $50 check, he or she converts it into convenient **denominations,** which are varieties of coins and currency, such as quarters, dimes, and $1 and $5 bills. Then the accountant issues the cash to the administrative assistant or other responsible person, who places it in a secure location. The accountant or owner and that person will agree on the limit of what can be considered petty cash.

REMEMBER

The Petty Cash Fund account is debited once when the fund is first established or if the fund is increased.

Payments from the Petty Cash Fund

The administrative assistant now takes the responsibility for the petty cash fund. He or she is designated as the only person who can make payments from it. In case of his or her illness, some other employee should be named as an alternate. A **petty cash voucher** must be used to account for every payment from the fund. The voucher is a receipt signed by the person who authorized the payment and by the person who received payment. Thus, even for small payments of $5 or less, there would have to be collusion between the payee and the administrative assistant for any theft to occur. Figure 8-11 shows what a petty cash voucher might look like.

Performance Objective 5

Complete petty cash vouchers and petty cash payments records.

Figure 8-11

```
                    PETTY CASH VOUCHER

  No. _1_                        Date _September 2, 19—_

  Paid to _Beck Delivery Service_              $ _2.00_

  For _Tip_

  Account _Miscellaneous Expense_

  Approved by                    Payment received by

  ___A. Rodriguez___             ___D. Stanton___
```

Petty Cash Payments Record

Some firms prefer to have a written record on one sheet of paper, so they keep a **petty cash payments record.** In a petty cash payments record, petty cash vouchers are listed along with the accounts that are to be charged. Special columns are included in the Distribution of Payments section for frequent types of expenditures. The petty cash payments record is not a journal.

Whitman Video made the following payments from its petty cash fund during September:

Sept. 2 Paid a $2 tip to Beck Delivery Service, voucher no. 1 (Miscellaneous Expense).
3 Bought pencils and pens, $3.09, voucher no. 2.
5 Paid for photocopying flyers for advertising, $5, voucher no. 3.
7 Paid postage on a customer's package, $2.90, voucher no. 4 (Delivery Expense).

10 Donna A. Whitman, the owner, withdrew $5 for personal use, voucher no. 5.

14 Reimbursed employee for a stamp, $.29, voucher no. 6.

21 Bought 1 ream of computer paper, $4.10, voucher no. 7.

22 Paid a $3 tip to Beck Delivery Service, voucher no. 8.

26 Paid postage on a customer's package, $3.80, voucher no. 9.

27 Paid $3.50 on a customer's package, voucher no. 10.

29 Bought memo pads, $4.40, voucher no. 11.

29 Paid for making duplicate keys, $2.60, voucher no. 12.

30 Paid a $3.20 tip to Beck Delivery Service, voucher no. 13.

30 Paid for removal of recycled paper, $5, voucher no. 14.

Figure 8-12 shows how these payments are recorded.

Figure 8-12

PETTY CASH PAYMENTS RECORD

Month of September 19–

	DATE	VOU. NO.	EXPLANATION	PAYMENTS
1	Sept. 1		Established fund, check no. 88, $50	
2	2	1	Beck Delivery Service—tip	2 00
3	3	2	Pencils and pens	3 09
4	5	3	Photocopy flyers	5 00
5	7	4	Postage on customer's package	2 90
6	10	5	Donna A. Whitman	5 00
7	14	6	Reimburse employee for stamp	29
8	21	7	Ream of computer paper	4 10
9	22	8	Beck Delivery Service—tip	3 00
10	26	9	Postage on customer's package	3 80
11	27	10	Postage on customer's package	3 50
12	29	11	Memo pads	4 40
13	29	12	Making duplicate keys	2 60
14	30	13	Beck Delivery Service—tip	3 20
15	30	14	Removal of recycled paper	5 00
16	30		Totals	47 88
17			Balance in Fund $ 2.12	
18			Reimbursed check no. 136 47.88	
19			Total $50.00	
20				
21				
22				
23				

Reimbursement of the Petty Cash Fund

To bring the fund back up to the original amount when the fund is nearly exhausted (for instance, at the end of the month), the accountant reimburses the fund for expenditures made. Consequently, the Petty Cash Fund may be considered a revolving fund. If the amount initially put in the Petty Cash Fund is $50 and at the end of the month only $2.12 is left, the accountant puts $47.88 in the fund as a reimbursement, thereby bringing the fund back up to $50 to start the new month.

PAGE __1__

OFFICE SUPPLIES	DELIVERY EXPENSE	MISCELLANEOUS EXPENSE	OTHER ACCOUNTS ACCOUNT	AMOUNT	
			DISTRIBUTION OF PAYMENTS		
					1
		2 00			2
3 09					3
			Advertising Expense	5 00	4
	2 90				5
			D. A. Whitman, Drawing	5 00	6
		29			7
4 10					8
		3 00			9
	3 80				10
	3 50				11
4 40					12
		2 60			13
		3 20			14
		5 00			15
11 59	10 20	16 09		10 00	16
					17
					18
					19
					20
					21
					22
					23

Bear in mind that the petty cash payments record is only a supplementary record for gathering information. A less formal way of compiling the information concerning petty cash payments might consist of collecting one month's petty cash vouchers, then sorting them by accounts, such as Office Supplies, Delivery Expense, and the like. Next, run a calculator tape for each account.

At any rate, the petty cash payments record or calculator tapes are not journals; they are simply used as a basis for compiling information for the journal entry. Remember, to change an account, we have to make a journal entry. At the end of the month, the accountant makes a summarizing entry to officially journalize the transactions that have taken place. The journal and T accounts of Whitman Video are shown below.

	DATE	DESCRIPTION	POST. REF.	DEBIT	CREDIT	
1	19–					1
2	Sept. 30	Office Supplies		1 1 59		2
3		Delivery Expense		1 0 20		3
4		Miscellaneous Expense		1 6 09		4
5		Advertising Expense		5 00		5
6		D. A. Whitman, Drawing		5 00		6
7		Cash			4 7 88	7
8		Reimbursed the Petty Cash				8
9		Fund, Ck. No. 136.				9
10						10

GENERAL JOURNAL   PAGE _____

Cash		D. A. Whitman, Drawing		Miscellaneous Expense	
+	–	+	–	+	–
	47.88	5.00		16.09	

Office Supplies		Delivery Expense		Advertising Expense	
+	–	+	–	+	–
11.59		10.20		5.00	

The Change Fund

Anyone who has ever tried to pay for a small item by handing a clerk a $20 bill knows that any firm that carries out numerous cash transactions needs a **Change Fund.**

Establishing the Change Fund

Performance Objective 6

Record the journal entry to establish a Change Fund.

Before setting up a change fund, one has to decide two things: (1) how much money needs to be in the fund, and (2) what denominations of bills and coins are needed. Like the petty cash fund, **the change fund is debited only once: when it is established or if the fund is increased.** It is left at the initial figure unless the person in charge decides to make it larger. The Change Fund account, like the Petty Cash Fund account, is an asset. It is recorded in the balance sheet immediately below Cash. If the Petty Cash Fund account is larger than the Change Fund account, it precedes the Change Fund.

The owner of Whitman Video, Donna Whitman, decides to establish a change fund; she decides this at the same time she sets up the company's petty cash fund. The entries for both transactions look like this:

	DATE	DESCRIPTION	POST. REF.	DEBIT	CREDIT	
1	19–					1
2	Sept. 1	Petty Cash Fund		5 0 00		2
3		Cash			5 0 00	3
4		Established a petty cash fund.				4
5						5
6	1	Change Fund		1 0 0 00		6
7		Cash			1 0 0 00	7
8		Established a change fund.				8
9						9

GENERAL JOURNAL PAGE _____

The T accounts for establishing the fund are as follows:

Change Fund		Cash	
+	−	+	−
100			100

Whitman cashes a check for $100 and gets the money in several denominations. She is now prepared to make change for any normal business transactions.

Depositing Cash

At the end of each business day, Whitman deposits the cash taken in during the day, but she holds back the amount of the Change Fund, being sure that it is in convenient denominations.

When she makes up the change fund depends on what time her business closes for the day and what time the bank closes. Let's say that on September 1, Whitman Video had $325 on hand at the end of the day.

$325 Total cash count
$-$ 100 Change fund

$225 New cash deposit

The T accounts look like this.

Cash		Rental Income	
+	−	−	+
225			225

The day's receipts are journalized as follows:

		GENERAL JOURNAL				PAGE ____	
	DATE	DESCRIPTION	POST. REF.	DEBIT		CREDIT	
1	19–						1
2	Sept. 1	Cash		2 2 5 00			2
3		Rental Income				2 2 5 00	3
4		To record revenue earned					4
5		during the day.					5

Recall that the amount of the cash deposit is the total cash count less the amount of the Change Fund, so that's how the deposit happens to be $225.

Cash Short and Over

There is an inherent danger in making change: Human beings make mistakes, especially when there are many customers to be waited on or when the business is temporarily short-handed. Because mistakes do happen, accounting records must be set up to cope with the situation. One reason that a business uses a cash register is to detect mistakes in the handling of cash. If, after subtracting the change fund, the day's receipts are less than the cash register reading, then a cash shortage exists. On the other hand, when the day's receipts are greater than the machine reading, a cash overage exists. Both shortages and overages are recorded in the same account, which is called Cash Short and Over. (The Cash Short and Over account may also be used to handle shortages and overages in the Petty Cash Fund.) Shortages are considered to be an expense of operating a business, and therefore shortages are recorded on the debit side of the account. Overages are treated as another form of revenue. Therefore, overages are recorded on the credit side of the account. No signs are placed on the account.

For example, let's say that on September 14, Whitman Video is faced with the following situation:

Cash Register Tape	Cash Count	Amount of the Change Fund
$387	$484	$100

After deducting the $100 in the Change Fund, Whitman will deposit $384 ($484 − $100). Note that this amount is less than the amount indicated by the cash register; therefore, a $3 cash shortage exists ($387 − $384). The following T accounts show how Whitman entered this transaction into the books:

Cash		Sales		Cash Short and Over	
+	−	−	+		
384			387	3	

The next day, September 15, the pendulum happens to swing in the other direction:

Cash Register Tape	Cash Count	Amount of the Change Fund
$459	$560	$100

The amount to be deposited is $460 ($560 − $100). This figure is $1 greater than the $459 in sales indicated by the cash register tape. Thus, there is a $1 cash overage ($460 − $459). The analysis of this transaction is shown in the following T accounts:

Cash		Sales		Cash Short and Over	
+	−	−	+		
460			459		1

Whitman Video's revenue for September 14 and 15 is recorded in the general journal as follows:

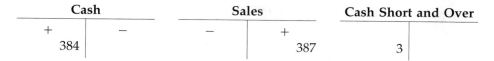

	DATE	DESCRIPTION	POST. REF.	DEBIT	CREDIT	
1	19–					1
2	Sept. 14	Cash		3 8 4 00		2
3		Cash Short and Over		3 00		3
4		Sales			3 8 7 00	4
5		To record revenue earned				5
6		during the day involving a				6
7		cash shortage of $3.				7
8						8
9	15	Cash		4 6 0 00		9
10		Sales			4 5 9 00	10
11		Cash Short and Over			1 00	11
12		To record revenue earned				12
13		during the day involving a				13
14		cash overage of $1.				14

As far as errors are concerned, one would think that shortages would be offset by overages. However, customers receiving change are more likely to report shortages than overages. **Consequently, the firm usually experiences a greater number of shortages than overages.** A firm may set a tolerance level for the cashiers. If the shortages consistently exceed the level of tolerance, either fraud is considered or somebody is making entirely too many careless mistakes.

COMPUTERS AT WORK

Staying Solvent: How to Use PCs to Keep the Cash Flowing

Whether you're a service provider, retail establishment or manufacturer, you need cash to pay suppliers for the goods and services you use as a part of your operations. You need cash to pay employees and meet tax, landlord, and other financial obligations. . . .

Computer software can help you manage the cash that flows into and out of your business, and in reporting it to others. What follows are basic cash flow principles, according to the SBA, which you can use with any computer program or no computer at all. . . .

CASHING IN • . . .The term "cash" usually refers not only to currency, but also to checks and checking accounts. Having adequate cash on hand can buy discounts with suppliers and leverage with customers, not to mention peace of mind.

Cash flows through the "operating cycle," from purchasing inventory through collecting accounts receivable. The operating cycle of any given business determines how quickly assets flow into cash. . . .

When you sell some of your inventory, unless it's a cash sale, your cash doesn't increase—accounts receivable increases. You usually collect receivables 30 days after the sale of inventory, which increases cash. Now your cash has completed its flow through the operating cycle and is ready to begin again.

CASH FLOW ANALYSIS • It's important to review the operating cycle of your business with periodic cash flow analyses. The cash flow forecast, in fact, has become an indispensalbe planning tool for many companies. . . . No matter how fast sales go up, expenses have a way of rising just as fast, and it can be difficult to know what cash is entering and leaving the business. The aim of cash flow management is to make sure you'll have enough cash to meet demands at any given time. . . .

The SBA recommends you have enough cash on hand each month to pay the cash obligations of the following month. . . .

POSITIVE PLANNING • To achieve a positive cash flow, you should have a sound business plan. Cash reserves can be increased by:

- Collecting receivables
- Tightening credit requirements
- Increasing the price of products or services
- Increasing sales
- Obtaining loans . . . .

CASH RESERVE • Always keep a cash reserve to cover expenses and as an added cushion for security. But it's unwise to keep more money on hand than is necessary to cover your obligations and any likely contingenices. Invest excess cash in an accessible, interest-bearing, low-risk account, such as a savings account, short-term CD, or treasury bill. Keeping excess cash on hand reduces both your growth and return on investment.

Source: Excerpted from Reid Goldsborough, "Staying Solvent," *PC Today*, April 1994, pp. 35–37.

Throughout any fiscal period, the accountant must continually record shortages and overages in the Cash Short and Over account. Let's say that Whitman's final balance is $21 on the debit side. Whitman winds up with a net shortage of $21.

At the end of the fiscal period, **if the account has a debit balance or net shortage, the accountant credits Cash Short and Over and debits Miscellaneous Expense.** The T account would look like this:

Cash Short and Over

Short		Over	
	3		1
	4		1
	3		2
	7		2
	5		1
	2		2
	3		1
	4		10
	31		

Bal. 21

Conversely, **if the account has a credit balance or net overage, the accountant debits Cash Short and Over and credits Miscellaneous Income.** This is an exception to the policy of recording accounts under their exact account title in financial statements. Rather than attaching plus and minus signs to the Cash Short and Over account immediately, we wait until we find out its final balance.

Computer Applications

Bank Reconciliation

There are many cash management software packages; for example, Microsoft® Money and Quicken™. These packages are capable of maintaining and reconciling dozens of bank accounts (personal or business), as well as managing mortgages, credit cards, and investments. They offer bill-paying schedules, electronic reminders, and the ability to graph revenue and expenses in a variety of charts. They are also capable of doing budgeting; and, with a few keystrokes allow the user to see schedules for potential savings or loans.

Figure 8-13 shows a bank reconciliation using an accounting software package. The software required only a few keystrokes to enter increases and decreases to bank information and the ledger balance of cash. These programs are very popular, but again, speed is only as valuable as the accuracy of the input.

Figure 8-13

Bank Reconciliation			Outstanding Deposits	
			Deposit Date	Amount
Bank balance	$8,966.00		10/31/9-	1,003.00
Add: Outstanding deposits	1,003.00			1,003.00
	9,969.00			
Less: Outstanding checks	1,474.00		Outstanding Checks	
Adjusted bank balance	8,495.00		Check Number	Amount
			916	461.00
Cash balance/company books	8,030.50		022	119.00
Add: Credit memos	615.00		023	827.00
	8,645.50		024	67.00
Less: Debit memos	150.50			1,474.00
Adjusted Cash balance	8,495.00			
			Credit Memos	
			Description	Amount
			Note/interest collected	606.00
			Error Ck. 2001/Davis	9.00
				615.00
			Debit Memos	
			Description	Amount
			Bank service charges	5.50
			NSF Check/Scott	125.00
			Cash withdrawal/Whitman	20.00
				150.50

CHAPTER REVIEW

R eview of Performance Objectives

1. **Describe the procedure for depositing checks.**

   The procedure for depositing checks consists of first endorsing each check and then completing a deposit slip. On the deposit slip record the date, the amount of currency to be deposited, the amount and ABA number of each check, and the total of the amount to be deposited. The checks to be deposited should accompany the deposit slip.

2. **Reconcile a bank statement.**

   The standard form for a bank reconciliation is as follows:

   Bank Statement Balance

   Add
   Deposit in transit
   Bank errors that understate bank statement balance

   Deduct
   Outstanding checks
   Bank errors that overstate bank statement balance

   Adjusted Bank Statement Balance

Ledger Balance of Cash

Add
Notes collected
Checkbook errors that understate ledger balance of cash
Bank credit memos

Deduct
Bank service charges
Checkbook errors that overstate ledger balance of cash
NSF checks
Bank debit memos

Adjusted Ledger Balance of Cash

3. Record the required journal entries directly from the bank reconciliation.

   Journal entries are required involving the Ledger Balance of Cash section. The entry for notes and interest collected is a debit to Cash and credits to Notes Receivable and Interest Income. The entry for a bank service charge is a debit to Miscellaneous Expense and a credit to Cash. The entry for an NSF check is a debit to Accounts Receivable and a credit to Cash.

4. Record journal entries to establish and reimburse Petty Cash Fund.

   The entry to establish a petty cash fund is a debit to Petty Cash Fund and a credit to Cash. The entry to reimburse the petty cash fund consists of debits to the items for which payments from the petty cash fund were made and one credit to Cash for the total payments.

5. Complete petty cash vouchers and petty cash payments records.

   A petty cash voucher is made out for each payment from the petty cash fund. In the petty cash payments record, each voucher is listed and a notation is made concerning the accounts involved. The petty cash payments record is used as a source of information for making the journal entry to reimburse the petty cash fund.

6. Record the journal entry to establish a Change Fund.

   The entry to establish the Change Fund is a debit to Change Fund and a credit to Cash.

7. Record journal entries for transactions involving Cash Short and Over.

   The Cash Short and Over account takes care of errors in making change. A debit to Cash Short and Over denotes a shortage; a credit to Cash Short and Over denotes an overage.

G lossary

ABA number The number assigned by the American Bankers Association to a given bank. The first part of the numerator denotes the city or state in which the bank is located; the second part denotes the bank on which the check is drawn. The denominator indicates the Federal Reserve District in which the check is cleared and the routing number used by the Federal Reserve Bank. **(342)**

ATM (automated teller machine) A machine that enables depositors to make deposits and withdrawals using a coded plastic card. **(343)**

Bank reconciliation A process by which an accountant determines whether there is a difference between the balance shown on the bank statement and the balance of the Cash account in the firm's general ledger. The object is to determine the adjusted (or actual) balance of the Cash account. **(348)**

Bank statement Periodic statement that a bank sends to the holder of a checking account listing deposits received and checks paid by the bank, debit and credit memos, and beginning and ending balances. **(347)**

Blank endorsement An endorsement in which the holder (payee) of a check simply signs her or his name on the back of the check. There are no restrictions attached. **(345)**

Canceled checks Checks issued by the depositor that have been paid (cleared) by the bank and listed on the bank statement. They are called canceled checks because they are canceled by a stamp or perforation, indicating that they have been paid. **(348)**

Cash funds Separately held amounts of cash set aside for specific purposes. **(341)**

Change Fund A cash fund used by a firm to make change for customers who pay cash for goods or services. **(358)**

Check register A checkbook containing columns—including a column for payee—like those in a cash payments journal. The cash column heading may contain the bank name. Check registers may be manual or computerized. **(346)**

Check writer A machine used to imprint the amount in figures and words on the check itself. Computer printers are also used to print checks. **(345)**

Collections Payments collected by the bank and added to the customer's bank account, in the form of a credit memorandum. **(350)**

Denominations Varieties of coins and currency, such as quarters, dimes, and nickels and $1 and $5 bills. **(355)**

Deposit in transit A deposit not recorded on the bank statement because the deposit was made between the time of the bank's closing date for compiling items for its statement and the time the statement is received by the depositor. **(350)**

Deposit slips Printed forms provided by a bank so that customers can list all items being deposited; also known as *deposit tickets*. **(342)**

Drawer The party who writes the check. **(345)**

Endorsement The process by which the payee transfers ownership of the check to a bank or another party. A check must be endorsed when deposited in a bank, because the bank must have legal title to it in order to collect payment from the drawer of the check (the person or firm who wrote the check). In case the check cannot be collected, the endorser guarantees all subsequent holders (*Exception:* an endorsement "without recourse"). **(343)**

Ledger balance of cash The balance of the Cash account in the general ledger before it is reconciled with the bank statement. **(348)**

MICR (Magnetic ink character recognition) The characters the bank uses to print the number of the depositor's account and the bank's number at the bottom of checks and deposit slips. The bank also prints the amount of the check in MICR when the check is deposited. A number written in these characters can be read by electronic equipment used by banks to process checks. **(343)**

NSF checks (Not Sufficient Funds) Checks drawn against an account in which there are *Not Sufficient Funds*; also known as *dishonored checks*. **(344)**

Outstanding checks Checks that have been written by the depositor and deducted on his or her records but have not reached the bank for payment and are not deducted from the bank balance by the time the bank issues its statement. **(350)**

Payee The person to whom a check is payable. **(345)**

Petty Cash Fund A cash fund used to make small immediate cash payments. **(354)**

Petty cash payments record A record indicating the amount of each petty cash voucher and the accounts to which they should be charged. **(355)**

Petty cash voucher A form stating who got what from the petty cash fund, signed by (1) the person in charge of the fund, and (2) the person who received the cash. **(355)**

Promissory note A written promise to pay a definite sum at a definite future time. **(352)**

Qualified endorsement An endorsement in which the holder (payee) of a check avoids future liability, in case the drawer of the check does not have sufficient funds to cover the check, by adding the words "Pay to the order of" and "without recourse" to the endorsement on the back of the check. **(345)**

Restrictive endorsement An endorsement, such as "Pay to the order of (name of bank), for deposit only," that restricts or limits any further negotiation of a check. It forces the check's deposit, because the endorsement is not valid for any other purpose. **(344)**

Service charge The fee the bank charges for handling checks, collections, and other items. It is in the form of a debit memorandum. **(350)**

Signature card The form a depositor signs to give the bank a copy of the official signatures of any persons authorized to sign checks. The bank can use it to verify the depositors' signatures on checks, on cash items that the depositors may endorse for deposit, and on other business papers that the depositors may present to the bank. **(342)**

QUESTIONS, EXERCISES, AND PROBLEMS

D iscussion Questions

1. Why is there generally a difference between the balance in the Cash account on the company's books and the balance on the bank statement?
2. What are the purposes served by endorsing checks?
3. Indicate whether the following items in a bank reconciliation should be (1) added to the Cash account balance, (2) deducted from the Cash account balance, (3) added to the bank statement balance, or (4) deducted from the bank statement balance.
   a. NSF check
   b. Deposit in transit
   c. Outstanding check
   d. Bank error charging the firm's account with another company's check
   e. Bank service charge
4. What is the purpose of the signature card?
5. Describe the function of a check register.
6. Why is it not necessary to make general journal entries for the bank statement portion of the bank reconciliation?
7. a. Explain the purpose of a petty cash fund.
   b. Describe the entries to establish and reimburse the fund.
8. a. What does a debit in Cash Short and Over represent?
   b. Where does a debit balance in Cash Short and Over appear in the financial statements?
   c. What does a credit in Cash Short and Over represent?
   d. Where does a credit balance in Cash Short and Over appear in the financial statements?

E xercises

Exercise 8-1 Fill in the missing amounts for the following bank reconciliation: P.O.2

Determine missing amounts on a bank reconciliation.

Cathy's Cooking
Bank Reconciliation
April 30, 19 —

Bank Statement Balance		$4,120.00
Add: Deposit in transit		(a)
		$4,350.00
Deduct: Outstanding checks		
No. 110	$ 60.00	
No. 124	(b)	
No. 127	220.00	410.00
Adjusted Bank Statement Balance		(c)
Ledger Balance of Cash		$3,880.00
Add: Note collected by bank		150.00
		(d)
Deduct: Bank service charge	(e)	
NSF check from customer	80.00	90.00
Adjusted Ledger Balance of Cash		(f)

P.O.2

Determine amount of outstanding checks.

Exercise 8-2 When the bank statement is received on November 4, it shows a balance of $2,000 on October 29, before reconciliation. After reconciliation, the adjusted balance is $1,600. If there was one deposit in transit amounting to $300, what was the total of the outstanding checks, assuming there was no other adjustment to be made to the bank statement?

P.O.2

Place items on a bank reconciliation.

Exercise 8-3 In reconciling a bank statement, indicate the placement of the following items by recording a check mark.

Item	Add to Bank Statement Balance	Subtract from Bank Statement Balance	Add to Ledger Balance of Cash	Subtract from Ledger Balance of Cash
a. A check-printing charge				
b. An outstanding check				
c. A deposit for $148 listed on the bank statement as $184				
d. A collection charge the bank made for a note it collected for its depositor				
e. A check written for $19.26 and recorded in the checkbook as $19.62				
f. A deposit in transit				
g. An NSF check received from a customer				
h. A check written for $429.30 and recorded in the checkbook as $42.93				

Exercise 8-4 The Bushnell Company's Cash account shows a balance of $699.41 as of October 31 of this year. The balance on the bank statement on that date is $1,149.40. Checks for $47.30, $326.95, and $416.00 are outstanding. The bank statement shows a check issued by another depositor for $146.00 (in other words, the bank erroneously charged Bushnell Company for a check written by another firm). The bank statement also shows an NSF check for $190.00 received from Bushnell's customer. Service charges for the month were $4.26. What is the actual balance of Cash as of October 31?

Exercise 8-5 The Ledger Balance of Cash section of the bank reconciliation for Merrick Company is shown below.

Ledger Balance of Cash			$7,468.00
Add: Note collected (principal $800, interest $32, signed by M. Williams)		$832.00	
Error in recording Ck. No. 3114 payable to Davis Company (recorded check for $16 too much)		16.00	848.00
			$8,316.00
Deduct: NSF check from L. Luge		$ 33.00	
Bank service and collection charges		8.00	41.00
Adjusted Ledger Balance of Cash			$8,275.00

Journalize the entries required to bring the general ledger up to date as of August 31 of this year.

Exercise 8-6 Make entries in general journal form to record the following:

a. Established a Change Fund, $100. Issued Ck. No. 745.
b. Established a Petty Cash Fund, $90. Issued Ck. No. 746.
c. Reimbursed the Petty Cash Fund for expenditures of $87: Store Supplies, $27; Office Supplies, $19; Miscellaneous Expense, $41. Issued Ck. No. 799.
d. Increased the amount of the Petty Cash Fund by an additional $25. Issued Ck. No. 802.
e. Reimbursed the petty cash fund for expenditures of $99.11: Store Supplies, $41.04; Miscellaneous Expense, $58.07. Issued Ck. No. 836.

Exercise 8-7 At the end of the day, the cash register tape lists $814.29 as total income from services. Cash on hand consists of $12.26 in coins, $487.00 in currency, $40.00 in traveler's checks, and $424.20 in customers' checks. The amount of the change fund is $150. In general journal form, record the entry to record the day's cash sales.

Exercise 8-8

a. Describe the entries that have been posted to the following accounts after the Change Fund was established.

Change Fund		Sales		Cash	
+	−	−	+	+	−
300			Jan. 2 1,422	Jan. 2 1,419	
			Jan. 3 1,410	Jan. 3 1,412	
			Jan. 4 1,554	Jan. 4 1,548	

Cash Short and Over	
Jan. 2 3	Jan. 3 2
Jan. 4 6	

b. How will the balance of Cash Short and Over be reported on the income statement?

 onsider and Communicate

As the new bookkeeper at a small business, you find the petty cash fund operation to be unorganized and ineffective. The amount of cash does not match the recorded amount of the fund, and there is no evidence how it was spent. Explain how the petty cash fund operation can be made more efficient in order to maintain an accurate accounting of its changes.

 hat If . . .

Your client's sales are too low to provide enough cash to pay the bills. She does not want her husband to know the trouble she is having, so she puts personal cash in with the business deposit. The register tape doesn't work, and she doesn't use prenumbered receipts. What if the IRS audits her books? Are sales understated or overstated? How might the amount she owes for her income tax be affected? How would you suggest she handle the cash deposits to avoid the possibility that the IRS will believe sales to be higher than they actually are?

A Question of Ethics

The business where you work sells used goods and carries a large inventory. All sales are recorded on prenumbered receipts, and cash refund policies are liberal to promote customer goodwill. You notice that several customers each day toss their sales receipt into the conveniently placed wastebasket. The records indicate several cash refunds are based on the discarded receipts. The owner of the firm is always the last to leave. You suspect that the owner records fictitious cash refunds to customers and pockets the cash. Is the employer behaving ethically? Legally? What is your risk if you are the employee balancing the prior day's activities and making the bank deposits?

P roblem Set A

P.O.2,3

Problem 8-1A Shereen's Tall Ladies' Shop deposits all receipts in the bank each evening and makes all payments by check. On May 31 its ledger balance of Cash is $3,370.50. The bank statement of May 31 shows a balance of $3,564.35. The following information pertains to reconciling the bank statement:

a. The reconciliation for April, the previous month, showed three checks outstanding on April 30: no. 451 for $97, no. 453 for $83.60, and no. 455 for $143. Checks no. 451 and 455 were returned with the May bank statement; however, check no. 453 was not returned.

b. Check no. 495 for $47, no. 512 for $33.75, no. 513 for $123.50, and no. 517 for $23 were written during May and have not been returned by the bank.

c. A deposit of $535 was placed in the night depository on May 31 and did not appear on the bank statement.

d. The canceled checks were compared with the entries in the checkbook, and it was observed that check no. 493 for $79 was written correctly, payable to S. L. Shereen, the owner, for personal use. However, the check was recorded in the checkbook as $97.

e. A bank credit memo for collection of a note signed by J. R. Gordon, $404, including $400 principal and $4 interest.

f. A bank debit memo for service charges, $4.

Instructions

1. Prepare a bank reconciliation as of May 31, assuming that the debit and credit memos have not been recorded.
2. Record the necessary entries in general journal form.

Instructions for General Ledger Software

1. Prepare a bank reconciliation as of May 31. Errors made by the company or the bank, as well as service charges, must be entered as debit or credit memos.
2. Print the bank reconciliation.
3. Record the necessary entries in the general journal.
4. Print the journal entries.

Problem 8-2A On April 1 of this year, the Cayle Company established a Petty Cash Fund, and the following petty cash transactions took place during the month:

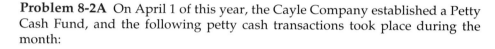

Apr.   1 Cashed check no. 306 for $90 to establish a Petty Cash Fund and put the $90 in a locked drawer in the office.
    3 Issued voucher no. 1 for printer ribbons, $17.80.
    5 Issued voucher no. 2 for taxi fare, $6 (Miscellaneous Expense).
    8 Paid $12.50 for an advertisement in high school football program, voucher no. 3.
  15 Paid $10.50 to have snow removed from office front sidewalk, voucher no. 4.
  21 Issued voucher no. 5 for delivery charge, $5.85.
  26 Bought postage stamps, $10, voucher no. 6 (Miscellaneous Expense).
  27 R. M. Cayle, the owner, withdrew $15 for personal use, voucher no. 7.
  28 Paid $6.20 for delivery charge, voucher no. 8.
  29 Paid $1.85 for postage, voucher no. 9 (Miscellaneous Expense).
  30 Issued check no. 378 for $85.70 to reimburse Petty Cash Fund.

Instructions

1. Make the entry establishing the Petty Cash Fund in the general journal.
2. Record the disbursements of petty cash in the petty cash payments record.
3. Journalize the summarizing entry to reimburse the Petty Cash Fund.

Problem 8-3A Jermaine Simpson, owner of Simpson's Detailing Shop, makes bank deposits in the night depository at the close of each business day.
    The following information for the last three days of June is available.

	June 28	June 29	June 30
Cash count	$1,025.50	$971.70	$1,178.15
Cash register tape	$ 926.70	$872.70	$1,076.40

Instructions

In general journal form, record the cash deposit for each day, assuming that there is a $100 Change Fund.

P.O.2,3

Problem 8-4A On September 30, Duncan and Company receives its bank statement. The company deposits its receipts in the bank and makes all payments by check. The debit memo for $147 is for an NSF check written by R. Wilson. Check no. 844 for $111, payable to Bronson Company (a creditor), was recorded incorrectly in the checkbook and journal as $1,110.

The ledger balance of Cash account as of September 30 is $2,820. Outstanding checks as of September 30 are no. 848, $357, and no. 849, $729. The accountant notes that the deposit of September 30 for $783 does not appear on the bank statement.

Baker National Bank

STATEMENT OF ACCOUNT	Duncan and Company 216 Williams Street Detroit, Michigan 48221	ACCOUNT NUMBER 172-36-4719 STATEMENT DATE *September 30, 19—*

SUMMARY		
	Balance Last Statement	$2,883.00
	Amount of Checks and Debits	$6,867.00
	Number of Checks	11
	Amount of Deposits and Credits	$7,953.00
	Number of Deposits	7
	Balance This Statement	$3,969.00

CHECKS/OTHER DEBITS	CHECKS	CHECK NUMBER	DATE POSTED	AMOUNT	CHECK NUMBER	DATE POSTED	AMOUNT
		837	9-04	516.00	843	9-09	1,863.00
		838	9-04	228.00	844	9-17	111.00
		839	9-05	438.00	845	9-17	42.00
		840	9-07	618.00	846	9-23	1,599.00
		841	9-07	417.00	847	9-28	282.00
		842	9-08	600.00			

OTHER DEBITS	DESCRIPTION	DATE POSTED	AMOUNT
	DM NSF check	9-30	147.00
	DM Service charge	9-30	6.00

DEPOSITS/OTHER CREDITS	DEPOSITS	DATE POSTED	AMOUNT	DATE POSTED	AMOUNT
		9-02	978.00	9-18	1,257.00
		9-05	1,236.00	9-24	1,194.00
		9-09	1,311.00	9-28	873.00
		9-14	1,104.00		

PLEASE EXAMINE THIS STATEMENT CAREFULLY. REPORT ANY POSSIBLE ERRORS IN 10 DAYS.

CODE SYMBOLS

CM Credit Memo   OD Overdraft

DM Debit Memo   EC Error Correction

Instructions

1. Prepare a bank reconciliation as of September 30, assuming that the debit memos have not been recorded.
2. Record the necessary journal entries.
3. Complete the bank form to determine the adjusted balance of cash.

Instructions for General Ledger Software

1. Prepare a bank reconciliation as of September 30. Errors made by the company or the bank, as well as service charges, must be entered as debit or credit memos.
2. Print the bank reconciliation.
3. Record the necessary journal entries.
4. Print the journal entries.

P roblem Set B

Problem 8-1B The Stetson Company deposits all receipts in the bank and makes all payments by check. On October 31 its ledger balance of Cash is $3,723.27. The bank statement on October 31 shows a balance of $3,920.51. You are given the following information with which to reconcile the bank statement:

P.O.2,3

a. A deposit of $425.17 was placed in the night depository on October 31 and did not appear on the bank statement.
b. The reconciliation for September, the previous month, showed three checks outstanding on September 30: no. 615 for $92.60, no. 621 for $132.50, and no. 625 for $41.92. Checks no. 615 and 621 were returned with the October bank statement; however, Ck. No. 625 was not returned.
c. Checks no. 629 for $62, no. 630 for $27.60, no. 633 for $112, and no. 636 for $22.64 were written during October but were not returned by the bank.
d. You compare the canceled checks with the entries in the checkbook and find that check no. 634 for $56 was written correctly, payable to M. M. Stetson, the owner, for her personal use. However, the check was recorded in the checkbook as $65.
e. Included in the bank statement was a bank debit memo for service charges, $3.75.
f. A bank credit memo was also enclosed for the collection of a note signed by T. R. Tremaine, $351, including $347 principal and $4 interest.

Instructions

1. Prepare a bank reconciliation as of October 31, assuming that the debit and credit memos have not been recorded.
2. Record the necessary entries in general journal form.

Instructions for General Ledger Software

1. Prepare a bank reconciliation as of October 31. Errors made by the company or the bank, as well as service charges, must be entered as debit or credit memos.
2. Print the bank reconciliation.
3. Record the necessary entries in the general journal.
4. Print the journal entries.

Problem 8-2B On June 1 of this year, the Sylvester Company established a Petty Cash Fund. The following petty cash transactions took place during the month:

P.O.4,5

June   1 Cashed check no. 821 for $80 to establish a Petty Cash Fund and put the $80 in a locked drawer in the office.
        3 Issued voucher no. 1 for delivery charges on outgoing parts, $10.50.
        5 Issued voucher no. 2 for taxi fare, $5.75 (Miscellaneous Expense).
        7 Bought postage stamps, $5, voucher no. 3 (Miscellaneous Expense).

9 J. Sylvester withdrew $7 for personal use, voucher no. 4.

14 Bought pens for office, $18.25, voucher no. 5.

19 Paid $6 for postage, voucher no. 6.

23 Paid $1.50 for paper clips, voucher no. 7 (Office Supplies).

27 Paid $12.50 for window cleaning service, voucher no. 8 (Miscellaneous Expense).

29 Paid $12.15 for correction tape, voucher no. 9.

30 Issued for cash check no. 935 for $78.65 to reimburse Petty Cash Fund.

Instructions

1. Make the entry establishing the Petty Cash Fund in the general journal.
2. Record the disbursements of petty cash in the petty cash payments record.
3. Journalize the summarizing entry to reimburse Petty Cash Fund.

P.O.7

Problem 8-3B Jennifer Scripps, owner of California Tans, a tanning salon, makes bank deposits in the night depository at the close of each business day. The following information for the first three days of May is available:

	May 1	May 2	May 3
Cash count	$497.50	$534.25	$504.75
Cash register tape	$424.00	$458.35	$431.00

Instructions

In general journal form, record the cash deposit for each day, assuming that there is a $75 Change Fund.

P.O.2,3

Problem 8-4B On September 2, Hanrahan's Fine Food receives its bank statement. The company deposits its receipts in the bank and makes all payments by check. The debit memo for $111.00 is for an NSF check written by C. P. Parks. Check no. 227 for $217.50, payable to Bingham Company (a creditor), was incorrectly recorded in the checkbook and journal as $172.50.

The ledger balance of the Cash account as of August 31 is $4,357.38. Outstanding checks as of August 31 are no. 241, $330; no. 242, $213.57; no. 243, $489.60. The accountant notes that the August 31 deposit of $497.07 did not appear on the bank statement.

Instructions

1. Prepare a bank reconciliation as of August 31, assuming that the debit memos have not been recorded.
2. Record the necessary journal entries.
3. Complete the bank form to determine the adjusted balance of cash.

Instructions for General Ledger Software

1. Prepare a bank reconciliation as of August 31. Errors made by the company or the bank, as well as service charges, must be entered as debit or credit memos.
2. Print the bank reconciliation.
3. Record the necessary journal entries.
4. Print the journal entries.

Safety National Bank

STATEMENT OF ACCOUNT	Hanrahan's Fine Food 240 Broad Street Dallas, Texas 75234	ACCOUNT NUMBER 824-341-680 STATEMENT DATE *August 31, 19—*

SUMMARY

Balance Last Statement	$3,461.40
Amount of Checks and Debits	$6,317.73
Number of Checks	14
Amount of Deposits and Credits	$7,584.51
Number of Deposits	7
Balance This Statement	$4,728.18

CHECKS/ OTHER DEBITS

CHECKS

CHECK NUMBER	DATE POSTED	AMOUNT	CHECK NUMBER	DATE POSTED	AMOUNT
227	8-03	217.50	234	8-08	360.00
228	8-03	501.00	235	8-09	1,288.80
229	8-03	372.60	236	8-12	112.20
230	8-05	411.60	237	8-14	115.47
231	8-06	708.75	238	8-22	548.13
232	8-06	479.67	239	8-25	290.61
233	8-08	733.50	240	8-26	57.60

OTHER DEBITS

DESCRIPTION	DATE POSTED	AMOUNT
DM NSF check	8-22	111.00
DM Service charge	8-31	9.30

DEPOSITS/ OTHER CREDITS

DEPOSITS

DATE POSTED	AMOUNT	DATE POSTED	AMOUNT
8-03	1,474.50	8-15	875.28
8-06	1,247.16	8-18	428.70
8-09	1,317.48	8-28	1,106.79
8-11	1,134.60		

PLEASE EXAMINE THIS STATEMENT CAREFULLY. REPORT ANY POSSIBLE ERRORS IN 10 DAYS.

CODE SYMBOLS

CM Credit Memo	OD Overdraft
DM Debit Memo	EC Error Correction

CHALLENGE PROBLEM

J. Farber owns two separate businesses—an established lumber yard and a hardware store opened at the beginning of the year. The hardware store frequently requires transfers of cash from the lumber yard to the hardware store checking account. The owner has authorized the transfers. The owner has one bookkeeper to handle all of the record keeping and banking activities of both businesses. He has now asked his CPA to look over the records of both businesses at year end. As staff accountant for the CPA firm, you have been asked to reconcile transfers from the lumber business to the hardware store.

A list of the checks and deposits is in your working papers.

There are no deposits in transit and all checks have cleared. Your tasks are:

1. To track the checks written by the lumber yard to the hardware store. The amounts are identified by date.
2. To prepare comments about the situation; that is, to make observations, draw conclusions, make suggestions, recommend changes (if any), and list implications of not making the changes you suggest (if any).

chapter 8

Payroll Accounting: Employee Earnings and Deductions

PERFORMANCE OBJECTIVES

After you have completed this chapter, you will be able to do the following:

1. Calculate total earnings based on an hourly, piece-rate, or commission basis.

2. Determine deductions from tables of employees' income tax withholding.

3. Complete a payroll register.

4. Journalize the payroll entry from a payroll register.

5. Journalize the entry to pay the payroll from a payroll register.

6. Maintain employees' individual earnings records.

At year end, when receiving a new client's accounting records so that I can prepare the tax returns, I am often surprised to see no payroll tax liability accounts. That usually means a big problem. When I ask the client to explain how they record the payroll entry each pay period, the answer is usually something like this: "Debit Payroll Expense and credit Cash, right?"

It is hard to explain that the payroll expense for each employee is his or her gross pay, not just the net amount of the check, and that all of the deductions withheld from all the employees' checks are liabilities. But clients understand immediately when I ask, "What would happen if you didn't pay the IRS all the money you withheld from your employees?"

The typical answer—"I'd get in trouble if I didn't pay"—is the best definition of a liability that I've heard yet!

Up to now, we've been recording employees' wages as a debit to Salaries or Wages Expense and a credit to Cash, but we've really been talking only about **gross pay:** the total amount of an employee's pay before deductions. We haven't said a word about the various deductions that we all know are taken out of our gross pay before we get to the **net pay,** or take-home pay. In this chapter, we will be talking about types and amounts of deductions and how to enter them in payroll records, as well as journal entries for recording the payroll and paying the employees.

Objectives of Payroll Records and Accounting

There are two primary reasons for maintaining accurate payroll records. First, we must collect the necessary data to compute the compensation for each employee for each payroll period. Second, we must provide information needed to complete various government reports.

The employer is required to keep records of the following information:

1. **Personal data on employee**   Name, address, Social Security number, date of birth

2. **Data on wage payments**   Dates and amounts of payments, and payroll periods

3. **Amount of taxable wages paid**   Total amount earned so far during the year

4. **Amount of tax withheld from each employee's earnings** Totals of required taxes (Social Security, Medicare, withholding) and of voluntary deductions (charitable contributions, medical insurance premiums)

Employer/Employee Relationships

Payroll accounting is concerned only with employees and their compensations, withholdings, records, reports, and taxes. *Note:* There is a distinction between an employee and an independent contractor. An **employee** is one who is under the direction and control of the employer, such as a secretary, bookkeeper, sales clerk, vice president, controller, and so on. An **independent contractor,** on the other hand, is someone who is engaged for a definite job or service, who may choose his or her own means of doing the work (*examples:* an appliance repair person, a plumber, a CPA firm). Payments made to independent contractors are in the form of fees or charges. Independent contractors submit bills or invoices for the work they do. The invoice is paid in a lump sum and is not subject to any withholding or payroll taxes by the person or firm paying that invoice. The independent contractor is responsible for paying his or her own taxes.

How Employees Get Paid

Employees may be paid a salary or wages, depending on the type of work and the period of time covered. Money paid to a person for managerial or administrative services is usually called a salary, and the time period covered is generally a month or a year. Money paid for either skilled or unskilled labor is usually called wages, and the time period covered is hours or weeks. Wages may also be paid on a piecework basis. In practice, the words *salaries* and *wages* are somewhat interchangeable. A company may supplement an employee's salary or wage by commissions, bonuses, cost-of-living adjustments, and profit-sharing plans. As a rule, employees are paid by check or in cash. However, their compensation may take the form of merchandise, lodging, meals, or other property as well. When the compensation is in these forms, one has to determine the fair value of the property or service given in payment for an employee's labor.

Performance Objective 1

Calculate total earnings based on an hourly, piece-rate, or commission basis.

Calculating Total Earnings

When compensation is based on the amount of time worked, the accountant of course has to have a record of the number of hours worked by each employee. When there are only a few employees, this can be accomplished by means of

Employee hours are electronically sent via the light pen to the computer files for accumulation and computation, saving time and money.

a time book. When there are many employees, time clocks are the traditional method. Today, many computer-operated time-keeping systems are available.

Employees may be paid weekly, biweekly, semimonthly, or monthly. Biweekly is every two weeks. Semimonthly is twice a month.

Wages

Let's take the case of John C. Logan, who works for Carson and Company. His regular rate of pay is $12 per hour. The company pays time-and-a-half for hours worked in excess of 40 per week. In addition, it pays him double time for any work he does on Sundays and holidays. Logan has a $\frac{1}{2}$-hour lunch break during an $8\frac{1}{2}$-hour day. He is not paid for the lunch break. His time card for the week is shown in Figure 9-1 on page 380.

Logan's gross wages can be computed by one of two methods. The first method works like this:

40 hours at straight time	$40 \times \$12$ per hour =	$480
2 hours overtime on Thursday	$2 \times \$18$ per hour =	36
1 hour overtime on Friday	$1 \times \$18$ per hour =	18
5 hours overtime on Saturday	$5 \times \$18$ per hour =	90
4 hours overtime on Sunday	$4 \times \$24$ per hour =	96
Total gross wages		$720

Figure 9-1

FYI

The Fair Labor Standards Act of 1938 (Wages and Hours Law) specifies that employers engaged in interstate commerce must pay their employees overtime at the rate of $1\frac{1}{2}$ times the regular rate for hours worked in excess of 40 hours per week. This act also prescribes rules for child labor, equal work for equal pay, and minimum wage levels.

TIME CARD

Name Logan, John C.

Week ending Oct. 7, 19—

Day	In	Out	In	Out	Hours Worked Regular	Overtime
M	7⁵⁷	12⁰⁰	12²⁰	4³²	8	
T	7⁵⁶	12⁰⁶	12³⁶	4³⁷	8	
W	7⁵⁷	12⁰²	12³¹	4³¹	8	
Th	8⁰⁰	12¹¹	12⁴⁰	6³²	8	2
F	8⁰⁰	12⁰³	12³³	5³³	8	1
S	7⁵⁹	1⁰²				5
S	7⁵⁵	12⁰⁴				4

The second method of calculating gross wages is often used when machine accounting is involved:

FYI

Minimum wages are set by Congress. Originally, the minimum wage was $.25 per hour.

52 hours at straight time: 52 × $12 per hour = $624
Overtime premium:
8 hours × $ 6 per hour premium = $48
4 hours × $12 per hour premium =   48

Total overtime premium   96

Total gross wages $720

Salaries

Employees who are paid a regular salary may also be entitled to premium pay for overtime. It is necessary to figure out their regular hourly rate of pay before you can determine their overtime rate. Let's consider the case of Myra A. Boyd, who gets a salary of $1,872 per month. She is entitled to overtime pay for all hours worked in excess of 40 during a week at the rate of $1\frac{1}{2}$ times her regular hourly rate. This past week she worked 44 hours, so we calculate her overtime pay as follows:

$1,872 per month × 12 months = $22,464 per year
$22,464 per year ÷ 52 weeks = $432 per week
$432 per week ÷ 40 hours = $10.80 per regular hour

Earnings for 44 hours:
40 hours at straight time   40 × $10.80 = $432.00
4 hours overtime   4 × $16.20 =   64.80

Total gross earnings $496.80

Piece Rate

Workers under the piece-rate system are paid at the rate of so much per unit of production. For example, Dean Huber, a stitcher, gets paid $.55 for finishing a buttonhole at a clothing assembler. If he finishes 88 buttonholes during the day, his total earnings are 88 × $.55 = $48.40.

Commissions and Bonuses

Some salespersons are paid on a purely commission basis. However, a more common arrangment is a salary plus a commission or bonus. Assume that Marta Graham receives an annual salary of $12,000. Her employer agrees to pay her a 5 percent commission on all sales during the year in excess of $120,000. Her sales for the year total $380,000. Her bonus amounts to $13,000 ($260,000 × .05). Therefore, her total earnings amount to $25,000 ($12,000 + $13,000).

Deductions from Total Earnings

Anyone who has ever earned a paycheck has encountered some of the many types of deductions that account for the difference between total earned and total received. Total earnings minus deductions equals net pay. The most usual deductions are for the following reasons:

1. Federal income tax withholding

2. State income tax withholding

3. FICA tax (Social Security and Medicare), employee's share

4. Purchase of US. savings bonds

5. Union dues

6. Medical and life insurance premiums

7. Contributions to a charitable organization

8. Repayment of personal loans from the company credit union

9. Savings through the company credit union

Employees' Federal Income Tax Withholding

The amount of federal income tax withheld from an employee's wages depends on the amount of her or his total earnings, marital status, pay period, and the number of exemptions claimed. An **exemption** is the amount of an individual's earnings that is exempt from income taxes (nontaxable). An employee is entitled to one personal exemption for himself or herself plus an additional exemption for each dependent. Each employee has to fill out an

Employee's Withholding Allowance Certificate (Form W-4), shown in Figure 9-2.

The employer retains this form as authorization to withhold money for the employee's federal income tax.

Figure 9-2

Form **W-4**	**Employee's Withholding Allowance Certificate**	OMB No. 1545-0010

Department of the Treasury
Internal Revenue Service
▶ **For Privacy Act and Paperwork Reduction Act Notice, see reverse.**

1 Type or print your first name and middle initial	Last name	2 Your social security number
John C.	Logan	543-24-1680

Home address (number and street or rural route)
6242 Baxter Drive

City or town, state, and ZIP code
Weston, South Dakota 57817

3 Marital Status
☐ Single ☒ Married
☐ Married, but withhold at higher Single rate.
Note: *If married, but legally separated, or spouse is a nonresident alien, check the Single box.*

4 Total number of allowances you are claiming (from line G above or from the Worksheets on back if they apply) **4** 3

5 Additional amount, if any, you want deducted from each pay . . . . **5** $

6 I claim exemption from withholding and I certify that I meet **ALL** of the following conditions for exemption:
● Last year I had a right to a refund of **ALL** Federal income tax withheld because I had **NO** tax liability; **AND**
● This year I expect a refund of **ALL** Federal income tax withheld because I expect to have **NO** tax liability; **AND**
● This year if my income exceeds $550 and includes nonwage income, another person cannot claim me as a dependent.
If you meet all of the above conditions, enter the year effective and "EXEMPT" here . . . . . ▶ **6** 19

7 Are you a full-time student? (**Note:** *Full-time students are not automatically exempt.*) . . . . **7** ☐Yes ☐No

Under penalties of perjury, I certify that I am entitled to the number of withholding allowances claimed on this certificate or entitled to claim exempt status.

Employee's signature ▶ *John C. Logan*   **Date** ▶ February 1   ,19

8 Employer's name and address (**Employer:** Complete 8 and 10 **only if sending to IRS**)	9 Office code (optional)	10 Employer identification number

---

Circular E, Employer's Tax Guide

Performance Objective 2

Determine deductions from tables of employees' income tax withholding.

Circular E contains withholding tables for federal income, Social Security, and Medicare taxes, as well as the rules for depositing these taxes. It is regularly updated to reflect changes in tax laws and withholding rates. Filing requirements for official employer reports are also described. Circular E is provided free of charge by the Internal Revenue Service. Accountants responsible for preparation of payroll registers and forms should be familiar with the contents of Circular E.

The **wage-bracket tax tables** cover monthly, semimonthly, biweekly, weekly, and daily payroll periods. The tables are also subdivided on the basis of married and unmarried persons. To determine the tax to be withheld from an employee's gross wages, first locate the wage bracket in the first two columns of the table. Next, find the column for the number of exemptions claimed and read down this column until you get to the appropriate wage-bracket line. A portion of the weekly federal income tax withholding table for married persons is reproduced in Figure 9-3.

Assume that John C. Logan, who claims three exemptions, has gross wages of $720 for the week. At first it appears that $720 could fall in either the $710–$720 bracket or the $720–$730 bracket. However, note the headings of the bracket columns: "At least" and "But less than." A strict interpretation of the $710–$720 bracket really means $710–$719.99. Therefore $720 must be included in the $720–$730 bracket. As can be seen from the table, $80 should be withheld.

Figure 9-3

MARRIED Persons—WEEKLY Payroll Period

And the wages are—		And the number of withholding allowances claimed is—										
At least	But less than	0	1	2	3	4	5	6	7	8	9	10
		The amount of income tax to be withheld shall be—										
$290	$300	$34	$28	$22	$15	$9	$3	$0	$0	$0	$0	0
300	310	36	29	23	17	11	5	0	0	0	0	0
310	320	37	31	25	18	12	6	0	0	0	0	0
320	330	39	32	26	20	14	8	1	0	0	0	0
330	340	40	34	28	21	15	9	3	0	0	0	0
340	350	42	35	29	23	17	11	4	0	0	0	0
350	360	43	37	31	24	18	12	6	0	0	0	0
360	370	45	38	32	26	20	14	7	1	0	0	0
370	380	46	40	34	27	21	15	9	3	0	0	0
380	390	48	41	35	29	23	17	10	4	0	0	0
390	400	49	43	37	30	24	18	12	6	0	0	0
400	410	51	44	38	32	26	20	13	7	1	0	0
410	420	52	46	40	33	27	21	15	9	2	0	0
420	430	54	47	41	35	29	23	16	10	4	0	0
430	440	55	49	43	36	30	24	18	12	5	0	0
440	450	57	50	44	38	32	26	19	13	7	1	0
450	460	58	52	46	39	33	27	21	15	8	2	0
460	470	60	53	47	41	35	29	22	16	10	4	0
470	480	61	55	49	42	36	30	24	18	11	5	0
480	490	63	56	50	44	38	32	25	19	13	7	0
490	500	64	58	52	45	39	33	27	21	14	8	2
500	510	66	59	53	47	41	35	28	22	16	10	3
510	520	67	61	55	48	42	36	30	24	17	11	5
520	530	69	62	56	50	44	38	31	25	19	13	6
530	540	70	64	58	51	45	39	33	27	20	14	8
540	550	72	65	59	53	47	41	34	28	22	16	9
550	560	73	67	61	54	48	42	36	30	23	17	11
560	570	75	68	62	56	50	44	37	31	25	19	12
570	580	76	70	64	57	51	45	39	33	26	20	14
580	590	78	71	65	59	53	47	40	34	28	22	15
590	600	79	73	67	60	54	48	42	36	29	23	17
600	610	81	74	68	62	56	50	43	37	31	25	18
610	620	82	76	70	63	57	51	45	39	32	26	20
620	630	84	77	71	65	59	53	46	40	34	28	21
630	640	85	79	73	66	60	54	48	42	35	29	23
640	650	87	80	74	68	62	56	49	43	37	31	24
650	660	88	82	76	69	63	57	51	45	38	32	26
660	670	90	83	77	71	65	59	52	46	40	34	27
670	680	91	85	79	72	66	60	54	48	41	35	29
680	690	93	86	80	74	68	62	55	49	43	37	30
690	700	94	88	82	75	69	63	57	51	44	38	32
700	710	96	89	83	77	71	65	58	52	46	40	33
710	720	97	91	85	78	72	66	60	54	47	41	35
720	730	99	92	86	⑧⓪	74	68	61	55	49	43	36
730	740	102	94	88	81	75	69	63	57	50	44	38
740	750	104	95	89	83	77	71	64	58	52	46	39
750	760	107	97	91	84	78	72	66	60	53	47	41
760	770	110	99	92	86	80	74	67	61	55	49	42
770	780	113	101	94	87	81	75	69	63	56	50	44
780	790	116	104	95	89	83	77	70	64	58	52	45
790	800	118	107	97	90	84	78	72	66	59	53	47
800	810	121	110	98	92	86	80	73	67	61	55	48
810	820	124	113	101	93	87	81	75	69	62	56	50
820	830	127	115	104	95	89	83	76	70	64	58	51
830	840	130	118	107	96	90	84	78	72	65	59	53
840	850	132	121	109	98	92	86	79	73	67	61	54
850	860	135	124	112	101	93	87	81	75	68	62	56
860	870	138	127	115	103	95	89	82	76	70	64	57
870	880	141	129	118	106	96	90	84	78	71	65	59
880	890	144	132	121	109	98	92	85	79	73	67	60
890	900	146	135	123	112	100	93	87	81	74	68	62
900	910	149	138	126	115	103	95	88	82	76	70	63
910	920	152	141	129	117	106	96	90	84	77	71	65
920	930	155	143	132	120	109	98	91	85	79	73	66

Employees' State Income Tax Withholding

Many states that levy state income taxes also furnish employers with withholding tables. Other states use a fixed percentage of the federal income tax withholding as the amount to be withheld for state taxes. In our illustration, we will assume that the amount of each employee's state income tax deduction amounts to 20 percent of that employee's federal income tax deduction.

Employees' FICA Tax Withholding (Social Security and Medicare)

The Federal Insurance Contributions Act provides for retirement pensions after a worker reaches age 62, disability benefits for any worker who becomes disabled (and for her or his dependents), and a health insurance program or Medicare after age 65. Both the employee and the employer have to pay **FICA taxes**. The employer withholds FICA taxes from employees' wages and pays them to the Internal Revenue Service.

FICA tax rates apply to the gross earnings of an employee during the **calendar year** (January 1 through December 31). After an employee has paid FICA tax on the maximum taxable earnings, the employer stops deducting FICA tax until the next calendar year begins. Congress has frequently changed the schedule of rates and taxable incomes. Taxable income increases automatically with growth in average earnings.

In this text, we will assume a Social Security rate of 6.2 percent of the first $60,600 for each employee and a Medicare rate of 1.45 percent of the total taxable earnings. Both tax rates apply to earnings during the calendar year. (Tables are available for Social Security and Medicare tax withholdings in the Internal Revenue Service Circular E, Employer's Tax Guide.)

Let's get back to John C. Logan, who had gross wages of $720 for the week ending October 7. Suppose that his total accumulated gross wages earned this year prior to this payroll period were $23,316. Logan's total gross wages including this payroll period were $24,036 ($23,316 + $720). Since the Social Security tax applies through the first $60,600, and the Medicare tax applies to all earnings, Logan's earnings will be subject to both taxes. For Logan's Social Security tax, multiply $720 by 6.2 percent ($720 × .062 = $44.64). For Logan's Medicare tax, multiply $720 by .0145 = $10.44.

Performance Objective 3

Complete a payroll register.

The Payroll Register

The **payroll register** is a form that summarizes the information about employees' wages and salaries for a given payroll period. In Figure 9-4 (see pages 386 and 387) we see a payroll register that shows the data for each employee on a separate line. This would be suitable for a firm, like Carson and Company, which has a small number of employees.

First, we'll show the entire payroll register, then we'll break it down to explain it column by column. The number at the foot of each column refers to the related text description.

The payroll period covers October 1 through October 7. The first part consists of employees' names, hours worked, earnings, and taxable earnings.

(1) **Total Hours**—taken from employees' time cards.

(2) **Beginning Cumulative Earnings**—the amount each employee has earned between January 1 and September 30 (the last day of the previous payroll period). It is taken from each employee's individual earnings record.

(3) **Regular Earnings**—hours worked up to and including 40. In other words, the first 40 hours multiplied by each employee's regular hourly rate.

(4) **Overtime Earnings**—hours worked in excess of 40 (relative to a 40-hour week) multiplied by each employee's overtime rate.

(5) **Total Earnings**—regular earnings plus overtime earnings.

(6) **Ending Cumulative Earnings**—beginning Cumulative Earnings plus Total Earnings.

(7) **Taxable Earnings**—consists of the amount of earnings that is subject to taxation, not the tax itself. We'll use these columns later to figure the amount of each tax. In other words, **Taxable Earnings is the base on which to figure the tax. Taxable Earnings multiplied by the tax rate equals the tax.**

(7A) **Unemployment Taxable Earnings**—in our illustration, consists of the first $7,000 of each employee's earnings during the calendar year beginning January 1. **Unemployment tax is paid by the employer only to the appropriate state.** Actually, states may use different maximum earnings and different rates. However, many states use $7,000, which is the amount used by the federal government. We will break the Unemployment Taxable Earnings down into three possibilities, as follows:

    a. **Employee's cumulative earnings including this pay period have not reached $7,000** When an employee's cumulative earnings so far during the calendar year (since January 1) are less than $7,000, we record the total earnings for the payroll period in the Unemployment Taxable Earnings column. For example, Silvano Anaya's cumulative earnings before this week were $6,460. Anaya's cumulative earnings after this week are $6,852 ($6,460 + $392). Because Anaya's total earnings are still less than $7,000, the entire $392 in wages earned during this pay period is listed in the Unemployment Taxable Earnings column. Note that the same situation applies to Arden Fife.

    b. **Employee's cumulative earnings before this week were less than $7,000 and after this week are more than $7,000** Next, look at the line for Dewey Brewer. Notice that his cumulative earnings before this week were $6,760. Brewer's new cumulative earnings (ending) are $7,235 ($6,760 + $475), putting him over the $7,000 maximum. Therefore, to bring Brewer up to the $7,000 limit, $240 ($7,000 − $6,760) of his earnings for the week are taxable. After this week, none of Brewer's earnings for the remainder of this calendar year will be taxable for unemployment.

    c. **Employee's cumulative earnings before this week were more than $7,000** After an employee's earnings top $7,000 during the calendar year, record a dash in the Unemployment Taxable Earnings column to indicate that the column has not been forgotten or overlooked. For example, John Logan's total earnings before the payroll period ended October 7 (beginning) were $23,316 (as shown in his individual earnings record in Figure 9-7). Since he had already earned more than $7,000 this year, we record a dash in the Unemployment Taxable Earnings column.

(7B) **Social Security Taxable Earnings Column**—we have assumed a Social Security tax rate of 6.2 percent of the first $60,600 paid to each employee

Figure 9-4

PAYROLL FOR

| | NAME | TOTAL HOURS | BEGINNING CUMULATIVE EARNINGS | BALANCE | | | | | ENDING CUMULATIVE EARNINGS |
				REGULAR	OVERTIME	TOTAL		
1	Anaya, Silvano P.	46	6 4 6 0 00	3 2 0 00	7 2 00	3 9 2 00	6 8 5 2 00	
2	Brewer, Dewey A.	45	6 7 6 0 00	4 0 0 00	7 5 00	4 7 5 00	7 2 3 5 00	
3	Delap, Debbie R.	49	23 1 0 0 00	4 0 0 00	1 3 5 00	5 3 5 00	23 6 3 5 00	
4	Dirksen, Carol B.	40	15 8 4 0 00	3 6 0 00	——	3 6 0 00	16 2 0 0 00	
5	Fife, Arden N.	40	6 1 2 6 00	3 8 4 00	——	3 8 4 00	6 5 1 0 00	
6	Garlini, Anthony N.	40	54 2 0 0 00	1 2 6 0 00	——	1 2 6 0 00	55 4 6 0 00	
7	Logan, John C.	52	23 3 1 6 00	4 8 0 00	2 4 0 00	7 2 0 00	24 0 3 6 00	
8	Lucero, Maria D.	40	26 4 0 0 00	6 0 0 00	——	6 0 0 00	27 0 0 0 00	
9	Moser, Donna G.	44	21 7 6 2 00	4 4 0 00	6 6 00	5 0 6 00	22 2 6 8 00	
10	Olson, Lavern H.	45	19 3 3 4 00	4 0 0 00	7 5 00	4 7 5 00	19 8 0 9 00	
11	Pearl, Thomas M.	40	37 4 0 0 00	8 5 0 00	——	8 5 0 00	38 2 5 0 00	
12	Taber, Martha R.	52	27 7 1 2 00	4 8 0 00	2 1 6 00	6 9 6 00	28 4 0 8 00	
13			268 4 1 0 00	6 3 7 4 00	8 7 9 00	7 2 5 3 00	275 6 6 3 00	
		(1)	(2)	(3)	(4)	(5)	(6)	

6,374.00 + 879.00 = 7,253.00

268,410.00 + 7,253.00 = 275,663.00

REMEMBER

Taxable Earnings is the base on which to figure the tax, not the tax itself.

FYI

On January 1, 1994, the cap or limit on the Medicare tax (health insurance portion of FICA) on both the employer and employee was lifted. All taxable earnings became subject to the 1.45 percent tax in existence at that time. The Omnibus Budget Reconciliation Act of 1993, signed August 10, 1993, is the enabling legislation. Its intent is to raise more funds, since more people will contribute when there is no limit.

during the calendar year. Only the first $60,600 for each employee is taxable.

a. **Employee's cumulative earnings including this pay period have not reached $60,600** When an employee's cumulative earnings so far during the year are less than $60,600, we record the total earnings for the payroll period in the Social Security Taxable Earnings column. For example, Silvano Anaya's cumulative earnings this year amount to $6,852. Because Anaya's total earnings are less than $60,600, the entire $392 of wages earned during this pay period is listed in the Social Security Taxable Earnings column. Note that this is true of all the employees.

b. **Employee's cumulative earnings before the week were more than $60,600** After an employee's earnings top $60,600 during the calendar year, record a dash to indicate that the column has not been forgotten or overlooked. (The same procedure is used for the Unemployment Taxable Earnings column.)

(7C) **Medicare Taxable Earnings Columns**—we have assumed a Medicare tax rate of 1.45 percent of all earnings paid to each employee during the calendar year. There is no cap on this portion of FICA.

(8) **Deductions**—deductions are amounts taken away (withheld) from total earnings.

(8A) **Federal Income Tax Deductions**—the amount of the federal income tax deduction for each employee can be located directly on the wage bracket tables. Although Garlini's earnings of $1,260 do not appear on the table presented here, an appropriate table is available in Circular E.

WEEK ENDED
October 7, 19–

	(7) TAXABLE EARNINGS			(8) DEDUCTIONS				
	UNEMPL.	SOCIAL SECURITY	MEDICARE	FEDERAL INCOME TAX	STATE INCOME TAX	SOCIAL SECURITY TAX	MEDICARE TAX	MEDICAL INSURANCE
	392 00	392 00	392 00	43 00	8 60	24 30	5 68	19 00
	240 00	475 00	475 00	55 00	11 00	29 45	6 89	19 00
	—	535 00	535 00	58 00	11 60	33 17	7 76	23 00
		360 00	360 00	38 00	7 60	22 32	5 22	19 00
	384 00	384 00	384 00	41 00	8 20	23 81	5 57	19 00
	—	1260 00	1260 00	215 00	43 00	78 12	18 27	25 00
	—	720 00	720 00	80 00	16 00	44 64	10 44	25 00
	—	600 00	600 00	62 00	12 40	37 20	8 70	23 00
	—	506 00	506 00	59 00	11 80	31 37	7 34	23 00
	—	475 00	475 00	55 00	11 00	29 45	6 89	19 00
	—	850 00	850 00	112 00	22 40	52 70	12 33	25 00
	—	696 00	696 00	88 00	17 60	43 15	10 09	25 00
	1016 00	7253 00	7253 00	906 00	181 20	449 68	105 18	264 00
	(7A)	(7B)	(7C)	(8A)	(8B)	(8C)	(8D)	(8E)

906.00 + 181.20 + 449.68 + 105.18 + 264.00 + 64.00 = 1,970.06

PAGE __68__

	(9) PAYMENTS			(10) EXPENSE ACCOUNT DEBITED		
OTHER	TOTAL	NET AMOUNT	CK. NO.	SALES SALARY EXPENSE	OFFICE SALARY EXPENSE	
—	100 58	291 42	931	392 00		1
UW 3 00	124 34	350 66	932	475 00		2
UW 3 00	136 53	398 47	933	535 00		3
—	92 14	267 86	934		360 00	4
—	97 58	286 42	935	384 00		5
UW 5 00	384 39	875 61	936		1260 00	6
UW 3 00	179 08	540 92	937	720 00		7
UW 3 00	146 30	453 70	938		600 00	8
—	132 51	373 49	939	506 00		9
AR 40 00	161 34	313 66	940	475 00		10
UW 4 00	228 43	621 57	941	850 00		11
UW 3 00	186 84	509 16	942	696 00		12
64 00	1970 06	5282 94		5033 00	2220 00	13
(8F)	(8G)	(9A)	(9B)	(10A)	(10B)	

1,970.06 + 5,282.94 = 7,253.00   5,033.00 + 2,220.00 = 7,253.00

(8B) **State Income Tax Deduction**—states imposing income taxes also provide wage-bracket tables. The state tax deduction for each employee can be located directly on the appropriate table. As stated previously, we are assuming a rate of 20 percent of the federal income tax.

(8C) **Social Security Tax Deductions**—for each employee's Social Security tax deduction, we first go back to the Social Security Taxable Earnings column and note the amount subject to tax. Next, multiply the Social Security taxable earnings by 6.2 percent. For example, Anaya's taxable earnings are $392, and his Social Security tax deduction is $24.30 (392 × .062).

(8D) **Medicare Tax Deductions**—for each employee's Medicare tax deduction, go back to the Medicare Taxable Earnings column and note the amount subject to tax. Next, multiply the Medicare taxable earnings by 1.45 percent. For example, Anaya's taxable earnings are $392, and his Medicare tax deduction is $5.68 ($392 + .0145).

(8E) **Medical Insurance Deductions**—consist of premiums paid by the employee through payroll withholding. The amount of the premium for each employee depends on the number of dependents claimed. For example, Anaya's premium is $19 per week.

(8F) **Other Deductions**—consist of employees' voluntary withholdings. In our illustration, UW represents the United Way, and AR stands for Accounts Receivable (employee pays charge account to the company). For example, Lavern Olson paid $40 on her charge account.

(8G) **Total Deductions**—consist of the combined total of each employee's deductions for taxes, insurance, and other. For example, Anaya's total deduction is $100.58 ($43.00 + $8.60 + $24.30 + $5.68 + $19.00).

(9) **Payments**—amount of each employee's payroll check (take-home pay).

(9A) **Net Amount**—consists of each employee's Total Earnings minus Total Deductions. For example, Anaya's net amount is $291.42 ($392 − $100.58).

(9B) **Ck. No.**—number of each employee's payroll check.

(10) **Expense Account Debited**—is used for distributing each amount into the appropriate salary expense account. Carson and Company uses Sales Salary Expense and Office Salary Expense. The sum of these two columns equals the total earnings.

(10A) **Sales Salary Expense**—amounts earned by employees involved in sales activities.

(10B) **Office Salary Expense**—amounts earned by employees involved in office activities.

REMEMBER

Taxable earnings multiplied by the tax rate equals the tax.

The Payroll Entry

Performance Objective 4

Journalize the payroll entry from a payroll register.

REMEMBER

The totals from the payroll register are the amounts used in the payroll entry.

Because the payroll register summarizes the payroll data for the period, it is used as the basis for recording the payroll in the ledger accounts. Since the payroll register does not have the status of a journal, a journal entry is necessary. Figure 9-5 shows the entry in general journal form. Note that the accountant records the total cost to the company for services of employees as debits to the salary expense accounts.

Also note that the total Social Security tax deductions ($449.68) and the total Medicare tax deductions ($105.18) are combined to become FICA Tax Payable of $554.86 ($449.68 + $105.18). The two tax deductions are combined into the one liability account because they are both paid together at the same time. The reason that Social Security and Medicare taxes are recorded separately in the payroll register is that they must be listed separately on each employee's W-2 form (Wage and Tax Statement). We will discuss W-2 forms in Chapter 10.

Figure 9-5

GENERAL JOURNAL   PAGE __31__

	DATE		DESCRIPTION	POST. REF.	DEBIT	CREDIT	
1	19–						1
2	Oct.	7	Sales Salary Expense		5 0 3 3 00		2
3			Office Salary Expense		2 2 2 0 00		3
4			Employees' Federal Income Tax				4
5			Payable			9 0 6 00	5
6			Employees' State Income Tax				6
7			Payable			1 8 1 20	7
8			FICA Tax Payable			5 5 4 86	8
9			Employees' Medical Insurance				9
10			Payable			2 6 4 00	10
11			Employees' United Way Payable			2 4 00	11
12			Accounts Receivable			4 0 00	12
13			Salaries Payable			5 2 8 2 94	13
14			Payroll register, page 68,				14
15			for week ended October 7.				15
16							16

To pay the employees, the accountant now makes the following journal entry:

17		7	Salaries Payable		5 2 8 2 94		17
18			Cash			5 2 8 2 94	18
19			Paid salaries for week				19
20			ended October 7. Issued				20
21			Ck. No. 667, payable to				21
22			special payroll bank				22
23			account.				23
24							24

Performance Objective 5

Journalize the entry to pay the payroll from a payroll register.

· · · · · · · · · · · · · · ·

R E M E M B E R

The amount shown as Salaries Payable is the employees' take-home pay.

· · · · · · · · · · · · · · ·

Special Payroll Bank Account

A firm having a large number of employees would probably open a special **payroll bank account** with its bank. One check drawn on the regular bank account is made payable to the special payroll account for the amount of the total net pay for a payroll period.

25		7	Cash-Payroll Bank Account		5 2 8 2 94		25
26			Cash			5 2 8 2 94	26
27			Issued Ck. No. 667,				27
28			payable to special payroll				28
29			bank account.				29
30							30

All payroll checks for the period are then written on the special payroll account. With the use of the special payroll account, if employees delay cashing their paychecks, then the checks do not have to be listed on the bank reconciliation of the firm's regular bank account. Balances of employees' Medical Insurance Payable, Employees' United Way Payable, and other employee deductions are paid out of the firm's regular bank account.

Small businesses that have just a few workers will not find it worthwhile to use a special payroll bank account. Instead, these firms will use their regular bank account to write the employees' payroll checks, crediting Cash directly rather than crediting Salaries Payable.

Paycheck

All the data needed to make out a payroll check are available in the payroll register. John C. Logan's paycheck is shown in Figure 9-6 at the top of the next page.

Employees' Individual Earnings Records

Performance Objective 6

Maintain employees' individual earnings records.

To comply with government regulations, a firm has to keep current data on each employee's accumulated earnings, deductions, and net pay. The information contained in the payroll register is recorded each payday in each **employee's individual earnings record.** Figure 9-7 below shows a portion of the earnings record for John C. Logan.

Figure 9-7

EMPLOYEE'S INDIVIDUAL EARNINGS RECORD

NAME John Charles Logan   EMPLOYEE NO. 5
ADDRESS 6242 Baxter Drive   SOC. SEC. NO. 543-24-1680
Weston, South Dakota 57816   PAY RATE $12.00
MALE X   FEMALE   EQUIVALENT HOURLY RATE $12.00
MARRIED X   SINGLE   DATE TERMINATED
PHONE NO. 663-2556   DATE OF BIRTH 9/19/51   CLASSIFICATION FOR WORKERS' COMPENSATION INSURANCE Sales floor

| | | | HOURS WORKED | | EARNINGS | | | | DEDUCTIONS | |
LINE NO.	PERIOD ENDED	DATE PAID	REG.	O.T.	REGULAR	OVERTIME	TOTAL	CUMULATIVE EARNINGS	FEDERAL INCOME TAX	STATE INCOME TAX
1	40	9/3	9/4	40	8	480 00	144 00	624 00	21 162 00	65 00	13 00
2	41	9/10	9/11	40	2	480 00	36 00	516 00	21 678 00	48 00	9 60
3	42	9/17	9/18	40	2	480 00	36 00	516 00	22 194 00	48 00	9 60
4	43	9/24	9/25	40	5	480 00	90 00	570 00	22 764 00	57 00	11 40
5	44	9/30	10/1	40	4	480 00	72 00	552 00	23 316 00	54 00	10 80
6	45	10/7	10/8	40	12	480 00	240 00	720 00	24 036 00	80 00	16 00
7										
8										

Figure 9-6

EMPLOYEE	TOTAL HOURS	O.T. HOURS	REG. PAY	O.T. PREM. PAY	GROSS PAY	FED INC. TAX	STATE INC. TAX	SOCIAL SECURITY TAX	MEDICARE TAX	OTHER	TOTAL DED.	NET PAY
John C. Logan	52	12	480.00	240.00	720.00	80.00	16.00	44.64	10.44	28.00	179.08	540.92

98-461
252

Payroll Account

Central National Bank

CNB

Carson and Company
610 First Avenue
Weston, South Dakota 57817

October 8 19 ____ No. 937

PAY TO THE
ORDER OF ___ John C. Logan ___ $ 540.92

Five hundred and forty and 92/100 ------------------- DOLLARS

Sandra C. Carson

⑆252⑉046⑈

Computer Applications

P ayroll software is usually available as a module depending on the sophistication and price of the software package. Some payroll modules integrate or automatically send totals to the general ledger and others do the work independently and require that the user make separate entries to the general ledger. Integration is quick and convenient; however, if an error has been made, the error will integrate and it can sometimes cause more problems than if the entries had been made independently.

DATE EMPLOYED 2/1/—

NO. OF EXEMPTIONS 3

PER HOUR X _____   PER DAY _____

PER WEEK _____   PER MONTH _____

SOCIAL SECURITY TAX	MEDICARE TAX	MEDICAL INSURANCE	OTHER CODE	OTHER AMOUNT	TOTAL	NET AMOUNT	CK. NO.	
38 69	9 05	25 00	UW	3 00	153 74	470 26	877	1
31 99	7 48	25 00	UW	3 00	125 07	390 93	889	2
31 99	7 48	25 00	UW	3 00	125 07	390 93	901	3
35 34	8 27	25 00	UW	3 00	140 01	429 99	913	4
34 22	8 00	25 00	UW	3 00	135 02	416 98	925	5
44 64	10 44	25 00	UW	3 00	179 08	540 92	937	6
								7
								8

Figure 9-8 illustrates a partial payroll register produced by an accounting software package. In addition to producing the payroll register, payroll packages maintain employee individual earnings records and produce checks, tax reports, and a variety of reports for managing personnel.

Even if you are unable to have a general ledger software package, it is an excellent investment in money and training time to install a payroll package, even if you only do payroll for a few employees. Payroll and report preparation is time consuming and requires absolute accuracy. Payroll software can eliminate some of the number crunching, but it is only as accurate as the input.

In addition to the obvious time-saving advantages of the electronic processing of payroll, software packages can provide password protection to limit access to confidential payroll information.

Figure 9-8

```
                        Harris Inc.
                     2020 South 400th
                     Seattle, WA  98003

                    Payroll Register (Detail)

                            June
                                                        Page 1
Employee  Category                      June
..............................................................
Anderson, Clara

    Wages
    Base Salary                      $1,161.54
                          Total: $1,161.54
..............................................................

    Deductions - Employee

    Medical Insurance                   $5.81
    Federal Income Tax                $202.15
    Federal Medicare Tax               $16.84
    Federal Social Security Tax        $72.02
                          Total:    $296.82
..............................................................

    Expenses - Employer

    FICA - Medicare Matching           $16.84
    FICA - Soc. Sec. Matching          $72.02
    FUTA                               $72.02
    Medical Insurance                   $5.81
    SUTA-WA                            $62.72
                          Total:    $229.41
```

CHAPTER REVIEW

R eview of Performance Objectives

1. **Calculate total earnings based on an hourly, piece-rate, or commission basis.**

   Earnings based on an *hourly basis* equal the hourly rate multiplied by the number of hours worked. Earnings based on a *piece-rate basis* equal the total number of products produced multiplied by the rate per unit of product. Earnings based on a *commission basis* equal the total number of units sold or the price of units sold multiplied by the commission rate.

2. **Determine deductions from tables of employees' income tax withholding.**

Using the appropriate income tax withholding table in IRS Circular E, first place the amount of earnings in the wage bracket. Next, on the same horizontal line, select the vertical column containing the number of exemptions claimed.

3. **Complete a payroll register.**

List the employees' names, hours worked, and beginning cumulative earnings. To the beginning cumulative earnings add the total earnings to get ending cumulative earnings. Unemployment Taxable Earnings is used for an assumed first $7,000 of each employee's earnings. Social Security Taxable Earnings is used for an assumed first $60,600. Medicare Taxable Earnings is based on total taxable earnings. Under the Deductions columns, list the income taxes withheld, the Social Security taxes withheld, the Medicare taxes withheld, and other deductions. The Social Security tax deduction equals the Social Security Taxable Earnings multiplied by an assumed rate of 6.2 percent. The Medicare tax deduction equals the Medicare Taxable Earnings multiplied by an assumed rate of 1.45 percent. Net amount equals total (gross) earnings minus total deductions. The Expense Account Debited columns are used to distribute Salary and Wages Expense to the appropriate accounts.

4. **Journalize the payroll entry from a payroll register.**

Totals are taken directly from the payroll register. For the following entry, it is assumed that one check is made payable to a special payroll bank account.

5. **Journalize the entry to pay the payroll from a payroll register.**

Totals are taken directly from the Net Amount column of the payroll register. A check may be written for each employee or one check for the total may be written to a special payroll account from which individual checks are written.

6. **Maintain employees' individual earnings records.**

In the employees' individual earnings records, list the personal data for each employee. Based on the information contained in the payroll register, record the earnings and deductions for each payroll period.

G lossary

Calendar year A twelve-month period beginning on January 1 and ending on December 31 of the same year. **(384)**

Employee One who works for compensation under the direction and control of the employer. **(378)**

Employee's individual earnings record A supplementary record for each employee showing personal payroll data and yearly cumulative earnings, deductions, and net pay. **(390)**

Employee's Withholding Allowance Certificate (Form W-4) This form specifies the number of exemptions claimed by each employee and gives the employer the authority to withhold money for an employee's federal income taxes and FICA taxes. **(382)**

Exemption An amount of an employee's annual earnings not subject to income tax; also called a *withholding allowance.* **(381)**

FICA taxes Social Security taxes plus Medicare taxes paid by both employee and employer under the provisions of the Federal Insurance Contributions Act. The proceeds are used to pay old-age and disability pensions and fund the Medicare program. **(384)**

Gross pay The total amount of an employee's pay before any deductions. **(377)**

Independent contractor Someone who is engaged for a definite job or service, who may choose her or his own means of doing the work. This person is not an employee of the firm for which the service is provided (*examples:* appliance repair person, plumber, freelance artist, CPA firm). **(378)**

Net pay Gross pay minus deductions. Also called *take-home pay.* **(377)**

Payroll bank account A special checking account used to pay a company's employees. **(389)**

Payroll register A multicolumn form prepared for each payroll period listing the earnings, deductions, and net pay for each employee. **(384)**

Taxable earnings The amount of an employee's earnings subject to a tax (not the tax itself). **(385)**

Wage-bracket tax tables A chart providing for amounts of deductions for income taxes based on amounts of earnings and numbers of exemptions claimed. **(382)**

QUESTIONS, EXERCISES, AND PROBLEMS

D iscussion Questions

1. What information is included in a wage-bracket withholding table? What is the title of the government form?
2. What information is included in an employee's individual earnings record, and what is its function?
3. For each employee, distinguish between gross earnings and net earnings for a payroll period.
4. How is an employee's individual earnings record related to the payroll register?
5. What is the difference between an employee and an independent contractor? Give three examples of independent contractors.
6. What is the purpose of the payroll register?
7. List three possible required deductions and four voluntary deductions from employees' total earnings.
8. Describe how a special payroll bank account is useful in paying the wages of employees.

E xercises

P.O.1

Calculate gross pay.

Exercise 9-1 Determine the gross pay for each employee listed below.

a. Gordon Dunlap is paid time-and-a-half for all hours over forty. He worked forty-five hours during the week. His regular pay rate is $9.80 per hour.

b. Marcia Eaton worked fifty-two hours during the week. She is entitled to time-and-a-half for all hours in excess of forty per week. Her regular pay rate is $12.60 per hour.

c. Diana Garate is paid a commission of 8 percent of her sales, which amounted to $8,526.

d. Robert Fisk's yearly salary is $31,616. During the week, Fisk worked forty-two hours, and he is entitled to time-and-a-half for all hours over forty.

Exercise 9-2 Raul Leon works for Vasquez Company, which pays its employees time-and-a-half for all hours worked in excess of forty per week. Leon's pay rate is $16.20 per hour. His wages are subject to federal income tax and a Social Security tax deduction at the rate of 6.2 percent and a Medicare tax deduction at the rate of 1.45 percent. He is married and claims three exemptions. Leon has a half-hour lunch break during an eight-and-one-half-hour day. His time card is shown below. Leon's beginning cumulative earnings are $36,482.

P.O.1,2

Determine gross pay and withholding.

TIME CARD

Name Leon, Raul

Week ending March 11, 19—

Day	In	Out	In	Out	Hours Worked Regular	Overtime
M	7:56	12:09	12:39	4:32	8	
T	7:52	12:05	12:35	5:04	8	1/2
W	7:59	12:20	12:40	5:03	8	1/2
Th	8:00	12:08	12:38	4:34	8	
F	7:56	12:09	12:39	6:33	8	2
S	8:00	11:01				3
S						

Complete the following:

a. _____ hours at straight time × $16.20 per hour $ _____

b. _____ hours overtime × $ _____ per hour   _____

c. Total gross pay $ _____

d. Federal income tax withholding (from tax tables in Figure 9-3, page 383) $ _____

e. Social Security withholding at 6.2 percent   _____

f. Medicare withholding at 1.45 percent   _____

g. Total withholding   _____

h. Net pay $ _____

Exercise 9-3 Using the income tax withholding table in Figure 9-3, page 383, for each employee of Regional Dollar Stores, determine the net pay for the week ended January 21. Assume a Social Security tax of 6.2 percent and a Medicare tax of 1.45 percent. All employees have cumulative earnings of less than $60,600.

P.O.2,3

Determine net pay.

Employee	Exemptions	Total Earnings	Social Security Tax Withheld	Medicare Tax Withheld	Federal Income Tax Withheld	Union Dues Withheld	Medical Insurance Withheld	Net Pay
a. Alden, C. A.	1	$492	$	$	$	$20	$30	$
b. Ehrlich, R. N.	2	541				20	26	
c. Harris, T. C.	3	684				—	30	
d. Menard, L. O.	0	427				20	30	
e. Yates, M. E.	2	568				20	30	

P.O.3

Locate errors in a payroll register.

Exercise 9-4 For the week ended September 7, the totals of the payroll register for Hanson, Inc., are presented below.

List six errors that exist.

	EARNINGS				TAXABLE EARNINGS		
BEGINNING CUMULATIVE EARNINGS	REGULAR	OVERTIME	TOTAL	ENDING CUMULATIVE EARNINGS	UNEMPL.	SOCIAL SECURITY	MEDICARE
245 754 00	6 724 00	1 220 00	7 494 00	253 248 00	2 456 00	7 944 00	7 944 00

P.O.3

Determine taxable earnings.

Exercise 9-5 For tax purposes, assume that the maximum taxable earnings for Social Security are $60,600 and no limit for Medicare. The maximum taxable earnings for the unemployment tax are $7,000. For the payroll register for the month of November, determine the taxable earnings for each employee.

EMPLOYEE	TOTAL EARNINGS	ENDING CUMULATIVE EARNINGS	TAXABLE EARNINGS		
			UNEMPL.	SOCIAL SECURITY	MEDICARE
Andrews, C. B.	4 420 00	59 610 00			
Crisp. T. N.	3 340 00	36 930 00			
Garcia, A. L.	2 960 00	32 170 00			
Norris, R. P.	1 310 00	5 040 00			
Seidel, C. K.	1 750 00	6 800 00			

P.O.3,4,5

Determine FICA withholdings and journalize the payroll entry and payment of the payroll.

Exercise 9-6 On January 21, the column totals of the payroll register for Romo Distributors showed that its sales employees had earned $13,620, its driver employees had earned $8,460, and its office employees had earned $6,220. Social Security taxes were withheld at an assumed rate of 6.2 percent, and Medicare taxes were withheld at an assumed rate of 1.45 percent. Other deductions consisted of federal income tax, $3,113; medical insurance, $1,472; union dues, $374. Determine the amount of Social Security and Medicare taxes withheld, and record the general journal entry for the payroll, crediting Salaries Payable for the net pay. All earnings were taxable.

Exercise 9-7 Bingham Laboratory has two employees. The information shown below was taken from their individual earnings records for the month of September. Determine the missing amounts, assuming that the Social Security tax is 6.2 percent and the Medicare tax is 1.45 percent. All earnings are subject to Social Security and Medicare taxes.

P.O.1

Determine missing amounts.

	Bates	Oliver	Total
Regular earnings	$1,690	$?	$?
Overtime earnings	?	76	?
Total earnings	$1,760	$?	$?
Federal income tax withheld	$ 327	$?	$?
State income tax withheld	?	79	?
Social Security tax withheld	109	82	?
Medicare tax withheld	26	19	?
Medical insurance withheld	96	96	?
Total deductions	$ 663	$520	$?
Net pay	$?	$796	$?

	DEDUCTIONS						PAYMENTS		WAGES EXPENSE
FEDERAL INCOME TAX	SOCIAL SECURITY TAX	MEDICARE TAX	UNION DUES	MEDICAL INSURANCE		TOTAL	NET AMOUNT	CK. NO.	DEBIT
9 4 9 00	4 2 9 53	1 1 5 19	1 9 3 00	2 9 2 00		1 9 7 8 72	5 5 1 5 28		7 4 9 4 00

Exercise 9-8 Assume the employees in Exercise 9-7 are paid from the company's regular bank account (check numbers 931 and 932). Record the payroll entry in general journal form, dated September 30.

P.O.4

Journalize the payroll entry.

C onsider and Communicate

Treadwell Company pays its employees weekly by issuing checks on its regular bank account. The accountant asks you about special payroll accounts. He presently feels that it would be too much trouble to have to reconcile another bank account. Respond to the accountant's concern.

W hat If . . .

What if the owner of a sole proprietorship takes money from the till and just signs his name and writes the amount on a piece of paper? When you say that you will charge the amount of money to his Drawing account, he tells you to charge it to Wages Expense. What accounts will be affected and how?

A Question of Ethics

Your regular hours of employment are 8:00 A.M. to 5:00 P.M. Due to road construction you have been arriving at work at 8:30 or 8:45 several days this past week, but you have worked past 5:00 P.M. each night or shortened your lunch hour to get in your regular eight hours each day. At the end of the week you sign off your time card showing that you were on the job from 8:00 A.M. to 5:00 P.M. each day for a total of 40 hours. Are you doing anything wrong?

Problem Set A

P.O.1,2

Problem 9-1A Dinah Perez, an employee of Kiersten Shipping Company, worked forty-four hours during the week of October 10 through 16. Her rate of pay is $10.20 per hour, and she receives time-and-a-half for all work in excess of forty hours per week. Perez is married and claims two exemptions on her W-4 form. Her wages are subject to the following deductions:

a. Federal income tax (use the table in Figure 9-3).
b. Social Security tax at 6.2 percent.
c. Medicare tax at 1.45 percent.
d. Union dues, $9.60.
e. Medical insurance, $32.70.

Instructions

Compute her regular pay, overtime pay, gross pay, and net pay.

P.O.3,4,5

Problem 9-2A Holland Company has the following payroll information for the week ended May 14:

Name	Earnings at End of Previous Week	Daily Time						Pay Rate	Federal Income Tax
		M	T	W	T	F	S		
Fornay, N. C.	6,566.00	8	8	8	8	8	0	8.60	35.00
Freeman, A. L.	6,624.60	8	8	8	8	8	0	7.30	28.00
Kahler, D. R.	5,254.20	0	8	8	8	8	8	7.30	28.00
McLeod, N. A.	8,647.00	8	8	8	0	8	8	9.75	41.00
Rudy, B. M.	5,254.20	8	8	8	8	8	8	7.30	34.00
Truitt, P. R.	7,356.30	0	8	8	8	8	8	8.60	35.00

Taxable earnings for Social Security are based on the first $60,600. All earnings are taxable for Medicare. Taxable earnings for federal and state unemployment are based on the first $7,000. Employees are paid time-and-a-half for work in excess of 40 hours per week.

Instructions

1. Complete the payroll register, page 34. The Social Security rate is 6.2 percent, and the Medicare tax rate is 1.45 percent.
2. Prepare a general journal entry to record the payroll. The firm's general ledger contains a Wages Expense account and a Wages Payable account.
3. Assuming that the firm transfers funds from its regular bank account to its special payroll bank account, make the entry in the general journal to record the payment of wages, Ck. No. 96. Begin payroll checks with No. 744.

P.O.2,3,4,5

Problem 9-3A The Ramsey Company pays its employees time-and-a-half for hours worked in excess of forty per week. The following information is available from time cards and employees' individual earnings records for the pay period ended September 21.

Name	Earnings at End of Previous Week	Daily Time						Pay Rate	Income Tax Exemptions
		M	T	W	T	F	S		
Gates, B. N.	6,416.00	8	8	8	10	0	0	8.70	1
Gray, W. C.	14,528.00	8	8	8	8	8	0	9.40	2
Hersel, R. A.	13,340.00	8	10	8	8	8	0	8.70	2
Karas, S. D.	16,112.00	8	8	8	8	8	4	12.50	3
Marci, M. F.	13,544.00	8	8	8	8	8	0	9.40	2
Steiner, L. E.	14,912.00	8	8	9	8	8	0	9.40	2
Vargis, S. P.	6,576.00	8	8	8	9	9	4	8.00	1
Wade, C. C.	15,484.00	8	8	10	8	8	0	9.40	1

Taxable earnings for Social Security are based on the first $60,600. All earnings are taxable for Medicare. Taxable earnings for federal and state unemployment are based on the first $7,000.

Instructions

1. Complete the payroll register, page 72, using the wage-bracket income tax withholding tables in Figure 9-3. The Social Security rate is 6.2 percent, and the Medicare tax rate is 1.45 percent. Assume that all employees are married.
2. Prepare a general journal entry to record the payroll. The firm's general ledger contains a Wages Expense account and a Wages Payable account.
3. Assume that the firm transfers funds from its regular bank account to its special payroll bank account. Make the entry in the general journal to record the payment of wages, Ck. No. 141. In the payroll register, begin payroll checks with Ck. No. 863.

Problem 9-4A For the Robledo Company the following information is available from the time books and employees' individual earnings records for the pay period ended December 22:

P.O.3,4,5,6

Name	Hours Worked	Earnings at End of Previous Week	Total Earnings	Class.	Federal Income Tax	Other Deduct.	
Bach, C. E.	44	22,950	501.40	Sales	52.00	AR	72.00
Ball, V. A.	40	27,410	512.00	Sales	55.00	UW	7.00
Church, J. P.	40	26,860	512.00	Sales	55.00	UW	7.00
Entzel, N. D.	44	22,490	471.50	Office	53.00		
Gram, J. W.	48	26,980	624.00	Office	67.00	UW	8.00
King, D. C.	40	59,680	1,060.00	Office	154.00	UW	10.00
Magana, R. G.	40	26,860	512.00	Sales	55.00	UW	7.00
Moody, P. M.	40	26,750	520.00	Sales	59.00		
Olson, T. B.	44	23,480	501.40	Sales	52.00	AR	62.00
Ross, K. C.	42	41,000	881.50	Sales	95.00	UW	8.00

Taxable earnings for Social Security are based on the first $60,600. All earnings are taxable for Medicare. Taxable earnings for federal and state unemployment are based on the first $7,000.

Instructions

1. Complete the payroll register, page 56, using a Social Security tax rate of 6.2 percent and a Medicare tax rate of 1.45 percent. (The total of Social Security tax deduction and Medicare tax deduction for D. C. King is $72.41. Check this figure.) Concerning Other Deductions, AR refers to Accounts Receivable, and UW refers to United Way.

2. Prepare a general journal entry to record the payroll and the payment to employees. Assume that the company transfers funds from its regular bank account to its special payroll bank account and issues Ck. No. 217. In the payroll register begin with check 114.

P roblem Set B

P.O.1,2

Problem 9-1B Lee Symmons, an employee of Herrington Distributing Company, worked forty-six hours during the week of February 8 through 15. His rate of pay is $11.60 per hour, and he gets time-and-a-half for work in excess of forty hours per week. He is married and claims one exemption on his W-4 form. His wages are subject to the following deductions:

a. Federal income tax (use the table in Figure 9-3).
b. Social Security tax at 6.2 percent.
c. Medicare tax at 1.45 percent.
d. Union dues, $9.60.
e. Medical Insurance, $32.90.

Instructions

Compute his regular pay, overtime pay, gross pay, and net pay.

P.O.3,4,5

Problem 9-2B Hanson Mobile Homes has the following payroll information for the week ended February 21:

Name	Earnings at End of Previous Week	Daily Time							Pay Rate	Federal Income Tax
		S	M	T	W	T	F	S		
Ames, A. C.	1,916.00	8	8	8	8	8			8.20	32.00
Beaty, D. R.	2,027.00			8	8	8	8	8	9.60	29.00
Colson, H. A.	1,916.00	8	8	8			8	8	8.20	32.00
Farris, P. N.	538.00				8	8			5.90	17.00
Oliver, L. B.	2,229.00	8	8	8			8	8	9.90	37.00
Thrush, G. W.	1,974.00	8	8		8	8	8	8	8.40	43.00

Taxable earnings for Social Security are based on the first $60,600. All earnings are taxable for Medicare. Taxable earnings for federal and state unemployment are based on the first $7,000. Employees are paid time-and-a-half for work in excess of 40 hours per week.

Instructions

1. Complete the payroll register, page 37. The Social Security rate is 6.2 percent, and the Medicare tax rate is 1.45 percent.
2. Prepare a general journal entry to record the payroll. The firm's general ledger contains a Wages Expense account and a Wages Payable account.
3. Assuming that the firm transfers funds from its regular bank account to its special payroll bank account, make the entry in the general journal to record the payment of wages, Ck. No. 72. Begin payroll checks with no. 206.

Problem 9-3B The Babson Company pays its employees time-and-a-half for hours worked in excess of forty per week. The information available from time cards and employees' individual earnings records for the pay period ended October 14 is shown below.

`P.O.2,3,4,5`

Name	Earnings at End of Previous Week	Daily Time						Pay Rate	Income Tax Exemptions
		M	T	W	T	F	S		
Brown, J. C.	12,916.00	8	8	8	8	8	0	8.75	2
Burke, K. A.	13,428.00		8	8	8	10	0	9.50	1
Collins, J. P.	13,114.00	8	8	10	8	8	0	8.90	1
Gonzales, S. P.	19,942.00	8	8	8	8	8	0	14.10	3
Martin, L. A.	14,096.00	8	8	8	8	8	4	9.50	3
Powell, N. B.	11,222.00	8	8	8	8	8	0	8.10	1
Thorn, J. C.	6,418.00	8	8	8	8	8	4	8.10	1
Weeks, P. W.	13,924.00	8	8	8	8	8	4	9.50	2

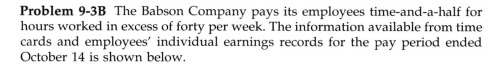

Taxable earnings for Social Security are based on the first $60,600. All earnings are taxable for Medicare. Taxable earnings for federal and state unemployment are based on the first $7,000.

Instructions

1. Complete the payroll register, page 72, using the wage-bracket income tax withholding tables in Figure 9-3. The Social Security rate is 6.2 percent, and the Medicare tax rate is 1.45 percent. Assume that all employees are married.
2. Prepare a general journal entry to record the payroll. The firm's general ledger contains a Wages Expense account and a Wages Payable account.
3. Assume that the firm transfers funds from its regular bank account to its special payroll bank account. Make the entry in the general journal to record the payment of wages, Ck. No. 198. In the payroll register, begin payroll checks with number 942.

P.O.3,4,5,6 **Problem 9-4B** For the Robledo Company the following information is available from Robledo's time books and the employees' individual earnings records for the payroll period ended December 22:

Name	Hours Worked	Earnings at End of Previous Week	Total Earnings	Class.	Federal Income Tax	Other Deduct.	
Bach, C. E.	44	22,950	494.50	Sales	53.00	UW	6.50
Ball, V. A.	40	27,410	510.00	Sales	55.00	AR	80.00
Church, J. P.	40	26,860	510.00	Sales	55.00	UW	6.50
Entzel, N. D.	44	22,490	460.00	Office	55.00	UW	5.00
Gram, J. W.	48	26,980	598.00	Office	65.00	UW	6.00
King, D. C.	40	59,750	1,050.00	Office	157.00	UW	12.00
Magana, R. G.	40	26,860	510.00	Sales	55.00	AR	54.00
Moody, P. M.	40	26,750	500.00	Sales	62.00	UW	6.00
Olson, T. B.	44	23,480	494.50	Sales	53.00	UW	6.50
Ross, K. C.	42	41,000	860.00	Sales	115.00	UW	8.00

Taxable earnings for Social Security are based on the first $60,600. All earnings are taxable for Medicare. Taxable earnings for federal and state unemployment are based on the first $7,000.

Instructions

1. Complete the payroll register, page 56, using a Social Security tax rate of 6.2 percent and a Medicare tax rate of 1.45 percent. (The total of Social Security tax deduction and Medicare tax deduction for D. C. King is $67.93. Check this figure.) Concerning Other Deductions, AR refers to Accounts Receivable and UW refers to United Way. Begin payroll checks with number 971.

2. Prepare a general journal entry to record the payroll and the payment to employees. Assume that the company transfers funds from its regular bank account to its special payroll bank account and issues Ck. No. 621. In the payroll register, begin the payroll check with Ck. No. 971.

CHALLENGE PROBLEM

You are responsible for putting out the payroll for December 15. Unfortunately, the computer went down before you printed a payroll register. Reconstruct the December 15 semimonthly payroll based on the following information, gathered from the records you do have, including the employees' checks that you did print. Assume a Social Security tax of 6.2 percent on $60,600 and a Medicare tax of 1.45 percent on all earnings. State and federal unemployment limits are $7,000.

Employee 1—Salesperson with salary of $2,000 per month
- Beginning cumulative earnings equal $22,000.
- Employee medical insurance (code MI) of $125 is deducted at the end of the month.
- Net pay is $773.50.

Employee 2—Salesperson with base monthly pay of $2,000 plus commission of 15 percent of sales

- Beginning cumulative earnings equal $5,825.
- Sales eligible for commission equal $3,500.
- Net pay is $1,179.34.

Employee 3—Controller with annual salary of $60,000

- Beginning cumulative earnings equal $55,000.
- Medical Insurance payment of $90 is deducted each pay period.
- Net pay is $1,643.75.

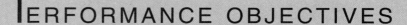

Chapter 10

Payroll Accounting: Employer's Taxes, Payments, and Reports

PERFORMANCE OBJECTIVES

After you have completed this chapter, you will be able to do the following:

1. Calculate the amount of payroll tax expense and journalize the related entry.

2. Journalize the entry for the deposit of employees' federal income taxes withheld and FICA taxes (both employees' withheld and employer's matching share).

3. Journalize the entries for the payment of employer's state and federal unemployment taxes.

4. Journalize the entry for the deposit of employees' state income taxes withheld.

5. Complete Employer's Quarterly Federal Tax Return, Form 941.

6. Prepare W-2 and W-3 forms and Form 940.

7. Calculate the premium for workers' compensation insurance, and prepare the entry for payment in advance.

8. Determine the amount of adjustment for workers' compensation insurance at the end of the year, and record the adjustment.

Whenever I hear a client announce, "I'm going to hire my first employee!" I inwardly groan. Little does the future employer know how her life will change if she decides to do the record keeping herself. I try to encourage her to attend one of the IRS-sponsored

workshops for small business owners. An excellent introduction to all business record keeping, these one-day seminars place special emphasis on the records of employers. Even when a client is planning to have someone else do the records, I still think it is good for the employer to know that she is responsible and will be liable if errors are made.

Many people have no idea how many payroll-related taxes there are—"SUTA, FUTA, FICA. What's that?" is usually the first response when I begin to explain all the payroll taxes on the employer. One hopes that, after learning the complexity of the job, the busy employer will hire a competent bookkeeper to make sure the records are kept and the payments are made properly and promptly.

In Chapter 9, we talked about the computing and recording of such payroll data as gross pay, employees' income tax withheld, employees' FICA tax withheld, and various deductions requested by employees. Now we will pay these withholdings and the taxes levied on the employer based on total payroll.

Employer's Identification Number

Everyone who works must have a Social Security number, a number that is a vital part of his or her federal income tax returns. For an employer, a counterpart to the Social Security number is the **employer identification number.** Each employer of one or more persons is required to have such a number, and it must be listed on all reports and payments of employees' federal income tax withholding and FICA taxes.

Employer's Payroll Taxes

An employer's payroll taxes are levied on the employer on the basis of the gross wages paid to the employees. Payroll taxes— like property taxes— are an expense of doing business. Carson and Company records these taxes in the **Payroll Tax Expense** account and debits the account for the company's FICA taxes as well as for state and federal unemployment taxes. In T account form, Payroll Tax Expense for Carson and Company would look like the following example.

Payroll Tax Expense

+	−
FICA (employer's matching portion) State Unemployment Tax Federal Unemployment Tax	Closed at the end of the year along with all other expense accounts

As you can see, **FICA tax (employer's share), state unemployment tax, and federal unemployment tax are included under the umbrella of Payroll Tax Expense.** In most states, the unemployment taxes are levied on the employer only.

Employer's Matching Portion of FICA Tax (Social Security Plus Medicare)

The FICA tax is imposed on both employer and employee. The firm's accountant deducts the employee's share from gross wages and records it in the payroll entry under FICA Tax Payable (the same liability account as shown in Chapter 9). Next, he or she determines the employer's share by multiplying the employer's tax rates (assumed to be 6.2 percent for Social Security and 1.45 percent for Medicare) by the taxable earnings (assumed to be $60,600 for Social Security and total earnings for Medicare). The same tax rates apply to both the employer and the employees.

The accountant gets the Social Security and Medicare taxable earnings amounts from the payroll register. In Figure 10-1 we present the Taxable Earnings columns taken from the same payroll register shown in Chapter 9 for the week ended October 7.

Before we look at the journal entry to record the employer's share of FICA tax, let's look at the entry in T account form below.

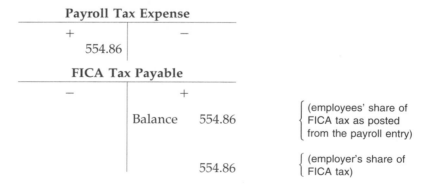

Payroll Tax Expense

+	−
554.86	

FICA Tax Payable

−	+	
	Balance 554.86	(employees' share of FICA tax as posted from the payroll entry)
	554.86	(employer's share of FICA tax)

Note particularly that **the FICA Tax Payable account is often used for the tax liability of both the employer and the employees.** This is logical because both FICA taxes are paid at the same time and the same place. There might be a slight difference between the employer's and the employees' share of FICA taxes, because of the rounding-off process. For the employees' share, the accountant uses the total of the employees' Social Security and Medicare tax deductions. For the employer's share, the accountant multiplies the total taxable earnings (Social Security and Medicare) by the tax rates.

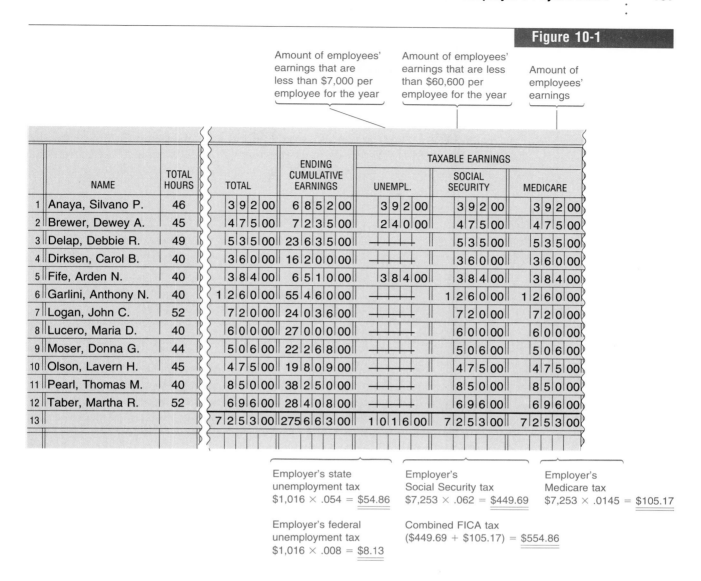

Figure 10-1

Amount of employees' earnings that are less than $7,000 per employee for the year

Amount of employees' earnings that are less than $60,600 per employee for the year

Amount of employees' earnings

	NAME	TOTAL HOURS		TOTAL	ENDING CUMULATIVE EARNINGS	TAXABLE EARNINGS		
						UNEMPL.	SOCIAL SECURITY	MEDICARE
1	Anaya, Silvano P.	46		392 00	6852 00	392 00	392 00	392 00
2	Brewer, Dewey A.	45		475 00	7235 00	240 00	475 00	475 00
3	Delap, Debbie R.	49		535 00	23635 00		535 00	535 00
4	Dirksen, Carol B.	40		360 00	16200 00		360 00	360 00
5	Fife, Arden N.	40		384 00	6510 00	384 00	384 00	384 00
6	Garlini, Anthony N.	40		1260 00	55460 00		1260 00	1260 00
7	Logan, John C.	52		720 00	24036 00		720 00	720 00
8	Lucero, Maria D.	40		600 00	27000 00		600 00	600 00
9	Moser, Donna G.	44		506 00	22268 00		506 00	506 00
10	Olson, Lavern H.	45		475 00	19809 00		475 00	475 00
11	Pearl, Thomas M.	40		850 00	38250 00		850 00	850 00
12	Taber, Martha R.	52		696 00	28408 00		696 00	696 00
13				7253 00	275663 00	1016 00	7253 00	7253 00

Employer's state unemployment tax
$1,016 × .054 = $54.86

Employer's Social Security tax
$7,253 × .062 = $449.69

Employer's Medicare tax
$7,253 × .0145 = $105.17

Employer's federal unemployment tax
$1,016 × .008 = $8.13

Combined FICA tax
($449.69 + $105.17) = $554.86

Employer's State Unemployment Tax (SUTA)

The employer's **state unemployment tax (SUTA)** is levied on the employer only in most states. The rate of the state unemployment tax varies considerably among the states. However, as we stated in Chapter 9, assume that Carson and Company is subject to a rate of 5.4 percent of the first $7,000 of each employee's earnings (same base amount as federal unemployment insurance). As shown in the portion of the payroll register illustrated in Figure 10-1, $1,016 of earnings are subject to the state unemployment tax. Accordingly, by T accounts, the state unemployment tax based on taxable earnings is as follows:

Payroll Tax Expense		State Unemployment Tax Payable	
+	−	−	+
(1,016 × .054) 54.86			(1,016 × .054) 54.86

Employer's Federal Unemployment Tax (FUTA)

The **federal unemployment tax (FUTA) is paid by the employer only.** Congress may from time to time change the rate. But for now, let's assume a rate of .8 percent (.008) of the first $7,000 earned by each employee during the calendar year. For the weekly payroll period for Carson and Company the tax liability is $8.13 ($1,016 of unemployment taxable earnings taken from the payroll register multiplied by .008, the tax rate). By T accounts, the entry is as follows:

Payroll Tax Expense		Federal Unemployment Tax Payable	
+		−	+
(1,016 × .008) 8.13			(1,016 × .008) 8.13

Journal Entry for Recording Payroll Tax Expense

Performance Objective 1

Calculate the amount of payroll tax expense and journalize the related entry.

R E M E M B E R

The sequence of steps for recording the payroll entries is: (1) record the payroll for the present period in the payroll register; (2) based on the payroll register, record the payroll entry in the journal; (3) based on the Taxable Earnings columns of the payroll register, record Payroll Tax Expense in the journal; (4) make a journal entry to pay the employees.

To make things clearer in the foregoing discussion, figures for the three employer's payroll taxes have been presented separately. Now let's combine this information into one entry, which follows the regular payroll entry. Carson and Company pays its employees weekly, so it also makes its Payroll Tax Expense entry weekly. The entry to record the employer's payroll taxes is journalized below.

	DATE		DESCRIPTION	POST. REF.	DEBIT	CREDIT	
17	Oct.	7	Payroll Tax Expense		6 1 7 85		17
18			FICA Tax Payable			5 5 4 86	18
19			State Unemployment Tax				19
20			Payable			5 4 86	20
21			Federal Unemployment Tax				21
22			Payable			8 13	22
23			To record employer's share				23
24			of FICA tax and employer's				24
25			state and federal				25
26			unemployment taxes.				26
27							27

Next, we will describe the entries for paying withholdings for employees' federal income tax and FICA tax and the employer's matching share of FICA tax. We will also show the entries paying the federal and state unemployment taxes as well as the withholdings for employees' state income tax.

Payments of FICA Tax and Employees' Federal Income Tax Withholding

After paying employees, the employer must make payments in the form of federal tax deposits. A deposit includes the combined total of three items: (1) employees' federal income taxes withheld, plus (2) employees' FICA taxes withheld, plus (3) employer's share of FICA taxes. These deposits put employers on a pay-as-you-go basis.

Deposits are made to authorized commercial banks or Federal Reserve banks. The deposits are forwarded to the U.S. Treasury. The timing of these deposits depends on the amounts owed. The calendar year is broken into days, semi-weekly periods, months, and **quarters** (3 consecutive months). The IRS will notify employers of their status before the beginning of each calendar year. Employers are divided into two major classes; they are either *monthly depositors* or *semi-weekly depositors*.

Monthly Depositor

An employer is a **monthly depositor** for a calendar year if the IRS has determined that the total amount of reported taxes for the four quarters in the lookback period is not more than $50,000. The **lookback period** is a measure of past tax liabilities used to determine the frequency of payment of present tax liabilities. The lookback period is the twelve-month period ending June 30 of the prior year.

Monthly depositors must deposit taxes accumulated on paydays during each month by the 15th day of the following month.

Semi-weekly Depositor

An employer is a **semi-weekly depositor** for a calendar year if the IRS has determined that the total amount of reported taxes for the four quarters in the lookback period is more than $50,000.

Semi-weekly depositors must deposit taxes accumulated on Wednesday, Thursday, and Friday paydays during each week by the following Wednesday, and deposit taxes accumulated on Saturday, Sunday, Monday, and Tuesday paydays during each week by the following Friday.

One-day Rule

The **one-day rule** requires that if an employer's accumulated tax is $100,000 or more on any day during a deposit period, either monthly or semi-weekly, the taxes must be deposited by the next banking day. If an employer has been a monthly depositor (has had less than $50,000 of undeposited taxes) and has hired more personnel, so that the undeposited taxes are now more than $50,000, the employer's status has changed. The employer now becomes a semi-weekly depositor for the remainder of the calendar year and for the next calendar year.

De Minimis Rule

The **de minimis rule** pertains to small employers whose undeposited taxes during the quarter (three-month period) are less than $500. The taxes must be deposited by the end of the following month or be mailed with their Form 941, described later in this chapter, due at the end of the month following the end of the quarter.

Cruise ship employees frequently receive their salaries in cash each week. But whether the payments are made in cash or by check, payroll records and reports must be kept.

Let's go back to Carson and Company, where taxes were previously paid up to date. Carson has been determined by the IRS to be a monthly depositor. Following are the totals for the October payrolls ending October 31:

Employee's federal income taxes withheld	$1,895.00
Employee's FICA tax withheld (Social Security and Medicare)	997.17
Employer's share of FICA tax (Social Security and Medicare)	997.17
Total undeposited federal taxes	$3,889.34

Carson and Company previously received a federal tax deposit card (pre-printed with the company's name and tax number) from the Internal Revenue Service. The accountant records the amount of the deposit and the name of the bank where the deposit is submitted (Figure 10-2).

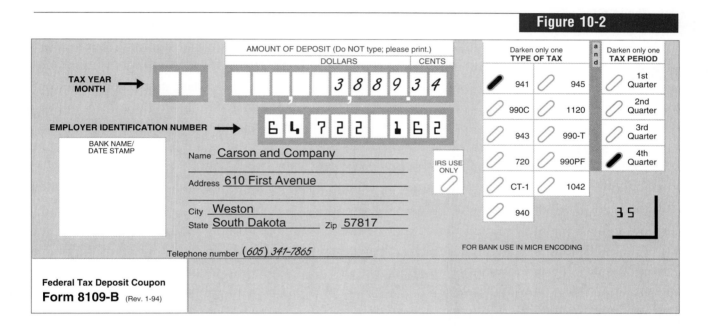

Figure 10-2

The entry in the general journal to record the deposit of accumulated FICA taxes and employees' federal income taxes looks like this:

	DATE	DESCRIPTION	POST. REF.	DEBIT	CREDIT	
1	19–					1
2	Nov. 30	Employees' Federal Income Tax				2
3		Payable		1 8 9 5 00		3
4		FICA Tax Payable		1 9 9 4 34		4
5		Cash			3 8 8 9 34	5
6		Issued check for federal tax				6
7		deposit.				7
8						8

Penalties for Failure to Deposit Federal Employment Taxes

If an employer fails to deposit Social Security, Medicare, and withheld income taxes on time with the appropriate financial institution or Federal Reserve bank, the employer may have to pay a penalty as well as being required to file monthly returns for these taxes in the future.

If employers do not withhold and collect federal employment taxes or withhold the taxes but do not pay them, employers may be subject to a penalty of 100 percent of the tax.

Penalties for a Late Tax Deposit of Federal Employment Taxes

The penalty for late deposit of federal employment taxes is based on the length of time the deposit is late. The following penalties apply for late deposits:

1. More than 1 day late but not more than 5 days late, the penalty is 2 percent of the underpayment.

2. More than 5 days late, but not more than 15 days late, the penalty is 5 percent of the underpayment.

3. More than 15 days late, the penalty is 10 percent of the underpayment.

4. If the deposit is not made within 10 days after the IRS issues the first notice demanding payment, the penalty is 15 percent of the underpayment.

Payments of State Unemployment Tax

As we stated previously, states differ with regard to both the rate and the taxable base for unemployment insurance. In our example, we have assumed the state tax is 5.4 percent of the first $7,000 paid to each employee during the calendar year. **The state tax is usually paid quarterly (every three months) and is due by the end of the month following the end of the quarter (same as the due dates for Form 941).** Here's the entry in general journal form made by Carson and Company for the first quarter (covering the months of January, February, and March). We will assume that $59,746 was taxable for the quarter. The amount of the tax is $3,226.28 ($59,746 × .054).

	DATE		DESCRIPTION	POST. REF.	DEBIT	CREDIT	
1	19–						1
2	Apr.	30	State Unemployment Tax Payable		3 2 2 6 28		2
3			Cash			3 2 2 6 28	3
4			Issued check for payment of				4
5			state unemployment tax.				5
6							6

The T accounts are as follows:

Cash				State Unemployment Tax Payable		
+	−		−		+	
	Apr. 30	3,226.28	Apr. 30	3,226.28	Mar. 31 Balance	3,226.28

The balance in State Unemployment Tax Payable is the result of weekly entries recording the state unemployment portion of payroll tax expense.

Payments of Federal Unemployment Tax

T he FUTA tax is calculated quarterly, during the month following the end of each calendar quarter. **If the accumulated tax liability is greater than an assumed $100, the tax is deposited in a commercial bank or Federal Reserve bank, accompanied by a preprinted federal tax deposit card,** like the form used to deposit employees' federal income tax withholding and FICA taxes. The due date for this deposit is the last day of the month following the end of the quarter, the same as the due dates for the Employer's Quarterly Federal Tax Return and for state unemployment taxes.

Here is the entry in general journal form made by Carson and Company for the first quarter. In our example, since the FUTA and state unemployment taxable earnings are the same (the first $7,000 for each employee), we will assume that $59,746 was taxable for the quarter. The amount of the tax is $477.97 ($59,746 × .008).

	DATE		DESCRIPTION	POST. REF.	DEBIT	CREDIT	
1	19–						1
2	Apr.	30	Federal Unemployment Tax				2
3			Payable		477 97		3
4			Cash			477 97	4
5			Issued check for deposit of				5
6			federal unemployment tax.				6
7							7

The T accounts are as follows:

Cash				Federal Unemployment Tax Payable		
+	−		−		+	
	Apr. 30	477.97	Apr. 30	477.97	Mar. 31 Balance	477.97

The balance in Federal Unemployment Tax Payable is the result of weekly entries recording the federal unemployment portion of payroll tax expense.

Deposits of Employees' State Income Tax Withholding

Performance Objective 4

Journalize the entry for the deposit of employees' state income taxes withheld.

Assume the withholdings for employees' state income tax are deposited on a quarterly basis, payable at the same time as state unemployment insurance. Also, as of March 31, the credit balance of Employees' State Income Tax Payable is $1,314.06. The entry in general journal form to record the payment for the first quarter looks like this:

	DATE		DESCRIPTION	POST. REF.	DEBIT	CREDIT	
1	19–						1
2	Apr.	30	Employees' State Income Tax				2
3			Payable		1 3 1 4 06		3
4			Cash			1 3 1 4 06	4
5			Issued check for state income				5
6			tax deposit.				6

The T accounts are as follows:

Cash		Employees' State Income Tax Payable	
+	–	–	+
	Apr. 30 1,314.06	Apr. 30 1,314.06	Mar. 31 Balance 1,314.06

Employer's Quarterly Federal Tax Return (Form 941)

Performance Objective 5

Complete Employer's Quarterly Federal Tax Return, Form 941.

The purpose of **Form 941** is to report the tax liability for withholdings of employees' federal income tax and FICA tax, as well as the employer's share of the FICA tax. Total tax deposits are also listed. As the title implies, the time period is a quarter, or three months. The due dates for filing Form 941, Employer's Quarterly Tax Return, are:

Quarter	Ending Date of Quarter	Due Date of Form 941
January-February-March	March 31	April 30
April-May-June	June 30	July 31
July-August-September	September 30	October 31
October-November-December	December 31	January 31

A completed Form 941 for Carson and Company is shown in Figure 10-3 on page 415. The form has three main sections, which may be completed in the order presented below. Bear in mind that the Internal Revenue Service has frequently changed the arrangement of and questions on Form 941.

Figure 10-3

Form **941**

Department of the Treasury
Internal Revenue Service   4141

Employer's Quarterly Federal Tax Return

▶ See Circular E for more information concerning employment tax returns.
Please type or print.

Your name, address, employer identification number, and calendar quarter of return. (If not correct, please change.)

Name (as distinguished from trade name)

Date quarter ended
December 31, 19—

Trade name, if any
Carson and Company

Employer identification number
64-7228162

Address and ZIP code
610 First Avenue
Weston, South Dakota 57817

OMB No. 1545-0029

T	
FF	
FD	
FP	
I	
T	

If address is different from prior return, check here ▶

IRS Use

1 1 1 1 1 1 1 1 1 1 1   2   3 3 3 3 3 3   4 4 4

5 5 5   6   7   8 8 8 8 8   9 9 9   10 10 10   10 10   10 10   10 10 10

If you do not have to file returns in the future, check here . . ▶ ☐   Date final wages paid . . . ▶

If you are a seasonal employer, see **Seasonal employers** on page 2 and check here . . ▶ ☐

1a	Number of employees (except household) employed in the pay period that includes March 12th . ▶	**1a**	*12*
b	If you are a subsidiary corporation AND your parent corporation files a consolidated Form 1120, enter parent corporation employer identification number (EIN) . . ▶ |**1b**| —		
2	Total wages and tips subject to withholding, plus other compensation . . . . ▶	**2**	*106,264 00*
3	Total income tax withheld from wages, tips, pensions, annuities, sick pay, gambling, etc. . . . ▶	**3**	*14,271 00*
4	Adjustment of withheld income tax for preceding quarters of calendar year (see instructions) . . ▶	**4**	
5	Adjusted total of income tax withheld (line 3 as adjusted by line 4—see instructions)	**5**	*14,271 00*
6a	Taxable social security wages (**Complete line 7**) $ *86,174 00* x 12.4% (.124) =	**6a**	*10,685 58*
b	Taxable social security tips $ x 12.4% (.124) =	**6b**	
7	Taxable Medicare wages and tips . . . . . $ *92,727 00* x 2.9% (.029) =	**7**	*2,689 08*
8	Total social security and Medicare taxes (add lines 6a, 6b, and 7)	**8**	*13,374 66*
9	Adjustment of social security and Medicare taxes (see instructions for required explanation) . . .	**9**	
10	Adjusted total of social security and Medicare taxes (line 8 as adjusted by line 9—see instructions) ▶	**10**	*13,374 66*
11	Backup withholding (see instructions).	**11**	
12	Adjustment of backup withholding tax for preceding quarters of calendar year . . . . ▶	**12**	
13	Adjusted total of backup withholding (line 11 as adjusted by line 12)	**13**	
14	**Total taxes** (add lines 5, 10, and 13)	**14**	*27,645 66*
15	Advanced earned income credit (EIC) payments made to employees, if any . . . . ▶	**15**	
16	Net taxes (subtract line 15 from line 14). **This should equal line IV below** (plus line IV of Schedule A (Form 941) if you have treated backup withholding as a separate liability)	**16**	*27,645 66*
17	**Total deposits for quarter,** including overpayment applied from a prior quarter, from your records. ▶	**17**	*27,645 66*
18	**Balance due** (subtract line 17 from line 16). This should be less than $500. Pay to IRS . . . . ▶	**18**	*0*

19 Overpayment, if line 17 is more than line 16, enter here ▶ $ _____ and check if to be:
☐ Applied to next return   **OR**   ☐ Refunded.

Record of Federal Tax Liability (You must complete if line 16 is $500 or more and Schedule B is not attached.) See instructions before checking these boxes.
Check only if you made deposits using the 95% rule ▶ ☐   Check only if you are a first time 3-banking-day depositor. . . . . . ▶ ☐

Show tax liability here, **not deposits.** IRS gets deposit data from FTD coupons.

Date wages paid		First month of quarter		Second month of quarter		Third month of quarter
1st through 3rd	A		I		Q	*2,238.70*
4th through 7th	B	*1,859.49*	J	*2,119.14*	R	
8th through 11th	C		K	*2,204.39*	S	*2,240.16*
12th through 15th	D	*2,029.86*	L		T	
16th through 19th	E		M	*2,296.47*	U	*2,218.75*
20th through 22nd	F	*2,113.10*	N		V	
23rd through 25th	G		O	*2,251.99*	W	*2,036.02*
26th through the last	H	*2,162.45*	P		X	*1,875.14*
Total liability for month	I	*8,164.90*	II	*8,871.99*	III	*10,608.77*

Do NOT Show Federal Tax Deposits Here

▶ **IV** Total for quarter (add lines **I, II,** and **III**). **This should equal line 16 above** . . . . ▶

Sign Here   Under penalties of perjury, I declare that I have examined this return, including accompanying schedules and statements, and to the best of my knowledge and belief, it is true, correct, and complete.

Signature ▶ *Sandra C. Carson*   Print Your Name and Title ▶ *Sandra C. Carson*   *Owner*   Date ▶ *Jan. 31, 19—*

For Paperwork Reduction Act Notice, see page 2.

FYI

If you have worked, it is wise to check contributions made to your own Social Security account. The Social Security Administration office near you will provide you with a form to request a printout of your quarters of contributions. It is important to be sure that errors were not made and that employers did make the contributions. It is interesting to find out whether firms going out of business used their accumulated payroll tax monies to pay other creditors or followed the law and made all of your and their contributions.

Heading

Once an employer has secured an identification number and has filed her or his first return, the Internal Revenue Service sends forms directly to the employer. These forms have the employer's name, address, and identification number filled in.

Record of Federal Tax Liability

For each payroll period, list the combined total of employees' federal income and FICA taxes withheld and employer's share of FICA. Carson and Company pays the full amount due rather than using the 95 percent rule, so the box is not checked. Carson and Company pays wages every week, resulting in thirteen paydays during the three-month period, as follows: October 7, 14, 21, 28, November 4, 11, 18, 25, December 2, 9, 16, 23, 30.

Questions Listed on Form 941

Read each question line by line.

1. Total number of employees during first quarter.

2. Total wages and tips subject to federal tax withholding.

3. Total federal income tax withheld—shown as credits in the Employees' Federal Income Tax Payable account.

4. Adjustments of federal income tax withheld—used to record corrections in income tax withheld in earlier quarters of the same calendar year.

6. a. Taxable Social Security wages paid—total of the Social Security Taxable Earnings listed in the payroll register for the three-month quarter; 12.4 percent equals the employees' 6.2 percent plus the employer's 6.2 percent.

   b. Taxable Social Security tips—refers to customer tips reported by employees; the employer withholds 6.2 percent.

7. Taxable Medicare wages and tips—total of the Medicare Taxable Earnings listed in the payroll register for the three-month quarter; 2.9 percent equals the employees' 1.45 percent plus the employer's 1.45 percent.

8. Total Social Security and Medicare taxes—shown as credits in the FICA Tax Payable account.

9. Adjustment of Social Security and Medicare taxes—used to record corrections in Social Security taxes reported on earlier returns.

11. Backup withholding—applies to payers (not employers) of interest, and dividends to recipients who have not given their Social Security numbers.

15. Advance earned income credit payments—pertains to payments made in advance to qualified employees for earned income credit. To be eligible for this credit, the filing status must be married filing a joint return, qualifying widow(er) with a dependent child, or head of household. Other requirements are having a child living in the home, having a twelve-month tax year, and earnings less than $21,245.

16. Net taxes—equals the total federal tax liability for the quarter (same amount as the total of the Record of Federal Tax Liability section).

17. Total deposits for quarter—total of the debits to the Employees' Federal Income Tax Payable and the FICA Tax Payable accounts for the three-month quarter.

Wage Withholding Statements for Employees (Forms W-2)

After the end of a year (December 31) and by the following January 31, the employer must furnish for each employee a Wage and Tax Statement known as **Form W-2.** This form contains information about the employee's earnings and tax deductions for the year. The source of information for completing Form W-2 is the employee's individual earnings record. John C. Logan's earnings record with his earnings up to October 7 was presented in Chapter 9 on page 390. The amounts used to complete Logan's W-2 form (in Figure 10-4) represent the amounts taken from his earnings record at the end of the calendar year, December 31.

Performance Objective 6

Prepare W-2 and W-3 forms and Form 940.

Figure 10-4

1 Control number	22222	For Official Use Only ▶ OMB No. 1545-0008								
2 Employer's name, address, and ZIP code		6 Statutory employee ☐ Deceased ☐ Pension plan ☐ Legal rep. ☐ 942 emp. ☐ Subtotal ☐ Deferred compensation ☐ Void ☐								

2 Employer's name, address, and ZIP code
Carson and Company
610 First Avenue
Weston, South Dakota 57817

7 Allocated tips — *0*
8 Advance EIC payment — *0*
9 Federal income tax withheld — *$3,642*
10 Wages, tips, other compensation — *$32,294*

3 Employer's identification number — *64-7228162*
4 Employer's state I.D. number — *464-729*
11 Social security tax withheld — *$2,002.23*
12 Social security wages — *$32,294*

5 Employee's social security number — *543-24-1680*
13 Social security tips — *0*
14 Medicare wages and tips — *$32,294*

19a Employee's name (first, middle, last)
John Charles Logan
6242 Baxter Drive
Weston, South Dakota 57817

15 Medicare tax withheld — *$468.26*
16 Nonqualified plans — *0*
17 See Instrs. for Form W-2
18 Other — *0*

19b Employee's address and ZIP code

20
21
22 Dependent care benefits — *0*
23 Benefits included in Box 10 — *0*

24 State income tax — *$728.40*
25 State wages, tips, etc. — *$32,294*
26 Name of state — *So. Dakota*
27 Local income tax — *0*
28 Local wages, tips, etc. — *0*
29 Name of locality — *0*

Copy A For Social Security Administration

Department of the Treasury—Internal Revenue Service

Form **W-2 Wage and Tax Statement**

Notice the squares in block 6. Satutory employees are life insurance and traveling salespersons; legal representatives include attorneys and parents; 942 employees include household workers; subtotal is used if the employer is submitting more than forty-one W-2 forms. Block 8 shows the total paid to employees as advance earned income credit (EIC) payments. For qualifying low-income taxpayers, the earned income credit is a deduction from income tax owed. Block 17 is used for miscellaneous items, such as sick pay not included in income, because the employee contributed to the sick pay plan. This block is also used for employer-provided group term life insurance of over $50,000. Block 18 may include the value of noncash fringe benefits, such as providing a vehicle for the employee.

The accountant will prepare at least four copies of W-2 forms for each employee.

Copy A—Employer sends to the Social Security Administration.

Copy B—Employer gives to employee to be attached to the employee's individual federal income tax return.

Copy C—Employer gives to employee to be kept for his or her personal records.

Copy D—Employer keeps this copy as a record of payments made.

If state and local income taxes are withheld, the employer prepares additional copies to be sent to the appropriate tax agency.

Employer's Annual Federal Income Tax Reports (Forms W-3)

Accompanying copy A of the employees' W-2 forms, Carson and Company sends **Form W-3,** Transmittal of Income and Tax Statements, to the Social Security Administration. This form is due on February 28, following the end of the calendar year.

For all employees, Form W-3 shows the total wages and tips, total federal income tax withheld, total FICA taxable wages, total FICA tax withheld, and other information. These amounts must be the same as the grand totals of the W-2 forms and the four quarterly 941 forms for the year. Carson and Company's completed Form W-3 is presented in Figure 10-5.

To sum up thus far: the employer must submit the following at the end of the calendar year: Employer's Quarterly Federal Tax Return, Form 941, for the fourth quarter by January 31; Wage and Tax Statments, Form W-2, for all employees by January 31; Transmittal of Income and Tax Statements, Form W-3, by February 28.

Some boxes deserve an explanation. Box 6, establishment number, may be used for a company that has separate establishments, and each establishment may file W-2 and W-3 forms separately. Box 8 is used for recording the amount of advance earned income credits shown on W-2 forms for qualified employees. Box 19 is used by a company that had more than one employer identification number (EIN) during the year.

FYI

The W-2 and W-3 forms, for example, are supplied in scored sheets that can be typed or can be run on printers linked to computers.

Figure 10-5

DO NOT STAPLE

1 Control number		

33333

For Official Use Only ▶
OMB No. 1545-0008

☐ Kind of Payer	▶	2 941/941E ☒ Military ☐ 943 ☐	3 Employer's state I.D. number *464-729*	5 Total number of statements
		CT-1 ☐ 942 ☐ Medicare govt. emp. ☐	4	*12*

6 Establishment number	7 Allocated tips *0*	8 Advance EIC payments *0*
9 Federal income tax withheld *$39,746*	10 Wages, tips, and other compensation *$361,424*	11 Social security tax withheld *$21,980.24*
12 Social security wages *$354,520*	13 Social security tips *0*	14 Medicare wages and tips *$361,424*
15 Medicare tax withheld *$5,240.65*	16 Nonqualified plans *0*	17 Deferred compensation *0*

18 Employer's identification number *64—7228162*	19 Other EIN used this year *0*
20 Employer's name *Carson and Company* *610 First Avenue* *Weston, South Dakota 57817*	21 Dependent care benefits *0*
	23 Adjusted total social security wages and tips *$354,520*
	24 Adjusted total Medicare wages and tips *$371,424*
	25 Income tax withheld by third-party payer *0*
22 Employer's address and ZIP code (If available, place label over Boxes 18 and 20.)	

Under penalties of perjury, I declare that I have examined this return and accompanying documents, and, to the best of my knowledge and belief, they are true, correct, and complete.

Signature ▶ *Sandra C. Carson*   Title ▶ *Owner*   Date ▶ *2/27/—*

Telephone number (optional) _____

Form **W-3** **Transmittal of Income and Tax Statements**

Department of the Treasury
Internal Revenue Service

Reports and Payments of Federal Unemployment Taxes

A s we stated previously, generally all employers are subject to the Federal Unemployment Tax Act. These employers must submit an Employer's Annual Federal Unemployment Tax Return, Form 940, not later than January 31 following the close of the calendar year. This deadline may be extended until February 10 if the employer has made deposits paying the FUTA tax liability in full. **Form 940** shows total wages paid to employees, total wages subject to federal unemployment tax, and other information.

R E M E M B E R

If the accumulated FUTA tax liability at the end of a quarter is greater than $100, a deposit must be made.

Using Carson and Company as our example, federal unemployment taxable earnings by quarter are as follows:

Federal Unemployment Tax	1st Quarter	2nd Quarter	3rd Quarter	4th Quarter	Cumulative Total
Taxable earnings	$59,746	$9,373	$14,514	$ 367	$84,000
Tax rate	× .008	× .008	× .008	× .008	× .008
Tax liability	$477.97	$74.98	$116.11	$ 2.94	$672.00

During the second quarter, many employees' total earnings had passed the $7,000 limit of taxable earnings, and the firm's tax liability was reduced accordingly. Since Carson's total accumulated liability ($74.98) was less than $100, a deposit was not made covering that quarter. However, due to an expansion of the company, three new employees were hired during the middle of the quarter.

For the third quarter, the tax liability amounted to $116.11. The total cumulative tax liability was now $191.09 ($74.98 second quarter plus $116.11 third quarter). Consequently, $191.09 was deposited on October 31.

By the end of the fourth quarter, each of the twelve employees' earnings has passed the $7,000 mark. The total liability for the quarter is $2.94. This amount will be paid by January 31, accompanied by the completed Employer's Annual Federal Unemployment Tax Return, Form 940.

The T account for Federal Unemployment Tax Payable is presented below. The credits to the account were part of the entries recording the federal unemployment tax portion of Payroll Tax Expense for each payroll period (like the entry on page 408).

Federal Unemployment Tax Payable

−		+	
April 30 deposit	477.97	1st quarter (liability)	477.97
Oct. 31 deposit	191.09	2nd quarter (liability)	74.98
		3rd quarter (liability)	116.11
Jan. 31 deposit	2.94	4th quarter (liability)	2.94

Employer's Annual Federal Unemployment (FUTA) Tax Return (Form 940)

Figure 10-6 on the next page shows a completed Form 940 for Carson and Company. Referring to the form, we are concerned with three sections. Bear in mind that this form has been changed from time to time.

Part I Line 1 Record total wages paid.

Line 2 Record certain other exempt wages—includes such items as agricultural labor, family employment, value of meals and lodging.

Line 3 Record exempt wages paid—wages paid to each employee over and above $7,000 for the calendar year.

Figure 10-6

Form **940**	Employer's Annual Federal Unemployment (FUTA) Tax Return	OMB No. 1545-0028

Department of the Treasury
Internal Revenue Service

▶ For Paperwork Reduction Act Notice, see page 2.

	T	
Name (as distinguished from trade name)	FF	
Calendar year 19—	FD	
	FP	
	I	
	T	

If incorrect, make any necessary change. ▶

Name (as distinguished from trade name)

Trade name, if any
Carson and Company

Address and ZIP code
610 First Avenue
Weston, South Dakota 57817

Calendar year
19—

Employer identification number
64-7228162

A Did you pay all required contributions to state unemployment funds by the due date of Form 940? (See instructions if none required.) ☒ **Yes** ☐ **No**

If you checked the "Yes" box, enter the amount of contributions paid to state unemployment funds ▶ *84,536.00*

B Are you required to pay contributions to only one state? ☒ **Yes** ☐ **No**

If you checked the "Yes" box: (1) Enter the name of the state where you are required to pay contributions ▶ *South Dakota*

(2) Enter your state reporting number(s) as shown on state unemployment tax return. ▶ *473-627*

C If any part of wages taxable for FUTA tax is exempt from state unemployment tax, check the box. (See the Specific Instructions on page 4.) ☐

Note: If you checked the "Yes" boxes in both questions A and B and did not check the box in C above, you may be able to use Form 940-EZ.

If you will not have to file returns in the future, write "Final" here (see general instruction "Who Must File") and sign the return. ▶

Part I   Computation of Taxable Wages (to be completed by all taxpayers)

			Amount paid		
1	Total payments (including exempt payments) during the calendar year for services of employees			1	*361,424* 00
2	Exempt payments. (Explain each exemption shown, attaching additional sheets if necessary.) ▶ _____			2	
3	Payments for services of more than $7,000. Enter only the excess over the first $7,000 paid to individual employees not including exempt amounts shown on line 2. Do not use the state wage limitation		3 *277,424* 00		
4	Total exempt payments (add lines 2 and 3)			4	*277,424* 00
5	**Total taxable wages** (subtract line 4 from line 1). (If any part is exempt from state contributions, see instructions.) ▶			5	*84,000* 00

Part II   Tax Due or Refund (Complete if you checked the "Yes" boxes in both questions A and B and did not check the box in C above.)

1	**Total FUTA tax.** Multiply the wages in Part I, line 5, by .008 and enter here	1	*672* 00
2	Total FUTA tax deposited for the year, including any overpayment applied from a prior year (from your records)	2	*669* 06
3	**Balance due** (subtract line 2 from line 1). This should be $100 or less. Pay to IRS. ▶	3	*2* 94
4	**Overpayment** (subtract line 1 from line 2). Check if it is to be: ☐ Applied to next return, or ☐ Refunded ▶	4	

Part III   Tax Due or Refund (Complete if you checked the "No" box in either question A or B or you checked the box in C above. Also complete Part V.)

1	Gross FUTA tax. Multiply the wages in Part 1, line 5, by .062	1	
2	Maximum credit. Multiply the wages in Part 1, line 5, by .054	2	
3	Credit allowable: Enter the smaller of the amount in Part V, line 11, or Part III, line 2	3	
4	Total FUTA tax (subtract line 3 from line 1)	4	
5	Total FUTA tax deposited for the year, including any overpayment applied from a prior year (from your records)	5	
6	**Balance due** (subtract line 5 from line 4). This should be $100 or less. Pay to IRS. ▶	6	
7	**Overpayment** (subtract line 4 from line 5). Check if it is to be: ☐ Applied to next return, or ☐ Refunded ▶	7	

Part IV   Record of Quarterly Federal Tax Liability for Unemployment Tax (Do not include state liability.)

Quarter	First	Second	Third	Fourth	Total for Year
Liability for quarter	*477.97*	*74.98*	*116.11*	*2.94*	*672.00*

Part V   Computation of Tentative Credit (Complete if you checked the "No" box in either question A or B or you checked the box in C above—see instructions.)

Name of state 1	State reporting number(s) as shown on employer's state contribution returns 2	Taxable payroll (as defined in state act) 3	State experience rate period 4 From—	To—	State experience rate 5	Contributions if rate had been 5.4% (col. 3 x .054) 6	Contributions payable at experience rate (col. 3 x col. 5) 7	Additional credit (col. 6 minus col. 7) if 0 or less, enter 0. 8	Contributions actually paid to the state 9
		84,000	*Jan. 1*	*Dec. 31*	*5.4*	*4,536*	*4,536*	*0*	*4,536*
10 Totals ▶		*84,000*						*0*	*4,536*

11 Total tentative credit (add line 10, columns 8 and 9 only—see instructions for limitations) ▶ *4,536* 00

Under penalties of perjury, I declare that I have examined this return, including accompanying schedules and statements, and to the best of my knowledge and belief, if it is true, correct, and complete, and that no part of any payment made to a state unemployment fund claimed as a credit was or is to be deducted from the payments to employees.

Signature ▶ *Sandra C. Carson*   Title (Owner, etc.) ▶ *Owner*   Date ▶ *1/31/—*

Form **940** (1990)

Line 5 Record the difference between total wages paid and exempt wages, which amount to the taxable wages (earnings).

Part II Line 1 Multiply taxable wages by .008 to determine amount of tax owed.

Line 2 Record the total amount of deposits made during the year—shown as debits in the Federal Unemployment Tax Payable account. As we stated previously, when the amount exceeds $100 at the end of any calendar quarter, the money must be deposited in an authorized financial institution (same as banks use for federal income and FICA taxes).

Line 3 Balance due—credit balance in Federal Unemployment Tax Payable account as of December 31.

Part IV Record the tax liability for each quarter—total credits in the Federal Unemployment Tax Payable account for each three-month period.

Performance Objective 7

Calculate the premium for workers' compensation insurance, and prepare the entry for payment in advance.

· · · · · · · · · · · · · ·
R E M E M B E R

Workers' compensation for the year is first estimated based on the anticipated year's payroll; debit Prepaid Insurance, Workers' Compensation, and credit Cash.

At the end of the year, when the actual payroll is known, the exact insurance premium is calculated; debit Workers' Compensation Insurance Expense and credit Prepaid Insurance, Workers' Compensation, for the amount paid at the beginning of the year.

If the amount of the actual payroll is greater than the estimated payroll, debit Workers' Compensation Insurance Expense and credit Workers' Compensation Insurance Payable for the difference between the actual premium and the estimated premium.
· · · · · · · · · · · · · ·

Workers' Compensation Insurance

Most states require employers to provide **workers' compensation insurance** or industrial accident insurance, either through plans administered by the state or through private insurance companies authorized by the state. The employer usually has to pay all the premiums. The premium rate varies with the amount of risk the job entails and the company's number of accidents. For example, handling molten steel ingots is much more dangerous than typing reports. Thus, it is very important that employees be identified properly according to the insurance premium classifications. For example, the rates as percentages of the payroll may be .15 percent for office work, .5 percent for sales work, and 3.5 percent for industrial labor in heavy manufacturing. These same rates may be expressed as $.15 per $100 of the salaries or wages for office work, $.50 per $100 for sales work, and $3.50 per $100 for industrial labor.

Generally, the employer pays a premium in advance, based on the estimated payrolls for the year. After the year ends, the employer knows the exact amounts of the payrolls and can calculate the exact premium. At this time, depending on the difference between the estimated and the exact premium, the employer either pays an additional premium or gets a credit for overpayment.

At Carson and Company, there are two types of work classifications: office work and sales work. At the beginning of the year, the firm's accountant computed the estimated annual premium, based on the predicted payrolls for the year, as follows:

Classification	Predicted Payroll	Rate (Percent)	Estimated Premium
Office work	$ 76,000	.15	$ 76,000 × .0015 = $ 114
Sales work	270,000	.50	270,000 × .0050 = 1,350
			Total estimated premium $1,464

As shown by T accounts, the accountant made the following entry.

Prepaid Insurance, Workers' Compensation		Cash	
+	−	+	−
Jan. 10 1,464.00			Jan. 10 1,464.00

Then, at the end of the calendar year, the accountant calculated the exact premium.

FYI

Workers' compensation laws protect employees and their dependents against losses due to death or injury incurred on the job. Some states require only the employer to pay and others require the employee to contribute also.

Classification	Exact Payroll	Rate (Percent)	Exact Premium	
Office work	$ 78,000	.15	$ 78,000 × .0015 = $ 117.00	
Sales work	283,424	.50	283,424 × .0050 = 1,417.12	
			Total exact premium	$1,534.12

Therefore, the amount of the unpaid premium is

$1,534.12	Total exact premium
1,464.00	Less total estimated premium paid
$ 70.12	Additional premium owed

Now the accountant makes an adjusting entry, similar to the adjusting entry for expired insurance; this entry appears on the work sheet. The accountant then makes an additional adjusting entry for the extra premium owed. By T accounts, the entries are as follows:

Performance Objective 8

Determine the amount of adjustment for workers' compensation insurance at the end of the year, and record the adjustment.

Prepaid Insurance, Workers' Compensation		Workers' Compensation Insurance Payable	
+	−	−	+
Jan. 10 Bal. 1,464.00	Dec. 31 Adj. 1,464.00		Dec. 31 Adj. 70.12

Workers' Compensation Insurance Expense	
+	−
Dec. 31 Adj. 1,464.00	
Dec. 31 Adj. 70.12	

Carson and Company will pay $70.12, the amount of unpaid premium, in January, together with the estimated premium for the next year.

Adjusting for Accrued Salaries and Wages

ssume that $800 of salaries accrue or build up for the time between the last payday and the end of the year. The adjusting entry is the same as that introduced in Chapter 4.

	DATE		DESCRIPTION	POST. REF.	DEBIT	CREDIT	
21			Adjusting Entry				21
22	Dec.	31	Salary Expense		8 0 0 00		22
23			Salaries Payable			8 0 0 00	23
24							24

Salaries Payable is considered a liability account, as are employees' withholding taxes and deductions payable. However, federal income tax and FICA tax levied on employees do not legally become effective until the employees are paid. Therefore, for the purpose of recording the adjusting entry, one includes the entire liability of the gross salaries and wages under Salaries Payable or Wages Payable. In other words, in the adjusting entry, such accounts as Employees' Income Tax Payable, FICA Tax Payable (employees' share), and Employees' Union Dues Payable, are not used.

Adjusting Entry for Accrual of Payroll Taxes

As we have seen, the following taxes come under the umbrella of the Payroll Tax Expense account: the employer's share of the FICA tax, the state unemployment tax, and the federal unemployment tax. The employer becomes liable for these taxes only when the employees are actually paid, rather than at the time the liability to the employees is incurred. From the standpoint of legal liability, there should be no adjusting entry for Payroll Tax Expense. From the standpoint of the income statement, however, failure to make this entry means that this accrued expense for payroll taxes is not included; thus the expenses are understated and the net income is overstated. The difference would be a rather inconsequential amount. Although the legal element is not consistent with good accounting practice, we have to abide by the law.

Computer Applications

ayroll software packages or modules related to general ledger packages do more than produce a payroll register, individual employee's earnings records, and checks. These packages can also generate information for 940 and 941 forms, W-2 forms, and a variety of personnel reports to assist management in analyzing its workforce.

PC Payroll Power

A number of software packages on the market offer a wealth of payroll capabilities. A few of the top programs include *QuickPay* 3.0 for DOS and Windows by Intuit, *M.Y.O.B.* 4.0 by Best!Ware, *One-Write Plus* 4.0 by Safeguard, *CA-Simply Accounting* for Windows and OS/2, *CA-BPI Accounting II* 4.0, and *ACCPAC Plus Accounting* 6.1 by Computer Associates.

Some, such as Intuit's QuickPay, focus on the most common payroll tasks and aim to do them faster and easier than anyone. Other programs strive to be comprehensive.

Accountants are likely to recommend, and owners are likely to feel comfortable with, systems they already know. *Quicken* and *QuickBooks* users can upgrade to QuickPay, *One-Write* users to One-Write Plus, and Simply Accounting users to one of CA's more powerful packages.

To find the best product for you, call the manufacturer and request product literature and a demo copy, if possible. As you examine the program, here are some questions to consider.

• How comfortable are you with accounting concepts? Do you prefer ease of use or power? (Despite claims to the contrary, most programs emphasize one or the other.)

• Does the software have any limitations, such as the number of departments, number of pay rates and categories, or number of time cards and time card entries per employee?

• Does your company have different types of pay rates (salaried, hourly, overtime)? Does it operate in multiple jurisdictions? Work in a specialized industry? (A program must take these variables into account.)

• Is your payroll situation simple, or do you offer a buffet of pay and benefit options? If not, will you provide more options in the future? Will your software "grow" with you?

• Will you run payroll on a single PC, tying it up periodically? Or on a network? Are you concerned about security and confidentiality issues?

• What payroll reports do you need? Do you want to do what-if analyses of your payroll? Does the program give you enough command over your data?

• What are the hidden costs of the payroll package: tax table updates, software upgrades, phone support, checks, forms, envelopes, even the ink in the printer?

Don't ignore the setup and maintenance time, either. When you're evaluating payroll software vs. a service bureau, be sure you're comparing apples to apples.

Source: Excerpted from *PC Today*, March 1994, p. 36.

Figure 10-7 on page 426 is an example of a report generated by a commercial software package to assist in completion of the 941 form. Notice that the report even suggests the location of the boxes on the forms where amounts are to be placed. As always, the accuracy of the numbers is more important than how good the printout looks. It is wise to run the manual payroll side by side with the computerized payroll until the employer is confident enough to run the payroll by computer only.

Figure 10-7

```
                          Harris Inc.
                        2020 South 400th
                        Seattle, WA  98003

                          941 Report

                          2nd Quarter
                                                              Page 1

                    Total Federal Wages and Tips (Box 2):     $3,125.00
                    Total Federal Tax Withheld (Box 3, 5):      $479.37

Total Social Security Wages (Box 6a):     $3,125.00  *  12.40%=   $387.50
  Total Social Security Tips (Box 6b):        $0.00  *  12.40%=     $0.00
Total Medicare Wages and Tips (Box 7):    $3,125.00  *   2.90%=    $90.63

        Total Social Security and Medicare Tax (Box 8):      $478.13

             Total Taxes Excluding Adjustments:             $957.50

                 Advanced Earned Income Credit:               $0.00

             Net Taxes Excluding Adjustments:               $957.50
```

CHAPTER REVIEW

R eview of Performance Objectives

1. **Calculate the amount of payroll tax expense and journalize the related entry.**

   Payroll tax expense consists of the employer's matching portion of FICA taxes, plus the state unemployment tax, plus the federal unemployment tax. The *FICA tax* consists of Social Security and Medicare taxes. *Social Security tax* equals total Social Security taxable earnings multiplied by .062 (6.2 percent assumed rate). Total *Medicare tax* equals earnings multiplied by .0145 (1.45 percent assumed rate). *State unemployment tax* equals unemployment taxable earnings multiplied by .054 (5.4 percent assumed rate). *Federal unemployment tax* equals unemployment taxable earnings multiplied by .008 (.8 percent assumed rate).

2. **Journalize the entry for the deposit of employees' federal income taxes withheld and FICA taxes (both employees' withheld and employer's matching share).**

   Payment of the combined amounts of employees' federal income tax withheld, employees' FICA tax withheld, and employer's FICA tax falls into two major brackets:

   a. **Monthly depositor** An employer who, during the lookback period (that is, the twelve months prior to June 30 of the prior year), did not report taxes of more than $50,000 must deposit taxes accumulated on paydays during each month by the 15th day of the following month.

   b. **Semi-weekly depositor** An employer who, during the lookback period (that is, the twelve months prior to June 30 of the prior year), reported taxes of more than $50,000 must deposit taxes accumulated on paydays during each month as follows:

1. Taxes accumulated on Wednesday, Thursday, and Friday paydays during each week are to be paid by the following Wednesday.
2. Taxes accumulated on Saturday, Sunday, Monday, and Tuesday paydays during each week are to be paid by the following Friday.

3. **Journalize the entries for the payment of employer's state and federal unemployment taxes.**

   State unemployment tax is paid on a quarterly basis. Payment is due by the end of the next month following the end of the calendar quarter.

   If the amount of the accumulated federal unemployment tax liability exceeds $100, pay the tax by the end of the next month following the end of the quarter. If the federal unemployment tax payable is less than $100 at the end of the year, pay it by January 31 of the next year.

4. **Journalize the entry for the deposit of employees' state income taxes withheld.**

   Employees' state income taxes withheld are paid on a quarterly basis. Payment is due by the end of the next month following the end of the calendar quarter.

5. **Complete Employer's Quarterly Federal Tax Return, Form 941.**

   Form 941 is illustrated on page 415.

6. **Prepare W-2 and W-3 forms and Form 940.**

   W-2 form (Wage and Tax Statement) is illustrated on page 417. W-3 form (Transmittal of Income and Tax Statements) is illustrated on page 419. Form 940 is illustrated on page 421.

7. **Calculate the premium for workers' compensation insurance, and prepare the entry for payment in advance.**

   Rates vary depending on the degree of physical risk involved in different occupations. The amount of the premium equals the predicted annual payroll multiplied by the premium rate. The entry is a debit to Prepaid Insurance, Workers' Compensation and a credit to Cash.

8. **Determine the amount of adjustment for workers' compensation insurance at the end of the year, and record the adjustment.**

   When the total annual payroll is known, the exact cost of workers' compensation insurance can be determined by multiplying the total payroll by the premium rate. Two adjusting entries are required. The first adjusting entry records the expired insurance as a debit to Workers' Compensation Insurance Expense and a credit to Prepaid Insurance, Workers' Compensation. The second adjusting entry records the difference between the estimated and the actual premiums. If the actual premium is greater than the premium that was paid in advance, the entry is a debit to Workers' Compensation Insurance Expense and a credit to Workers' Compensation Insurance Payable.

 **lossary**

De minimis rule A rule requiring an employer whose accumulated taxes are less than $500 during the quarter to deposit the taxes by the end of the following month or mail them with Form 941. **(410)**

Employer identification number The number assigned to each employer by the Internal Revenue Service for use in the submission of reports and payments of FICA taxes and federal income tax withheld. **(405)**

Federal unemployment tax (FUTA) A tax levied on the employer only, amounting to .8 percent of the first $7,000 of total earnings paid to each employee during the calendar year. This tax is used to supplement state unemployment benefits. **(408)**

Form 940 An annual report filed by employers showing total wages paid to employees, total wages subject to federal unemployment tax, total federal unemployment tax, and other information. Also called the *Employer's Annual Federal Unemployment Tax Return.* **(419)**

Form 941 A report showing the tax liability for withholdings of employees' federal income tax and FICA tax, as well as the employer's share of FICA tax. Total tax deposits made in the quarter are also listed on this *Employer's Quarterly Federal Tax Return.* **(414)**

Form W-2 A form containing information about employee earnings and tax deductions for the year. Also called *Wage and Tax Statement.* **(417)**

Form W-3 An annual report sent to the Social Security Administration listing total wages and tips, total federal income tax withheld, total FICA taxable wages, total FICA tax withheld, and other information for all employees of a firm. Also called the *Transmittal of Income and Tax Statements.* **(418)**

Lookback period A period of twelve months prior to June 30 of the prior year used to determine when and how often employers must pay accumulated federal employment taxes. **(409)**

Monthly depositor An employer whose total amount of reported taxes for the four quarters of the lookback period is not more than $50,000. Accumulated taxes must be deposited by the 15th day of the following month. **(409)**

One-day rule A rule requiring an employer whose accumulated taxes are $100,000 or more on any day during a deposit period, either monthly or semi-weekly, to deposit the taxes the next banking day. **(410)**

Payroll Tax Expense A general expense account used for recording the employer's matching portion of the FICA tax, the federal unemployment tax, and the state unemployment tax. **(405)**

Quarter A three-month interval of the year, also referred to as a calendar quarter, as follows: first quarter, January, February, and March; second quarter, April, May, and June; third quarter, July, August, and September; fourth quarter, October, November, and December. **(409)**

Semi-weekly depositor An employer whose total amount of reported taxes for the four quarters of the lookback period is more than $50,000. Taxes accumulated on Wednesday, Thursday, and Friday paydays during each week must be deposited by the following Wednesday, and taxes accumulated on Saturday, Sunday, Monday, and Tuesday paydays during each week must be deposited by the following Friday. **(410)**

State unemployment tax (SUTA) A tax levied on the employer and/or employee, depending on the state. Rates differ among the various states; however, they are generally 5.4 percent or higher of the first $7,000 of total earnings paid to each employee during the calendar year. The proceeds are used to pay subsistence benefits to unemployed workers. **(407)**

Workers' compensation insurance This insurance, primarily paid for by the employer, provides benefits for employees injured or killed on the job. The rates vary according to the degree of risk inherent in the job. The plans may be sponsored by states or by private firms. The employer pays the premium in advance at the beginning of the year, based on the estimated payroll. The rates are adjusted after the exact payroll is known. **(422)**

QUESTIONS, EXERCISES, AND PROBLEMS

D iscussion Questions

1. What payroll taxes are included under the Payroll Tax Expense account?
2. What is the purpose of Form 941? How often is it prepared, and what are the due dates?
3. What is the purpose of Form 940? How often is it prepared, and what is the due date?
4. List the correct sequence of the steps for recording payroll entries, and identify the specific source of information for each entry. Assume that the company uses a special payroll bank account.
5. How many copies are made of a W-2 form, and who uses the copies? What information is presented on a W-2 form?
6. Explain the deposit requirement for federal unemployment insurance.
7. Generally, what is the time schedule for payment of workers' compensation insurance premiums?
8. Explain the advantage of establishing a tax calendar.

E xercises

Exercise 10-1 Mason Company's partial payroll register for the week ended January 7 is shown below.

P.O.1

	NAME	TOTAL HOURS	BEGINNING CUMULATIVE EARNINGS	TOTAL EARNINGS	ENDING CUMULATIVE EARNINGS	TAXABLE EARNINGS		
						UNEMPL.	SOCIAL SECURITY	MEDICARE
1	Boyd, D. C.	46		742 00	742 00	742 00	742 00	742 00
2	Clark, L. O.	32		304 00	304 00	304 00	304 00	304 00
3	Falk, M. C.	40		380 00	380 00	380 00	380 00	380 00
4	Gunn, A. R.	40		380 00	380 00	380 00	380 00	380 00
5	Helm, R. D.	40		380 00	380 00	380 00	380 00	380 00
6	Judd, N. A.	37		352 00	352 00	352 00	352 00	352 00
7				2538 00	2538 00	2538 00	2538 00	2538 00
8								

Assume that the payroll is subject to a Social Security tax of 6.2 percent of the first $60,600 and a Medicare tax of 1.45 percent of earnings. Also assume that the federal unemployment tax is .8 percent of the first $7,000, and the state unemployment tax is 5.4 percent of the first $7,000. Give the entry in general journal form to record the payroll tax expense.

Journalize the entry for payroll tax expense.

Exercise 10-2 On January 14, at the end of the second week of the year, the totals of Broadmoor Floor Covering's payroll register showed that its store employees' wages amounted to $29,260, and its installers' wages amounted to

P.O.1

Journalize the entry for payroll tax expense.

$10,240. Withholdings consisted of federal income taxes, $3,980; Social Security taxes at the rate of 6.2 percent of the first $60,600; Medicare taxes at the rate of 1.45 percent of earnings; union dues, $410.

a. Calculate the amount of Social Security and Medicare taxes to be withheld, and write the general journal entry to record the payroll. Assume the company uses a special payroll account.

b. Write the general journal entry to record the employer's payroll taxes, assuming that the federal unemployment tax is .8 percent of the first $7,000 and the state unemployment tax is 5.4 percent of the same base and that no employee has surpassed the $7,000 limit.

P.O.1

Exercise 10-3 Briggs Diet Systems had the following payroll data for the week ended February 5:

TOTAL EARNINGS	ENDING CUMULATIVE EARNINGS	TAXABLE EARNINGS			DEDUCTIONS			
		UNEM-PLOYMENT	SOCIAL SECURITY	MEDICARE	FEDERAL INCOME TAX	STATE INCOME TAX	SOCIAL SECURITY TAX	MEDICARE TAX
6 5 2 0 00	71 7 2 0 00	6 5 2 0 00	6 5 2 0 00	6 5 2 0 00	7 1 7 00	1 4 3 00	4 0 4 24	9 4 54

Journalize the payroll entries.

a. Record the payroll entry as of February 5 in general journal form. The firm uses a special payroll bank account for wage payments.

b. Journalize the entry to record the employer's payroll taxes as of February 5. The employer matches the employee deductions for FICA. Assume rates of .8 percent for federal unemployment insurance and 5.4 percent for state unemployment insurance based on the first $7,000 for each employee.

P.O.1

Journalize the entry for payroll tax expense.

Exercise 10-4 The following information on earnings and deductions for the pay period ended December 14 is from McMaster Company's payroll records:

Name	Gross Pay	Beginning Cumulative Earnings
Bracken, R. A.	$ 224	$ 6,820
Butler, N. C.	640	28,100
Cooper, L. O.	1,100	54,900
Faraci, D. E.	730	38,700
Keyes, W. N.	1,070	53,600
Mayer, C. D.	220	6,710

For each employee, the Social Security tax is 6.2 percent of the first $60,600, and the Medicare tax is 1.45 percent of earnings. The federal unemployment tax is .8 percent of the first $7,000 of earnings of each employee. The state unemployment tax is 5.4 percent of the same base. Determine the total taxable earnings for unemployment, Social Security, and Medicare. Prepare a general journal entry to record the employer's payroll taxes.

Exercise 10-5 Selected columns of Flynn Company's payroll register for the month of January are shown below. The employees' FICA taxes are matched by the employer.

Payment Date	Employees' Federal Income Tax	Employees' Social Security Tax	Employee Medicare Tax
Jan. 7 (Tuesday)	1,084.00	480.00	112.26
14	1,214.00	537.54	125.72
21	1,302.00	576.66	134.85
28	1,302.00	576.66	134.85

Since Flynn Company qualifies as a large-sized employer, federal taxes are to be paid three days after the payroll payment date. Record the entry for first and second payments of federal taxes in general journal form. Assume that a deposit must be made if the federal tax liability exceeds $3,000.

Exercise 10-6 On September 15, Brooks Company's selected account balances are as follows:

Employees' State Income Tax Payable	$ 855
Employees' Federal Income Tax Payable	2,050
FICA Tax Payable (employer and employee)	2,420
State Unemployment Tax Payable	1,296
Federal Unemployment Tax Payable	192
Salaries Payable	605
Salary Expense	31,840
Payroll Tax Expense	1,954

In general journal form, prepare the entries to record the following:

Oct. 3 Payment of liabilities for FICA and federal income tax
  31 Payment of liability for state unemployment tax
  31 Payment of liability for federal unemployment tax
  31 Payment of liability for state income tax

Exercise 10-7 On September 30, Vivaldi Furniture's selected payroll accounts are as follows:

FICA Tax Payable

	Sept. 30 2,121.92
	Sept. 30 2,121.92

State Unemployment Tax Payable

	Sept. 30 1,328.94

Federal Unemployment Tax Payable

	Sept. 30 196.88

Employees' Federal Income Tax Payable

	Sept. 30 3,210.80

P.O.2

Journalize entries for payment of federal payroll taxes.

P.O.2,3,4

Journalize entries for payment of payroll taxes.

P.O.2,3

Journalize entries for payment of payroll taxes.

Prepare general journal entries to record payment of the taxes.

Oct. 3 Record payment of federal tax deposit of FICA and federal income tax.
31 Record payment of state unemployment tax.
31 Record payment of federal unemployment tax.

P.O.7,8

Journalize entries for workers' compensation insurance.

Exercise 10-8 Cooper Company received a premium notice on January 2 for workers' compensation insurance stating the rates for the new year. Estimated employees' earnings for the year are as follows:

Classification	Estimated Wages and Salaries	Rate Per Hundred	Estimated Premium
Office clerical	$ 92,000	.11	$ 101.20
Warehouse work	27,000	.92	248.40
Manufacturing	260,000	1.20	3,120.00
			$3,469.60

At the end of the year, the exact figures for the payroll are as follows:

Classification	Estimated Wages and Salaries	Rate Per Hundred	Exact Premium
Office clerical	$ 94,000	.11	$ 103.40
Warehouse work	26,000	.92	239.20
Manufacturing	268,000	1.20	3,216.00
			$3,558.60

a. Record the entry in general journal form for payment of the estimated premium.

b. Record the adjusting entries on December 31 for the insurance expired as well as for the additional premium.

C onsider and Communicate

During the first six months of the company's existence, the owner kept the books. The firm has four employees. The owner maintained a payroll register. She has heard of employee individual earnings records. However, she wonders why all the paperwork is necessary, since the employees' earnings and deductions are already in the payroll register.

W hat If . . .

You prepare the interim monthly financial statements. Your employer suggests that you record the payroll tax expenses only on the last of each quarter's financial statements. Your employer believes this will save time because you won't have to figure out what the amounts are for each month. Will this have any effect on the monthly interim financial statements if payroll is one of the business's major costs? If so, how?

A Question of Ethics

An employer prepares the payroll and correctly computes the necessary with-holding taxes. The employer is classified by the IRS as a monthly depositor, with accumulated employment taxes due by the 15th of the next month. Payday is the last day of the month. However, between the end of the month and the 15th day of the next month, the business bank account has been getting quite low; and this time, it looks as if the account will be below the amount that will be required to pay the federal tax deposit.

The employer has had to use the funds withheld from the employees to pay some of the business bills. He anticipates that enough of the customers who owe him money will pay their outstanding accounts receivable. If this assumption is true, the checking account will have enough in it to pay the federal deposit on the 15th of the month.

Is the employer acting ethically?

P roblem Set A

Problem 10-1A Hirsch and Company had the following payroll for the week ended March 21:

P.O.1

Salaries		Deductions	
Sales salaries	$7,380.00	Federal income tax withheld	$ 766.00
Office salaries	1,680.00	State income tax withheld	153.00
Total	$9,060.00	Social Security tax withheld	561.72
		Medicare tax withheld	131.37
		U.S. savings bonds	200.00
			$1,812.09

Assumed tax rates are as follows:

a. FICA: Social Security, 6.2 percent (.062) on the first $60,600 for each employee and Medicare, 1.45 percent (.0145) on all earnings for each employee. Assume no employees have reached the limit on Social Security.
b. State unemployment tax, 5.4 percent (.054) on the first $7,000 for each employee.
c. Federal unemployment tax, .8 percent (.008) on the first $7,000 for each employee.

Instructions

Record the following entries in general journal form:

1. The payroll entry as of March 21, assuming that Hirsch uses a payroll bank account.
2. The entry to record the employer's payroll taxes as of March 21, assuming that the total payroll is subject to the FICA tax (combined Social Security and Medicare) and that the $3,940 is subject to unemployment taxes.
3. The payment of the employees as of March 21.

Problem 10-2A Harris Insurance Agency has the following information for the week ended December 14:

P.O.1

NAME	BEGINNING CUMULATIVE EARNINGS	TOTAL EARNINGS	DEDUCTIONS	
			FEDERAL INCOME TAX	STATE INCOME TAX
Beem, M. A.	9 2 0 0 00	3 1 0 00	3 1 00	6 00
Clay, C. E.	37 9 0 0 00	7 6 0 00	9 9 00	2 0 00
Ebel, S. T.	59 7 0 0 00	1 0 8 0 00	1 7 7 00	3 5 00
Getz, R. R.	6 4 0 0 00	2 9 0 00	2 6 00	5 00
Hunt, N. C.	29 6 0 0 00	5 9 0 00	7 3 00	1 5 00
Marr, W. J.	47 4 0 0 00	9 5 0 00	1 4 9 00	3 0 00
	190 2 0 0 00	3 9 8 0 00	5 5 5 00	1 1 1 00

Assumed tax rates are as follows:

a. FICA: Social Security, 6.2 percent (.062) on the first $60,600 for each employee and Medicare, 1.45 percent (.0145) on all earnings for each employee.

b. State unemployment tax, 5.4 percent (.054) on the first $7,000 for each employee.

c. Federal unemployment tax, .8 percent (.008) on the first $7,000 for each employee.

Instructions

1. Complete the payroll register.
2. Prepare a general journal entry to record the payroll as of December 14. The company's general ledger contains a Salary Expense account and a Salaries Payable account.
3. Prepare a general journal entry to record the payroll taxes as of December 14.
4. Assuming that the firm uses a special payroll bank account, make the entry in the general journal to record payment of salaries, Ck. No. 317, as of December 16. Payroll checks begin with Ck. No. 923.

P.O.5

Problem 10-3A For the third quarter of the year, Romano Construction, of 7144 Stone Boulevard, San Francisco, California 94421, received Form 941 from the District Office of the Internal Revenue Service. The identification number for Romano Construction is 77-627116. Its payroll for the quarter ended September 30 is as follows:

NAME	EARNINGS	TAXABLE EARNINGS			FEDERAL INCOME TAX	SOCIAL SECURITY TAX	MEDICARE TAX
		UNEMPL.	SOCIAL SECURITY	MEDICARE			
Lamb, C. C.	3 2 7 6 00	9 4 2 00	3 2 7 6 00	3 2 7 6 00	2 9 7 00	2 0 3 11	4 7 50
Marr, G. L.	6 6 4 2 00		6 6 4 2 00	6 6 4 2 00	6 9 4 00	4 1 1 80	9 6 31
Pope, L. E.	7 6 0 0 00		7 6 0 0 00	7 6 0 0 00	8 3 6 00	4 7 1 20	1 1 0 20
Potts, W. A.	6 0 4 8 00		6 0 4 8 00	6 0 4 8 00	6 6 5 00	3 7 4 98	8 7 70
Rich, M. C.	4 1 0 0 00	7 6 0 00	4 1 0 0 00	4 1 0 0 00	3 7 2 00	2 5 4 20	5 9 45
Shell, V. A.	10 1 4 0 00		10 1 4 0 00	10 1 4 0 00	1 2 1 6 00	6 2 8 68	1 4 7 03
	37 8 0 6 00	1 7 0 2 00	37 8 0 6 00	37 8 0 6 00	4 0 8 0 00	2 3 4 3 97	5 4 8 19

The company has had six employees throughout the year. Assume that the Social Security tax is 6.2 percent of the first $60,600 and that the Medicare tax is 1.45 percent of earnings. The employer matches the employees' FICA (Social Security and Medicare) taxes. There are no taxable tips, adjustments, backup withholding, or earned income credits. Romano Construction has submitted the following federal tax deposits and written the accompanying checks:

On August 3 for the July Payroll		On September 3 for the August Payroll		On October 3 for the September Payroll	
Employees' income tax withheld	$1,341.00	Employees' income tax withheld	$1,365.00	Employees' income tax withheld	$1,374.00
Employees' Social Security and Medicare tax withheld	950.45	Employees' Social Security and Medicare tax withheld	967.66	Employees' Social Security and Medicare tax withheld	974.05
Employer's Social Security and Medicare tax contributed	950.45	Employer's Social Security and Medicare tax contributed	967.66	Employer's Social Security and Medicare tax contributed	974.04
	$3,241.90		$3,300.32		$3,322.09

Instructions

Complete Form 941 dated October 29 for the owner, Anthony Romano.

Problem 10-4A The Davis Company has the following balances in its general ledger as of March 1 of this year: `P.O.1,2,3`

a. FICA Tax Payable (liability for February), $1,315.18
b. Employees' Federal Income Tax Payable (liability for February), $714
c. State Unemployment Tax Payable (liability for January and February), $928.36
d. Federal Unemployment Tax Payable (liability for January and February), $137.54
e. Employees' Medical Insurance Payable (liability for January and February), $960.00

The company completed the following transactions involving the payroll during March and April:

Mar. 12 Issued check for $2,029.18 payable to Prudent Bank, for monthly deposit of February FICA taxes and employees' federal income tax withheld.

31 Recorded the payroll entry in the general journal from the payroll register for March. The payroll register had the following column totals:

Sales salaries	$7,146.00	
Office salaries	1,450.00	
Total earnings		$8,596.00
Employees' federal income tax deductions	$ 714.00	
Employees' Social Security tax deductions	532.95	
Employees' Medicare tax deductions	124.64	
Employees' medical insurance deductions	480.00	
Total deductions		1,851.59
Net pay		$6,744.41

31 Recorded payroll taxes. Employer matches the employees' FICA taxes. State unemployment tax is 5.4 percent. Federal unemployment tax is .8 percent. At this time, all employees' earnings are taxable for FICA and unemployment taxes.

31 Issued check for $6,744.41, payable to a payroll bank account.

Apr. 3 Issued check for $1,440, payable to Atlas Insurance Company, for employees' medical insurance for January, February, and March.

14 Issued check for $2,029.18, payable to Prudent Bank, for monthly deposit of March FICA taxes and employees' federal income tax withheld.

30 Issued check payable to Prudent Bank for deposit of federal unemployment tax for January, February, and March, $206.31.

30 Issued check for $1,392.54, payable to State Department of Revenue for state unemployment tax for January, February, and March. The check was accompanied by the quarterly tax return.

Instructions

Record the transactions in the general journal.

Instructions for General Ledger Software

1. Record the transactions in the general journal.
2. Print the journal entries.

P roblem Set B

P.O.1

Problem 10-1B The Beckett Optical Laboratory had the following payroll for the week ended February 28:

Salaries		Deductions	
Technicians' salaries	$5,566.00	Federal income tax withheld	$ 521.00
Office salaries	1,040.00	Social Security tax withheld	409.57
Total	$6,606.00	Medicare tax withheld	95.79
		Union dues withheld	160.00
		Medical insurance	384.00
		Total	$1,570.36

Assumed tax rates are as follows:

a. FICA: Social Security, 6.2 percent (.062) on the first $60,600 for each employee and Medicare, 1.45 percent (.0145) on total earnings. Assume no employees have reached the limit on Social Security.

b. State unemployment tax, 5.4 percent (.054) on the first $7,000 for each employee.

c. Federal unemployment tax, .8 percent (.008) on the first $7,000 for each employee.

Instructions

Record the following entries in general journal form.

1. The payroll entry as of February 28, assuming that Beckett uses a payroll bank account.
2. The entry to record the employer's payroll taxes as of February 28, assuming that the total payroll is subject to the FICA tax (combined Social Security and Medicare) and that $4,760 is subject to unemployment taxes.
3. The payment of the employees on February 28.

Problem 10-2B Browning Appraisal Service has the following payroll information for the week ended December 7.

P.O.1

NAME	BEGINNING CUMULATIVE EARNINGS	TOTAL EARNINGS	DEDUCTIONS	
			FEDERAL INCOME TAX	STATE INCOME TAX
Ames, C. P.	6 2 0 0 00	4 5 0 00	5 7 00	1 1 00
Bell, D. R.	6 8 0 0 00	4 7 0 00	6 4 00	1 3 00
Carr, N. O.	36 4 0 0 00	7 4 0 00	8 9 00	1 8 00
Dunn, G. M.	27 1 0 0 00	5 5 0 00	8 6 00	1 7 00
Eng, N. B.	59 5 0 0 00	1 1 1 0 00	1 3 5 00	3 7 00
Fry, C. A.	29 9 0 0 00	6 1 0 00	7 6 00	1 5 00
	165 9 0 0 00	3 9 3 0 00	5 0 7 00	1 1 1 00

Assumed tax rates are as follows:

a. FICA: Social Security, 6.2 percent (.062) on the first $60,600 for each employee and Medicare, 1.45 percent (.0145) on all earnings for each employee.
b. State unemployment tax, 5.4 percent (.054) on the first $7,000 for each employee.
c. Federal unemployment tax, .8 percent (.008) on the first $7,000 for each employee.

Instructions

1. Complete the payroll register.
2. Prepare a general journal entry to record the payroll as of December 7. The company's general ledger contains a Salary Expense account and a Salaries Payable account.
3. Prepare a general journal entry to record the payroll taxes as of December 7.
4. Assuming that the firm uses a special payroll bank account, make the entry in the general journal to record payment of salaries, Ck. No. 412, as of December 9. Payroll checks begin with Ck. No. 714.

Problem 10-3B For the third quarter of the year, Fisher Company, 6227 Fleming Avenue, Chicago, Illinois 60652, received Form 941 from the Internal Revenue Service. The identification number of Fisher Company is 76-421317. Its payroll for the quarter ended September 30 is as follows:

P.O.5

NAME	EARNINGS	TAXABLE EARNINGS			FEDERAL INCOME TAX	SOCIAL SECURITY TAX	MEDICARE TAX
		UNEMPL.	SOCIAL SECURITY	MEDICARE			
Daley, C. R.	5 5 6 2 00	1 4 2 0 00	5 5 6 2 00	5 5 6 2 00	5 4 5 00	3 4 4 84	8 0 65
Gray, A. R.	8 6 2 0 00		8 6 2 0 00	8 6 2 0 00	9 0 5 00	5 3 4 44	1 2 4 99
Hood, J. C.	4 9 1 4 00	2 2 1 6 00	4 9 1 4 00	4 9 1 4 00	4 8 1 00	3 0 4 67	7 1 25
Lee, F. N.	3 5 3 8 00	3 5 3 8 00	3 5 3 8 00	3 5 3 8 00	3 4 6 00	2 1 9 36	5 1 30
Mark, W. E.	7 6 0 0 00		7 6 0 0 00	7 6 0 0 00	8 3 6 00	4 7 1 20	1 1 0 20
Ogle, M. B.	5 0 5 0 00		5 0 5 0 00	5 0 5 0 00	4 9 4 00	3 1 3 10	7 3 23
	35 2 8 4 00	7 1 7 4 00	35 2 8 4 00	35 2 8 4 00	3 6 0 7 00	2 1 8 7 61	5 1 1 62

The company has had six employees throughout the year. Assume that the Social Security tax is 6.2 percent of the first $60,600, and that the Medicare tax is 1.45 percent of earnings. The employer matches the employees' FICA (Social Security and Medicare) taxes. There are no taxable tips, adjustments, backup withholding, or earned income credits. Fisher Company has submitted the following federal tax deposits and written the accompanying checks:

On August 3 for the July Payroll		**On September 3 for the August Payroll**		**On October 3 for the September Payroll**	
Employees' income tax withheld	$1,190.00	Employees' income tax withheld	$1,182.00	Employees' income tax withheld	$1,235.00
Employees' Social Security and Medicare tax withheld	890.51	Employees' Social Security and Medicare tax withheld	884.53	Employees' Social Security and Medicare tax withheld	924.19
Employer's Social Security and Medicare tax contributed	890.51	Employer's Social Security and Medicare tax contributed	884.53	Employer's Social Security and Medicare tax contributed	924.19
	$2,971.02		$2,951.06		$3,083.38

Instructions

Complete Form 941 dated October 31 for the owner, Brenda Fisher.

P.O.1,2,3

Problem 10-4B The Lacey Company has the following balances in its general ledger as of June 1 of this year:

a. FICA Tax Payable (liability for May), $1,706.56
b. Employees' Federal Income Tax Payable (liability for May), $976
c. Federal Unemployment Tax Payable (liability for April and May), $178.46
d. State Unemployment Tax Payable (liability for April and May), $1,204.64
e. Employees' Medical Insurance Payable (liability for April and May), $1,240

The company completed the following transactions involving the payroll during June and July:

June 13 Issued check for $2,682.56 payable to the First Security Bank for the monthly deposit of May FICA taxes and employees' federal income tax withheld.

30 Recorded the payroll entry in the general journal from the payroll register for June. The payroll register has the following column totals:

Sales salaries	$9,240.00	
Office salaries	1,914.00	
Total earnings		$11,154.00
Employees' federal income tax deductions	$ 976.00	
Employees' Social Security tax deductions	691.55	
Employees' Medicare tax deductions	161.73	
Employees' medical insurance deductions	620.00	
Total deductions		2,449.28
Net pay		$ 8,704.72

30 Recorded payroll taxes. Employer matches the employees' FICA taxes. State unemployment tax is 5.4 percent, and federal unemployment tax is .8 percent. At this time, all employees' earnings are taxable for FICA and unemployment taxes.

30 Issued check for $8,704.72 payable to a payroll bank account.

July 14 Issued check for $1,860, payable to Caring Insurance Company, in payment of employees' medical insurance for April, May, and June.

14 Issued check for $2,682.56, payable to First Security Bank for the monthly deposit of June FICA taxes and employees' federal income tax withheld.

31 Issued check for $1,806.96 payable to the State Tax Commission, for state unemployment tax for April, May, and June. The check was accompanied by the quarterly tax return.

31 Issued check for $267.69 payable to First Security Bank for the deposit of federal unemployment tax for the months of April, May, and June.

Instructions

Record the transactions in the general journal.

Instructions for General Ledger Software

1. Record the transactions in the general journal.
2. Print the journal entries.

CHALLENGE PROBLEM

The new payroll clerk has completed the monthly payroll for December 31 that includes a year-end bonus for long-time employees (see the Working Papers). You are asked to do the following:

a. Verify the clerk's work, because the supervisor noticed one error and there may be more. Pay close attention to the various limitations for taxable earnings and the bonuses.
b. Rewrite the payroll register correcting the errors.
c. If the errors affect the journal entries, rewrite the complete entry.
d. Write the clerk a brief memo that will explain the errors and clear up the misunderstandings.

Use the following federal income tax withholding percentages:

Employees Bak and Carr requested a flat rate of 28 percent.

Employees Larra and Ward requested a flat rate of 15 percent.

Chapter 11

Accounting for Notes

PERFORMANCE OBJECTIVES

After you have completed this chapter, you will be able to do the following:

1. Calculate the interest on promissory notes.

2. Determine the due dates of promissory notes.

3. Write journal entries for (a) notes given to secure an extension of time on an open account; (b) payment of an interest-bearing note at maturity; (c) notes given in exchange for merchandise or other property purchased; (d) notes given to secure a cash loan, when the borrower receives full face value of the note; (e) notes given to secure a cash loan, when the bank discounts the note; and (f) renewal of a note at maturity.

4. Complete a notes payable register.

5. Write journal entries for (a) adjustment for accrued interest on notes payable; (b) adjustment for Discount on Notes Payable; and (c) conversion of Discount on Notes Payable to Interest Expense.

6. Write journal entries to record (a) receipt of a note from a charge customer; (b) receipt of payment of an interest-bearing note at maturity; (c) receipt of a note as a result of granting a personal loan; (d) receipt of a note in exchange for merchandise or other property; (e) receipt of interest and renewal of a note at maturity; (f) discounting an interest-bearing note.

7. Complete a notes receivable register.

8. Write journal entry to record the adjustment for accrued interest on notes receivable.

One of the problems my clients have is the question of how to borrow money. Many people buy property and finance their purchase by paying an amount down and getting a mortgage. A mortgage is simply a long-term loan that is evidenced by a note payable. When they sign a note

for a mortgage, they are often confused because there are so many variables—15-year mortgages, 30-year mortgages, adjustable-rate mortgages, fixed-rate mortgages. Each kind of mortgage has advantages and disadvantages depending on the client's needs and ability to pay back the loan amount. I advise clients to avoid taking loans to pay for items that will wear out before they have paid off the loan. This is a situation many clients fall into when signing a note to refinance their homes, using the equity to buy everyday items that do not increase in value, but instead are used up or wear out before they are actually paid for.

Individuals and companies can expand their knowledge by carefully analyzing their current resources and future earnings potential. They should list their assets and liabilities as well as their expenses and revenues. If they come to me with this information, it is much easier and less expensive for the clients as I assist them in making decisions about a note before they sign it.

Credit plays an extremely important role in the operation of most business enterprises. We have seen that credit may be extended on a charge-account basis, with payment generally due in twenty-five to thirty days. This type of credit involves the Accounts Payable and Accounts Receivable accounts. Credit may also be granted on the basis of giving or receiving notes for specific transactions. This sort of credit involves the Notes Payable and Notes Receivable accounts. The notes, which represent formal instruments of credit, are known as promissory notes. A **promissory note** is a written promise to pay a certain sum at a fixed or determinable future time. It is customarily used as evidence of credit transactions for periods longer than thirty days. For example, promissory notes may be used for the sale or purchase of assets or merchandise on the installment plan and for transactions involving large amounts of money.

In this chapter, we will discuss transactions involving notes payable, where we have given a note to a creditor, and then notes receivable, where we have received a note from a debtor.

Promissory Notes

A promissory note, like a check, must be payable to the order of a particular person or firm, known as the **payee.** It must also be signed by the person or firm making the promise, known as the **maker.** In Figure 11-1, Adams Manufacturing Company is the payee, and Dodson Plumbing Supply is the maker.

Figure 11-1

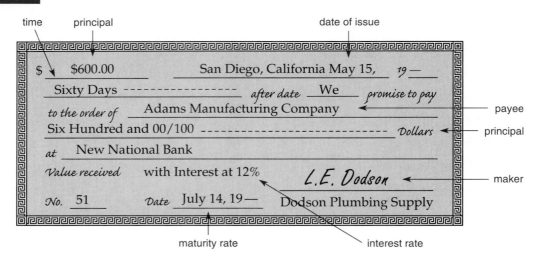

Notes offer advantages over an open account: (1) a note represents proof of the original transaction; (2) a note may bear interest and earn interest income; and (3) a note receivable may be pledged as security for a loan from a bank, which may grant more on the face value of a note than on the face value of open accounts (Accounts Receivable).

Calculating Interest

Performance Objective 1

Calculate the interest on promissory notes.

Interest is a charge made for the use of money. To the maker of the note, interest is an expense. The amount of interest a maker pays is expressed as a certain percentage of the principal of the note for a period of one year (or less). The following formula is used to calculate interest:

Interest = **Principal** of note × **Rate** of interest × **Time** of note
(in dollars)   (in dollars)   (as a percentage   (expressed as a
                                    of the principal)   year or fraction
                                                            of a year)

The **principal** is the face amount of the note. The *rate of interest* is a percentage of the principal, such as 10 percent or 11 percent. Since 1 percent equals $\frac{1}{100}$ or .01, then 10 percent equals $\frac{10}{100}$ or .10.

Time, or the length of life of the note, is expressed in terms of days or months. It is the period between the note's date of issue (starting date) and the **maturity date** of the note (the due date or interest payment date). It is stated in terms of a year or fraction of a year. Examples are

$$1 \text{ year} = 1 \qquad 6 \text{ months} = \frac{6}{12} \qquad 3 \text{ months} = \frac{3}{12}$$

$$90 \text{ days} = \frac{90}{360} \qquad 24 \text{ days} = \frac{24}{360}$$

The usual commercial practice is to use a 360-day year, thus making the denominator of the fraction 360. However, agencies of the federal government use the actual number of days in the year. All use this formula:

$$\text{Interest} = \text{Principal} \times \text{Rate} \times \text{Time}$$

Example 1 $2,000, 8 percent, 1 year.

Interest = $2,000 × .08 × 1 = $160

Example 2 $4,000, 9 percent, 3 months.

$$\text{Interest} = \$4{,}000 \times .09 \times \frac{3}{12}$$
$$= \$4{,}000 \times .09 \times 3 \div 12 = \underline{\$90}$$

Example 3 $6,000, 11 percent, 60 days.

$$\text{Interest} = \$6{,}000 \times .11 \times \frac{60}{360}$$
$$= \$6{,}000 \times .11 \times 60 \div 360 = \underline{\$110}$$

R E M E M B E R

Common practice is to use 360 days to compute interest on a note.

Determining Due Dates

Performance Objective 2

Determine the due dates of promissory notes.

A s we have said, the period of time a note has to run may be expressed in either days or months. If the time of the note is expressed in months, the maturity date is the corresponding day in the month after the specified number of months have elapsed. For example, a note dated March 15 with a time period of three months has a due date of June 15. In those cases in which there is no date in the month of maturity that corresponds to the issuance date, the due date becomes the last day of the month. For example, a three-month note dated March 31 would be due on June 30.

But suppose that the period of time a note has to run is expressed in days. When counting the number of days, begin with the day after the date the note was issued, since the note states "after date." The last day, however, is counted. Let us say that the due date of a promissory note is specified as 60 days after April 8. The calendar below shows that the due date is June 7.

R E M E M B E R

Do not count the day the note is issued when calculating the due date of a note.

April								May								June						
S	M	T	W	T	F	S		S	M	T	W	T	F	S		S	M	T	W	T	F	S
		1	2	3	4	5						1	2	3		1	2	3	4	5	6	7
6	7	8	9	10	11	12		4	5	6	7	8	9	10		8	9	10	11	12	13	14
13	14	15	16	17	18	19		11	12	13	14	15	16	17		15	16	17	18	19	20	21
20	21	22	23	24	25	26		18	19	20	21	22	23	24		22	23	24	25	26	27	28
27	28	29	30					25	26	27	28	29	30	31		29	30					

22 days
8th through the 30th
30 − 8 = 22 days left

+ 31 days

= 53 days have passed
60 − 53 = 7 days remaining
after May 31
June 7 due date

. . . .
R E M E M B E R
When counting the time period of a note, the date the note was issued is not counted, but the due date *is* counted.
. . . .

In summary, the due date is determined by the following steps:

1. Determine the number of days remaining in the month of issue by subtracting the date of the note from the number of days in the month in which it is dated.

2. Add as many full months as possible without exceeding the number of days in the note, counting the full number of days in these months.

3. Determine the number of days remaining in the month in which the note matures by subtracting the total days counted so far from the number of days in the note, as shown here.

April (30 − 8)   = 22 days left in April
May   = 31 days

Total days so far = 53 days
June (60 − 53)   =   7th day of June (due date)

Thus far, we have defined promissory notes, calculated interest on notes, and determined due dates of notes. As mentioned earlier, notes payable are notes given to a creditor (someone we owe), and notes receivable are notes given to us by a debtor (someone who owes us). The rules for calculating interest and determining due dates are the same for notes payable and notes receivable. In the next sections we will look at accounts and transactions related to Notes Payable. Later in the chapter, we will look at accounts and transactions related to Notes Receivable.

Notes Payable

Sometimes a business issues a note payable to a creditor at the time an account is due in order to extend the time available for payment of the debt. The amount due is removed from Accounts Payable and added to Notes Payable. A business may also issue a note payable at the time of a sale, rather than first charging the amount on open account (Accounts Payable), which usually requires payment in twenty-five to thirty days. If a business needs to borrow money, it may issue a note payable to a bank or to an individual to secure the loan.

Accounts Related to Notes Payable

Now let's see how transactions involving notes payable are journalized. Here are the accounts that are related to notes payable:

Notes Payable		Discount on Notes Payable		Interest Payable		Interest Expense	
−	+	+	−	−	+	+	−

Notes Payable is a liability account in which the accountant records the principal of the note.

Discount on Notes Payable is the contra-liability account. It is debited, along with Cash, when the accountant records a discounted note that is signed in one fiscal period and matures in the following fiscal period.

Interest Payable is the liability account in which the accountant records the amount of interest accrued on a note that began in one fiscal period and matures in a future fiscal period.

Interest Expense is the expense account in which the charges made for the use of money are recorded.

Transactions Involving Notes Payable

The following types of transactions involve the issuance and payment of notes payable:

1. Note given to a supplier in return for an extension of time for payment of an open account (charge account)

2. Note given in exchange for assets purchased

3. Note given to secure a cash loan

4. Note renewed at maturity

In our examples, we assume all the notes are due within one year, and thus they are classified on a balance sheet as Current Liabilities. However, if notes are due in a period longer than one year, that portion of the note due within one year is a Current Liability, and the remainder is classified as a Long-Term Liability. Interest Expense is classified on an income statement as Other Expense.

Note Given to Secure an Extension of Time on an Open Account

When a firm wishes to obtain an extension of time for the payment of an account, the firm may ask a supplier to accept a note for all or part of the amount due. For example, let's say that Dodson Plumbing Supply prefers to not pay its open account with Adams Manufacturing Company when it becomes due. Adams agrees to accept a 60-day, 12 percent, $600 note from Dodson Plumbing in settlement of the charge account. The entry that caused the account to be put on Adams's books in the first place came about when Dodson Plumbing bought merchandise on account on April 15, with terms 2/10, n/30.

Performance Objective 3a

Write journal entries for notes given to secure an extension of time on an open account.

R E M E M B E R

Accounts Payable is a controlling account. Notes Payable is not a controlling account like Accounts Payable and does not require the name of the maker following Notes Payable.

Payment by Note On May 15, Dodson Plumbing records the issuance of the note in its general journal shown below. *Note:* In the remaining general journals shown in this chapter, explanations like the one given for Notes Payable in the journal entry below are omitted for space reasons.

	DATE		DESCRIPTION	POST. REF.	DEBIT	CREDIT	
			GENERAL JOURNAL			PAGE ___	
1	19–						1
2	May	15	Accounts Payable, Adams				2
3			Manufacturing Co.		6 0 0 00		3
4			Notes Payable			6 0 0 00	4
5			Gave a 60-day, 12 percent				5
6			note in settlement of our				6
7			open account.				7
8							8

By T accounts, the transactions look like this:

Purchases		Accounts Payable		Notes Payable	
+	–	–	+	–	+
Apr. 15 600		May 15 600	Apr. 15 600		May 15 600

Observe that the above entry cancels out the Accounts Payable, Adams Manufacturing Company, account and substitutes Notes Payable. The note does not *pay* the debt, it merely changes the status of the liability from an account payable to a note payable. Adams prefers the note to the open account because, in the case of default and a subsequent lawsuit to collect, the possession of the note improves Adams's legal position. The note is written evidence of the debt and the amount owed. In addition, Adams is, in this case, entitled to 12 percent interest.

Payment of an Interest-bearing Note at Maturity

Performance Objective 3b

Write journal entries for payment of an interest-bearing note at maturity.

When a note payable falls due, payment may be made directly to the holder, or it may be made to a bank in which the note was left for collection. The maker of course knows the identity of the original payee, but he or she may not know who the holder of the note is at maturity. The payee may have transferred the note by endorsement to another party or may have left it with a bank for collection. When a note is left with a bank for collection, the bank usually mails the maker a **notice of maturity** specifying the terms and due date of the note. For example, Adams Manufacturing Company turned the note over to its bank, the New National Bank, for collection. Accordingly, the bank sent Dodson Plumbing a notice of maturity of the note.

Dodson Plumbing Supply pays the note on July 14. In general journal form, the entry is as follows:

	DATE		DESCRIPTION	POST. REF.	DEBIT	CREDIT	
GENERAL JOURNAL						PAGE ___	
1	19–						1
2	July	14	Notes Payable		6 0 0 00		2
3			Interest Expense		1 2 00		3
4			Cash			6 1 2 00	4

Because Interest = Principal × Rate × Time, we perform these calculations:

$$\text{Interest} = \$600 \times .12 \times \frac{60}{360} = \underline{\$12.00}$$

Cash		Notes Payable		Interest Expense	
+	–	–	+	+	–
Bal. 10,000	612	600		12	

In practice, if special journals are used, transactions like this one are recorded directly in the cash payments journal rather than in the general journal. However, to simplify the discussion of the entries, all transactions will be presented here in general journal form.

Note Given in Exchange for Assets Purchased

Occasionally, when the price of an item is high or the credit period is long, a buyer gives a note instead of buying the item on account. For example, Dodson Plumbing Supply issues a 90-day, 11 percent interest-bearing note for $3,500 to the Wexler Equipment Company in exchange for equipment purchased June 3 and records the transaction in the general journal as follows:

Performance Objective 3c
Write journal entries for notes given in exchange for merchandise or other property purchased.

	DATE		DESCRIPTION	POST. REF.	DEBIT	CREDIT	
1	19–						1
2	June	3	Store Equipment		3 5 0 0 00		2
3			Notes Payable			3 5 0 0 00	3

By T accounts, it looks like this:

Store Equipment		Notes Payable	
+	–	–	+
3,500			3,500

When Dodson Plumbing Supply pays the note at maturity, the entry in its books is the same as the entry it makes for the payment of any interest-bearing note. In general journal form, the entry looks like this:

. . . .
R E M E M B E R

Calculations are included to show how the amounts were determined. They would not normally appear in journal entries.
. . . .

	DATE	DESCRIPTION	POST. REF.	DEBIT	CREDIT	
1	19–					1
2	Sept. 1	Notes Payable		3 5 0 0 00		2
3		Interest Expense		9 6 25		3
4		Cash			3 5 9 6 25	4
5		($3,500 × .11 × 90/360)				5

Note Given to Secure a Cash Loan

Businesses frequently need to stock up on merchandise in large amounts in order to meet season demands. Sometimes their usual receipts from customers are not enough to cover the sudden volume of purchases. During such periods, business firms customarily borrow money from banks, through the medium of short-term notes, to finance their operations.

Borrowing from a Bank When Borrower Receives Full Face Value of Note

Performance Objective 3d

Write journal entries for notes given to secure a cash loan, when the borrower receives full face value of the note.

In one type of bank loan, a firm signs an interest-bearing note and receives the full face value of the note. The borrower repays the principal plus interest. For example, on June 11, Dodson Plumbing Supply borrows $1,650 from Finley National Bank for 120 days with interest of 10 percent payable at maturity. The entry to record the transaction is as follows:

	DATE	DESCRIPTION	POST. REF.	DEBIT	CREDIT	
1	19–					1
2	June 11	Cash		1 6 5 0 00		2
3		Notes Payable			1 6 5 0 00	3

Note Paid to the Bank at Maturity

After Dodson Plumbing Supply has paid the note and interest, its accountant makes the following entry on the books:

	DATE		DESCRIPTION	POST. REF.	DEBIT	CREDIT	
1	19–						1
2	Oct.	9	Notes Payable		1 6 5 0 00		2
3			Interest Expense		5 5 00		3
4			Cash			1 7 0 5 00	4
5			($1,650 × .10 × 120/360)				5

Borrowing from a Bank When Bank Discounts a Note

In another type of bank loan, the bank deducts the interest in advance, which is called **discounting a note payable.** For example, on June 19, Dodson Plumbing Supply borrows $8,000 for 90 days from Western National Bank; the bank requires Dodson Plumbing to sign a note. From the face value of the note, the bank deducts 11 percent interest for 90 days, so Dodson Plumbing actually gets only $7,780. This interest deducted in advance by a bank is called the **discount.** The principal of the loan left after the discount has been subtracted is called the **proceeds,** which is the amount the borrower has available to use. Since all the interest is deducted at the time the loan is made, the note must state that only the face amount is to be paid at maturity. The calculations are as follows:

$$\text{Interest} = \text{Principal} \times \text{Rate} \times \text{Time}$$

$$\text{Interest} = \$8,000 \times .11 \times \frac{90}{360} = \underline{\underline{\$220}}$$

As we said, the bank deducts the discount from the face amount of the note before making the money available to the borrower.

Principal	$8,000
− Discount	220
Proceeds	$7,780

Entry When Note Discounted at Bank Matures Before End of Fiscal Period

As long as a note begins and matures during the same fiscal period, the borrower may debit all the interest (or discount) to Interest Expense. The 90-day note that Dodson Plumbing Supply submits to the bank is dated June 19 and therefore matures September 17. Since Dodson Plumbing Supply's fiscal period is from January 1 to December 31, the company can include the entire amount of interest in Interest Expense. Accordingly, Dodson Plumbing records the transaction as follows:

	DATE	DESCRIPTION	POST. REF.	DEBIT	CREDIT	
1	19–					1
2	June 19	Cash		7 7 8 0 00		2
3		Interest Expense		2 2 0 00		3
4		Notes Payable			8 0 0 0 00	4

Note Paid to the Bank at Maturity

When the note becomes due, Dodson Plumbing Supply pays the bank just the *face value of the note* and records the transaction as follows:

	DATE	DESCRIPTION	POST. REF.	DEBIT	CREDIT	
1	19–					1
2	Sept. 17	Notes Payable		8 0 0 0 00		2
3		Cash			8 0 0 0 00	3

Entry When Note Discounted at Bank Matures After End of Fiscal Period

Now suppose that the time period of the note extends into the next fiscal period. Dodson Plumbing Supply must then record the discount as a debit to Discount on Notes Payable. Discount on Notes Payable is a **contra-liability account;** in other words, it is a deduction from Notes Payable. Recall that we defined the Accumulated Depreciation account as a contra asset—for example, a deduction from Equipment with the plus and minus signs switched around. Similarly, Discount on Notes Payable is another contra account—a deduction from Notes Payable with the plus and minus signs switched around. In T account form these accounts look like this:

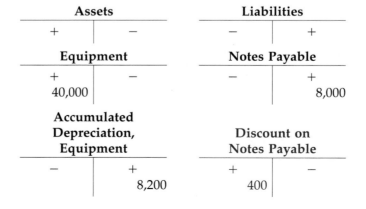

Also, on a balance sheet, the contra account is deducted as follows:

Assets					
Plant and Equipment:					
Equipment	$40 0 0 0 00				
Less Accumulated Depreciation	8 2 0 0 00	31 8 0 0 00			
Liabilities					
Current Liabilities:					
Notes Payable	$ 8 0 0 0 00				
Less Discount on Notes Payable	4 0 0 00	7 6 0 0 00			

At the end of the fiscal period, an adjusting entry must be made to record the amount of interest expense for the time between the date the note is issued and the end of the fiscal period. We will describe the adjusting entry on pages 454–455.

Let's say that, on December 1, Dodson Plumbing Supply borrows $2,500 from the Eastern State Bank for 120 days. The bank deducts 12 percent interest (in advance) for 120 days, $100, and gives Dodson Plumbing Supply $2,400. Dodson Plumbing Supply's fiscal period is from January 1 through December 31, so its accountant's entry in the general journal is like this:

	DATE	DESCRIPTION	POST. REF.	DEBIT	CREDIT	
1	19–					1
2	Dec. 1	Cash		2 4 0 0 00		2
3		Discount on Notes Payable		1 0 0 00		3
4		Notes Payable			2 5 0 0 00	4

In a discounted-note transaction, since all the interest is deducted at the time the loan is made, the note must state that only the face amount is to be paid at maturity. Payment of this note is discussed on page 457 as part of the end-of-fiscal-period adjustments.

Renewal of Note at Maturity

What if the maker (or borrower) is unable to pay a note in full at maturity? Then he or she may arrange to renew all or part of the note. At this time, he or she usually pays the interest on the old note. For example, assume that, on June 27, Dodson Plumbing Supply issues a 45-day note to Colvin, Inc., for $1,800, with interest at 10 percent. The original entry in general journal form is as follows:

	DATE	DESCRIPTION	POST. REF.	DEBIT	CREDIT	
1	19–					1
2	June 27	Accounts Payable, Colvin, Inc.		1 8 0 0 00		2
3		Notes Payable			1 8 0 0 00	3

REMEMBER

If a note payable discounted at a bank comes due *before* the end of the fiscal period, debit Interest Expense for the amount of the discount. If the note comes due *after* the end of the fiscal period, debit Discount on Notes Payable for the amount of the discount.

Performance Objective 3f

Write journal entries for renewal of a note at maturity.

Renewal of Note with Payment of Interest

When a firm renews an interest-bearing note, the accountant first makes an entry to pay the interest on the existing note, up to the present date. This entry occurs on August 11, the maturity date of the note:

	DATE		DESCRIPTION	POST. REF.	DEBIT	CREDIT	
1	19–						1
2	Aug.	11	Interest Expense		2 2 50		2
3			Cash			2 2 50	3
4			($1800 × .10 × 45/360)				4

The accountant then makes a separate entry for the issuance of the new note, to run for 30 days at 11 percent (the interest rate has been increased and the number of days decreased) as follows:

	DATE		DESCRIPTION	POST. REF.	DEBIT	CREDIT	
7	Aug.	11	Notes Payable		1 8 0 0 00		7
8			Notes Payable			1 8 0 0 00	8

Renewal of Note with Payment of Interest and Part Payment of Principal

R E M E M B E R

For a renewal of a note payable, debit the old note to take it off the books, and credit the new note to put it on the books.

On the other hand, what if the maker instead decides to pay only *part* of a note at maturity? Let us assume that, instead of taking the course of action we have just described, Dodson Plumbing Supply pays $600 on the principal of the note that is due (the old note), and also pays the entire interest on it. In other words, the maker pays the interest up to the present date for the old note, plus $600 to reduce the principal from $1,800 to $1,200, and issues a *new* note for $1,200.

	DATE		DESCRIPTION	POST. REF.	DEBIT	CREDIT	
7	Aug.	11	Notes Payable		6 0 0 00		7
8			Interest Expense		2 2 50		8
9			Cash			6 2 2 50	9
10							10
11		11	Notes Payable		1 2 0 0 00		11
12			Notes Payable			1 2 0 0 00	12

Ordinarily, small firms issue notes to relatively few creditors. These firms can record the details of the notes on stubs similar to check stubs, or they can just keep duplicate copies of the notes. However, if a firm issues many notes, it may be more convenient to keep a **notes payable register**. In an abbreviated form, here's an illustration of a notes payable register for Dodson Plumbing Supply through August 11:

Performance Objective 4

Complete a notes payable register.

NOTES PAYABLE REGISTER

DATE		PAYEE	AMOUNT	TIME	RATE	INTEREST	DUE DATE	DATE PAID	REMARKS
19—									
May	15	Adams Manu-							
		facturing Co.	600 00	60 days	12%	12 00	7/14	7/14	Open account.
June	3	Wexler Equipment							
		Co.	3500 00	90 days	11%	96 25	9/1	9/1	Bought equipment.
	11	Finley National							Loan, received
		Bank	1650 00	120 days	10%	55 00	10/9	10/9	full principal.
	19	Western National							Loan, discount
		Bank	800 00	90 days	11%	220 00	9/17	9/17	$220.
	27	Colvin, Inc.	1800 00	45 days	10%	22 50	8/11	Renewed	Open account.
Aug.	11	Colvin, Inc.	1800 00	30 days	11%	16 50	9/10		Renewed June 27 note.
		OR IF PARTIAL PAYMENT							
Aug.	11	Colvin, Inc.	1200 00	30 days	11%	11 00	9/10		Renewed June 27 note
									with part payment
									of $600.

Businesses frequently sign notes to buy long-lived depreciable assets. Keeping up with technology is vital if a business is to succeed—and it is also expensive.

More elaborate notes payable registers may include columns listing note numbers, addresses of payees, and similar information. An alternative would be to use spreadsheet software to manage notes.

At the end of the fiscal period, the firm may prepare a schedule of notes payable by listing the unpaid notes that appear in the notes payable register. This schedule is similar to a schedule of accounts payable. The total of the schedule is compared with the balance of Notes Payable.

End-of-Fiscal-Period Adjustments on Notes Payable

In the case of notes that start in one fiscal period and mature in the next, adjusting entries must be made both for accrued interest and for discounts on notes payable. Otherwise, neither the expenses incurred by the business firm during a fiscal period nor its liabilities at the end of the fiscal period would be correctly stated.

. . . .
R E M E M B E R

Accrual-basis accounting requires adjustment for notes spanning two or more fiscal periods, so that Interest Expense and Discount on Notes Payable are accurately reported in financial statements.
. . . .

Accrued Interest on Notes Payable

On all interest-bearing notes, interest expense *accrues*, or builds up, daily. Consequently, if any notes payable are outstanding at the end of a fiscal period, the **accrued interest on notes payable** (that is, the interest due but not yet paid) should be calculated and recorded. For example, assume that a firm has two notes payable outstanding as of December 31, the end of the current fiscal period.

$3,000, 60 days, 10%, dated December 10

$4,200, 90 days, 11%, dated December 2

We can diagram the period of each note like this:

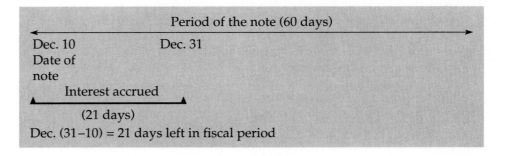

Interest = Principal × Rate × Time

$$\text{Interest} = \$3{,}000 \times .10 \times \frac{21}{360} = \underline{\$17.50}$$

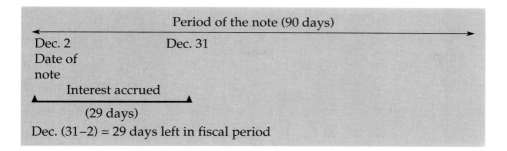

$$\text{Interest} = \text{Principal} \times \text{Rate} \times \text{Time}$$

$$\text{Interest} = \$4{,}200 \times .11 \times \frac{29}{360} = \underline{\$37.22}$$

In general journal form, the adjusting entry for the interest expense accrued on the two notes is as follows:

	DATE		DESCRIPTION	POST. REF.	DEBIT	CREDIT	
1	19–		Adjusting Entry				1
2	Dec.	31	Interest Expense		5 4 72		2
3			Interest Payable				3
4			($17.50 + $37.22)			5 4 72	4
5							5

Performance Objective 5a

Write journal entries for adjustment for accrued interest on notes payable.

Like all other adjustments, this one is first recorded in the Adjustments columns of the work sheet. By T accounts, it looks like this, assuming a balance of $825 before adjustment of Interest Expense:

Interest Expense			Interest Payable	
+	–		–	+
Dec. 31 Bal. 825.00				Dec. 31 Adj. 54.72
Dec. 31 Adj. 54.72				

On the balance sheet, Interest Payable is classified as a current liability.

R E M E M B E R

Any account name ending in Payable is always a liability account.

Discount on Notes Payable

Recall that, when a note payable is discounted at a bank, the bank deducts the interest (based on the principal of the note) in advance. **If the note begins and ends during one fiscal period, the interest is recorded as Interest Expense, and no adjustment is needed. But if the note extends into the next fiscal period, the interest is recorded as Discount on Notes Payable.** An adjusting entry will be needed to record the interest from the day the note started until the last day of the fiscal period.

Now let's recall our original entry (shown on page 456) made on December 1, in which the firm discounted its note at the bank.

R E M E M B E R

Discount on Notes Payable is a contra-liability account and a deduction from Notes Payable.

	DATE		DESCRIPTION	POST. REF.	DEBIT	CREDIT	
1	19–						1
2	Dec.	1	Cash		2 4 0 0 00		2
3			Discount on Notes Payable		1 0 0 00		3
4			Notes Payable			2 5 0 0 00	4

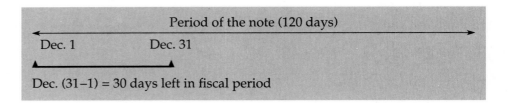

Period of the note (120 days)

Dec. 1   Dec. 31

Dec. (31–1) = 30 days left in fiscal period

Interest = Principal × Rate × Time

$$\text{Interest} = \$2{,}500 \times .12 \times \frac{30}{360} = \underline{\underline{\$25}}$$

Performance Objective 5b

Write journal entries for adjustment for Discount on Notes Payable.

Since 30 days elapse between December 1 and December 31, Dodson Plumbing's accountant has to make an adjusting entry to record the Interest Expense:

	DATE	DESCRIPTION	POST. REF.	DEBIT	CREDIT	
1	19–	Adjusting Entry				1
2	Dec. 31	Interest Expense		2 5 00		2
3		Discount on Notes Payable			2 5 00	3

In T accounts, it looks this way:

Interest Expense		Discount on Notes Payable	
+	–	+	–
Dec. 31 Adj. 25		Dec. 1 100	Dec. 31 Adj. 25

In addition to recording Interest Expense, the adjusting entry also serves to reduce the balance of Discount on Notes Payable to its correct amount. At

Figure 11-2

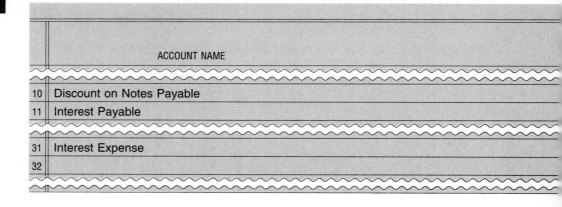

	ACCOUNT NAME
10	Discount on Notes Payable
11	Interest Payable
31	Interest Expense
32	

the end of the year, the Interest Expense account is closed along with all the other expense accounts. Figure 11-2 at the bottom of the page shows how these adjustments are recorded on a work sheet.

Now let's proceed one step further and make the entries for the final payment of the discounted note to the bank. These may be separated into two entries; the first is like the payment of any discounted note.

	DATE		DESCRIPTION	POST. REF.	DEBIT	CREDIT	
1	19–						1
2	Mar.	31	Notes Payable		2 5 0 0 00		2
3			Cash			2 5 0 0 00	3

The Discount on Notes Payable that was on the books has now become entirely an expense, so it is converted into Interest Expense.

8							8
9		31	Interest Expense		7 5 00		9
10			Discount on Notes Payable			7 5 00	10

In T accounts, it looks like this:

Interest Expense			**Discount on Notes Payable**		
+	−		+	−	
Dec. 31 Adj. 25	Dec. 31 Clos. 25		Dec. 1 100	Dec. 31 Adj. 25	
Mar. 31 75				Mar. 31 75	

Performance Objective 5c

Write journal entries for conversion of Discount on Notes Payable to Interest Expense.

Notes Receivable

Sometimes a business receives notes receivable from charge customers who wish to extend the time during which they can pay their accounts. A business may also receive a note as the result of lending money to an individual or a business. A note may be received in exchange for assets or merchandise. To raise cash a business may sell its notes receivable to a bank or finance company.

R E M E M B E R

A note receivable on the books of one company is a note payable on the books of the company signing the note.

	TRIAL BALANCE			ADJUSTMENTS			INCOME STATEMENT			BALANCE SHEET		
	DEBIT	CREDIT		DEBIT	CREDIT		DEBIT	CREDIT		DEBIT	CREDIT	
	1 0 0 00				(b) 2 5 00					7 5 00		10
					(a) 5 4 72						5 4 72	11
	8 2 5 00			(a) 5 4 72			9 0 4 72					31
				(b) 2 5 00								

Accounts Related to Notes Receivable

Now let's see how transactions involving notes receivable are journalized. Here are accounts related to notes receivable:

Notes Receivable			Interest Receivable			Interest Income	
+	−		+	−		−	+

Notes receivable is the asset account in which the accountant records a written promise made by a debtor to pay us a sum at a fixed or determinable future time. The credit is to Cash, Accounts Receivable, or Sales.

Interest Receivable is the asset account in which the accountant records the amount of interest accrued on a note that begins in one fiscal period and matures in a future fiscal period, specifically the amount accrued from the date the note is signed until the end of the fiscal period. The credit is to Interest Income.

Interest Income is the revenue account in which the accountant records the amount of interest earned by or accrued on a note that begins in one fiscal period and matures in a future fiscal period, specifically the amount accrued from the date the note is signed until the end of the fiscal period. The debit is to Interest Receivable or Cash.

Transactions Involving Notes Receivable

First, let's say that all notes received are recorded in a single current asset account: Notes Receivable. Second, we are going to use Dodson Plumbing Supply to illustrate such transactions. All notes are payable at Oliver Bank.

The following types of transactions involve the issuance and payment of notes receivable:

1. Notes from charge customers to extend time on their accounts

2. Receipt of payment of an interest-bearing note at maturity

3. Notes received as a result of granting personal loans

4. Notes received in exchange for merchandise or other property

5. Renewal of notes at maturity with receipt of interest

6. Renewal of notes with receipt of interest and partial payment of principal

FYI

Depending on the size of the note, many businesses require the maker to take out insurance on the note. Under conditions of the insurance, the payments would be made if anything should happen to the maker.

Notes from Charge Customers to Extend Time on Their Accounts

Performance Objective 6a

Write journal entry to record receipt of a note from a charge customer.

On March 7, Dodson Plumbing Supply sold $840 worth of merchandise to Hazen Plumbing and Heating, with the customary terms of 2/10, n/30, and made the original entry in its sales journal. On April 6, Hazen Plumbing and Heating sent Dodson Plumbing Supply a note for $840, payable within 30 days, at 8 percent interest. The note, dated April 6, was in settlement of the transaction of March 7. Dodson Plumbing Supply recorded this new development in its general journal as follows:

	DATE		DESCRIPTION	POST. REF.	DEBIT	CREDIT	
	GENERAL JOURNAL					PAGE ____	
1	19–						1
2	Apr.	6	Notes Receivable		8 4 0 00		2
3			Accounts Receivable, Hazen				3
4			Plumbing and Heating			8 4 0 00	4

REMEMBER

A note receivable and an account receivable differ only in the intensity of the promise they represent—a note is more formal.

Performance Objective 6b

Write journal entry to record receipt of payment of an interest-bearing note at maturity.

T accounts for the transactions look like this:

Accounts Receivable			Sales			Notes Receivable	
+	–		–	+		+	–
Mar. 7 840	Apr. 6 840			Mar. 7 840		Apr. 6 840	

Receipt of Payment of an Interest-Bearing Note at Maturity

On May 6, Hazen paid Dodson Plumbing Supply in full: principal plus interest. Dodson Plumbing Supply recorded the transaction in the general journal as follows:

	DATE		DESCRIPTION	POST. REF.	DEBIT	CREDIT	
1	19–						1
2	May	6	Cash		8 4 5 60		2
3			Notes Receivable			8 4 0 00	3
4			Interest Income			5 60	4
5			($840 × .08 × 30/360)				5

Let's look at the T accounts for this entry:

Cash			Notes Receivable			Interest Income	
+	–		+	–		–	+
May 6 845.60			Apr. 6 840.00	May 6 840.00			May 6 5.60

In practice, this transaction would be recorded directly in the cash receipts journal rather than in the general journal. But, for the sake of simplicity and clarity, we will use the general journal format to illustrate entries throughout this chapter.

Notes Received as a Result of Granting Personal Loans

Performance Objective 6c

Write journal entry to record receipt of a note as a result of granting a personal loan.

Let's say that Brenda Paine, an employee of Dodson Plumbing Supply, borrows $450 from her employer, for 3 months at 6 percent. Her note is dated April 8. In general journal form, the entry is as shown below:

	DATE		DESCRIPTION	POST. REF.	DEBIT	CREDIT	
1	19–						1
2	Apr.	8	Notes Receivable		4 5 0 00		2
3			Cash			4 5 0 00	3

When the loan reaches maturity, Paine pays the principal plus interest.

	DATE		DESCRIPTION	POST. REF.	DEBIT	CREDIT	
1	19–						1
2	July	8	Cash		4 5 6 75		2
3			Notes Receivable			4 5 0 00	3
4			Interest Income			6 75	4
5			($450 × .06 × 3/12)				5
6							6

Note Received in Exchange for Merchandise or Other Property

Performance Objective 6d

Write journal entry to record receipt of a note in exchange for merchandise or other property.

Business firms that sell high-priced durable goods in which the credit period is longer than the normal thirty days may accept notes from their customers fairly regularly.

On April 9, Dodson Plumbing Supply sold merchandise to C. T. Mills and Company for $920. Mills gave Dodson Plumbing a promissory note, promising to pay the full amount within 60 days; the note specified 7 percent interest. When this type of transaction occurs occasionally, the transaction is recorded in the general journal as follows:

FYI

It is extremely important to have collateral backing a note you receive. If the maker does not pay the note, there would be an asset, possibly the one the note was signed for, to repossess.

	DATE		DESCRIPTION	POST. REF.	DEBIT	CREDIT	
1	19–						1
2	Apr.	9	Notes Receivable		9 2 0 00		2
3			Sales			9 2 0 00	3

However, if this type of transaction were to occur frequently, Dodson Plumbing Supply would use a Notes Receivable Debit column in the sales journal to record such transactions.

Renewal of Note at Maturity with Receipt of Interest

If the maker of a note is unable to pay the entire principal at maturity, he or she may be allowed to renew all or a part of the note.

Now suppose that C. T. Mills and Company is not able to pay the note at maturity and offers to pay the interest on the current note and to issue a new note, for 30 days at 8 percent. Dodson Plumbing makes the entries in the general journal as shown below. Note that two entries are required. One entry records the interest on the old note. The second entry cancels the old note and records the new note.

Performance Objective 6e
Write journal entries to record receipt of interest and renewal of a note at maturity.

	DATE	DESCRIPTION	POST. REF.	DEBIT	CREDIT	
1	19–					1
2	June 8	Cash		1 0 73		2
3		Interest Income			1 0 73	3
4		($920 × .07 × 60/360)				4
5						5
6	8	Notes Receivable		9 2 0 00		6
7		Notes Receivable			9 2 0 00	7

Actually, there is only one Notes Receivable ledger account. However, when a note is renewed, it is customary for the debtor or maker to pay up the interest on the old note and then issue a new note.

R E M E M B E R

For a renewal of a note receivable, credit the old note to take it off the books, and debit the new note to put it on the books.

Renewal of Note with Receipt of Interest and Partial Receipt of Principal

Sometimes the maker of a note cancels the original note by paying the interest, plus part of the principal, and issuing a new note. Suppose that, as a substitute for the $920 note described above, Mills gives Dodson Plumbing $300 toward the principal and a new note for $620 in addition to the interest on the old note.

Dodson Plumbing records the transactions in the general journal as follows:

	DATE	DESCRIPTION	POST. REF.	DEBIT	CREDIT	
1	19–					1
2	June 8	Cash		3 1 0 73		2
3		Notes Receivable			3 0 0 00	3
4		Interest Income			1 0 73	4
5						5
6	8	Notes Receivable		6 2 0 00		6
7		Notes Receivable			6 2 0 00	7

Discounting Notes Receivable

I nstead of keeping notes receivable until they come due, a firm can raise cash by selling its notes receivable to a bank or finance company. This type of financing is usually called **discounting notes receivable,** because the bank deducts the interest from the maturity value of the note to determine the proceeds (that is, the amount of money received by the firm). The **maturity value** is the principal (face value) of the note plus interest from the date of the note until the due date.

In the process of discounting a note receivable, the firm endorses the note (as on a check) and delivers it to the financial institution. The financial institution gives out cash now in exchange for the privilege of collecting the principal and interest when the note comes due. The discount rate is the annual rate (percentage of maturity value) charged by the financial institution for buying the note.

A Discounted Note: Example 1 Dodson Plumbing Supply granted an extension on an open account by accepting a 60-day, 8 percent note for $1,080, dated April 20, from Cozart Hardware. To raise cash to buy additional merchandise, Dodson Plumbing sold the note to Oliver National Bank on May 5. The bank charged a discount rate of 7 percent. A diagram of the situation looks like this:

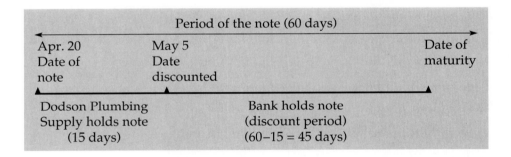

The **discount period** of the note consists of the interval between the date the note is given to the bank and the maturity date of the note. (In other words, the discount period is the time the note has left to run.) Now we ask: How many days are there in the discount period? For emphasis, let's repeat the diagram.

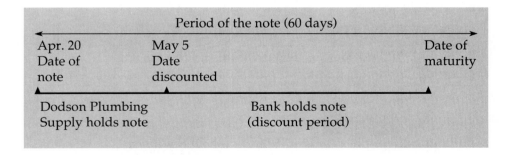

Next we determine the value of the note at maturity and deduct the amount of the bank's discount from it, using the following formula.

Principal ($1,080)
+ Interest to maturity date (8%, 60 days)

Value at maturity
− Discount (7%, 45 days)

Proceeds

After we set up the problem, we can complete the calculation:

Principal	$1,080.00	Interest = Principal × Rate × Time
+ Interest (8%, 60 days)	14.40	
Value at maturity	$1,094.40	Interest = $1,080 × .08 × $\frac{60}{360}$ = $14.40
− Discount (7%, 45 days)	9.58	
Proceeds	$1,084.82	Interest = $1,094.40 × .07 × $\frac{45}{360}$ = $9.576

Note that, in our calculations, we figure the discount on the value of the note at maturity ($1,094.40, 7 percent, 45 days). The proceeds are the amount that Dodson Plumbing Supply receives from the bank; this amount is therefore debited to Cash. *If the amount of the proceeds is greater than the amount of the principal, the difference represents Interest Income* because Dodson Plumbing Supply made money on the deal. *If the amount of the proceeds is less than the principal, on the other hand, the deficiency represents Interest Expense* because Dodson Plumbing Supply lost money in the deal. Look at the entry in Dodson Plumbing's general journal:

Performance Objective 6f

Write journal entry to record discounting an interest-bearing note.

	DATE		DESCRIPTION	POST. REF.	DEBIT	CREDIT	
1	19–						1
2	May	5	Cash		1 0 8 4 82		2
3			Notes Receivable			1 0 8 0 00	3
4			Interest Income			4 82	4

Payment of a Discounted Note by the Maker

The bank collects the principal plus the interest on a discounted note directly from the maker. A journal entry is not required.

A Discounted Note: Example 2 On April 25, Dodson Plumbing Supply received a 90-day, 6 percent, $900 note, dated April 24, from Niles Service Company. On May 4, Dodson Plumbing discounted the note at the Oliver National Bank. The discount rate charged by the bank is 7 percent. In handling discounted notes receivable, you should by all means follow a definite step-by-step procedure.

1. Diagram the situation.

R E M E M B E R

The discount period is the time the note is held by the bank.

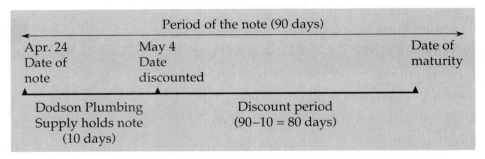

2. Determine the discount period.

April (30 − 24) = 6 days left in April
May   = 4 days
─────────────────────────────
Days held by= 10 days
endorser

Discount period (bank holds note),
(Total days − days held by endorser)
90 days − 10 days = 80 days
Proceeds

3. Record the formula.

Principal ($900)
+ Interest (6%, 90 days)
─────────────────────
Value at maturity
− Discount (7%, 80 days)
─────────────────────
Proceeds

4. Complete the formula.

Principal $900.00
+ Interest (6%, 90 days)   13.50 ⟶ Interest = $900 × .06 × $\frac{90}{360}$ = $13.50
─────────────────────   ───────
Value at maturity $913.50
− Discount (7%, 80 days)   14.21
─────────────────────   ───────
            Proceeds $899.29 ⟶ Interest = $913.50 × .07 × $\frac{80}{360}$ = $14.21

5. Make the entry, recognizing that the amount of the proceeds is a debit to Cash. If the amount of the proceeds is less than the principal, debit Interest Expense for the difference. The entry is shown at the top of the next page.

Figure 11-3

NOTES RECEIVABLE REGISTER

	DATE	MAKER	WHERE PAYABLE	AMOUNT	TIME	RATE	INTEREST	DUE DATE
1	19–							
2	Apr. 6	Hazen Plumbing/Heat.	Oliver Bank	8 4 0 00	30 days	8%	5 60	5/6
3	8	Brenda Paine	Oliver Bank	4 5 0 00	3 mos.	6%	6 75	7/8
4	9	C. T. Mills and Co.	Oliver Bank	9 2 0 00	60 days	7%	1 0 73	6/8
5	20	Cozart Hardware	Oliver Bank	1 0 8 0 00	60 days	8%	1 4 40	6/19
6	24	Niles Service Co.	Oliver Bank	9 0 0 00	90 days	6%	1 3 50	7/23
7	May 9	Martinez and Son	Oliver Bank	3 9 6 0 00	60 days	8%	5 2 80	7/8
8	June 8	C. T. Mills and Co.	Oliver Bank	9 2 0 00	30 days	8%	6 13	7/8
9		OR IF PARTIAL PAYMENT:						
10	June 8	C. T. Mills and Co.	Oliver Bank	6 2 0 00	30 days	8%	4 13	7/8
11								

	DATE		DESCRIPTION	POST. REF.	DEBIT	CREDIT	
1	19–						1
2	May	4	Cash		8 9 9 29		2
3			Interest Expense		71		3
4			Notes Receivable			9 0 0 00	4

Notes Receivable Register

Companies that have a significant number of notes receivable may find it worthwhile to set up a separate list to keep track of them. This list is called a **notes receivable register**. (See notes receivable register shown in Figure 11-3 at the bottom of the page). It is similar to the notes payable register presented earlier. Information is taken from the face of each note. Columns are included to record the specifics of each note. At the end of the fiscal period, the accountant makes a schedule of notes receivable by listing the unpaid notes that appear in the notes receivable register. Also, the total of the schedule is compared with the balance of the Notes Receivable account. The two should match.

Performance Objective 7

Complete a notes receivable register.

End-of-Fiscal-Period Adjustment on Notes Receivable

Accrued interest income on notes receivable runs parallel to accrued interest expense on notes payable. Whenever a firm receives *or* issues an interest-bearing note, the interest accrues or accumulates daily. As a result, any interest-bearing notes that overlap two or more fiscal periods require adjusting entries in order for the financial statements to present a true picture of the firm's net income and financial condition.

DISCOUNTED		DATE PAID	REMARKS	
BANK	DATE			
				1
		5/6	Open account.	2
		7/8	Employee loan.	3
		Renewed	Open account.	4
Oliver Bank	5/5	—	Discounted at 7%, $1,084.82 proceeds.	5
Oliver Bank	5/4	—	Discounted at 7%, $899.29 proceeds.	6
Oliver Bank	6/2		Discounted at 7.5%, $3,982.70 proceeds.	7
			Renewed April 9 note.	8
				9
			Renewed April 9 note with partial payment of	10
			$300 plus interest.	11

For example, if a firm has two notes receivable on December 31, the end of the fiscal period:

$4,000, 90 days, 8%, dated November 28

$5,200, 60 days, 7%, dated December 20

We can diagram the situation as follows:

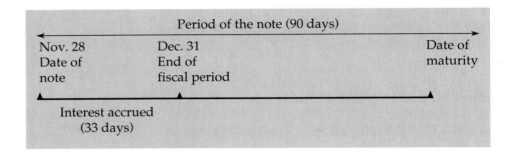

Nov. (30 − 28) =   2 days left in November
Dec.   = 31 days
——————————————————————
Total   33 days left in the fiscal period

Interest = Principal × Rate × Time

Interest = $4,000 × .08 × $\frac{33}{360}$ = $29.33

Figure 11-4

	ACCOUNT NAME	TRIAL BALANCE	
		DEBIT	CREDIT
2	Notes Receivable	9 2 0 0 00	
3	Interest Receivable		
30	Interest Income		6 1 9 70

Dec. $(31 - 20) = 11$ days left in the fiscal period

Interest = Principal × Rate × Time

$$\text{Interest} = \$5{,}200 \times .07 \times \frac{11}{360} = \underline{\underline{\$11.12}}$$

The maker doesn't ordinarily pay the interest until the note comes due. Since these notes have not matured, the interest income has been neither paid nor recorded ($29.33 + $11.12 = $40.45).

In the firm's general journal, the adjusting entry for the interest income accrued on the two notes looks like this:

Performance Objective 8
Write journal entry to record the adjustment for accrued interest on notes receivable.

	DATE	DESCRIPTION	POST. REF.	DEBIT	CREDIT	
1	19–	Adjusting Entry				1
2	Dec. 31	Interest Receivable		4 0 45		2
3		Interest Income			4 0 45	3
4		($29.33 + $11.12)				4

Like all other adjustments, the entry should first be recorded in the Adjustments columns of the work sheet. Here is a T account picture of the situation, assuming a balance in Interest Income of $619.70 before adjustment:

Interest Receivable		Interest Income	
+	–	–	+
Dec. 31 Adj. 40.45			Dec. 31 Bal. 619.70
			Dec. 31 Adj. 40.45

On the work sheet shown in Figure 11-4 below you can see the effect of this adjustment on the financial statements.

	ADJUSTMENTS		INCOME STATEMENT		BALANCE SHEET		
	DEBIT	CREDIT	DEBIT	CREDIT	DEBIT	CREDIT	
					9 2 0 0 00		2
(a)	4 0 45				4 0 45		3
		(a) 4 0 45		6 6 0 15			30

Computer Applications

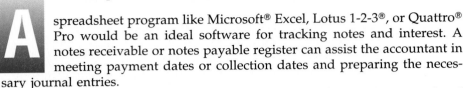

A spreadsheet program like Microsoft® Excel, Lotus 1-2-3®, or Quattro® Pro would be an ideal software for tracking notes and interest. A notes receivable or notes payable register can assist the accountant in meeting payment dates or collection dates and preparing the necessary journal entries.

Figure 11-5 shows a template or format of a register that can be saved and used to record details about notes payable or notes receivable. One of the major advantages of the spreadsheet is the ability to edit quickly and have totals recalculated instantly. This is possible because formulas have been embedded in the spreadsheet to control the mathematical operations to be applied to the entered numbers.

Figure 11-5

NOTES PAYABLE REGISTER

DATE	PAYEE	AMOUNT	TIME	RATE	INTEREST	DUE DATE	DATE PAID	REMARKS
May 15	Adams Mfg. Co.	600.00	60	12%	12.00	7/14	7/14	Open Account.
June 11	Wexler Equip. Co.	3,500.00	90	11%	96.25	9/1	9/1	Bought Equipment
27	Colvin, Inc.	1,800.00	45	10%	22.50	8/11	Renewed	
Aug. 11	Colvin, Inc.	1,800.00	30	11%	16.50	9/10	9/10	Renewed June 27 note.

CHAPTER REVIEW

R eview of Performance Objectives

1. Calculate the interest on promissory notes.
   The formula used to calculate interest is as follows:

   Interest = **Principal** of note × **Rate** of interest × **Time** of note
   (in dollars)   (in dollars)   (as a percentage   (expressed as a year
                                 of the principal) or fraction of a year)

2. Determine the due dates of promissory notes.
   The due date is determined by the following steps:
   1. Determine the number of days remaining in the month of issue by subtracting the date of the note from the number of days in the month in which it is dated.
   2. Add as many full months as possible without exceeding the number of days in the note, counting the full number of days in these months.
   3. Determine the number of days remaining in the month in which the note matures by subtracting the total days counted so far from the number of days in the note.

3a. Write journal entries for notes given to secure an extension of time on an open account.

May 15 Issued a 60-day, 12 percent note for $600, payable to Adams Manufacturing Company, in place of the open-book account. (See the general journal on page 446.)

3b. Write journal entries for payment of an interest-bearing note at maturity.

July 14 Paid at maturity the note given to Adams Manufacturing Company. (See the first general journal on page 447.)

3c. Write journal entries for notes given in exchange for merchandise or other property purchased.

June 3 Issued a 90-day, 11 percent note for $3,500 payable to the Wexler Equipment Company, for equipment. (See the second general journal on page 447.)

3d. Write journal entries for notes given to secure a cash loan, when the borrower receives full face value of the note.

June 11 Borrowed $1,650 from the Finley National Bank, giving in exchange a 120-day, 10 percent note (received full face amount). (See the second general journal on page 448.)

3e. Write journal entries for notes given to secure a cash loan, when the bank discounts the note.

June 19 Borrowed $8,000 from Western National Bank for 90 days; discount rate is 11 percent; issued a note for $8,000. (See the first general journal on page 450.)

3f. Write journal entries for renewal of a note at maturity.

Aug. 11 Cancelled note to Colvin, Inc. for $1,800 and issued an $1,800, 30-day, 11 percent note. (See the general journal on page 452.)

4. Complete a notes payable register.

For each note, list the date of the note, the payee, the amount, the time period, the interest rate, the amount of interest, the due date, the date paid, and relevant remarks. (See the notes payable register on page 453.)

5a. Write journal entries for adjustment for accrued interest on notes payable.

When the time period of the note spans two fiscal periods, record interest earned between the date of the note and the end of the fiscal period. A company has two notes payable outstanding as of December 31, the end of the current fiscal period: $3,000, 60 days, 10 percent, dated December 10; $4,200, 90 days, 11 percent, dated December 2. (See the general journal on page 455.)

5b. Write journal entries for adjustment for Discount on Notes Payable.

If a discounted note extends into the next fiscal period, the Discount on Notes Payable needs to be adjusted to reflect the portion of that discount which has become interest expense for the current fiscal period. (See the second general journal on page 456.)

5c. Write journal entries for conversion of Discount on Notes Payable to Interest Expense.

Upon payment of a discounted note spanning two fiscal periods, the remainder of the Discount on Notes Payable has become an expense and must be converted to Interest Expense. (See the second general journal on page 457.)

6a. Write journal entry to record receipt of a note from a charge customer.

Apr. 6 Received a note for $840 from Hazen Plumbing and Heating, in settlement of the sale of March 7, 30 days, 8 percent. (See the first general journal on page 459.)

6b. Write journal entry to record receipt of payment of an interest-bearing note at maturity.

May 6 Received a payment at maturity of principal plus interest on Hazen Plumbing and Heating's note. (See the second general journal on page 459.)

6c. Write journal entry to record receipt of a note as a result of granting a personal loan.

Apr. 8 Granted a loan to Brenda Paine, an employee, for $450 for 3 months, 6 percent, dated April 8. (See the first general journal on page 460.)

6d. Write journal entry to record receipt of a note in exchange for merchandise or other property.

Apr. 9 Received a note for $920 from C. T. Mills and Company for merchandise, 60 days, 7 percent, dated April 9. (See the last general journal on page 460.)

6e. Write journal entries to record receipt of interest and renewal of a note at maturity.

June 8 Received interest from C. T. Mills and Company on its note of April 9.

Then C. T. Mills agreed to renewal of the note by issuance of a new note, 30 days, 8 percent, dated June 8. (See the first general journal on page 461.)

6f. Write journal entry to record discounting an interest-bearing note.

May 5 Discounted at Oliver National Bank the note received from Cozart Hardware, dated April 20, $1,080, 8 percent, 60 days. The discount rate is 7 percent. (See the general journal on page 463.)

7. Complete a notes receivable register.

For each note, list the date, the maker, where the note is payable, the amount, the time period, the interest rate, the amount of interest, the due date, the date paid, and relevant remarks. (See Figure 11-3 on page 464.)

8. Write journal entry to record the adjustment for accrued interest on notes receivable.

The general journal on page 467 shows the adjusting entry for two notes: a $4,000, 90-day, 8 percent note dated November 28; a $5,200, 60-day, 7 percent note dated December 20.

G lossary

Accrued interest income on notes receivable When a note receivable begins in one fiscal period and matures in the following one, accrued interest represents interest income earned but not yet received—for example, from the date of the note until the last day of the fiscal period. **(465)**

Accrued interest on notes payable For notes payable beginning in one fiscal period and maturing in the following fiscal period, accrued interest is the unpaid interest expense from the date of issue of the note until the last day of the fiscal period. **(454)**

Contra-liability account A deduction from a liability, such as Discount on Notes Payable, which is a deduction from the balance of Notes Payable. **(450)**

Discount Interest deducted in advance by a bank that makes a loan. **(449)**

Discounting a note payable The process by which a bank deducts the interest from the face value of the note payable in advance, leaving the borrower with the remains, or proceeds. **(449)**

Discounting notes receivable The process by which a firm may raise cash by selling a note receivable to a bank or finance company. The bank deducts the interest from the maturity value of the note to determine the proceeds (amount of money) that the firm receives. **(462)**

Discount period The time between the date a note receivable is discounted and the date it matures. **(462)**

Interest A charge made for the use of money. Interest Expense is the account debited when interest is paid or owed to someone else; Interest Income is the account credited when interest is earned. **(442)**

Maker An individual or firm that signs a promissory note. **(442)**

Maturity date The due date of a promissory note. **(442)**

Maturity value The principal (face value) of a note plus interest from the date of the note until the due date. **(462)**

Notes Payable The liability account in which the accountant records a written promise to pay a creditor a sum at a fixed or determinable future time. **(445)**

Notes payable register An auxiliary record used for listing the details of notes issued. **(453)**

Notes Receivable The asset account in which the accountant records a written promise by a debtor to pay a sum at a fixed or determinable future time. **(458)**

Notes receivable register A supplementary record in which a firm lists details of notes received. **(465)**

Notice of maturity A notice specifying the terms and due date of a promissory note that has been left with a bank for collection; mailed by the bank to the maker. **(446)**

Payee The party receiving payment. **(442)**

Principal The face amount of a note. **(442)**

Proceeds The principal of a loan less the discount. **(449)**

Promissory note A written promise to pay a certain sum at a fixed or determinable future time. **(441)**

QUESTIONS, EXERCISES, AND PROBLEMS

D iscussion Questions

1. How can you determine the maturity date of a note?
2. What is the basic formula for the calculation of interest on a note? Explain each element.
3. Explain the difference in the entry for a note discounted at a bank in which the note matures before the end of the fiscal period and one in which the note matures after the end of the fiscal period. Is an adjusting entry required for each situation?
4. Explain the Discount on Notes Payable account. What is its classification?
5. Explain why it is necessary to make an adjusting entry for accrued interest on an interest-bearing note. Should the entry be reversed?
6. From the point of view of a creditor, what are the advantages of a note receivable over an account receivable?
7. Describe the formula for calculating the proceeds of an interest-bearing note receivable discounted at a bank. Define the terms.
8. List the advantages of notes payable and receivable.

E xercises

P.O.1,2

Exercise 11-1 Part A: Determine the interest on the following notes:

Determine interest amounts.

	Principal	Interest Rate (percent)	Number of Days
1.	$12,200	11.0	36 days
2.	1,200	10.0	45 days
3.	6,000	12.0	60 days
4.	9,600	10.5	90 days
5.	1,800	11.5	120 days

Part B: Determine the maturity dates on the following notes:

Determine maturity dates.

	Date of Issue	Time Period
1.	January 15	90 days
2.	February 12	3 months
3.	June 20	60 days
4.	September 10	120 days
5.	November 12	30 days

Exercise 11-2 Dovere Electrical Supply Company completes the following transactions in November. Record them in general journal form.

P.O.3c,f,5a

Journalize note renewal, interest payment, and adjusting entry.

a. Purchased merchandise for $18,300 on November 3, giving a 30-day, 11 percent note, dated November 3, to Miller Company in exchange for the merchandise.
b. On December 3, Dovere is unable to pay the principal of the note due but pays the interest due.
c. On December 3, Dovere renews the $18,300 note for 60 days at 11.5 percent, dated December 3.
d. On December 31, Dovere makes the adjusting entry for accrued interest.

Exercise 11-3 On September 20, S. L. Whittier issued a 120-day, 10 percent note, dated September 20, to Masterson Construction, a creditor, for $9,600. Write the entries in general journal form to record the following transactions. Assume that closing entries were made at the appropriate time.

P.O.3a,b,5a

Journalize note issuance, adjusting entry, reversing entry, and payment.

a. Issuance of the note on September 20.
b. Adjusting entry for accrued interest on December 31, the end of the fiscal year.
c. Reversing entry on January 1.

Exercise 11-4 On December 5, L. M. Carsten borrowed $6,400 from Ruston State Bank for 45 days, with a discount rate of 11 percent. Accordingly, L. M. Carsten signed a note for $6,400, dated December 5. The end of the fiscal year is December 31. Write entries in general journal form to record the following transactions. Assume the closing entries were made at the appropriate time.

P.O.3b,e, 5b,c

Journalize note issuance, adjustment payment, and conversion of Discount on Notes Payable to Interest Expense.

a. Issuance of the note on December 5.
b. Adjusting entry on December 31.
c. Payment of the note at maturity on January 19.
d. Conversion of the Discount on Notes Payable to Interest Expense for the current year.

Exercise 11-5 On March 9, the T. C. Yung Company received a 90-day, 12 percent note for $1,500, dated March 9, from B. L. Hyatt, a charge customer, to satisfy his open account receivable.

P.O.1,2

Calculate due date and interest.

a. What is the due date of the note?
b. How much interest is due at maturity?

Exercise 11-6 Given the data in Exercise 11-5, write entries in general journal form on the books of the T. C. Yung Company to record the following:

P.O.3a,b, 6a,b

a. Receipt of the note from Hyatt in settlement of his account.

Journalize issuance and payment of note on books of payee and maker.

b. Receipt of the principal and interest at maturity.

Given the same data, write entries in general journal form on B. L. Hyatt's books to record the following:

c. Issuance of the note by Hyatt in settlement of his account.
d. Payment of the note at maturity.

P.O.6d,f

Discount a note at the bank.

Exercise 11-7 On May 8, the Baginski Company received a 90-day, 10 percent note for $7,500, dated May 8, for merchandise sold to the Burr Company. Baginski endorsed the note in favor of its bank on May 28. The bank discounted the note at 9 percent, paying the proceeds to Baginski. Determine the following facts:

a. Number of days the Baginski Company held the note
b. Number of days in the discount period
c. Face value
d. Maturity value
e. Discount
f. Proceeds
g. Interest income or expense recorded by the payee (the Baginski Company)

P.O.6a,b,8

Journalize entries to receive a note, adjust for interest accrued, close, reverse, and record receipt of payment.

Exercise 11-8 Write entries in general journal form to record the following transactions for the Bonilla Company, whose fiscal year ends on December 31:

Dec.   3 The Bonilla Company received from BRB Enterprises an $8,000, 120-day, 10.5 percent note, dated December 3, as an extension of a charge account.
        31 The adjusting entry for accrued interest.
        31 The closing entry (for practice), assuming all other closing entries were made
Jan.   1 The reversing entry
Apr.   2 Receipt of the principal and interest at maturity

C onsider and Communicate

Your friend needs to buy a $900 component to upgrade some sound equipment. He has neither that much cash nor credit available. He has heard of promissory notes and asks for your help. Explain the concept of a promissory note, what it will mean when your friend signs it, and why your friend will pay more for the note at maturity than the original $900.

W hat If . . .

You loaned $15,000 to a close friend to buy an off-road vehicle. You planned to have him sign a note receivable, but in the excitement and rush to get the vehicle (which your friend is buying for an unbelievably low price) you forget to make arrangements for collateral or back up of the note with an asset owned by your friend. Furthermore, no papers were signed before the cash changed hands and the vehicle was purchased. What are the possible consequences of your behavior?

A Question of Ethics

You have a personal loan from your aunt for which you signed a note for $8,000. When you go to the bank to get a loan for a new house, the bank asks for a list of your liabilities. You are pretty sure that if you tell them about this personal note (which nobody outside the family knows about) they will not grant you the loan. You decide not to list the $8,000 note among your other liabilities. Are you acting in an ethical manner? Does the fact that this is just a loan within your family influence your response?

P roblem Set A

Problem 11-1A The following were among the transactions of Olandra and Company this year (January 1 through December 31):

P.O.3a,b,e, f,4

Jan.	30	Bought merchandise on account from Porento and Fitz, $2,860; terms net 30 days.
Mar.	1	Gave a 60-day, 11.5 percent note, dated March 1, for $2,860 to Porento and Fitz to apply on account.
Apr.	30	Paid Porento and Fitz the amount owed on the note of March 1.
May	5	Bought merchandise on account from Blandon and Company, $8,246; terms 2/10, n/30.
June	4	Gave a 45-day, 10.5 percent note, dated June 4, for $8,246 to Blandon and Company to apply on account.
July	19	Paid Blandon and Company the interest due on the note of June 4 and renewed the obligation by issuing a new 60-day, 11 percent note for $8,246 (2 entries).
Sept.	17	Paid Blandon and Company the amount owed on the note of July 19.
Oct.	15	Borrowed $15,300 from Runyon Bank for 60 days; discount rate is 11 percent. Accordingly, signed a discounted note for $15,300, dated October 15.
Dec.	14	Paid Runyon Bank at maturity of loan.

Instructions

1. Record these transactions in the general journal (page 36).
2. Immediately following each journal entry, record each note in the notes payable register (page 3).
   a. Fill in the date paid after journalizing the entry to pay the note, or fill in "renewed" if not paid.
   b. Show the calculation of each due date in the space provided below the notes payable register.

Instructions for General Ledger Software

1. Journalize the entries in the general journal.
2. Print the journal entries.

Problem 11-2A The following were among the transactions of Waldon and Company during the year ended December 31:

P.O.3b,c,d, e,f,5a,b

June	10	Gave a 30-day, 11 percent note, dated June 10, to Minter and Son, for $61,000, for an addition to the building.
	15	Borrowed $26,100 from Nindell National Bank, signing a 3-month, 11 percent note for that amount, dated June 15 (received full face value).
July	10	Paid the amount owed on the note given to Minter and Son.
	10	Gave a note to Williams and Jenkins for the purchase of office equipment, $9,242, at 10 percent for 120 days, dated July 10. The invoice was not previously recorded.

Sept. 15 Paid interest on the note given to Nindell National Bank; renewed loan by issuing note for 60 days at 11.5 percent, dated September 15.

Nov. 7 Paid amount owed on the 120-day note given to Williams and Jenkins.

14 Gave two notes to Morton Manufacturing in settlement of their November 14 invoice for merchandise, as follows: $11,200, 30 days, 10 percent, dated November 14; $11,200, 60 days, 11 percent, dated November 14. The invoice was not previously recorded.

14 Paid the note given to Nindell National Bank.

Dec. 14 Paid the amount owed on the 30-day note given to Morton Manufacturing.

17 Issued a 60-day, 10 percent note, dated December 17, payable to Garrison Company, in settlement of November 17 bill for merchandise, $18,950. The invoice was previously recorded.

18 Borrowed $30,000 from Aragon National Bank for 30 days; discount rate is 11 percent; issued a discounted note, dated December 18, for $30,000 (debit Discount on Notes Payable since the note extends into the next fiscal period).

Instructions

1. Record these transactions in a general journal (page 18).
2. Show the calculation of each due date.
3. On December 31, record the adjusting entries to account for accrued interest expense for the Morton and Garrison notes, as well as the adjustment of Discount on Notes Payable on the Aragon National Bank note.
4. On January 1, record the reversing entry. (Assume closing entries have been made.)
5. On January 13, record the payment of the note to Morton Manufacturing.
6. On January 17, record the payment of the note to Aragon National Bank.
7. On January 17, record the entry to expense the discount on the Aragon note.
8. On February 15, record the payment of the note to Garrison Company.

P.O.6a,b,d, e,f,7

Problem 11-3A Selected transactions of the Outdoor Center carried out this year are as follows:

Jan. 10 Sold merchandise on account to Osman Stores; 2/10, n/30; $5,230.

Feb. 9 Received a 30-day, 9 percent note from Osman Stores, $5,230, dated February 9, to apply on account.

Mar. 11 Received $2,269.23 from Osman Stores as part payment on its note dated February 9: $2,230 as part payment on the principal and $39.23 interest on $5,230 for 30 days at 9 percent. Received a new 30-day, 10 percent note, dated March 11, for $3,000.

Apr. 4 Sold merchandise to Fisher Sports, $2,790, receiving their 90-day, 9 percent note, dated April 4 (not previously recorded).

10 Received a check from Osman Stores for the amount owed on its note of March 11.

12 Discounted the note received from Fisher Sports at the Lundgren Bank; discount rate, 8 percent.

May 8 Sold merchandise on account to Laxtrom, Inc.; 2/10, n/30; $2,848.

June 7 Received a 45-day, 9 percent note for $2,848 from Laxtrom, Inc., dated June 7, to apply on account.

Instructions

1. Record these transactions in one of the following journals: a sales journal (page 37), a cash receipts journal (page 32), or a general journal (page 17).
2. Immediately after each journal entry, record each note receivable in the notes receivable register.
   a. All notes are payable at Lundgren Bank.
   b. Fill in date paid after journalizing the receipt of payment of the note, or fill in "renewed," or "discounted," when appropriate.
   c. Show the calculation of each due date in the space provided below the notes receivable register.

Instructions for General Ledger Software

1. Journalize transactions in either the sales journal, cash receipts journal, or general journal.
2. Print the journal entries from each journal.

Problem 11-4A Here are some selected transactions of Huntoon Grocery Supply carried out during the year ended December 31:

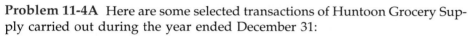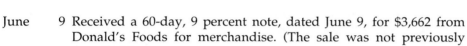

P.O.6a,b,c, d,e,f,8

June	9	Received a 60-day, 9 percent note, dated June 9, for $3,662 from Donald's Foods for merchandise. (The sale was not previously recorded.)
	21	Received a 30-day, 10 percent note, dated June 21, for $2,838 from Lindsey Restaurants, a charge customer, for a sale recorded previously.
July	1	Received a 90-day, 10 percent note, dated July 1, for $1,980 from Armstrong, Inc., a charge customer, for a sale recorded previously.
	21	Received a check from Lindsey Restaurants in payment of principal and interest on its note.
Aug.	8	Received payment of interest from Donald's Foods for its note of June 9 and a new 30-day, 9 percent note, for $3,662, dated August 8.
	20	Received a 60-day, 9.5 percent note, dated August 20, from C. T. Tamparo, a charge customer, for $3,010, for a sale recorded previously.
Sept.	7	Donald's Foods paid its note, dated August 8, principal plus interest.
	9	Discounted the note received from C. T. Tamparo, dated August 20, at the Hammond Bank; discount rate, 10 percent.
Dec.	6	Received a 60-day, 9 percent note, dated December 6, from C. L. Chan, a charge customer, for $2,642, for a sale recorded previously.
	8	Received a 30-day, 9.5 percent note, for a personal loan, dated December 8, from J. Brannon, an employee, for $380.

Instructions

1. Record these transactions in the general journal (page 47).
2. Show the calculation of each due date.
3. Dec. 31 Record the adjusting entry to account for accrued interest receivable for the Chan and Brannon notes, which are not due to be paid until the next fiscal period.
4. Jan. 1 Record the reversing entry. (Assume closing entries have been made.)
5. Jan. 7 Record the receipt of payment on the Brannon note on January 7 of the new fiscal year.

Problem Set B

P.O.3a,b,e,
f,4

Problem 11-1B The following were among the transactions of International Knit Shop this year (January 1 through December 31):

Jan. 25 Bought merchandise on account from Genoa Mills, $2,950; terms net 30 days.

Feb. 24 Gave a 45-day, 10 percent note, dated February 24, for $2,950 to Genoa Mills to apply on account.

Apr. 10 Paid Genoa Mills amount owed on the note of February 24.

May 4 Bought merchandise on account from Veldon Company, $8,300; terms net 30 days.

June 3 Gave a 30-day, 10.5 percent note, dated June 3, for $8,300 to Veldon Company to apply on account.

July 3 Paid Veldon Company the interest due on the note of June 3 and renewed the obligation by issuing a new 60-day, 11 percent note, dated July 3, for $8,300.

Sept. 1 Paid Veldon Company the amount owed on the note of July 3.

25 Borrowed $11,500 from Valley Bank for 90 days; discount rate is 11 percent. Accordingly, signed a discounted note for $11,500, dated September 25. (Use Interest Expense since the note will mature in the present fiscal period.)

Dec. 24 Paid Valley Bank at maturity of loan.

Instructions

1. Record these transactions in a general journal (page 27).
2. Immediately following each journal entry, record each note in the notes payable register (page 3).
   a. Fill in the date paid after journalizing the entry to pay the note, or fill in "renewed" if not paid.
   b. Show the calculation of each due date in the space provided below the notes payable register.

Instructions for General Ledger Software

1. Journalize the entries in the general journal.
2. Print the journal entries.

P.O.3b,c,d,
e,f,5a,b

Problem 11-2B The following were among the transactions of Richards Company during the year ended December 31:

May 24 Gave a 60-day, 10 percent note for $60,300, dated May 24, to DeClerk Builders for additional office space.

June 20 Borrowed $14,200 from First Forest Bank, signing a 3-month, 10 percent note for that amount, dated June 20 (received full face value).

July 15 Gave a note to Raines Custom Carpentry for shelving units, $12,600 at 10 percent for 90 days, dated July 15. The invoice was not previously recorded.

23 Paid the amount due on the note given to DeClerk Builders.

Sept. 20 Paid interest on the note issued to First Forest Bank; renewed loan by issuing new 60-day, 10.5 percent note, dated September 20.

Oct. 13 Paid amount owed on the note given to Raines Custom Carpentry.

27 Gave two notes to Chapman and Company in settlement of their October 27 invoice for merchandise, as follows: $12,300 note for 30 days at 11 percent, dated October 27; $12,300 note for 60 days at 11 percent, dated October 27. The invoice was not previously recorded.

Nov.   19 Paid the note given to First Forest Bank.

      26 Paid the amount owed on the 30-day note given to Chapman and Company.

Dec.   10 Issued a 60-day, 10 percent note, dated December 10, to McAusland and Son in settlement of November 11 invoice for merchandise, $11,460. The invoice was previously recorded.

      18 Borrowed $20,500 from Thornton Bank for 60 days; discount rate is 10 percent; signed a discounted note for $20,500, dated December 18. (Debit Discount on Notes Payable, since note extends into next fiscal period.)

      26 Paid amount owed on the 60-day note given to Chapman and Company.

Instructions

1. Record these transactions in a general journal (page 26).
2. Show the calculation of each due date.
3. On December 31, record the adjusting entries to adjust for accrued interest expense for the McAusland and Son note, as well as the adjustment of Discount on Notes Payable for the Thornton Bank note.
4. On January 1, record the reversing entry. (Assume closing entries have been made.)
5. On February 8, record the payment of the note to McAusland and Son.
6. On February 16, record the payment of the note to Thornton Bank.
7. On February 16, record the entry to expense the discount on the Thornton Bank note.

Problem 11-3B Here are some selected transactions carried out by Crystal Nursery this year:

P.O.6a,b,d, e,f,7

Jan.   6 Sold merchandise on account to Albin Gardens; 2/10, n/30; $4,850.

Feb.   5 Received a 30-day, 11 percent note from Albin Gardens for $4,850, dated February 5, to apply on account.

Mar.   7 Received $1,894.46 from Albin Gardens as payment on its note dated February 5: $1,850 as part payment on the principal, $44.46 as interest on $4,850 for 30 days at 11 percent. Received a new 30-day, 10 percent note for $3,000, dated March 7.

Apr.   6 Received a check from Albin Gardens for the amount owed on its note dated March 7.

      13 Sold merchandise to K. T. Frank, receiving her 60-day, 10 percent note, dated April 13, in the amount of $2,100 (not previously recorded).

      21 Discounted the note received from K. T. Frank at Kundert Bank; discount rate, 10 percent.

May   23 Sold merchandise on account to Hogan Company; 2/10, n/30; $1,366.

June   22 Received a $1,366 note from Hogan Company for 90 days at 11 percent, dated June 22.

Instructions

1. Record these transactions in one of the following journals: sales journal (page 37), cash receipts journal (page 32), or general journal (page 17).
2. Immediately after each journal entry, record each note receivable in the notes receivable register.
   a. All notes are payable at Kundert Bank.
   b. Fill in the date paid after journalizing the receipt of payment of the note, or fill in "renewed" or "discounted" when appropriate.

c. Show the calculation of each due date in the space provided below the notes receivable register.

Instructions for General Ledger Software

1. Journalize transactions in either the sales journal, cash receipts journal, or general journal.
2. Print the journal entries from each journal.

P.O.6a,b,c, d,e,f,8

Problem 11-4B Roger's Printing Company completed the following transactions during the year ended December 31:

June   14 Received a 60-day, 9 percent note, dated June 14, for $1,840 from Snapp Office Supply for the sale of services. (The sale was not previously recorded.)

26 Received a 30-day, 10 percent note, dated June 26, for $3,452 from Dawson, Inc., a charge customer, for a sale recorded previously.

July   7 Received a 90-day, 10 percent note, dated July 7, for $4,980 from Cole Office Supply, a charge customer, for a sale recorded previously.

26 Received a check from Dawson, Inc., in payment of principal and interest on its note.

Aug.   13 Received payment of interest from Snapp Office Supply for its note of June 14 and also a new 30-day, 10 percent note, dated August 13, for $1,840.

22 Received a 60-day, 9.5 percent note, dated August 22, for $2,600 from E. Morris and Company, a charge customer, for a sale recorded previously.

Sept. 12 Snapp Office Supply paid its note dated August 13, principal plus interest.

14 Discounted the note received from E. Morris and Company, dated August 22, at Harris Bank; discount rate, 10 percent.

Dec.   16 Received a 60-day, 10.5 percent note, dated December 16, for $5,820 from Largent and Ryan Company, a charge customer, for a sale recorded previously.

18 Received a 45-day, 10 percent note for a personal loan, dated December 18, from B. Jorn, an employee, for $450.

Instructions

1. Record these transactions in the general journal (page 47).
2. Show the calculation of each due date.
3. Dec. 31   Record the adjusting entry to account for accrued interest receivable for the Largent and Ryan Company and B. Jorn notes, which are not due to be paid until the next fiscal period.
4. Jan. 1   Record the reversing entry. (Assume closing entries have been made.)
5. Feb. 1   Record the receipt of payment from Jorn on February 1 of the new fiscal period.

CHALLENGE PROBLEM

Below are selected transactions from Listel Company. They have made several errors in journalizing.

Apr.   5 Borrowed $3,000 from Star Bank for 90 days, discount rate 9 percent. Signed a discounted note for $3,000 dated April 5.

June   30 Bought a new air conditioning system (Building) giving a 90-day, 9.5 percent note, dated June 30, to Weglin Company, $65,300.

July 4 Paid $3,000 note to Star Bank dated April 5.

Sept. 28 Paid the entire interest due to Weglin Company as well as $30,000 toward the principal. Issued a new $35,300, 120-day, 9.5 percent note, dated September 28.

Nov. 20 Borrowed $4,000 from Larson Bank for 45 days, discount rate 9.5 percent. Signed a discounted note for $4,000 dated November 20.

Dec. 31 Journalized the adjusting entries for the outstanding notes owed to Weglin Company and Larson Bank.

Journal entries as recorded by Listel Company:

GENERAL JOURNAL PAGE _____

	DATE		DESCRIPTION	POST. REF.	DEBIT	CREDIT	
1	19–						1
2	Apr.	5	Cash		3 0 0 0 00		2
3			Interest Expense			6 7 50	3
4			Notes Payable			2 9 3 2 50	4
5							5
6	June	30	Building		65 3 0 0 00		6
7			Notes Payable			65 3 0 0 00	7
8							8
9	July	4	Notes Payable		3 0 0 0 00		9
10			Discount on Notes Payable		6 7 50		10
11			Cash			3 0 6 7 50	11
12							12
13	Sept.	28	Notes Payable		30 0 0 0 00		13
14			Cash			30 0 0 0 00	14
15							15
16		28	Notes Payable		35 3 0 0 00		16
17			Notes Payable			35 3 0 0 00	17
18							18
19	Nov.	20	Cash		3 9 5 2 50		19
20			Interest Expense		4 7 50		20
21			Notes Payable			4 0 0 0 00	21
22							22
23			Adjusting Entries				23
24	Dec.	31	Interest Expense		9 1 8 92		24
25			Interest Payable			9 1 8 92	25
26							26
27		31	Discount on Notes Payable		4 4 33		27
28			Interest Payable			4 4 33	28
29							29

Instructions

1. Record the correct journal entries for those transactions that were recorded in error.

2. For those transactions that are correct, write "O.K." beside the date of the transaction.

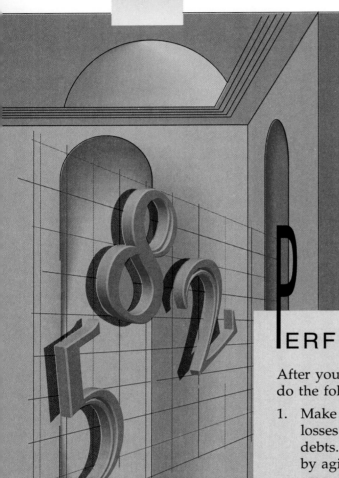

chapter 12

Accounting for Valuation of Receivables

PERFORMANCE OBJECTIVES

After you have completed this chapter, you will be able to do the following:

1. Make the adjusting entry to record estimated bad debt losses by using the allowance method of handling bad debts. (a) Determine the amount of the adjusting entry by aging Accounts Receivable. (b) Determine the amount of the adjusting entry by using a percentage of Accounts Receivable. (c) Calculate the amount of the adjusting entry by using a percentage of Sales or net sales.

2. Journalize the entries to write off accounts receivable as being uncollectible, using the allowance method of accounting for bad debt losses.

3. Journalize entries to reinstate accounts receivable previously written off, using the allowance method.

4. Journalize the entries to write off accounts receivable as being uncollectible, using the specific charge-off method.

5. Journalize entries to reinstate accounts receivable previously written off, using the specific charge-off method.

eceivables are balance sheet items. Nevertheless, most businesses expect some receivables to be uncollectible, which explains why they establish Bad Debts Expense to account for the amount estimated

PRACTITIONER'S CORNER

to be uncollectible for the period.

One of my first audit assignments gave me a good lesson in just how significant an impact on an income statement receivables can have. We were in the middle of a routine audit of a small savings and loan company. The company's management had prepared the financial statements. The income statement showed a decent profit, and the manager was looking forward to presenting this successful achievement to the board of directors at the next meeting. It was our job to make sure that management had fairly represented the company's health—or financial condition.

The audit was going smoothly until our team reached the receivable accounts. The Allowance for Doubtful Accounts account was obviously small. After investigation, we knew that an enormous amount of the receivables would never be collected. That was bad news for the manager because by the time the adjusting entry to reduce Accounts Receivable (via the allowance account) and to increase Bad Debts Expense rippled into the income statement, the profit was gone—in fact, the statement now showed a big loss. Not only did the manager lose his enthusiasm for the next board meeting, he made plans to find out who was responsible for underestimating Bad Debts Expense and overstating net income.

The use of credit for both buying and selling goods and services has become standard practice for businesses of all types and levels: retailers, wholesalers, and manufacturers.

Firms selling goods or services on credit inevitably find that not all the accounts receivable (charge accounts) are collected in full. Consequently, the unpaid accounts must eventually be written off as uncollectible or as bad debts. In this chapter, we'll discuss ways to provide for losses as well as to write off customer accounts that are no longer collectible.

We will examine two methods of accounting for uncollectible accounts: the allowance method and the specific charge-off method. The allowance method is consistent with the matching principle, in that it enables firms to match sales of one year with bad debt losses of the same year; and it is consistent with the accrual method of accounting required by generally accepted principles of accounting. The specific charge-off method traditionally has been used by small businesses. Now, in accordance with the Tax Reform Act of 1986, the specific charge-off method is the only method approved for federal income tax purposes. Many companies, especially larger firms, use the allowance method for their own accounting system of internal reporting, that is, for their own financial statements. They use the specific charge-off method for federal income tax reporting, that is, for their tax returns. The adjustments required on their tax returns are not entered in the companies' books. Incidentally, *write-off* and *charge-off* mean the same thing.

The Credit Department

Because it governs the extension of credit to charge customers, the Credit Department has to keep a watchful eye on present customers. The Credit Department evaluates the debt-paying ability of prospective customers, and determines the maximum amount of credit to be extended to each customer.

It's always bad, of course, if a business firm has high credit losses, since any firm needs to be paid for its sales on account. Surprisingly, it may be bad if a firm has no credit losses. Such a record may indicate that the firm is turning down applications for credit, even though most applicants would indeed pay their bills. It is the responsibility of the Credit Department to keep losses within acceptable limits.

Matching Bad Debt Losses with Sales

A basic principle of the accrual basis of accounting is that revenue for a fiscal period must be matched by the expenses incurred during that same period to earn that revenue. *In order to match up the bad debt losses of the year with the sales of the same year, the firm must make an estimate of the losses as a means of providing for them in advance.* The allowance method of accounting for bad debt losses provides the means for matching bad debt losses with the applicable sales in the company's financial statements.

The Allowance Method of Accounting for Bad Debts

Most big businesses use the **allowance method of accounting for bad debt losses** for financial reporting, which is consistent with the accrual method of accounting required by generally accepted accounting principles (GAAP). An adjusting entry is recorded first in the Adjustments columns of the work sheet—much like the adjustment for depreciation, which was described in Chapter 4. In general journal and T account form, the adjusting entry for the estimated bad debt losses for Morgan and Company is shown in the following examples:

	DATE		DESCRIPTION	POST. REF.	DEBIT	CREDIT	
1	19–		Adjusting Entry				1
2	Dec.	31	Bad Debts Expense		1 4 0 0 00		2
3			Allowance for Doubtful Accounts			1 4 0 0 00	3
4							4

Bad Debts Expense				Allowance for Doubtful Accounts		
+		–		–	+	
Adj.	1,400				Bal.	2,200
					Adj.	1,400
						3,600

The purpose of the adjusting entry is to increase Bad Debts Expense by the amount of the estimated loss and also to show a realistic figure for the book value of Accounts Receivable. **Allowance for Doubtful Accounts is classified as a deduction from Accounts Receivable. As such, it is a contra account, similar to Accumulated Depreciation.** Just as the book value of Equipment equals the cost of Equipment minus Accumulated Depreciation, Equipment, the **book value of Accounts Receivable** equals Accounts Receivable minus Allowance for Doubtful Accounts. Accountants also refer to the book value of Accounts Receivable as the **net realizable value of Accounts Receivable.**

Prior to the adjustments, the **Bad Debts Expense account has no previous balance, as the account is not used during the fiscal period.** The firm's accountant makes an adjusting entry to increase Bad Debts Expense and immediately closes the account along with all other expense accounts. Allowance for Doubtful Accounts, on the other hand, has a balance that is carried over from previous years and is not closed. Notice where these accounts appear in the partial work sheet shown in Figure 12-1 on pages 486 and 487.

Note that Accounts Receivable is recorded in the debit column, and Allowance for Doubtful Accounts is recorded in the credit column. The $1,400 adjustment is added to the previous credit balance of $2,200, resulting in $3,600 being recorded in the Balance Sheet Credit column. As you can see, Allowance for Doubtful Accounts is handled much like Accumulated Depreciation. Both are recorded as credits in the Adjustments and Balance Sheet columns of the work sheet; also, the adjustments are never reversed, because both accounts have previous balances after the first year of operations.

Bad Debts Expense and Allowance for Doubtful Accounts on Financial Statements

The Bad Debts Expense account appears on the income statement as an operating expense. Some firms subdivide operating expenses into selling expenses and general expenses, in which case they list Bad Debts Expense in the category of general expense. (*Reason:* The decision to grant credit is usually a function of the administrative rather than the sales staff.)

Performance Objective 1

Make the adjusting entry to record estimated bad debt losses by using the allowance method of handling bad debts.

R E M E M B E R

Allowance for Doubtful Accounts is a contra account. It is used to record an estimate of the accounts receivable that will not be collected in the future. Its signs are opposite of Accounts Receivable.

Accounts Receivable	
+	–

Allowance for Doubtful Accounts	
–	+

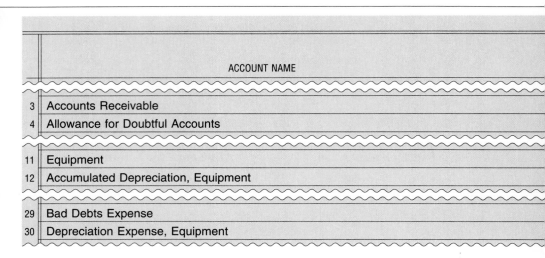

Figure 12-1

	ACCOUNT NAME
3	Accounts Receivable
4	Allowance for Doubtful Accounts
11	Equipment
12	Accumulated Depreciation, Equipment
29	Bad Debts Expense
30	Depreciation Expense, Equipment

FYI

Sometimes accountants use other account names, such as Allowance for Bad Debts, Allowance for Uncollectible Accounts, and Estimated Uncollectible Accounts instead of Allowance for Doubtful Accounts.

Allowance for Doubtful Accounts is listed immediately below Accounts Receivable in the Current Assets section of the balance sheet, as shown in Figure 12-2.

Figure 12-2

Morgan and Company
Balance Sheet
December 31, 19–

Assets			
Current Assets:			
Cash		$12 0 0 0 00	
Notes Receivable		8 0 0 0 00	
Accounts Receivable	$60 0 0 0 00		
Less Allowance for Doubtful Accounts	3 6 0 0 00	56 4 0 0 00	
Merchandise Inventory		96 0 0 0 00	
Supplies		4 0 0 00	
Total Current Assets			$ 172 8 0 0 00
Plant and Equipment:			
Equipment	$74 0 0 0 00		
Less Accumulated Depreciation	28 0 0 0 00	$46 0 0 0 00	

Estimating the Amount of Bad Debts Expense

Management—on the basis of its judgment and past experience—has to make a reasonable estimate of the amount of its uncollectible accounts. It stands to reason that any such estimate is modified by business trends. In a period of prosperity and high employment, one can expect fewer losses from uncollectible accounts than in a period of recession.

TRIAL BALANCE		ADJUSTMENTS		INCOME STATEMENT		BALANCE SHEET		
DEBIT	CREDIT	DEBIT	CREDIT	DEBIT	CREDIT	DEBIT	CREDIT	
60 0 0 0 00						60 0 0 0 00		3
	2 2 0 0 00		(e) 1 4 0 0 00				3 6 0 0 00	4
74 0 0 0 00						74 0 0 0 00		11
	22 0 0 0 00		(h) 6 0 0 0 00				28 0 0 0 00	12
		(e) 1 4 0 0 00		1 4 0 0 00				29
		(h) 6 0 0 0 00		6 0 0 0 00				30

The next question is: "For the adjusting entry, how does management estimate the dollar amount of bad debts expense?" The estimate can be made in several ways; we will present three methods here:

1. Aging Accounts Receivable

2. Using a percentage of Accounts Receivable

3. Using a percentage of Sales or net sales

Figure 12-3 illustrates the adjustment approaches to estimate the amount of bad debts expense.

Figure 12-3

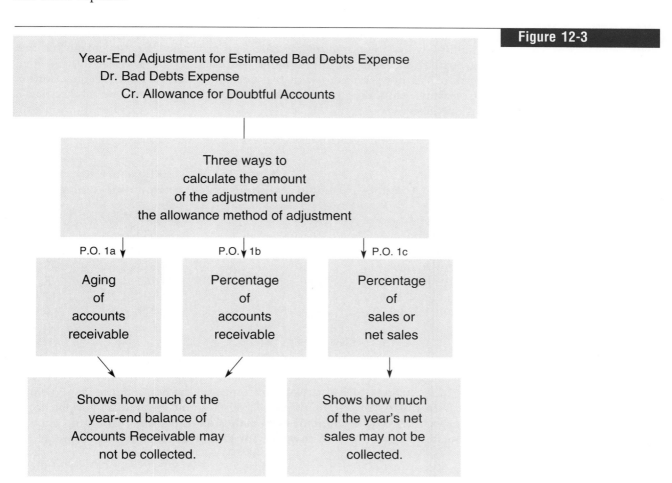

Determine the amount of the adjusting entry by aging Accounts Receivable.

Adjusting Entry Based on Aging Accounts Receivable

The most common technique for estimating the total uncollectible amount of Accounts Receivable is to **age** each charge customer's account by (1) determining the number of days old each account is and (2) determining the number of days the account is past due. As an example, we will use the accounts receivable of Deanna Gordon Company. Here is the partial aging schedule:

ANALYSIS OF ACCOUNTS RECEIVABLE BY AGE

CUSTOMER NAME	BALANCE	NOT YET DUE	DAYS PAST DUE					
			1–30	31–60	61–90	91–180	181–365	OVER 365
A. R. Anders	722.00	722.00						
B. N. Brandt	464.00				464.00			
C. L. Casey	136.90			136.90				
D. R. Dewey	914.00	914.00						
E. V. Eaton	593.10			593.10				
Total	90,000.00	78,200.00	4,030.00	3,280.00	1,975.00	1,260.00	834.00	421.00

Based on its past experience, a company can estimate that a given percentage of each age group of accounts will be uncollectible. Next, the accountant multiplies the total amount for each age group by the percentage for that group. This results in the amount estimated to be uncollectible for that group. We now continue with the Accounts Receivable of Deanna Gordon Company. Naturally, the older the account, the greater the possibility that it is uncollectible.

Age of Accounts	Amount	Estimated Percentage Uncollectible	Allowance for Doubtful Accounts
Not yet due	$78,200	2	$78,200 × .02 = $1,564.00
1 to 30 days	4,030	4	4,030 × .04 = 161.20
31 to 60 days	3,280	10	3,280 × .10 = 328.00
61 to 90 days	1,975	20	1,975 × .20 = 395.00
91 to 180 days	1,260	30	1,260 × .30 = 378.00
181 to 365 days	834	50	834 × .50 = 417.00
Over 365 days	421	80	421 × .80 = 336.80
Total	$90,000		$3,580.00

In the ledger of Deanna Gordon Company, the new balance in Allowance for Doubtful Accounts should be $3,580 (amount estimated by aging to be uncollectible). **The accountant now makes an adjusting entry large enough to make the balance of Allowance for Doubtful Accounts the same as the**

estimated uncollectible amount. Deanna Gordon Company had a credit balance of $320 in Allowance for Doubtful Accounts. We now make an adjusting entry to bring the balance of the account up to $3,580. The amount of the adjusting entry is $3,260 ($3,580 − $320).

Bad Debts Expense		Allowance for Doubtful Accounts	
+	−	−	+
Adj. 3,260			Bal. 320
			Adj. 3,260
			3,580

The adjusting data and their effect on the accounts are illustrated in Figure 12-4, which appears at the bottom of pages 490 and 491.

Bad Debts Expense ($3,260) will appear on the income statement in the general expense portion of Operating Expenses. Like all expenses, it will be closed at the end of the fiscal period into Income Summary.

Incidentally, aging Accounts Receivable is easily accomplished by existing computer accounting programs.

Adjusting Entry Based on Estimating Bad Debts as a Percentage of Accounts Receivable

Some business firms feel that the aging procedure is too time-consuming; they prefer a quicker but less exact method for estimating the amount of uncollectible Accounts Receivable. These firms take an average of the actual bad debt losses of previous years as a percentage of Accounts Receivable. For example, the John Lincoln Company calculated the amount of the adjustment for uncollectible accounts as follows:

Performance Objective 1b
Determine the amount of the adjusting entry by using a percentage of Accounts Receivable.

End of Year	Balance of Accounts Receivable	Total Actual Losses from Accounts Receivable (Accounts Receivable Written Off)
19x1	$22,000	$ 770
19x2	28,000	764
19x3	24,000	686
	$74,000	$2,220

The firm's average loss over three consecutive years was 3 percent.

$$\frac{2,220}{74,000} = .03 = \underline{\underline{3\%}}$$

Assume that, at the end of 19x6, the balance of Accounts Receivable is $29,600 and the credit balance of Allowance for Doubtful Accounts is $147. The amount

R E M E M B E R

The amount of the adjusting entry for bad debts should make the new balance of Allowance for Doubtful Accounts the same as the estimated uncollectible amount when based on aging of accounts or a percentage of Accounts Receivable.

of Accounts Receivable the company estimated to be uncollectible is $888 ($29,600 × .03 = $888). Since $888 is the desired figure, the amount of the adjustment is $741 ($888 − $147 = $741). As in the case of aging Accounts Receivable, when you figure the adjustment for bad debts as a percentage of Accounts Receivable, *you make an adjusting entry to bring the balance of Allowance for Doubtful Accounts up to the desired figure.* Notice how the adjusting entry looks in the following T accounts:

REMEMBER

No matter what method is used to determine the amount of the adjustment for bad debts, the resulting amount is an estimate only.

Bad Debts Expense		Allowance for Doubtful Accounts	
+	−	−	+
Adj. 741		Bal. 147	
		Adj. 741	
		888	

You would then record the adjustment in the work sheet (Figure 12-5) shown at the bottom of this page.

Figure 12-4

	ACCOUNT NAME
3	Accounts Receivable
4	Allowance for Doubtful Accounts
29	Bad Debts Expense

Figure 12-5

	ACCOUNT NAME
1	Cash
2	Notes Receivable
3	Accounts Receivable
4	Allowance for Doubtful Accounts
29	Bad Debts Expense

Adjusting Entry Based on Estimating Bad Debts as a Percentage of Sales

Some business firms prefer a simplified method for determining the amount of the adjustment for Bad Debts Expense. They multiply the current year's sales by a set percentage rate and then record the adjusting entry for the exact amount.

Estimate Based on Net Sales For example, the actual losses from sales on account for the C. A. Nelson Company have averaged approximately 1 percent of net sales (Sales less Sales Returns and Allowances and less Sales Discount). The firm makes virtually all sales on credit. On the basis of this information, the company computes the amount of the adjustment as 1 percent of net sales.

Performance Objective 1c

Calculate the amount of the adjusting entry by using a percentage of Sales or net sales.

Deanna Gordon Company
Work Sheet
For Year Ended December 31, 19—

TRIAL BALANCE DEBIT	TRIAL BALANCE CREDIT	ADJUSTMENTS DEBIT	ADJUSTMENTS CREDIT	INCOME STATEMENT DEBIT	INCOME STATEMENT CREDIT	BALANCE SHEET DEBIT	BALANCE SHEET CREDIT	
90 0 0 0 00						90 0 0 0 00		3
	3 2 0 00		(a) 3 2 6 0 00				3 5 8 0 00	4
		(a) 3 2 6 0 00		3 2 6 0 00				29

John Lincoln Company
Work Sheet
For Year Ended December 31, 19x6

TRIAL BALANCE DEBIT	TRIAL BALANCE CREDIT	ADJUSTMENTS DEBIT	ADJUSTMENTS CREDIT	INCOME STATEMENT DEBIT	INCOME STATEMENT CREDIT	BALANCE SHEET DEBIT	BALANCE SHEET CREDIT	
16 8 9 1 00						16 8 9 1 00		1
1 6 0 0 00						1 6 0 0 00		2
29 6 0 0 00						29 6 0 0 00		3
	1 4 7 00		(e) 7 4 1 00				8 8 8 00	4
		(e) 7 4 1 00		7 4 1 00				29

Here is the figure for net sales, as shown in the partial income statement:

C. A. Nelson Company
Income Statement
For Year Ended June 30, 19x7

Revenue from Sales:			
Sales		$ 652 0 0 0 00	
Less: Sales Returns and Allowances	$26 0 0 0 00		
Sales Discount	1 2 0 0 00	27 2 0 0 00	
Net Sales			$ 624 8 0 0 00

Now 1 percent of net sales is $6,248 ($624,800 × .01), **so the firm uses this amount directly for the adjusting entry, adding it to both accounts,** as shown in the T accounts below.

Bad Debts Expense		Allowance for Doubtful Accounts	
+	**−**	**−**	**+**
Adj. 6,248			Bal. 196
			Adj. 6,248
			6,444

Figure 12-6 shows how to record the adjustment in the work sheet.

Estimate Based on Net Credit Sales   Many companies that sell on both a cash and a credit basis compute the amount of their adjustment for bad debts on net credit sales only. As an example, we will use the Mallock Company.

Figure 12-6

	ACCOUNT NAME
3	Accounts Receivable
4	Allowance for Doubtful Accounts
20	Sales
21	Sales Returns and Allowances
22	Sales Discount
29	Bad Debts Expense

Charge sales, recorded in a sales journal, total $735,000. Sales Returns and Allowances and Sales Discounts relating to credit sales are $27,000 and $4,300, respectively. The Mallock Company records the adjustment for bad debts at $\frac{3}{4}$ percent of net credit sales. Look at the calculation and adjustment that follow:

Credit (charge) sales		$735,000
Less: Sales Returns and Allowances	$27,000	
Sales Discounts	4,300	31,300
Net credit sales		$703,700

$$\begin{array}{r} \$\,703{,}700 \\ \times\ .0075 \\ \hline \$5{,}277.75 \end{array}$$

By T accounts, the amount of the adjustment is added to both accounts and looks like this:

Bad Debts Expense			Allowance for Doubtful Accounts		
+		−	−		+
Adj. 5,277.75				Bal.	330.14
				Adj.	5,277.75
					5,607.89

Note that a firm using this simplified method multiplies net sales or net credit sales by the given percentage in order to determine the amount of the adjustment. **The present balance of Allowance for Doubtful Accounts is not involved in determining the amount of the adjustment.** If the given percentage does not adequately provide for the firm's losses (that is, if it yields either too little or too much), the firm merely changes the percentage.

C. A. Nelson Company
Work Sheet
For Year Ended June 30, 19x7

	TRIAL BALANCE		ADJUSTMENTS		INCOME STATEMENT		BALANCE SHEET		
	DEBIT	CREDIT	DEBIT	CREDIT	DEBIT	CREDIT	DEBIT	CREDIT	
	49 2 0 0 00						49 2 0 0 00		3
		1 9 6 00		(e) 6 2 4 8 00				6 4 4 4 00	4
		652 0 0 0 00				652 0 0 0 00			20
	26 0 0 0 00				26 0 0 0 00				21
	1 2 0 0 00				1 2 0 0 00				22
			(e) 6 2 4 8 00		6 2 4 8 00				29

COMPUTERS AT WORK

Analysis Tools

With a personal computer, you can make quick cash flow projections as well as take advantage of numerous other financial planning tools. A good spreadsheet program or a more specialized cash flow package can enable you to review projected cash inflows and outflows. By analyzing these projections you can see the fluctuations in cash flow and create management policies to avoid potential shortfalls. You can also create different kinds of reports to present to banks and others detailing your cash management. . . .

SPREADSHEETS • Spreadsheet programs also let you create cash flow projections. Spreadsheets are more flexible than specialized programs, but have a higher learning curve.

Stacy Kenworthy uses *Lotus 1-2-3 for Windows* to do cash flow analyses for clients. Kenworthy is technical director of the Executive Planning Service division of Alexander & Alexander, an Atlanta, Ga.-based consulting company. The Executive Planning Service, which has a staff of 15, specializes in planning and managing benefits for senior executives of Fortune 1000 companies.

Kenworthy uses Lotus to show how executives' benefits plans will affect their company's cash flow. Typically, planning and administering these plans is very complex. There are often several types of

benefits involved, some plans involve more than 3,000 executives, and there are numerous tax ramifications.

The cash flow calculations can also be complex. They involve projections through time, with different interest rate assumptions, different rate of return assumptions, and different product performance assumptions. . . .

The numerous American Red Cross offices around the country use Borland's *Quattro Pro* for cash flow analyses and other financial tasks. . . . Quattro Pro was chosen because of its flexible interface and support for a wide range of file formats, including Lotus 1-2-3. . . .

There also are checkbook managers such as Intuit's *Quicken,* accounting programs such as Teleware's *M.Y.O.B.,* other spreadsheet programs such as Microsoft Excel, other spreadsheet add-ons like Intex Solutions' *Forecast for Excel,* and other specialized financial planning programs such as Lord Publishing's *Ronstadt's Financials.* Whatever program you use, you'll be better armed to tackle the task of managing the flow of cash into and out of your business.

Source: Excerpted from *PC Today,* April 1994, pp. 36–37.

Closing the Bad Debts Expense Account

U p to now, we have seen that the firm's accountant first records the adjusting entry for bad debts in the appropriate columns of the work sheet. As an illustration, the T accounts for Mallock Company are repeated at the top of the next page.

Bad Debts Expense			Allowance for Doubtful Accounts	
+	−		−	+
Adj. 5,277.75				Bal. 330.14
				Adj. 5,277.75
				5,607.89

Next the firm's accountant closes Bad Debts Expense, along with all expenses, into the Income Summary account. **The Bad Debts Expense account is not used during the year, so the only entries in it are the adjusting entry and the closing entry.** This represents the beginning and the end of Bad Debts Expense for the fiscal period. In other words, the only entry in Bad Debts Expense is the adjusting entry, and, as we said, this account is immediately closed out. After the adjusting entry and closing entry have been posted, the accounts look like this:

Bad Debts Expense			Allowance for Doubtful Accounts	
+	−		−	+
Adj. 5,277.75	Clos. 5,277.75			Bal. 330.14
				Adj. 5,277.75
				5,607.89

Allowance for Doubtful Accounts

It is apparent that Allowance for Doubtful Accounts remains open. Rather than have the balance continually increase because of the successive adjustments on the credit side of the account, the accountant uses the debit side of the account to write off charge accounts that are considered definitely uncollectible.

We can consider Allowance for Doubtful Accounts as a reservoir: we fill it up at the end of the year through the medium of the adjusting entry by crediting the account. During the following year, we drain off the reservoir through the medium of write-offs by debiting the account. To avoid the possibility of the reservoir's "running dry," *the accountant should make the adjusting entry large enough to provide for all possible write-offs.*

REMEMBER

Allowance for Doubtful Accounts increases when the end-of-the-year adjustment is made (credit) and decreases as write-offs occur during the year (debits).

Uncollectible Accounts

Entry to Write Off a Charge Account in Full

uppose that a firm decides, after all attempts to collect a customer's debt have failed, that the account is definitely uncollectible. In such a case, the firm should write off the amount due. Let's get back to C. A. Nelson Company and assume that it decides that the account of a customer, C. N. Coe, is uncollectible. The accountant records the writeoff by making the following entry:

Performance Objective 2

Journalize the entries to write off accounts receivable as being uncollectible, using the allowance method of accounting for bad debt losses.

	DATE		DESCRIPTION	POST. REF.	DEBIT	CREDIT	
1	19x6						1
2	July	1	Allowance for Doubtful Accounts		1 7 1 40		2
3			Accounts Receivable, C. N. Coe			1 7 1 40	3
4			Wrote off the account as				4
5			uncollectible.				5
6							6

GENERAL JOURNAL PAGE 116

By T accounts, the entry looks like this:

Accounts Receivable					Allowance for Doubtful Accounts			
+		−			−		+	
Bal.	49,200.00	July 1	171.40		July 1	171.40	Bal.	6,444.00
Bal.	49,028.60				(Coe's write-off)			
							Bal.	6,272.60

The accountant also posts the entry to the account of C. N. Coe in the accounts receivable subsidiary ledger.

NAME C. N. Coe
ADDRESS 217 Barclay Road
Boston, MA 02101

	DATE		ITEM	POST. REF.	DEBIT	CREDIT	BALANCE
	19x4						
	May	1	Balance	✓			1 7 1 40
	19x6						
	July	1	Written off	J116		1 7 1 40	——

Note that the entry just shown does not change the net realizable value or book value of the Accounts Receivable.

Account Name	Balances Before Write-offs	Balances After Write-offs
Accounts Receivable	$49,200.00	$49,028.60
Less Allowance for Doubtful Accounts	6,444.00	6,272.60
Book value (net realizable value)	$42,756.00	$42,756.00

Also note that **the entry to write off an account does not involve an expense account.** The adjusting entry, which was made long before this time, provides for the expense. The estimated expense was recorded *during the year in which the sale was made,* even though this account is written off in a later year.

Rather than writing off each uncollectible account separately during the year, a firm may write off a number of accounts at the end of the year by using a compound entry.

Entry to Write Off a Charge Account Paid in Part

Sometimes a part payment is involved in a write-off of an account. When this happens, it may be due to a bankruptcy settlement. The federal laws governing **bankruptcy** legally excuse a debtor from paying off certain obligations. For example, on April 21, the C. A. Nelson Company received 10 cents on the dollar (10 percent) in settlement of a $442 account owed by its customer, R. E. Hays, a bankrupt. In general journal form, the entry is as follows:

	DATE		DESCRIPTION	POST. REF.	DEBIT	CREDIT	
1	19x6						1
2	Apr.	21	Cash		4 4 20		2
3			Allowance for Doubtful Accounts		3 9 7 80		3
4			Accounts Receivable, R. E. Hays			4 4 2 00	4
5			Settlement in bankruptcy,				5
6			wrote off account balance				6
7			as uncollectible.				7
8							8

Write-Offs Seldom Agree with Previous Estimates

The total amount of Accounts Receivable written off during a given year does not ordinarily agree with the estimates of uncollectible accounts previously debited to Bad Debts Expense and credited to Allowance for Doubtful Accounts. In the usual situation, the amounts written off as uncollectible turn out to be less than the estimated amount. At the end of a given year, there is normally a credit balance in Allowance for Doubtful Accounts. However, if (as sometimes happens) the amounts written off are greater than the estimated amounts, Allowance for Doubtful Accounts temporarily has a debit balance. The debit balance will be eliminated by the adjusting entry at the end of the year, which results in a credit to, or increase in, Allowance for Doubtful Accounts.

Collection of Accounts Previously Written Off

O ccasionally an account previously written off as uncollectible may later be recovered, either in part or in full. In such cases, the firm's accountant restores the account to the books, or reinstates it, by an entry that is the exact opposite of the write-off entry.

As an example, the C. A. Nelson Company sells merchandise on account to P. E. Mundt for $495 on May 5, 19x6.

The C. A. Nelson Company makes many futile attempts to collect, and the **statute of limitations** finally expires. Accordingly, three years later, in 19x9, the accountant for C. A. Nelson Company writes off the account of P. E. Mundt as uncollectible.

	DATE		DESCRIPTION	POST. REF.	DEBIT	CREDIT	
1	19x9						1
2	June	10	Allowance for Doubtful Accounts		4 9 5 00		2
3			Accounts Receivable,				3
4			P. E. Mundt			4 9 5 00	4

But on September 15, 19x9, P. E. Mundt suddenly pays his account in full! The entry to reinstate the account is the reverse of the entry used to write off the account.

	DATE		DESCRIPTION	POST. REF.	DEBIT	CREDIT	
1	19x9						1
2	Sept.	15	Accounts Receivable, P. E. Mundt		4 9 5 00		2
3			Allowance for Doubtful Accounts			4 9 5 00	3
4			Reinstated the account.				4

The way is now clear to record the collection of the account.

	DATE		DESCRIPTION	POST. REF.	DEBIT	CREDIT	
1	19x9						1
2	Sept.	15	Cash		4 9 5 00		2
3			Accounts Receivable,				3
4			P. E. Mundt			4 9 5 00	4
5			Collection of account in full.				5

Now suppose that P. E. Mundt had gone into bankruptcy and settled his account with the C. A. Nelson Company by paying it 5 cents on the dollar. The C. A. Nelson Company would realize that there was no hope of collecting any more, so the accountant would reinstate the account only for the amount collected, like this:

	DATE		DESCRIPTION	POST. REF.	DEBIT				CREDIT				
1	19x9												1
2	Sept.	15	Accounts Receivable, P. E. Mundt			2	4	75					2
3			Allowance for Doubtful Accounts							2	4	75	3
4			Settlement in bankruptcy.										4

The subsequent entry to record the cash payment would be as follows:

	DATE		DESCRIPTION	POST. REF.	DEBIT				CREDIT				
9		15	Cash			2	4	75					9
10			Accounts Receivable,										10
11			P. E. Mundt							2	4	75	11
12			Settlement in bankruptcy.										12

Specific Charge-off of Bad Debts

T he **specific charge-off method of accounting for bad debt losses** is a simpler system for writing off charge accounts determined to be uncollectible. No adjusting entry is made, since there is no attempt to provide for bad debt losses in advance or to match revenue with related expenses. Instead, when a firm decides that a specific customer account is never going to be paid, the accountant makes an entry in the general journal debiting Bad Debts Expense and crediting Accounts Receivable. Thus Allowance for Doubtful Accounts does not exist in the firm's charts of accounts. Traditionally, this method has been used primarily by small companies and professional enterprises. As we stated previously, the specific charge-off method is required for federal income tax reporting.

For example, on April 16, 19x5, the Rex Company sold merchandise on account to H. N. Rhodes for $79.10. Rhodes never pays his bill. Finally, three years later, on September 1, the account is written off as follows:

Performance Objective 4

Journalize the entries to write off accounts receivable as being uncollectible, using the specific charge-off method.

R E M E M B E R

The specific charge-off method is simple to do but can cause inaccurate matching of revenue and expenses; for example, a sale on account made in one fiscal period is found to be uncollectible in the next fiscal period. Nevertheless, this method is used for tax purposes for most businesses, even though they may use the allowance method for financial reporting.

	DATE		DESCRIPTION	POST. REF.	DEBIT				CREDIT				
1	19x8												1
2	Sept.	1	Bad Debts Expense			7	9	10					2
3			Accounts Receivable, H. N.										3
4			Rhodes							7	9	10	4
5			To write off an uncollectible										5
6			account.										6

By T accounts, the entries look like this:

Accounts Receivable				Sales				Bad Debts Expense		
+		−		−		+		+		−
19x5		19x8		19x5		19x5		19x8		
Apr. 16	79.10	Sept. 1	79.10	Dec. 31 Closed		Apr. 16	79.10	Sept. 1	79.10	

You can see that revenue does not match expenses for a particular year. The Rex Company counted the original sale of $79.10 in 19x5, thereby overstating true revenue for that year. It counted Bad Debts Expense three years later, in 19x8, thereby overstating expenses for that year. Note that the Rex Company did not use the account titled Allowance for Doubtful Accounts. On the balance sheet, Accounts Receivable is stated at the gross amount only; there is no book value or net realizable value.

Performance Objective 5

Journalize entries to reinstate accounts receivable previously written off, using the specific charge-off method.

As an illustration of reinstating an account previously written or charged off, let's go on and say that, on May 2, 19x9, H. N. Rhodes returns and pays his $79.10 bill. We will show the entries in general journal form.

			GENERAL JOURNAL					PAGE			
	DATE		DESCRIPTION	POST. REF.	DEBIT			CREDIT			
1	19x9										1
2	May	2	Accounts Receivable, H. N.								2
3			Rhodes		7 9 10						3
4			Bad Debts Recovered					7 9 10			4
5			Reinstated the account.								5
6											6
7		2	Cash		7 9 10						7
8			Accounts Receivable, H. N.								8
9			Rhodes					7 9 10			9
10			Collection of account in full.								10
11											11

By T accounts, the entries look like this:

Accounts Receivable				Bad Debts Recovered				Cash		
+		−		−		+		+		−
19x9		19x9				19x9		19x9		
May 2	79.10	May 2	79.10			May 2	79.10	May 2	79.10	

For a small company that uses the specific charge-off method alone, the account entitled Bad Debts Recovered is classified as a revenue account and would be listed in the Other Income section of an income statement. The Accounts Receivable account was placed back on the books, so that the firm would have a record of H. N. Rhodes's account. Note that this method of accounting is not consistent with the accrual method.

Federal Income Tax Requirement

All companies, except for financial institutions, are required to use the specific charge-off method for reporting on their federal income tax returns. A separate record should be maintained for reporting bad debt losses. For each account charged off, this record must contain the following:

1. A description of the debt, including the amount, and the date it became due

2. The name of the debtor

3. The efforts that have been made to collect the debt

4. Why it has been decided that the debt is worthless

Computer Applications

Aging accounts receivable is a tedious job when done manually, even when using a calculator. Spreadsheets or general ledger packages with accounts receivable modules can do the job much more quickly and accurately.

Figure 12-7 shows an aging schedule for Dodson Plumbing Supply's accounts receivable ledger prepared by an accounting software package. All amounts are current. If some accounts do not pay on time, the software program will count the number of days from the date of the sale to the current date and place the amount in the appropriate column, 31–60, 61–90 or 90+, total

Facsimile (fax) machines are common pieces of equipment in offices. Here an office worker prepares to fax a document to a client.

Figure 12-7

```
                     Dodson Plumbing Supply
                      1400 Jackson Avenue
                      San Diego, CA  92102

                        Aged Receivables

                           8/31/9-
                                                              Page 1
```

Name	ID#	Date	Total Due	Current	31 - 60	61 - 90	90+
Alvarez Construction							
	00000322	8/6/9-	$394.00	$394.00			
		Total:	$394.00	$394.00	$0.00	$0.00	$0.00
Barlow Building Supplies							
	00000327	8/23/9-	$384.00	$384.00			
	00000330	8/30/9-	$614.00	$614.00			
		Total:	$998.00	$998.00	$0.00	$0.00	$0.00
C. P. Landis Company							
	00000320	8/1/9-	$580.92	$580.92			
	00000331	8/31/9-	$375.50	$375.50			
		Total:	$956.42	$956.42	$0.00	$0.00	$0.00
Cozart Hardware							
	00000324	8/11/9-	$772.24	$772.24			
		Total:	$772.24	$772.24	$0.00	$0.00	$0.00
Cozart Hardware							
	00000328	8/24/9-	$293.22	$293.22			
		Total:	$293.22	$293.22	$0.00	$0.00	$0.00
F. A. Barnes, Inc.							
	00000332	8/31/9-	$861.00	$861.00			
		Total:	$861.00	$861.00	$0.00	$0.00	$0.00
Hazen Plumbing and Heating							
	00000326	8/20/9-	$710.00	$710.00			
		Total:	$710.00	$710.00	$0.00	$0.00	$0.00
Hewitt and Sons, Inc.							
	00000325	8/16/9-	$441.00	$441.00			
	00000329	8/28/9-	487.00	$487.00			
		Total:	$928.00	$928.00	$0.00	$0.00	$0.00
Milne, Inc.							
	00000321	8/3/9-	$116.00	$116.00			
		Total:	$116.00	$116.00	$0.00	$0.00	$0.00
Mitchell Service Company							
	00000323	8/9/9-	$961.00	$961.00			
		Total:	$961.00	$961.00	$0.00	$0.00	$0.00
	Grand Total:		$6,989.88	$6,989.88	$0.00	$0.00	$0.00
	Aging Percent:			100.0%	0.0%	0.0%	0.0%

the column, and compute the percentage of accounts receivable that are due in each time frame. This information can be linked to a word processing program and mail merge program to produce collection letters. However, none of these benefits can occur unless the program is set up, information is entered completely and accurately, and the person using the program is knowledgeable about program capabilities.

CHAPTER REVIEW

eview of Performance Objectives

1. **Make the adjusting entry to record estimated bad debt losses by using the allowance method of handling bad debts.**
   The adjusting entry is a debit to Bad Debts Expense and a credit to Allowance for Doubtful Accounts.
   (a) Determine the amount of the adjusting entry by aging Accounts Receivable.
   Classify each charge customer's account according to the number of days past due (thirty days, sixty days, and so on).
   Multiply the totals for each time period by a given percentage deemed to be uncollectible.
   Assuming that the Allowance for Doubtful Accounts has a credit balance, subtract the amount of the credit balance from the amount estimated to be uncollectible to get the amount of the adjusting entry.
   (b) Determine the amount of the adjusting entry by using a percentage of Accounts Receivable.
   Multiply the balance of Accounts Receivable by the given percentage. Next, assuming that Allowance for Doubtful Accounts has a credit balance, subtract the amount of the credit balance from the percentage amount to get the amount of the adjusting entry.
   (c) Calculate the amount of the adjusting entry by using a percentage of Sales or net sales.
   Multiply the amount of Sales or net sales by the given percentage and make the adjusting entry for the amount determined.

2. **Journalize the entries to write off accounts receivable as being uncollectible, using the allowance method of accounting for bad debt losses.**
   Debit Allowance for Doubtful Accounts and credit Accounts Receivable.

3. **Journalize entries to reinstate accounts receivable previously written off, using the allowance method.**
   Debit Accounts Receivable and credit Allowance for Doubtful Accounts (the opposite of a write-off).

4. **Journalize the entries to write off accounts receivable as being uncollectible, using the specific charge-off method.**
   Debit Bad Debts Expense and credit Accounts Receivable.

5. **Journalize entries to reinstate accounts receivable previously written off, using the specific charge-off method.**
   Debit Accounts Receivable and credit Bad Debts Recovered.

G lossary

Age (accounts receivable) To analyze the composition of accounts receivable by classifying the outstanding balance of each charge customer's account according to the amount of time it has been outstanding. One can then multiply the totals for each time period by a percentage deemed to be uncollectible. **(488)**

Allowance method of accounting for bad debt losses An adjusting entry is required to debit Bad Debts Expense and to credit Allowance for Doubtful Accounts. Write-offs of uncollectible accounts are debited to Allowance for Doubtful Accounts and credited to Accounts Receivable. **(484)**

Bankruptcy A federal law excusing a debtor from certain obligations incurred. **(497)**

Book value of Accounts Receivable The balance of Accounts Receivable after one has deducted the balance of Allowance for Doubtful Accounts; also called the *net realizable value of Accounts Receivable.* **(485)**

Net realizable value of Accounts Receivable The balance of Accounts Receivable after one has deducted the balance of Allowance for Doubtful Accounts; also called the *book value of Accounts Receivable.* **(485)**

Specific charge-off method of accounting for bad debt losses This method, used by small business firms, requires no adjusting entry. The accountant debits write-offs of uncollectible accounts to Bad Debts Expense and credits them to Accounts Receivable. This method is required for federal income tax reporting. **(499)**

Statute of limitations A law that limits the period of time during which the courts may force a debtor to pay a debt; usually three years for charge accounts. **(498)**

QUESTIONS, EXERCISES, AND PROBLEMS

D iscussion Questions

1. Explain the nature of Allowance for Doubtful Accounts, how it comes into existence, and what happens to it.
2. When the allowance method of accounting for bad debts is used to determine the amount of the adjusting entry, explain the difference between using a percentage of Accounts Receivable and a percentage of Sales.
3. Suppose that the estimate of bad debts is based on the aging method and that Allowance for Doubtful Accounts has a debit balance. Explain how this situation is handled.
4. When an account is written off under the allowance method of accounting for bad debts, why doesn't the book value of Accounts Receivable decrease?
5. Explain what is meant by aging the Accounts Receivable.
6. Which accounting principle is violated when the specific charge-off method of accounting for bad debts is used. How?
7. For each of the following items, indicate the normal balance; whether it would appear on an income statement or a balance sheet; and under which heading it should be shown:
   a. Discount on Notes Payable
   b. Bad Debts Expense
   c. Interest Receivable
   d. Notes Payable (due in six months)
   e. Allowance for Doubtful Accounts
   f. Interest Payable
8. Assume that a customer's account was previously written off as uncollectible and is paid at a later date. Under the allowance method, what journal

entries are made on the seller's books? What entry is made on the buyer's books?

Exercises

Problem 12-1 The Kinisky Company uses the allowance method of estimating losses from bad debts. Management analyzed its accounts receivable balances on December 31 and determined the following aged balances.

Age of Accounts	Balance	Estimated Percentage Uncollectible	Allowance for Doubtful Accounts
Note yet due	$110,000	1	____
30 to 60 days	18,000	2	____
61 to 120 days	9,000	5	____
121 to 365 days	1,200	30	____
Over 365 days	4,200	60	____
	$142,400		

P.O.1a

Estimate uncollectible accounts based on aging and make the adjusting entry.

Compute the estimate of the amount of uncollectible accounts. Write the adjusting entry for estimated credit losses on December 31. The credit balance of Allowance for Doubtful Accounts is $3,040.

Exercise 12-2 The Jubenville Company uses the allowance method of estimating losses from bad debts. Jubenville Company considers estimated losses to be 3 percent of Accounts Receivable. On December 31, the Accounts Receivable balance was $62,000, and Allowance for Doubtful Accounts had a credit balance of $320. Journalize the adjusting entry to record the estimated bad debt losses.

P.O.1b

Journalize the adjusting entry based on a percentage of Accounts Receivable.

Exercise 12-3 The Malgunas Company uses the allowance method of estimating losses due to bad debts. On December 31, before any adjustments have been recorded, the ledger contains the following balances:

Sales $180,000
Sales Returns and Allowances 27,000

P.O.1c

Journalize the adjusting entry based on a percentage of net sales.

The company estimates that bad debt losses will be $\frac{1}{2}$ percent of net sales. Journalize the adjusting entry to record the estimated bad debt losses. The Allowance for Doubtful Accounts account has a credit balance of $320.

Exercise 12-4 The Pennock Company uses the allowance method of handling losses due to bad debts. The Pennock Company's Accounts Receivable account has a balance of $82,000. Net sales for the year total $104,000. Write the adjusting entry to record the estimated bad debt losses under each of the following conditions. Assume that Allowance for Doubtful Accounts has a credit balance of $650.

P.O.1a,c

Journalize the adjusting entry based on (a) aging and (b) a percentage of net sales.

a. Aging of the charge accounts in the accounts receivable ledger indicates doubtful accounts of $6,175.
b. Bad debt losses are estimated at $\frac{3}{4}$ percent of net sales.

P.O.3

Journalize the write-off of an account using allowance method, compute net realizable value of Accounts Receivable, and prepare partial balance sheet.

P.O.1c,2,3

Allowance method: write off, reinstate, and collect on an account; journalize adjusting entry based on percentage of net sales.

P.O.4,5

Specific charge-off method: write off, reinstate, and collect on an account.

P.O.4,5

Journalize the write-off, the reinstatement, and the collection of an account using the specific charge-off method.

Exercise 12-5 On June 1, Richter Supply's Accounts Receivable balance was $26,436. The balance of the contra account Allowance for Doubtful Accounts was $1,630. On June 20, the account balance of Midano Bakery of $480 was written off.

a. Journalize the write-off of the Midano account using the allowance method.
b. Using T accounts, determine what is now the net realizable value of Accounts Receivable. How would this be shown in the financial statements (the period ends December 31, 19—).

Exercise 12-6 McCall Toy Shop had the following selected transactions this year. Assuming that McCall Toy Shop uses the allowance method of accounting for bad debt losses, record the three transactions in general journal form. Allowance for Doubtful Accounts has a credit balance of $346.

a. Wrote off the account of D. Yeckel as uncollectible, $280.
b. Reinstated the account of R. Nedved that had been written off during the preceding year, $65; received $65 cash in full payment.
c. Estimated bad debt losses to be 1 percent of sales of $80,150.

Exercise 12-7 Using the same data as in Exercise 12-6, assume that McCall Toy Shop uses the specific charge-off method of accounting for bad debt losses. Record transactions **a** and **b** in general journal form.

Exercise 12-8 With reference to Exercise 12-5:
a. Use the specific charge-off method of accounting for bad debt to write off the Midano account.
b. Reinstate the Midano account and collect the amount due.

Consider and Communicate

The owner of the business where you work is puzzled. He asks you how he can write off bad accounts. You know about both the allowance method and the specific charge-off method.

Explain why the allowance method of accounting for bad debts is preferable to the specific charge-off method for financial reporting.

What If . . .

A previously written off account receivable is paid in full by the customer. The bookkeeper records the entry as a debit to Cash and a credit to Allowance for Doubtful Accounts. Did the bookkeeper handle the transaction correctly? If the bookkeeper skips the entry to reinstate the account receivable first, are the records in error?

A Question of Ethics

As the company bookkeeper reviewing delinquent accounts receivable, you notice that a relative of yours has not paid his account in the amount of $250. You know that this relative has been experiencing financial difficulties, so you do not attempt to collect and do not include this account with the other past due accounts sent to a credit collection agency. Is your behavior ethical?

roblem Set A

Problem 12-1A The balance sheet prepared by C. L. Yung, Inc., for December 31 of last year includes $208,000 in Accounts Receivable and $13,203 (credit) in Allowance for Doubtful Accounts. C. L. Yung, Inc., uses the allowance method of writing off and adjusting for bad debt losses. The following transactions occurred during January of this year:

P.O.1a,2,4,5

Jan. 4 Sales of goods on account, $187,652.
   12 Sales returns and allowances related to sales of goods on account, $4,038.
   15 Cash payments by charge customers (no cash discounts), $174,841.
   20 Account receivable from Stock and Whitney written off as uncollectible, $1,488.
   31 By the process of aging Accounts Receivable, it was decided on January 31 that Allowance for Doubtful Accounts should be adjusted to a balance of $18,655.
   31 Closed Bad Debts Expense account.

Instructions

1. Record the entries in the general journal (page 36).
2. Record the balance on the Allowance for Doubtful Accounts ledger sheet.
3. Post the entries to the Allowance for Doubtful Accounts and Bad Debts Expense accounts.
4. Assume instead that C. L. Yung, Inc., uses the specific charge-off method of accounting for bad debt losses. Journalize entries to:

19x6
Jan.   20 Write off the Stock and Whitney account, $1,488
19x7
Oct.   18 Reinstate the Stock and Whitney account.
       18 Collect the Stock and Whitney account in full.

Problem 12-2A McIntyre Company uses the aging method of estimating bad debts as of December 31, the end of the fiscal year. Terms of sales are net 30 days. While in the process of completing the aging schedule, the accountant became very ill and was unable to finish the job. The accountant's report, as far as she had done it, appears as follows:

P.O.1a

Customer Name	Balance	Not Yet Due	Days Past Due			
			1–30	31–60	61–90	Over 90
Balance forward	$393,130.00	$251,300.00	$75,478.00	$40,013.00	$15,483.00	$10,856.00

The accountant had the following accounts left to analyze:

Account	Amount	Due Date
L. Green	$3,955.20	October 30
G. Haas	947.60	January 18 (next year)
E. Finch	6,674.40	November 16
L. Wold	9,702.60	January 25 (next year)
M. Powell	3,811.00	September 18
S. Newman	1,194.80	December 5

From past experience, the company has found that the following rates of estimated uncollectible accounts produce an adequate balance for Allowance for Doubtful Accounts.

Age of Accounts	Estimated Percentage Uncollectible
Not yet due	1.5
1–30 days	3.0
31–60 days	15.0
61–90 days	25.0
Over 90 days	45.0

Prior to aging Accounts Receivable, Allowance for Doubtful Accounts has a credit balance of $4,454.

Instructions

1. Enter the balance forward amounts and complete the aging schedule.
2. Complete the table for estimating an allowance for doubtful accounts.
3. Record the adjusting entry in the general journal (page 27).

P.O.1c,2,3

Problem 12-3A On January 1 of this year, Tauscher Company's Allowance for Doubtful Accounts account had a $2,030 credit balance. Tauscher uses the allowance method of writing off and adjusting for bad debt losses. During the year, Tauscher Company completed the following transactions:

Mar. 12 Wrote off the $895 account of Roy Company; the company had gone out of business, leaving no assets.

Apr. 15 Wrote off the account of M. Taubel as uncollectible, $540.25.

June 10 Received $250 unexpectedly from R. Falloon. The account had been written off two years earlier. Reinstated the account for $250 and recorded the collection of $250.

Sept. 14 Collected 15 percent of the $380 owed by J. R. Whitney, a bankrupt customer. Wrote off the remainder as worthless.

Oct. 19 Received $140 from M. Taubel as part payment of the account written off on April 15. He wrote a letter stating that he expects to pay the balance in the near future. Accordingly, reinstated the account for $540.25 and recorded the $140 payment.

Dec. 28 Journalized a compound entry to write off the following accounts: B. L. Tikkan, $298.50; R. M. Gretky, $378.80; K. C. Wuster, $281.72.

Dec. 31 Recorded the adjusting entry for estimated bad debt losses at $\frac{3}{4}$ percent of charge sales of $312,529.

Dec. 31 Closed the Bad Debts Expense account.

Instructions

1. Record the opening balance in the ledger account of Allowance for Doubtful Accounts.
2. Record the entries in the general journal (page 73).
3. Post the entries to the following ledger accounts: Allowance for Doubtful Accounts and Bad Debts Expense.

Problem 12-4A The following are among the transactions completed by Swan Construction Supply, which uses the allowance method of writing off and adjusting for bad debt losses:

`P.O.1b,2,3`

Jan.   17 Sold goods on account to H. L. Welch, $2,490, terms 2/10, n/30.

Feb.   18 Wrote off the account of Taubel, Inc., $1,412.18. The company went out of business, leaving no assets.

Mar.   10 Reinstated the account of G. Odem that had been written off in the preceding year; received $286.15 in full payment.

July   16 Received $188 unexpectedly from W. O. Harris. The account had been written off last year in the amount of $188. Reinstated the account and recorded the collection of $188.

Aug.   20 Recovered 10 percent of the $2,490 balance owed by H. L. Welch from the referee in bankruptcy and wrote off the remainder as worthless.

Sept. 16 Reinstated the account of Notman and Son that had been written off two years earlier and received $848.40 in full payment.

Dec.   22 Journalized a compound entry to write off the following accounts as uncollectible: B. T. Winfrey, $227; R. H. Rensvold, $881.32; B. G. Kundert, $1,485.94; L. Hikato, $1,640.26.

       31 On the basis of an analysis of accounts receivable, $5,239.50 of Accounts Receivable is estimated to be uncollectible. Recorded the adjusting entry.

       31 Recorded the entry to close the appropriate account to Income Summary.

Instructions

1. Open the following accounts, recording the credit balance as of January 1 of this fiscal year:

   114   Allowance for Doubtful Accounts $5,535.98
   399   Income Summary   _____
   536   Bad Debts Expense   _____

2. Journalize in the general journal (page 24) the transactions described above. After each entry, post to the three selected ledger accounts.
3. Prepare the Current Assets section of the balance sheet. Other pertinent accounts are: Cash, $13,252.49; Accounts Receivable, $92,326.18; Merchandise Inventory, $151,795.35; Supplies, $1,998.72; Prepaid Insurance, $778.68.

P roblem Set B

Problem 12-1B On December 31 of last year, the accountant for Domzalski, Inc., prepared a balance sheet that included $203,837 in Accounts Receivable and $12,996.54 (credit) in Allowance for Doubtful Accounts. Domzalski, Inc., uses the allowance method of writing off and adjusting for bad debts losses. Selected transactions occurred during January of this year, as follows:

`P.O.1a,2,4,5`

Jan.   5 Sales of goods on account, $185,538.

11 Sales returns and allowances related to sales of merchandise on account, $5,020.44.

17 Cash payments by charge customers (no cash discounts), $173,515.08.

24 Account receivable from Arms Company written off as uncollectible, $1,253.79.

31 By the process of aging Accounts Receivable, on January 31 it was decided that Allowance for Doubtful Accounts should be adjusted to a balance of $20,611.47.

31 Closed Bad Debts Expense account.

Instructions

1. Record the entries in the general journal (page 36).
2. Record the balance on the Allowance for Doubtful Accounts ledger sheet.
3. Post the appropriate entries to the Allowance for Doubtful Accounts and Bad Debts Expense accounts.
4. Assume instead that Arms Company uses the specific charge-off method of accounting for bad debt losses. Journalize entries to:

19x6

Jan.   24 Write off the Arms Company account, $1,253.79.

19x7

Aug.   12 Reinstate the Arms Company account.
       12 Collect the Arms Company account in full.

P.O.1a

Problem 12-2B Sakuma Company uses the aging method of estimating bad debts as of December 31, the end of the fiscal year. Terms of sales are net 30 days. While preparing the aging schedule, the accountant became very ill and was unable to finish the job. The accountant's report, as complete as he left it, appears as follows:

Customer Name	Balance	Not Yet Due	Days Past Due			
			1–30	31–60	61–90	Over 90
Balance forward	$369,906.60	$202,440.00	$99,120.00	$39,324.60	$15,708.00	$13,314.00

The accountant still had the following accounts left to analyze:

Account	Amount	Due Date
C. Peloza	$3,584.40	January 12 (next year)
J. Solter	2,430.80	December 18
W. Whyte	8,054.60	November 12
M. Yee	8,528.40	August 20
P. Tabor	1,565.60	October 15
B. Sheets	1,194.80	January 2 (next year)

From past experience, the company has found that the following rates of estimated uncollectible accounts produce an adequate balance for Allowance for Doubtful Accounts.

Age of Accounts	Estimated Percentage Uncollectible
Not yet due	2
1–30 days	4
31–60 days	15
61–90 days	20
Over 90 days	35

Prior to aging the accounts receivable, Allowance for Doubtful Accounts has a credit balance of $7,610.40.

Instructions

1. Enter the balance forward amounts and complete the aging schedule.
2. Complete the table for estimating an allowance for doubtful accounts.
3. Write the adjusting entry in general journal form.

Problem 12-3B On January 1 of this year, Geller Food Supply had a credit balance of $4,361.02 in Allowance for Doubtful Accounts. Geller uses the allowance method of writing off and adjusting for bad debt losses. During the year, the company completed the following selected transactions:

P.O.1c,2,3

Jan.   18 Wrote off as uncollectible a $518 account of Forbis Grocery, which had gone out of business, leaving no assets.

Mar.   13 Wrote off the account of Essen Caterers as uncollectible, $385.20.

Apr.   20 Collected 10 percent of the $1,530 owed by Bacha Company, which went bankrupt. Wrote off the remainder as worthless.

Sept.   12 Received $318.90 unexpectedly from Crews, Inc., whose account had been written off two years earlier. Reinstated the account and recorded the collection.

Oct.   21 Received $100.00 from Essen Caterers as part payment of the account written off on March 13. The owner wrote a letter saying that she expects to pay the balance soon. Accordingly, reinstated the account for $385.20 and recorded the $100 payment.

Dec.   30 Journalized a compound entry to write off the following accounts as uncollectible: R. K. Edwards, $403.54; Carlton Inn, $278.28; Durham's Drive-In, $602.40.

      31 Recorded the adjusting entry for estimated bad debt losses at $\frac{1}{2}$ percent of charge sales of $601,787.80.

      31 Closed the Bad Debts Expense account.

Instructions

1. Record the opening balance in the ledger account Allowance for Doubtful Accounts.
2. Record entries in the general journal (page 73).
3. Post entries to the following ledger accounts: Allowance for Doubtful Accounts and Bad Debts Expense.

Problem 12-4B The following transactions were among those completed by Hudspeth Wholesale Beauty Supply this year:

P.O.1b,2,3

Jan.   14 Sold goods on account to Kalina's Salon, $1,252.48, terms 2/10, n/30.

Feb.   10 Wrote off as uncollectible the account of Meng, Inc., $1,483.13. This company had gone out of business, leaving no assets.

Mar.   12 Reinstated the account of Tatafu, Inc., which had been written off in the preceding year; received $368.40 to satisfy account in full.

Aug.   20 Received $246.40 unexpectedly from Stice and Son, whose account had been written off last year in the amount of $246.40. Reinstated the account and recorded the collection of $246.40.

Sept.   14 Received 10 percent of the $1,252.48 balance owed by Kalina's Salon from the referee in the bankruptcy proceedings; wrote off the remainder as worthless.

Nov.   12 Reinstated the account of V. J. Weber that had been written off two years earlier and received $706.10 in full payment of the account.

Dec.   23 Journalized a compound entry to write off as uncollectible the following accounts: M. N. Swanson, $330.75; R. L. Vaa, $381.98; Pope and Ross, $895.53; The Hair Line, $2,684.81.

        31 On the basis of an analysis of accounts receivable, $5,183 of Accounts Receivable is estimated to be uncollectible. Recorded the adjusting entry.

        31 Recorded the entry to close the appropriate account to Income Summary.

Instructions

1. Open the following accounts, recording the credit balance as of January 1 of this fiscal year.

114	Allowance for Doubtful Accounts	$4,958.80
399	Income Summary	_____
536	Bad Debts Expense	_____

2. Record in the general journal (page 24) the transactions, as well as the adjusting and closing entries described above. After each entry, post to the three selected ledger accounts.

3. Prepare the Current Assets section of the balance sheet. Other pertinent accounts are: Cash, $15,078.06; Notes Receivable, $2,832; Accounts Receivable, $173,114.37; Merchandise Inventory, $327,845.34; Supplies, $1,850.30; Prepaid Insurance, $1,680.

CHALLENGE PROBLEM

Below is selected information from the Keene Company:

	12/31/x6	12/31/x7
Net Credit Sales	$250,000	$300,000
Accounts Receivable	48,000	65,000
Allowance for Doubtful Accounts (credit balance)	800	?

Instructions

For each situation do the following:

1. Write the correct entry for Keene Company to record either estimated Bad Debts Expense or actual Bad Debts Expense, depending upon the method used to value Accounts Receivable.

2. Determine the amount of the Allowance for Doubtful Accounts account at the end of December 19x7 based on situations A, B, C, and D.
3. Is the method acceptable for financial statement preparation and/or for income tax preparation?

Situation A The Keene Company ages Accounts Receivable to determine the amount of the adjustment for estimated Bad Debts Expense.
The following facts are available:

Age of Accounts	Balance	Estimated Percentage Uncollectible
Not yet due	$45,000	1
1 to 30 days	12,000	3
31 to 60 days	4,000	6
61 to 90 days	3,000	12
Over 90 days	1,000	30

Situation B The Keene Company uses a percentage of Accounts Receivable to determine the amount of the adjustment for estimated Bad Debts Expense. The firm's average actual bad debt losses over the prior three consecutive years was 3 percent. The firm feels that this is a reasonable estimate of Bad Debts Expense.

Situation C The Keene Company uses the percentage of Sales or net sales method to determine the amount of estimated Bad Debts Expense. The company determines that one-half of one percent (.005) of net credit sales will be uncollectible.

Situation D The Keene Company uses the specific charge-off method to determine the amount of estimated Bad Debts Expense. The following Accounts Receivable balances are considered to be uncollectible: ABC Co., $750; Southern, Inc., $1,200.

chapter Accounting for 13
Valuation of
Inventories

PERFORMANCE OBJECTIVES

After you have completed this chapter, you will be able to do the following:

1. Determine the overstatement or understatement of cost of goods sold, gross profit, and net income resulting from a change in the value of ending merchandise inventory.

2. Determine unit cost, the value of the ending inventory, and the cost of goods sold by the following methods: (a) specific identification; (b) weighted-average-cost; (c) first-in, first-out; and (d) last-in, first-out.

3. Journalize transactions relating to perpetual inventories.

4. Complete a perpetual inventory record card.

Getting a good inventory number is a challenge for many merchandising businesses. Unless a business owner understands the significance of the inventory valuation and its relationship to the balance sheet, current ratios, and the income statement, he or she may take too casual an approach to the whole job.

PRACTITIONER'S CORNER

Maintaining a proper cut-off point for counting inventory is one of the most common problems. For instance, if merchandise was purchased FOB shipping point and the goods have not been received, cost of goods sold will be overstated and gross profit will be understated. On the other hand, if goods have been shipped to a customer FOB destination (and were not counted) but the sale won't be recorded until the next accounting period because title or ownership hasn't passed, the gross profit will be misstated. Employees performing the physical count must coordinate with the accounting staff so that this kind of mistake isn't made.

It is a good idea to consider getting professional help if inventory is a significant asset in the company. The professionals have developed methods to avoid the kinds of mistakes that are so common. Furthermore, in states where personal property tax is significant, managers try to keep inventory amounts at a minimum and may prefer to order FOB destination because goods not yet received need not be counted as inventory. It will pay to watch inventory, to count it correctly, and to understand the relationship of inventory valuation to the balance sheet and the income statement.

One of the most important aspects of the operation of any merchandising business is the accounting for and valuation of the merchandise in stock. Let's look back briefly at what we have said so far. We defined *merchandise inventory* as goods purchased by the company and held for resale to customers in the ordinary course of business.

We have assumed that firms take a physical inventory at the end of their fiscal periods. At this time, the most up-to-date figure is included in the Adjustments columns of the work sheet. As we discussed in Chapter 7, Merchandise Inventory involves two adjusting entries:

a. The first entry closes off or "zeros out" the old value of the beginning merchandise inventory.

Contra accounts (like Sales Returns and Allowances or Purchases Discount) have signs opposite to the accounts to which they are connected.
. . . .

b. The second entry adds in or "enters" the new value of the ending merchandise inventory.

We are going to look at the valuation of inventories in two ways: First, some merchandising firms take a physical inventory of merchandise on hand and then attach a value to it. This is known as a **periodic inventory system,** as shown in the example above involving the two adjusting entries for Merchandise Inventory. Second, other merchandising firms keep running records of inventories by recording all transactions, so that at any given time they know what they have on hand and the current cost of each item. This is known as a **perpetual inventory system.**

The Importance of Inventory Valuation

Performance Objective 1

Determine the overstatement or understatement of cost of goods sold, gross profit, and net income resulting from a change in the value of ending merchandise inventory.

Merchandise Inventory is the only account that can appear on both major financial statements. On the balance sheet, it appears under Current Assets. On the income statement, it is listed under Cost of Goods Sold. Why is the valuation of merchandise inventory so important? In many businesses, merchandise inventory is the asset with the largest dollar amount. Furthermore, as a part of Cost of Goods Sold, it vitally affects the net income because the cost of goods sold is usually the largest deduction from sales. As a result, inventory valuation plays an important role in matching costs with revenue for a given period.

Differing costs of ending merchandise inventory can have a dramatic effect on net income. We can see this in the partial income statements that follow (Figures 13-1 through 13-4).

Figure 13-1

	YEAR 1	
Net Sales		$ 406 000 00
Cost of Goods Sold:		
Merchandise Inventory (beginning)	$ 168 000 00	
Purchases (net)	320 000 00	
Goods Available for Sale	$ 488 000 00	
Less Merchandise Inventory (ending)	184 000 00	
Cost of Goods Sold		304 000 00
Gross Profit		$ 102 000 00
Expenses		60 000 00
Net Income		$ 42 000 00

Now assume that, instead of setting $184,000 as the value for ending merchandise inventory, one could quite legally set its value at $164,000. The result would be a net income of only $22,000 (Figure 13-2), instead of $42,000. Of course, this would result in lower income taxes as well.

Figure 13-2

YEAR 1

Net Sales			$ 406 0 0 0 00
Cost of Goods Sold:			
Merchandise Inventory (beginning)	$ 168 0 0 0 00		
Purchases (net)	320 0 0 0 00		
Goods Available for Sale	$ 488 0 0 0 00		
Less Merchandise Inventory (ending)	164 0 0 0 00		
Cost of Goods Sold		324 0 0 0 00	
Gross Profit		$ 82 0 0 0 00	
Expenses		60 0 0 0 00	
Net Income		$ 22 0 0 0 00	

R E M E M B E R

The ending inventory of one year becomes the beginning inventory of the next year.

From Figures 13-1 and 13-2 we can see that, if the ending merchandise inventory is overstated (too high) by $20,000, the net income will be overstated (too high) by $20,000, because the two are directly proportional to each other. Similarly, **if the ending merchandise inventory is understated (too low), net income will be understated (too low).**

But there is something else you have to take into account. Since the *ending* inventory of one year becomes the *beginning* inventory of the following year, the net income of the following year is also affected, but in an opposite manner. Let's continue with our example into year 2. The $184,000 *ending* inventory of year 1 becomes the *beginning* inventory of year 2 (Figure 13-3).

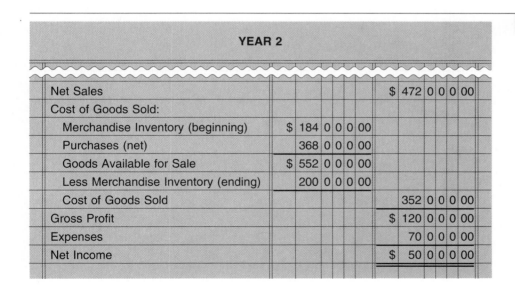

Figure 13-3

YEAR 2

Net Sales			$ 472 0 0 0 00
Cost of Goods Sold:			
Merchandise Inventory (beginning)	$ 184 0 0 0 00		
Purchases (net)	368 0 0 0 00		
Goods Available for Sale	$ 552 0 0 0 00		
Less Merchandise Inventory (ending)	200 0 0 0 00		
Cost of Goods Sold		352 0 0 0 00	
Gross Profit		$ 120 0 0 0 00	
Expenses		70 0 0 0 00	
Net Income		$ 50 0 0 0 00	

Now look at Figure 13-4 to see what happens when the $164,000 ending inventory of year 1 becomes the beginning inventory of year 2.

Figure 13-4

YEAR 2			
Net Sales			$ 472 0 0 0 00
Cost of Goods Sold:			
Merchandise Inventory (beginning)	$ 164 0 0 0 00		
Purchases (net)	368 0 0 0 00		
Goods Available for Sale	$ 532 0 0 0 00		
Less Merchandise Inventory (ending)	200 0 0 0 00		
Cost of Goods Sold		332 0 0 0 00	
Gross Profit			$ 140 0 0 0 00
Expenses			70 0 0 0 00
Net Income			$ 70 0 0 0 00

We can see that, if the beginning merchandise inventory is overstated by $20,000, the net income will be understated by $20,000, because the two are inversely proportional to each other. Similarly, **if the beginning merchandise inventory is understated, net income will be overstated.**

In other words, over a two-year period, the net income will be correct, since the overstatement of one year cancels out the understatement of the following year, and vice versa. We can summarize all this as shown in the following table:

Year	Ending Inventory of $184,000	Ending Inventory of $164,000
	Net Income	Net Income
1	$42,000	$22,000
2	50,000	70,000
Total	$92,000	$92,000

If *ending* inventory is *overstated*, net income for the period will be *overstated*.

If *ending* inventory is *understated*, net income for the period will be *understated*.

If *beginning* inventory is *overstated*, net income for the period will be *understated*.

If *beginning* inventory is *understated*, net income for the period will be *overstated*.

The Need for Inventories

irms that want to satisfy their customers have to maintain large and varied inventories, because all of us naturally would rather shop in stores that offer a wide selection. This assumes, of course, that the firm does not run out of goods at the end of the year. The successful firm has to buy enough merchandise in advance to satisfy the demands of its customers. Efficient purchasing also dictates that the firm take advantage of quantity discounts as well as special buys of seasonal or distressed goods. So, well-run businesses may keep fairly large stocks of merchandise on hand at all times.

Taking a Physical Inventory

Many merchandising firms, at a given moment in time, possess no record that shows the exact quantity and cost of merchandise on hand. They do make spot checks from time to time as part of inventory control, but they can determine *exact* amounts only by physically counting the goods on hand. Even stores that use computers or other means to maintain a perpetual inventory system need to take a physical inventory from time to time. Stores that carry a particularly wide array of merchandise in large amounts wait until their stock is reasonably low before they attempt to count it. Many department stores, for example, take a physical inventory of their stock toward the end of January, after the holiday rush and the postholiday special sales. Whether inventory is taken manually or electronically, only goods belonging to the firm should be counted. They must exclude goods that have been sold and are awaiting shipment, as well as goods held on a consignment basis. Merchandise sold on the basis of FOB destination should be included in the ending inventory of the seller while it is being transported, since the seller is paying the freight charges and thus still has title. Sometimes a firm must also count goods that it does not have on hand. This situation occurs when the supplier has turned the goods over to a transportation company and the goods are shipped FOB shipping point. Remember, this means that the buyer is paying the freight charges and, as a result, normally has title to the goods.

Methods of Assigning Costs to Ending Inventory

Performance Objective 2

Determine unit cost, the value of the ending inventory, and the cost of goods sold by the following methods:
(a) specific identification;
(b) weighted-average-cost;
(c) first-in, first-out; and
(d) last-in, first-out.

After the items have been described and counted, the unit costs are multiplied by the number of units at each cost. How does one determine unit cost? You might think that this is rather elementary. Indeed, it would be—*if* all the purchases of a given article had been made at the same price per unit. A firm usually buys a number of batches of a given item during the year, and the unit costs can vary. A can of shoe polish that cost 80 cents in January might cost 90 cents in October. Which unit cost should one assign to the goods on hand?

There are four main methods of assigning costs to goods in the ending inventory: (1) specific identification; (2) weighted-average-cost; (3) first-in, first-out; and (4) last-in, first-out.

Inventory Evaluation: Example   Dodson Plumbing Supply keeps an inventory of Deco single-handle kitchen faucets (#810) purchased from Adams Manufacturing Company. This year, Dodson Plumbing Supply sells eighty of these faucets and has twenty-six remaining in stock. The company started out the year with twenty-two in stock and bought more as the year went on, as follows:

Jan. 1	Beginning inventory	22 units @ $57 each = $1,254
Mar. 16	Purchase	30 units @ 62 each = 1,860
July 29	Purchase	36 units @ 65 each = 2,340
Nov. 18	Purchase	18 units @ 68 each = 1,224
	Total available	106 units $6,678

Now let's compute the cost of goods sold (eighty faucets) and the value of the ending inventory (twenty-six faucets). We will use the four different methods.

Specific Identification Method

When a firm sells big-ticket items (cars, appliances, furniture, jewelry, and so forth), it can keep track of the purchase price of each individual article and determine the exact cost of the goods sold. Such a firm uses the **specific identification method** of inventory control. Because the kitchen faucets have imprinted manufacture date codes, Dodson Plumbing Supply can identify each faucet with a separate purchase invoice listing the unit cost. When Dodson Plumbing takes inventory at the end of the year, it finds that there are twenty-six kitchen faucets left in stock; four of these were bought in March, ten were bought in July, and twelve were bought in November. Costs are assigned to the ending inventory as follows:

Mar. 16	Purchase	4 units @ $62 each = $ 248
July 29	Purchase	10 units @ 65 each = 650
Nov. 18	Purchase	12 units @ 68 each = 816
	Total	26 units $1,714

Dodson Plumbing Supply determines the cost of goods sold by subtracting the value of the ending inventory from the total available for sale:

Total kitchen faucets available (106 units)	$6,678
Less ending inventory (26 units)	1,714
Cost of goods sold (80 units)	$4,964

Weighted-Average-Cost Method

An alternative to keeping track of the cost of each item purchased is to find the **weighted-average-cost method** per unit of all like articles available for sale during the period. First, Dodson Plumbing Supply finds the total cost of the faucets it had on hand during the year by multiplying the number of units by their respective purchase costs.

Jan. 1	Beginning inventory	22 units @ $57 each = $1,254
Mar. 16	Purchase	30 units @ 62 each = 1,860
July 29	Purchase	36 units @ 65 each = 2,340
Nov. 18	Purchase	18 units @ 68 each = 1,224
	Total available	106 units $6,678

Next Dodson Plumbing finds the average cost per faucet.

Average cost per unit = Total cost ÷ Total units

Average cost per unit = $6,678 ÷ 106 units = $63 per unit

Value of ending inventory = Number of units × Average cost per unit

Value of ending inventory = 26 × $63 = $1,638

According to this method, the beginning inventory is *weighted* (that is, multiplied by the number of units it comprises). Each purchase thereafter is weighted by the number of units involved in that purchase. In other words, the more you buy at a time, the more that purchase influences the average cost.

Cost of goods sold = Total available − Ending inventory
$5,040   = $6,678   − $1,638

First-In, First-Out (FIFO) Method

The **first-in, first-out (FIFO) method** is based on the flow-of-cost assumption that merchandise sold should be charged against revenue in the order in which the costs were incurred. To determine the cost of goods sold, the accountant records the first (oldest) cost first, then the next-oldest cost, and so on. First-in, first-out is a logical way for a firm to rotate its stock of merchandise. Think of a grocery store selling milk. Because milk will sour, the oldest milk is moved up to the front of the shelf. As a result, the ending inventory consists of the freshest milk.

Again, let's return to Dodson Plumbing Supply's kitchen faucets. To repeat, 106 faucets were available for sale during the year:

REMEMBER

First-in, first-out refers to the way goods are sold. The ending inventory is assumed to consist of those items purchased most recently.

Jan. 1	Beginning inventory	22 units @ $57 each = $1,254
Mar. 16	Purchase	30 units @ 62 each = 1,860
July 29	Purchase	36 units @ 65 each = 2,340
Nov. 18	Purchase	18 units @ 68 each = 1,224
	Total available	106 units $6,678

Dodson Plumbing sold eighty units. The accountant calculates the total cost of the faucets on a first-in, first-out (FIFO) basis, like this:

Jan. 1	Beginning inventory	22 units @ $57 each = $1,254
Mar. 16	Purchase	30 units @ 62 each = 1,860
July 29	Purchase	28 units @ 65 each = 1,820
	Total	80 units $4,934

Dodson Plumbing has the twenty-six newest or most recently purchased units on hand in the ending inventory. The accountant records the ending inventory at the most recent costs, like this:

Nov. 18	Purchase	18 units @ $68 each = $1,224
July 29	Purchase	8 units @ 65 each = 520
	Total	26 units $1,744

The accountant now verifies the total cost of the eighty units sold:

Cost of goods sold = Total available − Ending inventory
$4,934 = $6,678 − $1,744

Last-In, First-Out (LIFO) Method

R E M E M B E R
Last-in, first-out refers to the way goods are sold. The ending inventory consists of the items purchased earliest.

The **last-in, first-out (LIFO) method** is based on the flow-of-cost assumption that the most recently purchased articles are sold first and the articles remaining in the ending inventory are the oldest items. As an example, think of a coal yard selling coal. When the coal yard buys coal from its supplier, the new coal is added to the top of the pile. When the coal yard sells coal to its customer, coal is taken off the top of the pile. Consequently, the ending inventory consists of those first few tons at the bottom of the pile. And, unless the pile is exhausted, they will never be sold.

Meanwhile, back at Dodson Plumbing, the firm sold eighty units. The accountant calculates the cost of the faucets on a last-in, first-out (LIFO) basis:

Nov. 18	Purchase	18 units @ $68 each = $1,224
July 29	Purchase	36 units @ 65 each = 2,340
Mar. 16	Purchase	26 units @ 62 each = 1,612
	Total	80 units $5,176

Dodson Plumbing has the twenty-six oldest units (or the units at the bottom of the pile) on hand in the ending inventory. The accountant records the ending inventory at the earliest costs, like this:

Jan. 1	Beginning inventory	22 units @ $57 each = $1,254
Mar. 16	Purchase	4 units @ 62 each = 248
	Total	26 units $1,502

The accountant now verifies the total cost of the eighty units sold:

Cost of goods sold = Total available − Ending inventory
$5,176 = $6,678 − $1,502

Comparison of Methods

If prices don't change very much, all inventory methods give just about the same results. However, in a dynamic market where prices are constantly rising and falling, each method may yield different amounts. Here is a comparison of the results of the sale of the kitchen faucets using the four methods we described:

Method	Cost of Goods Sold (80 Units)	Ending Inventory (26 Units)
Specific identification	$4,964	$1,714
Weighted-average-cost	5,040	1,638
First-in, first-out	4,934	1,744
Last-in, first-out	5,176	1,502

REMEMBER

Goods do not always move as described in the FIFO, LIFO, and weighted-average-cost methods. The goods are assumed to move as described for the purpose of costing.

REMEMBER

The method selected to cost inventory really has nothing to do with counting the inventory.

Assume that Dodson Plumbing sells the eighty kitchen faucets for $90 apiece. The four methods yield the following gross profits:

	Specific Identification	Weighted-Average-Cost	First-In, First-Out	Last-In, First-Out
Sales	$7,200	$7,200	$7,200	$7,200
Cost of goods sold	4,964	5,040	4,934	5,176
Gross profit	$2,236	$2,160	$2,266	$2,024

We can see from all this that the effects of the methods are as follows:

1. Specific identification matches costs exactly with revenues.

2. Weighted-average cost is a compromise between LIFO and FIFO, both for the amount of the ending inventory and for the cost of goods sold.

3. FIFO portrays the most realistic figure for ending merchandise inventory in the Current Assets section of the balance sheet. The ending inventory is valued at the most recent costs.

4. LIFO portrays the most realistic figure for the Cost of Goods Sold section of the income statement, because the items that have been sold will have to be replaced at the most recent costs.

Concerning the specific identification method, for Dodson Plumbing Supply we chose kitchen faucets as a realistic example. However, the firm carries a wide variety of products. Consequently, keeping track of the cost of each item of product may prove difficult and costly if computers and a system of scanning devices are not used. However, as we mentioned previously, for companies selling a few high-priced products, the specific identification method may be ideal for manual accounting, although computerized procedures are common. Additional examples of companies that are candidates for the specific identification method are heavy construction equipment and boats.

Tax Effect of LIFO

In a period of rising prices, LIFO yields the lowest gross profit and hence the lowest income tax, because the most recent costs are assigned to the cost of goods sold. For several decades, prices have kept going up in most industries, providing a built-in tax advantage for users of LIFO. In effect, a business using LIFO is postponing paying taxes. Since the money is not paid to the government, the business has the use of this money. Consequently, the money saved can be used to finance more inventories or to pay off interest-bearing debts. When prices fall, companies using LIFO are at a disadvantage from the standpoint of taxes.

Bear in mind that the cost figure determined by the different methods may have nothing to do with the physical flow of the goods. By physical flow, we mean the way that specific items are taken out of inventory and sold.

The **consistency principle** is a fundamental principle of accounting. We have seen that a firm can increase or decrease its gross profit, and likewise its net income and income tax, by changing the flow-of-cost assumption from one method to another—from FIFO to LIFO, for example. Although a firm may change its method of assigning inventory costs, it may not change back and forth repeatedly. Consistency in the method of determining cost of goods sold and the related cost of the ending inventory is necessary. For one thing, the government has said that a firm cannot switch back and forth in order to evade some of its income tax. In addition, the firm must use a single method of reporting in financial statements to its owners and creditors.

· · · · · · · · · · · · · ·
R E M E M B E R

The cost figure determined by the different methods may have nothing to do with the physical flow of goods.
· · · · · · · · · · · · · ·

Lower-of-Cost-or-Market Rule

All of the above methods for determining the cost of the ending inventory are based on the cost per unit. In our examples, prices were generally rising. However, sometimes the replacement cost of items in stock is *less* than the original market cost. The word *market* refers to the current price charged in the market. It is the price at which, *at the time of taking the inventory*, the items could be bought through the usual channels and in the usual quantities. The current prices may be quoted in catalogs or reflect contract quotations.

The **lower-of-cost-or-market rule** says that, under certain conditions, when the replacement or market cost is lower than the original cost, the inventory should be valued at the lowest cost. For example, the inventory of a store consists of twenty jean jackets originally purchased for $22 each (total, $440). At the time the inventory is being taken, the same type of jean jackets may be purchased (replaced) for $18 each (total, $360). Under the lower-of-cost-or-market rule, the inventory is valued at $360. In this example, the original cost of $22 may have been determined by the specific identification method, the weighted-average-cost method, or the FIFO method. Under the tax law, the cost may *not* be determined by the LIFO method, since this method already offers tax advantages.

Perpetual Inventories

Businesses such as equipment or appliance dealers that sell a limited variety of products of relatively high value maintain book records of their inventories on hand. They *record additions to or deductions from their inventories directly in Merchandise Inventory accounts.* This is known as the perpetual inventory system because the firms perpetually (or continually) *know* the *amount* of goods on hand. With computers, many firms have also adopted the perpetual inventory system for lower-value products. This system involves the following accounts, as illustrated by T accounts:

Performance Objective 3

Journalize transactions relating to perpetual inventories.

Merchandise Inventory		Cost of Goods Sold		Sales	
+	−	+	−	−	+
Record the purchase of merchandise at cost.	Record the sale of merchandise at cost.	Record the sale of merchandise at cost.			Record the sale of merchandise at selling price.

The adjusting entries at the end of the year are the only entries firms using the periodic system make in Merchandise Inventory. But firms using the perpetual inventory system make entries directly in the Merchandise Inventory account throughout the year. The perpetual inventory system enables the firm to do away with the Purchases and Purchases Returns and Allowances accounts.

To illustrate the perpetual inventory system, let's look at a series of entries in general journal form, with transactions recorded at the gross amount.

Feb. 14 Bought merchandise on account, from Floyd, Inc.; 2/10, n/30; $1,600.

	DATE	DESCRIPTION	POST. REF.	DEBIT	CREDIT	
1	19–					1
2	Feb. 14	Merchandise Inventory		1 6 0 0 00		2
3		Accounts Payable, Floyd, Inc.			1 6 0 0 00	3
4		Terms 2/10, n/30.				4
5						5

R E M E M B E R

Under the perpetual inventory system, when goods are bought for resale, Merchandise Inventory is debited instead of Purchases. Similarly, when the goods are sold, Merchandise Inventory is credited for the amount of its cost.

Merchandise Inventory		Accounts Payable	
+	−	−	+
1,600			1,600

Feb. 24 Paid the invoice within the discount period.

	DATE	DESCRIPTION	POST. REF.	DEBIT	CREDIT	
1	19–					1
2	Feb. 24	Accounts Payable, Floyd, Inc.		1 6 0 0 00		2
3		Cash			1 5 6 8 00	3
4		Purchases Discount			3 2 00	4
5		Paid invoice within discount				5
6		period.				6
7						7

Accounts Payable		Cash		Purchases Discount	
−	+	+	−	−	+
1,600			1,568		32

Mar. 5 Sold the merchandise on account to C. A. Drew for $1,900. (The cost of the merchandise is $1,600. Two entries are required to record a sale under a perpetual inventory system.)

	DATE	DESCRIPTION	POST. REF.	DEBIT	CREDIT	
1	19–					1
2	Mar. 5	Accounts Receivable, C. A. Drew		1 9 0 0 00		2
3		Sales			1 9 0 0 00	3
4		Sold merchandise on account.				4
5						5
6	5	Cost of Goods Sold		1 6 0 0 00		6
7		Merchandise Inventory			1 6 0 0 00	7
8		Relating to $1,900 sale to				8
9		C. A. Drew.				9

Accounts Receivable		Sales	
+	−	−	+
1,900			1,900

Cost of Goods Sold		Merchandise Inventory	
+	−	+	−
1,600		Bal. 1,600	1,600

For a firm using a perpetual inventory system, one can compare the Cost of Goods Sold account to an expense account: both are increased by debits, and both are closed at the end of the year.

Apr. 2 C. A. Drew returned merchandise having a sale price of $210 and a cost of $177.

	DATE		DESCRIPTION	POST. REF.	DEBIT	CREDIT	
1	19–						1
2	Apr.	2	Sales Returns and Allowances		2 1 0 00		2
3			Accounts Receivable,				3
4			C. A. Drew			2 1 0 00	4
5			Issued credit memo for				5
6			the return of merchandise.				6
7							7
8		2	Merchandise Inventory		1 7 7 00		8
9			Cost of Goods Sold			1 7 7 00	9
10			Merchandise returned				10
11			by C. A. Drew.				11

Accounts Receivable			Sales Returns and Allowances		
+		–	+		–
Bal. 1,900		210	210		

Cost of Goods Sold			Merchandise Inventory		
+		–	+		–
Bal. 1,600		177	1,600		1,600
			177		

Firms may take physical inventories both during and at the end of the year to verify the book value of the perpetual inventory. If there is a difference between the book value and the physical count, an adjustment is made to the Merchandise Inventory account. In this adjustment, Cost of Goods Sold is used as the offsetting account. Suppose the book value figure for Merchandise Inventory is $52,940 and the physical count shows $52,770 of merchandise on hand. The ending inventory is short by $170 ($52,940 − $52,770). After all attempts are made to reconcile the shortage, the adjusting entry looks like this:

	DATE		DESCRIPTION	POST. REF.	DEBIT	CREDIT	
1	19–		Adjusting Entry				1
2	June	30	Cost of Goods Sold		1 7 0 00		2
3			Merchandise Inventory			1 7 0 00	3
4							4

Figure 13-5

INVENTORY RECORD CARD

ITEM Kitchen Sinks, Briggs No. 729

MAXIMUM 40   MINIMUM 8

DATE	PURCHASED AT COST			SALES		
	UNITS	COST	TOTAL	UNITS	PRICE	TOTAL
1/2	Bal.					
2/6				4	$120	$ 480
2/22	30	$75	$2,250			
3/14				6	120	720
3/29				8	120	960
Total	30	—	$2,250	18	—	$2,160

Perpetual Inventory Record

Performance Objective 4

Complete a perpetual inventory record card.

When a firm uses the perpetual inventory system, Merchandise Inventory is a controlling account. The firm maintains an individual record in the subsidiary ledger for each kind of product, recording the number of units received as "units received" and the number of units sold as "units sold." The firm records the remaining balance after each receipt or sale. Companies may keep perpetual inventories by any of the four methods discussed earlier. For example, assume Dodson Plumbing Supply maintains a perpetual inventory on kitchen sinks, on a LIFO basis, as shown in Figure 13-5.

Scanning devices may be used to perpetually maintain inventories in lumberyards. Each bundle would be marked for scanning with information on type of lumber, size, grade, and number of pieces in the bundle.

LOCATION   Warehouse Sink Section

METHOD   LIFO

	COST OF GOODS SOLD			INVENTORY AT COST		
	UNITS	COST	TOTAL	UNITS	COST	TOTAL
				14	$72	$1,008
	4	$72	$288	10	72	720
				⎰ 10	72	720
				⎱ 30	75	2,250
	6	75	450	⎰ 10	72	720
				⎱ 24	75	1,800
	8	75	600	⎰ 10	72	720
				⎱ 16	75	1,200
	18	—	$1,338	—	—	

The ending balance of twenty-six units amounts to $1,920 ($720 + $1,200). Eighteen sinks were sold at $120 each for total sales of $2,160, and gross profit is $822.

Sales (from sales journal)	$2,160
Less Cost of Goods Sold	1,338
Gross Profit	$ 822

The weighted-average-cost flow can be used with a perpetual inventory system. Rather than computing the average price for each inventory item at the end of a period, a new average is calculated each time a purchase is made. This average method is called a **moving average.** When goods are sold, their cost is determined by multiplying the number of units sold by the moving-average cost existing at that time. Further discussion of moving averages is reserved for more advanced accounting courses.

Computer Applications

Some accounting software programs provide an inventory module to allow merchandising businesses to keep track of items bought, sold, and returned. The software will maintain counts of endless stock numbers, one assigned to each kind of merchandise. The program will maintain total units available, sold, purchased, and returned, and it will also trigger reorders when the number in stock reaches a certain point. Since the software also maintains the cost price of each item, it can easily produce a report of the value of ending inventory under either a LIFO, FIFO, or average cost method.

Figure 13-6 shows a report of inventory transactions showing quantities ordered, received, and sold, as well as the cost price and selling price. Figures

Figure 13-6

Inventory Transactions

12/31/9-

Date	Stock No.	Description	Quantity Sold	Selling Price	Quan. Ord.	Quan. Recd.	Cost Price
11/31	100	#3 battery			200	200	19.00
11/31	110	#5 battery			300	300	39.00
11/31	115	#10 battery			500	500	79.00
11/31	100	#3 battery	88	36.00			
11/31	110	#5 battery	65	69.00			
12/31	115	#10 battery	50	99.00			
12/31	100	#3 battery			100	100	22.00
12/31	110	#5 battery			100	100	41.00
12/31	115	#10 battery			150	150	80.00
12/31	100	#3 battery	118	36.00			
12/31	110	#5 battery	95	69.00			
12/31	115	#10 battery	118	99.00			
		Totals	534		1350	1350	

Figure 13-7

Inventory Valuation (Average Cost)

12/31/9-

Stock No.	Description	On Hand	Cost	Value At Cost	Retail Price	Value At Retail
100	#3 battery	114	20.29	2313.06	36.00	4104.00
110	#5 battery	265	39.56	10483.40	69.00	18285.00
115	#10 battery	502	79.24	39778.48	99.00	49698.00
	Total Inventory Value			52574.94		72087.00

Figure 13-8

Inventory Valuation (Last-in-First-Out)

12/31/9-

Stock No.	Description	On Hand	Cost	Value At Cost	Retail Price	Value At Retail
100	#3 battery	20	19.00	380 00	36.00	720.00
100	#3 battery	94	19.00	1786.00	36.00	3384.00
110	#5 battery	25	39.00	975.00	69.00	1725.00
110	#5 battery	235	39.00	9165.00	69.00	16215.00
110	#5 battery	5	41.00	205.00	69.00	345.00
115	#10 battery	20	79.00	1580.00	99.00	1980.00
115	#10 battery	450	79.00	35550.00	99.00	44550.00
115	#10 battery	32	80.00	2560.00	99.00	3168.00
	Total Inventory Value			52201.00		72087.00

Figure 13-9

Inventory Valuation (First-in-First-Out)

12/31/9–

Stock No.	Description	On Hand	Cost	Value At Cost	Retail Price	Value At Retail
100	#3 battery	14	19.00	266.00	36.00	504.00
100	#3 battery	100	22.00	2200.00	36.00	3600.00
110	#5 battery	165	39.00	6435.00	69.00	11385.00
110	#5 battery	100	41.00	4100.00	69.00	6900.00
115	#10 battery	352	79.00	27808.00	99.00	34848.00
115	#10 battery	150	80.00	12000.00	99.00	14850.00
	Total Inventory Value			52809.00		72087.00

13-7, 13-8, and 13-9 show how the same stock items are valued using three different methods—average cost, LIFO, and FIFO. If input is accurate, you can imagine the hours saved in maintaining current inventory information on a computer, as well as in producing a valuation report.

CHAPTER REVIEW

Review of Performance Objectives

1. **Determine the overstatement or understatement of cost of goods sold, gross profit, and net income resulting from a change in the value of ending merchandise inventory.**

   The amounts of the beginning and ending merchandise inventories appear in the Cost of Goods Sold section of the income statement.

2. **Determine unit cost, the value of the ending inventory, and the cost of goods sold by the following methods: (a) specific identification; (b) weighted-average-cost; (c) first-in, first-out; and (d) last-in, first-out.**

   (a) Specific identification: Used for high-value items when a firm can identify each item on hand with its respective price.

   (b) Weighted-average-cost: Number of units of each purchase × Unit price = Cost of each purchase. Cost of beginning inventory + Costs of each purchase = Total cost. Total cost ÷ Total units = Weighted-average cost per unit.

   (c) First-in, first-out (FIFO): Costs are charged against revenue in the order in which they were incurred. This method portrays the most realistic figure for the Current Assets section of the balance sheet.

   (d) Last-in, first-out (LIFO): Costs that are charged against revenue are the most recent costs. This method portrays the most realistic figure for the Cost of Goods Sold section of the income statement.

   In an era of rising prices, the LIFO method yields the lowest net income. Firms must be consistent in their use of inventory methods.

3. **Journalize transactions relating to perpetual inventories.**

   Perpetual inventories are book records of what a firm has in stock. The Merchandise Inventory account is a controlling account. Merchandise

Inventory is debited when goods are bought and credited when goods are sold. Cost of Goods Sold is a specific account, handled much like an expense account.

4. **Complete a perpetual inventory record card.**

   The perpetual inventory record card contains columns for the following information: date of purchase, number of units purchased, cost per unit purchased, total cost of purchase, number of units sold, selling price per unit of goods sold, total cost of goods sold, number of units in ending inventory, cost per unit of goods in ending inventory, total cost of goods in ending inventory.

G lossary

Consistency principle An accounting principle that requires that a particular accounting procedure, once adopted, will not be changed from one fiscal period to another. **(524)**

First-in, first-out (FIFO) method Process of assigning costs to merchandise sold, based on the flow-of-cost assumption that units are sold in the order in which they were acquired. Unsold units on hand at date of inventory are assumed to be valued at the most recent costs. **(521)**

Last-in, first-out (LIFO) method Process of assigning costs to merchandise sold, based on the flow-of-cost assumption that units sold are recorded at the costs of the most recently acquired units. Unsold units on hand at date of inventory are assumed to be valued at the earliest costs. **(522)**

Lower-of-cost-or-market rule When there is a difference between the original cost and the market price of goods, the lower price is used for determining the value of the ending inventory. The term *market price* means current replacement price. **(525)**

Moving average A modification of the weighted-average-cost method, used for computing the average cost of a perpetual inventory. The firm determines the moving-average unit price each time it buys more units. **(529)**

Periodic inventory system Determining the amount of goods on hand by periodically taking a physical count and then attaching a value to it. **(516)**

Perpetual inventory system A book record of the ending inventory showing the unit costs of the items received and the items sold. This gives the firm a running balance of the inventory on hand and the current cost of each item. **(516)**

Specific identification method Counting the actual cost of each individual item in the ending inventory. **(520)**

Weighted-average-cost method A method of determining the cost of the ending inventory by multiplying the weighted-average cost per unit by the number of remaining units. **(520)**

QUESTIONS, EXERCISES, AND PROBLEMS

D iscussion Questions

1. If the ending merchandise inventory of Year 1 is mistakenly understated by $3,000, what is the effect on the following?
   a. Year 1's net income   c. Year 2's net income
   b. Year 1's balance sheet
2. In periods of steadily rising prices, which of the three inventory methods (weighted-average-cost, FIFO, or LIFO) will give (a) the highest net income? (b) the lowest net income?

3. Explain the consistency principle. How can the consistency principle relate to inventory costing?
4. Do FIFO and LIFO result in different quantities? Explain.
5. What is meant by the specific identification method of pricing inventory? Give an example of a situation in which this method would be suitable.
6. List two reasons to justify the use of the LIFO inventory method.
7. When a perpetual inventory system is in use, what are the necessary journal entries for buying merchandise on account and selling merchandise on account?
8. List several computer devices used to count goods bought, sold, and returned.

Exercises

Exercise 13-1 An abbreviated income statement for Command and Company for this fiscal year is shown below.

P.O.1

Determine the effect of an error in ending inventory.

Net Sales		$ 155 0 0 0 00
Cost of Goods Sold:		
Merchandise Inventory, January 1	$ 132 0 0 0 00	
Delivered Cost of Purchases	25 0 0 0 00	
Goods Available for Sale	$ 157 0 0 0 00	
Less Merchandise Inventory, Dec. 31	37 0 0 0 00	
Cost of Goods Sold		120 0 0 0 00
Gross Profit		$ 35 0 0 0 00
Expenses		18 0 0 0 00
Net Income		$ 17 0 0 0 00

An accountant discovers that the ending inventory is overstated by $6,300. What effect does this have on cost of goods sold, gross profit, and net income in this fiscal year?

Exercise 13-2 Condensed income statements for Miracle Company for two years are presented below.

P.O.1

	19x7		19x6	
Net Sales		$91 0 0 0 00		$98 0 0 0 00
Cost of Goods Sold:				
Merchandise Inventory (beginning)	$13 0 0 0 00		$15 0 0 0 00	
Purchases (net)	47 0 0 0 00		49 0 0 0 00	
Goods Available for Sale	$60 0 0 0 00		$64 0 0 0 00	
Less: Merchandise Inventory (ending)	14 0 0 0 00		13 0 0 0 00	
Cost of Goods Sold		46 0 0 0 00		51 0 0 0 00
Gross Profit		$45 0 0 0 00		$47 0 0 0 00
Expenses		23 0 0 0 00		21 0 0 0 00
Net Income		$22 0 0 0 00		$26 0 0 0 00

Correct errors on comparative income statements.

After the end of 19x7, it was discovered that an error had been made in 19x6. Ending inventory in 19x6 should have been $12,000 instead of $13,000. Determine the corrected net income for 19x6 and 19x7.

a. Did the error understate or overstate cost of goods sold for 19x6?
b. Did the error understate or overstate net income for 19x6?
c. What is the amount of total net income for the two-year period with the error ($13,000) and corrected ($12,000)?

P.O.2

Calculate the value of ending inventory.

Exercise 13-3 The records of McLean Company show the following data as of January 31, the end of the fiscal year. Determine the value of the ending merchandise inventory.

a. Cost of goods on hand, based on physical count, $204,330.
b. Cost of defective goods (to be thrown away) included in (a), $328.
c. Cost of goods shipped out FOB destination on January 30, with an expected delivery date of approximately four days, $2,832; not included in (a).
d. Goods purchased January 28, FOB shipping point, delivered to the transportation company on January 31, $1,120.
e. Cost of goods sold to a customer on January 30, paid for in full and awaiting shipping instructions, $1,818; not included in (a) above.

P.O.2

Calculate the cost of goods sold and the inventory value, using FIFO.

Exercise 13-4 Environmental Systems keeps perpetual inventories on energy-efficient stoves, using the first-in, first-out method. Determine the cost of goods sold in each sale and the inventory balance after each sale for the following purchases and sales of energy-efficient stoves:

Jan.   1 Inventory of 35 units @ $430 each.
       25 Sold 16 units.
Mar.   4 Purchased 15 units @ $432 each.
       15 Sold 17 units.
June   5 Sold 10 units.
       22 Purchased 16 units @ $434 each.

P.O.2b,c,d

Compute the value of ending inventory and cost of goods sold using three methods.

Exercise 13-5 Rodger's Saw Shop maintains an inventory of radial saws. Purchases of the saws during the year were as shown below. (Round all computations to two decimal places.)

Jan.   1 Inventory of 25 units @ $250 each.
Mar.   8 Purchased 28 units @ $255 each.
May   15 Purchased 19 units @ $257 each.
      30 Purchased 12 units @ $258 each.

The ending inventory, by physical count, is 28 units. Determine the value of the ending inventory and the cost of goods sold by the following methods: weighted-average-cost; first-in, first-out; last-in, first-out.

P.O.2b,c,d

Calculate the cost of ending inventory using three methods.

Exercise 13-6 Price's Office Supplies has a July beginning inventory of model 37 desk lamps, consisting of 187 units at $87.50 each. Purchases and sales during July are as follows:

July   5 Sold 12 units.
      12 Purchased 8 units @ $88 each.
      14 Sold 15 units.
      25 Purchased 20 units @ $89 each.
      30 Sold 18 units.

Calculate the cost of the ending inventory under each of the following methods: weighted-average-cost; first-in, first-out; last-in, first out. (Round all computations to two decimal places.)

Exercise 13-7 Referring to Exercise 13-5, if the radial saws were sold during the year for $327 each, determine the gross profit using the weighted-average-cost; first-in, first-out; and last-in, first-out methods.

P.O.1

Calculate the gross profit using three methods.

Exercise 13-8 The Ducharm Company's fiscal year is from January 1 through December 31. The following figures are available:

P.O.3

Journalize adjusting entries under periodic and perpetual inventory methods.

Jan. 1 Inventory, $192,500 (by physical count).
Dec. 31 Inventory, $206,300 (by physical count).

a. Record the adjusting entries, assuming that the company uses the periodic inventory system.
b. Record the adjusting entry, assuming that the company uses the perpetual inventory system and that the book balance of the ending inventory is $206,820.

C onsider and Communicate

A person you work for in the accounting department is confused about FIFO and LIFO as methods of charging costs of goods against revenue. Explain, for each method, which units are used to calculate the cost of the ending inventory, which financial statement is emphasized, and which method results in a lower net income (assuming rising cost per unit).

W hat If . . .

What if you look at the inventory sheets and suspect that your assistant made some errors while computing the extensions for ending inventory for the period just ended. Should you redo all the calculations or just the ones that don't look right? If you let the errors go until the end of the next period, will the problem correct itself? What effect will such errors have on the income statement and balance sheet?

A Question of Ethics

A large computer retailer has taken year-end inventory and has valued 80 model XV computers at $800 each, or $64,000—the original cost of the model XV. Current technologies have allowed the supplier to reduce the cost of model XV to $600 although the computer store has not purchased any model XV's at this price. Is the owner doing anything unethical by valuing the 80 model XV's at the original cost of $64,000?

P roblem Set A

Problem 13-1A Brown Company, on January 1 of one year, had an inventory of TZ2717 of 15,000 gallons, costing $.89 per gallon. In addition to this beginning inventory, purchases during the next six months were as follows:

P.O.2b,c,d

Date		Quantity (gallons)	Cost per Gallon	Total Cost
Jan. 1	Inventory	15,000	$.89	$13,350
15		12,000	.90	10,800
Feb. 23		10,000	.91	9,100
Mar. 16		7,000	$.91\frac{1}{2}$	6,405
Apr. 21		12,000	.91	10,920
May 16		9,000	.92	8,280
June 3		10,000	.93	9,300
30		8,000	.94	7,520

The inventory on June 30 was 19,000 gallons. During this six-month period, Brown Company sold TZ2717 for $1.24 per gallon. Assume that no liquid was lost through evaporation or leakage.

Instructions

1. Find the value of the ending inventory by the following methods:
   a. Weighted-average-cost (Round to two decimal places.)
   b. First-in, first-out
   c. Last-in, first-out
2. Determine the cost of goods sold according to the three methods of costing inventory.
3. Determine the amount of the gross profit according to the three methods of costing inventory.

P.O.2b,c,d

Problem 13-2A Gold Distribution uses the periodic inventory system. Data pertaining to the inventory on January 1, the beginning of the fiscal year, as well as purchases during the year and the inventory count on December 31, are as follows:

	Model		
	PB80	**BB173**	**TB26**
Inventory, Jan. 1	12 @ $380	5 @ $621	22 @ $184
First purchase	18 @ 391	8 @ 618	30 @ 188
Second purchase	21 @ 394	10 @ 624	32 @ 189
Third purchase	15 @ 395	12 @ 630	34 @ 193
Fourth purchase	16 @ 396		36 @ 194
Inventory, Dec. 31	18	10	35

Instructions

1. Determine the value of the inventory on December 31 by the weighted-average-cost method. (Round to two decimal places.)
2. Determine the value of the inventory on December 31 by the first-in, first-out method.
3. Determine the value of the inventory on December 31 by the last-in, first-out method.

P.O.3

Problem 13-3A The Springer Company made the following selected transactions during the year:

Jan.   3 Bought merchandise on account from Welton Products; terms 2/10, n/30; $8,132.

        5 Received credit memo no. 681 from Welton Products for the return of merchandise bought on January 3, $521.

       12 Issued Ck. No. 1372 to Welton Products, in payment of the invoice dated January 3.

       15 Sold merchandise on account to E. Pemberton, $3,650. The cost of the goods sold was $2,592.

       29 Sold merchandise on account to M. Robbins, $4,886; the cost of the goods sold was $3,470.

Dec.   31 Made adjusting entries. The ending merchandise inventory determined by physical count is $142,482. The beginning inventory was $139,460. The balance in the inventory account under the perpetual inventory system is $142,902. Accrued interest on notes payable is $332. Accrued interest on notes receivable is $127. Allowance for Doubtful Accounts is to be increased by $1,470.

Instructions

1. Record the above transactions in the general journal (page 38), assuming that Springer Company uses the perpetual inventory system and records purchases at the gross amount.
2. Record the above transactions in the general journal (page 38), assuming that Springer Company uses the periodic inventory system and records purchases at the gross amount.

Instructions for General Ledger Software

1. Record the transactions in the general journal assuming the perpetual inventory system is used and purchases are recorded at gross amount. Print the journal entries.
2. Record the transactions in the general journal assuming the periodic inventory system is used and purchases are recorded at gross amount. Print the journal entries.
3. Both options are found on the problem menu.

Problem 13-4A The Shinbo Company's beginning inventory of F477 is 180 units at a cost of $47.50 each. Dates of purchases and sales for a three-month period are shown below.   P.O.2c,4

Shinbo Company maintains a perpetual inventory record using the first-in, first-out method. Data for the month of January were recorded in the Working Papers.

		Purchases		Sales	
Date	Units	Cost per Unit		Units	Price per Unit
Jan. 18	230	$48.30			
20				80	$56.00
31				145	56.00
Feb. 5	250	49.20			
14				135	57.00
22				185	57.00
26	220	50.35			
Mar. 4				75	58.00
11	160	52.60			
17				90	58.00
30				140	60.00

Instructions

1. Record the data for purchases and sales of item F477 and for cost of goods sold in a perpetual inventory record using the first-in, first-out method for the months of February and March.
2. Determine the total cost of goods sold during the three-month period.
3. Determine the total sales for the three-month period.
4. Determine the gross profit from sales of item F477 for the period.

P roblem Set B

P.O.2b,c,d

Problem 13-1B Eide Chemical's inventory of WN173 on January 1 of one year was 8,000 gallons, which had cost $.62 per gallon. In addition to the beginning inventory, the firm bought more WN173 during the next six months, as follows:

Date			Quantity (gallons)	Cost per Gallon	Total Cost
Jan.	1	Inventory	8,000	$.62	$4,960
	18		11,000	$.62\frac{1}{2}$	6,875
Feb.	6		13,000	.63	8,190
	25		11,000	.63	6,930
Mar.	8		13,000	$.63\frac{1}{2}$	8,255
	26		8,000	.65	5,200
Apr.	21		7,000	.65	4,550
May	30		5,000	.66	3,300
June	18		400	.67	268

Eide Chemical's inventory on June 30 was 11,000 gallons. During the six-month period, the firm sold WN173 at $.79 per gallon. Assume that no liquid was lost through evaporation or leakage.

Instructions

1. Find the value of the ending inventory by the following methods:
   a. Weighted-average-cost (Round to two decimal places.)
   b. First-in, first-out
   c. Last-in, first-out
2. Determine the cost of goods sold according to the three methods of costing inventory.
3. Determine the amount of the gross profit according to the three methods of costing inventory.

P.O.2b,c,d

Problem 13-2B Rainier Sound Components uses the periodic inventory system. Data for their inventories on January 1, the beginning of their fiscal year, as well as purchases during the year and the inventory count at December 31, are shown on the next page.

	Model		
	PB80	**BB173**	**TB26**
Inventory, Jan. 1	5 @ $532	5 @ $782	18 @ $432
First purchase	10 @ $546	9 @ $812	20 @ $440
Second purchase	12 @ $556	10 @ $814	32 @ $444
Third purchase	9 @ $558	7 @ $826	16 @ $448
Fourth purchase	8 @ $564		
Inventory, Dec. 31	7	6	25

Instructions

1. Calculate the value of the inventory on December 31 by the weighted-average-cost method. (Round to two decimal places.)
2. Calculate the value of the inventory on December 31 by the first-in, first-out method.
3. Calculate the value of the inventory on December 31 by the last-in, first-out method.

Problem 13-3B The Dawson Company carried out the following selected transactions during the year:

P.O.3

Jan. 3 Bought merchandise on account from Baugher, Inc.; terms 2/10, n/30; FOB destination; $14,300.

7 Received credit memo no. 1421 from Baugher, Inc., for the return of merchandise bought on January 3, $1,015.

12 Issued Ck. No. 2287, payable to Baugher, Inc., in payment of the invoice dated January 3.

22 Sold merchandise on account to Robin Company, $5,842; the cost of the goods sold was $4,627.

31 Sold merchandise on account to Grubiak Company, $6,418; the cost of the goods sold was $5,083.

Dec. 31 Made the following adjusting entries. The ending inventory determined by physical count is $286,418. The balance in the inventory account under the perpetual inventory system is $286,579. The beginning inventory was $259,128. Accrued interest on notes payable is $187. Accrued interest on notes receivable is $212. Allowance for Doubtful Accounts is to be increased by $1,852.

Instructions

1. Assuming that Dawson Company uses the perpetual inventory system, record the transactions in the general journal (page 28) with purchases recorded at the gross amount.
2. Assuming that Dawson Company uses the periodic inventory system, record the transactions in the general journal (page 28) with purchases recorded at the gross amount.

Instructions for General Ledger Software

1. Record the transactions in the general journal assuming the perpetual inventory system is used and purchases are recorded at gross amount. Print the journal entries.

2. Record the transactions in the general journal assuming the periodic inventory system is used and purchases are recorded at gross amount. Print the journal entries.
3. Both options are found on the problem menu.

P.O.2c,4

Problem 13-4B The Chung Company's beginning inventory of D520 is 180 units at a cost of $66 each. Dates of purchases and sales for a three-month period are as follows:

Date		Purchases Units	Cost per Unit	Sales Units	Price per Unit
Jan.	18	210	$67.50		
	20			80	$73.50
	31			170	73.50
Feb.	3	190	71.50		
	12			130	76.00
	18	210	72.00		
	28			160	82.00
Mar.	10			100	82.00
	13	110	73.30		
	23			70	82.00
	27			75	82.75

Chung Company maintains a perpetual inventory record using the first-in, first-out method. Data for the month of January are recorded in the Working Papers.

Instructions

1. Record the data for purchases and sales of item D520 and for cost of goods sold in a perpetual inventory record, using the first-in, first-out method for the months of February and March.
2. Calculate the total cost of goods sold during the three-month period.
3. Calculate the total sales for the three-month period.
4. Calculate the gross profit from sales of item D520 for this period.

CHALLENGE PROBLEM

Johnny's Music Store has taken inventory of the pianos, organs, and miscellaneous musical items that they sell retail. As the store's accountant, you gave your assistant instructions about taking the inventory and asked that unusual items be flagged for your review. Your assistant flagged the following items that need your review to determine if the time was correctly handled on the year-end inventory.

a. Last year's Model CX-2, Electronic Keyboard, is included in inventory at a cost of $468. (You happen to know that this outdated model can be purchased for $200, now that the new model is out.)

b. A purchase of 2 pianos at $750 each was sent by the supplier on 12/29, FOB destination. Shipment had not arrived and was not included in inventory.

c. A purchase of 2 organs at $950 each was sent by the supplier on 12/30, FOB shipping point. The shipment had not arrived and was not included in inventory.

d. You have received a credit memo for a defective amplifier, cost $237, from a supplier. The supplier issued the notice based on our promise to ship the defective unit back after the end of the year. The item is still in the warehouse, and the cost of $237 is included in the inventory.

e. A customer has paid $10,000 in full for a grand piano that cost $7,500. The customer requested we deliver at the end of the first week of the new year. The value of the grand piano is included in the inventory, as no one remembered to put a "sold" tag on it.

f. For the holidays, the shop owner has taken home the newest model of the Electronic Keyboards. Retail value $3,750, cost $2,770. This item was not counted in inventory.

g. According to the company's layaway policy, a sale is not recorded until the merchandise is paid for in full, and then delivery is made. A customer has paid 25 percent of the $5,000 price of a Spinet piano. The piano is set aside because the customer has put money down on it, and the $3,800 cost is not included in the inventory.

Instructions

1. What is the correct treatment for each item? Should you include it in inventory or exclude it? Why?

2. Was the item handled correctly by your assistant? If not correctly handled, what must be done to correct the inventory? Should you increase inventory and, if so, by what amount, or decrease inventory and, if so, by what amount?

Appendix B

Estimating the Value of Inventories

PERFORMANCE OBJECTIVES

After you have completed this appendix, you will be able to do the following:

1. Estimate the value of inventory by the retail method.

2. Estimate the value of inventory by the gross-profit method.

We can describe accounting as the eyes and ears of management. Managment sees and hears through the medium of financial reports that summarize the results of business operations. To function efficiently, management must have interim income statements and balance sheets prepared monthly. Management needs a physical inventory at the end of the year, because inventory balance figures are an integral element of financial statements. However, because it is both time-consuming and expensive to take a physical inventory, management finds it more expedient to estimate the value of the ending inventories each month and to use these estimates on the monthly financial statements. Let's take a look at the two most frequently used methods of estimating the value of inventories; the retail method and the gross-profit method.

Retail Method of Estimating the Value of Inventories

As its name implies, this method is widely used by retail concerns, particularly department stores. The retailer buys merchandise at cost, then adds the normal markup and prices the goods at the retail level. The **normal markup**—which is the normal amount, or percentage, that you add to the cost of an item to arrive at its selling price—covers operating expenses and profit. When a firm uses the retail method of estimating inventories, it must record the purchases-related accounts at both cost and retail values. The firm's accountant records retail values in supplementary records; he or she also records the physical inventory taken at the end of the previous year at both cost and retail values.

Performance Objective 1

Estimate the value of inventory by the retail method.

Example 1 Baldwin Company takes a physical inventory at the end of each year and estimates the value of the ending inventory at the end of each month for its monthly financial statements.

The accountant for Baldwin Company needs to determine the following information to estimate the value of the ending merchandise inventory at cost:

- Cost value and retail value of merchandise on hand at the beginning of the month. (The inventory at the beginning of a given month is the same as the inventory at the end of the preceding month.)

	AT COST	AT RETAIL
Merchandise Inventory (beginning)	41 2 0 0 00	68 6 0 0 00

- Delivered cost of purchases during the month, both cost value and retail value. The retail figures include the cost plus the company's standard markup, as shown.

	AT COST		AT RETAIL	
Purchases		82 7 4 5 00		137 9 0 8 00
Less: Purchases Returns and Allowances	2 3 0 0 00		3 8 0 0 00	
Purchases Discounts	1 9 0 0 00	4 2 0 0 00	3 2 0 0 00	7 0 0 0 00
Net Purchases		78 5 4 5 00		130 9 0 8 00
Add Freight In		4 3 5 5 00		7 2 5 9 00
Delivered Cost of Purchases		82 9 0 0 00		138 1 6 7 00

- Net sales for the month. All sales are recorded at retail price levels, as listed on sales slips and cash register tapes.

		AT RETAIL
Sales		151 6 5 0 00
Less: Sales Returns and Allowances	7 0 0 0 00	
Sales Discounts	2 6 5 0 00	9 6 5 0 00
Net Sales		142 0 0 0 00

The accountant can determine the cost value of the ending inventory by following these four steps:

1. Determine the dollar value of goods available for sale, at cost and at retail. The cost figures are the same as the Goods Available for Sale, which is part of the Cost of Goods Sold section in the income statement.

	At Cost	At Retail
Beginning Inventory	$ 41,200	$ 68,600
Plus Delivered Cost of Purchases	82,900	138,167
Goods Available for Sale	$124,100	$206,767

2. Find the ratio of the cost value of goods available for sale to the retail value of goods available for sale.

$$\frac{\text{Cost value of goods available for sale}}{\text{Retail value of goods available for sale}} = \frac{\$124,100}{\$206,767} = \underline{\underline{60\%}}$$

3. Determine the retail value of ending inventory.

Retail value of goods available	$206,767
Less net sales	142,000
Retail value of ending inventory	$ 64,767

Think of the retail value of the ending inventory this way: If the firm had $206,767 of goods available for sale, and $142,000 was actually sold, then the amount left over should be $64,767.

4. Convert the retail value of the ending inventory into the cost value of the ending inventory by using this formula and rounding to the nearest dollar:

$$\$64,767 \times 60\% = \$64,767 \times .6 = \underline{\$38,860}$$

Therefore, on its income statement for the month, Baldwin Company records the value of the ending inventory as $38,860. If the retail value is $64,767 and 40 percent of this figure represents markup, the remaining 60 percent must be the cost.

Example 2 Charnell Company had the following account balances, as shown in the following T accounts:

Merchandise Inventory			**Purchases**			**Sales**	
+	−		+	−		−	+
Bal. 210,160			720,327				985,000

Purchases Returns and Allowances		**Sales Returns and Allowances**	
−	+	+	−
	32,716	25,000	

Purchases Discount	
−	+
	14,082

Freight In	
+	−
37,911	

Retail value of beginning inventory, $296,000 (the accountant picks up this figure from a report dated the end of the preceding month).

Delivered Cost of Purchases = Purchases − Purchases Returns and Allowances − Purchases Discount + Freight In.

= $720,327 − $32,716 − $14,082 + $37,911

= $711,440 Delivered Cost of Purchases

Retail value of delivered cost of purchases, $984,000 (the normal markup is added to the cost figure).

Net Sales = Sales − Sales Returns and Allowances

= $985,000 − $25,000

= $960,000

Again, the information is obtained by following the four steps:

1. Determine the dollar value of goods available for sale, at cost and at retail.

	At Cost	At Retail
Beginning Inventory	$210,160	$ 296,000
Plus Delivered Cost of Purchases	711,440	985,000
Goods Available for Sale	$921,600	$1,281,000

2. Find the ratio of the cost value of goods available for sale to the retail value of goods available for sale.

$$\frac{\text{Cost value of goods available for sale}}{\text{Retail value of goods available for sale}} = \frac{\$921,600}{\$1,280,000} = 72\%$$

3. Find the retail value of ending inventory, as follows:

Retail value of goods available	$1,280,000
Less net sales	960,000
Retail value of ending inventory	$ 320,000

4. Convert retail value of ending inventory into cost value of ending inventory by using this formula:

$$\$320,000 \times 72\% = \$320,000 \times .72 = \underline{\$230,400}$$

In the above examples, there is a built-in assumption that the retailer will maintain the normal markup. In other words, we are assuming that the composition or mix of the items in the ending inventory, in terms of the ratio of cost price to retail price, will remain the same for the entire stock of goods available for sale.

Markups and Markdowns

In our examples, the retailers used normal markups, but some stores use additional markups and markdowns. Retailers impose additional markups on top of normal markups when the merchandise involved is in great demand. Because of the highly desirable nature of the goods (for example, up-to-the-minute fashion in clothes), a store may feel that it can get higher-than-normal prices for the goods. Conversely, a store uses markdowns to sell slow-moving merchandise during a clearance sale.

When a store using the retail inventory method imposes additional markups and markdowns, it must keep track of them, so that it can calculate the ratio of the cost value of merchandise available to the retail value of goods available. Look at the following example of how a store keeps track of markups and markdowns:

Step 1 Goods available for sale, at cost and at retail.

	At Cost	At Retail
Beginning Inventory	$ 60,000	$ 90,000
Plus Delivered Cost of Purchases	110,000	165,000
Plus additional markups		4,000
Goods Available for Sale	$170,000	$259,000

Step 2 Ratio of cost value of goods available for sale to retail value of goods available for sale is as follows:

$$\frac{\text{Cost value of goods available for sale}}{\text{Retail value of goods available for sale}} = \frac{\$170,000}{\$259,000} = \underline{\underline{66\%}}$$

Step 3 Retail value of ending inventory.

Retail value of goods available for sale	$259,000
Less net sales	200,000
Less markdowns	3,000
Retail value of ending inventory	$ 56,000

Step 4 Convert retail value of ending inventory into cost value of ending inventory:

$$\$56,000 \times .66 = \$36,960$$

End-of-Year Procedure

The only difference between the steps taken to prepare the end-of-the-year statement and the steps taken to prepare the interim or monthly statements is that, at the end of the year, there is a physical count of the merchandise, and consequently one begins with step 4.

However, to find out the magnitude of shoplifting, or to verify the accuracy of the evaluation of the physical inventory, some firms go through the full procedure of estimating the value of the inventory at the end of the year. Then they take a physical count of the goods on hand and compare this value with the value of the estimated inventory.

Gross-Profit Method of Estimating the Value of Inventories

Performance Objective 2

Estimate the value of inventory by the gross-profit method.

Sometimes a firm may find that the total of the retail prices of the beginning inventory and purchases is not readily available; in such cases, the firm naturally cannot use the retail method of estimating the value of the ending inventory. The **gross-profit method** is an alternative procedure that achieves the same objective. As the name implies, the key element in this method of estimating the value of inventories is the percentage of gross profit the firm makes over a given period of time.

The term *gross profit,* as used on income statements, represents net sales less cost of goods sold.

Net sales	$60,000
Less cost of goods sold	45,000
Gross profit	$15,000

You arrive at the figure for the percentage of gross profit by dividing the gross profit by the net sales, like this:

$$\text{Percentage of gross profit} = \frac{\text{Gross profit}}{\text{Net sales}} = \frac{\$15,000}{\$60,000} = \underline{\underline{25\%}}$$

A 25 percent gross-profit rate means that there is 25¢ of gross profit for every $1 of net sales. *Gross profit* is the profit earned on the sale of merchandise *before* expenses are deducted. You can compute the gross-profit rate or percentage by using figures from a recent income statement. Alternatively, you may compute the percentage of gross profit from income statements from past years, using averages of figures. The variation from year to year is usually relatively minor, unless marked changes have taken place in the buying and selling policies of the firm.

You need the following information for the current year:

- Sales (balance of account to date)
- Sales Returns and Allowances (balance of account to date)
- Sales Discounts (balance of account to date, if any)
- Beginning Merchandise Inventory (ending inventory of the previous period)
- Purchases (balance of account to date)
- Purchases Returns and Allowances (balance of account to date)
- Purchases Discount (balance of account to date)
- Freight In (balance of account to date)

Example On the night of April 29, the Ribling Quick Shop was destroyed by fire. However, a heroic salesclerk ran into the building and rescued the company's books and records of transactions. For insurance purposes, the owner must estimate the value of the inventory by the gross-profit method. The owner knows that the average gross-profit percentage for the past five years is 32 percent. By journalizing and posting the transactions of the current month, the company's accounts can be brought up to date from these sources:

- Sales (from sales journal, cash receipts journal, and invoices for April 29)
- Sales Returns and Allowances (from cash payments and general journal)
- Merchandise Inventory, December 31 (ending inventory of last fiscal period)
- Purchases (from purchases journal and invoices for April 29)
- Purchases Returns and Allowances (from general journal)
- Purchases Discount (from cash payments journal)
- Freight In (from purchases journal, cash payments journal, and invoices for April 29)

The owner of Ribling Quick Shop arranges these figures in the customary income statement format, extending from Sales to Gross Profit (see Figure B-1).

$$\text{Percentage of gross profit} = \frac{\text{Gross profit}}{\text{Net sales}} = \frac{\text{Gross profit}}{\$200,000} = \underline{\underline{32\%}}$$

$$\text{Gross profit} = .32 \times \$200,000 = \underline{\underline{\$64,000}}$$

Now we fill in the Gross Profit blank in the income statement (see Figure B-1 on page 548).

To find the value of the merchandise at the end (April 29), we should work backward. The cost of goods sold is the difference between net sales and gross profit, or $136,000 ($200,000 − $64,000). The equation is as shown here:

$$\text{Cost of goods sold} = \text{Net sales} - \text{Gross profit}$$

$$= \$200,000 - \$64,000$$

$$= \underline{\underline{\$136,000}}$$

Figure B-1

Ribling Quick Shop
Partial Income Statement
For Period January 1 through April 29, 19–

Revenue from Sales:					
Sales					$217 0 0 0 00
Less Sales Returns and Allowances					17 0 0 0 00
Net Sales					$200 0 0 0 00
Cost of Goods Sold:					
Merchandise Inventory, January 1, 19–				$ 72 0 0 0 00	
Purchases			$136 0 0 0 00		
Less: Purchases Returns and Allowances	$14 0 0 0 00				
Purchases Discount	2 4 0 0 00		16 4 0 0 00		
Net Purchases			$119 6 0 0 00		
Add Freight In			7 4 0 0 00		
Delivered Cost of Purchases				127 0 0 0 00	
Goods Available for Sale				$199 0 0 0 00	
Less Merchandise Inventory, April 29, 19–				63 0 0 0 00	
Cost of Goods Sold					$136 0 0 0 00
Gross Profit					$ 64 0 0 0 00

The value of the merchandise inventory on April 29 is the difference between the value of the goods available for sale and the cost of goods sold, or $63,000 ($199,000 − $136,000). The equation is as follows:

Value of ending inventory = Value of goods available for sale
− Cost of goods sold

= $199,000 − $136,000

= $63,000

Goods Available for Sale	$199,000.00
Less Merchandise Inventory, April 29, 19–	63,000.00
Cost of Goods Sold	136,000.00
Gross Profit	$ 64,000.00

roblems

P.O.1

Problem B-1 You are given the following information for Austin Stereo at the end of its fiscal year, October 31:

	At Cost	At Retail
Sales		$264,789
Sales Returns and Allowances		10,659
Purchases	$152,806	254,600
Purchases Returns and Allowances	7,026	11,712
Merchandise Inventory (beginning)	59,172	98,640
Freight In	8,042	13,534

Instructions

1. Determine the cost value of the ending merchandise inventory as of October 31, presenting details of your computations.
2. At the end of the year, Austin Stereo takes a physical inventory at marked selling prices and finds that the retail stock totals $98,889. There is a possibility that the difference between the estimated ending inventory and the actual physical inventory is due to shoplifting. Convert the value of the physical inventory at retail into its value at cost, and determine the amount of the loss.

Problem B-2 On May 10 of this year, a fire in the night destroyed the entire stock of merchandise of Clair's Crafts. Most of the accounting records were destroyed also. However, from assorted statements and documents, the firm's accountant was able to piece together the balances of several accounts. Over the past three years, the percentage of gross profit averaged 40 percent.

`P.O.2`

Merchandise Inventory, January 1 (beginning of fiscal year)	$128,859
Account balances, as of May 10	
Purchases	163,970
Purchases Returns and Allowances	984
Freight In	7,906
Sales	219,540
Sales Returns and Allowances	660

Instructions

Determine the cost value of the ending merchandise inventory as of May 10, giving details of your computations.

Problem B-3 On the morning of July 27, the owner of Sound Systems opened her store and discovered that a robbery had taken place over the weekend. A large part of the stock had been stolen. However, the following information for the period January 1 through July 27 was available. Each year during the past four years, the store had earned an average 34 percent gross profit on sales.

`P.O.2`

Merchandise Inventory, January 1 (beginning of fiscal year)	$190,389
Account balances, as of July 27	
Purchases	408,692
Purchases Returns and Allowances	10,986
Purchases Discount	8,244
Freight In	24,703
Sales	596,134
Sales Returns and Allowances	6,134

Instructions

Determine the cost value of the ending merchandise inventory as of July 27, giving the details of your computations.

chapter 14

Accounting for Valuation of Plant and Equipment

We described Plant and Equipment as an account classification in Chapter 7, in connection with the classified balance sheet. Because assets in this category have a useful life longer than one year, they are often referred to as long-lived or fixed assets. Such assets are originally purchased for use in the business, as opposed to merchandise, which is bought for the purpose of resale. Items most frequently classified as plant and equipment are equipment, furniture, machinery, tools, buildings, land improvements, and land.

Initial Costs of Plant and Equipment

T

he original cost of plant and equipment includes all normal expenditures necessary to acquire and install the plant and equipment. For example, the cost of a cash register includes not only its invoice price (less any discount for paying cash) but sales tax, freight charges, insurance costs while it is being transported, and costs of unpacking and assembling. Assuming that the buyer of the cash register pays these additional charges in cash, the accountant for the buyer debits Store Equipment and credits Cash. Suppose the firm bought a second-hand cash register and had to have it repaired before it could be used. The cost of the repairs would be debited to the relevant asset account, in this case Store Equipment.

The accountant should debit only normal and necessary costs to the asset accounts, which rules out expenditures that result from carelessness, vandalism, and other abnormal causes. For example, suppose that an employee dropped the cash register while unpacking it. The cost of the repair is not part

REMEMBER
Normal costs of the asset, such as its transportation and installation, are debited to the asset. Other expenditures, from abnormal causes, are expensed.

of the cost of the cash register; that cost is charged to an expense account, such as Repair Expense or Miscellaneous Expense. The cost is charged as an expense and not as an asset because the repair does not *add* to the usefulness of the cash register—it simply restores its usefulness.

Differentiating Costs of Land, Land Improvements, and Buildings

Performance Objective 1

Allocate costs to Land, Land Improvements, and Buildings accounts.

There is no legal recognition of the depreciation of land. Yet a buyer usually buys a package including the land, land improvements, and the building. In other words, the buyer pays one price for one package. So the question is: How should the price be allocated among the three elements?

When there is no qualified appraisal available, one accepts the ratio established by the county or municipal assessor. Suppose that someone buys some real property, including land and a building, for $500,000. The assessor valued this property for tax purposes at $300,000: $60,000 for the land and $240,000 for the building. The percentage the assessor allocated to the land is $60,000/$300,000 = 20 percent. The percentage allocated to the building is $240,000/$300,000 = 80 percent. Therefore, the value that the buyer should allocate to the land is $500,000 × .2 = $100,000; to the building, $500,000 × .8 = $400,000. For bookkeeping purposes, one separates land improvements from buildings because of the different lengths of life involved.

The accountant maintains separate accounts for the building, land, and land improvements.

Land

Suppose that someone buys a piece of land—just land, no building. The cost of the land includes the amount paid for the land plus incidental charges connected with the sale: real estate agents' commissions, escrow and legal fees, delinquent taxes paid by the buyer, plus any costs of surveying, clearing, draining, or grading the land. In addition, the municipality or county—either at the time of purchase or later—may assess the buyer for such improvements as the installation of paved streets, curbs, sidewalks, and sewers. The buyer debits these items to the Land account, since the items are considered to be as permanent as the land. If a business entity buys land for a building site and the land happens to have old buildings standing on it, the firm debits the cost of the structures as well as the costs of demolishing them to the Land account.

Land Improvements

An accountant uses the asset account **Land Improvements** to record expenditures for improvements that are (1) not as permanent as the land or (2) not directly associated with a building. Examples are driveways, parking lots, fences, and outdoor lighting systems.

Buildings

The cost of a building includes not only money spent for labor and materials, but also architectural and engineering fees, money spent for insurance premiums during construction, interest on construction loans during the period of construction, and all other necessary and normal expenditures applicable to the project.

> **R E M E M B E R**
> If land and building are bought as a package, the assets on the land must be separated for accounting purposes.

The Nature and Recording of Depreciation

When accountants use the term *depreciation*, they mean loss in usefulness of long-lived assets (assets that will last longer than one year). Examples of long-lived assets are buildings, office furniture, store fixtures, machines, computers, trucks, and automobiles. Assets lose their usefulness to companies for two reasons: (1) **physical depreciation**—simply wearing out or being used up, such as an automobile finally being beyond repair; and (2) **functional depreciation**—becoming obsolete or inadequate, such as a machine being outdated because a more efficient machine has been developed. As we said in Chapter 4, depreciation represents a systematic procedure for spreading out the cost of plant and equipment to the fiscal periods in which the company receives services from the assets.

> **R E M E M B E R**
> The purpose of depreciation is to spread the cost of plant and equipment over the years in which it is used to produce revenue—again, in keeping with the matching principle.

Determining the Amount of Depreciation

To determine the depreciation of a long-lived asset, one must take into account three elements:

1. The **depreciation base,** which is the full depreciation of an asset. Full depreciation is the total cost of an asset less the trade-in or salvage value.

2. The length of the useful life of the asset.

3. The method of depreciation chosen to allocate the depreciation base over the useful life of the asset.

Depreciation Base

When a business entity first puts an asset into service, it is hard to predict the amount of the trade-in or salvage (scrap) value, especially when such a trade-in probably will not take place for years. Many firms make estimates based on their own experience or on data supplied by trade associations or government agencies. If the firm expects the salvage value to be insignificant in comparison with the cost of the asset, the accountant often assumes the salvage value to be zero.

Useful Life

As we said, the length of an asset's useful life is affected not only by the amount of physical wear and tear to which it is subjected but also by technological change and innovation. For accounting purposes, the useful life of an asset is based on the expected use of the asset, in keeping with the company's replacement policy. An average car, for example, may have a useful life of five years. However, for reasons of competition, a car rental company may replace its cars every year in order to offer customers the latest models. A company operating a fleet of cars for its sales force may replace the cars every three years.

Calculating Depreciation

Performance Objective 2

Calculate depreciation by the straight-line method, units-of-production method, double-declining-balance method, and sum-of-the-years'-digits method.

The objective of recording depreciation is to spread out systematically the cost of a long-lived asset over the length of the asset's useful life. However, a firm need not use the same method of depreciation for all its assets.

The four most common methods of computing depreciation are the (1) straight-line method, (2) units-of-production method, (3) double-declining-balance method, and (4) sum-of-the-years'-digits method. Methods 3 and 4 represent **accelerated depreciation.** In accelerated depreciation, depreciation is speeded up, in that larger amounts of depreciation are taken during an asset's early life, and smaller amounts are taken during an asset's later life.

Straight-line Method

A firm that uses the **straight-line method** of calculating depreciation charges an equal amount of depreciation for each year of service anticipated. The accountant computes the annual depreciation by dividing the depreciation base (cost minus trade-in value, if any) by the number of years of useful life predicted for the asset. This is the type of depreciation we illustrated in Chapter 4. The percentage rate of depreciation per year is determined by dividing the number of years of useful life into 1. For instance, take an asset with an estimated life of eight years:

$$\frac{1}{8 \text{ years}} = .125 \qquad .125 \times 100 = \underline{\underline{12.5\%}}$$

One always applies the depreciation rate against the depreciation base (cost less trade-in value):

$$\text{Depreciation per year} = \frac{\text{Cost} - \text{Trade-in value}}{\text{Useful life (in years)}}$$

Example A neon sign costs $4,000 and has a useful life of eight years. The estimated trade-in value at the end of eight years is zero.

$$\text{Depreciation per year} = \frac{\$4,000 - 0}{8} = \frac{\$4,000}{8} = \underline{\underline{\$500}}$$

$$\text{Depreciation rate per year} = \frac{1}{8 \text{ years}} = .125 \qquad .125 \times 100 = \underline{\underline{12.5\%}}$$

Units-of-Production Method

The **units-of-production method** enables one to allow for an asset that is used a great deal more in one year than in another. You can obtain the depreciation charge per unit of production by dividing the depreciation base by the total estimated units of production.

$$\text{Depreciation per unit of production} = \frac{\text{Cost} - \text{Trade-in value}}{\text{Estimated units of production}}$$

Example A salesperson's car costs $16,200 and has a useful life of 60,000 miles. The estimated trade-in value at the end of 60,000 miles is $3,600. The car is driven 18,000 miles this year.

$$\text{Depreciation per mile} = \frac{\$16,200 - \$3,600}{60,000 \text{ miles}} = \frac{\$12,600}{60,000 \text{ miles}}$$

$$= \underline{\underline{\$.21}} \text{ per mile}$$

$$\text{Depreciation for 18,000 miles} = 18,000 \text{ miles} \times \$.21 \text{ per mile}$$

$$= \underline{\underline{\$3,780}}$$

Double-Declining-Balance Method

The **double-declining-balance method** is popular because it allows larger amounts of depreciation to be taken in the early years of an asset's life. Some accountants reason that the amount charged to depreciation of an asset should be higher during the asset's early years so as to offset the higher repair and maintenance expenses of the asset's later years. The total annual expense would then tend to be equalized over the entire life of the asset.

For an asset that has a life of three years or more, this method allows a firm to calculate depreciation by *multiplying the book value (cost less accumulated depreciation) at the beginning of the year by* twice *the straight-line rate.*

Trade-in or salvage value is not counted in determining depreciation by the double-declining-balance method until the end of the depreciation schedule. As with other methods, an asset may not be depreciated below its salvage value.

To compute depreciation by the double-declining-balance method, follow these steps:

1. Calculate the straight-line depreciation rate.

2. Multiply the straight-line rate by 2.

3. Multiply the book value of the asset at the beginning of the year by double the straight-line rate.

During the first year, the book value of an asset will be the same as its cost, since no depreciation has been taken. So, for the first year only, multiply the cost by twice the straight-line rate.

Example A firm's word processing equipment costs $30,000 and has a useful life of five years. The estimated trade-in value at the end of five years is zero.

1. Compute the straight-line depreciation rate:

$$\text{Straight-line depreciation rate} = \frac{1}{5 \text{ years}} = .2 \qquad .2 \times 100 = \underline{\underline{20\%}}$$

2. Twice the straight-line rate $= .2 \times 2 = .4 \qquad .4 \times 100 = \underline{\underline{40\%}}$

3. Depreciation per year $=$ Book value at beginning of year $\times$ .4.

Year	Book Value at Beginning of Year	Depreciation Expense	Book Value at End of Year
1	$30,000.00	$30,000.00 × .4 = $12,000.00	$30,000.00 − $12,000.00 = $18,000.00
2	18,000.00	18,000.00 × .4 = 7,200.00	18,000.00 − 7,200.00 = 10,800.00
3	10,800.00	10,800.00 × .4 = 4,320.00	10,800.00 − 4,320.00 = 6,480.00
4	6,480.00	6,480.00 × .4 = 2,592.00	6,480.00 − 2,592.00 = 3,888.00
5	3,888.00	3,888.00 × .4 = 1,555.20	3,888.00 − 1,555.20 = 2,332.80
Total		$27,667.20	

Under the double-declining balance method, book value never reaches zero. Therefore, a company typically switches over to the straight-line basis when straight-line depreciation exceeds double-declining-balance.

Year	Book Value at Beginning of Year	Depreciation Expense	Book Value at End of Year
1	$18,000.00	$18,000.00 × $\frac{1}{3}$ = $6,000.00	$18,000.00 − $6,000.00 = $12,000.00
2	12,000.00	12,000.00 × $\frac{1}{3}$ = 4,000.00	12,000.00 − 4,000.00 = 8,000.00
3	8,000.00	8,000.00 × $\frac{1}{3}$ = 2,666.67	8,000.00 − 2,666.67 = 5,333.33
4	5,333.33	5,333.33 × $\frac{1}{3}$ = 1,777.78	5,333.33 − 1,777.78 = 3,555.55
5	3,555.55	3,555.55 − $3,000 = 555.55	3,555.55 − 555.55 = 3,000.00
6	3,000.00	0	3,000.00 − 0 = 3,000.00
Total		$15,000.00	

Observe carefully that the trade-in or salvage value is not counted until the last year. When one uses the double-declining-balance method and there is a trade-in value involved, the book value gradually declines until it reaches the amount of the trade-in value. *An asset must not be depreciated beyond its trade-in value.* For example, take a delivery van costing $18,000 and with an estimated trade-in value of $3000 after six years. During the fifth year, the normal depreciation would be one-third of the book value at the beginning of the year. Calculate the depreciation for the year and the ending book value as follows:

Depreciation expense = $3,555.55 × $\frac{1}{3}$ = $\underline{\$1,185.18}$

Book value at end of year = $3,555.55 − $1,185.18 = $\underline{\$2,370.37}$

Obviously, if one calculates depreciation in this manner, the book value of the van ($2,370.37) dips below its established trade-in value ($3,000). Consequently, one must make an adjustment during this year so that the van's ending book value will be the same as its trade-in value. Even though its useful life was set at six years, the van is actually depreciated to the limit in five years.

REMEMBER

The double-declining-balance method is the only method in which one figures in the trade-in value at the end of the depreciation schedule.

Sum-of-the-Years'-Digits Method

The **sum-of-the-years'-digits method** yields a large proportion of depreciation during the early years of an asset's life. It does this on a reducing-fraction basis. To compute depreciation by this method, follow these steps:

1. Decide how many years the asset is likely to last. Then find the sum of the years' digits. For example, suppose the asset has an expected life of three years. Then add to find the sum of year 1, year 2, and year 3:

$1 + 2 + 3 = 6$ or $\dfrac{\text{Life}^2 + \text{Life}}{2} = \dfrac{3^2 + 3}{2} = \dfrac{9 + 3}{2} = \dfrac{12}{2} = \underline{\underline{6}}$

REMEMBER

The term *sum* in sum-of-the-years'-digits means the total of all the years of life in the order 1 + 2 + 3 and so on. The sum is used as the denominator (bottom part) of the fraction.

2. Record the years in reverse (or descending) order in the numerator (top) of the fraction and the sum of the years' digits in the denominator (bottom) of the fraction.

3. Multiply the decreasing fractions by the depreciation base (cost less trade-in value).

Example A printing press costs $16,800 and has a useful life of five years. The estimated salvage value at the end of five years is $600. The depreciation base is $16,200 ($16,800 − $600).

		Step 3	
Step 1*	**Step 2**	**Year**	**Depreciation Expense**
1	$\frac{5}{15}$	1	$\frac{5}{15} \times \$16,200 = \$ 5,400$
2	$\frac{4}{15}$	2	$\frac{4}{15} \times 16,200 = 4,320$
3	$\frac{3}{15}$	3	$\frac{3}{15} \times 16,200 = 3,240$
4	$\frac{2}{15}$	4	$\frac{2}{15} \times 16,200 = 2,160$
5	$\frac{1}{15}$	5	$\frac{1}{15} \times 16,200 = 1,080$
15	$\frac{15}{15}$		$16,200$

* Step 1 can be calculated as follows: $\dfrac{5^2 + 5}{2} = \dfrac{25 + 5}{2} = \dfrac{30}{2} = 15$

FYI

More and more court cases are requiring accounting clerks to explain how they arrived at certain totals. In one case, an accounting clerk did not understand the concept of depreciation and reported incorrect totals to the accountant. The consequences were expensive and embarrassing.

Comparison of Three Methods

You can see in the previous charts that the double-declining-balance method and the sum-of-the-years'-digits method yield relatively large amounts of depreciation during the early years of use of an asset. For this reason they are examples of *accelerated depreciation*, while straight-line depreciation yields an equal amount of depreciation for each year of service anticipated.

Depreciation for Periods of Less Than a Year

Businesses do not acquire (or get rid of) all their depreciable assets on the first and last days of their fiscal period. They buy and sell assets throughout the year. How, then, do they calculate depreciation? Remember that, when a business entity acquires a depreciable asset during the year, the accountant usually figures depreciation to the nearest whole month. If the firm held the asset for *less* than half a given month, the accountant doesn't count that month. But if the firm has held it for half of a given month or more, the accountant counts it as a whole month.

COMPUTERS
AT WORK

Using Financial Functions: Lotus 1-2-3 Provides Powerful Tools to Evaluate Business Options

The financial functions available in *Lotus 1-2-3* can generate information to help you make sound business decisions. They can be used to assess the viability of proposed business deals, depreciate assets, and compute the future value of cash flows for retirement and other purposes.

DEPRECIATING ASSETS • Depreciation is an accounting technique for charging part of the cost of an asset against earnings in the current period. The charge against earnings is the depreciation allowance. At the end of an asset's life, it is junked as having no value or some slight salvage value. The sum of the depreciation allowances across an asset's useful life should equal its cost less its salvage value.

Lotus 1-2-3 offers several functions to depreciate assets. These functions correspond to different accounting strategies for computing the charge against current income.

The most straightforward function, @SLN, computes the straight-line depreciation. This method allocates an equal charge in every year of an asset's useful life. The @SLN function requires three factors: an asset's cost, its salvage value, and its useful life. . . .

The @SYD, @DB, @DDB, and @VDB functions can all depreciate an asset faster than the @SLN function. The @SYD function computes the sum-of-the-years-digits depreciation allowance. To compute this function, you need an asset's cost, its salvage value, its useful life, and the depreciation period. . . .

The @DB function . . . computes the fixed declining-balance depreciation allowance. This function requires the same information as @SYD. However, @DB depreciates an asset faster than @SYD. . . .

The @VDB function computes depreciation based on the variable-rate declining-balance method. This depreciation function needs different information than the other ones because it can compute depreciation for more than one period at a time. The first three pieces of information are the same as for the other depreciation functions: cost, salvage, and useful life. The fourth and fifth factors designate the start and end periods, respectively, over which the function computes depreciation. . . .

Which function you use to depreciate assets depends on your objectives and accepted accounting practices. When computing depreciation for tax purposes, consult an accountant. . . .

Lotus 1-2-3's financial functions expedite many common business calculations. They may be intimidating at first, but with practice and the program's Help system, these powerful tools will help you make informed business decisions.

Source: Excerpted from Rick Dobson, "Using Financial Functions," *PC Today,* June 1994, pp. 28–30.

Capital and Revenue Expenditures

Performance Objective 3

Differentiate among capital expenditures, revenue expenditures, and extraordinary-repairs expenditures.

The term *expenditure* refers to spending, either by paying cash now or by promising to pay in the future for services received or assets purchased. After paying the initial price for an asset, one often has to pay out more, either to maintain the asset's operating efficiency or to increase its capacity. So there are two classifications of expenditures: capital and revenue.

Capital expenditures include the initial costs debited to plant and equipment; they also include any costs of enlarging or increasing the capacity of assets. You reap the benefits of capital expenditures during more than one accounting period. Examples are expenditures for buying a building, enlarging it, putting in air conditioning, and replacing a stairway with an elevator. All these expenditures result in debits to an asset account.

Revenue expenditures include the costs of maintaining the operation of an asset, such as the expense of making normal repairs. Examples are expenditures for painting, plumbing repairs, fuel, property taxes, and so on. These expenditures provide benefit only during the current accounting period and are recorded as debits to expense accounts.

Extraordinary-Repairs Expenditures

In accounting, **extraordinary-repairs expenditures** refer to a major overhaul or reconditioning that either extends the useful life of an asset beyond its original estimated life or increases its estimated salvage value. An accountant usually records expenditures for extraordinary repairs as debits to Accumulated Depreciation and credits to Cash or Accounts Payable.

For example, on January 3, Year 1, a firm bought a used car for $9,000. The car's estimated useful life is four years, and its trade-in value is $2,800; straight-line annual depreciation expense is $1,550. On January 6, Year 4, the firm puts in a new engine and has other major repairs done, for which it spends $1,740 in cash. The entry in general journal form is as follows:

	DATE		DESCRIPTION	POST. REF.	DEBIT	CREDIT	
1	Year 4						1
2	Jan.	6	Accumulated Depreciation,				2
3			Automobile		1 7 4 0 00		3
4			Cash			1 7 4 0 00	4
5			New engine installed in				5
6			company car.				6
7							7

This extraordinary repair extends the life of the car from the present one additional year to a total of three additional years. Here are relevant balances, together with the $1,740 payment as shown by T accounts:

Automobile		
+		−
Jan. 3, Year 1	9,000	

Accumulated Depreciation, Automobile			
−		+	
Jan. 6, Year 4	1,740	Dec. 31, Year 1	1,550
		Dec. 31, Year 2	1,550
		Dec. 31, Year 3	1,550

The car's book value before the extraordinary repair was $4,350 ($9,000 − $4,650). The accountant debits the Accumulated Depreciation account (rather than the asset account) to preserve the original cost figure in the asset account. Another reason is to partially offset the depreciation of previous years, since the estimated life is extended. In this example, the car that the firm bought cost $9,000, not $10,740. We can see this in the balance sheet as follows:

REMEMBER

When recording an extraordinary repair, debit accumulated depreciation. This maintains the original cost figure in the asset account, it increases the book value, and yields a new depreciation base.

Plant and Equipment:		
Automobile	$9,000.00	
Less Accumulated Depreciation	2,910.00	$6,090.00

When it comes to recording the remaining depreciation on this asset, the accountant now has a new cost base, which he or she uses to determine the new depreciation base. Assume that the trade-in value is still $2,800.

New book value ($9,000 − $2,910)	$6,090
Less trade-in value	2,800
New depreciation base	$3,290

$3,290 ÷ 3 years = $1,096.67

The adjusting entry for depreciation of the car at the end of Year 4 is:

	DATE		DESCRIPTION	POST. REF.	DEBIT	CREDIT	
1	Year 4		Adjusting Entry				1
2	Dec.	31	Depreciation Expense,				2
3			Automobile		1,096.67		3
4			Accumulated Depreciation,				4
5			Automobile			1,096.67	5
6			—				6
7							7

REMEMBER

For an extraordinary-repair cost, debit Accumulated Depreciation instead of Repair Expense, and credit Cash or Accounts Payable.

Assuming that no additional expenditures are made for extraordinary repairs, the adjusting entries for the remaining two years (Years 5 and 6) will be $1,096.67 for Year 5 and $1,096.66 for Year 6.

Prepare journal entries for discarding of assets fully depreciated, discarding of assets not fully depreciated, sale of assets involving a loss, sale of assets involving a gain, exchange of assets involving a loss on the trade, and exchange of assets involving a gain on the trade.

Disposition of Plant and Equipment

Sooner or later a business entity disposes of its long-lived assets by (1) discarding or retiring them, (2) selling them, or (3) trading them in for other assets. **If the assets are not fully depreciated, the account-ant must first make an entry to bring the depreciation up to date.** Let's look at some examples. (Ordinarily entries involving Cash would be recorded in the cash journals; however, for simplification and clarity, we shall present all the following entries in general journal form.)

Discarding or Retiring Plant and Equipment

When long-lived assets are no longer useful to the business and have no market value, a firm discards them.

Discarding of Fully Depreciated Assets A display case that cost $1,760 and has been fully depreciated is given away as junk. The present status of the accounts is as follows:

	Store Equipment			Accumulated Depreciation, Store Equipment		
	+		−		−	+
Bal.	1,760				Bal.	1,760

The journal entry to record the disposal of the asset looks like this:

	DATE		DESCRIPTION	POST. REF.	DEBIT	CREDIT	
6	July	10	Accumulated Depreciation,				6
7			Store Equipment		1 7 6 0 00		7
8			Store Equipment			1 7 6 0 00	8
9			Discarded a fully depreciated				9
10			display case.				10
11							11

Although fully depreciated assets are retained on the books as long as they remain in use, the firm may not take any additional depreciation on them. Once an asset is fully depreciated, the asset's book value will remain at its estimated salvage value unless an extraordinary repair is made or the company disposes of the asset.

Discarding an Asset Not Fully Depreciated A firm discards a time clock that cost $1,600. No salvage value is realized. Accumulated Depreciation up to the end of the previous year is $1,370; depreciation for the current year is $190. The present balances of the accounts are as follows:

	Office Equipment			Accumulated Depreciation, Office Equipment	
	+	−		−	+
Bal.	1,600			Bal.	1,370

Record the entry to depreciate the asset up to date:

	DATE		DESCRIPTION	POST. REF.	DEBIT	CREDIT	
12	Aug.	12	Depreciation Expense, Office				12
13			Equipment		1 9 0 00		13
14			Accumulated Depreciation,				14
15			Office Equipment			1 9 0 00	15
16			Depreciation on time clock				16
17			for the partial year.				17
18							18

The T accounts look like this:

	Depreciation Expense, Office Equipment			Accumulated Depreciation, Office Equipment	
	+	−		−	+
	190			Bal.	1,370
					190

The journal entry to record the disposal of the asset is as follows:

	DATE	DESCRIPTION	POST. REF.	DEBIT	CREDIT	
19	12	Accumulated Depreciation,				19
20		Office Equipment		1 5 6 0 00		20
21		Loss on Disposal of Plant and				21
22		Equipment		4 0 00		22
23		Office Equipment			1 6 0 0 00	23
24		Discarded a time clock.				24
25						25
26						26
27						27

The T accounts look like this:

	Accumulated Depreciation, Office Equipment			Loss on Disposal of Plant and Equipment			Office Equipment	
	−	+		+	−		+	−
	1,560	Bal. 1,370		40		Bal.	1,600	1,600
		190						

R E M E M B E R

A gain occurs when the amount received for an asset is greater than the book value. A loss occurs when the amount received is less than the book value. In order to calculate the book value, the depreciation must be brought up to date before a sale, disposal, or trade-in.

R E M E M B E R

Gains or losses from disposal of assets go in either the Other Revenue or the Other Expenses section of the income statement.

The book value of the asset is $40 ($1,600 − $1,560). Because the firm realized nothing from the disposal of the asset, the loss is for the same amount as the book value.

Loss on Disposal of Plant and Equipment is an expense account that appears under Other Expense in the income statement and is used when a firm sells or trades in an asset and receives an amount less than the book value of the asset.

Selling of Plant and Equipment

Naturally, it is very hard to estimate the exact trade-in or salvage value of a long-lived asset. It is quite likely that, when a firm sells or trades in such an asset, the amount realized will differ from the estimated amount.

Sale of an Asset at a Loss   Suppose that a firm sells a lathe for $250. This lathe originally cost $2,100; accumulated depreciation up to the end of the previous year (December 31) was $1,680. Yearly depreciation is $210. The lathe is sold on August 21.

The present balances of the accounts are as follows:

Factory Equipment		Accumulated Depreciation, Factory Equipment	
+	−	−	+
Bal. 2,100			Bal. 1,680

We record the depreciation of the asset to the present date:

	DATE	DESCRIPTION	POST. REF.	DEBIT	CREDIT	
1	19–					1
2	Aug. 21	Depreciation Expense, Factory				2
3		Equipment		1 4 0 00		3
4		Accumulated Depreciation,				4
5		Factory Equipment			1 4 0 00	5
6		Depreciation on lathe for				6
7		8 months, $140.				7
8		($210 × 8/12)				8

By T accounts, the situation looks like this:

Depreciation Expense, Factory Equipment		Accumulated Depreciation, Factory Equipment	
+	−	−	+
140			Bal. 1,680
			140

The entry, in general journal form, to record the sale of the lathe is as follows:

	DATE		DESCRIPTION	POST. REF.	DEBIT	CREDIT	
10	21		Cash		2 5 0 00		10
11			Accumulated Depreciation,				11
12			Factory Equipment		1 8 2 0 00		12
13			Loss on Disposal of Plant and				13
14			Equipment		3 0 00		14
15			Factory Equipment			2 1 0 0 00	15
16			Sold a lathe.				16

For purposes of illustration, let's record the above entry in the T accounts as follows:

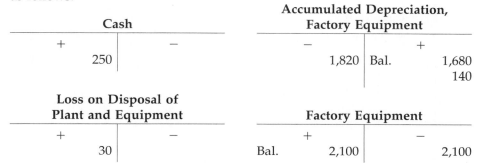

Cash			
+		−	
	250		

Accumulated Depreciation, Factory Equipment			
−		+	
	1,820	Bal.	1,680
			140

Loss on Disposal of Plant and Equipment			
+		−	
	30		

Factory Equipment			
+		−	
Bal.	2,100		2,100

Note that the book value of the lathe is $280 ($2,100 − $1,820). When the firm sells it for $250, the loss is $30, since the amount received for the item is $30 less than its book value.

Sale of an Asset at a Gain   Suppose that a firm sells an electronic analyzer for $400. The firm had originally paid $4,400; accumulated depreciation up to the end of the previous year, December 31, was $3,960. Yearly depreciation is $360. The electronic analyzer is sold on October 18. The present balances of the accounts are as follows:

Shop Equipment			
	+	−	
Bal.	4,400		

Accumulated Depreciation, Shop Equipment			
−		+	
		Bal.	3,960

We record the depreciation of the asset to the present date:

	DATE		DESCRIPTION	POST. REF.	DEBIT	CREDIT	
1	19–						1
2	Oct.	18	Depreciation Expense, Shop				2
3			Equipment		3 0 0 00		3
4			Accumulated Depreciation,				4
5			Shop Equipment			3 0 0 00	5
6			Depreciation on electronic				6
7			analyzer for 10 months.				7
8			($360 × 10/12)				8
9							9

FYI

Timber, oil, and mineral operations must account for the depletion or use of the natural resources they are taking from the land.

R E M E M B E R

The calculations shown in the explanation are for illustration and would not normally appear in practice.

By T accounts, the situation looks like this:

The general journal entry to record the sale of the electronic analyzer is as follows:

	DATE	DESCRIPTION	POST. REF.	DEBIT	CREDIT	
10	18	Cash		4 0 0 00		10
11		Accumulated Depreciation, Shop				11
12		Equipment		4 2 6 0 00		12
13		Shop Equipment			4 4 0 0 00	13
14		Gain on Disposal of Plant and				14
15		Equipment			2 6 0 00	15
16		Sold an electronic analyzer.				16

The T accounts look like this:

Cash

+ 400 | −

Accumulated Depreciation, Shop Equipment

− 4,260 | + Bal. 3,960 / 300

Shop Equipment

Bal. + 4,400 | − 4,400

Gain on Disposal of Plant and Equipment

− | + 260

The revenue account **Gain on Disposal of Plant and Equipment** appears under Other Income in the income statement and is used when a firm sells or trades in an asset and receives an amount greater than the book value for that asset.

The book value of the electronic analyzer is $140 ($4,400 − $4,260). When the firm sells the electronic analyzer for $400, the firm's gain is $260 ($400 − $140). The amount received for the item is $260 more than its book value.

Exchange of Long-lived Assets for Other Similar Assets Without Recognition of Gain or Loss

Often a business trades in one asset for another, using the old item as part payment for the new one. The trade-in allowance may differ from the book value of the asset. If the trade-in allowance is greater than the book value, the firm has a gain; if less than the book value, it has a loss. However, federal income tax laws state that when assets held for productive use are exchanged for similar assets, *no gain or loss is recognized*. In effect, the gain or loss is absorbed into the recorded cost of the new asset.

Exchange When Trade-in Value Is Less Than Book Value Suppose that a firm bought a delivery truck for $15,200. Four years later, the truck has an accumulated depreciation of $13,100 (Book value = $15,200 − $13,100 = $2,100). The firm buys a new truck, with a list price of $17,700, trading in the old one, for which they are allowed only $1,400, and paying the difference in cash. Assume that the depreciation for the year is already up to date. The present status of the accounts is as follows:

Delivery Equipment			Accumulated Depreciation, Delivery Equipment	
+	−		−	+
Bal. 15,200			Bal.	13,100

The firm's accountant records the transaction by the following steps:

1. Credit Cash, $16,300 (quoted price of new truck, $17,700 minus $1,400, which is the trade-in allowance on old truck).

2. Close or clear the account of the old asset: credit Delivery Equipment, $15,200.

3. Close or clear the Accumulated Depreciation account of the old asset: debit Accumulated Depreciation, $13,100.

4. Debit the account of the new asset for the difference between total debits and total credits, $18,400 ($16,300 + $15,200 − $13,100 = $18,400), which is the book value of the old asset plus the amount of cash or notes given.

The entry in general journal form with the steps labeled is shown below.

	DATE		DESCRIPTION	POST. REF.	DEBIT	CREDIT	
11	Nov.	(4)	Delivery Equipment		18 4 0 0 00		11
12		(3)	Accumulated Depreciation,				12
13			Delivery Equipment		13 1 0 0 00		13
14		(1)	Cash			16 3 0 0 00	14
15		(2)	Delivery Equipment			15 2 0 0 00	15
16			Bought a new delivery truck.				16

REMEMBER

No gain or loss is recognized when assets held for productive use are exchanged for similar assets—the gain or loss is absorbed into the recorded cost of the new asset.

You can see from this that, when you use the income tax method of accounting, the loss is absorbed in the cost of the new equipment. In this case, the accountant added the loss of $700 ($2,100 book value − $1,400 trade-in value) to the price of the new equipment, as follows:

Cost of old equipment	$15,200
Less accumulated depreciation	13,100
Book value	$ 2,100
Less trade-in allowance	1,400
Loss	$ 700
Quoted price of new equipment	$17,700
Plus loss absorbed in recorded cost of new equipment	700
Recorded cost of new equipment	$18,400

You can also use this technique to verify the cost recorded for the new equipment. For income tax purposes, the firm cannot count the $700 loss at this time; however, the firm does have an additional $700 that it can take in depreciation in the future.

Exchange When Trade-in Value is Greater Than Book Value A business bought a copier for $2,600. After some years, the business decides to trade it in on a new model. The old copier has an accumulated depreciation of $2,480 *on the date of the trade-in,* leaving a book value of $120. The new copier has a list price of $3,350; however, the salesperson gives the firm a generous trade-in allowance of $310 on the old equipment, and the firm pays the difference in cash. The present status of the accounts is shown in the following T accounts:

Office Equipment		Accumulated Depreciation, Office Equipment	
+	−	−	+
Bal. 2,600			Bal. 2,480

The firm's accountant records the transaction by the following steps:

1. Credit Cash, $3,040 (quoted price of new copier, $3,350, minus the $310 trade-in allowance on the old model).

2. Close or clear the account of the old asset: credit Office Equipment, $2,600.

3. Close or clear the Accumulated Depreciation account on the old asset: debit Accumulated Depreciation, $2,480.

4. Debit the account of the new asset for the difference between the total debits and credits, $3,160 ($3,040 + $2,600 − $2,480 = $3,160), which is the book value of the old asset plus the amount of cash or notes given.

Here is how one records the entries in general journal form with the steps labeled:

	DATE		DESCRIPTION	POST. REF.	DEBIT	CREDIT	
10	Nov.	(4)	Office Equipment		3 1 6 0 00		10
11		(3)	Accumulated Depreciation,				11
12			Office Equipment		2 4 8 0 00		12
13		(1)	Cash			3 0 4 0 00	13
14		(2)	Office Equipment			2 6 0 0 00	14
15			Bought a new copier.				15

The accountant records the cost of the new equipment at less than the list price, which indicates that a gain is involved. This gain has been absorbed in the price of the new equipment.

Cost of old equipment	$2,600
Less accumulated depreciation	2,480
Book value	$ 120
Less trade-in allowance of $310	
Gain	$310 − $120 = $190
Quoted price of new equipment	$3,350
Less gain absorbed in recorded cost of new equipment	190
Recorded cost of new equipment	$3,160

For income tax purposes, the firm does not count the gain at this time. However, the amount that the firm can take in depreciation in the future has been reduced by $190.

Plant and Equipment Records

Depreciation, which is regarded as an expense, vitally affects the net income of any business. Because net income is affected, the amount of income taxes owed is likewise affected. And not only Depreciation Expense, but also Loss (or Gain) on Disposal can affect net income. For income tax purposes, the business must be able to justify the amount of depreciation taken, as well as the gain or loss on disposal of assets.

Performance Objective 5
Maintain a plant and equipment subsidiary ledger.

We have discussed Plant and Equipment as a category on a classified balance sheet. Accountants use the term *plant* to include land, land improvements, and buildings.

The Store Equipment account represents a functional group; it includes all types of equipment used in the operation of a store. Examples of store equipment are display cases, cash registers, counters, and storage shelves. To account for the depreciation of each item of store equipment, accountants maintain a separate record for each item in the plant and equipment ledger. The record may be in the form of a computer file or a card file. We will illustrate a card.

Store Equipment is a controlling account; the plant and equipment ledger is a subsidiary ledger. This relationship is like that of Accounts Receivable, which is a controlling account, and the accounts receivable ledger, which is a subsidiary ledger with an account for each individual charge customer. Figure 14-1 shows a record card in a firm's plant and equipment ledger. Posting to the subsidiary ledger will also be marked by a check mark in the journal's Post. Ref. column when the asset accounts and the related accumulated depreciation accounts are debited or credited.

Account 128 is the number of the general ledger account for Store Equipment. Account 128-1 is the first piece of equipment listed under Store Equipment in the plant and equipment ledger.

The plant and equipment record enables the accountant to calculate the total amount of the adjusting entry to be recorded on the company's work sheet. The total of the adjusting entry is found by adding the fiscal period's depreciation for each separate asset contained in the plant and equipment ledger. The amount of depreciation for each asset is determined by the schedule of depreciation for that asset. Also, plant and equipment records are invaluable when a business has to submit insurance claims in the event of insured losses.

Figure 14-1

PLANT AND EQUIPMENT RECORD

ITEM Cash Register   ACCOUNT NO. 128-1

SERIAL NO. ND37-4163   MAKER Security, Inc.

FROM WHOM PURCHASED Rogers Equipment Company   ESTIMATED SALVAGE VALUE $100

ESTIMATED LIFE 5

DEPRECIATION METHOD Straight line   DEPRECIATION PER YEAR $300   DEPRECIATION PER MONTH $25   RATE OF DEPRECIATION 20%

DATE	EXPLANATION	ASSET DEBIT	ASSET CREDIT	ASSET BALANCE	ACCUMULATED DEPRECIATION DEBIT	ACCUMULATED DEPRECIATION CREDIT	ACCUMULATED DEPRECIATION BALANCE	BOOK VALUE
7/3/Yr. 1		1,600		1,600				1,600
12/31/Yr. 1						150	150	1,450
12/31/Yr. 2						300	450	1,150
12/31/Yr. 3						300	750	850

Depreciation for Federal Income Tax Reporting

Businesses are entitled to deduct depreciation expenses when calculating the amounts of income taxes owed to the federal government. However, the amount of depreciation recorded on a company's income statement may differ from the amount used for income tax purposes.

In 1981, Congress passed the Economic Recovery Act, which introduced the Accelerated Cost Recovery System (ACRS). ACRS provided for depreciation deductions that approximated the 150 percent declining-balance method.

In 1986, Congress passed the Tax Reform Act, which revised allowable depreciation under ACRS. The new schedule of allowable depreciation is called the **Modified Accelerated Cost Recovery System (MACRS).** Assets put into use after 1986 are divided into eight classes according to length of life. Depreciation for most property except real estate is approximated by the 200 percent (double) declining-balance method. For additional coverage of and practice with MACRS, refer to Appendix C.

Computer Applications

Accounting software is especially valuable for producing depreciation schedules for fixed assets. This task can be done manually, of course, but a software program can speed up the process and improve accuracy. There is very little to input in depreciation schedules.

Figure 14-2 shows a fixed assets report for Dodson Plumbing Supply for four of its fixed assets, each using a different method of depreciation. Figures 14-3, 14-4, 14-5, and 14-6 show depreciation schedules for double declining-balance method, MACRS, straight-line method, and sum-of-the-years'-digits method. The user simply selected the method to be used and then supplied the information shown at the top of each schedule; the program computed the rest. Notice that each schedule shows annual depreciation (including partial years since the dates acquired are in October), accumulated depreciation, and book value.

Figure 14-2

Dodson Plumbing Supply

Fixed Assets Report

12/31/9-

Asset Number	Asset Name	Date Acquired	Depr. Meth.	Useful Life	Original Cost	Salvage Value
200	Copier	10/03/9-	DDB	5	4500.00	500.00
201	Fax Machine	10/21/9-	MACR	5	1800.00	300.00
202	Laser Printer	10/06/9-	SL	4	2500.00	300.00
203	Office Desk	10/14/9-	SYD	5	2400.00	450.00

Figure 14-3

Dodson Plumbing Supply

Depreciation Schedules

12/31/9-

Asset Number. 200
Asset Name. . . . . Copier
Date Acquired 10/03/9-
Depreciation Method . . . . Double Declining-Balance
Useful Life 5
Original Cost 4500.00
Salvage Value 500.00

Year	Annual Depreciation	Accumulated Depreciation	Book Value
1994	450.00	450.00	4050.00
1995	1620.00	2070.00	2430.00
1996	972.00	3042.00	1458.00
1997	583.20	3625.20	874.80
1998	349.92	3975.12	524.88
1999	24.88	4000.00	500.00

Figure 14-4

```
                        Dodson Plumbing Supply

                        Depreciation Schedules

                             12/31/9-

Asset Number. . . . . . . . . . . . . 201
Asset Name. . . . . . . . . . . . . . Fax Machine
Date Acquired . . . . . . . . . . . . 10/21/9-
Depreciation Method . . . . . . . . . MACRS
Useful Life . . . . . . . . . . . . . 5
Original Cost . . . . . . . . . . . .     1800.00
Salvage Value . . . . . . . . . . . .      300.00
```

Year	Annual Depreciation	Accumulated Depreciation	Book Value
1994	360.00	360.00	1440.00
1995	576.00	936.00	864.00
1996	345.60	1281.60	518.40
1997	207.36	1488.96	311.04
1998	207.36	1696.32	103.68
1999	103.68	1800.00	

Figure 14-5

```
                        Dodson Plumbing Supply

                        Depreciation Schedules

                             12/31/9-

Asset Number. . . . . . . . . . . . . 202
Asset Name. . . . . . . . . . . . . . Laser Printer
Date Acquired . . . . . . . . . . . . 10/06/9-
Depreciation Method . . . . . . . . . Straight-Line
Useful Life . . . . . . . . . . . . . 4
Original Cost . . . . . . . . . . . .     2500.00
Salvage Value . . . . . . . . . . . .      300.00
```

Year	Annual Depreciation	Accumulated Depreciation	Book Value
1994	137.50	137.50	2362.50
1995	550.00	687.50	1812.50
1996	550.00	1237.50	1262.50
1997	550.00	1787.50	712.50
1998	412.50	2200.00	300.00

Figure 14-6

```
                    Dodson Plumbing Supply

                    Depreciation Schedules

                         12/31/9-

Asset Number. . . . . . . . . . . . 203
Asset Name. . . . . . . . . . . . . Office Desk
Date Acquired . . . . . . . . . . . 10/14/9-
Depreciation Method . . . . . . . . Sum-of-the-Years-Digits
Useful Life . . . . . . . . . . . . 5
Original Cost . . . . . . . . . .    2400.00
Salvage Value . . . . . . . . . .     450.00


             Annual            Accumulated          Book
Year       Depreciation        Depreciation        Value

1994          162.50              162.50           2237.50
1995          617.50              780.00           1620.00
1996          487.50             1267.50           1132.50
1997          357.50             1625.00            775.00
1998          227.50             1852.50            547.50
1999           97.50             1950.00            450.00
```

A Final Note

N ot all businesses have computers; not all of them require them. Not all accounting-related software packages provide the same features nor the same levels of sophistication. All require learning time, patience, and common sense. What is most important is that you know the basics of accounting, the accounting cycle, how information flows through the system, and that you continue to gain a feeling of confidence that you know how the information is generated. If you know these things, you will be better equipped to handle your accounting work either manually, by using a computer, or what is most likely, by using a combination of both methods.

Finally, you should learn to be proficient on the alpha-numeric keyboard, think when you input, proofread when you output, and never assume that the printout is always correct. Remember the computer term GIGO—Garbage In, Garbage Out.

CHAPTER REVIEW

R eview of Performance Objectives

1. **Allocate costs to Land, Land Improvements, and Buildings accounts.**

   Land includes amounts paid for the land plus incidental charges connected with the sale; for example, real estate agents' commissions, when the agent was retained by the buyer; legal fees; delinquent taxes paid by the buyer; surveying, clearing, and grading the land. *Land improvements* include costs of driveways, parking lots, trees and shrubs, and outdoor lighting systems.

Buildings include amounts paid for labor and materials, architectural and engineering fees, premiums for insurance during construction, and interest on construction loans during the period of construction.

2. **Calculate depreciation by the straight-line method, units-of-production method, double-declining-balance method, and sum-of-the-years'-digits method.**

   The depreciation base is the cost of the asset less the trade-in or salvage value.

   $$\text{Straight-line method} = \frac{\text{Cost} - \text{Trade-in value}}{\text{Useful life (in years)}}$$

   $$\text{Units-of-production method} = \frac{\text{Cost} - \text{Trade-in value}}{\text{Estimated units of production}} \times \text{Number of units produced}$$

   $$\text{Double-declining-balance method} = \text{Book value at beginning of year} \times \text{Twice straight-line rate}$$

   $$\text{Sum-of-the-years'-digits method} = \text{Reducing fraction} \times (\text{Cost} - \text{Trade-in value})$$

   Under the double-declining-balance method, the trade-in value is counted at the end of the schedule of depreciation. For the sum-of-the-years'-digits method, the numerator of the fraction is the years of the asset's life placed in reverse order. The denominator of the fraction is the sum of the years of the asset's life.

3. **Differentiate among capital expenditures, revenue expenditures, and extraordinary-repairs expenditures.**

   Capital expenditures include costs incurred to buy or increase the capacity of assets. Costs are debited to the asset accounts. *Revenue expenditures* include the costs of maintaining the operation of an asset, such as fuel, painting, and normal repairs. Costs are debited to expense accounts. *Extraordinary-repairs expenditures* include the costs of prolonging the life of an asset or increasing its estimated salvage value, such as a new engine for a truck or a new roof for a building. Costs are debited to accumulated depreciation accounts.

4. **Prepare journal entries for discarding of assets fully depreciated, discarding of assets not fully depreciated, sale of assets involving a loss, sale of assets involving a gain, exchange of assets involving a loss on the trade, and exchange of assets involving a gain on the trade.**

   When a firm changes its Plant and Equipment accounts, as a result of selling, exchanging, or discarding its assets, the accountant must close or clear the asset accounts along with their respective Accumulated Depreciation accounts. When a firm discards, sells, or trades in an asset that has not yet been fully depreciated, the accountant must first depreciate the asset up to the present date. When the amount received for the old asset is less than the asset's book value, the accountant debits Loss on Disposal of Plant and Equipment. When a firm receives more for an asset than its book value, on the other hand, Gain on Disposal of Plant and Equipment is credited.

   When a firm trades in one asset for a similar asset, the entry must include the following four steps:
   (1) Credit Cash or Accounts Payable for the difference between the quoted price of the new asset and the trade-in allowance.
   (2) Credit the account of the old asset.
   (3) Debit the Accumulated Depreciation account of the old asset.
   (4) Debit the account of the new asset for the difference between the total debits and the total credits. In other words, the recorded (adjusted) cost of the new equipment equals the price of the equipment plus the loss or minus the gain.

5. **Maintain a plant and equipment subsidiary ledger.**

   Plant and equipment records should consist of a controlling account and a subsidiary ledger. The subsidiary ledger should contain a card or electronic file for each piece of equipment, listing the date acquired, cost, and depreciation taken to date. For income tax purposes, a subsidiary ledger is a must.

G lossary

Accelerated depreciation Relatively larger amounts of depreciation recorded during the early years of an asset's use; decreasing in later years. **(554)**

Capital expenditures Costs incurred for the purchase of plant and equipment, as well as the cost of increasing the capacity of assets; the firm receives services or benefits from this plant and equipment for more than one accounting period. **(560)**

Depreciation base Total cost of an asset less the trade-in or salvage value. **(554)**

Double-declining-balance method An accelerated depreciation method that assigns greater amounts of depreciation in the early years of the asset's depreciable life and smaller amounts of depreciation as the asset gets older. (Book value at the beginning of the year multiplied by twice the straight-line rate.) **(556)**

Extraordinary-repairs expenditures Costs incurred for major overhauls or reconditioning of assets; repairs that either significantly prolong the life of the asset or increase its estimated salvage value. **(560)**

Gain on Disposal of Plant and Equipment When a firm sells or trades in an asset and receives an amount in excess of the book value for that asset, the gain is recorded in this account, which appears under Other Income in the income statement. **(566)**

Land Improvements An asset account covering expenditures for improvements that are (1) not as permanent as the land or (2) not directly associated with a building. These include driveways, parking lots, trees and shrubs, fences, and outdoor lighting systems. **(553)**

Loss on Disposal of Plant and Equipment When a firm sells or trades in an asset and receives an amount less than the book value for that asset, the loss is recorded in this expense account. **(564)**

Modified Accelerated Cost Recovery System (MACRS) An accelerated depreciation method utilizing the full cost of the asset to allow the business to recover its cost of plant and equipment for property placed in service on or after January 1, 1987 by deducting the cost of each asset on its federal income tax return. This method is used for tax purposes only and not for financial statement reporting. **(570)**

Revenue expenditures Costs incurred to maintain the operation of assets, such as normal repair expenses and fuel expenses. **(560)**

Straight-line method A method of depreciation that assigns equal amounts of depreciation each year of the asset's depreciable life. (Cost minus trade-in value divided by useful life [in years].) **(555)**

Sum-of-the-years'-digits method An accelerated method of depreciation that assigns greater amounts of depreciation in the early years of an asset's life and smaller amounts of depreciation as the asset gets older. (Reducing fraction multiplied by trade-in value.) **(557)**

Units-of-production method Method of depreciation that allocates the cost of depreciation based on its estimated productive ability. (Cost minus trade-in value divided by estimated units of production multiplied by the number of units produced.) **(555)**

QUESTIONS, EXERCISES, AND PROBLEMS

D iscussion Questions

1. How does the accountant's meaning of the term *depreciation* differ from the nonaccountant's meaning of the term?
2. Explain how an asset's estimated trade-in or salvage value is treated in computing depreciation under the sum-of-the-years'-digits method, the double-declining-balance method, and the straight-line method.
3. What is meant by disposition of an asset? List the situations involving disposition of assets.
4. Explain the two entries usually involved in the disposition of an asset.
5. Give examples of possible expenditures that should be included in determining the total cost of an asset, such as a machine.
6. Distinguish between expenditures for ordinary repairs and expenditures for extraordinary repairs.
7. List four things that an accountant should know about an asset in order to calculate the asset's depreciation.
8. Distinguish between capital expenditures and revenue expenditures. Give two examples of each type of expenditure for a truck.

E xercises

P.O.1

Record amounts debited to Land.

Exercise 14-1 Kramer Manufacturing Company purchased land adjacent to its factory for the installation of a holding area for equipment. Expenditures by the company were as follows: purchase price, $132,000; paving, $4,200; title search and other fees, $650; grading, $3,900; demolition of a shack on the property, $3,800; lighting, $11,200; signs, $1,950; broker's fees, $9,240; landscaping, $8,000. Determine the amount that should be debited to the Land account.

P.O.2

Determine depreciation using four methods.

Exercise 14-2 At the beginning of the fiscal year, Ortmeyer Tree Service bought a new chipper for $16,000, with an estimated trade-in value of $2,500 and an estimated useful life of five years. Determine the amount of the depreciation for the first and second years by the following methods:

a. Straight-line
b. Double-declining-balance method
c. Sum-of-the-years'-digits
d. Units-of-production (Useful life is 10,400 hours. Year 1 use is 2,050 hours; Year 2 use, 1,800 hours. Compute depreciation per hour, then depreciation for Year 1 and Year 2.)

P.O.3

Record an extraordinary-repair expenditure.

Exercise 14-3 Patterson Company owns a piece of machinery, bought for $8,000 with an estimated life of five years and an estimated trade-in value of $2,000; straight-line depreciation expense is $1,200. Record journal entries for the following transactions:

Jan. 12 Issued Ck. No. 5221 for $150 for inspection and lubrication of the equipment.
Oct. 15 Issued Ck. No. 5562 for $1,960 to replace the motor and rollers. Patterson estimates this repair to extend the life of the machinery about two years.

P.O.4

Exercise 14-4 On April 28, Recreation Plus discarded a video game that cost $6,600. The Accumulated Depreciation account shows depreciation of $6,600 as of the previous December 31. Make the entry in general journal form to record the disposal of the asset.

Exercise 14-5 On July 25, Reiger and Company discarded office equipment with no salvage value. The following details are taken from the subsidiary ledger: cost, $900; accumulated depreciation as of the previous December 31, $720; monthly depreciation, $15. Journalize entries to record the depreciation of the office equipment to date and to record the disposal of the office equipment.

Exercise 14-6 On June 20, Buster Communications sold editing equipment that cost $1,600 for $350. Accumulated depreciation up to the end of the previous year was $1,350. Monthly depreciation is $22.50. Make the necessary general journal entries.

Exercise 14-7 On September 20, Gilbert Florists traded in its old delivery van for a new one, which cost $16,000. Gilbert got a trade-in allowance of $3,000 on the old van and paid the difference in cash. The subsidiary account shows the following: cost (of old van), $12,000; accumulated depreciation as of last December 31, $9,600; monthly depreciation, $200. Without recognizing gain or loss, make entries in general journal form to record the depreciation of the old van to date and to record the trade-in and purchase of the new van.

Exercise 14-8 On June 25, Purkey Assemblers trades in a machine for a new one priced at $8,460, receiving a trade-in allowance of $1,500 on the old machine. Purkey makes a downpayment of $1,200 in cash and issues a 60-day, 9 percent note for the remainder. The subsidiary account shows the following: cost, $6,000 (of old machine); accumulated depreciation as of last December 31, $4,800; monthly depreciation, $100. Without recognizing gain or loss, make entries in general journal form to record the depreciation of the old machine to date and to record the trade-in and purchase of the new machine.

Record the disposal of a fully depreciated asset.

P.O.4

Record the update of depreciation and record the discarding of office equipment at a loss.

L.O.4

Record the update of depreciation and sale of an asset at a gain.

P.O.4

Record the update of depreciation and trade-in on a similar asset without recognizing a gain or loss.

P.O.4

Record the update of depreciation and trade-in on a similar asset without recognizing a gain or loss.

C onsider and Communicate

Margaret Connor owns a small catering service. The company owns a delivery van as well as ovens and large cooking containers. She is confused about the different traditional depreciation methods she may use for financial reporting. Briefly explain to her the features and benefits as well as the similarities and differences.

W hat If . . .

Your employer, who is ordering equipment for a new office, has signed the purchase orders for new equipment without looking at them carefully. As you complete an invoice for items for the employee lunchroom, you are tempted to change the order from one microwave to two microwaves and quietly take the second one home to compensate yourself for all the hard work you have done on your own time to get the new office ready. A trusted employee, you are sure that if your employer found out what you had done, there would be no real repercussions. What if you go ahead with this idea? How could it be discovered? Assume that you are the one who would accept shipment when the microwaves are delivered.

A Question of Ethics

As the accountant for a firm that owns several classes of equipment, you have decided to use the following methods of depreciation: straight-line on the building, units-of-production on the shop equipment, and double-declining-balance on the office equipment. Are you required to use the same method of depreciation for all of your depreciable assets? Is your action unethical and in violation of generally accepted accounting principles?

P roblem Set A

P.O.2

Problem 14-1A The Vasquez Company, at the beginning of a fiscal year, buys a machine for $50,000. The machine has an estimated life of five years and an estimated trade-in value of $5,000.

Instructions

Using the following three methods, determine the annual depreciation of the machine for each of the expected five years of its life and the book value of the machine at the end of each year. Use the columns provided in the Working Papers.

a. Straight-line method
b. Double-declining-balance method
c. Sum-of-the-years'-digits method

P.O.2,3

Problem 14-2A During a three-year period, Riverside Resort completed the following transactions pertaining to its mower:

Year 1

Jan.   10 Bought a used commercial-size mower, $9,600.
Oct.   15 Paid garage for maintenance and minor repairs to the mower, $327.
Dec.   31 Recorded the adjusting entry to record depreciation for the fiscal year, using the straight-line method of depreciation. The estimated life of the mower is four years, and it has an estimated trade-in value of $1,800.
        31 Closed the expense accounts to the Income Summary account.

Year 2

Feb.   5 Paid garage for tune-up and minor repairs, $180.
June   20 Bought a new tire, $98.
Dec.   31 Recorded the adjusting entry for depreciation.
        31 Closed the expense accounts to the Income Summary account.

Year 3

Jan.   5 Paid garage for a major overhaul to the mower transmission, $1,480. This expenditure extends the useful life of the mower an additional two years (total four years from the time of the overhaul).
Dec.   31 Recorded the adjusting entry for depreciation of the overhauled mower for the fiscal year.
        31 Closed the expense accounts to the Income Summary account.

Instructions

1. Record these transactions in the general journal (page 18).
2. After journalizing each entry, post to the following ledger accounts: Mower; Accumulated Depreciation, Mower; Mower Repair Expense; Depreciation Expense, Mower.

P.O.1,2,3,4

Problem 14-3A During a three-year period, Longhurst Commercial Landscaping completed the following transactions connected with a real estate purchase and its bulldozer:

Year 1

June   1 Bought a large lot for a warehouse for $42,000; real estate fees, $872; survey services, $2,300; land fill, $3,100.

       30 Bought a bulldozer, $110,200, paying $32,200 in cash and issuing a series of four notes for $19,500 each, to come due at six-month intervals. Payments are to include principal plus 9 percent interest to maturity of each note.

July   3 Paid transportation charges for the bulldozer, $3,200.

Dec. 31 Paid the principal, $19,500, plus interest of $877.50 on the first note.

       31 Made the adjusting entry to record depreciation on the bulldozer for the fiscal year (since June 30), using the double-declining-balance method at twice the straight-line rate ($22,680; verify this figure). The estimated life of the bulldozer is five years, and it has an estimated salvage value of $20,000.

       31 Closed the expense accounts to the Income Summary account.

Year 2

Mar. 25 Paid for maintenance and repairs to the bulldozer, $3,030.

June 30 Paid the principal, $19,500, plus interest of $1,755 on the second note.

Dec. 31 Paid the principal, $19,500, plus interest of $2,632.50 on the third note.

       31 Made the adjusting entry to record depreciation on the bulldozer for the fiscal year ($36,288; verify this figure).

       31 Closed the expense accounts to the Income Summary account.

Year 3

Apr. 20 Paid for maintenance repairs to the bulldozer, $2,875.

June 30 Paid the principal, $19,500, plus interest of $3,510 on the fourth note.

Sept. 29 Longhurst Commercial Landscaping decides to get rid of its bulldozer and use the services of an equipment rental firm in the future. Sold the bulldozer for $26,000, receiving cash. Made the entry to depreciate the bulldozer up to date ($16,329.60; verify this figure). Made the entry accounting for the sale of the machine.

Dec. 31 Closed the expense accounts to the Income Summary account.

Instructions

1. Record the transactions in the general journal (page 27).
2. After making each journal entry, post to the following ledger accounts: Equipment; Accumulated Depreciation, Equipment; Equipment Maintenance Expense; Depreciation Expense, Equipment; Interest Expense; Loss on Disposal of Plant and Equipment.

Problem 14-4A The general ledger of the McCready Advertising Agency includes controlling accounts for Office Equipment and for Accumulated Depreciation, Office Equipment. McCready's accountant also records the details of each item of office equipment in a subsidiary ledger. The following transactions affecting office equipment occurred during a three-year period:

P.O.2,4,5

Year 1

Jan.   5 Bought the following items from Osborn Office Supply for cash: Executive desk, $1,810; account no. 2619-1; estimated life, ten years; trade-in value, zero.

Executive chair, $425; account no. 2619-2; estimated life, ten years; trade-in value, zero.

Filing cabinet, metal; $219; account no. 2619-3; estimated life, fifteen years; trade-in value, zero.

(The above assets will be depreciated using the straight-line method.)

8 Paid Paulson Crafters $1,215 for a reception counter; account no. 2619-4; estimated life, ten years; trade-in value, zero; depreciation by straight-line method.

13 Purchased for cash a Hampson laminating machine from Keefer Office Machines, $830; serial no. GL1478; account no. 2619-5; estimated life, four years; estimated trade-in value, $100; depreciation by sum-of-the-years'-digits method.

Dec. 31 Made the adjusting entry to record depreciation of office equipment for the fiscal year (total depreciation, $651.60; verify this figure).

31 Closed the Depreciation Expense, Office Equipment, account into the Income Summary account.

Year 2

June 25 Bought a rug from Soudah Design on account, $1,840; account no. 2619-6; estimated life, eight years; trade-in value, zero; depreciation by double-declining-balance method at twice the straight-line rate.

Dec. 31 Made adjusting entry to record depreciation of office equipment for the fiscal year (depreciation for six months on the rug; total depreciation, $808.60; verify this figure).

31 Closed the Depreciation Expense, Office Equipment, account into the Income Summary account.

Year 3

June 24 Traded in the executive desk for a new one, which cost $2,100, from Hunter, Inc., account no. 2619-7, receiving a trade-in allowance of $525 on the old desk and paying the balance in cash. Expected life of the new desk is ten years, with a zero trade-in value. Use straight-line method of depreciation. Made the entry to depreciate the old desk up to date. Made the entry to record the exchange of assets, without recognizing gain or loss.

Dec. 31 Made the adjusting entry to record depreciation of office equipment for the fiscal year (depreciation for six months on the desk; total depreciation, $873.73; verify this figure).

31 Closed the Depreciation Expense, Office Equipment, account into the Income Summary account.

Instructions

1. Record the transactions in the general journal (page 21).
2. With the purchase of each new asset, open an account in the subsidiary ledger.
3. After each entry, post to the two controlling accounts and to the subsidiary ledger.
4. Make a list of balances at the end of year 3 in the subsidiary ledger accounts and compare the totals with the balances of the two controlling accounts.

P roblem Set B

P.O.2

Problem 14-1B At the beginning of a fiscal year, the Patterson Pickle Company buys a truck for $28,000. The truck's estimated life is five years, and its estimated trade-in value is $4,000.

Instructions

Using the following three methods, determine the annual depreciation for each of the estimated five years of life and the book value of the truck at the end of each year. Use the columns provided in the Working Papers.

a. Straight-line method
b. Double-declining-balance method
c. Sum-of-the-years'-digits method

Problem 14-2B During a three-year period, Lowe Cable Company completed the following transactions related to its service van:

P.O.2,3

Year 1

Jan.   5 Bought a used service van for cash, $18,600.
Oct.   20 Paid garage for maintenance and minor repairs to the van, $280.
Dec.   31 Recorded the adjusting entry for depreciation for the fiscal year. The estimated life of the van is four years, and it has an estimated trade-in value of $3,000. Lowe uses the straight-line method of depreciation.
       31 Closed the expense accounts to the Income Summary account.

Year 2

Mar.   12 Paid garage for a tune-up and minor repairs to the van's engine, $310.
June   18 Paid $250 for two tires for the van.
Dec.   31 Recorded the adjusting entry for depreciation for the fiscal year.
       31 Closed the expense accounts to the Income Summary account.

Year 3

Jan.   8 Paid garage for a major overhaul to the van transmission, $1,230. This expenditure extends the useful life of the van two additional years (total four years from the time of the overhaul).
Dec.   31 Recorded the adjusting entry for depreciation of the overhauled van for the fiscal year.
       31 Closed the expense accounts to the Income Summary account.

Instructions

1. Record these transactions in the general journal (page 27).
2. After journalizing each entry, post to the following ledger accounts: Van; Accumulated Depreciation, Van; Van Repair Expense; Depreciation Expense, Van.

Problem 14-3B During a three-year period, Swan Logging Company completed the following transactions pertaining to land and its self-loader:

P.O.1,2,3,4

Year 1

June   1 Bought acreage for a warehouse for $80,200; real estate fees, $7,265; $1,800 for land clearing; and $5,614 for grading.
       30 Bought a self-loader, $90,700, paying $30,700 in cash and issuing a series of four notes for $15,000 each, to come due at six-month intervals. Payments are to include principal plus interest of 9 percent to maturity of each note.
July   3 Paid transportation charges for the self-loader, $920.
Dec.   31 Paid the principal, $15,000, plus interest of $675 on the first note.
       31 Made adjusting entry to record depreciation for the fiscal year (since June 30). The estimated life of the loader is four years; it has a salvage

value of $10,000. Swan's accountant uses the double-declining-balance method ($22,905; verify this figure).

31 Closed the expense accounts to the Income Summary account.

Year 2

Feb. 15 Paid for normal maintenance and minor repairs to the self-loader, $492.

June 30 Paid the principal, $15,000, plus interest of $1,350 on the second note.

Dec. 31 Paid the principal, $15,000, plus interest of $2,025 on the third note.

Dec. 31 Recorded the adjusting entry for the fiscal year ($34,357.50; verify this figure).

31 Closed the expense accounts to the Income Summary account.

Year 3

Mar. 20 Paid for normal maintenance and minor repairs to the self-loader, $525.

June 30 Paid the principal, $15,000, plus interest of $2,700 on the third note.

Oct. 25 Swan Logging Company decided to get rid of its self-loader and use the services of an equipment rental firm in the future. Sold the self-loader for $18,400 cash. Made the entry to depreciate the loader up to date ($14,315.63). Made the entry to account of the sale of the self-loader.

Dec. 31 Closed the expense accounts to the Income Summary account.

Instructions

1. Record the transactions in the general journal (page 38).
2. After making each journal entry, post to the following ledger accounts: Equipment; Accumulated Depreciation, Equipment; Equipment Maintenance Expense; Depreciation Expense, Equipment; Interest Expense; Loss on Disposal of Plant and Equipment.

P.O.2,4,5

Problem 14-4B The general ledger of Zenorelli Temporary Services includes controlling accounts for Office Equipment and Accumulated Depreciation, Office Equipment. Zenorelli's accountant also records the details of each item of office equipment in a subsidiary ledger. During a three-year period, the following transactions affecting office equipment took place:

Year 1

Jan. 10 Bought the following from Rutherford, Inc., for cash:

Filing cabinet, $215; account no. 273-1; expected life, fifteen years; trade-in value, zero.

Executive desk, $1,960; account no. 273-2; expected life, twelve years; trade-in value, zero.

Executive chair, $540; account no. 273-3; expected life, twelve years; trade-in value, zero.

(The above assets will be depreciated using the straight-line method.)

11 Paid Young and Wolfe $1,130 for a custom-made service counter; account no. 273-4; expected life, ten years; trade-in value, zero; straight-line method.

12 Bought for cash a personal copier, serial no. R-9871B, account no. 273-5, from Nova Office Supplies for $810; estimated life, five years; estimated trade-in value, $150; sum-of-the-years'-digits method.

Dec. 31 Made the adjusting entry to record depreciation of office equipment for the fiscal year (total depreciation, $555.66; verify this figure).

31 Closed the Depreciation Expense, Office Equipment, account into the Income Summary account.

Year 2

June 29 Bought a rug from Regal Company on account; account no. 273-6; $640; estimated life, eight years; trade-in value, zero; double-declining-balance method.

Dec. 31 Made the adjusting entry to record depreciation of office equipment for the fiscal year (total depreciation, $591.66; verify this figure).

31 Closed the Depreciation Expense, Office Equipment, account into the Income Summary account.

Year 3

June 28 Traded in the executive chair for a new one from Gonzales Company, account no. 273-7. The new chair cost $610, has an estimated life of eight years, and has zero trade-in value. Zenorelli's Temporary Services received a trade-in allowance of $210 on the old chair and paid the balance in cash. Recorded the entry to depreciate the old chair up to date using the straight-line method of depreciation. Made the entry to record the exchange of assets, without recognizing gain or loss.

Dec. 31 Made the adjusting entry to record depreciation of office equipment for the fiscal year (total depreciation, $614.38; verify this figure).

31 Closed the Depreciation Expense, Office Equipment, account into the Income Summary account.

Instructions

1. Record the transactions in the general journal (page 32).
2. Each time Zenorelli buys a new asset, open an account in the subsidiary ledger.
3. After each entry, post to the two controlling accounts and to the subsidiary ledger.
4. Make a list of balances at the end of Year 3 in the subsidiary ledger accounts, and compare the totals with the balances of the two controlling accounts.

CHALLENGE PROBLEM

Mike's Motorcycle Shop owns various depreciable assets, which were purchased beginning in 1991. The only record you can find on December 31, 1996 (prior to any depreciation adjustments for 1996) is the general ledger account for Equipment, which has a balance of $56,000, and the general ledger account for Accumulated Depreciation, Equipment, which has a balance of $30,179, plus the information listed on the next page. You will need to prepare supporting schedules by asset classification and expense for each prior year before you can calculate the 1996 depreciation.

Depreciable Assets					
Asset	Bought	Method	Life	Cost	Salvage Value
Van #1	1/1/1991	DDB	5 yrs.	13,000	1,000
Office Desks	7/1/1991	SL	5 yrs.	2,500	500
Van #2	7/1/1993	DDB	5 yrs.	20,000	2,000
Display Ramps	7/1/1995	SYD	10 yrs.	5,500	–0–
Trailer	9/1/1995	DDB	5 yrs.	12,000	1,500
Computer	12/1/1995	SL	5 yrs.	3,000	–0–

Total Depreciation

1991	5,400
1992	3,520
1993	6,272
1994	7,923
1995	7,064

Instructions

1. Classify assets by type: Delivery Equipment, Showroom Equipment, or Office Equipment.
2. Recompute depreciation for 1991, 1992, 1993, 1994, and 1995. Round each year's depreciation expense to whole dollars.
3. Compute depreciation for 1996.

Appendix C

Modified Accelerated Cost Recovery System of Depreciation

PERFORMANCE OBJECTIVES

After you have completed this appendix, you will be able to do the following:

1. Calculate estimated annual depreciation using MACRS.

2. Journalize entries to record the purchase, annual depreciation, and sale of assets using MACRS.

The Tax Reform Act of 1986 introduced the Modified Accelerated Cost Recovery System (hereafter referred to as MACRS). MACRS calls for a change in the classification of assets and length of lives as stated in the Accelerated Cost Recovery System, which was passed by Congress and took effect as of January 1, 1981.

Recovery property is tangible property, such as equipment and buildings, that is subject to depreciation. The term *recovery* refers to the right of a business to recover its cost of plant and equipment by deducting the cost of each asset on its federal income tax return. Each asset's cost is deducted in the form of depreciation. **MACRS pertains to property placed in service on or after January 1, 1987.**

Property is depreciable if it meets the following requirements:

1. It must be used in business or held for the production of income.

2. It must have a determinable life, and that life must be longer than one year.

3. It must be something that wears out, decays, gets used up, becomes obsolete, or loses value from natural causes.

In general, if property does not meet all three of these conditions, it is not depreciable.

Classes of Property

Under MACRS, property falls into one of eight classes. Each of the classes has an officially recognized length of life. The table at the top of the next page shows the property classes and the types of assets for each class.

Depreciation or cost recovery is based on the full cost of each asset. This means that *the cost of an asset is not reduced by the asset's trade-in value or salvage value*. Companies can use either a straight-line method of depreciation, as defined by the Internal Revenue Service (IRS), or a declining-balance method involving schedules approved by the IRS. Generally, companies choose the method that gives them the greatest amount of tax-deductible depreciation in the early years.

Property Class	Description
3-year property	Certain horses and tractor units for use over the road
5-year property	Autos, trucks, computers, typewriters, and copiers
7-year property	Office furniture and fixtures and any property that does not have a class life and that is not, by law, in any other class
10-year property	Vessels, barges, tugs, and similar water transportation equipment
15-year property	Wharves, roads, fences, and any municipal wastewater treatment plant
20-year property	Certain farm buildings and municipal sewers
27.5-year residential rental property	Rental houses and apartments
31.5-year real property	Office buildings and warehouses

Schedules of Depreciation

Performance Objective 1

Calculate estimated annual depreciation using MACRS.

Depreciation for all three-, five-, and seven-year property is based on the 200 percent (double)-declining-balance method. During the first year, assets in these classifications may be depreciated for only half the year. Regardless of when the asset was acquired, whether on January 5 or August 12, only one-half year's depreciation may be taken on that asset. Taking only half a year's depreciation during the first year is called the **half-year convention.** The remaining half-year is taken in the year following the end of the recovery period unless the property is sold or otherwise disposed of before it has been fully depreciated. In that case, one-half of a year's depreciation may be taken during the year it was sold, regardless of when it was sold in that year.

Following are the approved schedules of percentage of cost allocated (written off or depreciated) each year for three-year, five-year, and seven-year property:

Year	Three-Year	Five-Year	Seven-Year
1	33.33	20.00	14.29
2	44.45	32.00	24.49
3	14.81	19.20	17.49
4	7.41	11.52	12.49
5	100.00	11.52	8.93
6		5.76	8.92
7		100.00	8.93
8			4.46
			100.00

To determine the depreciation for the year, multiply the cost of the asset by the percentage figure. The following examples compare allowable depreciation for five- and seven-year property according to the approved schedules with straight-line depreciation for five- and seven-year property as defined by the IRS.

Example for Five-Year Property

On April 2, a business purchased a pickup truck (five-year property) that cost $10,000.

MACRS Depreciation

Year	Depreciation Expense	Accumulated Depreciation	Book Value at End of Year
1	$10,000 × .2 = $ 2,000	$ 2,000	$10,000 − $ 2,000 = $8,000
2	10,000 × .32 = 3,200	$2,000 + $3,200 = 5,200	10,000 − 5,200 = 4,800
3	10,000 × .192 = 1,920	5,200 + 1,920 = 7,120	10,000 − 7,120 = 2,880
4	10,000 × .1152 = 1,152	7,120 + 1,152 = 8,272	10,000 − 8,272 = 1,728
5	10,000 × .1152 = 1,152	8,272 + 1,152 = 9,424	10,000 − 9,424 = 576
6	10,000 × .0576 = 576	9,424 + 576 = 10,000	10,000 − 10,000 = −0−
	$10,000		

Using the 200 percent declining-balance method with the truck's cost of $10,000, the percentages of MACRS depreciation were calculated by the following steps:

1. Calculate the straight-line rate:

$$\frac{1}{5 \text{ years}} = 1/5 = .2$$

2. Multiply the straight-line rate by 2:

$$.2 \times 2 = .4$$

3. Multiply the book value at the beginning of the year by double the straight-line rate:

Percentage amounts: *First year:* $10,000 × .4 = $4,000

One-half year: $4,000 × .5 = $2,000

$$\text{Percentage of cost} = \frac{\$2,000}{\$10,000} = .2 = 20\%$$

Second year: $8,000 × .4 = $3,200

$$\text{Percentage of cost} = \frac{\$3,200}{\$10,000} = .32 = \underline{\underline{32\%}}$$

Third year: $4,800 × .4 = $1,920

$$\text{Percentage of cost} = \frac{\$1,920}{\$10,000} = .192 = \underline{\underline{19.2\%}}$$

Straight-Line Depreciation (IRS Method)

$$\text{Straight-line depreciation rate} = \frac{1}{5 \text{ years}} = .2 \text{ per year}$$

Year	Depreciation Expense	Accumulated Depreciation	Book Value at End of Year
1	$10,000 × .2 × .5 = $ 1,000*	$ 1,000	$10,000 − $ 1,000 = $9,000
2	10,000 × .2 = 2,000	$1,000 + $2,000 = 3,000	10,000 − 3,000 = 7,000
3	10,000 × .2 = 2,000	3,000 + 2,000 = 5,000	10,000 − 5,000 = 5,000
4	10,000 × .2 = 2,000	5,000 + 2,000 = 7,000	10,000 − 7,000 = 3,000
5	10,000 × .2 = 2,000	7,000 + 2,000 = 9,000	10,000 − 9,000 = 1,000
6	10,000 × .2 × .5 = 1,000*	9,000 + 1,000 = 10,000	10,000 − 10,000 = −0−
	$10,000		

Fifteen- and Twenty-Year Property

or all fifteen- and twenty-year property, the 150 percent declining-balance method is used with the half-year convention.

For example, depreciation of a farm building (twenty-year property) for the first year, having a cost of $36,000, is figured like this:

Straight-line rate:

$$\frac{1}{20 \text{ years}} = \frac{1}{20} = \underline{\underline{.05}}$$

---

*The half-year convention is applied to the first year and to the year following the end of the recovery period.

Straight-line rate $\times$ 1.5:

$$.05 \times 1.5 = \underline{\underline{.075}}$$

$$\$36,000 \times .075 = \underline{\underline{\$2,700}}$$

$$\text{One-half year} = \frac{\$2,700}{2} = \underline{\underline{\$1,350}}$$

Twenty-Seven and One-Half- and Thirty-One and One-Half-Year Property

For all residential and nonresidential rental property, the straight-line depreciation must be used with *a midmonth convention.* In other words, half a month is taken during the first month of the first year of operation, regardless of the day of the month the property was purchased. Also, during the first year, all the full months are counted. For example, on November 3, a store building is purchased for $120,000 ($100,000 for building and $20,000 for land). Depreciation for the first year is calculated like this:

$$\text{One year's depreciation} = \frac{\$100,000}{31.5 \text{ years}} = \$3,174.60$$

$$\text{One month's depreciation} = \frac{\$3,174.60}{12 \text{ months}} = \$264.55$$

$$\text{One-half month's depreciation} = \frac{\$264.55}{2} = \$132.28$$

For the first year:

November (one-half month)	$132.28
December (one full month)	264.55
Total	$396.83

Exceptions to the Half-Year Convention

During any tax year, if the total property placed in service during the last three months (last quarter) of the year is greater than 40 percent of all property placed in service during that year, a midquarter convention is used instead of a half-year convention. (Incidentally, residential and nonresidential property is not counted.) The intent is to discourage companies from buying a lot of property during the last month of the tax year and then taking half a year's depreciation on that property.

Under the midquarter convention, all property placed in service during any quarter (three-month period) of a tax year is treated as being placed in service at the midpoint of that quarter. Since each quarter equals 25 percent, one-half quarter is 25 percent divided by 2, or 12.5 percent. This amount is then subtracted from the total percentage allowed for the number of quarters remaining in the year. The first quarter, which is 100 percent minus 12.5 percent, equals 87.5 percent. Here is a schedule of percentages to be applied to the full year's depreciation according to the quarter in which the assets are placed in service: first quarter, 87.5 percent; second quarter, 62.5 percent; third quarter, 37.5 percent; fourth quarter, 12.5 percent.

For example, Gordon Company's fiscal year extends from January 1 through December 31. Gordon bought a typewriter for $520 on February 5 and a computer for $5,400 on December 20. During the last three months, more than 40 percent of the property was purchased. (As a matter of fact, 91 percent was purchased during the last three months: $5,400 ÷ $5,920 = .91 = 91 percent.) Gordon Company must use the midquarter convention. The depreciation for each item is calculated like this:

Typewriter (purchased during first quarter) Five-year property using 200 percent declining balance:

Straight-line rate: $\frac{1}{5} = \underline{\underline{.2}}$

Double straight-line rate: .2 × 2 = $\underline{\underline{.4}}$

First year's depreciation: $520 × .4 = $\underline{\underline{\$208}}$

Depreciation allowed using the midquarter convention: $208 × .875 = $\underline{\underline{\$182}}$

Computer (purchased during fourth quarter) Five-year property using 200 percent declining balance:

Straight-line rate: $\frac{1}{5} = \underline{\underline{.2}}$

Double straight-line rate: .2 × 2 = $\underline{\underline{.4}}$

First year's depreciation: $5,400 × .4 = $\underline{\underline{\$2,160}}$

Depreciation allowed using the midquarter convention:
$2,160 × .125 = $\underline{\underline{\$270}}$

Sale of an Asset

Performance Objective 2

Journalize entries to record the purchase, annual depreciation, and sale of assets using MACRS.

The gain or loss on the sale of an asset must be computed using the MACRS schedules of cost recovery or depreciation. Referring back to our example of the pickup truck on page 587, let's say that the company sells the truck for $1,500 on May 7 during the fourth year of use. First, record depreciation for the fourth year. One-half year is allowed according to the half-year convention. Next, record the sale. These entries are shown in general journal form on page 591. We'll label the entries (1) and (2).

	DATE		DESCRIPTION	POST. REF.	DEBIT	CREDIT	
1	19–						1
2	May	7	Depreciation Expense, Truck		5 7 6 00		2
3			Accumulated Depreciation,				3
4			Truck			5 7 6 00	4
5			Recorded depreciation for				5
6	(1)		one-half year during the				6
7			fourth year of use,				7
8			($10,000 × .1152) ÷ 2				8
9							9
10		7	Cash		1 5 0 0 00		10
11			Accumulated Depreciation, Truck		7 6 9 6 00		11
12	(2)		Loss on Disposal of Plant and				12
13			Equipment		8 0 4 00		13
14			Truck			10 0 0 0 00	14
15			Sold light truck.				15

GENERAL JOURNAL   PAGE _____

The T accounts look like this:

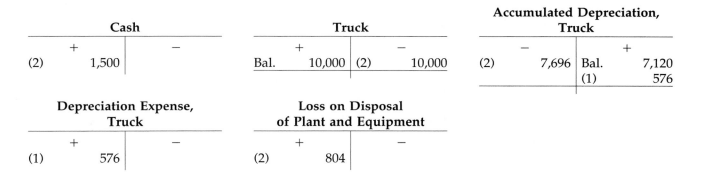

MACRS Versus Depreciation Methods

The actual lives of many assets differ significantly from the lives assigned to them by the IRS. For that reason, many firms use MACRS depreciation for federal taxes and straight-line depreciation, accounting method, for computing net income on their own financial statements. Assuming that the dollar amount of property acquisitions is about the same from year to year, using these two methods would show the highest net income to the owner(s) and the lowest net income to the IRS. Firms that follow this procedure maintain a double set of accounts for Depreciation Expense and Accumulated Depreciation, one for financial statement reporting and one for income tax reporting.

R E M E M B E R

Since lives of property under MACRS may differ from the actual useful lives of assets, a company may use MACRS for its federal income tax return and other methods of depreciation for financial reporting purposes.

P roblems

P.O.1

Problem C-1 On April 9, 19x4, Engle Company bought a computer for $6,000. No other plant and equipment was purchased during the year. Therefore, the midquarter convention does not apply.

Instructions

Determine the annual depreciation, the accumulated depreciation at the end of each year, and the book value at the end of each year using the MACRS schedule of depreciation.

P.O.1,2

Problem C-2 During a three-year period, Fister Company completed the following transactions pertaining to its office furniture. No other assets were acquired earlier in the year. Therefore, the midquarter convention does not apply.

Year 1

Aug. 16 Bought office furniture for cash, $8,500.
Dec. 31 Recorded the adjusting entry for depreciation for the fiscal year using the MACRS method.
     31 Closed the appropriate account to the Income Summary account.

Year 2

Dec. 31 Made the adjusting entry to record depreciation for the fiscal year using the MACRS method.
     31 Closed the appropriate account to the Income Summary account.

Year 3

Dec. 31 Made the adjusting entry to record depreciation for the fiscal year using the MACRS method.
     31 Closed the appropriate account to the Income Summary account.

Instructions

Record the transactions in general journal form.

P.O.1,2

Problem C-3 During a four-year period, Wiggins Company completed the following transactions related to its pickup truck. No other assets were purchased during the year. Therefore, the midquarter convention does not apply.

Year 1

Sept. 12 Bought a pickup truck for $15,000 from Clayton Cars, paying $4,000 in cash, with the remainder due in 30 days.
Oct. 11 Paid the balance due on the purchase of the pickup truck.
Dec. 31 Made the adjusting entry to record depreciation of the truck for the fiscal year using the MACRS method.
     31 Closed the appropriate account to the Income Summary account.

Year 2

Dec. 31 Made the adjusting entry to record depreciation for the fiscal year using the MACRS method.
     31 Closed the appropriate account to the Income Summary account.

Year 3

Dec.   31 Made the adjusting entry to record depreciation for the fiscal year using the MACRS method.

      31 Closed the appropriate account to the Income Summary account.

Year 4

May   19 Sold the truck for cash, $5,250.

Dec.   31 Closed the appropriate accounts to the Income Summary account.

Instructions

1. Record the transactions in general journal form.
2. Post to the following ledger accounts after journalizing each entry: Truck; Accumulated Depreciation, Truck; Gain on Disposal of Plant and Equipment; Depreciation Expense, Truck.

Statement of Cash Flows

PERFORMANCE OBJECTIVES

After you have completed this appendix, you will be able to do the following:

1. Classify cash flows as Operating Activities, Investing Activities, and Financing Activities.

2. Prepare a statement of cash flows.

The fourth major financial statement is the statement of cash flows. This statement explains in detail how the balance of Cash has changed between the beginning and the end of the fiscal period. Some accountants refer to the statement as the "where got, where gone" statement of cash.

Performance Objective 1

Classify cash flows as Operating Activities, Investing Activities, and Financing Activities.

Statement of Cash Flows

 he statement contains three main sections: Operating Activities, Investing Activities, and Financing Activities. Cash flows are subdivided as cash inflows and cash outflows.

Operating Activities

Cash involved in carrying out the company's operations

Cash inflows

- Selling of services or merchandise
- Miscellaneous income

Cash outflows

- Purchases of merchandise and supplies from suppliers
- Payments of salaries or wages
- Payments of rent, utilities, insurance
- Payment of interest to creditors

Investing Activities

Cash involved in buying or selling plant and equipment assets

Cash inflows

- Cash received from the sale of plant and equipment

Cash outflows

- Cash payments to buy plant and equipment

Financing Activities

Cash involved in changes in the owner's equity accounts

Cash inflows

- Investment of cash by the owner
- Borrowing from creditors

Cash outflows

- Withdrawals of cash by the owner
- Repayment of loans to creditors

Prepare the Statement of Cash Flows

The financial statements required to prepare the statement of cash flows consist of the income statement and statement of owner's equity for the fiscal period, the balance sheet at the end of the fiscal period, and the balance sheet at the end of the previous fiscal period. Based on the two balance sheets, we can prepare a comparative balance sheet for the two fiscal periods showing the increases and decreases in the various accounts.

Performance Objective 2

Prepare a statement of cash flows.

Bingham Company		
Income Statement		
For Year Ended December 31, 19x7		
Revenue from Sales:		
Net Sales	$ 647 0 0 0 00	
Less Cost of Goods Sold	500 0 0 0 00	
Gross Profit		$ 147 0 0 0 00
Operating Expenses:		
Salary Expense	$ 70 0 0 0 00	
Rent Expense	10 0 0 0 00	
Depreciation Expense, Equipment	6 0 0 0 00	
Supplies Expense	1 0 0 0 00	
Total Operating Expenses		87 0 0 0 00
Net Income		$ 60 0 0 0 00

Bingham Company

Statement of Owner's Equity
For Year Ended December 31, 19x7

R. A. Bingham, Capital, Jan. 1, 19x7		$ 120 000 00
Additional Investment, March 2, 19x7		10 000 00
Total Investment		$ 130 000 00
Net Income for the Year	$ 60 000 00	
Less Withdrawals	50 000 00	
Increase in Capital		10 000 00
R. A. Bingham, Capital, Dec. 31, 19x7		$ 140 000 00

Bingham Company

Comparative Balance Sheet
December 31, 19x6, and December 31, 19x7

	19x7	19x6	INCREASE OR DECREASE
Assets			
Cash	$ 12 000 00	$ 7 000 00	$ 5 000 00
Accounts Receivable	70 000 00	66 000 00	4 000 00
Merchandise Inventory	120 000 00	113 000 00	7 000 00
Supplies	3 000 00	4 000 00	(1 000 00)
Equipment	$ 72 000 00	$ 60 000 00	12 000 00
Less Accumulated			
Depreciation	(62 000 00) 10 000 00	(56 000 00) 4 000 00	(6 000 00)
Total Assets	$ 215 000 00	$ 194 000 00	$ 21 000 00
Liabilities			
Accounts Payable	$ 71 000 00	$ 69 000 00	2 000 00
Salaries Payable	4 000 00	5 000 00	(1 000 00)
Total Liabilities	$ 75 000 00	$ 74 000 00	$ 1 000 00
Owner's Equity			
R. A. Bingham, Capital	140 000 00	120 000 00	20 000 00
Total Liabilities and			
Owner's Equity	$ 215 000 00	$ 194 000 00	$ 21 000 00

Note the $5,000 increase in Cash. Now it's a matter of showing how this increase came about. First let's present the statement of cash flows.

Bingham Company

Statement of Cash Flows
For Year Ended December 31, 19x7

Cash Flows from (Used by) Operating Activities		
Net Income	$ 60 000 00	
Add (Deduct) Items to Convert Net Income		
from Accrual Basis to Cash Basis		
Depreciation	6 000 00	
Increase in Accounts Receivable	(4 000 00)	
Increase in Merchandise Inventory	(7 000 00)	
Decrease in Supplies	1 000 00	
Increase in Accounts Payable	2 000 00	
Decrease in Salaries Payable	$ (1 000 00)	
Net Cash Flows from Operating Activities		$ 57 000 00
Cash Flows from (Used by) Investing Activities		
Purchase of Plant and Equipment	$ (12 000 00)	
Net Cash Flows Used by Investing Activities		(12 000 00)
Cash Flows from (Used by) Financing Activities		
Cash Investment by Owner	$ 10 000 00	
Cash Withdrawals by Owner	(50 000 00)	
Net Cash Flows Used by Financing Activities		(40 000 00)
Net Increase (Decrease) in Cash		$ 5 000 00

- Cash flows involved in operating activities relate to changes in current asset and current liability accounts.
- Cash flows involved in investing activities relate to changes in plant and equipment accounts (with the exception of Accumulated Depreciation).
- Cash flows involved in financing activities relate to changes in owner's equity accounts.

Explanation of Items in the Statement of Cash Flows

Cash Flows from Operating Activities

The following list describes Bingham Company's cash flows from operating activities.

- Net income of $60,000 from the income statement included such items as selling services or merchandise, miscellaneous income, and payment of expenses like salaries or wages, utilities, interest.
- Depreciation of $6,000 was included as an expense on the income statement, but it did not result in paying cash to anyone. Since depreciation expense

was deducted on the income statement, we now add $6,000 back in. Depreciation expense will always be an addition under Cash Flows from Operating Activities.

- Accounts Receivable increased by $4,000. Of the amount shown as Sales on the income statement, $4,000 was in the form of additional charge accounts. So we deduct $4,000 from Cash Flows from Operating Activities.
- Merchandise Inventory increased by $7,000. Because the inventory increased by $7,000 during the year (more merchandise was bought than sold), we can assume the change resulted in a $7,000 decrease in Cash Flows from Operating Activities.
- Decrease in Supplies of $1,000 means that the company used up supplies bought in a previous fiscal period and included the entire amount of supplies used as Supplies Expense on the income statement. In other words, the $1,000 of Supplies Expense shown on the income statement did not result in a payment of cash in the current period.
- Increase in Accounts Payable of $2,000 in this case means that the amount listed as Purchases on the income statement (not shown since we included Purchases in Cost of Goods Sold) did not result in the payment of cash. So we add $2,000 to Cash Flows from Operating Activities.
- Decrease in Salaries Payable of $1,000 means that the amount listed as Salary Expense on the income statement is $1,000 less than the amount of cash spent by the company. So we deduct $1,000 from Cash Flows from Operating Activities.

Cash Flows from Investing Activities

Plant and Equipment increased by $12,000. We would have to look at the journal entry to determine how much cash was involved. In this case, we assume that the purchase of equipment resulted in a payment of $12,000 cash. So we deduct $12,000 from Cash Flows from Investing Activities.

Cash Flows from Financing Activities

- The owner's Capital account increased by $10,000. We would have to look at the journal entry to determine how much cash was involved. In this case, we assume that the investment was in the form of cash. So we add $10,000 to Cash Flows from Financing Activities.
- The owner's Drawing account increased by $50,000. We would have to look at the journal entries to determine how much cash was involved. In this case, we assume the withdrawals were in the form of cash. So we deduct $50,000 from Cash Flows from Financing Activities.

P roblems

P.O.1,2

Problem D-1 Moore Company has the following financial statements for 19x6 and 19x7. Assume the withdrawals were in the form of cash. Prepare a statement of cash flows for the year ended December 31, 19x7.

Moore Company
Income Statement
For Year Ended December 31, 19x7

Revenue:		
Income from Services		$ 134 0 0 0 00
Expenses:		
Wages Expense	$ 77 0 0 0 00	
Rent Expense	8 0 0 0 00	
Depreciation Expense, Equipment	5 0 0 0 00	
Supplies Expense	2 0 0 0 00	
Total Expenses		92 0 0 0 00
Net Income		$ 42 0 0 0 00

Moore Company
Statement of Owner's Equity
For Year Ended December 31, 19x7

B. N. Moore, Capital, January 1, 19x7		$ 94 0 0 0 00
Net Income for the Year	$ 42 0 0 0 00	
Less Withdrawals for the Year	40 0 0 0 00	
Increase in Capital		2 0 0 0 00
B. N. Moore, Capital,		
December 31, 19x7		$ 96 0 0 0 00

Moore Company
Comparative Balance Sheet
December 31, 19x6, and December 31,19x7

	19x7		19x6		INCREASE OR DECREASE
Assets					
Cash		$ 9 0 0 0 00		$ 6 5 0 0 00	$ 2 5 0 0 00
Supplies		5 0 0 0 00		2 5 0 0 00	2 5 0 0 00
Equipment	$ 100 0 0 0 00		$ 98 0 0 0 00		2 0 0 0 00
Less Accumulated					
Depreciation	(18 0 0 0 00)	82 0 0 0 00	(13 0 0 0 00)	85 0 0 0 00	(5 0 0 0 00)
Total Assets		$ 96 0 0 0 00		$ 94 0 0 0 00	$ 2 0 0 0 00
Owner's Equity					
B. N. Moore, Capital		$ 96 0 0 0 00		$ 94 0 0 0 00	$ 2 0 0 0 00
Total Liabilities and					
Owner's Equity		$ 96 0 0 0 00		$ 94 0 0 0 00	$ 2 0 0 0 00

P.O.1,2

Problem D-2 The financial statements for Ames and Company are presented below and on the next page. Assume the additional investment and the withdrawals were both in the form of cash. Prepare a statement of cash flows for the year ended December 31, 19x7.

Ames and Company
Income Statement
For Year Ended December 31, 19x7

Revenue:		
Income from Services		$ 270 000 00
Expenses:		
Wages Expense	$ 161 000 00	
Rent Expense	18 000 00	
Depreciation Expense, Equipment	12 000 00	
Supplies Expense	4 000 00	
Insurance Expense	1 000 00	
Total Expenses		196 000 00
Net Income		$ 74 000 00

Ames and Company
Statement of Owner's Equity
For Year Ended December 31, 19x7

S. T. Ames, Capital, January 1, 19x7		$ 150 000 00
Additional Investment		2 000 00
Total Investment		$ 152 000 00
Net Income for the Year	$ 74 000 00	
Less Withdrawals for the Year	70 000 00	
Increase in Capital		4 000 00
S. T. Ames, Capital,		
December 31, 19x7		$ 156 000 00

Ames and Company

Comparative Balance Sheet
December 31, 19x6, and December 31, 19x7

	19x7		19x6		INCREASE OR DECREASE
Assets					
Cash		$ 11 800 00		$ 2 800 00	$ 9 000 00
Accounts Receivable		32 000 00		26 000 00	6 000 00
Supplies		10 000 00		9 400 00	600 00
Prepaid Insurance		3 200 00		600 00	2 600 00
Equipment	$ 145 400 00		$ 145 400 00		———
Less Accumulated					
Depreciation	(36 000 00)	109 400 00	(24 000 00)	121 400 00	(12 000 00)
Total Assets		$ 166 400 00		$ 160 200 00	$ 6 200 00
Liabilities					
Accounts Payable		$ 10 400 00		$ 10 200 00	$ 200 00
Owner's Equity					
S. T. Ames, Capital		156 000 00		150 000 00	6 000 00
Total Liabilities and					
Owner's Equity		$ 166 400 00		$ 160 200 00	$ 6 200 00

Problem D-3 The financial statements for Chacara Company are presented below and on the next page. Assume the withdrawals were in the form of cash. Prepare a statement of cash flows for the year ended December 31, 19x6.

`P.O.1,2`

Chacara Company

Income Statement
For Year Ended December 31, 19x6

Revenue from Sales:		
Net Sales	$ 942 000 00	
Less Cost of Goods Sold	753 600 00	
Gross Profit		$ 188 400 00
Operating Expenses:		
Salary Expense	$ 86 900 00	
Rent Expense	18 000 00	
Depreciation Expense, Equipment	10 000 00	
Supplies Expense	4 700 00	
Insurance Expense	2 800 00	
Total Operating Expenses		122 400 00
Net Income		$ 66 000 00

Chacara Company

Statement of Owner's Equity
For Year Ended December 31, 19x6

C. L. Chacara, Capital, January 1, 19x6		$ 196 000 00
Net Income for the Year	$ 66 000 00	
Less Withdrawals for the Year	70 000 00	
Decrease in Capital		4 000 00
C. L. Chacara, Capital,		
December 31, 19x6		$ 192 000 00

Chacara Company

Comparative Balance Sheet
December 31, 19x5, and December 31, 19x6

	19x6		19x5		INCREASE OR DECREASE
Assets					
Cash		$ 9 400 00		$ 10 900 00	$ (1 500 00)
Accounts Receivable		56 000 00		48 600 00	7 400 00
Merchandise Inventory		104 600 00		104 400 00	200 00
Supplies		8 200 00		6 000 00	2 200 00
Prepaid Insurance		1 600 00		1 800 00	(200 00)
Equipment	$ 156 000 00		$ 156 000 00		
Less Accumulated					
Depreciation	(76 400 00)	79 600 00	(66 400 00)	89 600 00	(10 000 00)
Total Assets		$ 259 400 00		$ 261 300 00	$ (1 900 00)
Liabilities					
Accounts Payable	$ 62 700 00		$ 60 400 00		$ 2 300 00
Salaries Payable	4 700 00		4 900 00		(200 00)
Total Liabilities		$ 67 400 00		$ 65 300 00	$ 2 100 00
Owner's Equity					
C. L. Chacara, Capital		192 000 00		196 000 00	(4 000 00)
Total Liabilities and					
Owner's Equity		$ 259 400 00		$ 261 300 00	$ (1 900 00)

Index

Note: Boldface indicates a key term and the page where it is defined.

The Accounting Cycle

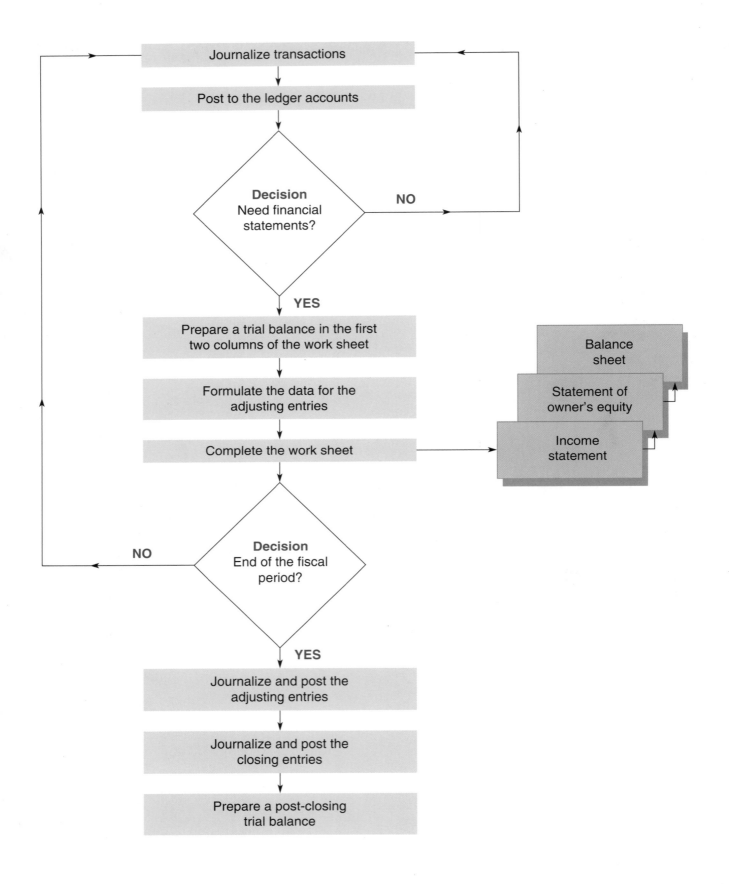